THE DIARY
OF VIRGINIA
WOOLF

Volume Five
1936-1941

Books by Virginia Woolf

The Voyage Out
Night and Day
Kew Gardens
Monday or Tuesday
Jacob's Room
The Common Reader: First Series
Mrs. Dalloway
To the Lighthouse
Orlando: A Biography
A Room of One's Own
The Waves
Letter to a Young Poet
The Common Reader: Second Series
Flush: A Biography
The Years
Three Guineas
Roger Fry: A Biography
Between the Acts
The Death of the Moth and Other Essays
A Haunted House and Other Short Stories
The Moment and Other Essays
The Captain's Death Bed and Other Essays
A Writer's Diary
Virginia Woolf and Lytton Strachey: Letters
Granite and Rainbow
Contemporary Writers
Collected Essays (four volumes)
Mrs. Dalloway's Party
The Letters of Virginia Woolf (six volumes)
Freshwater: A Comedy
Moments of Being
The Diary of Virginia Woolf (five volumes)
Books and Portraits
The Pargiters: The Novel-Essay Portion of The Years
Women and Writing
The Virginia Woolf Reader
The Common Reader: First Series Annotated Edition
The Complete Shorter Fiction of Virginia Woolf
The Common Reader: Second Series Annotated Edition
The Essays of Virginia Woolf, Vol. One (1904–1912)
The Essays of Virginia Woolf, Vol. Two (1912–1918)
The Essays of Virginia Woolf, Vol. Three (1919–1924)
Congenial Spirits: The Selected Letters of Virginia Woolf
A Moment's Liberty: The Shorter Diary of Virginia Woolf
A Passionate Apprentice: The Early Journals, 1897–1909

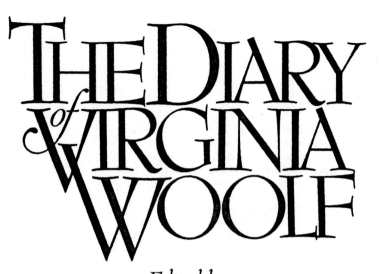

THE DIARY of VIRGINIA WOOLF

Edited by

Anne Olivier Bell

Assisted by Andrew McNeillie

VOLUME FIVE
1936-1941

A Harvest Book
Harcourt Brace & Company
San Diego   New York   London

cation may be
by any means,
:opy, recording,
ystem, without
blisher.

ies of any
:d to:
e & Company,
6277 Sea Harbor Drive, Orlando, Florida 32887-6777.

Library of Congress Cataloging-in-Publication Data
(Revised for volume 5)
Woolf, Virginia Stephen, 1882–1941.
The diary of Virginia Woolf.
Includes indexes.
CONTENTS: v. 1. 1915–1919.—v. 2. 1920–1924.—
v. 3. 1925–1930.—v. 4. 1931–1935.—
v. 5. 1936–1941.
1. Woolf, Virginia Stephen, 1882–1941—Diaries.
2. Authors, English—20th century—Biography. I. Title.
PR6045.072Z494   1977   828′.91203   [B]   77-73111
ISBN 0-15-626036-0 (v. 1)
ISBN 0-15-626040-9 (v. 5)

Printed in the United States of America

First Harvest edition 1985

C D E F G H I J

Contents

THE DIARY

Editor's Preface

Virginia Woolf was fifty-four on 25 January 1936, some three weeks after this final volume of her diary opens; its last page was written four days before she drowned herself on 28 March 1941. Inevitably it is a record of diminishing hope and confidence in both public and private affairs. These were the ominous years leading up to the second great war in Virginia's lifetime, with its initially sluggish and then all too terrifyingly swift development. Privately she had much to suffer: illness—her own, and more agitating because less expected, her husband's; deaths—sudden or lingering, of friends; violent and devastating, of her nephew; overdue, of her mother-in-law; the tangible dangers and destruction of war; the intangible but nonetheless disabling effects of her own vulnerable nature. But despite the horrors and sorrows of these years, this is by no means a wholly cheerless or dispiriting chronicle. Virginia's need to write—to gain a hold on reality by writing things down, served often enough as a safety-valve for despair; and her natural curiosity and capacity for enjoyment, and the pleasure she took in setting down her observations in apposite language, make these pages alive with high-spirited and vivid descriptions and reports.

The year 1936 was the year of Virginia Woolf's protracted struggle to revise and re-shape *The Years*—a book conceived with lively excitement in 1931 but which had now become an incubus, bringing her once more to the brink of the abyss. Her diary for this year is almost the scantest of the whole series; she could barely write. And when after four months' complete blank she returns to its blue pages, she refuses to look back and analyse her prostration but, asserting that it will be more helpful and healthy to write scenes, plunges into a long and vivacious account of Sibyl Colefax lurking furtively in Argyll House, the setting for her great social triumphs, now in the hands of the auctioneers. It is perhaps this perpetual interest in wholly external and non-threatening matters—the death of the old King, the abdication of the new, meetings with eminent men or visits to famous sights, gossip and parties, fulfilling for her the function of healthy and enjoyable exercise—that make Virginia Woolf's diaries so accessible to readers who may not primarily be interested in the creative processes of a great writer but are happy to follow her as a guide to her world and her times.

Virginia's long and agonising struggle with *The Years* was rewarded by its unexpected success; but its publication was attended by much premonitory anxiety and post-natal perturbation. She was easily—it often seems unwarrantably—cast down by adverse criticism, even when it came from sources she did not respect; she began now to believe that she had reached the limits of her success, and must henceforth make the best of being what she called 'an outsider'—a concept which she elaborates in *Three Guineas*, and which had for her a variety of meanings, but certainly implied a sense of becoming a back number, out of fashion, disregarded by the rising generation, although it also stood for freedom to write as and what she wished. *Three Guineas* indeed became for her a lifeline, absorbing and sustaining her in the aftermath of *The Years* and particularly during the dreadful time following the death of her nephew Julian Bell in the Spanish Civil War, when she would stride across the downs arguing with him about war, about male aggressiveness, about women's subjection and their claim for equality, justice, and liberty. In *Three Guineas* she said what she wished to say and, oddly enough, did not for once deeply mind what others said of it.

Virginia had given in to the pressure put upon her to write the life of Roger Fry; it was a courageous undertaking—a challenge in a totally new field for her, in which facts must determine ideas; and facts, in the shape of great quantities of documents, were heaped upon her. She had already begun reading her way through and making notes on them in the autumn of 1935 and, although she did not start the actual writing until March 1938, the evolution of this biography was woven into the fabric of her life for five years. Fascinated by the problems and dismayed by the drudgery involved, she alternately blessed and cursed its subject; and, seduced from her prescribed labours by the vision of a new work of the imagination, she had a hard fight to carry them through to the end. The new book was *Pointz Hall* (to be renamed *Between the Acts*), and 'oh! the relief of fiction' she wrote; 'taking four days holiday from Roger, writing PH'; 'one days happiness with PH'; 'taking a day or two with PH to rest myself from Roger'—so the pendulum swings, from the spring of 1938 until, in July 1940, she is finally free of *Roger Fry* and feels she can now write entirely to please herself. She 'finished' *Pointz Hall* in November 1940; began copying it and 'finished' it again on 26 February 1941, when she showed it to Leonard and some time later to John Lehmann, now his partner in the Hogarth Press. Despite their enthusiasm, she convinced herself it was not fit to publish, and a few days later, ended her life.

In the ordinary—or extraordinary—trials and reverses of her life, Virginia Woolf displayed a remarkable quality of resilience to which these pages bear witness. The prospect of disaster she dreaded; but when disaster struck, she rose manfully (if such an adverb is permissable) to whatever the situation might call for, showing courage, bringing comfort, coping capably and cheerfully: when Leonard was ill, when her sister was so tragically bereaved, she was their best support; when her London home was destroyed or enemy aeroplanes swooped low over her country garden her reactions were surprisingly robust; when her own head ached and her mind clouded she usually took a clear-sighted view of what she must do to recover serenity. *Between the Acts* was written under conditions of unusual stress: the approach of war, the actuality of war and, from the summer of 1940, the very present danger of death through war—the Woolfs' Sussex home was virtually in the front line of the expected German invasion, death was in the skies above them, and they had procured the means to end their lives should the Nazis come. Leonard Woolf wrote: 'Death, I think, was always very near the surface of Virginia's mind, the contemplation of death.' And it has been persuasively argued that this last book can be read as the longest suicide note in the English language. On the less abstruse evidence of eyewitnesses, of her letters, and of this diary, it does not seem to me that Virginia willingly or consciously contemplated bringing about her own death until after she had finished her book and had fallen into the depression which always followed the cessation of a sustained creative effort, and began to know that she was once again losing control of her mind. It is possible that 'this terrible disease—this madness' which dogged her life was a family propensity, linked to changes in the brain which might now be susceptible to treatment by drugs. But then . . . the prescription was the customary sustenance, seclusion, and sleep. Even at a late stage she was writing 'Oh dear yes, I shall conquer this mood'. But when she could no longer summon the strength or will to conquer it, was there not a certain valiancy in choosing death in the hope that Leonard, the 'inviolable centre' of her life, might continue his?

*   *   *

Like the preceding volumes, the record of Virginia Woolf's last years deals with daily delights and daily exasperations, great miseries and great joys. Now that we have her complete diary (the distinction is here made between Virginia Woolf and Virginia Stephen, whose various irregular journals are in the Berg Collection), it seems appropriate to recall the assertion by Quentin Bell in his introduction to the first published volume: 'it is a masterpiece'. The validity of this claim can now be left to the judgement of those who have read it all. But to another question there asked—'How true is it?'—a less prejudiced endorsement may confidently be given. These volumes have appeared during the lifetime of many people who played a part in them. Some have questioned Virginia's opinions or her taste; but none I think her veracity. Where it can be checked, her memory and her observation prove remarkably accurate. Those critics who find she falls short of (surely unattainable?) ideals of charity, humility, and social conscience, accept by implication that she tells the truth about her own feelings and attitudes. In short, hers is a reliable testimony. Living as she did near to the centre of the political, cultural, and social life of the nation, this is far more than an account of the doings of a narrow coterie in the years between 1915 and 1941—not that Bloomsbury, which contained such diverse figures as Maynard Keynes, Desmond MacCarthy, E. M. Forster or Roger Fry can in any true sense be considered centripetal. In these pages we meet a vast gallery of different characters and societies, from Fabians to Rodmell villagers, from H. G. Wells to the Countess of Oxford and Asquith, from Dame Ethel Smyth to the editor of *The New Statesman*. We are offered an enlightened and privileged view not so much of a group as of English history unfolding.

Since her death, interest in Virginia Woolf's life and work has increased immeasurably; her books are translated into almost every language; she is 'taught' in schools and universities; her person and personality are portrayed in books and plays about her and her contemporaries; she is perceived as a privileged, malicious, highbrow snob, as a fey loony, as a Rosa Luxembourg or Mme du Deffand or a Sappho dominated and crushed by her father and her husband. Although it is almost universally acknowledged that she had genius, there is a very wide diversity of opinion as to wherein it is manifested. In her novels? her criticism? or perhaps in her diaries? She has been shown to be a literary revolutionary, a political revolutionary, a feminist revolutionary; her writings are analysed in terms of their Christian, Celtic, Freudian, Marxist or astrological symbolism or content. Most of these are serious approaches to understanding and interpreting her many-sided talent. No doubt these diaries will be further quarried for material to support further argument. 'The germ of a theory is almost always the wish to prove what the theorist wishes to prove' wrote Virginia—and this is one reason why they have been transcribed and annotated with what may often seem excessive pedantry: to enable speculation to be based on accurate readings. But the reader of these diaries, whether specialist, Common, sophisticated or unsophisticated, is offered, to borrow the felicitous words of one critic, the rich and inexhaustible companionship of a writer of outstanding gifts, integrity, and—genius.

* * *

EDITORIAL NOTE

The principles and methods followed in this edition of *The Diary of Virginia Woolf* are fully explained in previous volumes, and hardly need repeating here; but to summarize:

Virginia Woolf's original manuscript diaries have since 1970 been preserved in the Henry W. and Albert A. Berg Collection of English and American Literature in the New York Public Library (Astor, Lenox, and Tilden Foundations) under arrangements made by Leonard Woolf in 1958. The diaries are listed (and the arrangement described) in the first volume of the present five-volume publication. The text for this—the final—volume is taken from Diaries XXV to XXX.

The transcription follows Virginia Woolf's rapidly handwritten pages as closely and completely as possible; omissions, where I have judged it proper to make them, are indicated. My uncertainties or failures in making out words are marked by square brackets (reserved for editorial interpolations) and question marks. I have followed the writer's own corrections where she has made them, occasionally retaining the cancelled word or words within angled brackets: ⟨ ⟩. Afterthoughts added in the wide margins of her pages are here printed as lateral insertions in the body of the text. Mis-spellings, which are comparatively rare, are preserved unless they appear purely inadvertent; after her sometimes phonetic spelling of proper names, the correct form is supplied in square brackets or a footnote. Virginia Woolf's almost invariable use of the ampersand is retained to suggest the pace of her writing, although it is unfortunate that in its printed form the symbol rather negates this intention.

For general convenience, the dating of entries has been standardised. Some dates have been corrected, supplied, or suggested on internal or external evidence—particularly that of Leonard Woolf's laconic pocket diaries, now in the Library of the University of Sussex.

I have distinguished paragraphs in Virginia Woolf's normally unindented pages where they suggest themselves; and I have very sparingly—for the unpremeditated nature of this writing should remain apparent—tidied up the punctuation, adding or eliminating a full-point, a bracket, an inverted comma or an apostrophe to clarify the sense. And where appropriate, I have bodied out her frequent abbreviations in the text.

Such annotations as I judge to be necessary are given at the foot of the page to which they relate, and are numbered in sequence within each month. These footnotes, which I have aimed to make relevant, accurate, concise, and interesting, are intended for a wide range of readers, and those who do not need them should resist the distraction of reading them. Some are inevitably dull, though I hope of use to scholars; but many do seem to me to furnish information essential to an understanding of Virginia Woolf's world, interests, and thought. Anyone of my generation and older may find I have been too expansive in elucidating references to historical and political events which are part of the fabric of our memories; but younger or more distant readers may need more explanation than we. I have attempted to identify every person to whom Virginia refers; the regular habitués of her world, with whom most readers of her diaries are by now probably familiar, I have relegated to Appendix I on p. 361; the irregulars and the minor players are normally introduced in footnotes on their first appearance; the index should discover them all. As more and more people crowd into her pages, with often less and less said about them, I have likewise reduced my particulars to the minimum.

Throughout my notes I have abbreviated Virginia and Leonard Woolf's names to their initials VW and LW. Virginia's own published writings are identified according to B. J. Kirkpatrick's indispensable *Bibliography of Virginia Woolf* (third edition, 1980); and books published by the Hogarth Press by J. Howard Woolmer's invaluable *A Checklist of the Hogarth Press, 1917-1938*; *M&M* denotes Majumdar and McLaurin's volume on Virginia Woolf in the *Critical Heritage* Series which usefully reprints critical reactions to her published work. A list of abbreviations regularly employed for books, journals, and collections will be found on p. 360; other books are cited by their author, full title, and date of publication in England, except for Virginia Woolf's own works, when reference is made, unless otherwise stated, to the Uniform Edition, published in London by the Hogarth Press and in New York by Harcourt Brace Jovanovich.

* * *

ACKNOWLEDGMENTS

Looking back over the ten years I have spent shepherding Virginia Woolf's diaries from manuscript to printed page, I am impressed by the benevolent cooperation of the innumerable people to whom I have applied for information, and on whom I have depended for support and encouragement, and it is hard to know where best to begin in expressing my appreciation and gratitude. Perhaps as most of my work has been done at home, those at home who have endured longest deserve it most: my husband; my children: Julian and Virginia who also made positive contributions in the form of maps and research, and Cressida, who preserved her independence; and Mr and Mrs Gosden (a prime source of Sussex lore) who during all these years have loyally and heroically lightened my burden of care for house and garden.

Beyond the home, the chief centres for Andrew McNeillie's and my activities have been the Library and Documents Centre of the University of Sussex and the London Library; at Sussex Elizabeth Inglis and John Burt, and at St James's Square ('If that's Mrs Bell, it must be Thursday') the Librarian Douglas Matthews have in particular assisted our researches with erudition, resource, and good humour. Peter Croft and Michael

Hall, Librarian and Modern Archivist respectively of King's College, Cambridge, and Richard Morphet of the Tate Gallery, have always been very helpful too. Dr Lola L. Szladits, the distinguished Curator of the Berg Collection, has since the beginning played a significant role in this enterprise as my notional monitor, rather an awesome figure; but in fact has always been human kindness itself. Nigel Nicolson, the editor with Joanne Trautmann of the six volumes of Virginia Woolf's letters which have been an indispensable accessory to our work, has been generous with his special knowledge of people and events. And once again I owe a particular debt of gratitude to Sir Henry Lintott to whom all intractable problems have been referred and to whose diligence and persistence is due the fact that so few remain unsolved; and who (to mis-quote) has generously and gratuitously corrected the punctuation, the grammar, the history, the geography, and the chronology of my notes in previous volumes and has not spared his services on the present occasion.

It seems a meagre way of thanking others who one way or another have helped me with this final volume—and many with previous volumes too—just to parade them in a list, and I hope I have thanked them all privately, and have not omitted anyone; but list them here I will, and thank them here I do:

Dr Igor Anrep; Mrs M. Bennett; Mr Stanley Burton, Lord David and the late Lady David Cecil; Mrs Richard Chilver; Mrs Jean Floud; Mr P. N. Furbank; Mr John Gere; Dr A. D. Harris; Professor and Mrs Matthew Hodgart; Professor John Humphrey; Professor John Haule; the late Mrs Walter Higgens; Professor Mitchell A. Leaska; Professor and Mrs Norman MacKenzie; Lady Lintott; Mrs Ruth Longman; Mr Peter Miall; Mrs Ian Parsons; Mrs Frances Partridge; Mr and Mrs Tim Pember; Sir Edward Playfair; the late Angela Richards, my dear cousin; Dr G. H. W. Rylands; Miss Daphne Sanger; Mr Desmond Shawe-Taylor; Mr Richard Shone; Dr Frances Spalding; the Hon. Piers St Aubyn.

I also wish to acknowledge the assistance I have received from officials and staff of the following:

Messrs Thomas Agnew & Sons; The National Book League; The Central School of Art and Design; The Courtauld Institute of Art; The London Borough of Enfield Library; The Fawcett Library; The Polytechnic of Central London; The Sussex Archaeological Society; *The Times.*

I have had essential and capable help in the preparatory work, the necessary typing, and the final checking of this volume from Sarah Matthews, Dominique Spedding, Victoria Walton, and Sandra Williams.

The Hogarth Press, that modest enterprise started by Leonard and Virginia Woolf in their dining room at Richmond nearly seventy years ago, survived and flourished and expanded and is now very properly, and also laudably, publishing these diaries, the last of Virginia Woolf's major works to be printed. I have been fortunate in working with members of so experienced and so sympathetic a firm, and am only sorry that my dilatoriness should have deprived Norah Smallwood of the satisfaction of seeing the completion, before her retirement, of an undertaking over which she has presided with beneficent omniscience from the beginning. But Hugo Brunner, her successor in this task, is happily for me equally a most considerate and constructive collaborator. Their transatlantic colleague, John Ferrone, of Harcourt Brace Jovanovich, has provided me with friendly support in a number of ways, and I am grateful to them all.

My respect and admiration for the printers of these volumes is the greater for knowing how difficult it must have been for them to resist correcting all the apparent errors and idiosyncrasies of the copy they had to set.

Virginia Woolf's copyrights were inherited by her surviving nephew and her niece Angelica, and it is they I have to thank for entrusting me with the responsible and arduous task of editing her complete diaries. That they are my husband and my sister-in-law does appear to make this all rather a family business; but I hope these volumes will be found none the worse for that, and that my labours will be judged on their merits and not on my connections—although these have undoubtedly been advantageous, not least because they have provided, from Virginia Woolf's own royalties, the necessary financial support to me and my assistant. Such an almost hermetic arrangement may well inspire mistrust: family Authorised Versions have not always a good reputation. But in the case of Virginia Woolf her family and heirs, headed by Leonard Woolf, by placing all her diaries and papers in public collections, and encouraging the publication not only of these diaries but of her memoirs and letters, have done what they can to ensure that her life, her personality, her thought, as well as her works, are freely accessible to the public—more so probably than of any major writer of this century.

My final grateful thought is for the house in which I have been fortunate enough to live and work for the past seventeen years and from which, as from these diaries, I now part with loving regret: Cobbe Place, Beddingham.

November 1983   ANNE OLIVIER BELL

The Ouse Valley

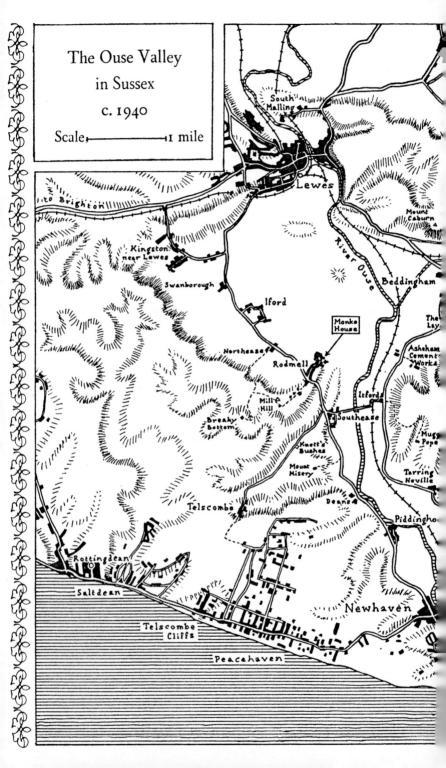

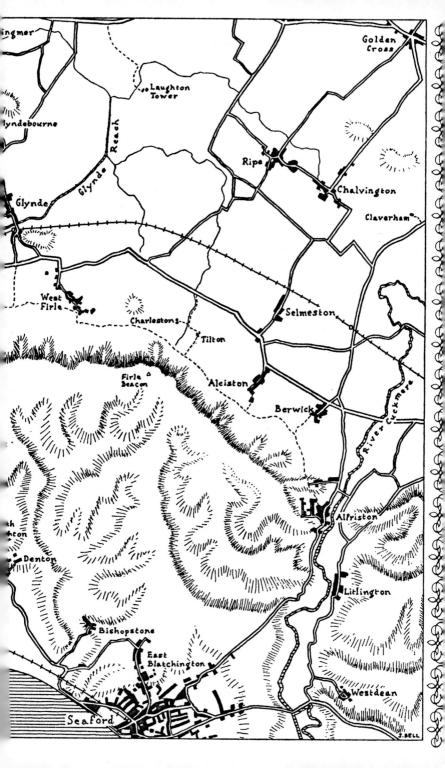

Central London

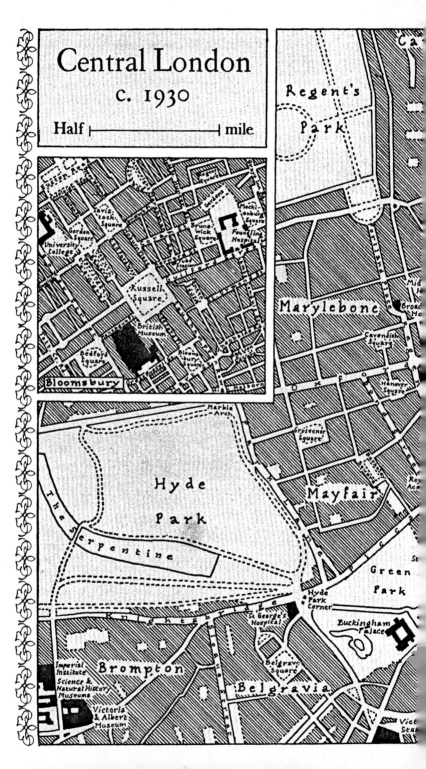

Central London
c. 1930

Half |————————————| mile

— 1936 —

1936

The Woolfs had been at Monks House since 20 December 1935; the weather was very cold and wet. On 29 December VW finished her first revision of The Years *which she had promised to have ready for the printer by the middle of February, and she ended the year in bed with a headache. Her diary for 1936 continues in the book she had begun on 28 December,* DIARY XXV.

Friday 3 January

I began the year with 3 entirely submerged days, headache, head bursting, head so full, racing with ideas; & the rain pouring; the floods out; when we stumbled out yesterday the mud came over my great rubber boots; the water squelched in my soles; so this Christmas has been, as far as country is concerned, a failure, & in spite of what London can do to chafe & annoy I'm glad to go back, & have, rather guiltily, begged not to stay here another week. Today it is a yellow grey foggy day; so that I can only see the hump, a wet gleam, but no Caburn.[1] I am content though because I think that I have recovered enough balance in the head to begin The Years, I mean the final revision on Monday. This suddenly becomes a little urgent, because for the first time for some years, L. says I have not made enough to pay my share of the house, & have to find £70 out of my hoard. This is now reduced to £700, & I must fill it up. Amusing, in its way, to think of economy again. But it would be a strain to think seriously; & worse—a brutal interruption—had I to make money by journalism. The next book I think of calling Answers to Correspondents. . . . But I must not at once stop & make it up.[2] No. I must find a patient & quiet method of soothing that excitable nerve to sleep until The Years is on the table—finished; In February? Oh the relief—as if a vast—what can I say—bony excrescence—bag of muscle— were cut out of my brain. Yet its better to write that than the other. A queer light on my psychology. I can no longer write for papers. I must write for my own book. I mean I at once adapt what I'm going to say, if I think of a newspaper.

1. Looking northwards from Rodmell across the Ouse Valley the view is dominated by the bare down of Mount Caburn, and punctuated by two 'humps' rising from the flat water-meadows on the near side of the river.
2. Ideas for this 'next book'—finally published in 1938 as *Three Guineas*—had been in VW's mind for several years (see *IV VW Diary*, 20 January 1931, and Index under *Woolf, Virginia*, §7, *Three Guineas*), although for the past twelve months and most of the coming year, while working on *The Years*, she suppressed her recurrent urge to start the actual writing of it. For VW's 'hoard', see *IV LW*, pp. 142-3.

JANUARY 1936

Saturday 4 January

The weather has improved, & we have decided to stay till Wednesday. It will now of course rain. But I will make some good resolutions: to read as few weekly papers, which are apt to prick me into recollection of myself, as possible, until this Years is over; to fill my brain with remote books & habits; not to think of Answers to C.ds; & altogether to be as fundamental & as little superficial, to be as physical & as little apprehensive, as possible. And now to do Roger; & then to relax.[3] For, to tell the truth, my head is still all nerves; & one false move means racing despair, exaltation, & all the rest of that familiar misery: that long scale of unhappiness. So I have ordered a sirloin & we shall go for a drive. L. is happier: will now do his trees.

Sunday 5 January

I have had another morning at the old plague. I rather suspect that I have said the thing I meant, & any further work will only muddle. Further work must be merely to tidy & smooth out. This seems likely because I'm so calm. I feel well, thats done. I want to be off on something else. Whether good or bad, I dont know. And my head is quiet today, soothed by reading The Trumpet Major last night, & a drive to the floods. The clouds were an extraordinary tropical birds wing colour: an impure purple; & the lakes reflected it, & there were droves of plover black & white; & all very linear in line & pure & subtle in colour. How I slept! Gray again today: but I shall not go to tea with Clive & Raymond. No news of Morgan. I cd. hardly listen to the news for fear they wd. begin We regret . . .[4]

Tuesday 7 January

I have again copied out the last pages, & I think got the spacing better. Many details & some fundamentals remain. The snow scene for example. & I suspect a good many unfaced passages remain. But I preserve my sense that its stated; & I need only use my craft not my creation. A pouring day—a day so wet that L. had to come in a mackintosh, & to spare him I drank my coffee in the dining room by candlelight.

---

3. After the death of Roger Fry in September 1934, VW had agreed to write his biography; a great deal of documentary material was entrusted to her and, from the autumn of 1935 until she began the actual writing in the spring of 1938, reading and taking notes from it became a staple element of her working life.

4. For Clive Bell, Raymond Mortimer, and E. M. (Morgan) Forster, see Appendix I. Forster, with gloomy foreboding, had undergone a preliminary prostrate operation in a London nursing home on 18 December 1935; it was successful, and the operation was completed in February.

No news of Morgan? Why? Joe's faithless.[5] All the angles of the twigs have white drops on them. Thats Hardy's gift by the way. minute obstinately individual observations. But how his reputation ever mounted, considering the flatness, tedium, & complete absence of gift of the T. Major, I cant say: & wd like to discover. I think he had genius & no talent. And the English love genius. I'm English enough too to feel my own past as a peasant expand his notes. Tom [T. S. Eliot], the American, cant; feels nothing I suppose. I think of taking sentences from great writers & expanding them. But then I'm always feathering round for some way of liberating my critical apprehensions which dont fit the strait jacket of the regular Times leader any longer. Anyhow this rain dissolves my guilt in wishing to go back. And I've had one or two sublime quiet evenings here—evenings of immunity, using that word in its highest sense.

The Woolfs returned to 52 Tavistock Square by car on the afternoon of Wednesday 8 January; it rained all the way.

Friday 10 January

London.

Back again. A great gale all yesterday & a dusk over everything & rain, so that the comfort I had expected was diminished. Origo to tea; & wants to dine next week.[6] All the same I will keep my hands on the reins. For, to tell the truth, this six weeks is going to be a most perilous enterprise. How on earth to finish, to get typed, to correct by the end of Feb? To show my state, I mistook 11 for 12 on my watch this morning; so shut up my book & stopped work with such relief that, when I discovered the mistake, I couldn't bring myself to do the extra hour & did Roger instead. How then am I going to finish? My head is so springless. What I plan is to finish this long last lap for *typing* say by Monday or Tuesday: send it to Mabel [*typist*], & then begin at the chapter I stopped at, & go through again, & so keep the whole reading till I've got it all retyped. But can I do this in the time? I'm going to space my days as carefully as I can, resting after lunch, & reading only with the skin of the eye. But its the chronic problem of people that is the crux (what a word). Heres Dadie asking us to Cambridge; & old Ethel on the alert; & the usual

5. Joe Randolph Ackerley (1896-1967), writer, and from 1935-59 literary editor of *The Listener*, was a close friend and confidant of Forster, on whose post-operational progress he had presumably undertaken to report.

6. Marchesa Iris Origo (b. 1902), writer, daughter of the late W. Bayard Cutting of Long Island and his wife Lady Sybil Cuffe (who subsequently married Geoffrey Scott and then Percy Lubbock); brought up in Florence, in 1924 she married the Marchese Antonio Origo. The Woolfs met her in London in the summer of 1935 and published her second book *Allegra* (*HP Checklist* 373) in October that year. She came to tea at Tavistock Square on 9 January.

letters. The C[ambridge]. U[niversity]. Lit. Soc, Dadie says, is asking me to lecture. Let it. A text for my letter.[7] Origo rather contorted: says Italy is blind red hot devoted patriotic: has thrown her wedding ring into the cauldron too. Anticipates a long war, & then the peace they cd have had a month ago. They are more set than on the great war. 2 meatless days a week.[8]

Saturday 11 January

This book is now becoming the oddest hop o' my thumb work: I peck & stop; peck & stop again. Think even of continuing this after tea. Its better than trying to work straight ahead. This is one of my pauses. Twelve o'clock—a very fine day. Asked to lecture to the Cambridge English Club. Shall I say anything of what I think of these invitations? I suppose not—not yet. Ann popped in suddenly after lunch; bare legs, socks, touseled hair: wanted to borrow the second vol. of War & Peace for Judith who's had her tonsils out. Something like a rugger blue, in a striped jersey, very tall, & vigorous. She says she has many friends in the colleges—young men—but we shouldn't know them.[9] Then I read Borrow's Wild Wales, into which I can plunge head foremost; then L. went to see Morgan, found him with the usual Bugger crew: & I to tea with Nessa; & Duncan came in, & we discussed the bugger crew; which Duncan dislikes when its self conscious, as at Raymond's, & I always liken to the male urinal. Then L. came— You see I leave out the quality of the talk . . . it was very sympathetic. We discussed journalism, the NS: its hard bright up to date reviews; D. had been dining with Colefax to meet Max. He becomes social—is so naturally, even though he goes on the wrong day & imagines S[ibyl]. having tea—bread & butter alone.[10] Home, & dine alone, & sleep over Mr Clarkson's memoirs. He had a

7. i.e.: 'Answers to Correspondents'. For G.H.W. ('Dadie') Rylands and Ethel Smyth, see Appendix I.

8. In October 1935, after the invasion of Abyssinia by Mussolini, sanctions were imposed against Italy by the League of Nations; to raise money for the prosecution of the war, the Fascists appealed to the patriotism of Italian women, inviting them to sacrifice their gold wedding rings. Ceremonies were held at war memorials throughout Italy on 18 December when, led by the Queen, women threw their rings into cauldrons and received steel rings in exchange.

9. Ann (b. 1916) and Judith (1918-72), VW's nieces, daughters of Adrian and Karin Stephen (see below, 9 February 1936, n. 1). Ann was in her first year at Newnham College, Cambridge, reading Natural Sciences; Judith was at Bedales School.

10. For Vanessa Bell and Duncan Grant, see Appendix I; when in London they lived in adjacent studios at 8 Fitzroy Street, W1. Sibyl (d. 1950), wife of Sir Arthur Colefax, KC, was an energetic London hostess who maintained a *salon* at their home, Argyll House, 211 King's Road, Chelsea. Max Beerbohm (1872-1956), author and caricaturist.

sexual kink, & a passion for fish—ran Sara Bernhardt's errands; & I suppose—but all details are lacking, made 40,000 wigs for one show.[11]

Monday 13 January

The precious days are ticking over. About 30 now left me, & how much to do! But my new method is working I think: each hour mapped in bed, & kept to, so far. Ann & Cr. Strachey to dine last night. Christopher a charming babbling humane boy, with a great deal of Oliver—in the voice chiefly—some of the Costello coarseness, of feature; but far more dash & vitality than a pure blooded Strachey. Laughter. Talk, of course, of Gumbo & Ray; Ray & Gumbo getting naked & swimming.[12] Yet, though the thought of R.'s nakedness makes me squirm, she has humanised her son. He eats 4 eggs, on equal terms, as he says, with her, for Sunday supper. And he was concerned that in Gumbo's new house, ordered from a catalogue, there is only a little box room for the servant. How very unlike Lytton! But he says that Oliver is also humane. Ann in her red; an ungainly girl; but silent, brooding, with opinions, chiefly medical & political. She sells the Daily Worker (3 copies) then breaks in on Cr. who is playing Bach on the piano, & demands eggs & biscuits for lunch at 3.30. Nessa, Clive, Duncan came in: but we drew the young on to chatter about B.B.[13]

I walked somewhere on the Sunday streets & L. went to Mrs W. & met Babs &c. with the Alsatian, which had to be returned. She had just bought it in Pug Row, if thats the name of the dog selling street in Whitechapel.[14] Fog—mitigated fog this morning.

11. *The Strange Life of Willy Clarkson* by Harry J. Greenwall (1936). Clarkson (c. 1860-1934), the wig-maker and theatrical costumier, had provided the disguises for VW and the other participants in the Dreadnought Hoax in 1910 (see *I QB*, pp. 157-60).

12. Christopher Strachey (1916-75) was Ann Stephen's first cousin, being the son of her mother's sister Rachel (Ray), *née* Costelloe (1897-1940) and Oliver Strachey (1874-1960), an elder brother of the critic and biographer Lytton Strachey (1880-1932); 'Gumbo'—Marjorie Colvile Strachey (1882-1964), a teacher, was his aunt; her new house was erected in the grounds of his parents' home, The Mud House, Friday's Hill, Haslemere. Christopher was at this time a first-year student of Mathematics at King's College, Cambridge.

13. Bernard Berenson (1865-1959), the eminent connoisseur and Italian art expert, was the second husband of Christopher and Ann's grandmother Mary, a matriarch fiercely and bountifully devoted to her two daughters by her first marriage, Ray Strachey and Karin Stephen, and their offspring, who from time to time were summoned to stay at the Berensons' villa *I Tatti*, near Florence, which Duncan and Vanessa had visited in 1920.

14. Marie Woolf (1850-1939) was LW's widowed mother; and Babs (Marjorie), the wife of his youngest brother Philip Woolf (1886-1965). The pet-selling street market is Club Row, in Bethnal Green.

JANUARY 1936

Thursday 16 January

Seldom have I been more completely miserable than I was about 6.30 last night, reading over the last part of The Years. Such feeble twaddle—such twilight gossip it seemed; such a show up of my own decrepitude, & at such huge length. I could only plump it down on the table & rush up stairs with burning cheeks to L. He said This always happens. But I felt, no it has never been so bad as this. I make this note should I be in the same state after another book. Now this morning, dipping in, it seems to me, on the contrary, a full, bustling live book. I looked at the early pages. I think there's something to it. But I must now force myself to begin regular sending to Mabel. 100 pages go tonight I swear.

Iris Origo to dine alone. At first I thought this too is going to be a wash out. But, chiefly owing to L.'s charm, & making myself a little drunk, we all chattered, more intimately than we should have done had John been there or William or Harold, & we both liked her.[15] And she is to come again. A genuine woman, I think, honest, intelligent &, to my pleasure, well dressed: also being a snob, I like her Bird of Paradise flight through the gay world. A long green feather in her hat suggests the image.

Sunday 19 January

I open this, forced by a sense of what is expected by the public, to remark that Kipling died yesterday; & that the King (George 5th) is probably dying today. The death of Kipling has set all the old war horses of the press padding round their stalls; & the papers have to eke out 5 or 6 columns with the very bare bulletin—condition causes anxiety—which they supplement with biographies of doctors, of nurses, pictures of Sandringham, remarks of old villagers, gossip about the little Princesses in their cherry coloured coats, a snow man, &c. But the fact remains that all the Princes have gathered together, & I suppose at any moment the butler may come in, just as theyre finishing dinner, & say King Edward 8th, upon which—but I need hardly invent that scene having already so many on my hands.[16]

Privately, I rang up Nessa at 6 yesterday & was alarmed by the agitated

---

15. Iris Origo dined on 15 January. For John Lehmann see Appendix I. William Plomer (1903-73), poet and novelist, was first published by the Woolfs in 1926 and became an established friend. Harold Nicolson (1886-1968), diplomat, politician, man of letters, and Vita Sackville-West's husband; from 1935-45 he was National Labour MP for West Leicester. Like Plomer, he was a dependably urbane and conversable guest.

16. Rudyard Kipling (b. 1865) died in London on 18 January; his ashes were buried in Poets' Corner, Westminster Abbey, on 23 January. The King was ill at Sandringham where the Royal family had spent Christmas.

& breathless way in which she said Not now: I'll ring later. This left me to imagine any number of catastrophes, but I find this morning that I interrupted the crisis of that London Group meeting, which went entirely against Nessa & Duncan's cabal; they dismissed the President, & elected Sickert. And now, at the same time that the King dies, Nessa & Duncan think of resigning & starting a new Group.[17] It is coldish snowy weather: the snow half melts half freezes; & I pad along, & Judith dined here, & we talked to James & Alix, walked by the Serpentine & must now lunch.[18]

I went up to an elderly stout woman reading the paper at The Times Book Club the other day. It was Margery Strachey. What are you doing? I said. Nothing! she replied. "I've got nowhere to go & nothing to do." And I left her, sitting reading The Times.[19]

Monday 20 January

This story I repeated to Duncan last night. He also had met Marjorie at The Times. She had flung her arms round him & kissed him. Another side of Marjorie's story. They were badly beaten, Nessa & Duncan; but both elected to the Cttee all the same. They had not arranged any speaker on their side, &, as neither of them spoke, & Nan & Ethel were silent, & the others had actually written out speeches, the result as they say was a foregone conclusion.[20]

And the King is not dead, but the same. It is a very fine bright day; I think I must force myself to go to Lewis's & get a dress made;

17. The London Group of artists had been formed in 1913 from a fusion of the Camden Town and Fitzroy Street Groups; Duncan Grant and Vanessa Bell had been members since 1919. Before Christmas they had learnt of what appeared to them an unscrupulous intrigue to oust the current President, Rupert Lee, and other officers of the Group, at the general meeting on 18 January 1936, and had made efforts to counter this. The meeting however resulted in what Vanessa described as 'a complete triumph for the enemy', when 75-year-old W. R. Sickert was elected President *pro tem.* as a façade for the intriguers' nominees. Vanessa and Duncan did resign, but rejoined during the war.

18. James Beaumont Strachey (1887-1967), psychoanalyst, Lytton's youngest brother and his literary executor; he was the general editor and principal English translator of Freud's collected papers, which were being published by the Hogarth Press. His wife Alix, *née* Sargant Florence (1892-1973) was also a psychoanalyst. They lived at 41 Gordon Square, Bloomsbury.

19. The Times Book Club, 42 Wigmore Street, was a circulating library; VW's subscription entitled her to be supplied with newly-published books on demand.

20. The American-born painters and lifelong companions Anna Hope (Nan) Hudson (1869-1957) and Ethel Sands (1873-1962) were among the original members of the London Group when it was founded in November 1913.

&—&— we are dining with Alice Ritchie. Sibyl is only too ready to come.[21]

Tuesday 21 January

The King died last night. We were dining with Alice Ritchie, & drove back past Buckingham Palace. It was a clear dry night, rather windy & rather cold. As we turned the corner & came by the Palace we saw cars drawn up all along the Mall. There were thin lights. On the white monument people were standing: only everybody seemed to be moving. There was a cluster like a swarm of bees, round the railings. Some people were plastered against the railings, holding on to the bars. There was a discreet frame, like a text, holding a bulletin. We had [to] drive on past the Monument before the policeman, who spoke with weary politeness, would let us stop. Then we got out, & walked back, crossing with difficulty because cars were passing all the time, & tried to shove our way through the crowd. But it was impossible. So I asked a policeman "What is the latest bulletin?" And he said, It has not been issued. So I said But what is the latest news. I havent heard. (We had only seen Strength diminishing on the placards as we drove out) to which he replied "His majesty's life is drawing to a peaceful close." This he said without conviction, as if he were reciting words put into his mouth, but with a certain official tolerance. There was some agitation & excitement; many foreigners talking German; a large proportion of distinguished looking men, in semi evening dress; everyone indeed looked rather tall; but by no means tragic; yet not gay; rather suppressing their excitement; & it was all very brightly lit. As we turned away, a firework—a silver gilt sputtering fizzing torch began bubbling up, like a signal, like a festival, but it was presumably a photographers light. The crowd clustering on the rails became chalky white for a few seconds; & then we got into the car & drove home. The streets were very empty. But save for the occasional placard—it was now "The King is Dying"—there was nothing out of the way. What I took for guns booming was only the banging of the loose door in the mews. But at 3 this morning, L. was woken by paper boys shouting in the street. The King had in fact died at 12.5. He was dead when we were outside the palace. There were one or two narrow lights in the little top windows, I remember. Otherwise all the white curtains were drawn.

Most of the men in Southampton Row wear black ties wh. are brand

---

21. Alice Ritchie (1897-1941) wrote two novels which had been published by the Hogarth Press; she now edited the journal of the International Alliance for Suffrage and Equal Citizenship, *International Women's News*; she lived in St George's Square, Pimlico. John Lewis & Co. Ltd., of Oxford Street, drapers and department store.

new, or dark blue ties, which are the nearest they can get. In the stationers the woman spoke with a subdued kindness as if we were both mourning a great uncle we had never seen. The woman in Dennisons said she often thought herself it was absurd only to sell plain labels by the thousand.[22] A very fine cold day. Sun shining.

Wednesday 22 January

The people of America are mourning, as if for their own King; & the Japanese are in tears. So it goes on. But as a matter of fact the Prime Minister [Stanley Baldwin]—we are only allowed official announcements on the BBC—& if you turn it on you only hear the ticking of a vast clock—was rather fitting; almost sincere, & very well conditioned. He gave out the impression that he was a tired country gentleman; the King another; both enjoyed Christmas at home; & the Queen is very lonely; one left the other taken, as must happen to married couples; & the King had seemed to him tired lately, but very kind, & quiet as if ready for a long journey; & had woken once or twice, on the last day & had said something Kind ('Kind' was the adjective always) & had said to his Secretary "How is the Empire?"—an odd expression. "The Empire, Sir, is well"; whereupon he fell asleep. And then of course, he ended with God Save the King.

The shops are all black. "We always carry a large stock" the woman at Lewis's said. But there'll be nothing doing after this rush at all. There'll be no work for us . . ." Mourning is to outlast the London Season. A black Ascot.[23]

[*Monday 27 January*]

I have done something so incredibly idiotic—left my last chapter at Monks yesterday—that I can hardly get over it. And there I was in the rush of the end. We went to Canterbury & I listened to a full service while L. lectured in the County Hotel. But I wont write my impressions. Almost smashed coming back—lights went out—we backed—a great car swung down, like a liner at sea, & was I thought on us. But missed. So home. Over to Nessa's: Quentin there. Duncan spent an hour blocked in his car outside Westminster. The death trudge goes on till 6 am. & I forgot to say we saw the coffin & the Princes come from

22. Dennisons were manufacturers of tags and labels, with showrooms in Kingsway.

23. The period of Court mourning was reduced from one year to six months at the behest of the new King, Edward VIII.

Kings X:[24] standing packed in the Square democracy, though held back
by Nessa, swarmed through; leapt the chain, climbed the trees. Then they
came, the coffin with its elongated yellow leopards, the crown glittering
& one pale blue stone luminous, a bunch of red & white lilies: after that
3 undertakers in black coats with astrachan collars: "our King" as the
woman next me called him, who looks blotched & as if chipped by a
stone mason: only his rather set wistful despair marked him from any shopkeeper—not an ingratiating face: bloated, roughened, as if by exposure to
drink life grief & as red as a fisherboys. Then it was over. & I shall not
try to see more. But the whole world will be afoot at dawn tomorrow.

Tuesday 28 January

The King is at this moment being buried, & if I go up I shall hear the
service. A fine mild morning. The sun is out, the streets almost empty.
An occasional hoot. No registered post this morning. And a tea party
this afternoon.[25]

The most extraordinary thing about writing is that when you've
struck the right vein, tiredness goes. It must be an effort, thinking wrong.
at 5 to one, after a sterile bitter morning, the vein flows. I think now I see
to the end.

[Sunday 9 February]

It is now the 9th of Feb & I have three weeks in which to finish my
book. Hence this stolen minute—stolen while waiting to go round to the
meeting at Adrian's—is the first I have had in wh. to make even this
elementary note.[1] I work 3 hours in the morning: 2 often after tea. Then
my head swells & I sleep.

24. Quentin Bell (b. 1910), painter, younger son of Clive and Vanessa Bell. King
     George V's body was brought by train from Sandringham to King's Cross on
     23 January; thence, draped with the Royal Standard and surmounted by the
     Imperial Crown, and followed on foot by the new King and his three brothers,
     the coffin was drawn on a gun-carriage (passing Tavistock Square) to Westminster
     Hall where for four days and nights it lay in state while an apparently inexhaustible
     host of mourners filed past. On 28 January it was taken to Windsor for burial in
     St George's Chapel.
25. VW's engagement diary only notes: 'Tea Origo Sibell William'; but LW's diary
     records that the party consisted of Iris Origo, William Plomer, Ethel Smyth,
     Elizabeth Cameron (Elizabeth Bowen, see below, 16 March 1936), and 'Kincaid'—
     perhaps C. A. Kincaid (1870-1954), formerly of the Indian Civil Service and
     author of numerous books on India.
  1. Adrian Leslie Stephen (1883-1942), VW's brother; he and his wife Karin, née
     Costelloe (1889-1953) were both practising psychoanalysts. They lived at 50
     Gordon Square, where a meeting was held on the afternoon of 9 February of a
     group, *For Intellectual Liberty*, formed the previous December as an English

Tuesday 25 February

And this will show how hard I work. This is the first moment—this
5 minutes before lunch—that I've had to write here. I work all the
morning: I work from 5 to 7 most days. Then I've had headaches.
Vanquish them by lying still & binding books & reading D. Copperfield.[2]
I have sworn that the script shall be ready, typed & corrected, on the 10th
March. L. will then read it. And I've still all the Richmond & El. scene to
type out; many corrections in that most accursed raid scene to make; all
this to have typed; if I can by the 1st which is Sunday; & then I must
begin at the beginning & read straight through. So I'm quite unable
either to write here, or to do Roger. On the whole, I'm enjoying it—
thats odd—though in the ups & downs, & with no general opinion.

Saturday 29 February

Leap Year day. A great deal of fuss about the marmots. In fact, these
weeks of solitude, seeing no one, only going round to Nessa, refusing all
parties—Sheppard, to see Greek Play, Ellis Roberts to meet Max, & so
on—have a space & quiet thats rather favourable to private fun.[3] I
become so absorbed in The Years that I take the other world as a kind of
amplification, variation in another key. Nothing interferes for the
moment; & I rush on; should in fact rush on this morning; but have done
so much copying—the Oxford Street scene—that I cant cut ice any more.
L. is lunching with the Robsons.[4] It is drizzling. It is a damp dismal day.

---

equivalent to a French organisation of anti-Fascist intellectuals, the *Comité de
Vigilance.*

2. Although VW had bound books in an amateur fashion since she was twenty, her
occupational therapy here was not bookbinding in the ordinary sense of the term:
she was pasting coloured paper over the red cloth covers of the 39 volumes of the
'Arden' edition of Shakespeare and labelling the spines in her elegant handwriting;
they are now the property of Lady Lintott.

3. Marmots: a sobriquet from the Woolfs' private language of love. J. T. Sheppard
(1881-1968), Greek scholar and Cambridge contemporary of LW's, since 1933
Provost of King's College, Cambridge; he had invited the Woolfs to his production
of the University's triennial Greek Play, Aristophanes' *The Frogs.* R. Ellis Roberts
(1879-1953), vice-President of the PEN Club, and one-time literary editor of the
NS&N and of *Life and Letters.*

4. The scene of Eleanor Pargiter in Oxford Street was one of 'two enormous chunks'
eliminated by VW in her final revision of *The Years*; it is reprinted by Grace Radin
in the *Bulletin of the New York Public Library*, Winter 1977. William Alexander
Robson (1895-1980), Reader in Administrative Law at the London School of
Economics 1933-46, was joint Editor with LW of the *Political Quarterly*; his
French wife Juliette Alvin (d. 1982) was a violoncellist and a pioneer in music
therapy.

All Duncan's pictures have been refused—to give a scrap of upper air news—by the Q. Mary. A great Bloomsbury agitation set on foot. But they think Sir Percy Bates when persuaded, gently, by the whole connoisseurship of London, may be bamboozled into relenting.[5] All the Cabinet has been murdered in Tokyo. Lydia is a great success at Cambridge. Clive in Paris. I read Quennel on Byron: dont like that young mans clever agile thin blooded mind: & very little else that counts. L. began this morning against Mabel again: because she asked for a rise. So I must face that with other accumulations during my hybernation. And now to lunch. & then to take tickets for Charlie Chaplin. And I've never recorded my request from Lady Oxford—that I shd. write an obituary of her writing; or my lunch there; & the little drawn up painted alert nervous brilliant woman, as hard as nails, but a good mimic.[6]

Wednesday 4 March

Well, I'm almost through copying the raid scene, I shd. think for the 13th time. Then it will go tomorrow, & I shall have I think one days full holiday—if I dare—before re-reading. So I'm in sight of the end: that is in sight of the beginning of the other book which keeps knocking unmercifully at the door. Oh to be able once more to write freely every morning, spinning my own words afresh—what a boon—what a physical relief & rest, delight after these last months—since October year more or less—of perpetual compressing & re-writing always at that one book.

The Dolls House last night. Lydia very good; an interesting play, wh.

5. Duncan Grant was among a number of artists commissioned in 1935 by the Cunard-White Star Line to provide decorations for their newest liner, the *Queen Mary*, which was being fitted out in Glasgow. He painted three large panels for the central lounge, two of which had recently been installed; however the Company's chairman, Sir Percy Bates, adjudged them inappropriate and rejected them. The ensuing outcry by 'the whole connoisseurship of London' failed to influence his decision. (See Richard Shone, *Bloomsbury Portraits* (1976), pp. 249-50.)

6. An abortive coup by junior officers of the Japanese Army in Tokyo on 26 February claimed the lives of the Prime Minister Admiral Okada and two other eminent public figures. For Lydia Lopokova (Mrs Maynard Keynes) see Appendix I; she was currently performing Ibsen at the Cambridge Arts Theatre. *Byron. The Years of Fame* by Peter Quennell (b. 1905), author and critic, was published in October 1935. 'Steady silent unselfish' Mabel Haskins had been the Woolfs' living-in cook and servant since May 1934; LW never liked her. Charlie Chaplin's latest film *Modern Times* was showing at the Tivoli in the Strand; the Woolfs went this evening. Lady Oxford, *née* Margot Tennant (1864-1945), was the widow of the Liberal Prime Minister H. H. Asquith; VW lunched with her on Monday 17 February; her two letters of request appear in VW's memoir 'Am I A Snob?', published in *Moments of Being*, 1976 (Kp A45).

throws light on some of my own efforts; but I wish I'd gone to Figaro instead. Not a good audience though, & I doubt if London will be as enthusiastic as Cambridge, which is Maynard's pocket borough. Old Garnett there, like a sheep whose coat has been half torn off. No one else known to me.[1]

Wednesday 11 March

Well yesterday I sent off 132 pages to Clark. We have decided to take this unusual course—that is to print it in galleys before L. sees it & send it to America.[2] I'm thus feeling more at ease; but rather slack, as we went to Hedda Gabler last night with Nessa Duncan & Mrs Grant. I did not get the full impact: my mind too much set, I suppose, on my own corrections. Jean F. Robertson however was sinuous seductive sinister in a curious metallic old dress. Blue.[3] A girl, who might have been an Ibsen lady, smiled at me. Now who is she? We cant place her. I am only writing this to mark time till lunch. Still, considering my languor, I think Ibsen comes pretty well out of it. (oh the rhythms that go on in my head. Thats one of the difficulties: I must break: want a usual [?] tone: must read Swift, I think). News is that we are going to stay one week end with David & Rachel: Morgan is again going on well. Nessa had trays of pure Chinese silk from Julian. She's taking a room for Angelica.[4] I'm pleased by the way that A. Bennett writing to his nephew seems, I think, to acquit me of authors' vanity. "We got on fine, the day after I'd slanged her publicly in

1. For Maynard Keynes, see Appendix I; he was responsible for the conception, financing, and building of the Arts Theatre in Cambridge which opened in February 1936 (after two gala evenings) with a cycle of four Ibsen plays which had now been transferred to the Criterion Theatre, London. His wife, Lydia Lopokova, played Nora in *A Doll's House* and Hilda Wangel in *The Master Builder*. Edward Garnett (1868-1937), writer and publishers' reader, was David ('Bunny') Garnett's father.
2. Normally LW would read VW's novels in typescript before sending them to her usual printers, R. & R. Clark of Edinburgh, who then supplied page proofs for final correction.
3. Jean Forbes Robertson (1905-62) played the title-rôle in *Hedda Gabler*, another of the Ibsen cycle transferred from Cambridge to the Criterion Theatre. Ethel Grant, née McNeil (1863-1948), was Duncan's widowed mother.
4. Lord David Cecil (b. 1902), younger son of the 4th Marquess of Salisbury, critic and biographer and at this time Fellow of Wadham College, Oxford; he had married Desmond MacCarthy's only daughter Rachel (1909-82) in 1932, and they had a house near Fordingbridge in Hampshire. Julian Bell (1908-37), poet, Clive and Vanessa Bell's elder son, had gone to China the previous autumn as Professor of English at the National University of Wuhan. Angelica Bell (b. 1918) was Vanessa's daughter by Duncan Grant; she had spent six months in France since leaving school and was now to live semi-independently at 64 Charlotte Street, a block away from her mother's studio.

15

the E.S. . . . . We had a great pow-wow at Ethel Sands. Virginia's all right . ." This might be my epitaph I think.[5]

I cant help feeling in the subcutaneous way one does feel such things that we are slightly on the up grade again: old Bloomsbury. Its rather a nicer feeling than being on the down grade perhaps. Nevinson, the painter, gave 50 centimes to the Fund to buy a Cézanne, in Roger's memory. Now that sort of meanness makes me angry. Its all of a piece with Grigson &c. And heres Hampson coolly applying to L. who is rushed & pumped & milked by every ninny on the European situation— for help about his miserable little contracts.[6] The European situation developed on Saturday. We were at Monks House. H[itler]. has broken his word again. proposes to re-enter the League. But I'm too languid: shall even consider having an afternoon off.[7]

Friday 13 March

Getting along rather better. So I steal 10 minutes before lunch. Never have I worked so hard at any book. My aim is not to alter a thing in proof. And I begin to suspect there's something there—it hasn't flopped yet. But enough of The Years—We walked round Ktn Gardens yesterday

5. *Letters to his Nephew* by the novelist Arnold Bennett (1867-1931) had just been published; VW abstracts phrases from two of them, dated 6 December 1926 and 2 December 1930. (For her own account of their 'pow-wow' at Ethel Sands's, see *III VW Diary*, 2 December 1930.) The debate between Bennett and VW on the contemporary novel dated back to 1923 (see *M&M*) and gave rise to her essay *Mr Bennett and Mrs Brown* (Kp A7). Bennett had 'slanged' VW in his 'Books and Persons' column in the *Evening Standard* of 2 December 1926 on grounds of her weakness in character-drawing, in construction, and of lack of vitality.

6. A letter signed by two dozen distinguished people (including VW) and published in the *Times* of 28 November 1934 had launched an appeal for funds to buy a picture worthy to hang in the National Gallery as a memorial to Roger Fry. (In the event the painting bought, and accepted by the Trustees in July 1936, was not the aimed-for Cézanne but Sisley's 'Les petits prés au printemps'.) C. R. W. Nevinson (1889-1946) had fallen out with Fry in the 'twenties over the management of the London Group, of which he was a founder-member, and thereafter cherished an unremitting hostility towards him and the 'Bloomsburies'. Geoffrey Grigson (b. 1905) the editor of *New Verse* and literary editor of the *Morning Post*, was (and is) a notoriously abrasive critic. John Hampson (John Hampson Simpson, 1901-55); after publishing his first two books in 1931 and 1932 (*HP Checklist* 256 and 290), the Woolfs rejected his third, and Chapman & Hall had published it.

7. The Woolfs went to Rodmell for forty-eight hours on Friday afternoon, 6 March. The following morning, in flagrant violation of the Versailles and Locarno Treaties, German troops marched unopposed into the demilitarized zone of the Rhineland; at noon in the *Reichstag* a defiant and ebullient Adolf Hitler paraded his own prospectus for European security, which included an offer to re-enter the League of Nations provided his other conditions were accepted.

.discussing politics. Aldous refuses to sign the latest manifesto because it approves sanctions. He's a pacifist. So am I. Ought I to resign. L. says that considering Europe is now on the verge of the greatest smash for 600 years, one must sink private differences & support the League. He's at a special L. Party meeting this morning.[8] This is the most feverish overworked political week we've yet had. Hitler has his army on the Rhine. Meetings taking place in London. So serious are the French that they're—the little Intelligence group—is sending a man to confer here tomorrow: a touching belief in English intellectuals. Another meeting tomorrow. As usual, I think Oh this will blow over. But its odd, how near the guns have got to our private life again. I can quite distinctly see them & hear a roar, even though I go on, like a doomed mouse, nibbling at my daily page. What else is there to do—except answer the incessant telephones, & listen to what L. says. Everything goes by the board. Happily we have put off all dinners & so on, on account of The Years. A very concentrated, laborious spring this is: with perhaps 2 fine days: crocuses out; then bitter black & cold. It all seems in keeping: my drudgery; our unsociability; the crisis; meetings; dark—& what it all means, no one knows. Privately . . . no, I doubt that I've seen anyone, or done anything but walk & work—walk for an hour after lunch—& so on. I must get back to H[ogarth]. P[ress]. MSS though.

Monday 16 March

I ought not to be doing this: but I cannot go on bothering with those excruciating pages any more. I shall come in at 3 & do some; & again after tea. For my own guidance: I have never suffered, since The Voyage Out, such acute despair on re-reading, as this time. On Saturday for instance: there I was, faced with complete failure: & yet the book is being printed. Then I set to: in despair: thought of throwing it away; but went on typing. After an hour, the line began to taughten. Yesterday I read it again; & I think it may be my best book. However . . . I'm only at the Kings death. I think the change of scene is whats so exhausting: the catching people plumb in the middle: then jerking off. Every beginning seems lifeless—& then I have to retype. I've more or less done 250: & theres 700 to do. A walk down the river & through Richmond Park did more than anything to pump blood in. Adrian though has had another queer seizure: suddenly became unconscious: & was then very sick. This

8. LW was a strong supporter of the League of Nations' collective security system; whereas Aldous Huxley (1894-1963), now a sponsor of the Peace Pledge Union, considered that imposition of sanctions against Italy following her invasion of Abyssinia had had the effect of 'forcing the Italians to rally round Musso'; and that such measures could only make the prevention of wars and the establishment of peace among nations more difficult to achieve.

reminds me of father falling down, & I thought he was on fire.[9] Politics have slightly died down. We had a meeting on Saturday: I went to E. Bowen & sat in her glass shining 'contemporary' room. Like a French picture—2 ladies sitting looking at the Lake. She is much like a picture. We discussed poor Rose M.'s terrible flurry about E. not wanting to see her. R. stopped me in T[orringto]n Sqre to gasp out this heart cry Does Eth no longer want to know me? I went to fetch something she had said she was out . . . there was a party . . reviewing young men. In fact they were BBC young men. But what a state of mind this shows![10]

Wednesday 18 March

It now seems to me so good—still talking about The Years—that I cant go on correcting. In fact I do think the scene at Witterings is about the best, in that line, I ever wrote. First proofs just come: so there's a cold douche waiting me there. And I cant concentrate this morning—must make up Letter to an Englishman. I think, once more, that is the final form it will take. because after all separate letters break continuity so [text ends][11]

Another pause. This wandering comes from having Karin to dinner last night; & Kot before that; the same as ever: rather heavier, yellower; & then E[lizabe]th Williamson afterwards; & tho' it wasn't late, I felt like a wet towel, sitting there. My brain wont grip. Also it is the first day of Spring—hot: swarming. And, God damn these persistent old women, I must go to tea with Mrs Grosvenor. Oh what vampires they are—my blood must feed that old wretch. I dislike going—no hat, want to lie & dream after tea. Then theres Lady Simon tomorrow. And Rodmell . . . . Then one week of peace I will have before a week end at the Cecils.[12]

9. See *Sir Leslie Stephen's Mausoleum Book*, edited by Alan Bell, 1977: '2 June [1900]. A giddy fit—pitched over as if I had been shot—[Dr] Seton calls it "stomachic vertigo" and seems to think little of it.'

10. Elizabeth Bowen (1899-1973), Anglo-Irish novelist, whose husband Alan Cameron worked in the BBC; they lived at 2 Clarence Terrace, overlooking the lake in Regent's Park. When she first came to London in the twenties she had received much kindness and encouragement from the successful novelist and journalist Rose Macaulay (1881-1958).

11. 'Letter to an Englishman': one of VW's titles for the work that grew into *Three Guineas* (see above, 3 January 1936, n. 2).

12. S. S. Koteliansky (1882-1953), pre-war emigrant from the Ukraine, collaborated with the Woolfs in translations from Russian writers which were published by the Hogarth Press in its early days in Richmond. Elizabeth Mary Williamson (1901-1980), favourite great-niece of Ethel Smyth and a woman of wide culture, was Demonstrator in Practical Astronomy at University College, London. The Hon. Mrs Norman Grosvenor (1858-1940) was the widowed mother of VW's friend

But Karin was very nice: so brisk headed; & somehow ⟨sad⟩ pathetic. Said she'd found Adrian unconscious & how awful it was. Yet they separated. A kind of suffering & capacity for something else in her, somehow, like a dog whose bones' been snatched away, but no longer snarls. E.W. very much to the point too.

Friday 20 March

Book again very good: very bad yesterday. And what a horrid evening. First Lady Simon & Harry: then Raymond:[13] then, longing for dinner, down I go to the Press, to see if my Macaulay's come: & theres a tap on the window. I thought it was a little dressmakers apprentice come with my dress. But it was oh dear—a girl, fainting. Can I have a drop of water? She was hardly able to walk. Sat on the area steps while I got one. Then I took her in: got L.: hotted soup. But it was a horrible thing. Shed been walking all day to get work, had neuritis—cdnt sew, had had a cup of tea for breakfast, lived in one room alone in Bethnal Green. At first she cd hardly speak—"I'm hungry" she said. Gradually livened. Half dazed. Said You look like brother & sister, both have long noses. I'm a Jewess—a curious stress on the word as if a confession. So's he I said. Then she perked up a little. But my God—no one to help her, she said. Friends? Oh they only think of enjoying themselves. May I take this home? taking a bun. We gave her tongue, 2 eggs, & 5/- Did you make this yourself—of the soup. Can you afford it—of the money. And a mere wisp—22—suffering. Never saw unhappiness, poverty so tangible. And felt its our fault. And she apologised. And what could we do. I shall stay in bed if I'm feeling bad & then go to the Labour Exchange. But I cant get any work. Think of one of our 'class': & this is what we exact.

Now its raining, & I suppose . . well, whats the use of thinking? As usual what was so vivid I saw it all the evening becomes stylised when I write. Some horror become visible: but in human form. And she may live 20 years . . . What a system.

[Marginal note:] Russian? No parents This was concealed. Very small, white, swollen hands: talked educated English—pattered. But a fact— She had to go. Knew she must go. Shuffled off to Bethnal Green. Used to make slips— pointing to L.'s waistcoat. Shook hands. And keep well she said

---

Susan Buchan (Lady Tweedsmuir). Shena Simon (1883-1972), wife and working partner of the Manchester industrialist, social reformer, and sometime Liberal MP Sir Ernest Simon, first met VW in 1933 and their ensuing friendship, though not close, was based on mutual respect.

13. VW's 'antiquated cousin' Harry Lushington Stephen, 3rd Bt (1860-1945), once a High Court Judge in India, had succeeded to the family baronetcy on the death of his brother in 1932.

Tuesday 24 March

A very good week end [*at Rodmell*]. Trees coming out, hyacinths, crocuses. Hot. The first spring week end. I slept. L. had a large [*Labour Party*] meeting. Clever people from Lewes. But I slept. Then we walked up to Rat Farm & looked for violets. Still spring here. Am tinkering—in a drowsy state. The approach of Easter that breaker up. Duncan going to Spain. Angelica coming back. We may do anything—perhaps go away with Morgan, whose book is out. Fat & blue. No time to read it yet.[14] And I'm so absorbed in Two Guineas—thats what I'm going to call it. I must very nearly verge on insanity I think. I get so deep in this book I dont know what I'm doing. Find myself walking along the Strand talking aloud. Old Mrs W[oolf]. in great spirits yesterday. Anxious to make out that Lady Oxford is not old: that a secluded life may be as good as a social one; & that parties are a natural pursuit for old women. So much of talk is always self-justification. But my five minutes is up, & I must go up. Miss Bernice Marks has been seeing Leonard.[15]

Sunday 29 March

Now its Sunday, & I'm still forging ahead. Done Eleanor in Oxford Street for the 20th time this morning. I've plotted it out now, & shall have done by Tuesday 7th April, I tell myself. And I cant help thinking its rather good. But no more of that. One bad head this week, lying prostrate. So I missed Nessa's potters party, at which Angelica made a sensation in a new hat. And we put off going to the Cecils this week end: but went instead to Richmond yesterday; saw the lovely view, with a piece of deep green grass, the gasometer, & the clouds: looking towards Ealing L. said. So home; then to the Master Builder, where I did not like Lydia's version; partly the ugly clothes; high boots, green skirt, red shawl. And she hasnt the compass; cant swing from the real to the poetic. Elizabeth [Bowen] Cameron was there with a cousin, who agreed. In fact they were very emphatic. Hated it. Asked us to meet the Master builder & drink beer at the Café Royal; but we refused, & came home; saw the Polish Prince coming, & only locked ourselves in just in time.[16] L. has a sore throat this morning. We think of going, & high time too, to

14. E. M. Forster's book was *Abinger Harvest*.
15. Bernice Marks, unidentified; possibly the fainting unemployed girl of the previous entry?
16. The part of the Master Builder (Holvard Solness) was played by D. A. Clarke-Smith. Count Potocki de Montalk, a fanatical anti-Semitic New Zealander who claimed descent from the Kings of Poland; arrayed in dingy flowing crimson robes, he was a familiar sight in Bloomsbury. In 1932 LW and others had organised an unsuccessful appeal on his behalf when he was sentenced to six months imprisonment for uttering an obscene libel. (See *IV VW Diary*, 13 February 1932.)

Monks House next Friday & digging ourselves in. Nessa & Angelica, Clive & Quentin will all be there [*at Charleston*].

I have left out Elizabeth Robins by the way—a great curse to me; for she came at a moment of high pressure; & I had to throw myself into her infinitely intense, exacting, pernickety demands.[17] No, she must explain—in fact had come from Brighton to explain. She cannot go to see the M.B. but she does go to plays—thats what I cant deny—with a friend. But my sight is going—now this is a secret. I dont mean I'm going blind. But I must spare my eyes. And I have a book to write. I want to keep all my strength for that. Could you explain do you think? Yes. yes. and then there['s] another thing, I could only tell you in confidence. I couldnt go & see her Hilda. *I'm* Hilda. I'm the person it was written for. . . All very intense. A small frozen humming bird—with rouged lips: intense blue eyes, very small, old; full of accents & intensities. We are to go to dinner or tea.

Wednesday 1 April

I forgot though to make L. an April fool, & he forgot too. The Ms. are lavender & silver. We went to tea with Gerald yesterday, which was like visiting an alligator in a tank, an obese & obsolete alligator, lying like our tortoises, half in & half out of the water. I wished I had gone to Downing St. to hear Baldwin on Newnham as I sat there in the very ugly de Vere Gardens room, with the dull covers, & the tea on wheeled waiters, & the old picture that Gerald bought 40 years ago at St. Ives over the fire. I doubt that he much enjoyed seeing us, or has any capacity for enjoying anything left. We talked publishers' shop, & she—her name I dont know —was vivacious in the strained way of a woman whose life is empty & who has perpetually to animate her husband. She is 'got up' but elderly; shrivelled; rather a nice woman, I suspect, but discontented.[1] And G. told me about his diseases, & threw cold water, sensible, business man's very

---

17. Elizabeth Robins (1862-1952), American actress, author, and feminist; she settled in England in 1888, and had known VW's parents. A pioneer interpreter of Ibsen on the London stage, she played Hilda Wangel in the first London performance of *The Master Builder* on 20 February 1893; her essay, *Ibsen and the Actress*, was published by the Hogarth Press in 1928 (*HP Checklist* 174). She now lived in Brighton, and at Maynard Keynes's behest, VW had written to ask her to see the production of *The Master Builder* at the Criterion Theatre in which Lydia Lopokova was playing Hilda (see *VI VW Letters*, nos. 3114 and 3116).

1. Gerald de l'Etang Duckworth (1870-1937), VW's surviving half-brother, eponymous founder of the publishing house which published her first novel in 1915; he had been married to Cecil Scott-Chad since 1921. Although VW did not go to Downing Street to hear the Prime Minister Stanley Baldwin speak on behalf of the Newnham College Building Fund, she made use of his reported words in *Three Guineas* (1938), pp. 88-95.

faded common sense—for he has failed as a business man—on all projects. Theres nothing in it—nothing in it, he kept saying. Also, nothing doing; nothing doing whatever. I think felt us perhaps more in the swim than himself. I doubt he has any sentiment about the past either: may like George's sons—I don't know. And keeps up with Sophie & Emma Vaughan.[2] So we went & walked in the park. If I can do 25 pages daily I shall be done by Tuesday next. And then the proofs. How its to come out in May, God knows. But I no longer bother much: am doing the difficult North & Sara; but philosophically.

Thursday 9 April

[*Monks House*]

Now will come the season of depression, after congestion suffocation. The last batch was posted to Clark at Brighton yesterday. L. is in process of reading. I daresay I'm pessimistic, but I fancy a certain tepidity in his verdict so far: but then its provisional. At any rate these are disgusting, racking at the same time enervated days, & must be thrown on the bonfire. The horror is that tomorrow, after this one windy day of respite—oh the cold North wind that has blown ravaging daily since we came, but I've had no ears, eyes, or nose: only making my quick transits from house to room, often in despair—after this one day's respite, I say, I must begin at the beginning & go through 600 pages of cold proof. Why oh why? Never again, never again. No sooner have I written that, than I make up the first pages of Two Guineas, & begin a congenial ramble about Roger. But seriously I think this shall be my last 'novel'. But then I want to tackle criticism too. Enough, though. The first task is to resume charge of life: to read Hogarth MSS. & to stir the waters. I've let them get a little stagnant, mildewed.

Dining at Charleston tonight, I'm glad to say. Clive's article on the Q.M. to be discussed. We met Nessa & Angelica in Lewes: & A. looked like the heroine in a Turgenev novel, in her frogged dress & little cap. Judith Bagenal already a woman of 45 with 6 children: husband a clergyman, I think, or Lecturer at the London School of Economics.[3]

2. Sir George Duckworth (1868-1934), Gerald's elder brother, had three sons. Sophia Farrell (c. 1861-1941), the family cook at Hyde Park Gate, was subsequently attached to one or other of the Stephen or Duckworth families until her recent retirement. Emma Vaughan (1874-1960) was a first cousin of both Gerald and VW; her early intimacy with VW had long since lapsed.

3. 'Inside the *Queen Mary*: A Business Man's Dream', by Clive Bell, *The Listener*, 8 April 1936. Judith Bagenal (b. 1918), the daughter of Barbara Bagenal (b. 1891), the Woolfs' apprentice-printer in the early days of the Hogarth Press at Richmond, and her husband the horticulturalist Nicholas Bagenal (1891-1974), was only a few weeks older than her friend Angelica; she did not marry until 1943.

I dont think I said we had taken Morgan to Abinger—a very very bitter cold day: his love, the stout policeman to see him off at Manchester Street. A silent drive, through suburbs, with raked roads: no view: all misted; then sharp to the right & left; up a lane, & there on a little hill was his house; & old Mrs F. columnar with the prominent grey eyes, the maid in apron & false teeth, the handy man & gardener in the distance, all there to welcome him. He has some nickname—"Tong?"—for his mother. And we had a look in at the scrupulous Victorian drawing room, with the silver kettle, & the Richmond drawings; one of Hannah More & Squirrel—& then left.[4]

And then there was Colefax—yes, instantly on us, the first day we arrived, for lunch: in a black beret, & grey tweed coat; dried, like one of the hams in Flint's shop [*in Lewes*]: not improved by sorrow I think, only posed. Poor woman, what a hard nature; so that to lose Arthur only liberates a little misty sentiment. And yet she's brave, I think: but still the hostess, the aspiring, restless, dissatisfied—running, running, like a dog behind a carriage, that always goes too fast. And how she snaps at the other running dogs—Mrs Wigram, Madame de Margerie. We had polite conversation about notables over the fire, & then she left. Rolls Royce: going on to customers, I think.[5]

There are no entries in VW's diary between 9 April and 11 June 1936. On 8 April she posted the final pages of her revised typescript of The Years *to Clark the printers, who were already returning earlier sections in galley proof for correction; however news that her American publishers Harcourt Brace were unable to publish the book until the autumn now provided a welcome respite to VW, whose concentrated work on the revision had already brought*

4. On 2 April, the day before coming to Rodmell, the Woolfs collected E. M. Forster from the nursing home in Manchester Street where he had been recovering from his prostrate operation, and drove him to West Hackhurst, his and his mother's home at Abinger Hammer. R. J. (Bob) Buckingham (1902-75) was a member of the Metropolitan Police Force whom Forster met in 1929 and who became his lifelong and constant friend. Forster invariably called his mother 'Mother'; the 'Tong?' overheard by VW could have been addressed to the cat Toma. George Richmond, RA (1809-96) '. . . sketched Thorntons and Forsters innumerable' (E. M. Forster, *Marianne Thornton* (1956), p. 77); some are listed in P. N. Furbank, *E. M. Forster. A Life*, Vol. II (1978), p. 291 and note. The picture of Hannah More, not apparently by Richmond, is illustrated facing p. 226 of M. G. Jones's *Hannah More* (1952), and is described by Forster himself in his essay on her in *Abinger Harvest* (1936).

5. Sibyl Colefax—who for some years had been running a business as an interior decorator—came to lunch at Monks House on Saturday 4 April; her husband, Sir Arthur (b. 1866), had died on 19 February 1936. Mrs Wigram was Ava, wife of Ralph Wigram (1890-1936) of the Foreign Office (see *IV VW Diary*, 17 and 22 April 1935); and Jenny de Margerie was the wife of Roland de Margerie, First Secretary at the French Embassy in London, 1933-39.

her close to nervous collapse, with familiar symptoms of headache and sleeplessness. She allowed herself four weeks absolute holiday, which she spent largely recumbent at Monks House. On 3 May the Woolfs returned to London, where VW was seen by her doctor, Elinor (Elly) Rendel, who endorsed LW's prescription of a change of scene. Accordingly from 8-20 May, setting out from Rodmell, they made a tour of the west country, driving via Weymouth and Lyme Regis to Cornwall, where they stayed three days with their friends Ka and Will Arnold-Forster near St Ives before returning to Rodmell via Shaftesbury; on 22 May they returned to Tavistock Square for a week, then went again to Rodmell for twelve days over Whitsun, and came back to London on 10 June. These past two months —and indeed the months to come—when VW's underlying anxiety and depression over The Years *produced a state of mind and body which brought her close to suicide, were later recalled by LW as 'a terrifying time'.*

Thursday 11 June

[*52 Tavistock Square*]

I can only, after 2 months, make this brief note, to say at last after 2 months dismal & worse, almost catastrophic illness—never been so near the precipice to my own feeling since 1913—I'm again on top.[1] I have to re-write, I mean interpolate & rub out most of The Years in proof. But I cant go into that. Can only do an hour or so. Oh but the divine joy of being mistress of my mind again! Back from MH. yesterday. Now I am going to live like a cat stepping on eggs till my 600 pages [*of proof correcting*] are done. I think I can—I think I can—but must have immense courage & buoyancy to compass it. This, as I say, my first voluntary writing since April 9th. after wh. I pitched into bed: then to Cornwall— no note of that; then back; saw Elly: then to M.H. Home yesterday for a fortnights trial. And the blood has mounted to my head. Wrote 1880 this morning.

Sunday 21 June

After a week of intense suffering—indeed mornings of torture—& I'm not exaggerating—pain in my head—a feeling of complete despair & failure—a head inside like the nostrils after hay fever—here is a cool quiet morning again, a feeling of relief; respite: hope. Just done the Robsons: think it good.[2]

I am living so constrainedly; so repressedly: I cant make notes of life.

1. It was after delivering the manuscript of her first novel *The Voyage Out* to Gerald Duckworth in 1913 that VW suffered the extended nervous breakdown which culminated in her suicide attempt in September that year.
2. See *The Years*, pp. 71-8.

Everything is planned, battened down. I do ½ an hour down here; go up, often in despair. lie down; walk round the square: come back do another 10 lines. Then to Lords yesterday [*MCC v. Oxford University*]. Always with a feeling of having to repress; control. I see people lying on sofa between tea & dinner. Rose M[acaulay]. E[lizabe]th Bowen. Nessa. Sat in the square last night. Saw the dripping green leaves. Thunder & lightning. Purple sky. N. & A[ngelica]. discussing $\frac{4}{8}$ time. Cats stealing round. L. dining with Tom & Bella.[3] A very strange, most remarkable summer. New emotions: humility: impersonal joy: literary despair. I am learning my craft in the most fierce conditions. Really reading Flaubert's letters I hear my own voice cry out Oh art! Patience. Find him consoling, admonishing. I must get this book quietly strongly daringly into shape. But it wont be out till next year. Yet I think it has possibilities, cd I seize them. I am trying to cut the characters deep in a phrase: to pare off & compact scenes; to envelop the whole in a medium.

Tuesday 23 June

A good day—a bad day—so it goes on. Few people can be so tortured by writing as I am. Only Flaubert I think. Yet I see it now, as a whole: I think I can bring it off, if I only have courage & patience: take each scene quietly: compose: I think it may be a good book. And then—oh when its finished!

Not so clear today, because I went to dentist & then shopped. My brain is like a scale: one grain pulls it down. Yesterday it balanced: today dips.

There are no entries in VW's diary between 23 June and 30 October 1936. Her state of health remained precarious, and the pressures of life in London where, as it seemed to VW, distracted and vociferous politicians were perpetually holding meetings in their flat, impelled the Woolfs to decamp to Rodmell earlier than usual, on 9 July. There they remained, LW going weekly to London, until 11 October. VW rested, read desultorily, played bowls and walked, and when possible laboured, an hour at a stretch, over her proofs of The Years, *which she still hoped to have ready for the Hogarth Press to publish in the autumn; but by the end of August it was apparent that this was beyond her powers. Her letters, mostly written to her relentless correspondent Ethel Smyth, best convey the tenor of her days during this time. Back in London, her health much improved, VW was able again to lead a relatively normal life; but the incubus of her unfinished proofs still oppressed her.*

3. LW's brother-in-law Sir Thomas Southorn (1879-1957) of the Colonial Service, had been appointed Governor of the Gambia after ten years in Hong Kong; he married LW's widowed eldest sister Bella (1877-1960) in 1921.

October 1936

Friday 30 October

I do not wish for the moment to write out the story of the months since I made the last mark here. I do not wish, for reasons I cannot now develop, to analyse that extraordinary summer. It will be more helpful & healthy for me to write scenes; to take up my pen & describe actual events: good practice too for my stumbling & doubting pen. Can I still 'write'? That is the question, you see. And now I will try to prove if the gift is dead, or dormant.

Tuesday 27th. On Tuesday I went to tea with Sibyl.[1] It was a very windy wet evening; leaves swirling along the pavement, people holding their hats & skirts. An oldish shabby man in seedy day clothes opened the door. He might have been a bailiff but was I suppose an auctioneer's assistant. "Lady Colefax?" I said. He shook his head. He thought I had come to see the furniture. Come this way, he said, & led me, or rather disappeared in front of me, into the servants quarters—that unknown region where so many meals have been prepared, when Fielding [*maid*] issued, so discreet, respectable & cordial. Now there were tables set out with dinner services, with bunches of knives & forks, all ticketed & labelled. Fielding came out from the hidden premises, still in her grey dress & apron, but looking blurred & flustered. "I dont know where to put you" she said, in an agitated way, & murmuring something about finding her ladyship, about people being still here, led me finally with apologies to the dining room. That brown festive & somehow succulent room was also up for sale. The walnut table had its ticket & the little glass trees on the mantelpiece & the chandelier. It is a nice warm room I thought sitting down on one of the brown chairs, & thinking how very shy I had been there; yet how glad after, that I had overcome the terror of hair & clothes, & how nimble my tongue became, & how little alarming it was to talk to Sir Arthur on my right, or George Moore or Noel Coward on my left. Yes, I had enjoyed myself in a mixed way there—the feeling was compounded of relief to find so little to frighten & of pleasure to find so much to say—when in peered, in the tentative calculating way of a stranger looking at things he may want to buy, an obviously alien gentleman: the sort of man in a brown overcoat that one sees at sales, but not at parties at Argyll House. And no sooner had he begun sizing up the furniture than two fashionable, dimly recognisable women, peered in; one of whom, the smaller, the vaguely pretty & familiar, recognised me to the extent of smiling & half extending her hand; but clearly my name

1. The widowed Lady Colefax was now leaving Argyll House, Chelsea, scene of her innumerable parties, and her surplus effects were to be sold by auction on the premises. The 'scene' which follows is used as the basis for the concluding pages of 'Am I a Snob?', read to the Memoir Club on 1 December 1936, and posthumously published in *Moments of Being*.

escaped her. And hers only tentatively seemed to me to be Ava Wigram. How sad—how very sad—she said (words I had used to the tremulous & flustered Fielding who seemed, as she agreed, about to burst into tears). 'Yes its sad, very sad . .' I echoed. And then she asked, had I come to see the things? for I was sitting in my chair as if waiting. No, I've come to see Sibyl I said . . & they prowled round: Ava I think surprised, perhaps displeased, at this assumption of superior intimacy. They were tentatively wandering, touching this & that, into the next room, when Sibyl herself peered in: hurried, furtive; summoned me, as if she lifted me, secretly, to some private assignation out of a world now all formal, no longer friendly. And so we crossed into the drawing room, where, with a sigh & some explanations, she shut the door & sank on the sofa.

My bare hand rested for a moment on her bare hand. This is sympathy, I felt: but it must not be emphasised or prolonged. She looked like a dried up bird; marks were cut on either side of her nose. Deep clefts ran under her eyes. But of course she talked facts. Who was that, in the dining room? Ava Wigram. Oh dear—she saw me then? No I think not.

But Sibyl, you must rest?

My dear, how can I rest? The Dr & surgeon said to me You must now take 6 months holiday. But I'm not Greta Garbo . . . Where's tea?

Tea, bread & butter & gingerbread, was brought.

No, everyone says Fielding is a help. I can tell you the truth. I've lived for 35 years with the Irish. She laughs. Then she cries.

But Sibyl, I said, trying to formulate some phrase of affection or regret, you have given . . . yes, passing this house, I've often thought that—seeing the lights.

Oh, in those days I was a millionaire. What could I do but give?

Then compliments to me, which I disdained. You've given to living people . . I've seen Arnold Bennett, George Moore, Noel Coward. . . .

Door opens . . .

Lady Mary Cholmondeley my lady.

Who? I dont know any such person . . Excuse me, I must go & see for myself . . .

And she wont wear spectacles, because of her appearance. I say I dont mind wearing them all day . . (but she doesnt). What were we saying? Yes, those you've named, they were the people I like to think of . . . Glad you've had some tea—this is wretched. No, I cant talk to anyone. I go on. I cant let myself talk, or I should sink into such depths . . . I should never recover. There are my old Aunts, the Wedgwoods. They knew us when we were young—when we were engaged. Yes. I go on, from thing to thing.

In comes Ava & the other woman. Society small talk. We shall see you again. . . .

My dear that woman. I dislike her.

I too, because she makes me dislike her: I dont like disliking people.

Thats true. Stories of Ava's meanness about the Lyttons & the house in North Street. A story about the house in North Street, how she got it for 700 less. And when I woke from the anaesthetic, Michael said to me the house is gone. I said Well, its not our year, thats all about it. Its not our year. After that I got the house for 700 less than I offered—because of the Lyttons, & its been lived in by a madman, its filthy.[2] No, I've always wanted to be able to say if theres anyone you want to meet, I'll arrange it. I wanted to bring people together . . . Now I'm going to do two things. To collect an anthology of love poems. Isnt it odd? When I was a girl of 18 I read a poem & thought I understood it all. At 18—knowing nothing of life. I'm going to collect an anthology for lovers. And in the nursing home I went through letters—little notes from A[rnold]. B[ennett]. from W[alter]. Raleigh.

To turn from dialogue to narrative.

She talked in a scattered nervous way, like a hen fluttering over the edge of an abyss. A brave hen. Her eyes were bright. And they say now that she has cancer in her breast. Nor could I always distinguish between the pose—I am going to show myself poetic & unworldly to Virginia—& the genuine gallantry. She has been too long exposed to artificial light to do without it. She is like a bat in a bright room when she is in darkness. She is blinded by darkness; I mean when she is alone, without the stimulus & direction of other peoples views she is uncertain. Flounders. With us it is just the opposite. But whether I imagined it or not, I still felt something genuinely rising from the depths in her: a desire to fight her adversity, a momentary desire to break down; but then she was up again & off again. When the door opened & Fielding croaked out "The car, m'lady" she was glad of the call to action & we swept through the wind swept fluttering lighted streets, sitting together in the Rolls Royce while she told stories, adequately indeed rather brilliantly, of George Moore & Wells, of Henry James & Carrie Balestier [Mrs Rudyard Kipling]. The machine had got going again, after its momentary paralysis, & she jumped out at Mount Street to pay a business visit. Then she was going to a concert & then to have a supper party

But in this hasty account I have forgotten to describe my farewell to Argyll House, as I walked with her out of the double doors, down the little path, & stood for a moment at the wrought iron gate.

Tuesday 3 November

Miracles will never cease—L. actually likes The Years! He thinks it so far—as far as the wind chapter [1908]—as good as any of my books. I will

2. The Wigrams lived in North (later Lord North) Street, Westminster, where Lady Colefax had bought no. 19, formerly the property of a Mr Brown, solicitor; she alleged that Mrs Wigram had incited the Lyttons to bid against her. Michael Colefax was her son.

put down the actual facts. On Sunday I started to read the proofs. When I had read to the end of the first section I was in despair: stony but convinced despair. I made myself yesterday read on to Present Time. When I reached that landmark I said This is happily so bad that there can be no question about it. I must carry the proofs, like a dead cat, to L. & tell him to burn them unread. This I did. And a weight fell off my shoulders. That is true. I felt relieved of some great pack. It was cold & dry & very grey & I went out & walked through the graveyard with Cromwell's daughters Tomb down through Grays Inn along Holborn & so back.[1] Now I was no longer Virginia, the genius, but only a perfectly insignificant yet content—shall I call it spirit? a body? And very tired. Very old. But at [the] same time content to go on these 100 years with Leonard. So we lunched, in a constraint: a grey acceptance; & I said to L. I will write to Richmond & ask for books to review. The proofs will cost I suppose between 2 & 300 pounds which I will pay out of my hoard. As I have 700 this will leave 400. I was not unhappy. And L. said he thought I might be wrong about the book. Then ever so many strange men arrived: Mr Mumford, mahogany coloured lean, with a very hard bowler & a cane; whom I put in the drawing room with a cigarette; Mr —— very heavy & large, who said Pardon me & knocked at the door. And Lord & Lady Cecil rang up to ask us to lunch to meet the Spanish Ambassador.[2] (I am making up 3 Guineas) Then, after tea, we went to the Sunday Times book show. How stuffy it was! How dead I felt—Oh how infinitely tired! And Miss White came up, a hard little woman, with a cheery wooden face, & talked about her book & reviews. And then Ursula Strachey came across from Duckworths & said you dont know who I am? And I remembered the moonlit river. And then Roger Senhouse tapped me on the shoulder.[3] We went home, & L. read & read & said nothing: I

1. The graveyard, to the north of the site of the Foundling Hospital (demolished in 1926), was known as St George's Gardens; Oliver Cromwell's granddaughter Mrs Gibson was buried here in 1727.

2. Sir Bruce Richmond (1871-1964) was from 1902-37 editor of the *TLS*; VW had been one of his regular reviewers until the earnings from her own books made such journalism unnecessary. The mahogany-coloured man was probably the American writer and sociologist Lewis Mumford (b. 1895) who was in London at this time. The strangers are named by LW as 'Read, Parker &c'. VW had known the Cecils— Lord Robert (see below, 17 November 1936) and his wife Nelly—since the beginning of the century; he was one of the architects of the League of Nations, of which the Deputy-Secretary-General from 1933-36, Señor Don Pablo de Azcárate y Florez (1890-1971), had recently been appointed Ambassador to London by the Spanish Republican Government. The Woolfs did not meet him now, though LW did later.

3. The fourth *Sunday Times* annual Book Exhibition was held at Dorland Hall, Lower Regent Street, from 2-16 November; the Hogarth Press had Stand A10

began to feel actively depressed; yet could make up The Years differently —I've thought of a scheme for another book—it should be told in the first person.—Would that do as a form for Roger?—& I fell into one of my horrid heats & deep slumbers, as if the blood in my head were cut off. Suddenly L. put down his proof & said he thought it extraordinarily good—as good as any of them. And now he is reading on, & tired out with the exertion of writing these pages I'm going up to read the Italian book.

Wednesday 4 November

L. who has now read to the end of 1914 still thinks it extraordinarily good: very strange; very interesting; very sad. We discussed my sadness .. But my difficulty is this: I cannot bring myself to believe that he is right. It may be simply that I exaggerated its badness, & therefore he now, finding it not so bad, exaggerates its goodness. If it is to be published, I must at once sit down & correct: how can I? Every other sentence seemed to me bad. But I am shelving the question till he has done, which should be tonight. Now I must copy out my Daily Worker article; then E. Watson is coming: then Ka to lunch.[4] It is one of the most puzzling situations I have ever been in. Of course we might appeal to Morgan.

Thursday 5 November

The miracle is accomplished. L. put down the last sheet about 12 last night; & could not speak. He was in tears. He says it is "a most remarkable book—he *likes* it better than The Waves." & has not a spark of doubt that it must be published. I, as a witness, not only to his emotion, but to his absorption, for he read on & on, can't doubt his opinion: what about my own? Anyhow the moment of relief was divine. I hardly know yet if I'm on my heels or head—so amazing is the reversal since Tuesday morning. I have never had such an experience before. Now it is pouring

---

there. Antonia White (1899-1980), journalist, advertising copy-writer and author; her autobiographical novel *Frost in May* was published in 1933. Lytton Strachey's niece Ursula (b. 1911) and his last love Roger Senhouse (1900-70) were both in publishing: she worked for Duckworth; he was a partner in Secker and Warburg.

4. Elizabeth Watson (1906-1955), painter, a charming and persuasive Communist friend of Quentin Bell, had prevailed upon VW to contribute an article to the *Daily Worker*: 'Why Art To-Day Follows Politics' was published on 14 December 1936 (Kp C347). 'Ka' Arnold-Forster, *née* Cox (1887-1937), with whom the Woolfs had stayed at her home at Zennor in Cornwall earlier in the year, had been a particularly dependable friend to them both during VW's previous serious breakdown in 1913-14.

& we go down to Lewes for the fireworks.[5] Eth Watson & Ka yesterday
& to the Book Show & walk along V[ictoria?] Street & so on.

Monday 9 November

I must make some resolutions about this book. I find it extremely
difficult. I get into despair. It seems so bad. I can only cling to L.'s
verdict. Then I get distracted: I tried, as an anodyne, to take up an
article; a memoir: to review a book for the Listener. They make my mind
race. I must fix it upon The Years. I must do my proofs & send them off.
I *must* fix my mind on it all the morning. I think the only way is to do
that, & then let myself do something else between tea & dinner. But
immerse in The Years all the morning—nothing else. If the chapter is
difficult, concentrate for a short time. Then write here. But dont dash off
into other writing till after tea. When it is done, we can always ask
Morgan.

Tuesday 10 November

On the whole it has gone better this morning. Its true my brain is so
tired of this job it aches after an hour or less. So I must dandle it, &
gently immerse it. Yes I think its good; in its very difficult way.

Yesterday Barnes came to tea; a very white & black professional young
man. Strained: on a leash: much burdened with his job; & the moral
strain of keeping the BBC up to Cambridge standards. A nice old
fashioned Cambridge young man.[6]

Before that I met L. at the Red Lion & down came Kingsley looking,
I thought pale lead coloured, ravaged, unwholesome. My pity of course
came to the surface; & of course he asked me to review Chesterton's
Au[tobiograph]y wh. he held in his hand. No doubt I could make a living
that way if I chose.[7] In fact the old fountains only want this paving stone
of a book off them to spring up. I wonder if anyone has ever suffered so
much from a book, as I have from The Years. Once out I will never look
at it again. Its like a long childbirth. Think of that summer, every morning

---

5. Guy Fawkes Day—November 5th—is by tradition celebrated with spectacular
   enthusiasm by the various Bonfire Societies in Lewes.

6. George Barnes (1904-60), half-brother of Mary Hutchinson (see below, 10
   December 1936), was from 1930-1935 assistant secretary of the Cambridge University Press, and had now joined the BBC Talks Department, which he was later to
   direct.

7. Kingsley Martin (1897-1969) was editor of the *New Statesman & Nation* from 1931
   to 1960. G. K. Chesterton had died in June this year; his *Autobiography* and *A
   Chesterton Omnibus* were reviewed in the *NS&N* of 21 November 1936 by Kingsley
   Martin himself. The meeting place was the Old Red Lion pub at the corner of Red
   Lion Street and Holborn, across the road from the *NS&N* offices.

a headache, & forcing myself into that room in my nightgown; & lying down after a page: & always with the certainty of failure. Now that certainty is mercifully removed to some extent. But now I feel I dont care what anyone says so long as I'm rid of it. And for some reason I feel I'm respected & liked. But this is only the haze dance of illusion, always changing. Never write a long book again. Yet I feel I shall write more fiction—scenes will form. But I am tired this morning: too much strain & racing yesterday. The Daily Worker article. Madrid not fallen. Chaos. Slaughter. War surrounding our island. Mauron over, & G. Brennan. Dine with Adrian tonight.[8]

Wednesday 11 November

Armistice day—completely forgotten. by us. I'm going along quietly, rather ashamed of my extreme deliberation. Cant review Miss Weeton either. Joe [Ackerley] will only allow me 800 words of unsigned; 1500 of signed. An amusing illustration of the virtues of capitalism. Its the advertisement, not the article, they want. And its the advertisement I dont want. But anyhow the book is bad mostly; & to compress Miss W. into 800 words would not be worth doing in the eyes of eternal truth, or any other. No. The desire to review dies out in me when I have the book. Rather an interesting experiment in its way. Again I am confirmed in my project of some private sheet.[9]

Dined with Adrian last night: a solid man called Rickman there.[10] A. & K[arin] very busy & friendly & both enjoying life more than they did, as I think. A. very tenuous & frail & distinguished. On the whole well in the thick of things, not so aloof as of old. A good deal of p[sycho]. a[nalysis]. talked; & I liked it. A mercy not always to talk politics. L. by

8. The Spanish Civil War had broken out in July when VW was unwell at Rodmell; in early November Madrid (whence the Government had moved to Valencia) came under siege by the insurgent forces of General Franco, and on 9th suffered heavy bombardment. (It did not fall until March 1939.) Gerald Brenan (b. 1894), writer, had lived in Andalusia since 1920 (the Woolfs stayed with him in 1923), but had [now returned to England because of the war. Charles Mauron (1899-1966), Provençal intellectual and a close friend of Roger Fry, who encouraged him to undertake translations (of E. M. Forster, of VW) and to write on aesthetics (see *HP Checklist* 131, 372) when he was forced to relinquish his career as a scientist because of progressive loss of sight.

9. Joe Ackerley, literary editor of *The Listener*, had sent VW a copy of *Miss Weeton: Journal of a Governess, 1807-1811*, edited by Edward Hall, 1936; she did not review the book, but quotes from it in *Three Guineas*, pp. 137-8.

10. Dr John Rickman (1891-1951) was a pioneer of psychoanalysis in Great Britain; from 1931 he edited the *British Journal of Medical Psychology*, and contributed two volumes to those published by the Hogarth Press and the Institute of Psycho-Analysis (*HP Checklist* nos. 172, 409).

the way put down Bertie's book just before we went, & said "Now my mind is made up." He had become an isolationist. I feel I was, for other reasons, these many months: but for different reasons—those I want to explore. But not here.[11] R[ickman].'s family had always lived in Lewes & he remembered the violent Guy Fox days, when you had to wear goggles & wet straw. K. is pleased to make £800: a very dissatisfied woman, since she always emphasises this fact. But I'm no longer so censorious either. Have done 110 pages, & those the worst. Or so I hope.

[*Friday 13 November*]

Another moment of depression, largely caused by dining with Alix & James last night I think.

Tuesday 17 November

Lord Cecil to tea. He has grown large, but still has the angular twisting movements of a thin man. His face is moon shaped; brown & pink—it used to be lank & cadaverous. He is more genial. Indeed, much expanded, & at his ease. A man of the world. A little frieze of still brown hair, very fine, at the back of his head. Bright merry eyes. In good spirits, in spite of the world. But he said, I think there is more vitality both in men & in institutions, than one expects. We have failed (the L. of N.) no matter we must try again. I'm convinced by Winston. An alliance of France England & Russia. B. Russell—insane! Complete insanity! To tell us we are to submit to Hitler! Do what Hitler tells us! What do you think, Sally? Caressed Sally [*dog*] with his long pointed fingers.[12] Had been speaking

11. Bertrand Russell, in his recently published book, *Which Way to Peace?*, argued for the extreme pacifist position; in Chapter 3 he defined 'Isolationism' as 'the doctrine that Great Britain ought to fight in defence of the British Empire . . . it maintains that every State is justified in defending its own territory, but not in engaging in war for any other cause.' LW, who had already reached the painful conclusion that rearmament was a necessity to counter the growing threat of Fascism, did not in fact support an isolationist foreign policy, but favoured a system of strong international alliances.

12. Lord Robert Cecil (1864-1958), third son of the third Marquess of Salisbury and husband of VW's old friend Lady Eleanor (Nelly) Cecil, was created Viscount Cecil of Chelwood in 1923, when Baldwin put him in charge of League of Nations affairs, to which, in office or out (he resigned in 1927 over the Conservative government's refusal to agree to parity with America in naval disarmament), he devoted his great energies, influence, and intellectual powers; he was President of the League of Nations Union from 1923-45. Winston Churchill (1874-1965), at this time in the political wilderness, preoccupied with the growing menace to peace from the resurgent power and convergent tactics of Hitler and Mussolini, was an advocate of rearmament and alliances to strengthen the authority and effectiveness of the League.

33

in M[ancheste]r. When he repeated B[ertie].s arguments people's faces fell flat. The L. Mayor of M. said to him We want Dalton as leader. Atlee's not a colourful man. Said the peoples political sense is unerring & right.[13] One working man said to another, Vansittart has far too much say in things. Quite true. V. ruled Simon. Simon the worst F[oreign]. S[ecretary]. ever been. Hoare a complete disappointment. They shd. have put in Halifax. Not a genius but courageous. Eden young, poor, ambitious: his only interest politics. Human nature being what it is, therefore . . . No, has no opinion of Eden. Shd. have resigned. The country sees through him. Very difficult to know when to resign, as I found.[14] Phil Baker shd. do half what he does, & should drink wine. Everyone loves him—the boys at the Treasury will do anything for him. But dictates letters as he drives.[15]

Had been taken to see Mussolini. An absurd fellow. There he sat at the end of a very long room, making eyes at me (he made eyes). That doesnt impress me. The F.S. should submit his facts to the P[ermanen]t. officials but shd. control them. They write jargon, as my father used to say. Gave the impression of extreme well being: a saucepan gently simmering on the comfort & consideration of 70 years. Best type of Eng. Governing class I suppose: the flower of 19th Century civilisation: urbane, broadminded, kind & hopeful. Much more cheerful than the intellectuals. Is it that he has not so much mind? Compare him with Bertie or Aldous. Inclined to mock the earnest intellectual. Very nice of him to come of course. I was flattered. And it was raining & he went home in the Tube. Very poor he said. Had sacrificed 5 or 6000 a year when he gave up the bar. Cdn't afford a car. Anything else? Knows human nature from one angle. Likes

13. Clement Attlee (1883-1967), deputy-leader since 1931, succeeded George Lansbury as Leader of the Labour Party on the latter's resignation in October 1935 (see *IV VW Diary*, 2 October 1935); his unassuming and laconic style did not inspire popular enthusiasm. Hugh Dalton (1887-1962), a more flamboyant character, was a Fabian Socialist educated at Eton and King's College, Cambridge, where he studied economics under Maynard Keynes; a Labour MP and member of the party's National Executive, he now acted as opposition spokesman on foreign affairs.

14. Sir Robert Vansittart (1881-1957) was Permanent Under-Secretary of State at the Foreign Office from 1930-38, the influential if controversial adviser to three successive Foreign Secretaries: Sir John Simon (1873-1954), Sir Samuel Hoare (1880-1950), and Mr Anthony Eden (1897-1977). The latter finally resigned in February 1938 because of irreconcilable differences with the then Prime Minister Mr Neville Chamberlain, who thereupon appointed Lord Halifax (1881-1959) to the office.

15. Philip Noel-Baker (1889-1982), an old friend of the Woolfs, was a tireless worker for peace and disarmament and a close associate of Lord Cecil in his League of Nations activities. A Labour MP from 1929-31, he had been re-elected to the House of Commons in a bye-election in July 1936.

it. Not much deluded I shd. say. Less of a fanatic, or more concealed than of old. Winston on side of Franco, because he has friends in that camp. But the people dont respect Winston. He changes his mind & policy. Baldwin a complete failure. He shd. have resigned when Hoare did. Awful Mansion House speech.[16] No leaders. Young men on L[abour]. side kept back till theyre over 40. I wanted to ask him to call me Virginia but refrained. Thats about all. And Chapman coming today. Mauron dined on Sunday; another nice man. telling humorous stories of Roger: his car: Josette.[17]

Tuesday 24 November

Here I am cleft as usual in my little stick. So free & so cabined. The future. What I'm to write. Yes I think I can write &c. Began 3 Gs. yesterday. & liked it. Today the old symptoms—t. of l., cant get rid of it—the swollen veins—the tingling; the odd falling; feeling of despair. Brain not fully blooded. Hot & cold. I'm glad, how odd, that I'm lunching with Clive to meet Mme de Polignac. That I've a new black felt hat, bought yesterday after having Ethel S. to lunch. Glad too that Helen Anrep is dining with me: that I shant be alone, alone I fall into those trances, comas, which are I suppose t. of l: but so frustrating [?], when I want to be clear & to read.[18] A curious throbbing this disease produces. But I've been on the whole vigorous & cheerful since the wonderful revelation of L.'s that night. How I woke from death—or non being—to life! What an incredible night—what a weight rolled off!

Yeats' anthology out.[19] Am I jealous? No: but depressed to feel I'm not a poet. Next time I shall be one. And I've touched ground. Whatever happens I dont think I can now be destroyed. Only work work is essential. Roger . . . . &c.

Very cold & dank. We came up on Sunday through the fog. Figures suddenly emerged. The kind man with a paper. I walked by his side

16. By tradition, the Prime Minister's speech at the annual Lord Mayor's Banquet in the City of London presents a wide-ranging review of Government policy. On 9 November 1936 Mr Baldwin, who was temperamentally averse to the problems of foreign affairs, confined himself to platitudinous utterances on the subject of peace and war.

17. R. W. Chapman (1881-1960), Secretary to the Delegates of the Oxford University Press 1920-42, and editor of Jane Austen's novels and letters, came to tea with the Woolfs on 17 November. Josette Coatmellec was a consumptive Frenchwoman whose love affair with Roger Fry ended in her suicide; see *II VW Diary*, 14 June 1924.

18. For Helen Anrep, see Appendix I; she and Gerald Brenan dined with VW this evening; LW was out. For Clive Bell's luncheon party, see below 25 November 1936. 't. of l.': VW's term for the menopause.

19. *The Oxford Book of Modern Verse*, edited and introduced by W. B. Yeats.

leading the car. It crashed into a wall. The wing buckled. Walked by the kerb all through Wimbledon & Wandsworth. The kerb ended. Here I was lost in a trackless mist. & so on & on. A little boy emerged—a street ruffian. People lined the pavement watching the lost cars. Another man led us; offered me a rest. In the car I looked & found the paper was The Blackshirt.[20] Out again. Just as we thought we must find a garage & come home by tube a bus driver told us that in 200 yards it would be clear. So, miraculously, it was. Glass clear—lit up, & so home.

I have also written my memoir [*Am I a Snob?*]. Indeed The Years has taught me something about scenes. But are they worth doing? I want a spell of private writing—with Nessa perhaps. Dotty much praised. My hackles rise—that she shd. lend herself to puffing, shd. print her photograph. Old E. says this is a detail. I daresay she's right—with all her faults she has scope, proportion. She touched me by giving me her little notebook of the woman in the train, well bound, with an inscription.[21] When I'm low, how this touches me. But I will not be low. Up & off again, like the gull in the poem. Meredith's.[22] I wish I cd. invent a way of dashing down criticism, as I do here.

Wednesday 25 November

L.'s birthday. Lunch with Clive. The Princess. a waxy solid handsome lady with kind eyes. Not formidable. Ros. Eddy Ld Berners.[23] Talk all

20. *The Blackshirt* was the weekly organ of the British Union of Fascists.
21. Dorothy (Dotty) Wellesley—Lady Gerald Wellesley (1891-1956)—had sponsored and edited the 'Hogarth Living Poets' series; she was a particular friend and admirer of W. B. Yeats, in whose idiosyncratic anthology her own verse was given inordinate exposure, a feature of his selection generally unfavourably noticed in the press; the puff and photograph have not been discovered. In Ethel Smyth's autobiographical *Streaks of Life* (1921) she refers to 'my notebook, still a cherished possession' in which she took down the words of her heroine in the episode called 'An Adventure in a Train'; its present whereabouts are untraced.
22. See the last stanza of Meredith's 'Juggling Jerry' (1859):
    'I mind it well, by the sea-beach lying,
        Once—it's long gone—when two gulls we beheld,
    Which, as the moon got up, were flying
        Down a big wave that sparked and swelled.
    Crack, went a gun: one fell: the second
        Wheeled round him twice, and was off for new luck:
    There in the dark her white wing beckon'd:—
        Drop me a kiss—I'm the bird dead-struck!'
23. The Princesse de Polignac, *née* Winnaretta Singer (1865-1943), inheritor of an immense fortune from her American father's sewing-machine patents and widow of Prince Edmond de Polignac, was a notable patron of the arts and sciences in Europe. She was an old friend of Ethel Smyth's, and Clive Bell had dined with her

very brilliant. The usual sense of having done with that when it was half over. And the different changes of light. The intimacy. Then the super-ficiality. Very cold. An eyeless grey day. The same subjects recur. Sybil. Ld. B's jokes, the same. Ros. muffled & tentative. I, rather too erratic. The P[rincess]. out of things. And I must lunch with her & Ethel tomorrow.

Friday 27 November

Lunch, again with the Princess, at Claridges, where in all my 54 years I have never been. Like a private house—sumptuous yet refined. The French—little Polignac niece—a singer: Nadia Boulanger, the Conductor —wear black. Sir R. Storrs. Like George [Duckworth]: stolid, second rate, a snob, & very vain.[24] Also disapproving. The genial man gone cold, like red beef congealed. And what a lot to eat! Half left on our plates. Ethel talking with admirable racy English. The smart white faced lady in pearls listening. How she went to prison. The Ps not very vital. Boulanger the one I liked—a vital shabby governess type. French, very, so erect & smart, not dowdy, only shabby: one cheap brooch in the right place. Little P. devitalised, pretty, said F. women must have men. B[oulanger] says they rule France through influence. Its true they cant get passports officially: but unofficially get everything run everything. Storrs masculine. Only has wine at night. Reads seasonally: Dante: Homer: Shakespeare.

K. Martin, approached by one of the King's circle, was asked to write an article, revealing the facts from the King's side.	Is writing his memoirs—a conceited man—a non-entity I think, but wants to come here. Why? P. tactfully puts a shade over Ethel. Ethel the only one with brains (except B.) (I think I must read Dante of a morning.) So not a very exciting or formidable affair. I walked home; in my black

the preceding November in Paris; but previous attempts by both Ethel and Clive to bring her and VW together had miscarried, and this was in fact their first meeting. Clive's other guests were the novelist Rosamond Lehmann (Mrs Wogan Philipps), second of John Lehmann's three elder sisters; the Hon. Edward Sackville-West (1901-65), Vita's cousin and the heir to the Sackville titles, a writer and musician; and the composer, author, painter and eccentric Lord Berners (1883-1950).

24. Marie-Blanche de Polignac, *née* di Pietro (d. 1958), was not in fact a niece of the Princess but the wife of Comte Jean de Polignac, a kinsman of her late husband; she was a soprano, and the hostess of a musical *salon* in Paris. Nadia Boulanger (1887-1979), French composer and teacher; she conducted the London Symphony Orchestra at the Queen's Hall on 24 November, and was giving further concerts at the Wigmore Hall in December. Sir Ronald Storrs (1881-1955), an authority on the Near East and formerly Governor of Jerusalem and the Judea, of Cyprus, and of Northern Rhodesia, was an urbane man of the world and connoisseur; his memoirs, *Orientations*, were published in 1937.

Then he was told to wait. Finally he came out after the great splash with a very inaccurate version. The King's men told him in strict secrecy about the sexual difficulty.

velvet; not a bad day. Happy to be so unconcerned.

L. has a confidential story about the King & Mrs Simpson, told him in secret by K. Martin.[25] Dined alone, read Sir T. Browne's letters. I am getting back to solid food again. My wits fritter easily, but not so easily. I must work, as I told Sally G. who suffers I think considerably & shd. break off her engagement instead of being psycho-analysed. Ott. after tea—& am I to tell her about Stephen Tennant & Lytton's letters?[26] She will erect herself & puff out her cobra hood if I do.

Sunday 29 November

On the contrary, she was attenuated, & abashed. She put up no fight; was all shyness & anguish, & agreed with me about S.T. & the letters. Only had forgotten there was anything intimate. St. came in by chance; had a little rucksack. So she took pity on him &c. Age is coming on her. much shrivelled; all the down worn off.

Monday 30 November

There is no need whatever in my opinion to be unhappy about The Years. It seems to me to come off at the end. Anyhow to be a taut real strenuous book: with some beauty & poetry too. A full packed book. Just finished it; & feel a little exalted. Its different from the others of course: has I think more 'real' life in it; more blood & bone. But anyhow, even if there are appalling watery patches, & grinding at the beginning, I dont think I need lie quaking at nights. I think I can feel assured. This I say sincerely to myself; to hold to myself during the weeks of dull

25. As the result of a self-imposed press silence, the British public at large was ignorant of the facts and/or speculations concerning the new King's private life, and of the constitutional crisis threatened by his determination to marry the twice-divorced American, Mrs Wallis Simpson; the first reference to the matter—the 'great splash'—in the London papers was on 3 December. Kingsley Martin's leader 'King and Country' appeared in the *NS&N* of 5 December 1936; it advocated the solution of a morganatic marriage.

26. Elizabeth (Sally) Graves (b. 1914), came down from Somerville College, Oxford, in 1935, and met the Woolfs later that year; LW encouraged her to write *A History of Socialism* which the Hogarth Press published in 1939. She married R. C. Chilver, a civil servant, in January 1937. For Lady Ottoline Morrell, see Appendix I. The Hon. Stephen Tennant (b. 1908), painter and aesthete and a nephew of Margot Asquith; Ottoline had apparently let him have letters written to her long ago by Lytton Strachey in which he repeated indiscreet stories concerning Virginia and Leonard's engagement.

anticipation. Nor need I care much what people say. In fact I hand my compliment to that terribly depressed woman, myself, whose head ached so often: who was so entirely convinced a failure; for in spite of everything I think she brought it off, & is to be congratulated. How she did it, with her head like an old cloth I dont know. But now for rest: & Gibbon.[27]

Monday 7 December

Now, we are—without a King? With a Queen? What? The Simpson affair is on the surface. It was on Wednesday 2nd Dec that the Bishop commented on the Kings lack of religion. On Thursday all the papers, The Times & D[aily] T[elegraph]. very discreetly, mentioned some, domestic difficulties; others Mrs Simpson.[1] All London was gay & garrulous—not exactly gay, but excited. We cant have a woman Simpson for Queen, that was the sense of it. She's no more royal than you or me, was what the grocer's young woman said. But today, before the PM. makes his announcement to the House, we have developed a strong sense of human sympathy; we are saying Hang it all—the age of Victoria is over. Let him marry whom he likes. In the Beefsteak Club however only Lord Onslow & Clive take the democratic view. Harold [Nicolson] is glum as an undertaker, & so are the other nobs.[2] They say Royalty is in Peril. The Empire is divided. In fact never has there been such a crisis. That I think is true. Spain, Germany, Russia—all are elbowed out. The marriage stretches from one end of the paper to another. Pictures of the D. of York & the Princesses fill every cranny. Mrs Simpson is snapped by lime light at midnight as she gets out of her car. Her luggage is also photographed. Parties are forming. The different interests are queueing up behind Baldwin, or Churchill. Mosley is taking advantage of the crisis for his ends. In fact we are all talking 19 to the dozen; & it looks as if this

27. VW had been invited to write on Edward Gibbon to mark the bicentenary of his birth (8 May 1737); her article, 'The Historian and "The Gibbon"', appeared in the *TLS* on 24 April 1937 (Kp C348).

1. The address to his Diocesan Conference on 1 December by the Bishop of Bradford, in which he regretted that King Edward was not a more regular churchgoer and adverted to the religious nature of his forthcoming coronation, was reported in some Northern provincial newspapers on 2 December, and this released the flood of comment and news on the subject of the King and Mrs Simpson which thenceforth poured from the National press.

2. On Sunday evening, 6 December, after driving up from Rodmell, the Woolfs went round to Clive Bell's flat in Gordon Square. He was now a member of the Beefsteak Club, as were Lord Onslow (5th Earl, 1876-1945), Chairman of Committees and Deputy-Speaker of the House of Lords, and Harold Nicolson, an active member of the House of Commons. The latter left a vivid record of day-to-day social and political movements during the abdication crisis: see his *Diaries and Letters 1930-39* (1966), edited by Nigel Nicolson, who gives a convenient summary of the facts.

one little insignificant man had moved a pebble wh. dislodges an avalanche. Things—empires, hierarchies—moralities—will never be the same again. Yet today there is a certain feeling that the button has been pressed too hard: emotion is no longer so liberally forthcoming. And the King may keep us all waiting, while he sits, like a naughty boy in the nursery, trying to make up his mind.

Coming past the Palace last night there were crowds waiting in the cold—it is very cold—cant write—with eyes fixed on the windows. Two or 3 lights were burning in upper windows.

Tuesday 8 December

Now what am I to do about these proofs? send them off? But how exercise patience & courage? What shall I write? Sketches I think . . .

Thursday 10 December

The chops & changes of the Crisis wd. be worth investigating, had I time. It is a foggy cold morning, as damp & dismal as can be. I have just turned on my electric light. Has the King abdicated? I think so. At 3.30. Baldwin will speak. Each day has been different—jud[g]ing from the papers & shop sampling. The Times reiterates No one has hurried the King. We sympathise but . . . it is for his Majesty to decide. The Rothermere press & Churchill, who was shouted down in the House, have subsided. No more talk of coercing the King. Mrs Simpson at Cannes says she is ready to withdraw from an unhappy & untenable position. Cars, black cars, drive constantly to & from Fort Belvedere where the King is immured, some (Labour Party gossips) say drinking: the papers say consulting a vet, about a dog who has hurt her paw. Baldwin goes down constantly: the King is rude & drunk. Last night the Queen & Pss Mary went. A brake laden with luggage was seen to leave the fort. No royal engagements are kept. It is a time of mourning. The Q. visits old curiosity shops & is said to have bought a gold frog. Meanwhile 'the people' have swung round to a kind of sneering contempt. "Ought to be ashamed of himself" the tobacconists young woman said. Timmy the Q's sec: told George Bergen that abdication is settled. Maynard says no: the difficulties, legal &c, are too great. Bergen says Timmy says he is now merely haggling for a sufficient income. K. George left him nothing; & he has lavished money & jewels on Simpson.[3] All the royal dukes are in &

3. The American painter George Bergen—in England at this time—was through his friendship with both Duncan Grant and 'Timmy'—the Hon. Gerald Chichester (1886-1939), a private secretary to Queen Mary since 1926—the channel for gossip between the Court and Bloomsbury. A dependable and detailed account of the whole business of the abdication is given by Frances Donaldson in her biography, *Edward VIII*, 1974; from this it appears that VW's reports are in the main well-founded.

out & the Chancellors & solicitors with their black boxes. Last night Mary [Hutchinson] on the telephone said that to her certain (through Lady Diana [Cooper] & Lord Brownlow) knowledge the King some weeks ago, finding Mrs S. cooling, became mad with rage; also was entirely possessed against all friends advice, of some bourgeois (her word) obsession about marriage: insisted, after 2 years of license, that the marriage service was essential—though Mrs S. did not wish it—& went to Baldwin. Baldwin, Mary says, then learnt of the situation for the first time. The rest followed.[4] She says all his friends think him insane. He could have gone on with Mrs S. as mistress till they both cooled: no one objected. Now he has probably lost her, & thrown away the Kingdom & made us all feel slightly yet perceptibly humiliated. Its odd, but so I even feel it. Walking through Whitehall the other day, I thought what a Kingdom! England! And to put it down the sink . . . Not a very rational feeling. Still it is what the Nation feels. The Times is discreetly sarcastic at his expense: has a curl of disdain in its tone; quotes, in its leader this morning, letters which beginning earlier in the week with hysterical sympathy, now say Our sons & brothers gave their wives & lovers & also their lives for the country. And cant the King do even this—? But everything now hardens into the certainty that the King cant do this, & will follow his luggage to Cannes. Rather an ignominious flight—I feel again. He will live in America, Bergen says, Timmy says: & the Q. wants him to abdicate. I gather that Lady Diana, en route for [Fort] Belvedere, called on Jack [Hutchinson] in his nursing home, to ask his advice. He advised that the King should professedly give her up: abstain from her society for one year; & then revert to her. But apparently the King's little bourgeois demented mind sticks fast to the marriage service. Mrs S. gives him, unlike all the other mistresses, physical relief: her time synchronises with him. And it is said that she is now a little cooling; so what will they do in Kentucky? I am reluctant to end this page, because it is I think the last entry I shall make in this book on the subject of Edward the Eighth. If I write tomorrow, it will be in the reign, I suppose of Albert the First—& he's not, so Mary says, a popular choice. Let it be. This

4. Mary Hutchinson, *née* Barnes (1889-1977) was the wife of St John (Jack) Hutchinson, KC (1884-1942); her long affair with Clive Bell, which began early in the war, had ended ten years earlier; but although moving in a more sophisticated social milieu than the Woolfs, the Hutchinsons always remained on friendly terms with them and Bloomsbury. The sempiternal beauty and charmer Lady Diana Cooper (b. 1892) and her husband Duff Cooper, MP (1890-1954), at this period Secretary of State for War, had been guests of the King during his summer holiday cruise off the Dalmatian coast with the then not divorced Mrs Simpson. Lord Brownlow, 6th Baron (1899-1978) was Personal Lord in Waiting to King Edward VIII; at the King's request, he accompanied Mrs Simpson when she left England for Cannes on 3 December in an attempt to escape the attentions of the press.

afternoon I shall go down in the fog to the hub of the universe, & hang about the H. of C.

Thursday 10 December

This is the first hour, or since it is 5.30, & the abdication was announced at 4, the first hour & a half, of the new reign.[5] Yes, I thought, its silly buying sachets at Stags & Mantles: I will go to Westminster. A bus took me to the top of Whitehall. There traffic was turned off & I dismounted. Whitehall was full of shuffling & trampling. People going both ways. Not a thick crowd—a moving crowd. A very beautiful yellow brown light: dry pavements: still lamps lit. Lines of light at Parliament Sqre. & the houses of Parliament in silhouette. The lamp burning in the watch tower. Opposite the Horse Guards there was Ottoline, black, white, red lipped coming towards me. She intercepted my impulse to escape. We turned & walked on. Then Bob Trevelyan loomed up. We three stood & talked. They said it was dreadful ... I'm very sad ... Its a pity. Has he abdicated? I asked. No, but they say he will. No one knew if he had or hadn't. A stir of uneasy feeling . . most people half sad, yet also ashamed, yet also excited. Bob left us, not before tho' he's hummed & hawed & said that Hawtrey didnt think so badly of the D. of York.[6] Then on we wandered down the yellow brown avenue. We looked up at the beautiful carved front of —what office? I dont know. Thats the window out of which Charles the First stepped when he had his head cut off said Ottoline, pointing to the great lit up windows in their frame of white stone. So my mother always told me. I felt I was walking in the 17th Century with one of the courtiers; & she was lamenting not the abdication of Edward—still though people shuffled this way & that— but the execution of Charles. Its dreadful, dreadful, she kept saying. Of

Bob raising his eyebrows & qualifying in his usual way.

also, Under wh. King Bezonian? Speak or die?

---

5. The Instrument of Abdication was signed by the King on the morning of 10 December; that afternoon his Message to Parliament announcing his decision was read in the Commons by the Speaker, and the Prime Minister Mr Baldwin then gave a plain and straightforward account of the sequence of events which led to it and of his own part in them. King Edward VIII's reign formally ended with the passage through both Houses of Parliament of the Abdication Bill the following day, 11 December, when he was succeeded by his brother Albert, Duke of York, as King George VI.

6. The poet and classical scholar R. C. (Bob) Trevelyan (1872-1951) was an old friend of the Woolfs, and had shared a house with Roger Fry in the 'nineties. He, LW, and R. G. Hawtrey (1879-1975), economist and Treasury official, were all at Trinity College, Cambridge, and 'Apostles'. The quotation in the margin is from *II Henry IV*, V, iii.

course Portland's glad he should go.[7] Poor silly little boy—He always lost his temper. No one could ever tell him a thing he disliked. But to throw it away . . . . Still he hadn't yet, so far as we knew, thrown it away. 'It' seemed then, looking at the curved street, & at the red & silver guards drawn up in the court-yard with the Park & the white government buildings behind, very stately, very lovely, very much the noble & severe aristocratic Stuart England . . However, nothing seemed to happen. And she had a tea party: so we hailed a taxi. Have you any news? the man said. No. I dont know . . What do you think? I say he should. We dont want a woman thats already had 2 husbands & an American when there [are] so many good English girls . . We were thus driving & talking when a newspaper car drove by with the word Abdication very large on a placard. It stopped near us; & the first papers in the bale were bought by Ottoline & me.

This is the first moment of the new reign, I said to Milly, at the open door of number 10: but she was agitated because some unexpected visitor—a man in a coat—had come—[8]

Sunday 10 December

Then we had the Broadcast.[9] "Prince Edward speaking from Windsor Castle"—as the emotional butler announced. Upon which, with a slight stammer at first, in a steely strained voice, as if he were standing with his back against the wall, the King (but that is already vanishing & attaching itself to York) began: "At long last . . I can speak to you . . . . . The woman I love . . . I who have none of those blessings . . ." Well, one came in touch with human flesh, I suppose. Also with a set pigheaded steely mind . . . a very ordinary young man; but the thing had never been done on that scale. One man set up in the Augusta Tower at Windsor addressing the world on behalf of himself & Mrs Simpson. Out in the Square there was complete emptiness. All the life had been All the withdrawn to listen, to judge. Miss Strachan [*clerk*] wdn't omnibuses listen, for fear of sympathising. And then Edward went on were empty. in his steely way to say the perfectly correct things, about the Constitution, the P. Minister, her majesty my mother. Finally he

7. Charles I was beheaded in 1649 on a scaffolding erected in front of the Banqueting House in Whitehall. Portland—the 6th Duke (1857-1943)—was Lady Ottoline's half-brother.
8. Millie—Mildred Ellis—was Lady Ottoline's long-established and trusty parlourmaid. Since 1927 the Morrells had lived at 10 Gower Street, Bloomsbury.
9. HRH Prince Edward (as he was now styled) broadcast to the nation from the Augusta Tower of Windsor Castle at 9 pm on 11 December; he was introduced by the Director General of the BBC, Sir John Reith (1889-1971). The closing words were spoken by the BBC's chief announcer Stuart Hibberd (1893-1983).

wound up, God Save the King with a shout; after which I heard his sigh go up, a kind of whistle. Then silence. Complete silence. Then Mr Hibbert saying. And now we shut down. Good night everybody. Goodnight; & we were tucked up in our beds.

The Woolfs drove to Monks House for Christmas on 18 December, and were to remain there until 16 January. On Christmas Eve they drove some fifteen miles north to Fletching, where Edward Gibbon is buried in the mausoleum of his friend the Earl of Sheffield in the north transept of the church. On Christmas day they had lunch and tea with the Keyneses at Tilton; and on New Year's Eve they dined at Charleston.

Thursday 30 December

There in front of me lie the proofs—the galleys—to go off today . . a sort of stinging nettle that I cover over. Nor do I wish even to write about it here.

A divine relief has possessed me these last days—at being quit of it— good or bad. And, for the first time since February I shd. say my mind has sprung up like a tree shaking off a load. And I've plunged into Gibbon & read & read, for the first time since Feb. I think. Now for action & pleasure again & going about. I cd. make some interesting perhaps valuable notes, on the absolute necessity for me of work. Always to be after something. I'm not sure that the intensiveness & exclusiveness of writing a long book is a possible state: I mean, if even in future I do such a thing—& I doubt it—I will force myself to vary it with little articles. Anyhow, now I am not going to think can I write? I am going to sink into unselfconsciousness & work: at Gibbon first: then a few little articles for America; then $\left\{ \begin{array}{l} \text{Roger} \\ \text{3 Guineas} \end{array} \right\}$ Which of the 2 comes first, how to dovetail, I dont know. Anyhow even if The Years is a failure, I've thought considerably; & collected a little hoard of ideas. Perhaps I'm now again on one of those peaks where I shall write 2 or 3 little books quickly: & then have another break. At least I feel myself possessed of skill enough to go on with. No emptiness.

& in proof of this will go in, get my Gibbon notes & begin a careful sketch of the article.

— 1937 —

1937

VW's niece Judith Stephen came for two nights to Monks House on 2 January, and, other than Charlestonians, further visitors were the Robsons, the Keyneses, and Rosamond Lehmann and her husband who came to tea on 10 January; on 8 January the Woolfs went to tea with Elizabeth Robins in Brighton. With the following entry VW begins a new book, DIARY XXVI.

Sunday 10 January

Another windless perfectly brilliant day. And Tommie is dead & buried yesterday, just as Clive was saying that no one had died lately. Also there's Tonks dead in Chelsea.[1] But Tommie's death is a queer piece of work. We said on the whole perhaps it was a good thing, because for the past 3 or 4 years we had scarcely seen him: when we did he seemed ravaged by his own misery; couldn't work, had been a failure; tore everyone & everything to bits in a kind of egotistic rage. Rosamund L. said he would sit on the lawn there by the hour denouncing women, complaining of his own lot. And he had grown immensely fat, white unwholesome looking, & was said to drink.

Duncan said he spent most of his time in the public houses near Tottenham Court Road, drinking. And Julia said no one could live with him, though she loved him. Everybody said one thing or another, as if he had cocked a snook at them & gone off. My own intercourse with him broke over that bust, when I took a shudder at the impact of his neurotic clinging persistency, & perhaps behaved, though I didn't think so at the time, unreasonably, perversely. But he was such an egotist; such a man for confiding, & getting wound up in the miserable intricacies of his own psychology. I remember his launching out on the history of his own suffering, which began, of course, with his mother & father, misunder-

---

1. Henry Tonks (1862-1937), Slade Professor of Fine Art in the University of London 1917-30; he sat next to VW at a dinner (see *IV VW Diary*, 6 March 1935) which recalled to her his visit to Gordon Square to criticise Vanessa's pictures thirty years before. He died at his Chelsea home on 8 January. The Hon. Stephen (Tommy) Tomlin, sculptor, died on 5 January. VW met him first in 1924, and in the summer of 1931 reluctantly agreed to sit to him; the original plaster of his portrait head of her is at Charleston, and lead casts are at Monks House and in the National Portrait Gallery. In 1927 he married Oliver Strachey's elder daughter Julia Strachey (1901-1979), but they had not lived together for some years.

standing him as a child. Then there was Garrow's death;[2] then the difficulties with Julia; how she fell in love with someone; how he still loved her. But the odd thing was that he had, years ago, great sensibility; a human charm, & sympathy—for instance when Duncan was ill at Cassis —I remember how he came into the drawing room at 37 [Gordon Square] with his arms open: Nessa kissing him in tears. And then when Carrington killed herself he came round that evening to break the news so that I shouldn't get the shock first hand. Yes. I remember his curious squashed face, his suppleness, something eager & friendly & warm, quivering about him. Here he sat in the drawing room, when we lit the stove for the first time & the room was full of smoke: & he talked about me then: my work; not himself. He was extremely loquacious. Anything set him off. And he had a great gift for making people love him: Angus, Eddy, Barbara.[3] But there was something twisted, deformed in him: some shudder & profound distaste, & uneasiness. Lately he had tried, I think, living alone in the country; didn't like it; used to haunt public houses; deserted the respectable. N. & D. say they hadn't seen him for a long time. And then he catches some germ, goes to a nursing home in Boscombe, from the [Augustus] Johns where he was staying; the only person he wanted to see was Oliver [Strachey]: & so died aged 35. A tragic, wasted life: something wrong in it; & wrong that we shouldn't feel it more .Yet one does, by fits & starts, this very fine spring morning.

Adrian, who rang up, said it was a very good thing his death. That he was in a hopeless state. He had not heard of the death, only had overheard someone say "Poor Tommie".

I have scribb[l]ed this down, because it is an off morning. I am trying to screw myself to send an article to the N.S. on fishing.[4] My Gibbon wants polishing; & I've got out of the mood. So let me go on to Elizabeth Robins & Octavia Wilberforce, before Quentin & Angelica come to our last roast turkey.[5]

2. Tomlin, who abandoned the study of law at Oxford to become a sculptor, was the second son of the High Court Judge Lord Tomlin (1867-1935); his elder brother George Garrow Tomlin (b. 1898) was killed in a flying accident in 1931.

3. For Duncan Grant's illness at Cassis, see *III VW Diary*, 23 January 1927; for Lytton Strachey's devoted companion Carrington's suicide, see *IV VW Diary*, 12 and 17 March 1932. Angus Davidson (1898-1980), who had worked in the Hogarth Press for three years until 1927 as potential manager, was now living in Cornwall writing a biography of Edward Lear (published 1938). Eddy was Edward Sackville-West (see above, 25 November 1936, n. 23); and Barbara, Barbara Bagenal; she had been a contemporary of Carrington's at the Slade and was a close friend.

4. VW's article 'Fishing', animated by the book *My Sporting Life* (1936) by Major J. W. Hills, MP (see below, 18 January 1937, n. 9), did not appear in the *NS&N* and was first published posthumously in *The Moment*, 1948 (Kp A29).

5. Elizabeth Robins, until her return to America in 1940, shared a house in Brighton with Dr Octavia Mary Wilberforce (1888-1963); the latter was the great-grand-

They live in one of those rounded houses in Brighton—Montpelier Crescent—a shaped crescent; a solid, clean, rather unsophisticated house. Miss R. sat alone in her own room, a back room, with well polished tables, rather solid books, covers on things, a sketch of W. Wilberforce over

little glass stands for table legs

the fire; a large coal fire; everything spick & span; documents on the writing table; as if she had good housemaids. She is old, but gnarled. Her face is perhaps slightly rouged, but crinkled. Her hair is curled & grizzled. Her eyes L. said, a faun's eyes: very intense: suddenly intensifying, like an actresses. All her movements angular, intense, grown rather rigid. She examined us, very tensely, but compactly, about her book.[6] And Lord knows if we told the truth, or if it was any good what we said, for she is past her prime; but has had an interesting highly charged past evidently; she held much in reserve. I suspect she has had a great many emotional & physical experiences, which have crystallised into packed & solid views; on life, on religion, or rather the dislike of religion; on work, on sex. She was launching into a panegyric, very tense too & stylised, upon O.W: when in she came—a very fresh coloured healthy minded doctor, in black, with loops of silver chain, good teeth, & a candid kind smile which I liked. Opposite my plate she had put a little china statue of W.W[ilberforce].: opposite L.'s another of Hannah More. This led us—she & me—to discuss our, I think mythical, relationship: from that we slipped to education —she had none: to families—she had 9 in family; & they coerced her, though unwanted, through pressure of antiquated family feeling & propriety, to stay at home. Only through a great struggle did she break off & become a doctor. People in Brighton, where she has practised for 13 years, play Bridge sometimes 6 or 7 hours a day; dont have children; their husbands go to London to work in offices. They sometimes take a drive —& so on. I had the flushed & exuberant feeling which means I liked being there & talking & we broached many scraps of memories. How

daughter of William Wilberforce (1759-1833), 'The Emancipator', whose widowed sister Sarah became the second wife of VW's great-grandfather 'Master' James Stephen (1758-1832); she had no children by him. Hannah More (1745-1833; see below), the 'bishop in petticoats', was a good friend of both Wilberforce and Stephen.

6. Elizabeth Robins had written a book about her brother called *Raymond and I* which Macmillan had offered to publish but on terms unsatisfactory to her. In December 1936 she had sent the manuscript to the Woolfs, and it was this book they were now to discuss with her. They agreed that the Hogarth Press should publish it, but in the event Colonel Robins objected to its appearing in his lifetime, and it was not until the year after his death in 1955 that LW—to whom Elizabeth Robins had bequeathed the copyright—published it with an explanatory foreword. At his suggestion, Macmillans then brought out an American edition (see LWP, Sussex, I.Q.4).

father asked E.R. to come when he gave his Forgotten Benefactors talk. "But I couldn't say what it made me feel. . . . It was tremendous. Very courageous of him. I couldn't think how he had the courage. No I could never say what I felt about that speech".[7] So she clips & cuts off. And about 7 we went out into the dark crescent, & I thought, Now what are they saying about us? & hoped I had made a good impression. O. said I must have great knowledge of other peoples lives to write A R. of O. That pleased me, having read that morning something about my 'lyrical emptiness'.[8] Oh but I'm going to think of Cleopatra's Needle when I get on to my old nightmare: & so canter past it. I think I can too. And L. is giving Sally a run after her bath: I must go & work in this extraordinary hot spring morning. Work, work, work—thats my final prescription—so have written to [Bruce] Richmond.

The Woolfs returned to Tavistock Square on the afternoon of Saturday 16 January. VW has misdated the following entry Sunday Jan. 18th.

Sunday 17 January

Home again. Poor L. grumbling, making Mabel a peg on which to hang his misery oh dear. But rather a good evening all the same. Not a nice morning though: proofs; dust. How quiet London is however. Not a sound. I must make up my mind to work, & break through the enchanted circle of [*illegible*]. First I must tidy up: throw away all the old Years litter get things clean & fresh. Lunch with Clive tomorrow to meet I dont know who. That great mystery rather amuses me. I think Jack Hills & Violet Dickinson.[9] A great many MSS to read. I shall also go to the Nat Gall. & to the Zoo.

Raymond:
Mary Baker:
Virginia Brett:
Tom Eliot:

7. Cf Sir Leslie Stephen's *Mausoleum Book*, edited by Alan Bell, 1977, p. 98: 'On 20 October 1895 I gave a lecture at the Ethical Society upon "Forgotten Benefactors". . . . the intention was to speak of Julia [his wife] without mentioning her name.' The lecture was published in vol. II of his *Social Rights and Duties*, 1896.

8. Although the phrase 'lyrical emptiness' is not actually used, the thought is expressed in a discussion of VW's writing in the chapter on 'The Romantic Novel' in Philip Henderson's book *The Novel Today* (1936) which she may have read.

9. John Waller (Jack) Hills, MP (1867-1938) was the widower, and Violet Dickinson (1865-1948) originally the friend, of VW's half-sister Stella Duckworth who died in 1895, and thus were both among her oldest friends. Clive's guests in fact were, besides Raymond Mortimer and T. S. Eliot, his rich American flame Mary Baker (see *IV VW Diary*, 18 July 1932) and the Hon. Virginia Brett, eldest daughter of the 3rd Viscount Esher.

Thursday 21 January

News that Miss West is dying of pneumonia.[10] A melancholy walk with L. in the rain. The usual thoughts: & this too; that I was too aloof, & never friendly eno', & never asked her to dine. I must conquer this aloofness if I possibly can. So little one can do; but at least do it if possible. Such a mute relationship. I pass her room, & think I might have gone in; & now never shall.

[Friday 22 January]

Miss West died yesterday. And Miss Howlett reproaches Miss Bevan, ill at Worthing. And Miss Hepworth is now seeing L. about a job.[11] It pours. Last night I turned Nessa to steel by talking about J.'s essay on Roger—a most curious transformation: as if some tigress lay in a cave, growling.[12] Vita to lunch today. Polishing Gibbon. Will now I think do the A. Artists [?] leaflet—& then? Oh some stuff for the NS?[13]

Saturday 23 January

A dripping foggy day: Miss West's funeral at Golders Green. The same table, the same flowers: a little purple coffin: a large eagle like parson: & a scatter of brown, dowdy, very old & feeble spinsters: Miss Howlett chief mourner. Miss Howlett with knotted hands: an old pink [?] face; blue steady aged eyes. Nothing dingier & less forcible cd. be imagined. And we were forced to wail through hymn 478 or some such number; about saints receiving their due; alleluia. Only the hired man from the undertaker, or one of the crematorium servants sang: once a

---

10. Margaret West had been ('far and away the best': *VI VW Letters*, no. 3214) manager of the Hogarth Press since early in 1933.

11. Miss Rosa Howlett had shared a home with Margaret West; Miss Bevan had worked under her at the Hogarth Press; Miss Barbara Hepworth was to replace Miss Bevan as assistant manager and traveller.

12. Before he went to China in 1935, VW encouraged Julian Bell to write down his recollections of Roger Fry; he did so in the form of 'A Letter to A.', which he described as 'by way of being my last testament on a number of subjects', and sent it home in March 1936, hoping the Woolfs might publish it entire in their *Hogarth Letters* series. VW who was then not well had it typed, but it was not until June that she read it, and in a letter to Julian of 28 June (unpublished, King's College, Cambridge) both praised and criticised and explained why they could not publish it. She did not hear from him again until the end of the year, when he admitted that he had been hurt by her response. The essay was in the end published by the Hogarth Press in the posthumous volume *Julian Bell: Essays, Poems and Letters*, 1938 (*HP Checklist* 426).

13. This could be read as 'American articles leaflet' or 'Allied Artists leaflet'; but neither can be satisfactorily explained. For Vita Sackville-West, see Appendix I.

woman piped up: but gave out. L. & I sat grimly. The attendant then touched a spring, & the little coffin slid through; after which we gathered in the cloister & inspected the wreaths. Miss Howlett then was led forward, & formally shook hands, & thanked us for our letters. As for Miss West, had she been a kitten or a puppy I think one wd. have felt as much. And yet there was something alive, humorous, kindly, & even merry in the basement room where she sat surrounded with neat papers; a spotted horse; a carved wooden flower, & a piece of green linoleum. Miss L. came up and said she was left executor of what little money belonged to Margaret. One of the wreaths was what L. called a best seller's wreath. Miss Delafield was there.[14] But I think on the whole Miss W. enjoyed the H.P. She liked literary parties, & had an unselfish, quite disinterested temper. But its the service—the unreality.

Thursday 28 January

Sunk once more in the happy tumultuous dream: that is to say began 3 Guineas this morning, & cant stop thinking it. My plan is to write it out now, without more palaver, & think perhaps it might be roughed in by Easter; but I shall allow myself, make myself, scribble a little article or two between whiles. Then I hope to float over the horrid March 15th [*publication date of* The Years]: wire today to say Years havent reached America. I must plate myself against that sinking in mud. And so far as I can tell, this method is almost too effective.

& ended it 12 Oct. 1937 (provisionally that is)

L. seeing Miss Lange upstairs;[15] dining with Hutchinsons to meet Wells; & now must rush up to lunch.

Friday 29 January

Wells rather shrunk. Hair still brown, but has the dyed appearance of hair that is brown on an old face. Lines more marked: skin less plumped out. He was very affable: put both hands on top of L.'s to signalise his regret I suppose for their quarrel. Budberg is a sympathetic broad faced slow moving soft eyed slav; dignified & sincere I think. Not a nonentity. Even able to impress her slow broken English upon H.G.'s little sparrow

14. Miss Lorna Lewis was one of Margaret West's circle of women friends, as was E. M. Delafield (1890-1943), author of the best-selling *Diary of a Provincial Lady* (1931)—*not* published by the Hogarth Press, though her *Ladies and Gentlemen in Victorian Fiction* was to be, in June 1937 (*HP Checklist* 407).

15. Miss Lange was to succeed Miss West as manager of the Hogarth Press; she had previously worked for the publishing houses Longman, Green & Co., and Rich & Cowan.

chirp.[16] He sat by me, & was [a] little apprehensive of the highbrow at first I think. We made talk about Scotland; then he laughed at Compton Mackenzie, always dressing up:[17] then switched off on to the poverty of authors, & instanced Arnold [Bennett]. He totted up A.'s expense & receipts. Then we got on to Russian politics, so, somehow to Tom Eliot. Tee Ess he called him with a hiss of despite; & then proceeded to say how he, which I think meant we, had been the death of English literature. Afraid of being vulgar, thats what was at the root of it. And Tom's religion. By that we came to the Archbishop. I wonder—if I had any brains in my foolish little head, I wish they would reveal this to me: does Cosmo Gordon Lang ever alone at dead of night face his Trinity? We all have to—But does he . . . & so on.[18] He likes to be listened to; & to chatter on, loosely generally, as he said to me when the gentlemen came upstairs. We've had a loose general kind of talk. Then he lay back in the arm chair, put his tiny hands & still tinier feet together, & chirped away. Sometimes Budberg interrupted with her solemn intoning: attacked Germany; defended France. It was old man's talk; mellower than I remembered; mischievous; eyes a little bleared; kindly in his way; merry. Had been warned off the air for some joke; off the Daily Mail for another joke. He gives the impression that on the whole he is a detached satisfied little man; conscious of his lack of distinction; prone to snap at any pretence; introduced "my father the professional cricketer";[19] content I think with his position, & immensely interested still. He wished to live to be 170. is 70. Had one seen him behind a counter he wd. have seemed the very type of busy little grocer. I couldnt ever detect any mass behind his pointed beak. And I suspect that when he faces his Trinity at dead of night there are a good many books that he thinks justly, trash: & he shuffles his hands among the loose innumerable pages; & then snaps at Culture; but remembers that he has done a vast mass of work, & thinks it wont all die; & is amused at the place he has made—from Bromley Kent to Regents Park: the Baroness; & I suppose the greatest circulation in the whole world. A humane man in some corner; also brutal; also entirely without poetry.

This I scribble with the snow darkening my skylight; we are not going

16. The Woolfs had not seen H. G. Wells since his 'quarrel' with LW (see *IV VW Diary*, 25 March 1932); since then he had settled into a stable alliance with the Russian Baroness Moura Budberg (1892-1974), though in separate houses; his was at 13 Hanover Terrace, Regent's Park.

17. Compton Mackenzie (1883-1972) was a very successful and cosmopolitan author; he chose to live in the Outer Hebrides.

18. The Most Rev. Cosmo Gordon Lang (1864-1945) had been Archbishop of Canterbury since 1928.

19. Wells's father, besides being a professional cricketer, had been an unsuccessful shopkeeper in Bromley.

to Rodmell: I need not present prizes to the young Animal Fanciers; & we are waiting to see if Mr Rich of Rich & Cowan will tell us about Miss Lange.

Slight uneasinesses pass like vapour already over me: prelude to The Years. Miss Bevan has read the proofs but says nothing; Miss West presumably had read & did say nothing. And I must expect that attitude on my friends part. And I must dig myself deep in 3 Guineas ... so that the other voices are scarcely heard. It will be immensely depressing; but I've no doubt I can survive.

Friday 12 February

Why should I write here? Only that I am devilishly anxious. L. is going to a Harley St specialist at 4 today to get a report: whether the sugar means diabetes or prostate gland or nothing serious. And I must face facts: how to keep cool, how to control myself, if it is a bad report. Work is my only help. That is the conclusion I came to last night. Probably it is only a question of treatment. Anyhow we shall soon know, unless he keeps us hanging about.

It is a very fine cold day & we are going straight on down to Rodmell where there is a L. party meeting & Q. to dinner. I have been writing hard since Jan 28th at 3 Guineas, & must simply keep at it. Even if I dont manage to finish it,—& I expect I shall—it is the one support. I have got it into trim—that is I can I think pour all I want to rather roughly & quickly into this form. Various people skim in and out: but that becomes very dim. We had too the anxiety about Julian—he tells C. Mauron that he means to enlist for Spain. Cornford's son was killed there last week.[1] But I cant feel that now anything like so much as I did before this happened. Nessa was in one of her entirely submerged moods on Monday when we went in. Always that extraordinary depth of despair. But I must fight, thats my instinct. And happily these statements may be extreme; but we are faced with a horrid afternoon; & cant ignore it. Odd tho' how

---

1. Propelled by emotions and reasons both personal and political, Julian Bell resigned his professorship at Wuhan University, and sailed for Marseilles at the end of January 1937. He had asked his mother to go out and meet him in France, but it was from Charles Mauron that she first learnt, early in February, of his already fixed intention to go on directly to Spain to join the International Brigade. Although their correspondence had been very full and intimate, Julian's decision came as a great shock to Vanessa, and she implored him to return to England to discuss his future plans with her and others; and this in the event he did (see below, 12 and 14 March 1937). John Cornford (1915-1936), poet and communist, the son of VW's old pre-war Cambridge friends Francis and Frances Cornford, was killed on the Cordoba front at the end of December, fighting with the International Brigade. (See Stansky & Abrahams, *Journey to the Frontier*, 1966).

any kind of action—that we have to get ready & go—makes thinking impossible. I feel like the man who had to keep dancing on hot bricks. Cant let myself stop. Hence I suppose I write here; wh. explains why Tolstoy & his wife kept diaries.

Monday 15 February

Oh it was heavenly driving down to Rodmell on Friday evening with that weight off us! I walked Harley Street up & down up & down for an hour; people looked at me; I bought a paper; dropped my handkerchief; always returned to the swing doors of 149. People kept on going in & out. & I hardly could make myself turn my back. At last just before 5 L. came in his new light overcoat, & smiled. Well he was quite composed. And the whole thing at once fell into different proportions. Graham thinks its only a case of diet: eats too great a whack of sugar; wdn't even examine him for diabetes; said nothing about prostate gland; found all organs very healthy; told him to continue eating as before until Hensman communicated. And L.'s symptoms are almost over.[2] So as I say we drove down, in that odd relieved state which seems as much physical as mental; as if one's body could unfurl; & become warm & sleepy. Got to MH. only at 7.30. had to dine hurriedly; Q. rang up to say his car had broken down. The meeting. N. Lyons sprightly & talkative;[3] Q. came at 9.30; in gum boots wet through; had dinner at 10.30: went back over the downs in the rain. And over us brooded the same delicious ease & content, as if another space of life had been granted us.

On Sunday the O. had 2 little mildly appreciative notes about The Years; & I observed, with pleasure, that all praise & blame & talk about that book seems like tickling a rhinoceros with a feather. This is true; & remarkable. I connect it partly with my 1932 philosophic revelation: one doesnt matter: also with my present absorption in Three Guineas.[4]

Thursday 18 February

200	I have now written for 3 weeks at 3 Guineas, & have done
38	38 pages. Now I've used up that vein momently & want a
1600	few days change. At what? Cant at the moment think. And
600	a kind gentleman from the Motor Union has troubled my
7:600	peace with a copy of the Saturday Review (USA) in which I

2. LW's specialists were Dr George Graham of Harley Street and Mr J. Stuart Hensman of Chester Street.

3. A. Neil Lyon (1880-1940), author and journalist, of Rock Cottage, Southease.

4. The references to 'Mrs Woolf's new novel . . . so long and pleasurably anticipated' occur in the 'Books and Authors' column of the *Observer*, 14 February 1937. For her 'philosophic revelation' see *IV VW Diary*, 2 October 1932: '. . . all this flitter flutter of weekly newspapers interests me not at all. These are the soul's changes.'

am called a maker of films & laces; a sitter in shaded drawing rooms, & so on.[5] Now I will use a few minutes to lay this demon. I am quite sure that the next lap of my life will be accompanied with whistlings & catcalls in this strain. If I live another 15 years & go on writing they will probably change their tune. The question I have now to settle is what 'attitude' to adopt. This kind of sneer has an inhibiting effect for the moment. Of course reason tells me that it is the Proletarian growl trying to rationalise itself. But I must be quit of the need even of defending myself. I want to forge ahead, on my own lines. To do this I must always have a book or article on foot: except when we can escape, as I hope in June, to other settings. But in London where I am exposed all day & every day to criticism some plating of resolution is absolutely needed. And I think I've got it by the tip of the tail—a new kind of indifference. I experiment with snubs & sneers. How little they matter in the sum! how little they count with other people—how little the goodness or badness of my books affects the world. And there is the world—represented by picture galleries, the Caledonian Market, Gibbon, Nessa, going to MH., walking, planning new arrangements of the room, & always throwing my mind 2 or 3 miles ahead.

Stephen Spender came to tea & dinner the other day [16 February]. Rather a beautiful if too conventionally poetic young man: sunk cheeks, large blue eyes, skin always burning; great enthusiasm, but now tempered, & rather metalled because, having married, his friend, the male, joined the F Legion, is fighting in Spain; Inez, who is political in the Oxford way only, sits at Brussels studying Spanish MSS.[6] Stephen finds this intolerable. Why then did you marry, we asked, more or less. To stabilise himself; because he dreaded the old Brindled Tom puss life of William [Plomer], safe by the fireside. Now is torn two ways: so Inez sits there, in order, should he be killed in Spain—but he's only broadcasting—she may have her job to fall back on. A curious interpretation of marriage, dictated by the guns. I like him: told him not to fight. He said it was the easiest thing to do. I said give up speaking—he said But it brought in money. He argued that we cannot let the Fascists overrun Spain: then it'll be

5. By Herbert J. Muller in his article 'Virginia Woolf and Feminine Fiction', *Saturday Review of Literature* (New York), 6 February 1937; see *M&M*, pp. 360-66.

6. The poet Stephen Spender (b. 1909) had made a somewhat impromptu marriage in December 1936 to Agnes Mary ('Inez') Pearn, a student of Spanish poetry whom he met while speaking at an Aid for Spain meeting at Oxford. His friend and companion of many years, T. A. R. (Tony) Hyndman, thereupon joined the International Brigade, and Spender was now going to Spain to take up what proved to be a delusory broadcasting post in Valencia. For his own account of these matters, see his autobiography, *World Within World*, 1951 (where Hyndman is called 'Jimmy Younger').

France; then us. We must fight. L. said he thought things had now gone so far it did not matter. Fighting did no good. S. said the C.P. which he had that day joined, wanted him to be killed, in order that there might be another Byron. He has a child's vanity about himself. Interesting to me at the moment, as I'm working out the psychology of vanity. Then he went to speak about Spain at the Friends House, & we to Uncle Vanya. A very cold night. I have left out my lunch with Christabel, & various other entertainments. Oh yes, I'm rather nervous about March 15 but can hold myself very much aloof. We were dining with the MacCarthys, but 'the eldest Miss Cornish died suddenly last night at St George's Hospital—so she must put you off'.[7]

Friday 19 February

The difficulty wh. now faces me is how to find a public, a way of publishing, all the new ideas that are in me? I've written this morning 3 descriptions for Nessa's pictures: they can be printed by us no doubt, & somehow put into circulation. But then theres in my drawer several I think rather good sketches; & a chapter on biography. Clearly I have here in the egg a new method of writing criticism. I rather think so. I feel that I want some private way of producing these studies; these adumbrations. If one writes them for a paper the attitude changes. Theyre not Times articles or N.S. articles: yet I dont want to keep them till theyre books, or flutter them out separately . . . Lord knows. Anyhow I like the fruitful sense it gives me.[8]

Yesterday Ethel Sands in black & silver fur to tea; early; had been to Eltham House:[9] on top of her Eth Williamson, striding, masculine, shooting her linen as it used to be called. Ethel flitting by the rich dusk of high liberal life; full of swerving half sentences; betwixt & between.

7. Chekhov's *Uncle Vanya*, with Harcourt Williams in the name part, was being performed at the Westminster Theatre. VW had been to lunch with Christabel—now Lady Aberconway (1890-1974)—on 10 February. The dinner with Desmond and Molly MacCarthy (see Appendix I) was cancelled because of the death of the latter's sister Margaret Warre-Cornish.

8. VW and Vanessa Bell were apparently planning a collaborative work to consist of 'incidents' described by VW and illustrated by Vanessa; by 24 February 1937 (see below) this project seems to have acquired the title 'Faces and Voices', though it never in fact materialised; nor at this time did the chapter on biography—'a possible leader on Biography' also referred to on 20 February—though VW's perennial interest in the subject achieved published form in her essay 'The Art of Biography' in the *Atlantic Monthly* in 1939 (Kp C359).

9. Eltham House was the grand Kent mansion recently completed for Stephen Courtauld on the site of Eltham Palace (residence of English Kings from Henry III to Henry VIII) where his architect's incorporation of the spendid Tudor Great Hall, the only relic of its royal past, had given rise to controversy.

Talked of her own funeral: this was my private joke with her—Then L. came & we talked about India. E. had been impressed by the Eng. Civilian: most of all by the rains: how the temp. fell, like this, she drew her finger along the table cloth. Then I forget—I flirted with old Ethel: about her golden wedding present. Nan [Hudson] used to know about water gilding. The Sinclairs see no danger ahead for England.[10] One of her nephews tho' says this is his last winter's hunting. Eth has a telescope wh. she will sell us cheap. Off she went. Ethel stayed on. We discussed the young; catastrophe; she went, with the usual sweetness, to sit with Nan who has laryngitis. Molly's sister scalded her foot & died of heart failure.

Saturday 20 February

I turn my eyes away from the Press as I go upstairs, because there are all the Review Copies of The Years packed & packing. They go out next week: this is my last week end of comparative peace. What do I anticipate with such clammy coldness? I think chiefly that my friends wont mention it, will turn the conversation rather awkwardly. I think I anticipate considerable lukewarmness among the friendly reviewers—respectful tepidity; & a whoop of red Indian delight from the Grigs who will joyfully & loudly announce that this is the long drawn twaddle of a prim prudish bourgeois mind, & say that now no one can take Mrs W. seriously again. But violence I shant so much mind. What I think I shall mind most is the awkwardness when I go, say to Tilton or Charleston, & they dont know what to say. And since we shant get away till June I must expect a very full exposure to this damp firework atmosphere. They will say its a tired book; a last effort . . . Well, now that I've written that down I feel that even so I can exist in that shadow. That is if I keep hard at work. And there's no lack of that. I discussed a book of illustrated incidents with Nessa yesterday; we are going to produce 12 lithographs for Xmas, printed by ourselves. As we were talking, Margery Fry rang up to ask me to see Julian Fry about Roger.[11] So that begins to press on me. Then

I suppose what I expect is that they'll say now Mrs W. has written a long book all about nothing

10. Sir Archibald Sinclair, 4th Bt (1890-1970), MP and Leader of the Parliamentary Liberal Party, was Ethel Sands's nephew.

11. Margery Fry (1874-1958), JP, prison reformer, educationist, was the most devoted of Roger Fry's six sisters, and was left his literary executor. Having asked her to write his life, she collected for or directed towards VW relevant documents, information, and, as in this case, people. Her nephew Julian Edward Fry (b. 1901), Roger's only son, educated at Bedales School and from 1919-22 at King's College, Cambridge, had then left England permanently to become a cattle-rancher in British Columbia. In 1929 he had married Eva Hambleton—a marriage which was later dissolved.

L. wants if possible to have 3 Gs. for the autumn: & I have my Gibbon, my broadcast, & a possible leader on Biography to fill in chinks.[12] I plan to keep out of literary circles till the mild boom is over. And this, waiting, under consideration is after all the worst. This time next month I shall feel more at ease. And its only now & then I mind now . .

Sunday 21 February

Isherwood & Sally [Chilver] last night. I[sherwoo]d rather a find: very small red cheeked nimble & vivacious. We chattered. He lives in a pension at Brussels; is heir to an E[lizabe]than house near Manchester; & likes my books.[13] The last put some colour into my cheeks. He said Morgan & I were the only living novelists the young—he, Auden, Spender I suppose—take seriously. Indeed he admires us both I gathered warmly. For M.'s books he has a passion. "I'll come out with it then Mrs Woolf—you see, I feel youre a poetess: he does the thing I want to do . . . a perfect contraption." But I was satisfied with my share of the compliment wh. came very pat in these days of depression. Auden & he are writing away together. He does the prose, A. the poetry. A. wants innumerable blankets on his bed; innumerable cups of tea; then shuts the shutters & draws the blinds & writes. Id. is a most appreciative merry little bird. A real novelist, I suspect; not a poet; full of acute observations on character & scenes. Odd how few 'novelists' I know: it wd. interest me to discuss fiction with him. Sally rather smudged & pale: but then Id. & I were such chatterboxes. Suddenly he said he must meet John Andrews at Rules & motor to Croydon. has to fly to Paris for one day today.[14] Such is the life of the young when theyre not preparing revolutions. One of the most vital & observant of the young: & a relief after the mute dismals of the others. In fact both he & Sally now think things are going well in England, & that Madrid wont fall. So we chop & change. I've now 'done' 8 incidents. Julian Fry alas for tea.

12. George Barnes had asked VW to give a talk for the BBC in April in a series called 'Words Fail Me'; see below, 3 April 1937.

13. Christopher Isherwood (b. 1904), two of whose books had already been, and two more were to be, published by the Hogarth Press, was living a nomadic life on the continent with his German lover, trying to evade the latter's conscription into the *Wehrmacht*. He was at present in London for rehearsals at the Mercury Theatre of *The Ascent of F6*, the second of three plays which he wrote in collaboration with his friend the poet W. H. Auden (1907-1973). Isherwood was due to inherit both Marple Hall and Wybaslegh Hall (where he was born) near Stockport in Cheshire on the death of his uncle.

14. John Andrews, unidentified; Rules Restaurant, Maiden Lane; Croydon—London's airport.

FEBRUARY 1937

[Monday 22 February]

Julian Fry last night. Stories about his ranch. The condition of the beef trade. Unfinished work: thin cows sent to England. Stories of dances: driving home; "lit up": we gave him the honk honk honk & the ra ra ra; my wifes passionate: they say a man marries a woman like his mother: no dont send me that letter. I like to know of it (Roger's praises) but if it were there in an envelope I cdn't read it. Stayed from 5:15 to 12. & oh I was sleepy after talking to G. Sturgeon in R[ichmon]d Park.[15] No time. The translator coming

[? Tuesday 23 February]

That extraordinary scribble means, I suppose, the translator coming. Madame or Mlle Youniac(?) Not her name.[16] And I had so much to write about Julian, who is half a sensitive suppressed intellectual, living with rather acute affections & perceptions in Roger's shade. (I was devoted to him: but he wanted me to hate my public school. And I never got enough of the open air, till Joan took us to Failand. Even then I was afraid of lambs. And then I drank too much after bump suppers at Cambridge . . Oh Roger always had so many things on hand. One felt one didnt come up to his standard. Then there was Champco: & the Ott. I didnt develop that side of me till later. But I had a few days quite alone with him—let me see (he's very precise) that was July 1934. We drove from Dieppe to Dijon. I had the impression that he was much happier. At Norwich one day the car punctured; & we didnt meet & so on, & I said to Eva, a few years ago he'd have been raging & ramping—now he was as calm as anything.)[17] What I meant was, this the shady civilised side is only half of Julian: the other is the ordinary Colonial, which I like too; all this expert talk about cattle; & the coyotes, & how they ride. A good rider is a man who can jump into the saddle of an unbroken horse, & sit him while he breaks in two. How Julian did this, & cdn't catch onto the saddle & fell: & Eva wdn't let him mount; but he has a great affection for that horse. A boy of 16 is now in charge. The reason they wear high heeled

15. The Woolfs had been for a walk in Richmond Park on Sunday afternoon with LW's youngest sister Flora and her husband George Sturgeon.
16. Marguerite Yourcenar (b. Brussels 1903), whose translation of *The Waves* was published in Paris as *Les Vagues* in 1937 (Kp D27).
17. Because of their mother's illness and incapability, Julian Fry and his sister Pamela had as children been cared for by Joan Mary Fry (1862-1955), another of Roger Fry's sisters, and at one time lived with her in lodgings on a farm near their grandparents' home, Failand House, near Bristol. Both Elspeth Champcommunal, widow of a French painter, and Lady Ottoline Morrell had been close friends of his father's during Julian Fry's youth.

boots is so that they dont catch in the stirrups. Only through wearing those boots was he now here. All the beef is sold to the liners going to China. Beef is always good on ship—not mutton. And he likes riding all day after his cattle; & thinks, at night, if he has rounded them up that he has done something. Doubts sometimes crop up I suspect; about his wife too. But one doesnt know how one makes these decisions. Roger always gave him very good advice. rather casually I gather. And he drank a bottle of claret, 2 glasses of vermouth, & got a little "lit" as he would call it. And he wd. have stayed talking about Canada till one. I suppose the stimulus of society. So I've no time or room to describe the translator, save that she wore some nice gold leaves on her black dress; is a woman I suppose with a past; amorous; intellectual; lives half the year in Athens; is in with Jaloux &c, red lipped, strenuous; a working Fchwoman; friend of the Margeries; matter of fact; intellectual; we went through The Waves. What does "See here he comes?" mean & so on.[18]

And the Dr. says L. is quite normal! So all that might have been spared us.

[Wednesday 24 February]

Dearest Virginia, I am back when you get this, alive Westminster: will you send word to 19 North Street when & where I can come & see you? 6 o'clock or dine alone Sibyl . . . Paris. 12. 23.II.1937. This significant & illegible card has just been brought me by L. & I copy it as material for a memoir: raw matter to serve in writing the history of my own times: also to fill 5 minutes before luncheon. I'm off again, after 5 days lapse (writing Faces & Voices) on 3 Guineas; after a most dismal hacking got a little canter, & hope now to spin ahead. Odd that one sometimes does a transition quite quickly. A quiet day for a wonder—no one seen yesterday: so I went to Caledonian market, cdn't find spoon shop; bought yellow gloves 3/- & stockings 1/- & so home. Started reading French again: Misanthrope & Colette's memoirs given me last summer by Janie: when I was in the dismal drowse & cdn't fix on that or anything.[19]

Today the reviewers (oh d—n this silly thought) have their teeth

---

18. Edmond Jaloux (1878-1949), French novelist and influential literary critic, and an admirer of VW's novels: see his *Au Pays du roman* (1931) and the weekly *Les Nouvelles littéraires* no. 593 (1934); after her death he described her as 'un des très grands écrivains de ce temps . . . une des lumières spirituelles de l'Europe.' The Margerie family moved in literary as well as diplomatic circles in London and Paris.

19. Jane-Simone (Janie) Bussy (1906-60), painter, daughter of the French painter Simon Bussy (1870-1950) and his wife Dorothy, née Strachey (1866-1960); in 1934 she had given VW French lessons, and in July 1936 sent her a copy of Colette's *Mes Apprentisages* (1936). *Le Misanthrope* (1666) by Molière.

fixed in me; but what care I for a goosefeather bed &c. In fact, once I get into the canter over Three Gs. I think I shall see only the flash of the white rails & pound along to the goal.[20]

Sunday 28 February

I'm so entirely imbued in 3 Guineas that I can hardly jerk myself away to write here. (here in fact I again dropped my pen to think about my next paragraph—universities—how will that lead to professions & so on.) Its a bad habit. Yesterday it was effectively broken by Desmond who came punctually at one, & stayed till 7.15. nor did we stop talking all that time. Nor was I once bored or wished it to stop. A greater tribute to D. cdn't be paid. What did we talk about? The Amberley Papers: the Russells: her self conscious control: how she lies on the floor in an attitude calculated to attract, but pretends to ignore it.[21] Now I like nothing better than conscious allurement, D. said. I said was he no longer attracted. And he cried out No, its all gone—all gone. As a man in a train said, I'm not impotent, but I've had enough. This may have been to shut off all thoughts of the nameless American lady. Anyhow, he was well lit—dear old Desmond—as round as a marble: a paunch pendant; but nearly bald: with an odd 18th Century look, as if he had been dining at the Club with Johnson—a kind of Goldsmith or Boswell; a congenial spirit. And as full of human kindness as a ripe grape with juice. I think he had set himself now not to write a great book but to be nice to other people. What can I do for you, was his last remark on the stairs. Alas, he carried off The Years, wh. means—well, never mind. We talked—so easily & merrily. I went back to old talks with Lytton—talking shop about Kipling's style: he had the same quotation—about the man who cut his throat & looked like a robin redbreast—that I had.[22] Then how Jack Squire has imposed another false self upon his true self, which is sensitive, unhappy. He dresses up as Dr Johnson, but a Johnson without the power of speech. Lives now with

20. 'What care I for a goose-feather bed
       With the sheet turned down so bravely-O?
    For tonight I shall sleep in a cold open field
       Along with the Raggle-taggle gipsies-O!'
                    Song.
21. *The Amberley Papers. The Letters and Diaries of Lord and Lady Amberley*, edited by Bertrand and Patricia Russell, was published by the Hogarth Press in March 1937 (*HP Checklist* 405). Patricia ('Peter') Russell, *née* Spence, was Russell's third wife, whom he married in 1936; she was some forty years younger than him.
22. See *Something of Myself* (1936) by Rudyard Kipling, p. 87: 'When the fog thinned, I looked out and saw a man standing opposite the pub where the barmaid lived. Of a sudden his breast turned dull red like a robin's, and he crumpled, having cut his throat.'

Miss Warrender & drinks: she teaches him not to drink & he teaches her to drink.[23] So to the death of Margaret Cornish after scalding her foot in St George's Hospital. He was rung up as he was working at 2: went to the hospital; saw she was dying, so red & panting. Told her not to be afraid. Molly too deaf to hear so went home. D. & Cecilia [*her sister*] sat there. Her breathing was like a saw going up & down. And they prolonged it with oxygen; so that she lay tortured till 6 when they heard the stump of the nurses bringing early tea, & the voices of children like birds, & then she died. Dear old Desmond, infinitely human & sensible—a good send-off from him to the other world. So to Rachel & Michael. & so—but now its one, on a snowy Sunday. We were prevented from going to MH. Miss Bevan strained the car. Its axle has to be mended.[24] But a wet dreary week end anyhow.

Monday 1 March

I wish I could write out my sensations at this moment. They are so peculiar & so unpleasant. Partly T[ime] of L[ife]? I wonder. A physical feeling as if I were drumming slightly in the veins: very cold: impotent: & terrified. As if I were exposed on a high ledge in full light. Very lonely. L. out to lunch. Nessa has Quentin & dont want me. Very useless. No atmosphere round me. No words. Very apprehensive. As if something cold & horrible—a roar of laughter at my expense were about to happen. And I am powerless to ward it off: I have no protection. And this anxiety & nothingness surround me with a vacuum. It affects the thighs chiefly. And I want to burst into tears, but have nothing to cry for. Then a great restlessness seizes me. I think I could walk it off—walk & walk till I am asleep. But I begin to dislike that sudden drugged sleep. And I cannot unfurl my mind & apply it calmly & unconsciously to a book. And my own little scraps look dried up & derelict. And I know that I must go on doing this dance on hot bricks till I die. This is a little superficial I admit. For I can burrow under & look at myself displayed in this ridiculous way & feel complete submarine calm: a kind of calm moreover which is strong eno' to lift the entire load: I can get that at moments; but the exposed moments are terrifying. I looked at my eyes in the glass once & saw them positively terrified. Its the 15th March approach[ing] I suppose—the

23. The increasingly aberrant poet and man of letters Sir John (Jack) Collings Squire (1884-1958), editor of *The London Mercury* from 1919-34, parted from his wife, was now largely sustained by the wealthy and philanthropic Miss Alice Warrender, (c. 1857-1947), founder of the Hawthornden Prize, at her Buckinghamshire home.
24. Rachel (Lady David Cecil, 1909-82) was Desmond MacCarthy's daughter and Michael (1907-73), a farmer, his elder son. LW had taught Miss Bevan to drive his car in order to travel books for the Hogarth Press.

dazzle of that head lamp on my poor little rabbits body wh. keeps it dazed in the middle of the road. (I like that phrase. That gives me confidence.)

normal ———— 2nd March

at Misanthrope

Tuesday 2 March

I'm going to be beaten, I'm going to be laughed at, I'm going to be held up to scorn & ridicule—I found myself saying those words just now. Yet I've been absorbed all the morning in the Un[iversit]y part of 3 Gs. And the absorption is genuine; & my great defence against the cold madness that overcame me last night. Why did it suddenly point itself like a rain cloud & discharge all its cold water? Because I was switched off doing Pictures in the morning; & then at the play, I suddenly thought the Book Society has not even recommended The Years.[1] Thats true; but the B.S. is not an infallible guide. Anyhow these days of waiting must be a dull cold torture. I shall be happy eno' this time next month I've no doubt. Meanwhile, suffer me now & again to write out my horror, the sudden cold madness, here. It is partly T. of L. I think still. And it wont be anything like so bad in action as in prospect. The worst will be that the book will be treated with tepid politeness, as an effusive diluted tired book. All my other books have stirred up strife; this one will sink slowly & heavily. But when thats said, need I fear more? I may get praise from some people—indeed I think there must be some 'seriousness' in it. And I can feel a little proud that I have faced the music; that we have sold 5,000 before publication; that we shall get some money; that I'm doing my share, & not merely subsiding into terrified silence. Also my own psychology interests me. I intend to keep full notes of my ups & downs, for my private information. And thus objectified, the pain & shame become at once much less. And I have proved to my own conviction that I can write with fury, with rapture, with absorption still. Now the BBC want a story.

1. On 1 March the Woolfs went to see the Cambridge Arts Theatre production of Molière's *The Misanthrope*, brought for a fortnight's season to the Ambassadors Theatre, with Lydia Lopokova as Célimène and scenery and costumes by André Derain.

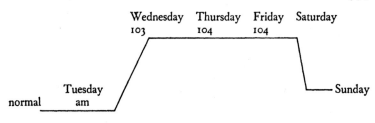

Wednesday   Thursday   Friday   Saturday
103   104   104

Tuesday   Sunday
am
normal

Sunday 7 March

As will be seen on the last page my spiritual temperature went up with a rush; why I dont know, save that I've been having a good gallop at 3 Guineas. Now I have broached the fatal week & must expect a sudden drop. Its going to be pretty bad, I'm certain; but at the same time I am convinced that the drop needn't be fatal; that is, the book may be damned, with faint praise; but the point is that I myself know why its a failure, & that its failure is deliberate. I also know that I have reached my point of view, as writer, as being.

We have sold 5,300 before publication

As writer I am fitted out for another 2 books—3 Gs & Roger; (let alone articles); as being the interest & safety of my present life are unthrowable. This I have, honestly, proved this winter. Its not a gesture. And honestly the diminution of fame, that people aren't any longer enthusiastic, gives me the chance to observe quietly. Also I am in a position to hold myself aloof. I need never seek out anyone. In short either way I'm safe, & look forward, after the unavoidable tosses & tumbles of the next ten days, to a slow, dark, fruitful spring, summer & autumn.

This is set down I hope once & for all. And please to remember it on Friday when the reviews come in.

To Cockfosters yesterday, & saw the old tramp woman on the bank, lighting a damp fire & eating dry bread. I took What shall we do then in my pocket. A curious comment. Saw also the monument to the birth of George Earl Grey in 1702.[2] Had buttered toast & jam & saw the girl

2. The Woolfs took a train to Cockfosters and walked round Trent Park, which at this period belonged to the Under-Secretary of State for Air, Sir Philip Sassoon (whom VW had once met lunching with Lady Colefax in 1929); he had transformed and embellished the house and grounds, the seat of much of his lavish hospitality. The great obelisk commemorating the birth in 1702 of the son of Henry Grey, Duke of Kent, came from Wrest Park in Bedfordshire, and was re-erected at Trent Park by Sassoon when he lent the house to Prince George—newly created Duke of Kent—and Princess Marina for their honeymoon in 1934. VW was probably reading *What Then Must We Do?*, Tolstoy's graphic description of poverty in Moscow in the 1880's and his analysis of its causes.

65

going to the vicarage to rehearse a religious drama. Many people. Ethel Sands, Shaw Desmond. Eth Bowen. Miss Loeb at Clive's.[3]

Monday 8 March

What I noticed on the walk to Cockfosters were: the father mother & small boy: (to whom the school took off their caps, one said I gave her the glad eye) the father saying "I've a large book waiting for you" The son piping up "I've got some stamps already"—the father, "I've torn off lots of stamps" upon wh. I thought of L. if he had a son. Then the wall round the park; how we had to walk as the car is still broken. how at every gate or even fence there was a notice This is Private . . Private road: I thought how I cursed the possessors of great parks who made me walk along the road, shaved every second by a car or a lorry; then the tramps. It was a wet cold day: had been raining in the night; the grass border very damp. The middle aged woman was trying to make a fire: a man in townish clothes was lying on his side in the grass. Both had stupid coarse broad rather truculent faces, as if they wd fire off oaths if one spoke or even looked too long. When we came back after an hour the woman had got the fire to burn, & the man was sitting up, among some old clothes & bits of dirty paper; also I think a small perambulator of some sort. She was cutting a slice of bread off a loaf, but there was no butter. At night it became very cold, & as we sat down to our duck L. said he wondered how they [s]pent the night. I said probably they go to the workhouse. This fitted in with What shall we do then, wh. I read in the train. But incidentally I'm not so much impressed as I expected by it. Vivid, but rather wordy so far.

Wednesday 10 March

The fatal day is approaching—in fact I think if I can slip out after tea & buy a paper I may have the experience tomorrow—when my little reputation lies like an old cigarette end. But I'm too jaded with 3 Gs. to care to find even the right metaphor. In my perhaps cowardly wish to ⟨store⟩ have next week as an empty compartment, I've crammed this too full: had Christabel yesterday, must have Nan Hudson today: & to my dismay L. suddenly wants to have Mrs R. & Elaine tomorrow: & the

3. Both LW and VW confuse the names of Shaw Desmond (1877-1960), a prolific Irish writer, and Desmond Shawe-Taylor (b. 1907), a regular literary and music critic for the *NS&N*; he was a friend of Ethel Sands, and no doubt VW here refers to him. Janice Loeb was a young and vivacious American art student who became a close friend of Clive Bell, with whom the Woolfs dined on 5 March.

Bagenals are dining.[4] On Friday we get off—the doomed discarded ridiculed novelist. What care I? I begin to whistle, but I'm too jaded.

Friday 12 March

Oh the relief! L. brought the Lit Sup to me in bed & said Its quite good. And so it is; & T. & Tide says I'm a firstrate novelist & a great lyrical poet.[5] And I can already hardly read through the reviews: but feel a little dazed, to think then its *not* nonsense; it does make an effect. Yet of course not in the least the effect I meant. But now, my dear, after all that agony, I'm free, whole; round. Can go full ahead. And so stop this cry of content; sober joy. Off to MH. Julian back today.

I use my last 5 minutes before lunch to note that though I have slipped the gall & fret & despair even of the past few weeks wholly today, & shan't I think renew them; I have once more loaded myself with the strain of 3 Gs. at which I have been writing hard & laboriously. So now I'm straining to draw that cart across the rough ground. It seems therefore that there is no rest; no sense of Its finished. One always harnesses oneself by instinct; & cant live without the strain. Now The Years will completely die out from my mind.

Car mended. But rain pouring.

The Woolfs drove to Rodmell on Friday 12 March, returning to London on Monday afternoon, 15 March.

Sunday 14 March

I am in such a twitter owing to 2 columns in the Observer praising The Years that I cant, as I foretold, go on with 3 Guineas. Why I even sat back just now & thought with pleasure of people reading that review. And when I think of the agony I went through in this room, just over a year ago . . . . when it dawned on me that the whole of 3 years work was a complete failure: & then when I think of the mornings here when I used to stumble out & cut up those proofs & write 3 lines, & then go back & lie on my bed—the worst summer in my life, but at the same time the most illuminating—its no wonder my hand trembles. What most pleases me tho', is the obvious chance now since de Selincourt sees it, that my

4. The Bagenals, see above, 9 April 1936, n. 3; the Woolfs seldom saw them now. Elaine (b. 1931) was the eldest child of LW's friend and colleague W. A. Robson and his wife Juliette (see above 29 February 1936, n. 4).

5. *The Years* was reviewed in the *TLS* dated 13 March 1937 (*M&M*, pp. 368-70); and in *Time and Tide* dated 13 March 1937, by Theodora Bosanquet (*M&M*, pp. 367-68). Although VW has three times referred to the approaching publication date of *The Years* as 15 March, it appears in fact to have been issued on Thursday 11 March 1937.

intention in The Years may be not so entirely muted & obscured as I feared.[6] The TLS spoke as if it were merely the death song of the middle classes: a series of exquisite impressions; but he sees that it is a creative, a constructive book. Not that I've yet altogether read him: but he has pounced on some of the key sentences. And this means that it will be debated; & this means that 3 Gs. will strike very sharp & clear on a hot iron: so that my immensely careful planning won't be baulked by time of life &c. as I had made certain. Making certain however was an enormous discovery for me, though. If there's one triumph I applaud—excuse this flamboyant language—it is the afternoon when Desmond came, & Nan Hudson was there: & I almost cracked with the wish to talk to him about The Yrs & Nan sat on, like some tepid bread poultice; & I summoned my forces, & got her to talk to me about her own life & Ethel (that was a chink) instead of letting the agonising hour go to ruin.

Now at any rate money is assured: L. shall have his new car; we will be floated again; & my last lap—if I've only 10 years of life more—should be fruitful. Work—work. But at the moment, the relief is so great, not I think an ignoble fame-gratified relief—that I feel myself rocking up & down, like a bush a huge fowl sat on. Still I must remember that I'm bound to get a good many shrewd knocks. And much of The Years is very feeble—for example the scene in the college still makes me blush.

Dinner at Charleston last night. Julian grown a man—I mean vigorous, controlled, as I guess embittered, something to me tragic in the sadness now, his mouth & face much tenser; as if he had been thinking in solitude. Nessa said he hasn't altogether given up his idea of Spain: all depends on getting a job here. I felt him changed: taut, tense, on the defensive: yet affectionate: but no longer spontaneous. He comes to tea today. And L. was irritated by the intense "self centredness" of my family: Nessa only cares for her children: Julian can't even let her know his decision, so inconsiderate; all "on the make". This is partly due to his family complex; but there's some truth in it.

And now I can put my philosophy of the free soul into operation. Thats what I'm thinking—needn't go to the writers auction on 20th.[7] All the falsities can drop off.

Monday 15 March

Spending a lazy morning. Tired in the head. Too much talk—Julian & Bunny—why do we live in such a way that the sight of our oldest

6. Basil de Selincourt reviewed The Years in The Observer, 14 March 1937 (M&M, pp. 371-5).
7. This was an exhibition and sale of autographed books and manuscripts organised by the International Association of Writers for the Defence of Culture at Foyle's Bookshop, Charing Cross Road.

friends & nephews back from China gives us a little shock of regret—I
mean misery for the quiet evening gone?[8] Julian set & rather self centred.
Can only think what he ought to do. Still if what he ought to do is
something for the world at large, one must excuse this grinding of an iron
upon a Granite slab. Anyhow, being too tired to write, I've been thinking
cd. I recast the rejected section of The Years for the Uniform Edition?
Why do I bother? Only I rather suspect its needed for the whole argument impression. But there it is, safe; & I needn't consider this seriously
at the moment. Keep it at the back of my mind, & judge
5,300 I think from reviews—save that they're all so scatter brained—
sold before how far the book misses fire on that account. We are stay-
publication ing till 3.30: L. has rung up the Press & about 25 more
Years have been ordered. A good sale possible I think. Say 10, or 11, or
12,000.

Brooding over Gibbon. Perhaps a weeks break to finish that wd be
good. I dont think I shall much mind the chitter chatter; shall be glad
when this following week is over; all reviews out & forgotten; & then
Lord the pleasure of coming here for 10 quiet days at Easter. And they
shall be quiet too—that I swear. We have done our duty by family &
society quite sufficiently.

Wednesday 17 March

The communist press began its little snigger yesterday. John Brophy
in D.T. a tired anaemic middle class book.[9] So be it. That sneer is already
rubbed out. But I'm too jaded to tackle the Professional chapter of 3 Gs.
so write here. Yesterday we had Buxton to lunch, who had never heard of
me or my agonies; & then I fetched my new lustre, & walked in the rain
all across Hyde Park, now pink with coronation seats. This morning
Austen Chamberlain is dead, & its an off day for me. No reviews I hope.
L.'s irritation bad; will go to Hensman. No I cant write; & think shall I
look at my Gibbon? Very wisely I have kept the week empty: save for the
persistent Hayward tomorrow.[10] But we know that the Spectator is giving

8. Julian Bell and David ('Bunny') Garnett (see Appendix I) came to tea at Monks
   House on Sunday.
9. John Brophy reviewed *The Years* together with other novels in the *Daily Telegraph*
   of 16 March 1937: 'Mrs Woolf's work seems to lack the spring and surge of true
   creation. It is work deserving respect. . . . But all the characters . . . are muffled and
   hid from the reader by the author's cultured but petrifying observation.'
10. Charles Roden Buxton (1875-1942) was chairman of the Labour Party Advisory
    Committees on international and imperial questions, to both of which LW was
    secretary. He had met VW with LW several times (see her description of him,
    IV VW Diary, 5 October 1933). Sir Austen Chamberlain (1863-1937), elder
    statesman of the Conservative Party, died suddenly in London on 16 March; VW

a whole page to The Years: that the E. Standard is giving 2 columns: Desmond promises 2 cols on Sunday: & theres the NS. on Friday—so my peace is only that of a grasshopper under a leaf. No, I dont seriously fidget any more; because its plain there are 2 lines of criticism: one the Communist; the other the free mind. Had there been only the one, I shd. have been damned. As it is I'm discussed (as usual) & no one has yet seen the point—*my* point.

Friday 19 March

Now this is one of the strangest of my experiences—'they' say almost universally that The Years is a masterpiece. The Times says so. Bunny.

Something about a master-piece, & how Mrs W. since To the L has more to give us than any living novelist . . . astonishing fertility.

&c: Howard Spring:[11] If somebody had told me I shd. write this, even a week ago, let alone 6 months ago, I shd. have given a jump like a shot hare. How entirely & absolutely incredible it would have been! The praise chorus began yesterday: by the way I was walking in Covent Garden & found St Pauls, CG for the first time, heard the old char singing as she cleaned the chairs in the ante hall; then went to Burnets [*of Garrick St.*]: chose stuff; bought the E. Standard & found myself glorified as I read it in the Tube. A calm quiet feeling, glory: & I'm so steeled now I dont think the flutter will much worry me. Now I must begin again on 3 Gs.

Hensman is now come, I suppose—not that I'm much upset by that: as I dont seriously think this irritation matters. At the same moment, Miss Strachan has broken out into spots. L. suggests fleas. I heard him describing fleas just now in the Press. I have toiled a little at 3 Gs. but cant concentrate sufficiently: fly up into easy flights, because I'm praised no doubt.

knew him from the time—1902-5—when her half-brother George Duckworth had acted as his (unpaid) private secretary. For the persistent Hayward, see below, 19 March 1937, n. 12.

11. Howard Spring reviewed *The Years* in the *Evening Standard* of 18 March (*M&M* pp. 382-5); David Garnett in the *NS&N*, 20 March (*M&M* pp. 382-5); and J. S. in 'Books of the Week' in *The Times* of 19 March under the heading 'Time and Mrs Woolf': '. . . this is a book that might be called, in more exacting times, a master-piece. . . . Ten years ago, in "To the Lighthouse", Mrs Woolf showed that she had more to give the reader, both of her mind and his own, than any other contemporary novelist. Once again she liberates the imagination, exciting and inspiring it with that beautifully economical and resourceful prose . . . Mrs Woolf's incomparably fertile [novel] . . .' etc.

Yesterday at Hayward's we heard a strange story.[12] He lives in Bina
Gardens, called Bina from Rubina, the builders favourite daughter. He
sits askew in a 3 cornered chair. Cant get up. His room is an uncreative
room: spick & span: too tidy. Carrington painted him a book case: the
books all ranged in sizes. 2 glass horses on the Victorian mahogany table:
flowers separately springing: a dish of carefully arranged fruit. The story
was about his landlord: in prison for writing indecent letters to the girls
at Roedean—addressed To the Head Girl—therefore opened by the
headmistress. These he concocted in the kitchen while Mrs Baker? cooked
John's dinner. He interviewed all the lodgers & stated the facts. He liked
telling this: partly to impress me, I think; & give a kick at Dryden &
editing. Wont see more of the spring he said than Walls Ice Cream van.
Has a great thick soft red lip: frozen green eyes; & angular attitudes like
a monkey on a string. Said how Tom gave it as his opinion that Anglo
Catholics may not, owing to Church Law, use contraceptives. Hence the
indecent letters, I suppose. Another feather in the cap of Tom's Church.
Now I must creep upstairs to see if Hensmans gone. My treat is to go to
the Caledonian market.

Monday 22 March

No I didnt. It rained. And I left my umbrella apparently in a bus. And
my brain is tired—yes, it was a strain, holding myself erect through the
suspense of last week. Now I've a holiday from reviews till Wednesday
(Listener) then till Sunday, & Desmond does it. And all 3 Gs. is held up—
yet I have it pressing for speech. Can I describe old Kot. yesterday. L.
looked at the telephone, thinking he was mad. Had been 'ill'. Mere solitude
mania I think. Calmed down. Gave us tea on hard chairs in basement.
abused Ott & Murry.[13] So shall now stop writing for a day.

Thursday 25 March

Yes, 2 days lying down, & cant write today. But a divine holiday. No
reviews. Listener not done it. And sales great. A rush before Easter: 280
sold yesterday. Nessa to tea. But I will not write: am only waiting for my
signature to dry. B. Richmond asked one for Ormond St. hospital. Boat
Race at 11.30. Then we go tomorrow. No letters about Years, save one
from Ly Simon. Kot, Hayward, Margery Fry all in favour of Years. No

12. John Davy Hayward (1905-65), bibliophile, bibliographer, editor; VW met him
first in 1925 in Cambridge during his final year at King's College; since then he
had become a close friend of T. S. Eliot. He suffered from muscular dystrophy.
13. Koteliansky's antipathy towards John Middleton Murry (1889-1957) stemmed
from his devotion to Murry's dead wife, Katherine Mansfield.

one else has yet read, or spoken. And its very fine, clear & cold. The Dss of Bedford lost.[14]

On four successive days from 21 March LW noted 'V. headache'. On Thursday 25 March they drove to Rodmell for Easter, and stayed there until Sunday 4 April.

Saturday 27 March

No, I am not going to titivate Gibbon—that is condense by a thousand words. Too much screw needed, & my brains unstrung. Merely scribbling here, over a log fire, on a cold but bright Easter morning; sudden shafts of sun, a scatter of snow on the hills early; sudden storms, ink black, octopus pouring, coming up; & the rooks fidgetting & pecking in the elm trees. As for the beauty, as I always say when I walk the terrace after breakfast, too much for one pair of eyes. Enough to float a whole population in happiness, if only they wd. look. Curiously a combination, this garden, with the Church, & the cross of the Church black against Asheham Hill. That is all the elements of the English brought together, accidentally. We came down on Thursday, packed in the rush in London; cars spinning all along the roads: yesterday at last perfect freedom from telephones, & reviews, & no one rang up. I began Lord Ormont & his Aminta, & found it so rich, so knotted, so alive, & muscular after the pale little fiction I'm used to, that, alas, it made me wish to write fiction again. Meredith underrated. I like his effort to escape plain prose. And he has humour & some insight too—more than they allow him now. Also Gibbon. And so I'm well fitted out; but cant write more than this without the old tightening & throbbing at the back of the head.

Sunday 28 March

Again I take my tiny little flutter, with the accursed Xtian bells ringing—however, dulled as they are with 500 years or more at Rodmell I cant seriously dislike them. A June morning. A log fire & a June morning. No review by Desmond: so that sword hangs suspended. L. thinks he's jealous. I dont think that—suspect some perplexity. Q. rings up. L. will go to tea. I shant. I shall lapse into dreams. What luck if I cd. strike a good vein! Reading Othello was it once at Asheham—I remember sitting in the garden there, so sublime.

Yesterday a reporter for the N. York Times rang up: was told he cd. look at the outside of 52 if he chose. At 4.30 as I was boiling the kettle a

14. The Duchess of Bedford (1865-1937), known as 'The Flying Duchess', wife of the 11th Duke, was a pioneer aviator, making record flights to India and the Cape. On 22 March she took off from Woburn for a short solo flight to the east and was never seen again.

huge black Daimler drew up. Then a dapper little man in a tweed coat appeared in the garden. I reached the sitting room—saw him standing there looking round. L. ignored him. L. in the orchard with Percy [Bartholomew, *gardener*]. Then I guessed. He had a green note book & stood looking about jotting things down. I ducked my head—he almost caught me. At last L. turned & fronted him. No Mrs W. didnt want that kind of publicity. I raged. A bug walking over ones skin—cdn't crush him. The bug taking note. L. politely led him back to his Daimler & his wife. But they'd had a nice run from London—bugs, to come & steal in & take notes.[15]

Monday 29 March

The misery is passing off in its usual way—a drowsy slackness this morning. And there is nothing much to stir it. I read a great deal yesterday—White's Selborne, & the London Spy.[16] A very cold night. No, this is hardly worth writing out. A man in an overcoat took notes in the field yesterday, & then someone banged on the door. I sat tight. L. was at Charleston. Julian, he says, very depressed. Today Ethel S. writes that she has read The Y. but will not comment till she has re-read. I suppose dislikes it. Well—& will look in on Wednesday. No. My policy is to lie low & invite no visitors till the summer is over—a luxurious couching like a fox on its nest. Meredith is an influential writer: how wd it be to counter him with H. James? a kind of medical mixture? And my books are waiting at Lewes: Southey's commonplace book; Leaves of Grass: Clarendon's history in 6 vols—rather a leap in the dark—all for £1-8.[17]

Tuesday 30 March

No good playing Schubert if one thinks L. minds the noise. And I dont really want it either. Cold grey day—reading rather better todays over

---

15. For VW's further reactions to this intrusion, see *II QB*, Appendix B: 'Fantasy upon a gentleman who converted his impressions of a private house into cash' (MHP, Sussex, A/19).
16. *The Natural History and Antiquities of Selborne* (1798) by Gilbert White; VW had Miall and Warde-Fowler's edition of 1901: see *Holleyman*, VS II, p. 8. *The London Spy* by Edward Ward, first published in monthly parts from 1698, throws much light on the life of London's coffee houses and taverns of the period.
17. These books—probably ordered from a bookseller's catalogue—were Robert Southey's *Commonplace Book*, published posthumously in 4 volumes, 1849-51, by his son-in-law the Rev. John Wood Warter (see *Holleyman*, VS I, p. 15); *History of the Rebellion and Civil Wars in England* by Edward, Earl of Clarendon, 6 volumes, 1705-6 (*Holleyman*, MH V, p. 6); and Walt Whitman's *Leaves of Grass* (1855).

the fire. Yesterday I walked to the Bridge [*at Southease*] & back over the hanger. This is a Gilbert White word.[18] Odd thing in White is the change of proportion. 1770 proportions. Thus the downs become majestic mountains; a tortoise as large as an elephant; an oak a forest &c. A very pleasing change, like a slow motion picture: a magnifyer of things. Everything six times its present size. Thats one of the great charms to us. Then the clear bell like sentences. Had no scientific instruments: only his eyes. Question when & how science suddenly developed. 18th Cent. practically middle ages.

Ethel rings up to say she has re-read Years, under Miss Hudson's direction, & finds it no longer unintelligible, but superb—How can this be true of any mind? Yet I'm a little relieved. For one thing it makes it unnecessary to argue. I shall accept. Also shows The Years has selling power—if Miss Hudson can spontaneously enjoy.[19] Today our last of seclusion. Possible London post this evening. Q. to dine. L.P. meeting. I am resting my brain entirely till we go back. But Thursday will be a bit of a rub—all the way to Minstead & back with the talk thrown in: but when one's dying one must. Janet dying I mean. How strange to lie there calmly contemplating the distant but inevitable end—& Emphie watching too. But I rather suspect she is happy in her quiet composed way—save for Emphie—reading W[ordswor]th & Me[redi]th I expect, as she used, out of her carefully annotated copies. She read them with me in the Park at Firle 30 years ago I suppose.[20]

Wednesday 31 March

Thank goodness, better today. Clear & stable—at least I'm sunning myself on that ledge at the moment. But I will not write till Monday. A hot June morning. Little gummy noises under the trees as if buds were popping, twigs exploding. Rooks cawing. Trees still clear & coloured. Letters began last night. Lord Olivier. "Being out of sorts & unable to tackle serious books I read The Years"—that sort of drivle. And the visitors beginning—Hugh [Walpole], Sally Graves party. Today a shifty apologetic letter from Sparrow asks me not to read his review, of

18. *Hanger*: a wood on the side of a steep hill or bank (OED).
19. Miss Alice Hudson, JP, one-time Mayor of Eastbourne, of Wootton Manor, near Polegate; VW had once been to tea with her when Ethel was staying there (see *IV VW Diary*, 12 September 1935).
20. Janet Elizabeth Case (1862-1937) had taught VW Greek in the early years of the century and remained a respected and trusted friend; she now lived in retirement with her sister Emphie at Minstead in the New Forest, slowly dying from Graves's disease. She had stayed with VW at Firle before the latter's marriage; and later at nearby Asheham in 1914 when she was ill.

wh he's not proud. L. says 'little swine . .'²¹ Ethel engrossed by Dotty.
So be it. Q. last night pleased me, praising The Y. as poetry—like To the
L the oddest novel he'd ever read. A good meeting. Fenders & pokers
brought by Mr Macer Wright. Louie enchanted.²² But cant write as the
above shows. Hand wont hold pen.

Friday 2 April

How I interest myself! Quite set up & perky today with a mind
brimming, *because* I was so damnably depressed & smacked on the cheek
by Edwin Muir in The Listener & by Scott James in the Life & Letters on
Friday. They both gave me a smart snubbing: EM says The Years is dead
& disappointing—so in effect did S. James. All the lights sank; my reed
bent to the ground. Dead & disappointing—so I'm found out & that
odious rice pudding of a book is what I thought it—a dank failure. No
life in it. Much inferior to the bitter truth & intense originality of Miss
Compton Burnett.¹ Now this pain woke me at 4 am. & I suffered acutely.
All day driving to Janet & back I was under the cloud. But about 7 it
lifted. There was a good review, of 4 lines, in The Empire review [*not
traced*]. The best of my books: did that help? I dont think very much. But
the delight of being exploded is quite real. One feels braced for some
reason; amused; roused; combative; more than by praise. Of course I was
pleased when L. said none of our friends read The Listener. Anyhow,
my spirits rose, calm & steady; & I feel once more immune, set on my
own feet, a fighter.

No one has written to me. So I feel that buffeting is over, & I can make

---

21. Sydney Olivier (1859-1943), 1st Baron Olivier, Fabian socialist, Governor of
Jamaica 1907-13, and ex-Labour Government Minister; like LW, he was a member
of the Labour Party Advisory Committee on imperial affairs, and his books were
published by the Hogarth Press. For Hugh Walpole, see below, 9 April 1937.
John Sparrow (b. 1906), Fellow of All Souls, had reviewed *The Years* in *The
Spectator* of 19 March 1937: '[Mrs Woolf] has neither retreated nor advanced
along the path of her own development . . . She has turned aside and written an
ordinary book . . .'.

22. Mr Macer Wright was local organiser of the Rural Industries Bureau. Louie
Everest, *née* West (1912-77) came to Monks House as maid of all work in July
1934 and remained until LW's death in 1969; she and her husband, a farm worker,
lived out in a nearby cottage LW had bought in 1929.

1. Edwin Muir reviewed *The Years* in *The Listener*, 31 March 1937 (see *M&M*, pp.
386-88); and R. A. Scott James in the April issue of *The London Mercury* (of which
he was editor): 'Mrs Woolf has not removed from the picture the sense of dreariness
and fatuity, however brightly coloured the strands with which the pattern is
woven . . .' Ivy Compton Burnett (1892-1969) had recently published her seventh
novel, *Daughters and Sons*.

a fresh start. Still only Desmond to come—if he is to come: & then perfect freedom.

A very interesting visit to Janet. Both of them as spry & gay & even charming to look at as possible. Janet rounded & mellowed, with the beautiful——telephone: Keynes's: Maynard is reading The Years. & is enthusiastic. Well that does please me, all the same— For one thing it gives more ply to 3 Guineas. Now I'm making up my Broadcast: whose date we've tried to change: but to continue with J. & E. A little thatched sunny house, full of nice furniture. Emphie with those lustrous eyes, as if she had always lived her life. She is completely at her ease; voluble; human, spontaneous. Flitting as usual from room to room interrupting, but as naturally as a bird, one eye spilling tears; but no gloom about—a natural gaiety & fun. Its true Janet is apparently dying; but they dont know how long she'll be at it. Such a bore, she said, to have got this ulcer just as we'd planned to have a nice old age together. So many things we wanted to do. They had meant to go to Holland & look at birds. Nor was this a pose; no stiffness about it, quite natural. So we had a sip of talk with Janet—then with E.: E. says she can't believe in death ending things— whats 70 years? So short—so short—Whats it all for I ask if it ends now? Oh no we go on—I'm convinced of that. It cdn't be possible otherwise— so senseless—all the time balancing one elbow in a grey jumper on the edge of the table; a tear running. Now Janet dont believe this—she dont go to Church. I do. I'll just see if she's ready for you. Yes, we've always been poor. But then we made up our minds—we wdnt go to Theatres, we wdnt have clothes. We'd have good food—my mother always said that was so important for the young—& then we had to earn our livings. That was so interesting—made you know interesting people. Very few girls in our time had to work.

With Janet gossip, rather straitened, owing to time, about the past; the present; her belief, owing to Heard's book, in some sort of life in common, not as individuals. Some mystic survival. The young wanting it. No religion. Katherine Asquith offering to come: but I doubt if she wants visits. Quite happy, some discomfort, cant sit or walk.[2]

What is so odd is the switch over from thinking oneself a bad writer (after Muir) to thinking oneself a great writer (after Myanard). On the whole, being a bad writer gives one a greater feeling of freedom: but not the same glory. Difference between one's back to the wall & soaring with pinions through the dominions . . —soaring

2. Gerald Heard (1889-1971), influential writer on scientific and philosophical subjects; his book referred to by Janet Case was probably *The Social Substance of Religion* (1931). Katherine Asquith, *née* Horner (1885-1976), widow of the Liberal prime minister's eldest son Raymond, had been one of her pupils.

with supreme dominion—how does it go?—the most liquid line in poetry.[3]

Saturday 3 April

Now I have to broadcast on the 29th. It will go like this: cant be a craft of words. am going to disregard the title & talk about words. why they won't let themselves be made a craft of. They tell the truth: they arent useful. That there shd. be 2 languages: fiction & fact. Words are inhuman ... wont make money, need privacy—Why. For their embraces, for ⟨their⟩ to continue the race. A dead word. The purists & the impurists. There are only impressions; not fixations. I respect words too. Associations of words. Felicity brings in absent thee. We ⟨have to⟩ can easily make new words. Squish squash: crick crack: But we cant use them in writing[4]

Sunday 4 April

Another curious idiosyncracy. Maynard thinks The Years my best book: thinks one scene, E[leanor]. & Crosby, beats Tchehov's Cherry Orchard—& this opinion though from the centre, from a very fine mind, doesn't flutter me as much as Muir's blame; it sinks in slowly & deeply. Its not a vanity feeling; the other is: the other will die as soon as this weeks number of The Listener is passed. L. went to Tilton & had a long quiet cronies talk. Maynard not well; cramp in the muscle of the heart. His toes curl up. Lydia anxious. Queer, since he said at Xmas he had never been so well. Talk of what to do for Julian, who strikes everyone as depressed. Oh & no papers this morning—what a curious spite against me, to keep me mildly frizzling all day. But after all, *if* Desmond does me he will only be mildly avuncular & depressing. Most likely he wont do me. Oh to be quit of reviews! Reading Balzac with great pleasure. Novel reading power is coming back.

Maynard said that he thought The Years very moving[;] more tender than any of my books; did not puzzle him like The Waves; symbolism

---

3. See the last verse of Thomas Gray's *The Progress of Poesy*, published 1757:

> 'O Lyre divine! what daring Spirit
> Wakes thee now? Tho' he inherit
> Nor the pride, nor ample pinion,
>   That the Theban eagle bear
> Sailing with supreme dominion
>   Thro' the azure deep of air:'

4. VW's broadcast, given on 29 April, was entitled 'Craftsmanship' and was published in *The Listener* of 5 May 1937 (Kp C349). The word associations with 'felicity' stem from the last scene of *Hamlet*.

not a worry; very beautiful; & no more said than was needed. hadnt yet finished it. But how compose the 2 opinions; its my most human book: & most inhuman? Oh to forget all this & write—as I must tomorrow.

The Woolfs returned to London on Sunday afternoon, 4 April.

Friday 9 April

"Such happiness wherever it is known is to be pitied for tis surely blind."[5] Yes, but my happiness isn't blind. That is the achievement, I was thinking between 3 & 4 this morning, of my 55 years. I lay awake so calm, so content, as if I'd stepped off the whirling world into a deep blue quiet space, & there open eyed existed, beyond harm; armed against all that can happen. I have never had this feeling before in all my life; but I have had it several times since last summer: when I reached it, in my worst depression, as if I stepped out, throwing aside a cloak, lying in bed, looking at the stars, those nights at Monks House. Of course it ruffles[?], in the day but there it is. There it was yesterday when old Hugh came & said nothing about The Years.[6] He has grown fatter, coarser. I did not feel him so genial: a little vulgarised I think by Hollywood. Isherwood came. We chattered, about the Royal family: Hugh is to report the Coronation for the Daily Mail, & will get £200 for 2,000 words. Then he told us the true story of Frank Vosper & Mr Willes—sodomy—a sudden impulse— over the ships side: how his face grew; he was afraid of being a monstrosity. This is what I milk Hugh for. But his stories will get a little battered. He has Mr Davidson, the parson in the barrel ⟨to lunch⟩ calling.[7] Not much real interest in human nature in Hugh. Always

5. Lines 55-6 from Wordsworth, 'Elegiac Stanzas suggested by a Picture of Peel Castle, in a Storm, painted by Sir George Beaumont'.

6. Hugh Walpole (1884-1941), the highly successful and popular novelist with whom VW had been friendly since 1929; because of her ill-health and his long absence in Hollywood, they had not now seen each other for some two years.

7. Frank Vosper (1899-1937), actor and author, disappeared on 6 March from the French liner *Paris* on her voyage from New York to Plymouth; his body was recovered from the sea near Beachy Head on 21 March, and an inquest was held at Eastbourne, the jury returning an open verdict of Found Drowned on 6 April. Vosper and his travelling companion Peter Willes had been drinking in the stateroom of a beauty queen, Miss Europe 1935, before his disappearance. The Rev. Harold Francis Davidson (1875-1937), Rector of Stiffkey in Norfolk, charged under the Clergy Discipline Act in the Consistory Court in 1932 and found guilty of moral offences, sought to raise money for an appeal by being exhibited in a barrel on the promenade at Blackpool. His appeal being dismissed, sentence of deprivation was pronounced in October 1932. He died in July 1937 after being mauled by a lion at a Skegness amusement park, where he was hired as an attraction.

something irking him. Still the party went very briskly, & when it was over I walked round the Square, the first summer evening walk, & admired our patriotic beds of red, white & blue hyacinths. We go to France in May.

Wednesday 14 April

I *must* make myself correct Gibbon & send today. But after those months of correction, correction almost makes me cry out in agony. So to ease myself I'm taking 10 minutes rapid writing. I've done, that is scribbled down, my BBC essay—with some exhilaration. Old Ethel came to tea [*on 9 April*], & left her thorns in my flesh. Said I was the strongest of women, by way of hinting that L. & I had kept her away at Rodmell on a pretext. But I did *not* write & tell her so; No: I'm sunk in privacy in quiet. How strange! It would be flat, if I were not active in the head. Not a letter this morning: only 10 or 11 perhaps about The Years since it came out. Nobody talks to me about it, nobody now writes about it. It seems to have sailed out of sight. And I have some foolish shrinking from meeting anyone who would talk, or not talk of it. Yet it sells—best of all my novels. H[arcourt] B[race]. in America have sold 12,000 before publication—easily my record. Honestly I do not know what to think of this book: is it good or bad? Honestly I am floored—& so will not think, but cut back as quick as I can to 3 Guineas. Fresh as June dawn in my head again. Another run ahead of me.

Sold I think 9,300

And tonight Kingsley Martin, Stephen Spender & Julian dine. K.M. in an agitated voice on the phone asks L. why I wont write for NS. is it money? They propose to increase my fee & also offer more space. So what am I to say then? The truth?

Thursday 15 April

And Stephen says The Years is the best of my books, & Kingsley also —but that don't please me. Stephen does. Not so much as it should. Yet soon I can cast up my accounts about The Years: add, subtract & cast up & say no more. A long close political argument. Julian, KM, Stephen— all calling each other by Xtian names. What is our duty? What is the responsible man like KM to do? Cant be a pacifist; the irresponsible can. I sat there splitting off my own position from theirs, testing what they said, convincing myself of my own integrity & justice. K.M. very neurotic, dark eyed, melodramatic. A much travelled too easily agitated superficial man—all froth & feeling—self questioning—not rooted. Julian peppery & pithy—making his strange faces, suddenly hooting with laughter—uncouth rather, yet honest, yet undisciplined, yet keeping something up his sleeve. Obstinately set on going to Spain—wont argue; tight; hard fisted—has amusing phrases "joining for duration of the quarrel". Harry Pollitt cuts up rough when asked to arrange Tony's & Stephen's amours—not unnaturally, as KM. said: being in control of the CP in this war—being ravaged by deaths: pestered also by relations. The CP will only accept those who are devoted to The Cause.[8] KM. lives much in the military area; so we discussed hand grenades, bombs, tanks, as if we were military gents in the war again. And I felt flame up in me 3 Gs. wh. has been submerged by Gibbon & BBC—that I should revise now, but cant screw this morning, after all that chatter. Stephen runs on too fluent, too formless; but as I say gave me a shock of pleasure. Says The Years gives him the sense of time; & is so precise—but he will write upon it in The Left Review.[9] So thats the young on my side. *Against*: Vita; Elizabeth Williamson; Hugh Walpole; For: Maynard, Hayward, Kot, Nessa, Stephen; I refer only to the speakers not to the writers, whom to differentiate would take a whole morning. The complete absence of fan mail is curious. But America is now just beginning. And did I say that they sold—oh I think I did: & am rambling. Reading Balzac: reading A. Birrell's memoirs;[10] & now shall shut my Gibbon rather reluctantly: I wd. like to finish. Shall I begin another article? Scott's letters?

Wednesday 21 April

What a mercy to use this page to uncramp in! after squeezing drop by drop into my 17 minute BBC: wh. is alternately 25 & then 15 minutes. Curse the BBC. Also the N.S. They come pestering, & instead of lounging at MH. I made up an article on Gibbon's Aunts. Why? Partly because of pressure, unconscious, from Leonard.[11] However, on the whole MH was a good week end. Very cold wind. Went to tea at Charleston; & there found the whole family for once. Unfortunately Julian is dog obstinate about driving an ambulance; which casts a shadow over Nessa, & us too. There he'll be keeping us all on the tenterhooks— But it wont be for 2 months, & what's the use of looking ahead? On Monday we drove, round London, deviously, through the half dead old villages, to Ickenham: where Sally was almost surgically mated; the after

8. Harry Pollitt (1890-1960) was Secretary of the Communist Party of Great Britain from 1929-56, and was deeply involved in the political, practical, and personal problems of the British volunteers fighting for the Government in Spain. For Spender's particular problems, see above, 18 February 1937, n. 6.

9. Spender did not review *The Years* in the *Left Review* (nor did anyone else), but he expressed his admiration for it in a long letter to VW dated 26 April 1937 (LWP, Sussex).

10. *Things Past Redress* (1937) by Augustine Birrell.

11. It was published as 'Reflections at Sheffield Place' in the *NS&N*, 19 June 1937 (Kp C350).

marriage taking over 20 minutes. L. & the stableman & Mr Lloyd assisted: I, prudently, & chastely sat in the car & showed Mitz to the children.[12] Then home to find Vita waiting—tomato red with one blue yellow eye: unconscious, easy & lazy as usual. We argued about Ethel. As she approached The Years—might have been written by somebody else—no wild poetry—in came L. to say Willie [Robson] must have his tea. So that argument was scotched. She went off to Curtis Brown; then to her first night of the Edwardians at Richmond; then Julian came with my glass fish: & then at last unpacked the car, slept over the fire.[13]

Summer time began on Sunday: & I look up & see my clock still an hour late.

These little articles ruin ones time; today spoilt because I must finish off the talk & send to The Listener. Never again. Yet of course there's a certain thrill about writing to read aloud—I expect a vicious one. And it could have been a good article. Its the talk element that upsets it. And in the pouring rain we went to Nessa's; saw the D. of Kent pass in his emblazoned car, & then bought some of Julian's Chinese pots.

[*Tuesday 27 April*]

Yes, that'll be nice—to sit out of doors & drink, in some French town, away from all this. I ought to buy a dress; from Murray; but can't be bothered. Opera last night: Raymond, Molly & Shaw Taylor: not as fine as it used to be; & a faded arty opera, Ariane.[14] BBC rehearsal at 3: then Memoir Club. Sales slackening. Coronation impending. But on the 7th we're off. BBC have asked L. to do a whole series. Never again will I read even one talk.

Thursday 29 April

L. is talking about stock. "This oughtn't to be here at all . . ." I have just done my BBC. Never again never again: "Somebody hasnt checked

---

12. The Woolfs had bought their pedigree spaniel Sally from Mr Lloyd of Swakeleys Farm, Ickenham, in June 1935. Mitz was LW's ubiquitous marmoset, a certain magnet to strangers, if generally repellent to friends.

13. Curtis Brown: literary agents. A dramatisation by Edward Knoblock of V. Sackville-West's novel *The Edwardians* (1930) was first performed at the Richmond Theatre on 19 April. The orange glass fish, now at Monks House, was among the considerable number of artefacts shipped home from China by Julian Bell.

14. Ronald Murray had made clothes for VW since 1933. The opera, *Ariane et Barbebleue* by Paul Dukas, was performed at Covent Garden by a French company under Philippe Gaubert. The Woolfs and their party had a box; and Mr Shawe-Taylor recalls VW's admiring exclamation on noticing Molly MacCarthy using her elegant lorgnette opera-glasses: 'Molly, what a hold you have on life! Spectacles upon a golden stalk!'

it properly" Well, we've decided to let the H.P. lapse or change next June. Yes I think, owing to Miss Lang[e']s incompetency, that is now definite. Many things have happened—a crowd of little engagements—the pleasantest, indeed a happy one, was the Memoir Club meeting. We dined in a kind of sitting room behind the Etoile—& soon kindled, though it was a wet night: D[uncan]. had a cold; Bunny the whooping cough; & Morgan dined with Forrest Reid.[15] But Desmond was babbling as a nightingale—never have I known him in such jubilant good temper as this year. As if he worked only to enjoy to radiate. And my thimble of vanity was filled instantly because Maynard said my Gibbon was 20 times better than anyone elses; & praised The Years—a lovely book: & D. said he is going to write a long essay on me altogether. (but he wont) And then Molly & I kissed; & Maynard suggested that D. should give the L.S. lecture on L.S.: & we had a nice slice of savoury meat; & so round to the Studio. D. read a good account of his adventure at Florence, when he misrepresented Maynard.[16] And then old Desmond 'obliged'. That is he had a few notes in his hand, took a comfortable chair, & gave us with perfect ease & fluency & form a character of Wilfred Blunt & his own shooting. & so to the Trevelyans—how Sir G.O. came hopping loping like a great gorilla across the wood in the middle of the shoot to say Alfred Lyall's poems are as near poetry as anything I can stand. Oh but it was beautifully done—& stopped when it might have gone on without boring us.[17] Then Morgan read his condemned introduction to the Lawrence letters, which Bunny is now to do.[18] And then we went off in the rain. Desmond said We're not a day older, & we enjoy our society as much as

15. The *Etoile* restaurant, 30 Charlotte Street; the meeting was on 27 April. Forrest Reid (1876-1947), the Belfast writer, was an old friend of Forster's.

16. Desmond MacCarthy did give the Leslie Stephen Lecture on Leslie Stephen at Cambridge on 27 May 1937 (published CUP, 1937). Duncan Grant's (unpublished) memoir recalled the occasion in 1920 when he, Vanessa Bell and Maynard Keynes were staying with the Berensons at *I Tatti* near Florence and, at a party given for Keynes to meet the Governor of the Bank of Italy, he (Duncan) unwittingly was taken for '*il gran' economista Inglese*' by the assembled bankers, while Maynard happily held forth upon painting to the collectors and *cognoscenti*.

17. Cf 'Shooting with Wilfred Blunt' in the posthumous collection *Memories* (1953) by Desmond MacCarthy. Sir George Otto Trevelyan (1838-1928), statesman and historian and father of R. C. (Bob) Trevelyan, was a keen shot. Sir Alfred Lyall (1835-1911), Etonian and eminent in the Indian civil service, was the author of *Verses Written in India* (1899).

18. After T. E. Lawrence's death in 1935, his brother and executor invited E. M. Forster to edit a volume of his letters; Forster's own anxieties and ill-health led him to relinquish this task, which then fell to David Garnett (his edition was published in 1938). See P. N. Furbank, *E. M. Forster: A Life*, vol. II (1978), pp. 207, 211.

we ever did. And Morgan said I felt so fond of everyone, I almost wept —I think he said that. Anyhow, it was a great success; & no nonsense about it.

Yesterday oh how Margery Fry snubbed me, by announcing, as she came into the room, that the reviews of The Y. had been so sniffy she was afraid it must have influenced the sales. This was said exactly as Dora Sanger says things. But I had hold of myself, & got some sparks out of her & then David & Rachel came, & I had the best bath of understanding praise yet had: D. said The Ys had helped him more than any book he had read; & was profoundly human, moving, & a triumph. & R. chimed in with perspicacious quotation. And I kindled & thought it genuine. BBC tonight: have put off the supper party & shall get through no doubt tolerably. I rested my brain on Lotta Leaf last night, so slept & am freshened.[19]

Friday 30 April

So we have reached the last day of this agitating month—far better than I could have foreseen. Doesnt the Lit Sup this morning finish its Centenary article by a reference to that great artist V.W. & The Years, & head it with the same immortal name? Why do they go out of their way to be polite, I wonder?[20] If it weren't for Julian going to Spain I should be wholly content on our French journey.

The BBC was moderately successful: that is I got my pecker up & read with ease & emotion; was then checked by the obvious fact that my emotion did not kindle George Barnes who [is] long & weary & reminds me of Adrian in his weary days (A. is no longer so weary—he had tea the other day & I found him sympathetic). But the bright bubble, the fly in the eye, & all the other effects—premonitory shivers & disgusts of that BBC gently subsided & vanished as I walked home through the cold streets alone, & thought that very few people had listened: the world much as usual. So great was the relief that I was very cordial to Barnes, & would have agreed to do another had he asked me. Remember, however, to refrain from that folly.

19. Dora Sanger (1865-1955), whose virtues invariably aggravated VW, was the widow of the universally beloved lawyer C. P. Sanger. *Walter Leaf, 1852-1927. Some Chapters of Autobiography.* With a Memoir by Charlotte M. Leaf (1932); she and her sisters Madge Vaughan and Katherine Furse were old Stephen family friends.

20. *TLS*, 1 May 1937: 'A Century of English Letters/Procession of the Novelists from Dickens to Virginia Woolf'. The article concludes: 'It may be that art is going to be pushed aside for a time under the stress of political and social indignations or anxieties: therefore let us welcome the latest manifestation of a great artist, Virginia Woolf, whose title fittingly and symbolically closes this retrospect, *"The Years"*.'

A very cold grey day; the Busmen threaten to strike tonight; streets laced across; camps & latrines in all the parks, like the Crimea; poles with silver hatchets along the pavements.[21] The Queen told David [Cecil] that she went all ice at the thought of the Coronation; said the monarchy hadnt the same position as in the days of Victoria. They went to grand party— Harold's—at B.P.: & agreed that the food was bad, & the wine delicious. King George's hair curls; Queen Eth is growing fat; jewels were worn, & the Band played The Merry Widow in a back room. There are miles of corridors to be walked. Many guests came in taxis. They had Lord S.'s car.[22] All the fiddles are tuning up. Barnes told me the BBC is having 150 microphones & observers along the route. I shall try to listen in from some French café. Seats are still to be had; my hairdresser's assistant bought one for 15/- in the New Zealand Stand. Hugh Walpole is to be knighted. We are giving a youthful party—Spenders, Chilvers, Julian, Plomer on Monday: cut Sibyl & the Bob Cecils lunch, & leave on Friday—that is one week, in which I must settle the question of clothes. In the past month & a half I have written Gibbon; Gibbon's Aunts; & the BBC, thus making I hope about £60: but oh such hard work. Gibbon remains to be copied out—the last turn of the screw. When I come back I shall instantly pounce on 3 Guineas & see what I can do.

Allington sneers at me on the BBC—too clever "for myself who am only a simple person"—& wrist watches were not invented in 1880—so the deans have their vanity, & if I say what I mean in 3 Guineas I must expect considerable hostility.[23] Yet I so slaver & silver my tongue that its sharpness takes some time to be felt. This maundering must cease: I must face the weekend drive down, so calm & happy, now its all over.

L.'s doctor says the eczema is much better: a disease afflicting printers oddly enough: a man, Dr Rau, intelligent enough to play with theories he cant answer. Ewart refuse for some inscrutable reason to put in our new watercloset: Norris's mechanations suspected; with what else can I fill this last blue inch?—sales of The Y. about 10,250; Amberleys going on for 300. Mr Pritchard thought me very original & amusing last night [on the BBC]. Stephen Spender thinks The Y. my best book: poetical in

---

21. London's 25,000 busmen went on strike from midnight on 30 April; they failed to secure their objectives and returned to work on 28 May. Streets and parks were being got ready for the approaching coronation of King George VI.

22. The dinner party at Buckingham Palace on 15 March is described by Harold Nicolson: *Diaries and Letters 1930-39* (1966), pp. 296-9. Lord S. = 4th Marquess of Salisbury, Lord David Cecil's father.

23. The Very Rev. Cyril Argentine Alington (1872-1955), Dean of Durham since 1933 and previously headmaster of Eton, broadcast on 'Taste in Fiction' in the series *Book Talk* on 15 April; part was published (but with no reference to VW) in *The Listener*, 28 April 1937.

the right sense; Nessa's show early next week. Shall I buy one? Am rather stingy at the moment. Now I shall stop[24]

Tuesday 4 May

The day mother died in 1895—that $\frac{37}{42}$ 42 years ago: & I remember it—

at the moment, watching Dr Seton walk away up Hyde Park Gate in the early morning with his head bowed, his hands behind his back. Also the doves swooping. We had been sent up to the day nursery after she died; & were crying. And I went to the open window & looked out. It must have been very soon after she died, as Seton was then leaving the house. How that early morning picture has stayed with me! What happened immediately afterwards I cant remember.[1]

I'm jaded after our youthful party—they stayed till 12.45. The Bus strike on, so that they couldn't get buses—had to walk. The streets look odd, all aflutter with banners—white in Bond Street, red at Selfridges; & no omnibuses; a lower level in the streets; all taxis & innumerable private cars; & droves & herds trudging the pavement. I went to Murray's smart new shop in Grosvenor Street; should never have faced it if I hadnt known him in his shabby days: a lovely 18th Century library turned into a work room with long trestle tables, & some big tree on the garden wall outside. Women—middleaged fat thin short paraded like Ascot horses for my very shy & incompetent observation. I felt the lure of clothes again. Ordered a dress—was tempted to get a coat too. But cant yet feel rich again: tho' they say The Years is in its 4th printing in America: only an advt. though, & H.B. not so scrupulous as we are. Then had to ford my way along Oxford Street, but the legs & shoulders so pressing & bothering I took to the back streets; finally the Tube; was shoved in at one door, pressed out behind a stout kind man who said "Barge after me"—why "barge"? to what social strata does that word belong? Public school, I think (by the way no letters about my BBC except private ones)

24. LW's new doctor was Dr Leo Rau, a German refugee with Berlin and Scottish qualifications. Ewarts of Euston Road were sanitary engineers and Norris & Sons a local firm of builders. George Pritchard was a partner in the firm of solicitors, Dolmann and Pritchard, the Woolf's friendly tenants on the ground and first floors of 52 Tavistock Square. '32 Recent Paintings by Vanessa Bell' were shown at Alex. Reid & Lefevre, 1A King Street, St James's; VW went on 6 May and bought a 'divinely lovely' picture (see *VI VW Letters*, no. 3246).

1. Julia Stephen died on 5 May 1895 (VW has mistakenly dated this entry *Tuesday May 5th*); see also *II VW Diary*, 5 May 1924 and *Moments of Being*, p. 84 for similar recollections of the morning of her death.

The party though—jaded as I am I must refer to the party. Sally: Julian; bell rings: the Spenders; Chilver: William. So we were crowded— no fire: a hot spring night. Julian was bitter at dinner against the B[loomsbur]y habit of education. He had been taught no job; only a vague literary smattering. But I wanted you to go to the Bar, I said. Yes, but you didn't insist upon it to my mother, he remarked, rather forcibly. He now finds himself at 29 without any special training. But then he objected, as I thought, to all professions. An argument in favour of my ½ professions. Sally agreed. Downstairs we found Inez; controlled; small: of the Greek horse type; a little fixed & rigid; shy I daresay; in a red dressing gown dress: very silent; precise. William immensely fat; as if just taken off the Brighton pier: jubicund: much Hugh gossip & banter; H. is becoming a Knight, tho' I know you'll laugh. I was in favour of his Autobiography Julian against it.² The Chilver sat all inhibited & nerve drawn, so I had to give him claret & sit by him & make party talk, about carpentering & bulbs. He wd. like to leave the Air Ministry & become a carpenter—make good chairs—but of course wont & cant, though Sally urges. Another aspect of the professional question. Air Ministry long hours, hard work; but regular & safe. Julian now all in favour of a settled job: even the Treasury. He is learning the mechanics of lorries. Hadn't even been taught that at Cambridge—only the eternal Pope—wh. I scrambled through as a child. Poor old Julian—rather on a crazy edge of life I feel. And then there was some well informed political talk to which Inez contributed, dispassionately, sensibly. I daresay there's something to her; but why they chose to connect themselves forever—she & Stephen—God knows. Seemed to me completely separate: he critical, polite, unintimate with her.

Every moment till we go seems now numbered like stones in a building—& thats why I shall be so relieved on Friday—no numbers of any stones for almost 3 weeks— And then— Still more must this be true of L. who, with every moment plotted has to endure the actual presence of Mrs Jones, who stumped round on foot just now, employed by Dr Jones. Reminds me of Mrs Cartwright & the General strike, arriving on a rusty bicycle.³ Desmond is going to do L.S. on the 26th May. Shall I go? in my new dress? Nothing from the TLS about Gibbon:

---

2. Hugh Walpole sent VW his autobiographical *The Apple Trees* for Christmas in 1932 (see lot 107 in Sotheby Sale, 27 April 1970); in her letter of thanks (*V VW Letters* no. 2687) she wrote: '. . . of all literature . . . I love autobiography most.'

3. Mrs Jones was Katherine, wife of Dr Ernest Jones (1879-1958), pioneer of psychoanalysis in England, and editor of the British Psycho-Analytical Library which since 1924 had been published by the Hogarth Press. Mrs Cartwright had been secretary to the Press from 1925-31.

but Dadie writes that G. Trev. approved. Odd how recognition eddies about. Now to write to Susie Buchan.[4]

The Woolfs crossed to Dieppe from Newhaven by the night boat on Friday 7 May, and toured Western France by car as far south as Albi; they recrossed the channel on Sunday night, 23 May, and after some twenty-four hours at Monks House, returned to London. LW's diary (LWP, Sussex) details their itinerary. The ensuing chronicle of their tour is typewritten on five pages which have been inserted in Diary XXVI; VW's very slapdash typing has been corrected.

Tuesday 25 May

These are the rough and rapid chronicles of our last French voyage which to fill this distracted morning I will try to copy here.

For example: the first vines are to be seen at La Chemille; that is on Sunday the 8th May 1937, driving from Dieppe on a fairly fine morning. Also the road ahead looked like a white steeple. Then at *rising straight up.* Uzerche where we stayed we saw a woman sewing a white cloth on the banks of the river. She called the cows which obeyed. The river had a fresh lip. The flowers were like an Elizabethan meadow. A man chopped wood in the wood above. I could hear the hollow sounds. No other sound. And a boy showed us the way, opening the door of a great barn. Also that day we punctured and the man at the garage, talking about Mitz who was always our introduction to humanity, said how he'd been in Gambia, and longed to be there not in this dead alive French village; where his wifes parents made him live.

So to Souillac. There it became two hundred years ago. There we sat on the banks of the Dordogne in the evening and saw the man in the great hat and gaiters, and women washing clothes on the shingle. There was a cabin built against the rock like a scene in a play; and a man sitting there while the women went in and out. All this I said happened two hundred years ago. The castle was Cromwell Road; but had a chapel and soft brown roofed barns. Roofs here like high felt hats pulled down with

4. George Macaulay Trevelyan (1876-1962) was Regius Professor of Modern History at Cambridge; replying on a postcard to George Rylands, VW wrote: 'I never thought to take in a real historian.' (*VI VW Letters*, no. 3243). Susan Buchan, now Lady Tweedsmuir (1882-1977), whose husband was Governor-General of Canada, was a very old friend of VW's; no letter to her of this date survives.

a dent in the middle. Chapel reminded me of times of Rousseau. Man went fishing. Peasants employed perhaps by the great house. Sudden violent storm—as usual. Climate here 'temperamental'.

The perfect day.—May—I forget what. Hot. To the Caves [Les Eyzies]. The brownish red tracings of prehistoric animals half rubbed out by children who used to play here, until someone from Paris came and looked for these pictures. All this country very classical with its poplars in straight decorous groves; and the hills beyond. Then I had a bad time in an antiquity shop—very nasty people the old furniture sellers everywhere. Liars and spiders catching tourists. Had to buy a five shilling plate to be quit and not popular at that. The cupboards only cost £3 but couldnt be sent. Man did bad drawings of Paris life— youthful memories, stupid and imitative. The vanity of an artist and the avarice of a peasant. But I saw their bedroom which interested me. W.C. opening out of it. Then it became very hot. A town crier went round Souillac beating a drum announcing a play by Loti. Both were upset from eating truffle perhaps. Great day at Meyronne, where I wish to live—up in the castle. An old woman shredding salsify. Talked about wild boars— sometimes killed; quite tame; they eat them. Church full of flowers for the Pentecôte. The farm with the great pigeon house; all these old things not preserved but used and allowed to fall into decay.

Sunday was the fête. People in bright clothes. Villages full of black men, standing about. The lady like the Princesse Lointaine going into the ruins.[5] Farm carts in the cloister. A little girl who lived in the cloister and caught snails for Mitz. On 17th May I was thinking about action; how far directed or dictated by publicity motives, therefore largely impure, while we took in petrol at Villefranches: on road to Albi. Cold cloudy day. Left Souillac in a state of wild distraction. Madame like Sibyl C. at a party, doing accounts, answering questions about cheese, about bills, &c. Umbrellas open on the Place; people dining out there. Very bad dinner owing to crowd the night of the feast. At last the diners were so many we got up and left. Bank Holiday in France. Then to Najac— sordidly medieval; bossed; with great beams; and muffled grinning heads; round a mediaeval fountain. No place for human beings to live in—the middle ages. Houses perched on top of cliff. River flattened out beneath. An unreal dead crawling quiet, as if they were inhabiting an old shell. The old men gossiping with their pointed walking sticks. No life; no shops; dirt and misery. Albi on a very wet bank holiday. A flashy hotel; circle of blue and red electric light in the hall which went in and out. Bad dinner. The worst hotel yet found. Walked in the rain. Cathedral magnificent—like factory in red: firm, fluted, rock-like, painted within. And so on. Rain all night. Room thick with dust. Walls stained—bugs

5. *La Princesse lointaine* (1895), poetic drama by Edmond Rostand.

possible. Off to Rodez now in a northern hill country. Houses changing. Still the helmets.

At Rodez the best hotel in the world. Spirits sprung up. A long walk after tea. Sat and looked at the mountains, over the very green flat nightingale valley. No Coronation movies. Reading *Elle et Lui*, a very good best seller [*by George Sand*]. Cant stop reading. They say May is always stormy. Oh a very fine rust red cathedral at Rodez. In a valley—I suppose, stopping for petrol. The Dordogne running through a meadow; very steep green brushed hills; mob headed trees. Cold and grey.

Reading Beckford by [Guy] Chapman [1937]—but why write about this cold egotist? this nugatory man? A chirp of birds and grass hoppers. Aurillac first class hotel. Dinner of character; fried eggs, ham and rice. Choc. cream with biscuits floating. Aubergines with chopped bacon and gravy; also stuffed with cheese dressing. Am forgetting English words like artichoke. Rather a dirty sky. Now on to Toulle [Tulle].

Cold, cold and wet; slept in the village of Treysac—but how do you spell it [Treignac]? Went walking to the top of the mountain to find the druid stones; all drenched green under trees; cuckoo calling; a little shepherds farm; rain coming down in full flood; as we went up following arrows, paths twisting; divine views all misted and shrouded; green lit. Had to stop, wet to skin, plod back; change; dine for 2/-; but left hungry, so to bed; no chairs; clean little place, should be seen again so lovely was it even then; still raining—now we are driving to Gueret and now I am thinking about 4 dimensional character: different aspects to be given— not the one personal intensity. But what on earth do I mean? Not I hope to excuse my own limitations; see Desmond in *Sunday Times*; who as usual depresses me beyond reason.[6] Conversation at Vallensay [Valençay] about Talleyrand. D. of Valensay. No he's not very good, not very bad. Has no children, divorced—his wife was an American. Mlle Worth— some such name. Comes here. Keeps birds, zebras for his pleasure; has a hotel at Paris. But you should see his zebras. Great nephew of the great Talleyrand. Very rich.[7]

Lost spectacles at Beaugency—the perfect town on the Loire. Maintenon 50 miles from Paris; old claws of ruin against the bright evening sky after dinner. Birds singing; many nightingales, very fine and pure. All

6. Desmond MacCarthy's long review, entitled 'The Ever-Rolling Stream', appeared in the *Sunday Times* of 9 May 1937. '. . . of the drama of the will in action out of which stories are made . . . she knows nothing. What an extraordinary, what a fatal, limitation, you would say, in a novelist! And yet (it is the mark of the artist to make his limitations also serve his end) she succeeds in being one.'

7. The owner of the Château de Valençay in 1937 was Boson Talleyrand-Périgord, duc de Valençay et de Sagan (1867-1952); he had been married (from 1901-1904) to the daughter of Levi P. Morton, American banker, sometime Vice-president of the USA, and Minister to France.

silent and unspoilt. But this has rapidly changed. 50 miles an hour. C'est un oustiti—un petit singe. Est-ce qu'il est dangereux? The same talk we've had at every town: shows the poverty of the human race. Blazing hot taking in petrol. Lunch Rouen in a sq. off the Cathedral. No salt, the English say. I give them salt. Now petrol running out. Hot sun, but this Brighton Road empty, flat, uninhabited. Boudanville 8k. Le Havre 73k. Mitz here gave her last representation as I hope. Last petrol taken. Anxious about Maynard to the extent of dreading post or buying a paper. Old wounds twinging.[8] Still a very good end to journey. No bad news of Maynard at Dieppe; a good hotel the Rhine; man who talked fluently and intelligently after dinner about South Africa; mines; diamonds—how different from rubies; about fish; about soles and the French taking fish from Grimsby; about cooking; his wife used to cook; now lives at residential hotel; a biologist; round; chubby; spry; very objective and interesting about facts; would like to talk to innumerable people in hotels about their jobs. Night boat; calm sea; arrive at New-haven; the Customs find cigars in the other car; pass us; we breakfasted at the Bridge Inn; on eggs and bacon; so to M.H. all very private and quiet; and glad of chairs and intimacy and the garden lush with grass and fruit trees not standing the comparison at all badly. Sally jumped at L.; deserted Percy. Now to London for two days and another week here.

Monday 1 June

Monks House.

I have at last got going with 3 Guineas—after 5 days grind, re-copying & to some extent re-writing, my poor old brain hums again—largely I think because I had a good long walk yesterday & so routed the drowse— it was very hot— At any rate I must use this page as a running ground— for I cant screw all the 3 hours; I must relax & race here the last hour. Thats the worst of writing—its waste. What can I do with the last hour of my morning? Dante again. But oh how my heart leaps up to think that never again shall I be harnessed to a long book. No. Always short ones in future. The long book still wont be altogether downed—its rever[b]erations grumble. Did I say—no the London days were too tight, too hot, & distracted for this book—that H. Brace wrote & said they were happy to find that The Years is the best selling novel in America? This was confirmed by my place at the head of the list in the Herald Tribune. They have sold 25,000—my record, easily. (now I am

---

8. At Guéret on 21 May VW picked up a letter dated 16 May from Vanessa, telling her that Maynard Keynes was seriously ill at Cambridge—too ill to be moved to hospital.

Monday 14th
Jun. The Years
still is top of
the list.

Monday. 12th
July The Years
still top of the
list. & has
been weekly.

Aug. 23rd:
Years now 2nd
or 3rd. 9
editions

Yesterday,
Oct. 22nd, it
was last on
the list.

dreaming of 3 Guineas) We think if we make money of buying perhaps an annuity. The great desirable is not to have to earn money by writing. I am doubtful if I shall ever write another novel— Certainly not unless under great compulsion such as The Years imposed on me. Were I another person, I would say to myself, Please write criticism; biography; invent a new form for both; also write some completely unformal fiction: short: & poetry: Fate has here a hand in it, for when I've done 3 Gs—wh. I hope to have written, not yet for publication tho', in August, I intend to put the script aside, & write Roger. What I think best wd. be to work hard at 3 Gs for a month—June: then begin reading & rereading my Roger notes.

By the way, I have been sharply abused in Scrutiny, wh., L. says, calls me a cheat in The Waves & The Years; most intelligently (& highly) praised by Faulkner in America—& thats all.[1] (I mean thats all I need I think write about reviews now; I suspect the clever young man is going to enjoy downing me—so be it: but in private Sally Graves & Stephen Spender approve: so, to sum up, I dont know, this is honest, where I stand; but intend to think no more of it. Gibbon was rejected by the N. Republic, so I shall send no more to America. Nor will I write articles at all except for the Lit Sup: for whom I am going now to do Congreve.)[2]

It has been August hot; Nessa came over & we had a long natural gossip. Maynard has been very ill but is better. Must rest for 6 months. Duncan in France. We stay here for one weeks perfect solitude. Then a London season, very hectic I guess. I should make a note of Desmond's queer burst of intimacy the other evening. He came, was waiting, the evening we arrived—last Tuesday that is; read us his L[eslie]. S[tephen]. lecture, a rather laboured but honest but perfunctory lecture: after which he & I sitting in the twilight with the door open, L. coming in & out, discussed his shyness: he says he thinks it made him uncreative. Could he have told his intimate friends his private life it would (for some reason) have freed, enriched him. But he was shy; afraid of sinking in our opinion. Not surface shy of course; but heart shy. Reference to his

1. 'When she had written *To the Lighthouse* there were three courses open to Mrs Woolf. Either she could enlarge her scope, do something fresh; or she could stop writing altogether; or she could cheat by way of technique. She chose the last of these alternatives.' Wilfred M. Mellers (then an undergraduate of Downing College, Cambridge) reviewing *The Years* in the June issue of *Scrutiny* (see *M&M*, pp. 395-9). Faulkner's notice has not been traced.

2. See *TLS*, 25 September 1937: 'Congreve's Comedies: Speed, Stillness and Meaning' (Kp C352).

mistresses. He then asked if I thought he had still power to write a good book. What could he do with his wretched stump of life? I said write your private thoughts, not autobiography. And tell us your private life. He said Oh yes, I'll come & talk to you. And I'll write it you. I felt something uneasy, trying to express itself; egotistical, weak I daresay. I think I see why he has been so fluent, so friendly, so embarrassingly anxious to be on some warmer footing, this last few months. Its his pressing need to write a good book somehow to assert himself before the stump of life is thrown on the fire. But how far am I sincere in thinking that he can? Isnt there a fatal softness, flabbiness; now gone too far? But how can one judge? Thats my note—not altogether satisfactory, & leaving it unshaded—the picture of D. now in my mind—my affection, my unintimate, but all the same genuine affection for him. He repudiated Maurice Baring or—some titled lady I think—as 'friends'. Said his most intimate friend was G. Moore: but was shy with him. Could not ask him that is, if he had found marriage disappointing. D. is decided that he has. Mrs M. a woman who will drag in education.[3]

Lady Simon, too, another visitor those crowded days, will drag in education. She sent me a report, private, of the meeting at Newnham to discuss the great question if gowns should be worn. This is connected with the question, is it time to ask the U[niversit]y to admit us? And she says, next time, if ever, you are asked to lecture, please print your answer; her wish being that the question should be frankly & rashly posed—by me, in default of Girton & Somerville. Well, perhaps, if I can bring off 3 Gs.[4] But can I. Down here—now cold—I scribble & traverse miles of argument as I walk through Tristrams Grove to Piddinghoe. Mr Gwynne's cows wear brown holland coats.[5] Oh so hot yesterday: today the air splintered into arrows & the sun muffled & whitened. Mary H. asks me to dine to meet the Duff Coopers. Courage bids me say Yes. But my hair? & my dress?

3. Maurice Baring (1874-1945), diplomat, man of letters and of the world, whose writing was held in particularly high esteem by Ethel Smyth—an estimation not shared by VW. Desmond MacCarthy and the philosopher G. E. Moore (1873-1958) were both at Trinity College, Cambridge, and Apostles; in 1916 Moore had married Dorothy Ely (1892-1977).

4. Lady Simon (who came to tea with VW on 27 May) was a member of the Governing Body of Newnham from 1924-39. Women at Cambridge were not admitted to full and equal membership of the University until 1947; in 1937 the tactics of attaining this objective were under discussion at both women's colleges; VW adverts to the matter in *Three Guineas*, p. 55 and note. Since Oxford women had obtained full equality in 1920, the reference to Somerville is perplexing.

5. Neville Gwynne, of Deans, Piddinghoe—about two miles down the Ouse valley from Rodmell—was one of the principal local landowners; he kept a herd of Jersey cows.

*The Woolfs returned to Tavistock Square on the afternoon of Sunday 6 June,
and dined that evening with Clive Bell.*

Friday 11 June

Brain rather dried up after 6 days strenuous London. Tuesday dinner
to meet Duff Cooper; Wednesday Ethel Smyth; Thursday Nessa &
dressmaker; Friday Harcourt Brace.[6] So I'm running in a circle, having
got on to the university chapter a difficult one. Very very hot. Very
noisy. The hotel dancing: buses everywhere; a hop & frying [?]. And on
top, Julian gone to Spain on Monday: & on Tuesday, news that Wogan
was wounded, a man with him killed.[7] So, a strain: which I cannot now
go into: & it must last—how long? A year? Who knows? Anything to
keep talking, inventing, distracting.

Wednesday 16 June

Apostle Night last night: a good one L. says. Sydney's son made one
of the best young man speeches.[8] But I have not heard much gossip yet,
since it lasted till one; & the morning is given to business. Just finishing
the education section: much re-arranged. Then I shall have a few days
flutter, I think. Congreve perhaps.

Helen dined with me: & the night before I dined with the Camerons,
& heard Tony's version of Mary: looks like a gnat, or a jerboa; prominent
startled blue eyes, hands held like a jerboas. A pale pretty Shelley
imitation American girl there, who sat on the floor, at my feet, &
unfortunately adores & worships & gave me primroses one day in the
winter & her poems. Not a type from which I now get much kick.[9]

6. VW (but not LW) dined with the Hutchinsons on 8 June with Duff Cooper and his
wife Lady Diana; he had just been appointed First Lord of the Admiralty by
Neville Chamberlain, who succeeded Baldwin as Prime Minister on the latter's
resignation on 28 May. Donald Clifford Brace (1881-1955), founder and vice-
President of VW's American publishers Harcourt Brace & Co., lunched with the
Woolfs on 11 June.

7. Julian Bell, immovably set on going to Spain despite the rational and emotional
opposition of his mother and friends, had compromised to the extent of joining the
non-combatant organization Spanish Medical Aid as an ambulance driver. The
Hon. Wogan Philipps (Rosamond Lehmann's husband), also a member of SMA,
suffered concussion and a broken arm during an insurgent air raid to the north-west
of Madrid.

8. The annual Apostles' dinner was held in London. John Conrad Waterlow (b. 1916),
scholar of Eton and now a medical student at Trinity College, Cambridge, was the
son of the Woolfs' old friend the diplomat Sir Sydney Waterlow.

9. At dinner at the Camerons (Elizabeth Bowen and her husband) on 14 June, VW
met William Plomer's friend Anthony (Tony) Butts (1900-41), rich old-Etonian

93

Yes. London is hectic. But I'm going to reserve the next few days for moodiness. Cant always be on the hop without shaking my brains dry. No news of Julian; cant go to MH this week end because Sally may accouche. We have laid down a mattress & clothes' drying screens to protect her.

I've seen: the Hutchinsons: Diana [Cooper] beautiful, veiled, easy going. Desmond there. Then Ethel Smyth: with her rough old claws scratching. Sniffing out 3 Gs. Then to the Coronation film, bits & bits; some good; others not. Then to Herbert's on Sunday; oh the ugliness of that perfectly self-satisfied passive stockbrokers life: the Wyandottes, the orchard, the picture—the coloured photograph—the mats, the maids, Freda soft & motherly with a cat for a child: unreal, padded, easy . . & we walked at Staines. Then Adrian after dinner, on a visit of friendship. Then the Bowen, Bowras, Butts; then Helen . . . Now lunch.[10]

Sunday 20 June

An odd thought strikes me, now that I think so much of conduct &c. (for 3 Gs). Why does one secretly desire the misfortunes of one's friends? It is a cold grey day, & secretly I'm pleased that the Bells are at Charleston & we in London: I mean I'm glad that they should have a bad week end. Yet this kind of gladness is not so pleasant as the other. But after splitting meanings in my Congreve, I dont take this page in order to continue.

I have turned on my electric fire—now the sun's out. Willie [Robson] is upstairs, & Mabel comes in to say, shall she buy sausages? I'm rather cross, since I had hoped to have one unravished day. Cant get on with my 4 Congreve plays. Last evening Ann Watkins forced her way in: offered me—I could see the bait put on the hook—£1000 & all expenses if I wd. go to USA & lecture 3 times weekly for 3 months. What about I asked. That they didn't mind. The more personal the better: for instance, about my experience of publishing, bringing in my marriage—a happy one. At this, your husband, who is sitting in the audience, will cry BOO!

---

playboy and painter whose elder sister Mary Butts, an extravagantly Bohemian character whom he mistrusted and was ashamed of, had died in March, aged 44. (VW's description refers to his, rather than to his sister's, appearance.) The 'Shelley imitation' was May Sarton (b. 1912), an American who came to England in 1936 and later, through fellow-lodgers in Bloomsbury, met Elizabeth Bowen. For VW's acknowledgement of her tribute, see *VI VW Letters*, no. 3234; and for May Sarton's own account of her relations with VW see *I Knew A Phoenix*, 1954.

10. Herbert Woolf (1869-1949), LW's elder brother, a stockbroker, and his wife Alfreda lived at Cookham Dean in Berkshire. VW disappointingly fails to record her impression of Elizabeth Bowen's friend the ebullient Oxford wit and scholar Maurice Bowra (1898-1971)—presumably a fellow-guest at dinner on 14 June—whose name she merely notes.

Well we declined. I was to repeat the same lecture—not to read it, but to speak it. That was very important. And Aldous & Gerald Heard, those apostles of the inner life & peace & goodness, are touring the States doing this in duet.[11] Lord lord! what an example for the Soul . . . & what a good quote for my book. I was amused by her perfectly frank commercialism. Money—money—money. Couldnt help liking her—so fat, so coarse, like a bathing woman still touseled & blowsy from the sea. "I've had a chequered career" she said. And told us how she had lectured to "nice young women . . . when I wasn't one at all myself" she said. No: I dont think she'll even be able to sell my stories for me. What they want & Don Brace wants is that I should come over & exhibit my person, & make money for Don & for Ann. And what would they spend the proceeds of my personality on? Drink I should say, looking at Ann's cheeks. Don would presumably buy his daughter a new dress. And I dont want a thousand myself, if I pay for it by hearing a gramophone forever braying in my head. She was honestly disappointed; & I cdn't finish my Congreve. And must now write & thank Margaret Keynes for a nice trusty old world letter about The Years.[12]

I must add, we are waiting for Sally to give birth: so havent gone away: but is she even pregnant? L. asks again & again. He has made her a bed behind screens in his study. But she leaps & laughs.

Tuesday 22 June

Isnt it shameful to write here first thing, not to tackle Congreve? But my brain after talking to Miss Sarton, to Murray, to Ann [Stephen] gave out after dinner, so that I cdn't read Love for Love. And I won't do 3 Gs. till Monday—till I've had a quiet breather. Then the Prof. Chapter: then the final . . .

So now to draw the blood off that brain to another part—according to H. Nicolson's prescription, which is the right one. I wd. like to write a dream story about the top of a mountain. Now why? About lying in the snow; about rings of colour; silence . . . & the solitude. I cant though. But shant I, one of these days, indulge myself in some short releases into that world? Short now for ever. No more long grinds: only sudden intensities. If I cd. think out another adventure. Oddly enough I see it

11. Ann Watkins was a New York literary and lecture agent. Heard and the Huxleys had sailed for America (where they were all to settle) in April 1937; in October Aldous and Heard embarked on a lecture tour, giving 'a sort of Mutt and Jeff on war and peace and religion and so on'. (See *The Letters of Aldous Huxley*, edited by Grover Smith, 1969, p. 426).

12. Margaret Keynes, *née* Darwin (1890-1974), wife of Maynard's brother the surgeon and bibliophile Geoffrey Keynes, wrote from the R.M.S. *Queen Mary*; her letter is in MHP, Sussex. For VW's reply see *VI VW Letters*, no. 3263.

now ahead of me—in Charing X road yesterday—as to do with books: some new combination. Brighton? A round room on the pier—& people shopping, missing each other—a story Angelica told in the summer. But how does this make up with criticism? I'm trying to get the 4 dimensions of the mind . . life in connection with emotions from literature— A days walk—a mind's adventure: something like that. And its useless to repeat my old experiments: they must be new to be experiments.

Ann is a great sea monster. Her hair is bound with a fillet bought at Woolworth. She is sunburnt, sea kissed. What I mean is she's like the figure head of the Aurora Jane. She & Richard (engaged?) ask us to supper on Monday.[13] This pleases us, who are now teased & tried by invitations of every sort. The young are pretty ruthless though. Fierce & egotistical, also very sensitive. Ann said she shd. have taken a First: owing to politics took a third. I gave her 5gs. but she didn't think it cost me much—certainly hadn't read The Years.

Sarton had: disappointed; but a 'greater book' than Waves. Waves her cup o' tea. Her cup o' rose water—that is, she's fine drawn, wd. be poetic, more gushing though in letter than in speech. She has a shrewd American vein: she ran a theatre for 3 years in N. York; but it failed so she took to poetry, & the Zoo: that is lives, for the summer, in Julian Huxley's lodging at Whipsnade, writing a novel for Kot, & we had to promise to dine there.[14] Ann Watkins is now hot on the scent of magazine articles, & wants another talk. But here my gorge rises. No I will not write for the larger paying magazines: in fact, couldn't. In this way I put 3 Guineas daily into practice. For here's Rosemary Beresford coming, & I shall tactfully cross-examine her about Eng. Lit. at Cambridge. Ann thinks Pernel far too conservative. Miss Cristal wants a chapel. Miss C. wont let them have gramophones. But they're allowed out at night.[15]

13. Richard Llewelyn-Davies (1912-81), son of Crompton and nephew of Margaret Llewelyn Davies, old friends of the Woolfs; he had been at Trinity College, Cambridge, and was now pursuing his studies at the Architectural Association and living in rooms (in the same house as E. M. Forster) at 26 Brunswick Square. He and Ann Stephen married in 1938.

14. May Sarton—who came to tea with VW on 21 June—had been lent his apartment at the Zoological Society's country outpost at Whipsnade by Julian Huxley, secretary to the Society from 1935-42. Through the Huxleys she had met Koteliansky, then acting as reader to the Cresset Press, which published her first novel, The Single Hound, in 1938.

15. Rosemary Beresford (b. 1916) was the elder daughter of J. B. Beresford (1888-1940), civil servant, man of letters, Treasury colleague and close friend of the Woolfs' eccentric old friend Saxon Sydney-Turner (1880-1962); she had just left Newnham College, Cambridge, of which Pernel Strachey (1876-1951) was Principal. Edith Margaret Chrystal (1887-1963) was College Tutor and Director of Studies in Theology there.

We're a poor college, she said casually, therefore cant join clubs. But I doubt if she sees the force of my arguments. She is absorbed in politics— communism—& Richard. According to her the scheme is to accept L[abour]. P[arty]. policy, of gradual revision: Edu[catio]n, wages; socialism; but to be ready to enforce it by force. Force may ⟨produce⟩ win what cant be won except by force. She instanced the Fr. Revn. I denied it. Its the glory of death in battle, not in childbirth that appeals to them; the spectacular; the limelight. But I shall investigate further on Monday.

Wednesday 23 June

Its ill writing after reading Love for Love—a masterpiece. I never knew how good it is. And what exhilaration there is in reading these masterpieces. This superb hard English! Yes, always keep the Classics at hand to prevent flop. I cant write out my feeling, though; must decant it tomorrow in an article. But neither can I settle to read poor Rosemary's verses, as I should with a view to this evening. How could L.S. in DNB. deny C[ongreve]. feeling, passion [?]—more in that one play than in all Thackeray: & the indecency often honesty. But eno'—

I went shopping, whitebait hunting to Selfridges yesterday, & it grew roasting hot, & I was in black—such astonishing chops & changes this summer—often one's caught in a storm, frozen, or roasted. As I reached 52, a long trail of fugitives—like a caravan in a desert—came through the square: Spaniards flying from Bilbao, which has fallen, I suppose.[16] Somehow brought tears to my eyes, tho' no one seemed surprised. Children trudging along; women in London cheap jackets with gay handkerchiefs on their heads, young men, & all carrying either cheap cases, & bright blue enamel kettles, very large, & saucepans, filled I suppose with gifts from some Charity—a shuffling trudging procession, flying—impelled by machine guns in Spanish fields to trudge through Tavistock Sqre, along Gordon Square, then where?—clasping their enamel kettles. A strange spectacle—they went on, knowing wh. way: I suppose someone directed them. One boy was chatting—the others absorbed—like people on the trek. A reason why we cant write like Congreve I suppose.

16. Bilbao finally fell to the rebel Spanish forces on 18 June; but as the pressure of the Fascist attack increased, some 4000 Basque children had been evacuated in the *Royal Oak* which landed them at Southampton on 23 May. In the following weeks the refugees were dispersed to various country centres, and the party observed by VW was presumably in transit, making its way on foot from one London railway terminus to another.

JUNE 1937

Thursday 24 June

A letter from Ott. praising my NS. Gibbon article [*Reflections at Sheffield Place*]. Now I have observed that any of my friends who disliked The Years always praise my articles, by way of urging me to give up fiction, & I suppose to make amends to me for not liking The Years. She has been *very* ill; almost thought she wd have "waved us adieu" but is recovering at Tunbridge Wells. Pipsy reads Emma to her, & she reads H James to herself.[17]

I bought my 4 amber tubes as theyre called on Wednesday 23rd June. I want to see how long they last uncracked.

Last night was a hard & fruitless grind: that is, I cant see why Saxon shd have dropped Rosemary [*omission*] into our mill; nor was there much point in bringing the Finn—a flaxen honest girl, who spoke very little English, & couldn't understand a third of what we said. Saxon himself maintained almost complete silence—benevolent, but self indulgent; lazy. Why? I asked again & again, and should have had even harder work if Ann & Richard Ll. D. hadn't come in; Karin & Adrian on top, rather unharmoniously. So we tumbled & tossed. Poor little RB [*omission*], going to teach Eng. Lit. to children in the provinces. So I lashed out at teaching Eng Lit. Ann very spontaneous, ardent & rough, at the same time sensitive—a very attractive combination, with the beauty of a ships figure head—a little blown back & battered. Richard I suppose selfish, but amiable enough. Rebecca West asked us to dine that night. Well—I dont know if that wd have done better. Odd that Saxon was so insistent for so little reason.[18]

Friday 25 June

To the Albert Hall meeting last night. The last I swear.[19] Inaudible. Megaphone to those behind merely vociferates split words. A little family gossip. Nessa Duncan Morgan. Oh but I liked being introduced to Auden, who wanted Stephen to bring him up. A small rough haired terrier man: slits for eyes; a crude face; interesting, I expect, but wire

17. Since suffering a stroke in May, Lady Ottoline Morrell had been in Dr A. J. D. Cameron's private clinic in Tunbridge Wells, being treated for an agglomeration of ailments. 'Pipsy' was her husband, Philip Morrell (1870-1943).

18. Rebecca West (1892-1983), novelist, literary critic, and political writer.

19. A meeting organised by the National Joint Committee for Spanish Relief and denominated 'Spain and Culture' was held at the Albert Hall on 24 June for the purpose of raising funds for the Basque refugee children. The Woolfs were among the notable writers, artists, and performers invited to sit on the platform behind the speakers.

haired, yellowish white. Charles Trevelyan &c. Then speeches. Then semi jocular money collecting; then an auction of pictures. One by Picasso: one by Kapp. All very stagey empty & unreal. Wogan with his arm in a sling: looked tragic when unwatched, so I thought, listening to the Basque children singing on the gramophone. Robeson sang: a sympathetic, malleable, nigger, expressive, uninhibited, all warmth & the hot vapours of African forests.[20] I took several snubs & benedictions; thus:—Bunny cold, Morgan indifferent, Auden warm, Sally friendly; Kingsley Martin uneasy—a man I dont like—so voluble, histrionic, & he drove us home, taking a hand off the wheel to gesticulate—a different style of driving from Leonard's. I'm hurrying. Cant analyse. Off to MH. No puppies. A finer day. Olaf Stapledon has sent me his new book: wh. flatters me, as 3 papers say it's a masterpiece; the 4th says its bad. But am I more genially disposed because he says he admires me?[21] Oh for this perfect soul business: how can we pretend to it? Starting my Congreve: going to do it in 3 days at MH. Then back to 3 Gs. refreshed.

Monday 28 June

Home is the hunter, home from the hill, & the Wolves are back from Monks House.[22] And much refreshed into the bargain. Three solitary nights. Think of that! Was there ever such a miracle? Not a voice, not a telephone. Only the owl calling; perhaps a clap of thunder, the horses going down to the Brooks, & Mr Botten [*farmer*] calling with the milk in the morning. A hot sulphurous week end, as if a cloud of white dust were over Lewes. The red grasses cut. Hay in black marks on the hill.

20. Sir Charles Trevelyan, 3rd Bt (1870-1958), R. C. (Bob) Trevelyan's elder brother, had been a Labour MP and public servant. The money-collecting (some £1500 was raised) was the speciality of Isobel Brown, who possessed almost irresistable powers of persuasion. Edmond X. Kapp (1890-1978), artist and caricaturist. Paul Robeson (1898-1976), the American negro singer and actor, was described by Vanessa (letter to QB) as 'the real star of the evening—he is superb to look at . . . & his voice fits his looks'.

21. On 9 March 1937 Olaf Stapledon (1886-1950), author of the best selling *Last and First Men* (1930), wrote to VW: 'Thank you. My work is so crude compared with yours. Your appreciation cheers me a lot.' (LWP, Sussex)—though what occasioned his letter is obscure. He had now sent her an inscribed copy of *Star Maker*, described by his publisher as a 'Cosmological Fantasy'. On 15 July 1937, replying to VW's (lost) letter of thanks, he expressed his pleasure that 'some of the ideas in it fall in line with your own thought'. (MHP, Sussex.)

22. 'This be the verse you grave for me:

> *Here he lies where he long'd to be;*
> *Home is the sailor, home from sea,*
> *And the hunter home from the hill.*'

From *Requiem* by Robert Louis Stevenson.

Some, in the meadows, still up to my knees, & able to cover me as I lay on the river bank yesterday. We got very hot trying to move a chair—for L. this time; but it stuck; Louie & I butted like rams; L. hauled like a horse. There it stuck half way up the stairs & was only moved, down again, by Percy in his best Sunday brown coat. (By the way he talks of leaving).[23] Up at 7.30 this morning, picked a rose, & drove up through Wimbledon, as Wandsworth Bridge is mending. Wimbledon all lush & pastoral; a crowd in Portland Road, but back by 10.30, & at work on the Second Guinea by 11. It is now started, that very difficult chapter, but I was heartened by reading some of the first: saw it as 3 Chapters suddenly; & if I can drive my pen hard, might have it done by August. But theres a terrible lot of reasoning (for me) & fitting in of the right quotations. Roger waiting too. Letters from Altounyan, Mary Fisher—Willy is dead: saw it on Friday's placard—& the dossier from Ethel Smyth.[24]

[*Tuesday 29 June*]

Mrs Woolf will you do me a great service? chirped up that bright little bird Isherwood at Richard's last night. It was to send a message to a conference of Int. Libertarians at Madrid. He was going with Auden & Stephen & Miss Townsend Warner. But he rang up just now to ask for Hugh Walpole's number & said that the whole thing is probably forbidden by the F.O. owing to various incompetences.[25] It was a hard youthful comfortless but honest & genuine evening, dining in R.'s front room with no blinds: a chicken he & Ann had cooked; asparagus fried by mistake—but he a very attentive quick witted host. And wine &c. And a cat & flowers. White walls, no colour. All tidy & bare. Ann in pink, handsome truculent, concealing some sensibilities, I suppose, of a feminine kind. An odd vessel for passionate love—I mean for tender

23. Percy Bartholomew had been LW's gardener for nine years and continued as such until after the war.

24. Ernest Altounyan (1889-1962), an English-born and -educated half-Armenian doctor who aspired to be a poet; since 1919 he had worked at his father's hospital in Aleppo, making intermittent contact with his English friends, among whom he counted the Woolfs. Mary (b. 1913) was the only child of the historian H. A. L. Fisher, Warden of New College, Oxford, and the niece of Admiral Sir William Fisher—both first cousins of VW, who had not seen the latter since 1910 when she participated in the 'Dreadnought Hoax' (see *I QB*, pp. 157-61 and his Appendix E)—an insult to the Senior Service he was unable to forgive. 'Dossier' presumably refers to Ethel Smyth's usual prolix letter.

25. The Second International Writers' Congress was to be held in Spain in July. In the event the Foreign Office refused to issue visas to the English delegates, though the more determined—including Stephen Spender and the poet and novelist Sylvia Townsend Warner (1893-1978)—got through without.

considerate love. But there it is I suppose making her sometimes sharp. But much more mature. In came, or down from his room came, Morgan with the bright bird. Morgan on taking his coat off—a very hot night—revealed a round barrel. Has he suddenly grown a fat man? Rather silent, hopping pecking, skimming away as usual. Talk of the A[lbert] H[all] meeting & Madrid mostly. Morgan rose to £5 on the wings of Miss Brown. Rather glad of bed & sleep. But a good evening in its hard adolescent way. And Richard maybe not a desirable son in law, as Adrian says. I wonder: but cant wonder, must lunch. In full flush of 2nd Guinea now. Years still top. Even higher. 7th printing. But what does that mean? That I can buy a book case?

Sunday 11 July

A gap: not in life, but in comment. I have been in full flood every morning with 3 Gs. Whether I shall finish by August becomes doubtful. But I am in the middle of my magic bubble. Had I time I wd. like to describe the curious glance of the world—the pale disillusioned world—that I get so violently now & then, when the wall thins—either I'm tired or interrupted. Then I think of Julian near Madrid. & so on. Margaret Ll. Davies writes that Janet is dying, & will I write on her for The Times—a curious thought, rather: as if it mattered who wrote, or not.[1] But this flooded me with the idea of Janet yesterday. I think writing, my writing, is a species of mediumship. I become the person. Then Society: Saxon's Club dinner: Old Sir Wm. & Beresford. And the Nefs, Sybil, Butts, Sarton—so many faces. I cdn't face the Bussys, tho' I shd. have liked to meet Matisse, Pernel & the rest. But the clock strikes one.[2]

1. Margaret Llewelyn Davies (1861-1944), who until her retirement in 1921 had for over thirty years been the General Secretary of the Women's Co-operative Guild, was an old friend equally of the Woolfs and Janet Case. VW agreed to her request (see *VI VW Letters*, no. 3272); Janet Case died on 15 July, and VW's tribute: 'Miss Janet Case: Classical Scholar and Teacher. By an Old Pupil' appeared in the *Times* on 22 July 1937 (Kp C351).

2. 'Society' had been particularly exigent since VW last wrote in her diary: on 30 June the Woolfs had driven to Whipsnade to dine with May Sarton; they spent the weekend at Rodmell, and on 5 July a cultured pair from Chicago who had visited Monks House four years earlier—John Ulric Nef (b. 1899), the distinguished academic and author and his literary wife Elinor Castle Nef—came to tea at Tavistock Square, coinciding with Lady Colefax and Tony Butts; on the 6th the Woolfs dined with Helen Anrep, and the following day did *not* go to the Bussy's cocktail party to meet Matisse (a one-time fellow-student of Simon Bussy, the French painter who had married Lytton Strachey's sister Dorothy in 1903). On Friday 9 July Saxon Sydney-Turner gave a dinner at the Oxford and Cambridge Club for the Woolfs to meet the Beresfords and the retired Treasury Counsel Sir William Graham-Harrison.

JULY 1937

Monday 12 July

To stop myself from thinking about 3 Gs. I will chatter here. A cold July: a grey skylight. Alone with Nessa in the studio last night. We are very gingerly in our remarks about Julian, & Madrid, I notice; but she begins to discuss politics. Always I feel the immeasurable despair just on tother side of the grass plot on wh. we walk—on wh. I'm walking with such energy & delight at the moment. The reaction from last ⟨summer⟩ years 9 months gloom & despair I suppose.

I went to Stoke Newington yesterday & found a study table in white stone on wh. James Stephen was carved, large & plain, as I suspect he was large & plain. A long inscription about Wilberforce & wife & family neatly filled with green moss on top of the study table. Next door to the old Church, which might be in a hollow under the downs, is Clissold Park, & one of those white pillared houses in which Grandpapa studied The Times while She cut roses[3]—now it smelt of Clissold Park mothers; & cakes & tea; the smell—unpleasant to the nose—of democracy. Clissold Park runs to greyhounds [?], unlike Hyde Park. There is a stag, & some say a Kangaroo. I was much refreshed by all this.

Monday 19 July

Just back from MH. but I *cant* & *wont* write anything—too hithered & dithered. Also, I screwed my head tight—too tight—knocking together a little obituary of Janet for The Times. And couldnt make it take the folds well; too stiff & mannered. She died. Three notes from Emphie this morning. She died on Thursday, shut her eyes, "& looks so beautiful". Today they are cremating her, & she had had printed a little funeral service—with the death day left blank. No words; an adagio from Beethoven, & a text about gentleness & faith, wh. I would have included had I known. But what does my writing matter? There is something fitting & complete about the memory of her, thus consummated. Dear old harum scarum Emphie will have her solitary moments to herself. To us she will always be a scatter brain; yet to me very touching, & I remember that phrase in her letter, how she ran into Janet's room at midnight, & they had a nice little time together. She was always running

---

3. The family vault and table-tomb in Stoke Newington churchyard was erected by VW's *great*-grandfather James Stephen (1758-1832), brother-in-law and friend of William Wilberforce; the inscription was added at his death. His parents had moved in 1774 from the city to 'a very pleasant and genteel house situated in a garden, on the North side of Church Street', where his beloved mother died the following year. See *The Memoirs of James Stephen*, edited by Merle M. Bevington, Hogarth Press 1954, pp. 141 and 152 (where the inscription is recorded in full).

in. Janet was the steadfast comtemplative one, anchored in some private faith wh. didn't correspond with the worlds. But she was oddly inarticulate: no hand for words. her letters save that the last began "My beloved Virginia" always cool & casual. And how I loved her, at Hyde Pk Gate; & how I went hot & cold going to Windmill Hill: & how great a visionary part she has played in my life, till the visionary became a part of the fictitious, not of the real life.

An august Sunday: I thought of the Forest lying green in the sun, & Janet dead. But I thought—not much. Too hot & harrassed with fitting phrases. And I was badly beaten at bowls. The kitchen a great success—now green & cool, & the new window shows a square of flowers. Why, all these years, I never thought to lay out £20 on a new cupboard, paint & window, I dont know. Last year of course I was carefully drawing my poor limp horns in. And now Elizabeth Bowen thinks The Years—oh, all I wanted it to be. And Olaf Stapledon also, & so on. I'm now coming in for measured slow sound praise—a long article by Delattre pleased me—my deepest & strongest book—so that I can discount old Ethel, who hedges—& Vita who never hedges, but takes great rough leaps over all subtleties.[4] I am scribbling to avoid my Congreve: to avoid deciding whether to finish *that* off this last 10 days, or storm the last section of 3 Gs. Cant make up my mind.

On Friday we went to Worthing. Mrs W. very plaintive. Would even like to try Dr. Alexander—have I noted—no I leave out all the interesting facts—that L. is trembling less & less—can drink his coffee steady—& has, at 56, cured a disease that has, I guess, moulded his life wrongly since he was 5. All his shyness, his suffering from society, his sharpness, & definiteness, might have been smoothed. I mean by this something mostly superficial, but possibly constricting underneath also.[5] Mrs. W however was plaintive, & Alice solid, like a large tree in shape, & Harold, the gayest of the Wolves, said, No one ought to live after 80. Like a good fellow he does his share & more of the necessary chatter. But has now bought a farm, in order to become a venerable & protected member of

---

4. Floris Delattre, Professeur at the Sorbonne, had published a book on VW in 1932; the article here referred to, 'Le Nouveau Roman de Virginia Woolf' appeared in *Etudes Anglaises IV*, Juillet 1937; it concludes: 'Virginia Woolf s'y révèle un très grand poète impressioniste, d'une spontanéité toujours jaillissante, et, à la lettre, un des quelques artistes foncièrement originaux dont s'enorgueillit l'Angleterre d'aujourd'hui.'

5. On the recommendation of Bernard Shaw, LW, who suffered all his life from a nervous trembling of the hands, had been going three or four times a week since early June to Dr. F. M. Alexander (1869-1955), who had developed a technique for the control of the use of the self known as the 'Alexander Method'. Although he considered him a remarkable man and definitely benefitted from his treatment, LW did not continue with it after the summer at Rodmell. See *I LW*, pp. 101-2.

society, not a hated rentier.[6] Then a meeting at MH. where the Major, who talks to mice, & holds toads in his hand, treated us to the most drivelling murmured muddle I ever heard—about force, & religion, which is heredity, & I may say with your permission, what I mean is, its all a question of thinking isnt it, & you cant talk to a Spaniard, but you can to a Mahommedan, & thats what I feel, religion's at the back of it, & one has to take orders, as I see it, but Sir, if I may say so, its a question of heredity—but I cant reproduce the shell shock Major; & cd. only keep from howling by fixing my eyes on a cigarette. L. summed up in a masterly flight—thats what I mean: & so concluded. Q. & I were dumb.[7]

During the evening of Tuesday 20 July VW learned of the death of Julian Bell in Spain. In the following days and weeks she devoted herself to the support of her grief-stricken sister, whom she and LW drove to Charleston on 29 July, then installed themselves at Monks House, from whence VW went over almost daily to be with Vanessa. Julian, struck by a shell fragment while driving his ambulance on the Brunete front on 18 July, died that evening in the Escorial hospital. VW wrote out her thoughts about him on 30 July: see MHP, Sussex, A8, published, with omissions, in II QB, Appendix C.

Friday 6 August

Monks House, Rodmell.

Well but one must make a beginning. Its odd that I can hardly bring myself, with all my verbosity—the expression mania which is inborn in me—to say anything about Julian's death—I mean about that last 10 days in London. But one must get into the current again. That was a complete break; almost a blank; like a blow on the head: a shrivelling up. Going round to 8 [*Fitzroy Street, Vanessa's studio*] that night; & then all the other times, & sitting there. When Roger died I noticed: & blamed myself: yet it was a great relief I think. Here there was no relief. An incredible suffering—to watch it—an accident, & someone bleeding. Then I thought the death of a child is childbirth again; sitting there listening.

No no, I will not go back to those days. The only thing was a kind of comfort in being there with Nessa Duncan, Quentin & Angelica, &

---

6. Harold Sidney Woolf (1882-1967) was Mrs Woolf's third son; he married Alice Bilson in 1913.

7. Major Gardner lived at Thatched Cottage, Rodmell, with his children Paul and Diana; the latter was a member of the Rodmell Labour Party, and introduced her father into the meeting at Monks House.

losing completely the isolation, the spectator's attitude in being wanted; & spontaneous. Then we came down here last Thursday; & the pressure being removed, one lived; but without much of a future. Thats one of the specific qualities of this death—how it brings close the immense vacancy, & our short little run into inanity. Now this is what I intend to combat. How? how make good what I protest, that I will not yield an inch or a fraction of an inch to nothingness, so long as something remains? Work of course. I plunged on Monday into Congreve, & have about done him this morning. And undoubtedly that sets the wheels running. Directly I am not working, or see the end in sight, then nothingness begins. I have to go over though every other day to Charleston. We sit in the studio door. It is very hot, happily. A hot bank holiday—a child killed at the top; aeroplanes droning. The thought of Julian changing so queerly, no so usually: now distant, now close; now of him there, in the flesh; now some physical encounter—kissing him surreptitiously: & so on. And then I had some relief when Tom rejected his essays, for I felt then I had not been merely spiteful, merely jealous.[1] But how it curtails the future: how it reduces ones vision to ones own life—save for Q. & Angelica. A curiously physical sense; as if one had been living in another body, which is removed, & all that living is ended. As usual, the remedy is to enter other lives, I suppose; & the old friction of the brain; but now I must sum up, & try to get my accounts, that is my plans for working, in being again.

Well, theres 3 Guineas to finish: the last chapter, now I suppose its stiff & cold. But I will try that tomorrow: then polish off Congreve: then earn £200, so they say, with a story: & so to Roger this autumn.

Will another novel ever swim up? If so, how? The only hint I have towards it is that its to be dialogue: & poetry: & prose; all quite distinct. No more long, closely written books. But I have no impulse; & shall wait; shant mind if the impulse never formulates; tho' I suspect one of these days I shall get that old rapture. I dont want to write more fiction. I want to explore a new criticism: One thing I think proved; I shall never write to 'please' to convert; now am entirely & for ever my own mistress.

Rodker is nibbling at the Press. At the first nibble, through John, we

1. Before his departure for Spain, Julian Bell had assembled three long polemical essays—including the 'Letter to A.' rejected by the Woolfs (see above, 22 January 1937, n. 12)—which, he wrote to his brother, were 'meant to cause pain to intellectuals, thought if possible, but pain anyway', and asked his mother to send them to T. S. Eliot in the hope that his firm, Faber and Faber, would publish them as a book. After his death, Eliot wrote to VW to tell her, and through her Vanessa, that although he himself found them very interesting, they could not do so. In the event they were published by the Hogarth Press in *Julian Bell: Essays, Poems and Letters* in 1938.

both shied so strongly, that I suspect we shall end by reducing the Press to ourselves, & keeping it for ever, reduced. Rodker is a communist. Any other hand in the Press is suspect at once.[2] Today we go to Charleston: Clive is in France with Janis [Loeb]; Duncan has been in London; Nessa is alone today. A very hot day—I add, to escape from the thought of her.

"I shall be cheerful, but I shall never be happy again"
"I thought when Roger died that I was unhappy—"

Wednesday 11 August

I have half an hour over, & may as well spend it here. 'Here' I always write about writing: I'm rather ashamed. But its to set a flame to the effort & the grind of the day this summer. Now we are in the worst of the time—I think I can recognise that. We dont talk so freely of Julian. We want to make things go on. Angelica & Q. come over to play bowls. We beat up talk. Its unreal. We provide amusement, L. & I: this makes us rather quarrelsome when we're alone—the strain I suppose. The unbecoming stage of sorrow. And we are never alone. Graham on Saturday: Mrs W. & Ada on Sunday: the children:[3] on Monday I went by train to Charleston. Thus I left L. alone: have I the right to leave L. alone, & sit with Nessa? She was again in the submerged mood. An atmosphere of deep grey waters; & I flopping like a dilapidated fish on top. Very hard work. Then A[ngelica] came to sleep & yesterday was an odious London day. L. silent; house grimy; waking up: heat; heavy rough, burnt up heat. A. late; tea; drive back: great thunderstorm, dine at C[harleston]. Nessa better. But now begins the visitor crises, so bothering this summer. Are the Maurons coming? Then Judith & Adrian. I hate these decisions, & L. is silent. So I write here, not about this, but about my writing, which is the only flame the day strikes. Actually [?] I'm offered £200 for 1,500 words in the Cosmopolitan. Shall I, shant I?[4] Why make money? Another car, I suppose; another table; some new records & a dress. Familiar tune: Nessa's children; my envy of them, leading to work. But no use in thinking—I mean in analysis. I shall have a long walk this afternoon, to

2. John Rodker (1894-1955), poet, printer, and publisher of limited editions of contemporary writers.

3. John Graham, whose book *The Good Merchant* the Hogarth Press had published in 1934, was a young schoolmaster who 'was a soldier and a champion runner, but has turned literary' (see *VI VW Letters*, no. 3198). Ada de Jongh was Mrs Woolf's sister-in-law. 'The children' were Quentin and Angelica.

4. She did: 'America Which I Have Never Seen Interests Me Most in this Cosmopolitan World of To-day' was published in *Hearst's International Combined with Cosmopolitan*, New York, April 1938 (Kp C355).

Piddinghoe: walk myself serene; play bowls, read; & not think of little arrangements; I bought a 6d. Jeans on the Mysterious Universe: I'm reading George Sand quietly; a long novel that L. thinks good carefully for the Press: shd. read Congreve to complete my study, but have had no time—only got back from Charleston late. Have Auden McNeice in Iceland from The Times [*Book Club*]; also some French George Sand memoirs.[5] So I can browse along. And a huge box of Roger's articles. Endless unwritten letters—sympathy about Julian who stalks beside me, in many different shapes.

Tuesday 17 August

Not much to say. Its true, the only life this summer is in the brain. I get excited writing. 3 hours pass like 10 minutes. This morning I had a moment of the old rapture—think of it!—over copying The Duchess & the Jeweller, for Chambrun NY. I had to send a synopsis. I expect he'll regret the synopsis. But there was the old excitement, even in that little extravagant flash—more than in criticism I think.[6]

At Charleston yesterday in the rain. I take the train to Lewes; shop; 4.35 bus; reach Charleston for tea. Its true that I cannot write about Nessa: have to keep myself from thinking about her.

Happily—if thats the word—I get these electric shocks—Cables asking me to write. Cha[m]brun offers £500 for a 9,000 word story. And I at once begin making up adventures—10 days of adventures—a man rowing with black knitted stockings on his arms.

Do I ever write, even here, for my own eye? If not, for whose eye? An interesting question, rather. I'm musing on the nature of Auden's egotism. Suspect its something to do with uneasiness. He wants to write straight from the heart: to discard literature; egotism may be his way of

5. The books referred to are: *The Mysterious Universe* (1930) by James Jeans; *Histoire de ma vie* by George Sand, first published 1854-55; *Letters from Iceland* (1937) by W. H. Auden and Louis MacNeice. The long novel was probably *Mile End* by Kathleen Nott, which the Hogarth Press published in 1938 (*HP Checklist* 435).

6. Late in July VW received a cable from the New York literary agent Jacques Chambrun offering her $1000 for a story; she sent him a synopsis of 'The Duchess and the Jeweller' which he approved, but later rejected on grounds that it was 'a psychological study of a Jew' and thus, because of widespread racial prejudice in America, unacceptable to his (unnamed) client. After further vexatious dealings and LW's intervention, Chambrun contrived matters so that two stories—'The Shooting Party' as well as 'The Duchess and the Jeweller'—appeared in successive issues of *Harper's Bazaar* both in London and New York in the Spring of 1938 (Kp C353, 356). In the end VW received a total of $960 for the two (see LPW, Sussex, II D 1a).

orienting himself. What I mean I dont quite know. perhaps that it seems to him thats being honest, simple, naked, taking off literary clothes.

A letter from Tom; uneasily egotistic also. Or do I impute this? Eddy Playfair & the Maurons impend.[7] The weather has broken. A great rain storm last night. [Southease] Bridge up as we drove back: a ship coming up. The river men running about in great coats with sticks like conspirators in the 17th Century. We talked at Charleston about America. Nessa made A. read aloud a description of a flood in Dr Heynes [?] book. She has read this with interest. She has a considerable detached imaginative power. This may help. Then A. & Q. But now & then she looks an old woman. She reminds me of father taking Thoby's arm: so she asks Q. to help her.[8] How can she ever right herself though? Julian had some queer power over her—the lover as well as the son. He told her he could never love another woman as he loved her. He was like her; yet had a vigour, a roughness, & then as a child, how much she cared for him. I mean, he needed comfort & sympathy more I think than the others, was less adapted to get on in the world—had a kind of clumsiness, of Cambridge awkwardness, together with his natural gaiety. And thats all lost for the sake of 10 minutes in an ambulance. I often argue with him on my walks; abuse his selfishness in going but mostly feel floored by the complete muddle & waste. Cant share the heroic raptures of the Medical Aid, who are holding a meeting next week to commemorate the six who were killed. "Gave their lives" as they call it.[9]

I think I mean lack of judgement: obstinate & emotional. Eddie Playfair agreed. We shd. have respected him more if he had stayed in England & faced drudgery.

[*Wednesday 25 August*]

In London yesterday, & write here because I cannot force myself on with Congreve. I suspect its a failure. Or am I a failure? Not a question I intend to ask: since clearly one must act. In London yesterday, I began:

7. T. S. Eliot wrote to VW on 16 August to explain why he had not written when Faber and Faber returned Julian's essays—he was in Wales without a typewriter and with a festering thumb. Edward Wilder Playfair (b. 1909), now working in the Treasury, was one of Julian Bell's closest friends at King's College, Cambridge; he stayed with the Woolfs for the week-end of 21 August, when the Maurons and Helen Anrep were at Charleston.

8. Julian Thoby Stephen (1880-1906) was VW's elder brother whose death from typhoid fever was, like Julian's, untimely. Dr Heynes [?] book: unidentified.

9. A meeting to mark the anniversary of the departure of the first British Medical Unit for Spain, and to commemorate 'six gallant members who have given their lives in the cause of Spanish democracy' was held at Friends House, Euston Road, on 23 August 1937.

& saw Dr Hart & Archie Cochran about Julian.[10] Rather a physical distress than mental; about his wounds: as if one felt them bodily. Nothing new: only that he was conscious when they got him to hospital, & anxious to explain that the road was dangerous: then anxious to get on with the operation. He became unconscious, talked in French about military things apparently . . . & died 4 hours later. Why do I set this down? It belongs to what is unreal now. What is left that is real? Angelica in a yellow handkerchief picking dahlias for the flower show: that Edgar took a gun: & shot Churchill's white dog:[11] Nessa seemed 'better': that is could laugh & seem interested. But the reality is very shallow this summer. We had Eddie Playfair this week end & the Maurons & Helen [Anrep] for bowls & tea. I am dried up with talk, with compacting my 2 £200 efforts; one on USA: one a story; the Jeweller; now must do Congreve. Very hard work in its way, packing & pressing. I shall soon long for the space & irresponsibility of fiction.

Our telescope came last week. The erudite Eddy focussed it. We have seen Jupiter minus the waiting women: & a plaster cast of the moon. Fog driving home from Charleston last night. The robber caught at South Heighton.

Much forced talk with Hart & Cochran. Cochran a nice simple but rather tense (naturally) practical reddish young man; giving his account stiffly kindly: Hart a Jew; neurotic, rather shiny nosed, intellectual, with the professional surgeons manner. A conflict of sympathy, tragedy, professional manner, & social politeness. Queer rather. A very fine day. Now can I tackle Congreve?

Sunday 29 August

Yes I am tackling Congreve, because I want to be quit of all articles & ready for 3 Gs on the 1st.

How far would this energy of the mind carry me—could I take this narcotic successfully if Leonard died, if Nessa died? I come out here at 10 & dont wake to anything but Congreve till one. Go in with my head swaying like a captive balloon. The thing is theres no richness & security when I wake. No depth of happiness to refresh myself in. Considerable agility & gaiety & chatter. Mrs Curtis, William Plomer, Janie, Q. & A., over yesterday. Mrs C. reminds me of Jean Thomas: something spurious

10. The Woolfs drove to London on the morning of 24 August, returning to Sussex to dine at Charleston that evening. Archibald Cochrane (b. 1909), a contemporary of Julian's at King's College, Cambridge, and Dr Philip d'Arcy Hart (b. 1900), had both volunteered for the British Medical Unit in Spain and were attached to the Escorial Hospital where Julian died.
11. Edgar Weller was employed as chauffeur by Maynard Keynes; Churchill was a keeper on the Tilton estate.

—showing off. She's a highly successful liver: had £200: therefore borrowed, ran Langford Grove; lodges 10 people on top of Firle down; is adventurous, stack full of go & slapdash; but somehow not convincing as a character. Too smooth & slick & so on.[12] A useful phrase when I'm writing in a hurry. A very hot August again. Bowls have become a passion. I gave up a walk to play. But then I'm anxious to vary the day. How independent I feel myself of tradition; & what to do next. Simply trust to life? I think Roger said he trusted life on the whole. I mean, no cut & dried rules possible. I must think out some autumn plans one of these days. We saw the Ring of Saturn last night, like a cardboard collar. The man is still at large. Mrs Curtis pretends that she is elemental: I think thats it, sets a meal out for him & entertains cosmopolitanly. Why does any showing off mildew everything? William was portentously stout, red, & healthy. He lives at Brighton for the breezes he says, & finds Cape's MSS. distracts him from novel writing. But in fact, as the chatter was so incessant I had no gossip or silent listening with him. And now there is little to add, except that the British Ambassador in Japan has been shot: Santander has fallen; there is war between China & Japan; Clive is at Grenoble, & for 2 days I've had no letters, nor yet heard if my Jeweller is commissioned[13]

Thursday 2 September

With this odd mix up of public & private I left off: & finished my Congreve, the end too crowded, but forced myself to take it to the post just as Q. & A. & Janie drove up to tea. And todays a holiday: letter writing; reading, how strangely—to hear his voice so clear from the other side of the grave—Julian on War.[1] I hear his sharp quizzical laugh now & then: something like Clive; shrewd & biting. But as usual, the whirl of things, of things half grasped & sweeping on, like a staircase that for ever passes the platform—bewilders me. Why could he never

12. Elizabeth Curtis, headmistress of Angelica's former school, Langford Grove, had rented America Farm on the downs above Firle for the summer. Jean Thomas was the proprietor of the nursing home for nervous and mental cases at Twickenham in which VW—in 1910, 1912 and 1913—had been a patient.

13. William Plomer acted as publisher's reader to Jonathan Cape Ltd. Sir Hughe Knatchbull-Hugesson, British Ambassador to China, travelling from Nanking to Shanghai on 26 August, was hit by machine-gun fire from Japanese aircraft (the Sino-Japanese war, never formally declared, had erupted on 7 July 1937). Santander, on the northern coast of Spain, fell to the Nationalists on 26 August.

1. See 'War and Peace: A Letter to E. M. Forster', published by the Hogarth Press in the memorial volume *Julian Bell . . .*, 1938. VW thought it 'the best thing I've ever read of his . . . and at last I think I understand his point of view.' (*VI VW Letters*, no. 3305).

force himself to think to the bottom of his idea? But I'm stopping in the middle; write here to make myself take breath. 5 past 12.

Sunday 12 September

I opened this—then thought of 3 Gs: then of Julian's essay: so wasted 5 minutes; & all I had to say was that The Duchess & the Jeweller is a firm commissn: therefore I have made £400 by these 2 stories, & we bought two fountains at Hand X going to M. in the wet.[2] Now time up.

Sunday 26 September[3]

Tom & Judith here: therefore I am not writing the end of 3 Gs: which has kept me completely submerged from 10 to one every morning; & driven me like a motor in the head over the downs to Piddinghoe &c every afternoon from 2 to 4. Then we play bowls from 5 to 6. Then read. Then cook dinner. Then wireless. Then read. Then chocolates. Then bed. And so it begins again. But there have been so many interruptions, the specimen day is the exception. We went to Sissinghurst—unrecorded: with Eve A. & Q.: Vita with that silent goodness, & Harold too, a sense of the human understanding unspoken, & now that Gwen is not there, for me more unbroken. Many improvements: men digging; an Elizabethan drain being dug up. Lady S.'s money now supplies Vita with enough to store the house, which is too museum like perhaps. The red amber stood in the light: Persian pots: too many possessions. & then Vita shows that she inherits the magpie gift of her mother, but stabilised & dignified by the old honourable yet rather null Sackvilles. I'm drawing upon Pepita for this illuminating sketch.[4]

Not a happy summer. That is all the materials for happiness; & nothing behind. If Julian had not died—still an incredible sentence to write—our happiness might have been profound. "Our"—L.'s & mine, now that The Years has sold between 40 & 50,000 in America; now that we are floated financially, & perhaps to shift the Press & take a new house, & privately as happy & rounded off as can be—but his death—that extraordinary extinction—drains it of substance. I do not let myself think.

---

2. On 9 September the Woolfs drove *via* Handcross to Dorking to have tea with Margaret Llewelyn Davies.

3. VW has misdated this entry: *Sunday 27 September.*

4. The excursion to Sissinghurst was on Thursday 16 September. Eve Younger was a long-standing friend of Angelica's who often stayed at Charleston. Gwen was Harold Nicolson's sister—the Hon. Mrs Francis St Aubyn—who for some years past had been Vita's most intimate friend. Vita's mother, the wealthy Lady Sackville, had died in January 1936; Vita's account of her and of *her* mother, *Pepita*, was published by the Hogarth Press in October 1937 (*HP Checklist* 419).

That is the fact. I cannot face much of the meaning. Shut my mind to anything but work & bowls. Now theres Tom & Judith, & I think I have solved the week end problem, & made it a reasonable & even enjoyable habit, as it should be—having friends in the house. Tom in some ways—with his sensitive, shrinking, timid but idiosyncratic nature—is very like myself. This morning, as Priestley's play is praised, he is uneasy, as I shd be, & insinuates, as I should, distrust of critics, yet reads them, as I do, furtively.[5] Tom is liverish looking, tired; but revives under the effect of Judith's fresh & downright & able but not sophisticated, or I daresay, highly aesthetic, youth. She is a whopper: a strapper; yet with the usual complexities I think, submerged. I should however write a pack of letters; to Vita (who sent me Nessa's little message: to me so profoundly touching, thus sent secretly via Vita that I have 'helped' her more than she can say) & to Chambrun, my employer: & to the Fabian [*untraced*], & others, for with the autumn letters begin, & publicity puts its rather heavy, not altogether unacceptable fingers on me. More letters than usual of praise & demands therefore.

The Woolfs returned to Tavistock Square on Sunday 10 October.

Tuesday 12 October

London.

Yes we are back at Tavistock Square; & I've never written a word since Sept. 27th. That shows how every morning was crammed to the margin with 3 Guineas. This is the first morning I write, because at 12, ten minutes ago I wrote what I think is the last page of 3 Gs. Oh how violently I have been galloping through these mornings! It has pressed & spurted out of me, if thats any proof of virtue, like a physical volcano. And my brain feels cool & quiet after the expulsion. I've had it sizzling now since—well I was thinking of it at Delphi I remember.[1] And then I forced myself to put it into fiction first. No, the fiction came first. The Years. And how I held myself back, all through the terrible depression, & refused, save for some frantic notes, to tap it until The Years—that awful burden—was off me. So that I have deserved this gallop. And taken time & thought too. But whether it is good or bad how can I tell? I must now add the bibliography & notes. And have a weeks respite. This may be provided by Mr Davis of Harpers Bazaar, coming to tea today to discuss a story suggested by that maroon coloured sharper, as we suspect him, M. Chambrun—whom I have not described—the agent

5. *Time and the Conways* by J. B. Priestley was at the Duchess Theatre.
1. See *IV VW Diary*, Delphi, 2 May 1932: '. . . the male virtues are never for themselves . . . (I'm thinking of the book again).'

who cabled about the Duchess & the Jeweller, offered £200, & I think will somehow wriggle out.

So nothing was said here of the last weeks at Monks House. The weather was very fine. That objective statement sounds a little odd.

Nessa went to Paris. Last night she came here, for the first time. We have the materials for happiness, but no happiness. All this summer, I find myself saying that verse, Lowell's, about those whose coming steps we listen for: the verse about the nephew killed in the war. When Thoby died I used to walk about London saying to myself Stevenson's verses: You alone have crossed the melancholy stream.[2] Both doggerel I suppose: yet they say themselves spontaneously. With Thoby though I felt we were the same age. With Julian it is the old woman, saying that she wont see the young again. It is an unnatural death, his. I cant make it fit in anywhere. Perhaps because he was killed, violently.

Yours the undiminished gladness undecaying dream.

I can do nothing with the experience yet. It seems still emptiness: the sight of Nessa bleeding: how we watch: nothing to be done. But whats odd is I cant notice, or describe. Of course I have forced myself to drive ahead with the book. But the future without Julian is cut off. lopped: deformed.

We have decided, gradually, completely, not to sell the Press; but to let it die off, saving for our own books. This is a good conclusion I think. It keeps the right to adventure; cuts off some money. We cd not face writing for publishers. Thus I carry out my own theories anyhow. And we get fresh scope for experiment & freedom.

Wednesday 13 October

George Davis came & commissioned a story I think. On top of him Philip Hart the Dr who was with Julian when he died. The facts now seem to be: Julian was brought in with a very bad wound—looked deathly white. He asked H. What chance have I? Hart told him 80 per cent recover. A lie. He had only the chances of a miracle. He was very brave. After the operation, H. saw him comfortably in bed. Went back 2 hours later & found him dozing half conscious. And so he remained till he died that night. Hart said Julian & the other man lay under the ambulance. They might, & could have taken cover in a trench. But it is

2. 1937 was the year of the great Paris International Exhibition: Vanessa made a short visit to see the '*Chefs d'oeuvre de l'art français*'. For Lowell's verse, see below, 19 October 1937, n. 5. Robert Louis Stevenson, 'In Memoriam F.A.S.', verse 3:

'Came and stayed and went, and now when all is finished,
   You alone have crossed the melancholy stream,
Yours the pang, but his, O his, the undiminished
   Undecaying gladness, undeparted dream.'

impossible to take precautions always. Julian was hit by a side splash from a shell: the other man not touched. It was as if he were killed at once. The mind of a person so wounded is only on immediate things. He said nothing about Nessa. Was anxious to get on with the operation.

This does not tally altogether with the other accounts: P.H. & the others thought he was alone, & so on.[3] But now there is no more to be discovered. Hart was tormented by some sense of guilt. That they had not kept J. from the front. They would have done so later. This was his first experience. Things are now much more dangerous. The Ambulance is almost as dangerous as the Army. And so he went. He said that the worst fighting is about to come. A long talk. Like Tisdall [*VW's dentist*] to look at. A nice, sensitive thin man, an enthusiast. If we allowed arms thro we shd save thousands of lives.

& then I go upstairs & find L. enraged with the L. Party which sent a deputation to the F.O. & was diddled by Vansittart. So we shant let arms through: we shall sit on the fence: & the fighting will go on— But I am not a politician: obviously. can only rethink politics very slowly into my own tongue.[4]

Tuesday 19 October

It came over me suddenly last night, as I was reading The Shooting Party,—the story that I'm to send to America, H[arper's]. B[azaar]., that I saw the form of a new novel. Its to be first the statement of the theme: then the restatement: & so on: repeating the same story: singling out this & then that: until the central idea is stated.

This might also lend itself to my book of criticism. But how I dont now, being very jaded in the brain, try to discover.

What happened was this: when I finished the S.P. I thought, now that the woman has called a taxi; I will go on to meet, say, Christabel, at T. Square who tells the story again: or I will expatiate upon my own idea in telling the story; or I will find some other person at the S.P. whose life I will tell: but all the scenes must be controlled, & radiate to a centre. I think this is a possible idea; & wd. admit of doing it in short bursts: cd. be a concentrated small book: cd. contain many varieties of mood. And

---

3. Portia Holman (1903-83) read economics at Cambridge, and went on to study medicine. She was a friend of Julian Bell's and encountered him in Madrid where she was working with the British Medical Aid Unit. The Woolfs had talked to her in London in July, and again in Sussex early in September when she stayed at Charleston.

4. The policy of Non-Intervention in the Spanish Civil War, formally agreed to by all the Great Powers though patently disregarded by Germany, Italy and Russia, was strictly observed by Great Britain.

possibly criticism. I must keep the idea at the back of my mind for a year or two, while I do Roger &c.

This struck me just as the Spenders came to dinner. I was depressed. Why do I resent Stephen now that Julian's dead?—the incredible words? Just before they came I found the lines in Lowell: Biglow papers: Its hard to see the young go fust, all brimming full of gifts & graces . . . whose coming steps there's some that wont, no, not lifelong leave off ⟨expecting⟩ awaiting. (something like that).[5] Then Stephen comes in: not Julian. Last time they dined, it was to meet Julian. Well, one must not think of this. Julian wd. have said, "But my dear—once he said sweetheart—(I suspect his word for his loves) its clear that you've got to go on & comfort Nessa." Thats what he wd say at this moment. Oh Lord!

Well: I will go to Maples about chaircovers; to Highgate to see Roger's house; & dream today, because I must unscrew my head & somehow freshen up if I am to write, to live, to go through the next lap with zest, not like old sea weed. Stephen talked mostly about a new magazine: another; to run 6 numbers; L. to write politics in each: as the unifyer [?]. & the H.P. to publish. But he wont; & the H.P. won't. So it fizzled out. Then there was a good deal of politics: Inez a precise, horse headed woman, at last emerged. Talked of her Spanish book. Still an Oxford student. They had been seeing Ottoline. Not much gossip. A fog.

Friday 22 October

I am basking my brains. No I didnt go to Paris. This is a note to make. Waking at 3 I decided I would spend the week end at Paris. Got so far as looking up trains, consulting Nessa about hotel. Then L. said he wd. rather not. Then I was overcome with happiness. Then we walked round the square love making—after 25 years cant bear to be separate. Then I walked round the Lake in Regents Park. Then . . . you see it is an enormous pleasure, being wanted: a wife. And our marriage so complete.

5. James Russell Lowell (1819-1891), the American poet and sometime Ambassador in London, was VW's *soidisant* godfather. The relevant lines from *The Biglow Papers*, Second Series, 1867, read:

". . . An I set thinkin' o' the feet
Thet follered once an' now are quiet,—
          (*two lines omitted*)
Whose comin step ther' 's ears thet won't,
No, not lifelong, leave off awaitin'."

and:

" 'Tain't right to hev the young go fust,
All throbbin full o' gifts an' graces,
Leavin' life's paupers dry ez dust
To try an' make b'lieve fill their places."

To return to facts (tho' this 'fiction' is radiant still under my skin): walked to see Roger's Highgate birthplace: suddenly L. developed the idea of making the young Brainies take the Press as a Cooperative company (John [Lehmann]; Isherwood; Auden; Stephen). All are bubbling with discontent & ideas. All want a focus; a manager: a mouthpiece: a common voice. Wd. like L. to manage it. Couldnt we sell, & creep out? Thats the idea—& yet keep the soul, tran[s]lated into this on the whole appropriate body? Anyhow, John was heard in the Press: consulted; interested; fights shy of money; £6,000: will lunch with I. & discuss. And now telephones he will come on Monday. So that fats a frizzling. Off now, not to Paris, but to the Grocer with the Cupid, so to MH, Q. & the L.P. meeting: a fair exchange for Paris, where, too, I shd. have met & mixed with Nick, Barbara, Saxon, & the Easdales.[6] Nick, the lout with a veneer of 2nd hand Bloomsbury, came to tea, & considerably exacerbated me. He is having lectures on ways of improving his intercourse with Judith. Duncan gave me a green brooch. A fine day.

Monday 25 October

A terrific gale this week end. We went to Cuckmere, via Seaford. The sea over the front: great spray fountain bursting to my joy over the parade & the lighthouse. Right over the car. Then we walked down to the sea at Cuckmere; the birds came up like shots out of a catapult. We cd. not stand against the wind, the breath pressed out of us; nor see. We stood behind a shed, & watched the waves: a yellow rough light on them; pounding; a great curled volume roughened of water. Why does one like the frantic the unmastered? And the brooks streaked with white & blue lines; where the wind I suppose raised a long streak of drops. Also the drops were like the spurt made by a stone falling—shaped something like pinched up glass. The light over the marsh steel blue & tawny.

So to Charleston, wet & soaking. Saw Q. & Kapp as dry & merry as sandhoppers, & so bought muffins, toasted them, had tea; & a tree fell in Princes gap on top of Bannister's lorry. Also the branch fell in the churchyard over the vegetables.[7]

A meeting on Friday: Mr Hancock, Lyons &c. The new garden ready, save for the basins still to be embedded. The view is now clear through

6. The Woolfs intended to stop at Crawley on their way to Rodmell to buy a leaden Cupid for their garden, but either didn't stop, or didn't buy. The Easedales were friends and country neighbours in Kent of the Bagenals; the Hogarth Press had published the precocious verses of the daughter, Joan Adeney Easedale (b. 1918).

7. Yvonne Kapp, *née* Cloud (b. 1903), who wrote under her maiden name, was separated from her husband the artist Edmond Kapp.

the walled garden to the down. Talk of Drawbell building: also building at Knotts Bushes—my Tristram's Grove.[8]

Monday 1 November

A damp depressed morning. So why not write here? Pouring; vanity hurt by the preference given to Morgan by Day Lewis in the Book Society News [*not traced*]. Why not V.W? Yes, thats the mean little worm that will nibble when I wake talk tired after yesterday. We went to Philip's for lunch. We had dined at the Hotel—the 87th birthday party.[1] So hot the clothes stuck to one. Abrahamson soliloquised. Most of the daughters in law munching like cows in a field. And poor Connie Ross in brown, with a trickle of ribbons, poised on an armchair like a much battered moth, the moth that has been attracted out of the even damper garden by the light & the noise. And we played whist. Then yesterday we went to Philip's; a soft warm late summer morning: stopped at Milton's cottage. Persuaded the cultivated man to show us round. Babs said "We want to consult you about Cecil".[2] The poor little boy wont say whats the matter. He takes no interest in anything. Wont turn & wave to her, or write to her; drudges on at Latin. Babs uninhibited. Simple. And the many ponies followed us round the garden. Not a happy family exactly. No high spirits. Attenuated critical children. Education weighing on Philip & Babs. A beautiful sweep of 18th century view.

So home. Wyndham Lewis Auby: hot mean reading. Exacerbates. Yet diminishes vitality. Thank God, it will be out of the house today.[3] Dinner with Clive: Janis: Nessa, Angelica. I think poor old Clive even a little on the bare wheels; no blown up tires. That to me is very ominous [?]—if Clive's spirits should give way—if he were to give up his enjoyment of life! We discussed education; dreams; N. & A. stitched at some private garment. A. alternately silent & decisive. Duncan came in. Not much boasting. I feel that N. has, with her bad eye, given up all hope of

---

8. F. R. Hancock had been the Labour Party Parliamentary candidate for Lewes Constituency (a Conservative stronghold); in 1931 he built himself a house—VW dubbed it 'Hancock's Horror'—on the down above Rodmell. J. W. Drawbell (1899-1979), newspaper publisher and editor, was to build an even more conspicuous eyesore, rather higher up Mill Lane than Hancock's.

1. The family gathering for Mrs Woolf's 87th birthday party on 29 October included her nephew Sir Martin Abrahamson (1870-1962) and her old friend Constance Ross, mother of her fourth son Edgar Woolf's wife Sylvia.

2. Chalfont St Giles—to which Milton retired during the plague year 1665—is on the way to Waddesdon, Bucks, where LW's youngest brother Philip was the manager of the Rothschild estate. The Woolfs went to Sunday lunch with him and his wife Marjorie (Babs) and their children Cecil, Philippa, and Marie.

3. *Blasting and Bombardiering* (1937) by Percy Wyndham Lewis (1882-1957).

painting at the moment. She is querulous sometimes about my "success". When I told her the actual figures—40,000—she was, I think, relieved (as I shd. have been in her place) to find them less than reported.

An odds & ends evening, neither one thing nor another. I am revising the 1st Guinea: shall send them all off, to be typed: show to L.: then provide notes. But no more this morning. The Co-operative Press hangs: I think the young are eager to bite. Pepita begins to boom; also Sally Bowles. Dick Sheppard died at his desk yesterday; just elected Rector some where. A pity, I expect; if peace is a cause, he had some gift that way.[4]

On Saturday I "saw"; by wh. I mean the sudden state when something moves one. Saw a man lying on the grass in Hyde Park. Newspapers spread round him to keep off the damp. A cheap attaché case; & half a roll of bread. This moved me. So uncomplaining: a positive statement. He was asleep. Others lying near. The last time I 'saw' was at MH. last week end, when Louie was discussing the building at Knotts Bushes. My mother used to take us that way when we were children. She used to tell us how she walked from Telscombe to Newhaven to shop—a vision of the little caravan, absolutely private silent, unknown, going over the downs, talking. Ought one only to write about what one "sees" in this way? These sights always remain. Isherwood, now Christopher, & John, beg me to write a story for New Writing. A compliment. Suggestion: "Portrait of a Young man" but I'm so fed up with short stories[5]. Todays the day of the deputation to the H of C. But the PM has the gout. Must I go? Cant I get out of it?

Wednesday 3 November

Yes, I did get out of it: much to my regret next morning when I read that the deputation had been received by the PM in the Cabinet room at Downing Street.[6] What a chance of "seeing" to have missed! But I had

---

4. Christopher Isherwood's *Sally Bowles* had just been published by the Hogarth Press (*HP Checklist* 411). The Very Rev. H. R. L. ('Dick') Sheppard (1880-1937), Dean and Precentor of St Paul's Cathedral and a founder in 1936 of the Peace Pledge Union, died suddenly on 31 October. He had recently been elected Lord Rector of Glasgow University by the students in preference to Winston Churchill and others.

5. *New Writing* was a twice-yearly miscellany in book form of contemporary imaginative writing from England and abroad, edited by John Lehmann. Four issues had already appeared. See below, 3 May 1938.

6. A deputation representative of the signatories to a petition for 'An international enquiry into the fundamental causes of rivalry and unrest among nations' was received by Mr Chamberlain on 1 November; VW was among those reported (in *The Times* of 2 November) to have been present.

the sense to weigh my own peace over the fire with a book; & my freshness the next morning which sped me through the revision. So I cry quits.

To Southwark & Lambeth, walking, yesterday. A great autumn for long City walks this. I discovered St James Garlick hill: & St Mary's Lambeth.[7] A quiet day. Missed seeing David Cecil too. On the other hand Rosemary Hodgson rang up fr. The Daily Express to ask me to write a signed article. Its your name they want—& shant have. L. is writing a strong Letter to the Listener who cut his phrase about privacies [?].[8]

Tuesday 30 November

Yes, its actually the last day of November; & theyve passed like a streak of hounds after a fox because I've been re-writing 3 Guineas with such intentness, indeed absorption, that several times 5 minutes past one has shown on the clock & I still at it. So I've never even looked at this stout volume. I have left out Cambridge: Peter & Prudence; the shiny busts; the bitter cold silent city; the chatter at Ann's; Newmarket; Oh & people innumerable. Or so I think, for I have not time to re-read.[9] A great strain; but how merciful a compulsion, so that I need not go into the sensation I have on drinking tea at 8 [*Fitzroy Street*] with Nessa. No, no, I will not describe that: dont I dread it? But I make myself all the same stay on when she's alone. Innumerable people: the Hutchinsons, Katie Lewis, Adrian, Cecil Duckworth, Gerald's relics still littering the drawing room. Some extravagances: Oxford Walpole bought off Hopkins at the Book Show: Vita there, signing, dabbing her lips red, with Gwen in attendance; my profound distaste for Harold's Dufferin, its falseness; equal exacerbation from Wyndham Lewis & Nevinson's autobiographies; strong effect of mean minds;[10] & buying with some recklessness, fur

7. From the Wren church of St James Garlickhithe, on the corner of Garlick Hill and Upper Thames Street, to St Mary's, by Lambeth Palace on the south bank of the Thames, is about a two-mile walk.

8. LW's article, 'Does Education Neutralise Thought?' appeared in *The Listener* on 22 December 1937; his 'strong letter' is in LWP, Sussex, I.R.

9. The Woolfs drove to Cambridge for the night on 12 November, when LW addressed the New Peace Movement in the Audit Room at King's on 'The Colonial Problem'. They saw, among others, F. L. ('Peter') Lucas (1894-1967), Fellow of King's and University Lecturer in English, and his second wife Prudence; and next morning Ann and Judith Stephen. They drove to Newmarket for lunch before returning to London.

10. The Hutchinsons dined with the Woolfs on 27 November. Adrian Stephen and Katherine (Katie) Lewis came to tea on 28 November; she was the younger daughter (1878-1961) of the rich and eminent Victorian solicitor Sir George

boots, leather waistcoat, underclothes; for money once more brims the pot. I could make £100 by choosing books for the Pelicans, with Morgan & Hugh & Aldous, but have refused, by way of a snub to Lane for shifting, sans apology, from Leonard to me. And I'm paid 200 by Cosmopolitan, 120 by H[arper's]. B[azaar]: another 120: then 25: which adds up to 465. £465 for a handful of old sketches.[11] This a little shames me in comparison with Nessa's sales: but then I reflect, I put my life blood into writing, & she had children.

200
120
120
25
___
465

At Duncan's show, we met the Bugger boys, Joe, Morgan, William; & savoured the usual queer scent.[12] Joe the slave of The Listener. And what will the slaves say when 3 Gs. comes out? in March I suppose. Then the Webbs ask us to lunch to meet the Shaws. We fight shy; & are now asked to Liphook. A very foggy November: a trail of brown every day, keeping us at home of an evening. And one of these foggy evenings, Ethel Smyth came, & then Madame de Polignac, like a perfectly stuffed cold fowl (K. Lewis, with her white hands, plump, with emeralds, had that look too). Another evening Lady Simon came, commends my secret & nefarious projects: not to get anyone else into trouble. &c. And so the month has run through my fingers, with a walk or two: many letters & some divine quiet evenings. L. in his stall, I in mine, reading Chateaubriand now, bought in 6 fine vols for one guinea at Cambridge: also much random trash as usual, & many lives & some blue books for my little harlequin book; but no poetry I observe—no Shakespeare, because by instinct I suppose, & here must change by force to white paper, I want prose to quiet my brain. Or am I lazy? Now the sacred hour comes, luncheon: a wet damp

---

Lewis whose London home had been a centre for art and society. VW's younger half-brother Gerald Duckworth died on 28 September 1937; the Woolfs visited his widow Cecil in de Vere Gardens, Kensington, on 4 November. The 5th *Sunday Times* Book Show opened on 8 November; VW's extravagance was probably the 2-volume *Supplement to the Letters of Horace Walpole* edited by Paget Toynbee, 1918 (see *Holleyman*, VS. V, p. 46). V. Sackville West was signing copies of *Pepita*, on display at the Hogarth Press stand. *Helen's Tower* by Harold Nicolson, just published, was a life of his uncle, the 1st Marquess of Dufferin & Ava. C. R. W. Nevinson's autobiography was called *Paint and Prejudice* (1937).

11. See *VI VW Letters*, no. 3330 to Denys Kilham Roberts, declining his invitation (letter, MPH Sussex, 24 November 1937) to participate in the choice of books for the *Pelican* series which Allen Lane, founder of *Penguin* sixpenny paperback books, started this year to complement his more popular list. The £25 was perhaps paid by the *TLS* for 'Congreve ...' (Kp C352); for the others, see above, 11 August 1937, n. 4 and 17 August 1937, n. 6.

12. 'Recent Works by Duncan Grant' at Thomas Agnew & Sons, Bond Street; VW went to the private view on 11 November.

day; & I must alas lavish my after tea time upon Eth Bowen, for all that I like her, a source of regret.

Wednesday 15 December

And then I had one of my little dips into the underworld—a temperature, sofa, 3 days recumbent, Monks House in a snowstorm; no walking; foot & mouth still dominant; back to our party. Young Newnham, all most free & easy, vigorous & inspiriting—Nat & Harry & George & Margaret & Ann Williams & Elizabeth somebody else [*friends of Ann and Judith Stephen*]—all sitting on the floor; & then—writing, writing; the 1st chapter taken on Monday to the Chancery Lane typist; cold & rain; visits from Mrs Woolf & Herbert, from John yesterday; the Press question looms & lapses; offers from Rodker & Secker & even Miss Lange wd. like to buy; & our views change: secretly we both wish to fade, not to sell; but John is eager to buy, yet stingy; must consult Isherwood & Stephen; & settle by mid January; Vita, who dined [*on 13 December*], more matronly & voluptuous than ever, wont go in with them: a parcel of hot headed & ignorant boys;—well, no use trying to pull this five minutes before lunch sentence together so I stop it. I have spent £35 on a picture by Duncan, nervously; Karin has taken a house in Regents Park & is transported; Adrian & Katie Lewis hit it off very well at tea; Nessa & Angelica go on Sunday to Cassis. Christmas is on us, & owing to Lord Ivor's gossip, I am once more riddled by invitations from Sybil.[1] I hope to find an Italian oil jar & a column waiting upstairs.

Saturday 18 December

Oh this cursed year 1937—it will never let us out of its claws. Now its L.'s kidneys: Rau says he may have a chill, or it may be something wrong with the kidneys; possibly the prostate gland—that perennial horror. Its more likely, he says, to be a chill; but cant tell for a fortnight. So we go away with that hanging over us— And once more my only refuge is work. So I wont expatiate. The great cat is playing with us once more.

How much do I mind death? I wondered last night, when I did not go to Helen's painters party, & concluded that there is a sense in which the end could be accepted calmly. Thats odd, considering that few people are more immensely interested by life: & happy. Its Julian's death that makes one sceptical of life I suppose. Not that I ever think of him as

1. No picture by Duncan Grant now at Monks House corresponds to the titles of the three priced at £35 in Agnew's catalogue of his show. Adrian and Karin Stephen moved to 26 York Terrace, Regent's Park. Lord Ivor Spencer Churchill (1899-1956), connoisseur and collector.

dead: which is queer. Rather as if he were jerked abruptly out of sight, without rhyme or reason: so violent & absurd that one cant fit his death into any scheme. But here we are, on a fine cold day, going to mate Sally at Ickenham: a saner proceeding than to analyse here. In fact I'm still spinning over 3 Gs. Finished the 2nd today for typing.

Helen's party, Mabel said, viewing it from the pantry where she washed up till 2.30 am, was crowded noisy drunk. Several young people fell down tipsy. The fumes of punch made her head ache. This is a jaundiced pantry view; but so would mine have been I daresay had I gone. And I've promised to guarantee £25 for 2 years. Why? Helen's rather exacerbating partisanship, when she dined with Joe here & was the old cantankerous Helen of Bernard St. made me ask this question.[2]

The Woolfs drove to Monks House on 22 December. On Christmas day the Keyneses came to lunch. On 28 December LW took to his bed with a temperature, but the following day drove to London to see Dr Rau, who sent him to be X-rayed; he ended the year in bed at Tavistock Square, awaiting the results.

2. The 'painter's party' was given by Helen Anrep in Duncan and Vanessa's adjacent studios at 8 Fitzroy Street on 17 December to publicise and raise support for the recently opened 'School of Drawing and Painting' (later known as 'The Euston Road School'). Mrs Anrep—who since Roger Fry's death had moved from their home in Bernard Street to Charlotte Street, dined with the Woolfs on 16 December.

— 1938 —

1938

VW here begins DIARY XXVII at 52 Tavistock Square.

Sunday 9 January

Yes, I will force myself to begin this cursed year. For one thing I have 'finished' the last chapter of Three Guineas, & for the first time since I dont know when have stopped writing in the middle of the morning.

How am I to describe 'anxiety'? I've battened it down under this incessant writing, thinking, about 3 Gs—as I did in the summer after Julian's death. Rau has just been, & says there is still a trace of blood: if this continues, L. will have to go next week to a nursing home & be examined. Probably it is the prostate. This may mean an operation. We shall know nothing till Tuesday. What use is there in analysing the feelings of the past 3 weeks? He was suddenly worse at Rodmell; we came up on Wednesday:—the 28th or thereabouts [*29 December*]; since when its been a perpetual strain of waiting for the telephone to ring. What does the analysis show &c? He went to the hospital to be X rayed; has been, is still, in bed. There is a sense in which feelings become habitual, dulled; but only laid under a very thin cover. I walk; work, & so on. Nessa & Angelica & Duncan all at Cassis, which shuts off that relief, but why should she have this forced on her? Anyhow, they come back in a fortnight I suppose.

Harry Stephen, Judith, I think our only visitors. A dead season. No one rings up. Fine today. And the result of writing this page is to make me see how essential it is to steep myself in work; so back to 3 Guineas again. Then the time passes. Writing this it flags.

Tuesday 11 January

Rung up last night: Specimen completely normal.
So the claws relax for the moment.
Ideas: An Ode to Whitaker.[1]

Specimen lecture in USA: both in rhymed prose.

---

1. *Whitaker's Almanack*, founded by Joseph Whitaker in 1868, contained 'an account of Astronomical and other Phenomena, and a vast amount of Information respecting the Government, Finances, Population, Commerce, and General Statistics of the various Nations of the World'. VW had frequent recourse to it in writing *Three Guineas*.

Saturday 15 January

In the 5 minutes left me before starting for MH. I cant describe the relief of hearing at 8 on Wednesday: Specimen perfectly normal. You can go away— Thats where we are at this moment of a wet & windy January. Definitions, explanations can wait. And I've just taken the last pages of the last guinea to Chancery Lane [*to be typed*], so deserve one days pause.

The Woolfs drove to Monks House on 15 January, returning to London on Sunday 23 January; the following day VW ran a temperature and spent several days in bed.

Tuesday 1 February

Nor can I begin analysing now. Still fairly relieved: shall be more so when the 4 weeks test is over next week. But influenza since last Monday has downed me. And 3 Gs. A week at MH. hard at work. Nessa & Angelica back—dinner at Charleston. Wet, but open fields at last.[1] So home: then temperatures; bed; complete submersal, on the sofa &c. Now down for final corrections. 3 Gs. to be shown up to L. tonight. And I feel quite confident once in a way, & only frustrated because it cant now come out till mid May, & I must remain dumb under the shadow of The Years & Miss Storm Jameson's bitter disappointment till then.[2] Never mind. I can make it more compact & the notes shorter & sharper in the time added. This is only a run of my pen—the usual treat. Now for sofa.

Thursday 3 February

Tomorrow is Julian's birthday: his 30th I suppose. And I've been reading what Charles has to say of him. Nobleness his sign mark: & naturalness. Thats true too. A complete lack of self-consciousness; a directness won for him by our flounderings; & yet when he had gained the open world he had to make his choice. Had to be killed in Spain— an odd comment upon his education & our teaching. I dont think Charles, who has many very precise bees in his bonnet, quite sees to the bottom of the crisis, but then my vision—how Julian wanted a profession—his

1. Vanessa and Angelica returned from France on 17 January and the Woolfs dined with them at Charleston on 22nd. Foot and Mouth Disease restrictions had been in force in the Rodmell area since before Christmas.
2. (Margaret) Storm Jameson (b. 1891), writer, President of the English Centre of the International PEN Club from 1938-45; where or how her disappointment was expressed has not been discovered.

innate desire for self assertion, to be a figure, perhaps thats tinged by some obfuscation of my own.[3]

Judith brought a Leslie Humphries to tea the other day—I still in my dressing gown after my first walk. A very nice couple.[4] They're free too; but more balance to them, I rather think. Anyhow I spurted my ideas for a new society at Newnham to Judith; who at once enlarged them to consist of dinners in private rooms with a subject for discussion—say Hazlitt, for whom she has a passion. This is putting flesh & blood on the ideas in 3 Gs. a work wh. L. is now reading.

One always has to allow for the extreme diminution of force: the effect on a second person is so much slighter than one expected. My satire seems to him mild. But the final verdict has not yet been given. I have now to do the notes. A love letter from Philip: the Press business practically through: John our partner: his first interview with Miss Lange yesterday: the Cecils today; Nessa afterwards; Monks House; still fine day.[5]

Friday 4 February

A ten minutes spin here. L. gravely approves 3 Gs. Thinks it an extremely clear analysis. On the whole I'm content. One cant expect emotion, for as he says, its not on a par with the novels. Yet I think it may have more practical value. But I'm much more indifferent, thats true: feel it a good piece of donkeywork, & dont think it affects me either way as the novels do.

David Cecil to tea—a thin slip of a man: like the stalk of a bluebell. Said he begins, at 36, to feel stale. Therefore accepts Clark lectureship, on Hardy, & would like a Provostry at Wadham.[6] A dried analytic mind. Not much room or verge in him. No juice: interesting as a type; & until Nessa & Leonard came in & were judicial—she very set & almost stern—

3. Charles Mauron's essay on Julian Bell's character and mind was published as the Preface to Part II of the memorial volume, 1938.

4. Leslie Alfred Humphrey (1917-1949) went from Winchester to Trinity College, Cambridge, in 1935, and took his degree in Natural Sciences in 1938.

5. Philip Morrell's long letter dated 31 January 1938 and his even longer response to VW's reply (*VI VW Letters*, no. 3362) are in MPH, Sussex; he had been ill, 'and at those times . . . I feel it sad that we should live so estranged . . . and I think of old days—at Garsington and at Richmond—when you seemed to me as in a different way you still do, the most wonderful creature in the world.'

The agreement (outlined in *VI VW Letters*, no. 3345) whereby John Lehmann became LW's partner in the Hogarth Press, buying VW's share for £3000, was signed on 23 February, and came into effect in April.

6. Lord David Cecil delivered the six Clark Lectures at Cambridge in the Easter term of 1941 on 'Thomas Hardy, the novelist: A Critical Appreciation'. The Warden of Wadham was due to retire in 1938; Maurice Bowra was elected to succeed him.

I enjoyed my intimacy. Again, what is Desmond, why is he, whom all our swains adore, so melancholic & superficial? The façade. Could he have broken it, would he have written better? Old questions. Now to Rodmell

Monday 7 February

(Mother's birthday) where we had by the way a perfect week end, still, brisk spring: crocuses in the garden; birds rapturous; Q. to dine; Hubbard to ask L. advice about divorce. That dour gra[s]ping Dedman daughter has made his life Hell for 14 years; & now he finds romance in Doris Thompsett. Oh the lives of the poor![7] But (save for a twinge at the imminence of the sample, & thinking of Nessa) I was very happy: relieved of my book; & tossing ideas as I walked over the downs. For instance: an illustrated sheet to be called The Outsider: a barrel organ tune about The Shrivelled Thorn Furze tree on the downs, through which I see the bungalows: rhymed burlesque. A good idea. But I must do the notes to 3 Gs first.[8]

Nessa, D. & A. dining here.

In the period between VW's last diary entry and the next, the Woolfs again went to Monks House, from Friday to Monday, on 19 February and 4 March; the intervening days at Tavistock Square were very fully occupied with work on Three Guineas, *with negotiations over John Lehmann's partnership in the Hogarth Press, with seeing friends and going to the theatre and concerts.*

Thursday 10 March

Relieved of my book? What nonsense. Here am I working 5 hours a day to finish off those notes, those proofs, & severely warned by L. today that unless I send off both in 6 days from this very Thursday, we must postpone till the autumn. But I've done my due today; & have said nothing here for so long: nothing about the Press; how 10 days ago I signed my rights away to John; how the last week has been June weather; & then all the people: & yesterday I went to Bunhill Fields Burial Ground; & we met Nessa & D. & A. at the 3 Sisters: & Hugh [Walpole]

7. Jack Hubbard was a Rodmell farm worker; he did not get his divorce; for Doris Thomsett, see below, 5 September 1938, n. 4.

8. The concept of 'the Outsider' (see *Three Guineas*, chapter 3), and the possibilities of an Outsider's Society or paper, frequently exercised VW's reflections at this period.

& Saint Denis.[1] I dont think I can add at this moment; & shall owl round the corner to buy a surreptitious packet of cigarettes.

The new Radio came yesterday. We dine alone & shall try it. Bobo came to tea: a yellow pariah dog, still amorous, flinching from the name of Clive.[2]

Reading scraps only; shall I ever force myself to this hard task again—& again? Yet no sooner is one idea fledged, than another cackles. Morgan told me he wrote 11 letters daily. And I none. Maynard & Lydia in residence. Two steps up into the great new room. M. recumbent, but with a stock of ideas. Bentham the origin of evil. Lydia like a peasant woman, wringing her hands, on a stool. Oh why was I born in this age? It is a terrible age. This refers to the Russian spy trials, which reflect the middle ages. A veil of insanity everywhere: & whats to be done, save keep pegging round one's little plot?[3]

Saturday 12 March

Hitler has invaded Austria: that is at 10 last night his army crossed the frontier, unresisted. The Austrian national anthem was heard on the wireless for the last time. We got a snatch of dance music from Vienna.[4] This fact, which combines with the Russian trials, like drops of dirty water mixing, puts its thorn into my morning: a pernickety one spent

1. Bunhill Fields off the City Road, which between 1695 and 1852 was the main burial ground of the Non-Conformists, contains the graves of Defoe, Blake and Bunyan. Chekhov's *The Three Sisters*, with John Gielgud and Peggy Ashcroft, opened at the Queen's Theatre on 28 January 1938; its French director Michel Saint-Denis (1897-1971), whom the Woolfs met at dinner with Vanessa in February, founded the London Theatre Studio at which Angelica had been a student since the summer term of 1936.

2. Beatrice ('Bobo') Mayor, *née* Meinertzhagen (1885-1971), playwright; she and Clive Bell had an affair in the 'twenties. Quentin Bell heard VW use the term 'pariah-dog' in addressing her old friend, clearly intending a compliment; perhaps the elegant *sound* of the word diverted her mind from its true meaning.

3. Keynes, still semi-convalescent after his severe illness the previous year, had acquired the lease of the house (no. 47) next to his own at 46 Gordon Square, and had thrown the adjoining first floors together to form one vast room; the Woolfs had tea there on 28 February. Jeremy Bentham (1748-1832), utilitarian philosopher, economist and jurist. In the series of trials staged in Moscow from early in 1937, great numbers of Stalin's political and military opponents were found guilty of treason, terrorism, or espionage, and exterminated.

4. Hitler's military plan to incorporate Austria into the German Reich was put into operation on 11 March to forestall the Austrian Chancellor's attempt to ascertain, through a plebiscite, the wishes of his people concerning the Fuehrer's demand for a Nazi presence in the Government of Austria. Within hours of the invasion, an all-Nazi cabinet was announced in Vienna.

over notes. The strength of the ray emitted from Vienna can therefore be judged. Privately I'm, as usual at the proof stage, bored with the book which was like a spine to me all last summer; upheld me in the horror of last August; & whirled me like a top miles upon miles over the downs. How can it all have petered out into diluted drivel? But it remains, morally, a spine: the thing I wished to say, though futile. Three USA papers have rejected it; but the Atlantic will pay £120 for 12,000 words.[5] Their cable came when Morgan was here—blown in like thistledown— a very round & voluminous down he is now: but with a breeze behind him: he likes, I think, & very naturally, the praise which now comes from the young. And do I grudge it that *he* should be the best living novelist? He handed me a cutting, about Rose's book, in which he is thus saluted. And so, jealous as I am, rather mean always about contemporaries, I got my dejection, to run into the dirty drop. He had been staying with Charles Trevelyan, & had his novelists bag full of small odds & ends there collected: Charles a good sort; dislikes his daughters pets; theyre sick on the carpet; Lady T.'s tapestry; the face & shield of the ancestral knight hollow; Macaulay's books: all noted with a view to the whole, much as I do. Then Rose as usual rang up. Do you like my book? Havent yet read it. Well I do wonder what people will make of it &c. Privately I know they dont take much stock of it. But this reminds me that our last Leonard & Virginia season is perhaps our most brilliant: all the weeklies I think single out Isherwood, Upward, & even Libby Benedict for the highest places.[6] Yes: if there is success in this world, the Hogarth Press has I suppose won what success it could. And money this year will fairly snow us under. £4,000 about from The Years: then Pepita &c &c. In fact we have asked Mr Wicks [*Lewes builder*] to estimate for a library at MH. in spite of Hitler. But its all a little—my earnings—in the air. To solidify them I bought 2 pairs of American shoes, with rubber soles, yesterday: item: a paper holder, now holding my great notebooks: item: a chair. & negotiated the exchange of my embroidered table—The delight of money; buying freely. Yet, puritanically, I spend next to nothing on dress. Mabel's lugubrious sister copies very cheaply. The delight of spending is to say I want this & buy it

5. A summary of *Three Guineas* entitled 'Women Must Weep' was published in the *Atlantic Monthly* in May and June 1938 (Kp C357).

6. Rose Macaulay's *The Writings of E. M. Forster* had just been published by the Hogarth Press (*HP Checklist* 434). The Trevelyans lived on their family estate at Wallington, Northumberland, which Sir Charles—a great-nephew of Lord Macaulay—made over to the National Trust in 1941. The Hogarth Press books commended by the weeklies were Christopher Isherwood's *Lions and Shadows*, *Journey to the Border* by Edward Upward, and *The Refugees* by Libby Benedict (*HP Checklist* nos. 431, 439, and 427).

outright, especially small articles of furniture & stationery. Perhaps in a fortnight I shall start Roger.

Tuesday 22 March

The public world very notably invaded the private at MH. last week end. Almost war: almost expected to hear it announced. And England, as they say, humiliated. And the man in uniform exalted. Suicides. Refugees turned back from Newhaven. Aeroplanes droning over the house. L. up to his eyes in the usual hectic negotiations. The Labour Party hemming & hawing. And I looked at Quentin & thought Theyll take you. And then, just as in private crises, a sudden lull. The tension relaxes, whether really or only because no one can keep it up; again the Torso case, the private English disputes come to the surface.[7] And it was like June—& so remains—bland sunny blue; with the thought of Julian dead, somehow not pointless; but I keep thinking why is he not here to see the daffodils; the old beggar woman—the swans;—a useless thought: but one that comes so near the surface at Charleston, as if we were all thinking, & might see him.

I am drowsing away my last 20 minutes, having once more tried to recast the last page. Now I must ward off the old depression: the book finished, whats the use of it, feeling. So yesterday I went to Wapping Old Stairs, & roamed through Shadwell & Whitechapel; a change, as complete as France or Italy. Then Tom to dinner, & to Stephen's Judge. A moving play: genuine; simple; sincere; the mother like Nessa. Too much poetic eloquence. But I was given the release of poetry: the end, where they murmur Peace freedom an artist's, not an egoist's end. He gave me a copy, & wants me to write an opinion.[8] I like him always: his large sensitive sincerity better than the contorted nerve drawn brilliancy of the others . . . And a certain richness; but only about 50 people there. And I'm too eye dazzled to write more.

Miss Hepworth's friend the bookseller finds the proofs of 3 Gs exciting.

Saturday 26 March

On Monday the galleys will go. So I can then seriously turn my mind off onto Frys, Highgate, the past. And this is a fact. And would have

7. The discovery early in February of the headless and limbless body of a man in the River Severn at Haw Bridge in Gloucestershire, and the death or disappearance of two others in the neighbourhood, had provided a fruitful subject for speculative journalism. (The mystery remained unsolved.)
8. Stephen Spender's play *Trial of a Judge*, in a production by the Group Theatre, was given a week's run at the Unity Theatre Club in Camden Town; the inscribed copy he gave VW was sold at Sotheby's, 27 April 1970, lot 95.

been accomplished yesterday were it not that Pippa comes to dinner, to lay more facts before us; & Hugh Jones afterwards:[9] hence jaded yesterday; wind & rain & cold; so to Kew, perversely, with Ann, who stayed till 8. A fine figure, athletic, hardheaded; emotional too I guess. living at Brunswick Sqre with Richard. On Monday they go to Corsica for a family jaunt together. Influenza has attacked Flossie & Clive. Dinners supplied to 8 F. Street.[10] How dull I'm grown: what they call objective: it needs a good brain to be objective. The crisis still shakes our telephone, the voice of Kingsley appealing to L. to have his mind made. The crisis has once more set it violently in motion. But the lull is hushing us; not very profoundly though. When the tiger, ie Hitler, has digested his dinner he will pounce again. And privately, I have no letters. I must take up life again on Monday: by which I mean ask E. Bowen to tea, buy a new dress off Murray, arrange one or two parties, & not let myself be submerged in Roger quite so completely as in 3 Gs. But that submersal was a remedy; an anodyne. How could I have toiled along these last months without? As usual I have drawn too many words from my well, & want to fill it from some good book. Mandeville The Bees, I think.[11] No sooner do I say this than I am pelted with MSS. Vast meritorious novels, that one cant skimp. My insatiable appetite for reading will glut itself on Roger. Then what? Oh my Outsider papers: The TLS is now a paper like another, not my paper. And some attempts at brief scenes. And the Odyssey. And a few days doing nothing between tea & dinner: the unconscious is asking for a rise.

[Thursday 31 March]

But I have too much drudgery donkey work, now correcting proofs of notes, to write, or to invite: Rose & Jeremy Hutchinson dining tonight.[12] And the nibs are wrong. And I detest my own now paralytic hand. Two pages of Roger written: then that cup dashed down by proofs. Then there'll be page proofs. Walking in the City the great relief.

9. Philippa (Pippa) Strachey (1872-1968), an active campaigner for women's causes for over thirty years, was Secretary to the London & National Society for Women's Service; she dined with the Woolfs on 24 March. Philip Hugh-Jones (b. 1917), son of Philip Morrell and Alice Jones, his wartime secretary and subsequently on the staff of the *NS&N*, was at this time an undergraduate at King's College, Cambridge.

10. Flossie (Mrs Riley), a sister of VW's Mabel Haskins, was Vanessa's daily cook and servant.

11. VW quoted Bernard de Mandeville, *The Fable of the Bees; or Private Vices, Publick Benefits* (1714) in *Three Guineas* (note 34 to Chapter 1), presumably from her 1924 2-volume edition by F. B. Kaye (see *Holleyman*, VS V, p. 74).

12. Jeremy (b. 1915), son of St. John and Mary Hutchinson, was still an undergraduate at Magdalen College, Oxford.

Leather Lane & Neville's Court—both new ground—& the Cut with
its stale fish—yesterday. Then Ethel Smyth. Then K. Martin with his
eternal article after dinner. Then MH & LP tomorrow. So its not yet
possible to dive into darkness. And I've just bought E. FitzGerald on
Sevigne, & may broach her.[13] Very hot again. No letters again. Colefax
snubbed short. L. writing his play—the one he's brewed these 10 years
& more. This is his only free week. Then accounts. John still abroad.
He was in Vienna for the Hitler coup. Sheilah Grant Duff to come
tonight. Oh & Judith & Ann about the place, with Richard, & a minute
figure called Shawn.[14]

Tuesday 12 April[1]

Anyhow, on April 1st I think, I started Roger; & with the help of his
memoirs have covered the time till Clifton.[2] Much of it donkey work; &
I suppose to be re-written. Still there is 20 pages put down, after being so
long put off. And it is an immense solace to have this sober drudgery
to take to instantly & so tide over the horrid anti climax of 3 Gs. I didnt
get so much praise from L. as I hoped. He had to swallow the notes at a
gulp though. And I suspect I shall find the page proofs (due tomorrow)
a chill bath of disillusionment. But I wanted—how violently—how
persistently, pressingly compulsorily I cant say—to write this book; &
have a quiet composed feeling; as if I had said my say: take it or leave it;
I'm quit of that; free for fresh adventures—at the age of 56. Last night I
began making up again: Summers night: a complete whole: that's my
idea.[3] E. Bowen to tea; cut out of coloured cardboard but sterling &

13. *Dictionary of Madame de Sevigné* by Edward Fitzgerald ('. . . a Dictionary of the
   Dramatis Personae figuring in her Correspondence whom I am always forgetting
   and confounding'), edited and annotated by his great-niece Mary Eleanor
   FitzGerald Kerrich, 2 vols, 1914; VW's copy, with her pencilled index on the
   endpapers of each volume, she gave to QB.
14. LW's play *The Hotel*—about 'the horrors of the twilight age of Europe'—was
   published by the Hogarth Press in 1939. Shiela Grant Duff (b. 1913), well-
   connected and idealistic, worked as a journalist in Central Europe after leaving
   Oxford; she had become increasingly alarmed by the drift of British foreign
   policy and the dangers of appeasement, particularly with regard to Hitler's mount-
   ing threats to Czechoslovakia (see her autobiographical *The Parting of the Ways;
   A Personal Account of the Thirties*, 1982). Sean Llewelyn Davies was an Irish
   cousin of Richard's.
1. VW has misdated this entry: *Tuesday April 11th.*
2. Roger Fry's memoir is in the Fry Papers, King's College, Cambridge.
3. This is the first allusion in VW's diary to what was to develop into a new book,
   variously entitled *Poyntzet Hall, Poyntz Hall*, or *Pointz Hall*, but finally *Between
   the Acts*, the first page of the first draft of which is dated 2 April 1938 and headed
   'Summer Night'; see *Virginia Woolf: Pointz Hall. The Earlier and Later Typescripts*

sharpedged; Lennox Robinson (bright blue tweeds) called:[4] we have John on us now—John saddened & hammered by his experiences at Vienna. K[ingsley] M[artin]. still rings up, at inordinate length: I've time to change & write a letter while they talk; its about emigrating now from our doomed Europe. "If it weren't that I feel I must stay by the paper"— Also W. Robson is back; gave me the vertebrae of a cow, with his usual kind simplicity, made into a brooch; Easter is on us: Bells at Charleston; hard blue dry weather with a cold wind. Margery F. dines tomorrow; Roger surrounds me; & then to MH on Thursday, & that infernal bundle of proofs.

Am I right though in thinking that it has some importance—3 Gs— as a point of view: shows industry; fertility; & is, here & there as "well written" (considering the technical problems—quotations arguments &c) as any of my rather skimble skamble works? I think there's more to it than to A Room: which, on rereading, seems to me a little egotistic, flaunting, sketchy: but has its brilliance—its speed. I'm suspicious of the vulgarity of the notes: of a certain insistence.

Wednesday 13 April

But the proofs have not come; & thus I have had a mitigated respite, which has been spent (am) reading R.'s letters; trying to decide what to leave out in the School fragment; & collecting the Clifton dossier. Now I shall not be so literal; but what am I to be? And I a little resent so much fact seeking. Also resent being told by some French scribbler [*not identified*] that I cant externalise; so to contradict him wish to be intelligent —so wd like to read 3 Gs & see if I am intelligent—& so on. A very fine clear day. A spring without any paralell. so enduring: so constantly unexpected this sun. All the trees are now full out. And no checks. The hyacinths over. So in MH we shall get the full blast. Summer time last Sunday. And today (oh these pens—I'm always throwing them away & hoping for a better one) . . . we may go into society; to a party at Susan Lawrence's. Why? God knows, having rejected so many others.[5] Probably our Press takings this year will beat all others: £2,500?

---

of BETWEEN THE ACTS, edited by Mitchell A. Leaska, New York, 1983. LW published a 'rather rough typescript heavily corrected in handwriting' as 'The Moment: Summer's Night' in the posthumous collection *The Moment* (Kp A29); but from the evidence of the typescript in the Berg this appears to be a later (1940) attempt by VW to form 'a complete whole' of her idea.

4. Lennox Robinson (1886-1958), Irish writer and director of the Abbey Theatre, Dublin.

5. Susan Lawrence (1871-1947), ex-MP and one-time chairman of the Labour Party; Margery Fry dined with the Woolfs and went with them to the party.

Tuesday 26 April

We had our Easter at MH; but as for the sun, it never shone; was colder than Christmas; a grudging lead-coloured sky; razor wind; winter clothes; proofs; much acute despair; curbed however, by the aid of divine philosophy; a joy in discovering Mandeville's Bees (this really a fruitful book; the very book I want) then Q. rings up; to warn you: Have you had a letter from Pipsy? Ottoline is dead. They told her P. might die, & the shock killed her; & hes asking you to write about her.[6] (with Mr Wicks & Mr Muzzell [*builders*] exploring the attics for the new room). So I had to write; the horrid little pellet screwed my brain; leaves it giddy. Yet in spite of that here am I sketching out a new book; only dont please impose that huge burden on me again, I implore. Let it be random & tentative; something I can blow of a morning, to relieve myself of Roger: dont, I implore, lay down a scheme; call in all the cosmic immensities; & force my tired & diffident brain to embrace another whole—all parts contributing—not yet awhile. But to amuse myself, let me note: why not Poyntzet Hall: a centre: all lit. discussed in connection with real little incongruous living humour; & anything that comes into my head; but "I" rejected: 'We' substituted: to whom at the end there shall be an invocation? "We" . . . composed of many different things . . . we all life, all art, all waifs & strays—a rambling capricious but somehow unified whole—the present state of my mind? And English country; & a scenic old house—& a terrace where nursemaids walk? & people passing —& a perpetual variety & change from intensity to prose. & facts—& notes; &—but eno'. I must read Roger: & go to Ott's memorial service, representing also T. S. Eliot at his absurd command. 2.30 at Martins in the Fields.

[? *Wednesday 27 April*]

Ottoline's burial service. Oh dear, oh dear the lack of intensity; the wailing & mumbling, the fumbling with bags; the shuffling; the vast brown mass of respectable old South Kensington ladies. And then the hymns; & the clergyman with a bar of medals across his surplice; & the orange & blue windows; & a toy Union Jack sticking from a cranny. What all this had to do with Ottoline, or our feelings? Save that the address was to the point: a critical study, written presumably by Philip

6. Lady Ottoline Morrell died early on 21 April at the International Clinic, Tunbridge Wells, from whence Philip Morrell wrote to VW that day, wondering 'whether as one of her oldest friends you would like to send some short account of her to the Times. . . .' (MPH, Sussex). VW's obituary tribute appeared in the early editions only on 28 April 1938 (Kp C354), two days after the memorial service; see Appendix II.

& delivered, very resonantly, by Mr Speiaght the actor:[7] a sober, & secular speech, which made one at least think of a human being, though the reference to her beautiful voice caused one to think of that queer nasal moan: however that too was to the good in deflating immensities. P.'s secretary buttonholed me, & told me to sit high up. The pew was blocked by a vast furred lady who said "I'm afraid I cant move"—as indeed seemed the fact. So, I stationed myself rather behind; near eno' though to see the very well set up back of P. in his thick coat; & his red Rams head turned now & then looking along the ranks: also I pressed his hand, simulated I fear, more emotion than I felt when he asked me, had I liked the address? & so slowly moved out on to the steps—past Jack & Mary, Sturge Moores, Molly, &c: Gertler having tears in his eyes; various household staffs;[8] was then pounced on & pinioned by Lady Oxford: who was hard as whipcord; upright; a little vacant in the eye, in spite of make up which made it shine. She said she had expostulated with Ott. about the voice. Mere affectation. But a wonderful woman. Tell me, though, why did her friends quarrel with her? Pause— She was exigeante, Duncan volunteered at last. And so Margot refused to ask further; & modulated into stories of Symonds & Jowett, when I bantered her on her obituary. Mine, of Ott. for the Times, has not appeared nor do I much regret.[9] So to Nessa's where we recounted the story; & yet I'm left fumbling for a house I shant go to. Odd how the sense of loss takes this quite private form: someone who wont read what I write. No illumination in Gower Street. an intimacy ⟨checked⟩ abolished.

[*Thursday 28 April*]

Walked in Dulwich yesterday & lost my brooch by way of a freshener when confronted with the final proofs just today (April 28th) done; & to be sent this afternoon: a book I shall never look at again. But I now feel entirely free. Why? Have committed myself. am afraid of nothing. Can do anything I like. No longer famous, no longer on a pedestal; no

7. Robert Speaight (1904-76), creator of the part of Becket in *Murder in the Cathedral*, was first introduced to T. S. Eliot by Lady Ottoline at one of her Thursday tea-parties.

8. T. Sturge Moore (1870-1944), poet, eldest brother of the philosopher G. E. Moore. Mark Gertler (1891-1939), painter, towards whom, early in his career, Ottoline had extended an almost maternal benevolence.

9. In *The Times* of 22 April 1938, the obituary notice of Lady Ottoline was followed by a personal tribute by Lady Oxford. However, VW's allusion to 'her obituary' may refer to Margot Asquith's request (see above, 29 February 1936 and 'Am I A Snob' in *Moments of Being*) that VW should prepare a tribute to *her* for *The Times* to keep on file against her death.

longer hawked in by societies: on my own, for ever. Thats my feeling: a sense of expansion, like putting on slippers. Why this shd. be so, why I feel myself enfranchised till death, & quit of all humbug, when I daresay its not a good book, & will excite nothing but mild sneers; & how very inconsequent & egotistical V.W. is—why why I cant analyse: being fluttered this morning. Lady Simon this afternoon—Well I've done my bit for that cause, & cant be bullied. And then, when they badger me, I can say Refer to 3 Gs.

Rain & dark. A lost dog in the Square; political lull. Income Tax up to 5/6. Our earnings prodigious. Income last year about £6,000. John much impressed. Press worth £10,000. & all this sprung from that type on the drawing room table at Hogarth House 20 years ago. I can now give all my mind to Roger; also blow a few private bubbles of a morning; & dont wait publication day with any expectations. I shall I feel forget this book completely. Yet I never wrote a book with greater fervour; under such a lash of compulsion. And it stood me in good stead. Now America wants Common Reader articles (Penguin republishes in the autumn) will pay £50: & I think of Walt Whitman: Walpole's Letters; & White's Selborne. 3 Gs. has won me the right to go back to that world: no doubt a more 'real' world: but debarred by brambles for 4 years.[10]

[Friday 29 April]

The difficulty is that I get so absorbed in this fantastic Pointz Hall I cant attend to Roger. So what am I to do? This however is only my first day of freedom; & I have been rendered self-conscious by a notice of T[hree]. G[uineas]. on the front page of the new bloated TLS.[11] Well it cant be helped; & I must cling to my 'freedom'—that mysterious hand that was reached out to me about 4 years ago.

Meanwhile, Lady Simon came to tea, & of course looks forward to my castigation at their expense—for so I suspect it will be; a very nice salt of the earth dowdy but decisive woman, with whom I'm on impersonal

10. *The Common Reader* was published by Penguin Books as a Pelican Book (price 6d) in October (Kp A8d). America's wants were transmitted by the agent Ann Watkins; VW did not write on Whitman; her article on Walpole based on the Yale edition of *Letters of Horace Walpole to the Rev. William Cole* (1937) and called 'Two Antiquaries' was rejected by the *Atlantic Monthly* (see below, 7 August 1938) but appeared in the *Yale Review* (Kp C358); she did write on 'White's Selborne' later, but not for America (Kp C361).

11. Under the heading 'News and Notes' on the newly designed front page of the *TLS* dated 30 April 1938 it was reported that 'Mrs Woolf has retired from partnership in the Hogarth Press ...' which '... is shortly to publish a new book by [her] entitled "Three Guineas" in which the author develops certain trains of thought which ran through "The Years" ...' etc.

good terms. Yet she alluded yesterday to my daughter, the most gifted of my children who died.[12] And off she went in chocolate brown fur & puce to investigate elementary schools in Suffolk.

A fine day for once. Dog loose in square. L. & I have our week's treat this afternoon. I'm in a dazed state, hovering between 2 worlds like a spiders web with nothing to attach the string to. Why not write about Scott's diaries, so bring in the immortal novels? My Times obit. on Ott. printed in early editions, omitted by mistake, they say, from the later. A thousand from H[arcourt]. B[race].: the last fruit I suppose from The Years. This makes about 3,000 from them. Can I therefore buy a chair? & 2 dresses? Oh how odd to see the blue sky at the top of the skylight again!

Tuesday 3 May

Pouring now; the drought broken; the worst spring on record; my pens diseased, even the new box; my eyes ache with Roger, & I'm a little appalled at the prospect of the grind this book will be. I must somehow shorten & loosen; I *cant* (remember) stretch out a long painstaking literal book: later I must generalise & let fly. But then, what about all the letters? How can one cut loose from facts, when there they are, contradicting my theories? A problem. But I'm convinced I cant physically, strain after an RA portrait.

What was I going to say with this defective nib? Heres L. to ask me what I think Libby Benedict looks like? I guess fat & Jewish: she's thin & Jewish. I think I suspect our first breach with John. It'll be over his fashion complex. HP must be in the movement. Wants to reject the Kabbalah (a powerful Arnold Bennett novel) because its old fashioned. And what line am I to take about a story for New Writing: when I dont mean to be a signpost to that gang of elderly novelties? These are our problems. Mrs Nicholls also a problem.[1] A flashy underworld flibberti-gibbet on the surface; daughter of a Hastings Dr: has a child: the child has tonsils. Mrs N. very "naive": has kept underworld company. Lange has waddled off; gooselike; into what line of life we dont know. I have very few letters. And we take our treat on Friday now, & went to St Albans, in the grey blizzard; & saw Roman pavements, guarded by men in overcoats, attending upon imbecile sons. Had tea, & heard the local

12. The Simons' daughter Antonia, an exceptionally intelligent child, died at the age of twelve in 1929 after three years' illness.

1. *The Kabbalah* was an earlier title for *Mile End* by Kathleen Nott, published by the Hogarth Press in October 1938 (*HP Checklist* 435). For the line VW took about *New Writing*, see *VI VW Letters*, no. 3385: 'shouldnt anyhow have time'. Mrs Norah Nicholls started work as office manager at the Hogarth Press on 2 May in succession to Miss Lange.

ladies discussing the Empire Day celebrations, which are to include a red white & blue cake decorated with flags. What will they say to 3 Gs? But I'm philosophic, fundamentally; & feel, as I've said, oddly quit of it all. A Row in the papers about Wyndham Lewis's rejected portrait of Tom:[2] & Tom has to be represented at Ott's funeral. Clive at Charleston. Sunday evening alone with Nessa: oh dear— That signifies my desperation: Julian not there, I mean. The wound bleeding; & nothing to be said. So I will buy a chair this wet day, in order to keep moving.

Monday 9 May

This is written to fill up the usual distracted relics of Mondays broken morning: drove up [*from Rodmell*] in the clear May morning light: sun out wonderously; laburnum all chipped by the bitter spring: but pink on the may, & various fine shades of gold red & bluebell blue on the trees all the same. Found here that Richard cant dine & go to A.'s play this evening (she had a triumph, dancing, Nessa says [;] is mentioned in the Times): also Miss Phyllis Bentley's lecture on me; shall I tell her anything true about The Years for example?[3] Then Tom in Portugal; then Mary Hutch. whom I met in a shoe shop; then Morgan asking some literary help about a quotation in a pageant. Then I ring up Sally & mercifully secure her for tonight: find Mabel has moved the drawing room chair here—oh what comfort I now sit in after 10 years moderate discomfort; but her chair, her long promised chair, has stuck. A rather patchy week end: bitter cold, Q. didnt come; I had no good nonsense book; & giddy in the head; cant settle either to my Play (Pointz Hall is to become in the end a play) or to Roger's Cambridge letters. The truth is we want a holiday; & have to dribble along rather jaded, trying odds & ends to keep moving, until June 8th or so, when we escape. However on Sunday, we walked, rather slowly to save my head, from Tarring Neville toward Bishopstone, along the long Down road made by primeval carts; & half the down was blue purple with some grass: & then the gorse blazing silky, nutty, hares racing; home to bowls & the silly clever imitation & oh how she makes me detest my own writing—May Sarton's book this

2. On 21 April the Selection Committee of the Royal Academy rejected Wyndham Lewis's portrait of T. S. Eliot (now in the Municipal Art Gallery, Durban); the ensuing *furore*, during which Augustus John resigned from the Academy, an institution Lewis described as a 'disgusting bazaar', enabled the latter to attract welcome attention to himself.

3. In the London Theatre Studio students' end of term show, playing for a week in their converted chapel in Islington, Angelica Bell danced in six mimed scenes based on Goya's *Desastros della Guerra* and acted in *La Malguerida* by Benavente; her appearances were briefly noticed by *The Times* of 7 and 9 May respectively. Phyllis Bentley (1894) was the Yorkshire-born writer; her lecture on VW, untraced.

refers to, ungrammatically.[4] A social week ahead: Bella back; lunch Clive; to Philip [Morrell] to choose a ring & emotionalise; 2 plays of A[ngelica']s & God damn it, Saturday at Ray's. L. rather on edge about that. Now lunch.

Thursday 12 May

Lunch Clive (balderdash, respectability rampant; hard superficiality) to Philip's after tea. Shook hands with Grey Millie. Two interesting things: that Ott. confided everything in M. whom she had had all M.'s life: the other the vast importance she attached to her Memoirs. To be saved in a fire before anything. They were her justification; the proof to herself I suppose & the world that Ott was not what they thought. Sat in the upper room with P. kindly, I wary. Simple. Some little reserve; touched hands over the ring. He pressed things on me. I felt rather uncomfortable: a vulture feeling; didnt want to take so much. But took the big green ring & pearl earrings, shawl & fan. A kind of ripple of laughter at myself "doing well out of Ottoline". But thats not the whole. P. has been left out of it all as he said. O. when dying last summer, suddenly named Hacket, a vulgar Irish peasant, P. says, joint lit. executor with Bob. G. Hardy & Hope.[5] I advised P. to write a solid memoir at once. He will, but am I to add a chapter? We had out the great box with all the orange bound books she used to keep on a stool—all full. Whats to be done? And then the great bedspread? Julian [*daughter*] despises the old curiosity shop side of O. Wont look at these things. O. not a good mother—didn't want children. P. rather battered—simple, cheerful, with a vast black satin cravat. Had a bad heart, from an old rowing strain. The specialist thinking Ott. an ordinary wife said "Do you want the truth?" Yes. "Well any shock will kill you. How old? 67. You wont see 68—except you live like a potato." She burst into tears, which she seldom did. Then he recovered, she got ill—paralysed—some nerve affection. They then told her of the Drs. death: she was sick all night; recovered; & suddenly died in the early morning. She had written though a letter of farewell to the duke as if expecting this.[6] Drawing room littered &

4. On 19 May VW replied to an apprehensive enquiry from May Sarton that she had still not had time to read her novel *The Single Hound* (see *VI VW Letters*, no. 3386).

5. Ottoline met the Irish writer Francis Hackett (1883-1962) and his Danish wife Signe in 1936 and rapidly formed a close intimacy with them. Her friendships with Hope Mirrlees (1887-1978) and with the Hon. Robert Gathorne-Hardy (1902-73) were of some twenty years' duration, and it was the latter who finally undertook the editing and publication of her memoirs (2 volumes, 1963, 1974).

6. Ottoline, already undergoing dietary treatment, suffered a stroke in May 1937 on learning of Philip Morrell's heart condition; thenceforward she was under the care

unkempt. A lovely thrush egg blue evening; domes & chimneys very pure & sharp walking home with my green shagreen box the shawl & the fan. O.'s last gifts.

Friday 20 May

Time & again I have meant to write down my expectations, dreads, & so on, waiting the publication on—I think June 2nd—of 3 Gs—but haven't, because what with living in the solid world of Roger, & then (again this morning) in the airy world of Poyntz Hall I feel extremely little. And dont want to rouse feeling. What I'm afraid of is the taunt Charm & emptiness. The book I wrote with such violent feelings to relieve that immense pressure will not dimple the surface. That is my fear. Also I'm uneasy at taking this role in the public eye—afraid of autobiography in public. But the fears are entirely outbalanced (this is honest) by the immense relief & peace I have gained, & enjoy this moment. Now I am quit of that poison & excitement. Nor is that all. For having spat it out, my mind is made up. I need never recur or repeat. I am an outsider. I can take my way: experiment with my own imagination in my own way. The pack may howl, but it shall never catch me. And even if the pack—reviewers, friends, enemies—pays me no attention or sneers, still I'm free. This is the actual result of that spiritual conversion (I cant bother to get the right words) in the autumn of 1933—or 4— when I rushed through London, buying, I remember, a great magnifying glass, from sheer ecstasy, near Blackfriars: when I gave the man who played the harp half a crown for talking to me about his life in the Tube station. The omens are mixed: L. is less excited than I hoped; Nessa highly ambiguous; Miss Hepworth & Mrs Nicholls say "Women owe a great deal to Mrs Woolf" & I have promised Pippa to supply books. Now for R.'s letters & Monks H—at the moment windy & cold.

Tuesday 24 May[7]

I'm pleased this morning because Lady Rhondda writes that she is "profoundly excited & moved by 3 Gs." Theo Bosanquet who has a review copy read her extracts. And she thinks it may have a great effect, & signs herself my grateful Outsider.[8] A good omen; because this shows

---

of a Dr A. J. D. Cameron, spending long periods in his clinic at Sherwood Park, Tunbridge Wells. Dr Cameron, whose treatments by injection of Prontosil was occasioning serious misgivings in the medical world, committed suicide at Sherwood Park on 19 April 1938; Ottoline died there on 21 April. The duke was her half-brother, the 6th Duke of Portland.

7. VW has misdated this entry *Tuesday May 17th.*

8. Margaret Haig Thomas, Viscountess Rhondda (1883-1958), founder and editor of the weekly *Time and Tide;* her letter to VW dated 23 May 1938 is in MHP, Sussex;

that certain people will be stirred; will think; will discuss: it wont altogether be frittered away. Of course Ly R. is already partly on my side; but again as she's highly patriotic & citizenlike she might have been roused to object. Its on the cards that it will make more splash among the ink pots than I thought—feeling very dim & cold these last weeks, & indifferent too: & oblivious of the great excitement & intensity with which (certainly) I wrote.

But as the whole of Europe may be in flames—its on the cards. One more shot at a policeman, & the Germans, Czecks, French will begin the old horror. The 4th of August [1914] may come next week. At the moment there is a lull. L. says K. Martin says we say (the P.M.) that we will fight this time. Hitler therefore is chewing his little bristling moustache. But the whole thing trembles: & my book may be like a moth dancing over a bonfire—consumed in less than one second. Morgan rang up yesterday about Rosamond's great meeting for writers to protest against Spain, for wh. she has hired the Queens Hall. But hasnt asked us.[9] What is he to do? Thinks it foolish. So I let fly a few, guarded hints as to my own attitude. We must attack Hitler in England. "Thats what I'm always saying" he said "But how?" "Oh I'm in touch with Pippa & Newnham . . ." He seemed to sympathise. Anyhow he wont speak at QH. or send a message. Now for the [*Chelsea*] Flower Show; dinner at the Hutch. What am I to wear?

Aeroplanes growling overhead in the cloudy blue sky. They look like sharks, seen through our wavy window. No rain. No fruit. Vegs. dried up.

Wednesday 25 May[10]

Too tired after a dreary dinner at the Hutchinsons to write: so let me scribble. Ka is dead. I read it by chance in the [News] Chronicle yesterday before going to the flower show. No flowers, no mourning.[11] Why did

for VW's reply, see *VI VW Letters*, no. 3387. Lady Rhondda's close friend and companion Theodora Bosanquet (d. 1961) reviewed *Three Guineas* in *Time and Tide* of 4 June 1938 (see *M&M*, pp. 402-3).

9. A public meeting 'In defence of freedom against Fascism' organised by the Association of Writers for Intellectual Liberty and supported by Hugh Walpole, Philip Guedalla, Rose Macaulay, Compton Mackenzie and Cecil Day Lewis among others, was held at the Queen's Hall on 8 June 1938.

10. VW has misdated this entry *Wednesday, May 18th*.

11. Ka Cox—whom VW had known since before either of them was married—died of a heart-attack at her home in Cornwall on 22 May; she had married Will Arnold-Forster (1885-1951) in 1918, and their only child Mark was born in 1920 (and died in 1980). Ka's troubled relationship with Rupert Brooke is documented in Christopher Hassall's biography of the poet (1964).

she die? And what do I feel? Oh that one could feel more for the deaths of ones friends! But it comes & goes, feeling. Always at first visual—Ka lying drawn & white, there with the flat sea underneath—the ships passing. And Will pretending, poor little dried squeezed man—all her thought would be for him. Her passion for the boy—that she had left him, unknowing what he was to become, unable to go on educating protecting planning for Mark. I remember going there one spring morning when he was asleep in the perambulator at the door. And she came hurrying out agitated lest we should wake him. Her own identical life ended when Rupert died. So I think. After that she was acting a part very carefully & deliberately chosen. Maternity, Will, public life. Hence some squint; she was never natural, never with me at least. And I was self-conscious; remembering how she had seen me mad. She used to come to Asheham, to Holford: condescending, patronising, giving up her own pleasures to tend me & help L. I dont think I was ever at my ease with her. Yet we had an old affection; remembered things—Rupert &c—that we never spoke of. She had that irritating Quack Quack in her voice; as if she always must be impressing me with her busyness, her social standing even among the county families; her responsibilities: how she was a JP on some Education Co[mmi]ttee; doing actual things with important real people, while we frittered our time away writing books in London. She protested too much—a sign of dissatisfaction I suppose—with Will? She had to transform him into something noble, unconventional, brilliant, good; from the material which was none of those things really. But she liked Cornwall; so did I. She liked the view that day she took us to—the promontory all silver & blue—the lovely moor —the badger & the foxes barking round the house, & the long drives over Zennor Moor; seeing the gipsy woman in her tent; I daresay alone she was happier than she ever got said. In her house—a singularly ugly house in some ways—with a kind of formality & no luxuriance—she was too much the hostess who keeps open house. But at the same time that was her role: to help; to lift lame dogs; to entertain; to arrange; manage; receive confidences. And what was wrong with all that? Only that after Rupert's death she was playing a part. Yet this is superficial. For there was a trustiness in her; a stable goodness; a tenderness under the assumption— Children, she wd. say & irritated me—& a good deal of fortitude, patience; a determination to oar her way—Bruin I called her, at the Vienna Café one day with Rupert—Bruin oaring her way—with a beavers tail, & short clumsy paws. He liked the image. It conveyed her thickness, breadth. She was very broad cheeked; & her face was long drawn out. In spite of her clumsiness & sturdiness she was very pale. She had thinned & wrinkled last time we stayed there. She wore 2 or 3 good Rings—cameos with heads on them. She chose bright pure colours for her clothes; wore a coloured handkerchief round her hair; often stuck

it with a silver pin: an individual looking woman; derived partly from a
John painting; but also practically equipped for her car driving, committees; her endless meetings in St Ives & Truro; she took her place very
capably on the Bench: had a great shrewdness & capacity & some humour,
only suppressed by Will's acidity. Now I come to think of it, she had
managed her life with great ⟨composure⟩ individuality. There was her
cottage at Aldbourne; her ability to make excursions, take charge of
situations, oar her way courageously where she wished. I wonder, did
she know she was dying? & what did she think of it all? And why? As
usual, I regret: that she sent me cream at Christmas, & in the flurry of
L.'s illness I never wrote & thanked; that she suggested coming, &
absorbed in Nessa last autumn, I did not arrange it. But this is always so;
& can't be helped. And I am thinking of her with affection—old Ka. The
deep silence between us was threaded with something that could vibrate,
& does: chiefly through the eye at this moment. I can imagine a half
smiling So goodbye Children & dont bother. Old Ka's all right . . . But
Mark?

Thursday 26 May

Ka had a seizure & died without regaining consciousness. This is
from a typed form sent by Chris A.F. [*her brother-in-law*] this morning.
She is buried today—rainy & dark: & I shall not go to the service. Will
is in Canada.

My usual 5 minutes for notes. The PH mood used up. Roger at
Cambridge difficult to recover. 3 weeks before Scotland, & rather
anxious (though its true I'm more indifferent than ever before) during
these 3 coming out weeks. Mercifully we shall be away mostly. And I
think to fill in the time quietly by forcing myself to do a Horace Walpole
sketch for America. Why not? It means close reading; alien matter; &
just time to do it. I cant broach another R. chapter—too tired of facts.

Friday 27 May

Its odd to be working at half cock after all those months of high
pressure. The result is half an hour every day to write here. Roger I'm
retyping; & shall then sketch Walpole. I have just been signing in bright
green ink those circulars. But I will not expatiate on the dreariness of
doing things one ought to do. A letter, grateful, from Bruce Richmond,
ending my 30 year connection with him & the Lit Sup.[12] How pleased

12. VW signed and forwarded to her friends an appeal for funds to support the library
of the London and National Society for Women's Service at 29 Marsham Street,
SW1. Sir Bruce Richmond, now retired and living near Salisbury, wrote flatter-
ingly to VW on 26 May of her long connection with the *TLS* (MHP, Sussex).

I used to be when L. called me "You're wanted by the Major Journal!" & I ran down to the telephone to take my almost weekly orders at Hogarth House! I learnt a lot of my craft writing for him: how to compress; how to enliven; & also was made to read with a pen & notebook, seriously. I am now waiting for today week—when thats over, my swell will subside. And cant I prophesy? On the whole I shall get more pain than pleasure; I shall mind the sneers more than I shall enjoy Ly Rhondda's enthusiasm. There'll be many sneers—some very angry letters. Some silences. And then—3 weeks yesterday—we shall be off. And by July 7th when we come back—or sooner, for we dread too many hotels—it will be over, almost entirely; & then for 2 years I think I shall publish nothing, save American articles. And this week of waiting is the worst, & its not very bad—nothing in the least comparable to the horror of The Years: (that deadened into indifference so sure was I of failure). As for sales, I am not very hopeful; 6 thousand I daresay; the shops are tepid.

Today I'm had in a corner by a persistent Miss Neilsen, my evening ruined. L. went to his Jury this morning, only to be told "You will be pleased to hear that you're discharged." So thats over.[13]

Saturday 28 May

A pouring wet day as dark as November. May—this spring has been blotted from the calendar. Heres my daily canter: which will take the form I suppose of a temperature Chart. The Buzz is beginning, though the little gadfly only emerges from its shell next Thursday. Mrs Lynd in Harper's Bazaar sneers, says I preach sitting still on a sofa; & Miss Osler or some such name writes to thank & praise—my grand work &c &c.[14] These first rumours always give the shape of whats to come: I can foretell that those who dislike will sneer at me for a well to do aesthete; & those who approve will echo Rhondda's "most exciting" profoundly moving. All reviews & letters will ring changes on those notes; now I have to send a copy to Pippa, with my heart beating: after that it will beat to the time

13. Elizabeth Nielson, a Danish-American from Michigan, was an aspiring pioneer of the American doctoral dissertation upon the works of Virginia Woolf (though in the event her subject was rejected as too modern). At her meeting with the Woolfs she 'chattered loudly and wildly . . . but try hard as I could, I simply could not collect myself'. (Letter to VW, 16 October 1938, MHP, Sussex). LW was summoned for Jury duty at the Law Courts on 23 May, excused until the 25th and again until the 27th.

14. Reviewing *Three Guineas* in the June 1938 issue of *Harper's Bazaar*, Sylvia Lynd wrote: 'To sit on one's sofa and keep one's head, what pleasant advice is this. But alas . . . .' &c. Mary Geraldine Ostle, formerly Registrar of the Froebel Society and editor of *The Notebooks of a Woman Alone* (1935), wrote 'gratefully', a letter of four typed pages (MHP, Sussex).

of sneer enthusiasm, enthusiasm sneer. And I rather think I shall sum it all up in 6 months in a pamphlet; & if my facts are challenged get 29 M[arsham]. S[treet]. to reply.

To the Caledonian market in my new pinching shoes yesterday, where I bought 6 tea spoons & some flowers. Miss Nielsen came; a daneish bee haunted American lit. prof., entirely distracted by Einstein, & his extra mundane influence upon fiction. L. threaded the maze to the muddle in the centre. I gave up on the outskirts. Rather genuine, naive, a little like Christabel; & as usual much more likeable than her letters. One cant dislike people in the flesh. But she ruined my reading of Walpole to wh. I now happily turn.

L. lunching with Robsons.

Monday 30 May

Nessa's birthday—the 58th [*59th*] I think it must be. She is at Charleston, with A. & Q. now that A.'s time at Islington is done. Oh dear—Julian not there. And it rains hard—she says she is glad to be away. How could she have lived through the suspense last summer? what torture . . . so I thought, as I walked to Gough Square yesterday, by way of freshener before the Robson children & Tom at tea.[15] A great spread; mostly eaten. The little boy crammed his mouth with sweets, & added one that Sally had already sucked. Tom came, most respectable; swallow tails & grey silk tie, having he explained to slip into his evening service in time to take round the plate—a churchwarden in South Kensington. Very friendly; & elaborate description of his triumphal progress through Portugal as Brit. Rep. on some prize giving commission. And then he spoke at Salisbury on George Herbert, in aid of the Cathedral, staying with the Richmonds. I was amused at the careful analysis he gave Juliette —a very sympathetic Frog—no humbug—no clothes—giving dinner to 30 people off cold food & so on—of his own plays failure, & of Priestley's artistic nonentity, scrupulously, painfully conscientious in detail; with his wild hazel eyes.

But I meant to record the chart: Observer has a friendly forecast: says 3 Gs. is poetic; profound; in my essayists vein; so that brings in another note—poetry. beautifully written & lucidly argued.[16] No word from Pippa. L. says I must expect some very angry reviews from men. I add, From women too. Then there'll be the clergy. But I think I can sit calm as a toad in an oak at the centre of the storm. And am training myself to inhabit that centre[;] read quietly: Walpole; Johnson; & stodge away at

15. Dr Johnson's house is located in Gough Square, off Fleet Street. The Robson children, Elaine and Philip, were aged about seven and three respectively.

16. The anonymous column-writer of 'Books and Authors' in the *Observer* of 29 May 1938 indulged in a bit of fine writing on the prospect of a new book by VW.

Roger. I possess my soul—now thats a thing one can do. I am not forcing myself to buy a new dress from Murray—a great victory for the shabby city haunting V. Its true—people cant really "get at one".

Tuesday 31 May

A letter from Pippa. She is enthusiastic.[17] So this is the last load off my mind—which weighed it rather heavy, for I felt if I had written all that & it was not to her liking I should have to brace myself pretty severely in my own private esteem. But she says its the very thing for which they have panted; & the poison is now drawn. Now I can face the music, or donkeys bray or geeses cackle by the Reviews so indifferently that (truthfully) I find myself forgetting that they'll all be out this week end. Never have I faced review day so composedly. Also I dont much mind my Cambridge friends either. Maynard may have a gibe; but what care I? And I shant send copies to my family, & so they need say nothing. What the bemedalled Wolves, with whom we dined last night, will say I dont know, but would find probably amusing. And the old Prostitutes, Hugh, Compton Mackenzie, Guedalla, Storm Jameson &c who are meeting next week to declare their belief in Liberty—well, they're not going to show it save on the platform, & can hardly deny me the right they preach.[18] So I expect a good deal of fun one way & another: some teasing of venerable gents; some innuendos, some digs at the Lynds & Squires; as well as a fountain of effusion from the faithful. But its the fun I shall enjoy: Hugh's elaborate defence of his creative zest for honours & cheques.

The dinner last night was a severe middleclass patriarchal grind: T[om] & B[ella] had been to Court. "He looked the type of a beautiful man" Mrs W. said—"in all his medals & cocked hat & Bella with her tiara, & no flowers—they wd. have hidden the medals". A very long dinner, hard chairs & very forced cheery talk. But we get off easily.[19]

Friday 3 June

Rodmell

This is the coming out day of 3 Gs. And the Lit Sup has 2 columns & a leader; & the Referee a great black Bar Woman declares sex war; or some such caption. And it makes so much less difference than any other

17. Philippa Strachey's letter on *Three Guineas*—'I have read it with rapture—It is what we have panted for for years and years'—dated 30 May 1938, is in MHP, Sussex.
18. See above, 24 May 1938, n. 9.
19. LW's brother-in-law Sir Thomas Southorn, Governor and C.-in-C. The Gambia 1936-42, had been created KCMG in the New Year Honours.

cackle on coming out day that I've written quietly at Poyntz Hall; haven't even troubled to read R. Lynd, nor look at the Ref: nor read through the Times article.[1] Its true I have a sense of quiet & relief. But no wish to read reviews, or hear opinions. I wonder why this is? Because its a fact I want to communicate rather than a poem? I daresay something of the kind. Mercifully we have 50 miles of felt between ourselves & the din. L. has been talking to Mrs Ebbs about the school, & finally won her over by praising her new chintz covers, hideous as they are.[2] Then I found a grass snake sunning itself in the hedge, but when L. came, it was gone. Then Mrs Curtis wired to ask us to go to Macbeth at Glyndebourne. Refused. It is sunny, warm, dry & like a June day but will rain later. Oh it pleased me that the Lit Sup says I'm the most brilliant pamphleteer in England. Also that this book may mark an epoch if taken seriously. Also that the Listener says I am scrupulously fair, & puritanically deny myself flights.[3] But thats about all.

Anyhow thats the end of six years floundering, striving, much agony, some ecstasy: lumping the Years & 3 Gs together as one book—as indeed they are. And now I can be off again, as indeed I long to be. Oh to be private, alone, submerged.

I talked to Nessa about Julian on Wednesday. She can hardly speak. What matters compared with that? Yet I was always thinking of Julian when I wrote.

Whit Sunday 5 June

This is the mildest childbirth I have ever had. Compare it with The Years! I wake knowing the yap will begin & never bother my head. Yesterday I had T. & Tide, & various London obscurities: today Observer: Selincourt: A terrible indictment.[4] Sunday Times, N. Statesman, & Spectator, reserved for next week presumably. So the temperature

1. *Three Guineas* was the subject of a long critical review (see *M&M*, p. 400), and was discussed in a leading article, in the *TLS* dated 4 June 1938. The *Sunday Referee* of 29 May carried the banner headlines: 'WOMAN STARTS NEW SEX-WAR/Says Men's Clothes are "Barbarous"'. Robert Lynd's review was in the *News Chronicle* of 3 June 1938.
2. Mrs Ebbs, wife of the Rev. John Webber Ebbs, Rector of Rodmell, was a member of the Board of Management of the Church of England village school, which practically adjoined Monks House garden—a possible source for controversy.
3. See 'The *Listener*'s Book Chronicle' (unsigned), 2 June 1938: 'Mrs Woolf seems to have put an almost puritanical restraint on her pen lest its charms seduce attention from reason and logic. . . . She thinks of everything and is too fair-minded and sincere to want to trip her readers up.'
4. For the *Time & Tide* review, see above, 24 May 1938, n. 8; for Basil de Selincourt in the *Observer*, 5 June 1938, see *M&M*, p. 403.

remains steady. I foretell a great many letters on Tuesday night: some anonymous & abusive. But I have already gained my point: I'm taken seriously, not dismissed as a charming prattler as I feared. The Times yesterday had a paragraph headed "Mrs Woolf's call to women. A serious challenge that must be answered by all thinkers"—or something like that; prefacing the Lit Sup. advt: unknown before I think; & must be some serious intention behind it. A note of ecstasy from Ethel half way through.

Walked on the racecourse: bought ⟨stockings⟩ cakes in Lewes. Charleston & Bunny to tea today, yesterday the first hot summer day. People in tails & white shirts tripping about Lewes. Glyndebourne in full flower. Mrs Curtis asked us. We refused. Windy today, but still fine, & the sun still active—after I suppose 2 months drought ⟨damp⟩ & darkness. The ugliest spring on record. So we were wise to save our holiday, though I'm so rested now, & writing gaily at P.H. that I dont want very much: to look at the sea however wd. be a relief: we shall attempt Skye, for if we dont now we never shall. L. says we are old. I say we are middle aged.

Saturday 11 June

Only five minutes to record the merciful fact that the N.S. is out (K. John prattling is foolish but as L. says well meaning) & now, save for the Sunday Times, the ink splash is over, & I can count it on the whole a good deal better than I expected. On the whole 3 Gs is taken seriously: many high compliments; some snarls (Spring in the E. Standard has his hackles up) but generally kind, rather surprised, & its over—[5] Off we can go to Scotland for a holiday that I dont really need, but still a freshener before Roger wont come amiss. No book ever slid from me so secretly & smoothly. Letters begin from America, about the extract in the Atlantic. None, save Pippa Ray & an amusingly tepid one from Judith, who likes it very much but thinks the end diffuse.[6] No thanks: no enthusiasm from the young for whom I toiled. But thats as I expected, & as it should be. Ray & Pippa are the prime relief. Nothing from Pernel, or Vita. Sales began slowly; but today & yesterday, 300 sold. I think 10,000 will go off. And its hit the crest of the wave. Tom being given his degree at Cambridge: walking in procession with the other

5. 'The New Lysistrata', K. John's review of *Three Guineas* in the *NS&N* of 11 June 1938, is in part reprinted in *M&M*, p. 405. Howard Spring, under the heading 'A Woman Pacifist Says: Men Want War' in the *Evening Standard* of 9 June 1938, found 'Mrs Woolf's aloofness a little too inhuman' and 'an annoying sense of superiority in what she writes'.

6. The letters from Ray Strachey ('it is simply *perfect*') and Judith Stephen are also in MHP, Sussex.

bigwigs: Trinity feast; Tattoo; honours List—if anyone reads it, the illustration is pat to hand.[7] Quit of all this, I've written an article on Walpole, very fast & free, for America. Walked several good walks. Weather much recovered, though unstable. Mrs Ebbs put the School meeting off. We go up this evening after tea. Bowls. Bells. & the garden being planted by L. with some little help from me. And I must go in to cold mutton.

The Woolfs left London for a motoring holiday in the North of England and Scotland on Thursday 16 June, returning to Tavistock Square on Saturday 2 July. LW's diary (LWP, Sussex) records their itinerary and the hotels at which they stayed. VW, as was her custom, made brief pencil notes en route which she typed out at home on 5 July (see below) and inserted in her diary. Her obvious typing errors have been corrected.

Thursday 16 June

Baldock. Stop to light a pipe on the Icknield Way, a scrubby street of yellow villas. Now St James Deeping. After Croyland, a magnificent moulded Church. Now very hot; flat; an old gent fishing. Spread out and exposed. River above road level. On now to Gainsborough. Lunch at Peterborough: factory chimneys. Railway gate opened; off again. Gainsborough. A red Venetian palace rising among bungalows; in a square of unkempt grass. Long windows, leaning walls. A maze of little lanes. A strange forgotten town.

Sunday [*19 June*] at Housesteads [*Northumberland*]. Thorn trees; sheep. The [Roman] wall and white headed boys in front. Miles and miles of lavender campagna. One thread coloured frail road crossing the vast uncultivated lonely land. Today all cloud and blue and wind. The wall is a wave with a sharp crest, as of a wave drawn up to break. Then flat. Bogs under the crest. Waiting now for the rain to stop, for it blew and rained that day on the wall. Now a few miles from Corbridge waiting in the middle of the moor. Very black. Larks singing. Lunch deferred. A party of ninety lunching at the Inn at Piercebridge [*on 17 June*]. A sense of local life 18th century inn diners to celebrate some sport. So on to a Manse in a garden; a very solid private house that takes in residents. Hot ham, and fruit, but real cream, looking over an ugly range. The country early today was fen Wash country. Then the Pennines. These

7. At a ceremony at the Senate House on 9 June 1938, Lord Baldwin, Chancellor of Cambridge University, conferred Honorary Degrees on (among others) Anthony Eden and T. S. Eliot; it so happened that Lord Baldwin in his ceremonial robes was the subject of the third illustration to *Three Guineas*, entitled 'A University Procession'. Queen Mary attended the Aldershot Military Tattoo on 10 June; and the King's Birthday Honours were announced on 9 June.

are shrouded in a heat mist. Larks singing. L. now looking for water for Sally. (but this should precede the wall).

Sunday [*19 June*]. Sitting by the road under the Roman wall while L. cleans sparking plugs. And I have been reading translations of Greek verse, and thinking idly.[8] When one reads the mind is like an aeroplane propeller invisibly quick and unconscious—a state seldom achieved. Not a bad Oxford introduction, trying to be in touch, up to date; scholarly but Oxford. Cows moving to the top of the hill by some simultaneous sympathy. One draws the others. Wind rocks the car. Too windy to climb up and look at the lake. Reason why the hills are still Roman—the landscape immortal . . . what they saw I see. The wind, the June wind, the water, and snow. Sheep bedded in the long turf like pearls. No shade, no shelter. Romans looking over the border. Now nothing comes. Also I'm thinking with an occasional rasp of Vita's letter—'misleading', could beat me down with fisticuffs. Well let her.[9] But none of this very serious. All the wild white flowers along the grass border in violent agitation. Many buried camps. Grass still takes their shape. Why dig up? Not I think an impressive reconstruction of the past—too like the foundations of farm buildings, when they do. The outpost feeling though from the little watchtowers remains. Forts to fight from; the wall to look from. In one well a glass bottle was dug up. And the latrines and the treasure house.

[*Monday 20 June*] Scotch border: Monday ten to eleven. Sitting in the car looking across a vast spread emerald tinted little hills rising a great flow of green land. Some bars of trees otherwise grass, uncultivated, no roads. Carter Fell behind; ripples of hills in the distance; a few single scattered trees. One red brown field; some tent shaped hills. Board has Scotland written on it—a moor road. How Scott must have come this way—near Jedburgh. Burke Sir Walter.[10] A cold windy day with blue slabs consequent floating colours. A novelist should be able to describe two spinsters sisters opening letters at breakfast—letters with stamped addresses. "How awfully stupid—I said the 18th" (a fragment from the

---

8. I.e.: *The Oxford Book of Greek Verse in Translation*, edited and with introductions by T. F. Higham and C. M. Bowra, 1938.

9. Vita had written to VW about *Three Guineas*: 'You are a tantalising writer because at one moment you enchant one with your lovely prose and next moment exasperate one with your misleading arguments . . .' See *VI VW Letters*, no. 3422 where VW quotes her own words back at Vita, and no. 3405, VW's direct reply, dated from the George Inn, Chollerford, on 19 June.

10. See Leslie Stephen on Sir Walter Scott in the *DNB*: 'On 18 May [1831] he persisted . . . in attending an election at Jedburgh, to protest for the last time against parliamentary reform. A mob of weavers from Hawick filled the town and grossly insulted him. He was taken away at last amid a shower of stones and cries of "Burke Sir Walter!" '

breakfast table at Chollerford. These old ladies caught me smoking a cigar. They played patience ferociously; but not on Sunday. Then they read solid books.)

Tuesday [*21 June*]. Now in Midlothian. Stopping for petrol. On the way to Stirling. Scotch mist driven across the trees. Normal Scots weather. Great hills. Ugly puritanical houses. The Hydro [Hotel, Melrose] built 90 years ago. A woman called and said she had seen Mrs Woolf walking in Melrose on Saturday. Second sight as I was not there. Galashiels a manufacturing town. Hideous. Fragments of talk overheard at the Hydro Melrose. Soft voiced old Scotch ladies sitting in their accredited places by the fire under the window. "I was wondering why you walked about with an umbrella." One who is stitching, "I wonder if I should wash it and begin again. I'm working on a dirty ground."

Here I interpose. We stopped at Dryburgh to see Scott's grave. It is under the broken palanquin of a ruined chapel. Just enough roof to cover it. And there he lies—Sir Walter Scott Baronet, in a caddy made of chocolate blancmange with these words cut large and plain on the lid. As Dame Charlotte who is buried beside him is covered with the same chocolate slab it must have been his taste. And theres something fitting in it. For the Abbey is impressive and the river running at the bottom of the field, and all the old Scots ruins standing round him. I picked a white syringa in memory but lost it. An airy place but Scott is much pressed together. The col. by his side, and Lockhart his son in law at his feet. Then there's Haig's stuck about with dark red poppies.[11]

But the old ladies are discussing Dr John Brown whose brother was a doctor in Melrose. Soon ones head would ache and ones senses fuddle. One would eat too many cakes at tea and theres a huge dinner at 7. "I think he's very nice—her husband. She's got a personality of her own. A very nice cir-r-cle. Where do they live? Retired to Perthshire. . . . I'm three stitches out . . . Miss Peace came along to the reading room with her friend and wanted a fire. Couldnt she have rung the bell or something? Out you come! (unpicking the knitting.) Theres so much opened up now. Two years ago was the Centenary (of Dryburgh?). I went to the meeting. There was a service—most interesting. All the Ministers. Five on the platform. Possibly the Moderator. At any rate it was very nice and

---

11. The tombs of Sir Walter Scott and his wife Charlotte, and of his son-in-law and biographer J. G. Lockhart, lie in the ruined North transept chapel in the remains of Dryburgh Abbey in Berwickshire. Nearby is the burial place of the Haigs of Bemersyde: Field-Marshal Earl Haig (1861-1928), C.-in-C. of the British Expeditionary Force in the 1914-18 war, was President of the British Legion, in support of which red poppies are sold on Armistice Day each year.

it was a beautiful day and the place was very full. The birds joined in the music. Alan Haig's birthday. There was a service at Dryburgh. I like D. I've not been to Jedburgh—awfully pretty." No, I don't think I can write it all out. The old creatures are sitting on a sofa not much older than I am I daresay. Yes, they're about 65. "Edinburgh's nice—I like it. We have to go away before we appreciate it. You have to go away from your birthplace. Then when you go back everything changed. A year does it—2 years do it. I should leave it (of the work) and see the effect afterwards. What church d'you go to? Church of Scotland—not to St Giles. It used to be the Troon. We go to St Giles. It was St George's parish—my husband was an elder in St George's parish Charlotte Square. D'you like Waugh? I like him in a way. I don't *hear* him and its a common complaint. He gives very hard sermons—you cant take anything away. The choir's beautiful. I cant get a sitting from which you can hear. I feel it infra dig rushing with the crowd. The crowd hasnt reached—I've just got to sit still—I'm having a service—I hear the prayers the young men the music. It was pretty well where they come in from the Thistle chapel. They passed me bang. I rose and moved along. There are some seats the people never come to, and often the best seats. I like St Giles, a lovely old place. The old lady whose seat I had told me the church was all renovated. Chambers did it, and when it came to the opening not a seat retained for the Chambers family. Badly arranged. Someone provided seats for them.[12] A stupid thing. Always some higher church alteration. I like the episcopal. If it be episcopal let it be; if Church of Scotland, let it be Ch. of Scotland. Dr Waugh's brother is at Dundee. He would like Roseneath. Someone said that the minister at Roseneath is delicate."

Wind rages trees leafless bannocks and a blue pound note the only changes. Glencoe. Menacing. Leaf green hills, islands floating, a moving string of cars; no inhabitants, only tourists. . . Ben Nevis with stripes of snow. The sea. Little boats; feeling of Greece and Cornwall. Yellow flags and great foxgloves no farms villages or cottages; a dead land over-run with insects. An old man who could not get up from his chair, two other ladies, her legs overflowing her shoes; all dress for dinner, and sit in the drawing room. This was the good inn at Crianlarich [*on 21 June*]. Lake with hanging stalactites green trees in the middle: bowl of the hills. Hills with velvet leaf green. The Bannington of Eaton Place. She had found winter green for her father-in-law, a botanist. Sky light at 11. Bad review of Three Guineas by G. M. Young. Pain lasted ten minutes:

12. The restoration of the disfigured and degraded St. Giles's Church was due to the energy and generosity of William Chambers, one of the founding brothers of the Edinburgh publishing house; he died three days before the re-opening ceremony in 1883.

over then.[13] Loch Ness swallowed Mrs Hambro. She was wearing pearls.[14]

From 'the good inn at Crianlarich' the Woolfs drove in stages via Loch Ness to the Isle of Skye; they stayed three days (24-26 June) at Portree before continuing their tour by Spean Bridge and Ben Nevis; at Oban the persistent rain determined them to abandon Scotland. By 30 June they reached Ambleside, and the following morning visited Dove Cottage, Wordsworth's home from 1799-1808. That night they spent at Newark and the following afternoon, after lunching in Cambridge, they reached home.

[*In handwriting:*] And then, sick of copying, I tore the rest of it up— a lesson, next journey, not to make endless pencil notes that need copying. Some too I regret: some Boswell experiments in Inns. Also the woman whose grmother worked for the Wordsworths & remembered him an old man in a cloak with a red lining muttering poetry. Sometimes he wd pat the children on the head, but never spoke to them. On the other hand, H. Coleridge was always drinking at the pub with the men[15]

Tuesday 5 July

A thunderstorm, still further to distract my already distracted brain. How am I to calm & contract back again to Roger? We returned on Saturday. Now this morning I settled to a difficult passage in P.H. Pippa rings up. 20 minutes with her about 3 Gs. L. comes in & asks me to choose 3 quotes for the Observer. Nessa brings Maynard on Julian.[1] Lightning. Torrents. Yet I must slide beneath all this if I'm to make a

13. *Sunday Times*, 19 June 1938: 'Women in the Modern World/Mrs Woolf's Survey' by G. M. Young, who concluded that 'bound up with the wit, the philosopher, the critic whom you cannot admire more than I do, is a pamphleteer of 1905' whose 'Guild of Outsiders' he saw as 'the endeavour of belated sex-egotism' to arrest women's advance towards a better society.

14. Winifred Hambro, wife of the chairman of Hambro's Bank (a Sussex resident), lost her life when the speedboat carrying her and her family burst into flames on Loch Ness on 29 August 1932; local gossip blamed the Monster: see *VI VW Letters*, no. 3406.

15. Hartley Coleridge (1796-1848), S. T. Coleridge's eldest son, whose intemperance cost him his Oxford fellowship, spent the greater part of his time wandering about the Lake district where he became 'much better known to the people than poet Wordsworth' (*DNB*).

1. Quotes from reviews of *Three Guineas* in the *Daily Mail*, in *Country Life*, in *The Queen* and in *Reynolds News* were used in a Hogarth Press advertisement in the *Observer* on 10 July 1938. Maynard Keynes's brief obituary of Julian Bell in the 1937 Annual Report of King's College, Cambridge, was reprinted as the Foreword to the memorial volume now in preparation by the Hogarth Press.

job of the summer lap. I think I will read Roger tonight, & so slide down into the water, & I will use this final half hour of a ruined morning to type out my Skye notes—not that theyre worth it, save as an authentic relic, like a sprig or leaf torn from a hedge & pressed between the pages of a book. My hand staggers. I will type.

Thursday 7 July

Oh the appalling grind of getting back to Roger, after these violent oscillations: 3 Gs. & P.H. How can I concentrate upon minute facts in letters? This morning I have forced myself back to Failand in 1888. But Gumbo [Marjorie Strachey] last night threw cold water on the whole idea of biography of those who have no lives. Roger had, she says, no life that can be written. I daresay this is true. And here am I sweating over minute facts. Its all too minute & tied down & documented. Is it to be done on this scale? Is he interesting to other people in that light? I think I will go on doggedly till I meet him myself—1909—& then attempt something more fictitious. But must plod on through all these letters till then. I think contrast the 2 all the time. My view, his & other peoples. And then his books. Meanwhile Freud (son) & John Lunch:[2] Sarton to tea; & I'm so raddled & raked with people, noise, telephones—cant copy my Skye notes: have endless letters to write, long for peace; holiday seems over; & what can I recover from all this litter? 3 G's selling well[:] 5,400 I think. But if I get into that mood I cant do anything at Roger. I must order & lay my mind out in pigeon holes. Now to change for lunch.

Sunday 17 July

No time— Time wasted writing an angry letter to John about New Writing: letter shown to L. & torn up.[3] My new clock says its just on one: & my new clock cant lie. So I note: 3 Gs has struck the rock of rage, I think; & sells very little—almost on 6,000—wont reach the 8. . . Then oh the rush of people. Susie telling me in strict confidence of her un-utterable gilded fly boredom. Memoir Club. Desmond dined. Molly ill. Bunny read. Last night at the Robsons. Old French woman in skimpy

2. Martin Freud (1889-1967), Sigmund Freud's eldest son, managed the *International Psychoanalytischer Verlag* which published his father's works in Vienna; he had been forced to leave Austria in May following the *Anschluss*. The Hogarth Press had been Freud's English publishers since 1924.

3. When lunching with the Woolfs and Martin Freud on 7 July, John Lehmann again asked VW to contribute to *New Writing*; she again refused (*VI VW Letters*, no. 3414). In reply he wrote (14 July 1938, MHP, Sussex): 'I don't feel you are quite fair . . .' and '. . . it is very perverse of you to complain about being inhibited by a manifesto when that is just what I was trying to avoid.'

black; beautiful eyes, playing Beethoven & looking round like Mitz at Juliette: their faces playing: voluptuous absorption & sorrow & exaltation. Lovely brown swollen cello— Old lady wd have been congenial to Roger. Rothenstein tomorrow to discuss Roger.[4] I'm stuck in a bristle of dates. Cant get on. Wet, black cold—worst July on record—Morgan's pageant. Kathleen Knott & Eddie dined. Ben & Judith & Rose [Macaulay] afterwards.[5] Still letters come about 3 Gs. On the whole I'm pleased at the splash in the inkpots & hidden references in papers—indirect results. Not a word said of it by any of my family or intimates

Tuesday 19 July

What about yesterday as a specimen day? Work at Roger—fearful niggling drudgery till 15 to 1. Robson to lunch. Isherwood wants to see me at 3. I slip out; buy flowers for Madame Alwin, pate de foie for Adrian. Back at 3.15. peep in at Stephen Spender, Chris [Isherwood] & John & L. all talking in J.'s room. Receive present of deaths head [*moth*] in box from Jack [Hills]. Sit down upstairs. Visit Adrian, tea on balcony. Dog playing cars passing—Judith there. Ann to marry on Thursday. No invitations. Karin in & out. Look at house. Gossip & home. Will R[othenstein]. to dine. A respectable, suppressed, but I dont think quite such a snake as Duncan makes out. Only dimmed, tamed; kindly, fairly obstinate: I think on his guard. No enthusiasm for life:—too much high nobility. But of course instructed, experienced, & kind. Only . . . Compared with R[oger]. how blunted, tolerant, & a little plausible. Wished to make out a case, to some extent. Gave me letters. So to bed with sore lips. Nothing vivid about R. & Paris. all dim now. Wdn't eat— abstemious. Fetched by a chauffeur & car. respectable. But not so slimy as they said.

Mercifully no one—I repeat *no one*—today. Today Julian was killed last year. And its hot again. Angelica's first night in Regents Pk Lysistrata. So we go on. I shant say anything to Nessa. Oh dear—And shall I buy

---

4. The 'rush of people': Susan Buchan (Lady Tweedsmuir) had tea with VW on 14 July; the Memoir Club meeting was on 12th. At the Robsons', the old French-woman was Mme Henri Alvin, Juliette's mother. Sir William Rothenstein (1872-1945), Principal of the Royal College of Art from 1920-35, was a fellow-student of Roger Fry's in Paris in 1892, and in his *Men and Memories* (1931-32) recalled their early association.

5. The Woolfs did not go to any of the three performances of E. M. Forster's village pageant, *England's Pleasant Land*, given this week at Milton Court, near Dorking. Kathleen Nott was the author of *Mile End* (see above, 3 May 1938, n. 1); she and E. W. Playfair dined on 14 July. Among the after-dinner arrivals was Benedict Nicolson (1914-78), Vita and Harold's elder son, at this time a temporary attaché at the National Gallery at the outset of his career as an art-historian.

Desmond [?] a case? & myself a Chair? Or what? We go—this is an event for us—to the Ballet at Drury Lane in proper seats tonight.[6] 3 Gs selling very slowly. Abusive or sneering letters the last 2 days.

Friday 22 July

If I were not rather proud of my abstracting power, how could I keep my head now, called on to write Roger a m: to interview Origo, [Lady] Simon &c. about 3 Gs. 5 to 7.: to combat John & the young generation this evening; to sympathise with Adrian, see Bussys, Rothensteins; give tea to Virginia Richards aged 8; & have Elizabeth Bowen, &c skirmishing in & out?[7] Nor do I suspect that Rodmell will be a shelter. Mary threatens to come & stay. So I must exercise my new muscles; be adept at making compartments; filling them, like a pipe, full but not too full. I'm getting more adept at leaping from swing to swing this summer. better than last anyhow. Its odd how one's friends torment one. Oh & Richard Hughes duns me for a written opinion on his book. Also theres Vita & her poem. And I have written to say that she must withdraw her charges.[8]

Weather steamy but no longer blue. Sat in Gordon Sqre last night & D. & V. were we thought unreasonable about R. & W. Rn. & the Grafton. What a kettle of fish![9] And 3 Gs. is once more selling: has now broached the 6 thousand. But my new clock says it's 2 mins. to one. The man came, like a doctor, to regulate. Ann was married yesterday. I gave her £15; L. £10. Thats all I've time for.

Tuesday 26 July

Its very true that I have no time. I have simply dedicated the last fortnight to people—seeing people—not a day free from it. Always an

6. Angelica's first professional engagement was as a member of the chorus of Robert Atkins' production of *Lysistrata* at the Open Air Theatre, Regent's Park. The ballets *Don Juan*, *Carnaval*, and *7th Symphony* were performed at the Theatre Royal, Drury Lane, on 19 July by the 'Ballet Russe de Monte Carlo' under the direction of René Blum and Massine.

7. Virginia Richards was VW's nominal god-daughter; VW had known her mother as Noel Olivier before she married a fellow-doctor in 1920.

8. Richard Hughes (1900-76), author of *High Wind in Jamaica* (1929) and now *In Hazard* (1938). V. Sackville-West had sent her poem *Solitude* to the Woolfs; but her remarks about *Three Guineas* still rankling (see above, 16 June 1938), VW replied that she could not read it impartially (see *VI VW Letters*, nos. 3421, 3422, 3423). *Solitude* was published by the Hogarth Press in November 1938 (*HP Checklist* 438).

9. This refers to the dissension which arose between Roger Fry and William Rothenstein in 1911 over Fry's plans for a second Post-Impressionist exhibition at the Grafton Galleries; see Mary Lago's Introduction to her abridgement of Rothenstein's *Men and Memories* (1978) and VW's *Roger Fry*, chapter 7, §111.

engagement. If you let it fill your sails there's something to be said for it. But I'm doing it deliberately & so . . . well: here's a list: Elizabeth Bowen Saturday; Lehmann Sunday; Nessa & Duncan; Monday I will keep free after tea: in comes Angelica: but we talked about Julian, & I adored her sobriety & depth; am in doubts if she'll stick at acting; today our Bussy dinner & others in afterwards; then Vita (oh she wired Horrified by your letter), to lunch: put off Noel & Virginia; D. asks me to tea to fetch my glass; then shall we go to Lysistrata in Regents Park: so we reach Thursday through this lit up gallery of many faces. And phones—& books. Buchan & Susie present theirs: Hughes his. And its now one. I'm staggering through Beaufort St.[10]

Wednesday 27 July

Yesterday we had John to tea, & the Bussys to dinner, Chilvers in after dinner. Rather hard bilingual work. Simon praised W. Rothn. Inclined to laugh at B[loomsbur]y. He said they had never noticed his work. D[oroth]y. said this. Clive & Roger ignored him. Thought R[oger]. an illuminé; his best work on Cézanne. Threw things over. Marchand dropped—put his hands out—down on the ground. But very learned & charming. Is Matisse sincere? asked him meeting in the street, 1910.[11]

On 28 July the Woolfs drove to Rodmell for their summer respite.

Thursday 4 August

Monks House

What a very silly thing I did—not that it was my fault. I thought I knew the voice, asking for Mrs Woolf: & so got let into conversation with a woman called Coralie Anderson, a Dublin broadcaster, from New Zealand, at Newhaven: & had the idiotic good manners to say she could come to a dull family tea party today: that is, a strange woman, of the most insensitive kind, may, indeed will, walk in, on top of Mrs Woolf Edgar & Sylvia today. And L. will be glum; & Mrs W. resent the interruption.[1] The fact was, Vita was there: hence I answered the telephone. And this is how we escape

No: she had the tact not to come.

10. VW's 'glass': a mirror with a frame designed by Duncan Grant and worked in *gros point* by his mother, now at Monks House. The books presented were *Sir Walter Scott* (1932) and *Oliver Cromwell* (1934) by John Buchan, and *In Hazard* (1938) by Richard Hughes. From 1892 until his marriage in 1896 Roger Fry shared a house at 29 Beaufort Street, Chelsea, with R. C. (Bob) Trevelyan, to whom VW wrote on 22 July to ask for his memories of this period.

11. Roger Fry owned several paintings by Jean Marchand (1883-1941) and saw quite a lot of him in the early 1920s.

1. Edgar Woolf (1883-1941) was LW's third brother, and Sylvia was his wife.

to the peace of the country. Came down on Thursday; almost mute with botheration: 6 from Charleston on Sunday; Angus [Davidson] & Eddie [Playfair]; then Vita on Tuesday for the night & yesterday; & now this incongruous assembly. Yet we are very happy. I should add that we found a new gable thrown out in the roof, workmen hammering, Mr Wicks started work, without warning, & says he will be here 3 weeks which means 5. Two days ago L. had the brilliant idea of converting half the library into an open air verandah with glass doors, in which we can sit on a hot night & survey the stars. This is now in progress. We shall have a balcony & rails.

It has been very hot with a strong hot wind. And I'm taking a gallop in fiction, after bringing Roger to his marriage. Rather a jerk & an effort, my work at the moment. Switching from assiduous truth to wild ideas. But I liked seeing Vita, so free & easy again. We sat out here & discussed her loves; death; father Darcy on death; Ben's tears, on being scolded by Vita; Willy Maugham; Clive, who's writing a book, secretly, on war; Julian; Nessa; looking so ill; so many women have lost sons & lovers; I forget how it went. Also she brought a basket of peaches & half a bottle of Chateau Yquem from her mothers cellar. Nigel only got a third. He & Harold mind. She doesnt. And off she went in her great black car that impresses Mrs Bartholomew so, to entertain Mrs Rubens & her final husband, who likes fishing. She has a daily visitor—not to sleep though. She was much like old times.[2]

I cant unstring my mind after trying to write about a lily pool. P.H. is to be a series of contrasts. Will it come off? Am I in earnest? Its to end with a play. L. is writing his in the garage room. I note he doesnt like to be asked when will it be done? He has, amusingly, all an artists sensibilities. And now?—Well there's always a heap of Roger's papers—old paper cuttings—to go through. And I might, of course, revise the last chapter: Beaufort Street; but am waiting for Bob's notes. What an undertaking! R.'s 2 lives enough for 6 books: emotion & art.[3]

2. The Very Rev. Martin d'Arcy, S. J. (1888-1976), Master of Campion Hall, Oxford, subtle, worldly and influential priest. Harold Nicolson was staying with W. Somerset Maugham at Cap Ferrat; Vita wrote to him on 3 August of her visit to Monks House, passing on VW's esteem for Maugham's autobiographical *The Summing Up* (1938); see Harold Nicolson, *Diaries and Letters 1930-39* (1966). Clive Bell's 'book' was his controversial pamphlet *Warmongers*, published by the Peace Pledge Union in September 1938, which argued the extreme pacifist position. Nigel (b. 1917) was the Nicolsons' younger son; he had just left Oxford. Olive Rubens, whose installation at Knole by Vita's father was the proximate cause of her mother's departure thence in 1919, married Brig. Gen. J. J. H. Nation four years after Lord Sackville's death in 1928.

3. On 7 August VW wrote to thank R. C. Trevelyan (*VI VW Letters*, no. 3430) for the notes he had sent, and to ask for more—particularly for recollections of Roger

AUGUST 1938

Saturday 7 August

I rather enjoy doing PH. Thats something, for it wont please anyone, if anyone should ever read it. Ann Watkins by the way says the Atlantic readers haven't read enough of Walpole to understand my article. Refused. Thats another reason then for my Outsider to be born. The Times Lit Sup this week has an article discussing, among other views, Mrs Woolf's view on intellectual harlotry. I rather think the book wh sells slowly is sinking in.[4]

Yesterday I saw 6 tanks with gun carriages come clambering down the hill & assemble like black beetles at Rat Farm. Small boys playing idiotic games for which I pay. Harold is very dismal, Vita says: predicts war, but not this week. A lull at the moment. And terrifically hot. A great purple black cloud massed itself behind Mrs W. Sylvia & Edgar as they sat out here; then thunder: then rain, at last. And we had lights lit. Why they so rub the country bloom off—these family Woolves—I dont know. Always a dusty feeling of Earls Court & offices. Oh & the commonplaceness of the talk—mostly about furniture at Lexham: lovely silver mirrors, most artistic overmantels, suites of dining room chairs, coffee cups. She lies awake counting them, deciding who's to have what, & so falls asleep. Why is it all so low in tone, even as human life? Sylvia might be one slice of bread off the eternal loaf.[5] Workmen tapping. The verandah being cut open. Yesterday the men about the wireless. Too many gadgets & dodges perhaps in this house. And the children shrieking. But we go to Charleston for tea: & Bob has written, revising in some respects my chapter: upon which I start work again tomorrow. I plan, a short chapter on marriage; then a difficult one on R.'s early work; some discussion of his theories & development; so to Hampstead & America. So to the Post I[mpressionists]. & ourselves. That will make the break in the book. A change of method. Then the Omega: before the war. Then the Dalmeny, Bernard Street. Consummation. So (here at least) the end is in sight. I may have it written over by Xmas; re-written by next August. Out in spring of 1940?

Fry's wife Helen, who from 1910 (the year VW first met him) until her death in 1937 was confined in an asylum. Trevelyan and his wife Bessie both obliged (see MHP, Sussex).

4. For VW's article on Walpole, see above, 28 April 1938, n. 10. The *TLS* article on 6 August 1938, the first of three 'on the present state of the world of letters', enlists VW's expression 'intellectual harlotry' (*Three Guineas*, p. 179) as a sub-heading, and quotes from her 'brilliant book'.

5. 101 Lexham Gardens, Kensington, was the large house inhabited by Mrs Woolf and her family in the days of their prosperity, before her husband's untimely death in 1892.

Wednesday 17 August

No I won't go on doing Roger—abstracting with blood & sweat from the old Articles—right up to lunch maybe. I will steal 25 minutes . . . In fact I've been getting absorbed in Roger. Didnt I say I wouldn't? Didnt L. say theres no hurry? Except that I'm 56; & think that Gibbon then allowed himself 12 years, & died instantly. Still why always chafe & urge & strain at the leash? What I want is a season of calm weather. Contemplation. I get this sometimes about 3 am when I always wake, open my window, & look at the sky over the apple trees. A tearing wind last night. Every sort of scenic effect—a prodigious toppling & cleaving & massing, after the sunset that was so amazing L. made me come & look out of the bathroom window—a flurry of red clouds; hard; a watercolour mass of purple & black, soft as a water ice; thin hard slices of intense green stone; blue stone, & a ripple of crimson light. No: that wont convey it: & then there were the trees in the garden. & the reflected light: our hot pokers burning on the edge of the steep.

I'm too tired in the head & fingers to sum up. We have been sociable in a scattered way. Seen Edgar's new house,—& Mr Colbourne's Alsatians, routing Gwen's pocket handkerchief from a tub of rags, jumping through fiery hoops, & also retrieving L.'s bandanna from a distant field. All dogs can do this, Mr C. said. A dog at its prime at 3. Dogs entirely changed by education. For this, see 3 Gs. (wh. stops selling, between 6 & 7000: but still wrings letters from schoolmasters. Oh & I must answer one of them).[6]

I began Mme de Sevigne last night.[7] Then there was the sunset, & then some music on the new set. The window, with the round top, is going in today. Less noise than I expected.

The old woman who lived up at Mt Misery drowned herself 3 days ago. The body was found near Piddinghoe—my usual walk. Her son died; she turned queer; had been a midwife in Brighton; lived in the broken windowed half of Mr Bradfield's house. She used to moon over the downs with a dog. Once she came to the shop late on Sunday to beg 2d of paraffin—she was alone in the dark. They threatened to turn her out—farm wanted. She had killed her dog. So at last off she goes, on Monday perhaps when the tide was high in the afternoon, & jumps in. Louie says her brother found a drowned woman the other day at Barcombe Mills—

6. The Woolfs went to tea with the Edgar Woolfs at Buxted on 11 August; and on 15th met Vita Sackville-West and Gwen St Aubyn at a dog show at Uckfield.

7. VW had the fourteen-volume edition of the letters of Madame de Sévigné in the collection *Les grands écrivains de la France*, Paris 1862-66 (*Holleyman*, MH V, p. 6); she sometimes made notes as she read through them (see Brenda R. Silver, *Virginia Woolf's Reading Notebooks* (1983), XVI, XXXVII, LIV. Her essay 'Madame de Sévigné' was published posthumously in *The Death of the Moth* (Kp A27).

a horrid sight. So I order dinner hastily & come out here to brew more Roger.[8] But I wont go into my doubts—partly due to reading B.J. by his wife & thinking it richer & warmer & more important than Morgan on Goldie.[9] So, at supper, we discussed our generation: & the prospects of war. Hitler has his million men now under arms. Is it only summer manoeuvres or—? Harold broadcasting in his man of the world manner hints it may be war. That is the complete ruin not only of civilisation, in Europe, but of our last lap. Quentin conscripted &c. One ceases to think about it—thats all. Goes on discussing the new room, new chair, new books. What else can a gnat on a blade of grass do? And I would like to write PH.: & other things. I worry a little over the young generation & its complacent compromises. This is partly of course that we sold the HP share very cheap: that Mrs Lehmann [*John's mother*] lives in far greater style than we do; that the young in short have an eye to the main chance, a bitter tongue, & a fawning way of asking sympathy. Thats my nettle under the mattress; but a very little frail one—not so stinging as a row that once lasted a whole month here with Colefax. I mean one of those nagging worries that I say aloud when I'm walking.

Tonight we dine off the first grouse at Charleston. Q.'s birthday. Oh & we went to Pulborough & saw A. act—but I forget—I may have written this down—so casual am I in what I say or dont say:[10] & have half a mind one of these days to explain what my intention is in writing these continual diaries. Not publication. Revision? a memoir of my own life? Perhaps. Only other things crop up. Pippa says Waller [Jack Hills] has been desperately ill. Logan [Pearsall Smith] has recovered—as Logan would.

Monday 22 August

The first, I think, really soaking wet day since we came. We therefore went into Lewes about the threat of the Sewage Pump. They want to plant it on us: 'they' being instigated by Jansen & Botten so L. suspects. The village cabal against us is roused by the L.P. & the Village Council matter, & they are rumoured (Percy says) to be going to seize our field

8. The inquest on Mrs Kathleen Shearer, aged about 45, of Shepherd's Cottage, Mount Misery, Southease, found that she committed suicide while the balance of her mind was disturbed. No independent record has been found of Louie's other gruesome report.

9. *Memorials of Edward Burne-Jones* by G. B.-J., 2 volumes, 1904. E. M. Forster's biography of his, and Roger Fry's, Cambridge friend Goldsworthy Lowes Dickinson (published 1934), was necessarily reticent and restricted.

10. The Woolfs and the Bells went to Pulborough on 13 August to see a performance of *Gammer Gurton's Needle* given by the London Village Players, a travelling company formed for the summer by students of the London Theatre Studio.

for a play ground. This delightful sample of village life—the egg under the microscope—doesn't please: such is human nature.[11] Also I am in the wars, or shall be. Maynard sends for us on Wednesday; is said by Lydia to be very critical of 3 Gs: & a note in the Observer (Hayward) says that Miss Wilson is preparing a counter-blast; & no-one can better correct, contradict & amplify than she.[12] Now the thing to remember is that I'm an independent & perfectly established human being: no one can bully me: & at the same time nothing shall make me shrivel into a martyr or a bitter persecution maniac. The one specific is to write a thorough good book—i.e. Roger. I've not got the words right about the soul. I mean I stand on my own feet. Maynard & the rest can only puff: & the honesty of my intention in 3 Gs is bound to see me through. But this is written in too great detail. In fact I must now, as we cant play bowls, read my Roger chapter: after the criticism I must . . . but not here. All Charleston & William Plomer yesterday: a lovely thin blue day. Bowls. Nessa painted. better I think. Clive talked. I liked him—he has some shiver of sensibility still.

[Tuesday 23 August]

Its odd to be as nervous as I am at the idea of seeing Maynard to-morrow, & his heckling: dear old Hitler. But I wont be nervous; I'll go & walk on the terrace for 10 minutes before lunch. The worst of this kind of controversy is that it adds so much friction to my work on Roger: I have to urge my mind on, while the surface is all worried & flurried into tufts & vapours of replies [&] arguments. So it kindles, like a meteor, & burns, instead of keeping cool & dark & solid as I had hoped this summer. The price I pay, though, for having views. Never mind. Now the terrace —& a treat this afternoon [*a drive to Tunbridge Wells*].

Sunday 28 August

The character of this summer is extreme drought. Brooks dry. Not a mushroom yet. By the way Maynard never said a word. Some were unsaid. As for instance, Lydia: we all put up with you Virginia, said

11. Chailey Rural District Council were proposing to locate a sewage pumping station on the field adjoining Monks House which LW bought in 1928 specifically to protect his amenity; he refused to sell the required plot. (He had similar—and similarly successful—struggles with the local council in 1951 and 1957: see *II LWP, Sussex*, I 4b). Guy Janson of South Farm and Jasper Botten of Rodmell Place were the principal farmers in Rodmell.

12. John Hayward, reviewing *Jane Austen and Some Contemporaries* by Mona Wilson in the *Observer* of 21 August 1938, does indeed say what VW says he does; but Miss Wilson apparently did no more than contemplate her counterblast to *Three Guineas*.

significantly, kissing me at parting. M. tired, extended, rather grim. But emotion had to be restrained. Sunday is the devils own day at M.H. Dogs, children, bells . . . . there they go for evensong. I cant settle anywhere. Beaten after 3 hard fights at bowls. Bowls is our mania. Reading rather scamped. I'm strung into a ball with Roger—got him, very stiffly to the verge of America. I shall take a dive into fiction; then compose the chapter that leads to the change. But is it readable—& Lord to think of the further compressing & leavening.

Ding dong bell . . . . ding dong—why did we settle in a village? And how deliberately we are digging ourselves in! And at any moment the guns may go off & explode us. L. is very black. Hitler has his hounds only very lightly held. A single step—in Cheko Slovakia—like the Austrian Archduke in 1914 & again its 1914.[13] Ding dong ding dong. People all strolling up & down the fields. A grey close evening. Dr Chavasse died on Friday, while Nessa & Q. were here—she to paint the view—he my table. Oh thank God, Ding dong—no, its begun again.[14]

I should call it a very free summer, happy compared with last. However, I cant go into that. I mean Julian's ghost. How could he ever become a ghost—My dear Aunt—then the burst of laughter; & how he gripped the sides of the chair. Angelica announces that she is giving up the stage. That I think revives Nessa. At any rate they are free—more united—& go to Cassis. I ponder—as usual—a flight to the Maurons. But shall I get there?[15] Sybil [Colefax] meanwhile thrusts herself on us, for dinner; we have the Jones's at Seaford: visits to London; must say good bye to Bella. The autumn mists assemble. And I'm irritable with work & noise. We dine at Charleston. Now its as quiet as the grave . . all grey; the chestnut leaves hanging heavy; birds on the telegraph posts.

Letters fret me. Never one thats disinterested. Requests always to speak, write, lecture, see people. Thats Fame—dogs again. Thats because Miss Emery is with the dead I suppose. Yap Yap.[16] Perhaps the house would be better & Madame de Sevigne—who may inspire me, as good writing does, to write to Ethel—so no more.

13. In pursuance of his resolve to unite all Germans within a greater Reich, Hitler, after the annexation of Austria, had increased his pressure on Czechoslovakia, exploiting the grievances of the Sudeten Germans within, and mobilising his army upon, her borders, estimating that Britain, France and Russia would present no effective deterrence to his plans to attack by 1 October 1938.

14. Dr H. S. Chavasse, who died on 26 August, was for over fifty years a general practitioner in Warwickshire; he and his wife had retired to Rodmell the previous autumn.

15. Roger Fry's friends Charles and Marie Mauron still lived in the *mas* at St Rémy-de-Provence which he bought in 1931 and shared with them.

16. Miss Kathleen Emery, the Woolfs' neighbour across the intervening path to the churchyard, bred dogs.

Wednesday 31 August

War seemed round the corner again. Question what Hitler will do, when he'll do it. Cabinet Ministers summoned. &, of course, Kingsley Martin ringing up, & annoyed that L. isn't in London to hold his hand, & make it write an article. I say As if articles mattered! We were in London yesterday. Streets fuller than last time, perhaps, by reason of the Crisis. K.M. to lunch—stout & dark & brown & black & theatrical. 3 possibilities. One of them European war. But not at once. A game of bluff on H[itler]'s part, possibly. Anyhow he doesn't want a European war now. So may isolate the shindy; & we may rat with the French at the last moment. If theres a war, "my own solution is suicidal"—while he munches mutton chops, & sweeps up fragments, scraping his knife & fork round in a way I hate. But cant hate anyone in the flesh. So he burbled on: with his own article, & his own figure, histrionically arrayed, in the centre. Some bye-references, with an eye to me, on the Prostitution of Journalists. I walked off, bought a pewter plate, a scissors, & a lustre globe, encouraged by a letter from Brace reporting enthusiasm for 3 Gs in our office, good advance orders, & great praise.[17] Also encouraged by the E[uropea]n situation: gather rosebuds while we may. So we came back to find the roof painted a first coat of white; men erecting L.'s new Crystal Palace greenhouse in the orchard; & the fireplace ready in the new room.

Sally was mated on Monday, with much coyness: we had tea with Mrs Jones, Hugh, & a sturdy girl who's going to teach a school in Bexhill. Mrs Jones like a pricked air ball flopped on the floor. Hugh the spit of Philip.

Thursday 1 September

A very fine clear September day. Sybil threatens to dine, but may put us off—should a Cabinet Minister crop up. Politics marking time. A violent attack on 3 Gs in Scrutiny by Q. Leavis. I dont think it gave me an entire single thrill of horror. And I didnt read it through. A symbol though of what wiggings are to come. But I read eno' to see that it was all personal—about Queenie's own grievances & retorts to my snubs.[1] Why I dont care more for praise or wigging I dont know. Yet its true. A slight distaste for my biog. of Roger this morning: too detailed & flat.

17. See Donald Brace to VW, 23 August 1938, MHP, Sussex (LVP).

1. *Scrutiny*, September 1938; see *M&M*, pp. 409-19. Mrs Leavis begins: 'This book is not really reviewable in these pages because Mrs Woolf implies throughout that it is a conversation between her and her friends, addressed . . . to "women of our class" '; but her verdict is that 'this book is not merely silly and ill-informed, . . . it contains some dangerous assumptions, some preposterous claims, and some nasty attitudes'.

But I must take it up tomorrow, & lay aside P.H. I fear. Quentin over to finish his table. We have settled to keep the roof Cornish cream colour. I found a new walk down Telscombe valley to the river yesterday.

Oh Queenie was at once cancelled by a letter from Jane Walker—a thousand thanks . . . 3 Gs ought to be in the hands of every English speaking man & woman &c.[2]

Monday 5 September

Its odd to be sitting here, looking up little facts about Roger & the M[etropolitan] M[useum]. in New York, with a sparrow tapping on my roof this fine September morning when it may be the 3rd Aug 1914 . . . What would war mean? Darkness, strain: I suppose conceivably death. And all the horror of friends: & Quentin . . . All that lies over the water in the brain of that ridiculous little man. Why ridiculous? Because none of it fits. Encloses no reality. Death & war & darkness representing nothing that any human being from the Pork butcher to the Prime Minister cares one straw about. Not liberty, not life . . . merely a house-maids dream. And we woke from that dream & have the Cenotaph to remind us of the fruits. Well I cant spread my mind wide eno' to take it in, intelligibly. If it were real, one cd. make something of it. But as it is it merely grumbles, in an inarticulate way, behind reality. We may hear his mad voice vociferating tonight. Nuremberg rally begun: but it goes on for another week. And what will be happening this time 10 days? Suppose we skim across, still at any moment, any accident may suddenly bring out the uproar. But this time everyone's agog. Thats the difference. And as we're all equally in the dark we cant cluster & gossip; we are beginning to feel the herd impulse: everyone asks everyone, Any news? What d'you think? The only answer is, wait & see. Sybil fresh from London, can only titivate this answer into shapes that reveal her own complicity, but utter ignorance. The talk, when she came that wet evening [*1 September*] all the way from London to dine, turned most satisfactorily upon the Windsors; & how, as he came late into Willy Maugham's lunch party, he said, "Her Royal Highness was detained by the American sailors . . ." That is what he will have her called.[3]

2. Dr Jane Harriet Walker, CH (1859-1938), an eminent specialist in the treatment of consumption and its social causes, wrote to VW on 31 August (MHP, Sussex) declaring that *Three Guineas* (which she had reviewed for the Journal of the Medical Women's Federation) 'ought to be read and re-read by every grown up man and woman in the English speaking world' and suggesting that it should be published as a *Penguin* 'special'.

3. Harold Nicolson was a house-guest of W. Somerset Maugham at Cap Ferrat when the latter entertained the Duke and Duchess of Windsor on 5 August 1938 (see Nicolson's *Diaries 1930-39*, p. 351); Lady Colefax's reference to the sailors supplements his account of the dinner party.

Old Mr Thomsett meanwhile after driving horses to the brooks & about the fields for 74 years has died in the hospital. & L. is to read his will on Wednesday. He left it all—how much?—to Doris; & Annie thinks the other children will protest. L. made his will for him. I like this in L.[4]

Saturday 10 September

I dont feel that the crisis is real—not so real as Roger in 1910 at Gordon Square, about which I've just been writing; & now switch off with some difficulty to use the last 20 minutes that are over before lunch. Of course we may be at war this time next week. Seven ships are mobilised today. The Papers each in turn warns Hitler in the same set grim but composed words, dictated by the Govt. presumably, that if he forces us we shall fight. They are all equally calm & good tempered. Nothing is to be said to provoke. Every allowance is to be made. In fact we are simply marking time as calmly as possible until Monday or Tuesday, when the Oracle will speak. And we mean him to know what we think.[5] The only doubt is whether what we say reaches his own much cumbered long ears. (I'm thinking of Roger not of Hitler—how I bless Roger, & wish I could tell him so, for giving me himself to think of—what a help he remains—in this welter of unreality.) All these grim men appear to me like grown up's staring incredulously at a child's sand castle which for some inexplicable reason has become a real vast castle, needing gunpowder & dynamite to destroy it. Nobody in their senses can believe in it. Yet nobody must tell the truth. So one forgets. Meanwhile the aeroplanes are on the prowl, crossing the downs. Every preparation is made. Sirens will hoot in a particular way when there's the first hint of a raid. L. & I no longer talk about it. Much better to play bowls & pick dahlias. They're blazing in the sitting room, orange against the black last night. Our balcony is now up. Today Morgan comes, & we have our

4. Thomas Henry Thomsett, who lived across the road from Monks House, had been a carter on Rodmell Place farm since he was fifteen; he was 72 when he died. The Woolfs both went to his funeral in Lewes on 7 September. One of his daughters, Annie (Mrs Penfold), had worked for them for five years until her marriage in 1934; the other, Doris, looked after one of their brothers, Jacky, who was deaf and dumb.

5. On 7 September the pro-Nazi Germans in the Sudetenland broke off their spurious negotiations with the Czechoslovak Government for self-determination; France, by treaty bound to assist Czechoslovakia now threatened by German invasion, called up her reservists; and on 9 September France's ally Great Britain announced that the first mine-sweeping flotilla and four mine-laying destroyers of the Royal Navy were to be brought into full commission. Hitler was expected to speak on the Czech crisis, which he had successfully fomented, at the conclusion of the Nazi Party Congress at Nuremberg on 12 September.

crowded Memoir Club week end. It is at Tilton, in the afternoon, to suit Maynard, who is going to read. Q. & Molly lunch here tomorrow, & I've no doubt we shall all behave as if the moment were eternal—as Roger said to Goldie. What other attitude—but its not one—is possible to even moderately adult people? As far as I can judge the villagers share it. Whats the use of war? We dont want war. Thats Louie's verdict. But our candidate, our little Mr Black who dined here the other night, has the brains of a rabbit, reminds me of Tisdall, will only talk of his daughter's pet mice—she breeds many coloured mice which she sells for 5d to a local breeder, & his other girl makes posters depicting mice, while he himself collects matchboxes—well, he's the average politician, I suppose: & he's all for war, at once. Why? to build a new state . . . & what kind of new state? One in which mice & matchboxes are collected.[6]

Sunday 11 September

Morgan here. He is writing in the garden. L. in his room. I have been sorting old cuttings out here. Molly & Q. will soon come. A very fine clear spruce blue day. The news as black as possible. Hitler has at any rate cursed, & Goering spat: nothing said till tomorrow. And now in to the house to tidy rooms & hair. Easy & intimate with M[organ]. about GLD[ickinson] & Roger &c. He wears a new tie given by Stephen Tennan[t]

Monday 12 September

Papers all say that we shall know the truth, one way or the other, tonight. But Maynard yesterday thought Hitler may say nothing for some days. The Cabinet all occupied whenever they emerge—sitting all day—in making plain without actual statement that we shall fight if France fights. Press all harmonious. So there's nothing to do but wait.

Memoir Club meeting had its little sensation. M[olly] & Q. lunched. After lunch, as she came down stairs, M. tripped & fell over the loose tile. Lay very white in great pain. Cdnt move. Obviously a bad twist. After a time we managed to hop her to the terrace—sat & talked; but when we had to go, she couldn't move. Ankle swollen. So we took her, after various telephones, to [Dr] Tooth's substitute: & he—a blue serge red faced knobby man—was afraid the bone was hurt. Then the X ray: the man out: at last to Tilton; carried her in. Maynard read a very packed profound & impressive paper so far as I could follow, about Cambridge

6. Frederick W. Black of Seaford, who for a short time succeeded F. R. Hancock as the Labour Party's parliamentary candidate for Lewes Constituency, dined at Monks House on 7 September. C. J. Tisdall was VW's London dentist (see also 13 October 1937 above).

youth; their philosophy; its consequences; Moore; what it lacked; what it gave. The beauty & unworldliness of it.[7] I was impressed by M. & felt a little flittery & stupid. Then he had to rest; it turned grey & cold. M. had to be slowly conveyed—a bed made on the ground floor at Charleston. Nevertheless a very human satisfactory meeting. Tea: Lydia presiding, "Now boys & girls sit down." Hot cakes. Ham sandwiches. No politics. Bunny, Desmond, Q. & Lydia, ourselves Morgan Clive Nessa (in big hat: much more herself than ever yet). Rachel is to have a baby. Molly very much more composed: brave; matter of fact; & heard what we said. But we are off now to lunch with William [Plomer] at Brighton, taking Morgan.

Tuesday 13 September

No war yet anyhow. Hitler boasted & boomed but shot no solid bolt. Mere violent rant, & then broke off. We listened in to the end. A savage howl like a person excruciated; then howls from the audience; then a more spaced & measured sentence. Then another bark. Cheering ruled by a stick. Frightening to think of the faces. & the voice was frightening. But as it went on we said (only picking a word or two) anti-climax. This seems to be the general verdict. He darent cross the line. Comes up to it & stands bawling insults. Times very scathing & sarcastic. How can people stand this nonsense? Negotiations to go on, under threat that he will use force if &c.[8]

Immense relief last night at Monk's House, after a gloomy dinner. Very hot. Jaded with Brighton. Lunch with Wm & Morgan at a place where he knew the waitress. I depressed by praise of Morgan's Credo: silence on all my friends part about my own.[9] But the impersonal attitude worked well. I let myself sink like a bag from a balloon: & felt, if dejected, light & free. A good piece of work that, for it leaves me free to go on my way in silence. Not from journalists or schoolmasters though. A great packet of reviews from USA. All summer in a day again. Oh we enjoy being alone, save that I'm too jaded to do Roger. Wicks here about the tiles. John tomorrow. London & farewell to Charleston on Thursday. Peaceful if depressed: anyhow a week or 2 without war.

7. This was posthumously published as 'My Early Beliefs' in *Two Memoirs* (1949) by J. M. Keynes.

8. At the Nuremberg rally on 12 September Hitler, while ranting and threatening the Czechs, appeared to allow further time for negotiations on the claims of the Sudeten Germans for self-determination.

9. Forster's article 'Two Cheers for Democracy', published in the New York *Nation* in July 1938, was retitled 'Credo' and reprinted (with additions) in the *London Mercury*, September 1938; it was published by the Hogarth Press as a sixpenny pamphlet entitled *What I Believe* in May 1939.

SEPTEMBER 1938

Odd this new public anxiety: how it compares with private: how it blinds: but too stupid to write. And lunch waiting this roasting hot morning.

.

Wednesday 14 September

Things worse today. Rioting in Prague. Sudeten ultimatum. It looks as if Hitler meant to slide sideways into war. Raises riots: will say cant be stopped. This came on the 9.30 wireless last night. This morning more marking time. No one knows.[10] Headachy, partly screw of Roger: partly this gloom. So I'm stopping Roger; as we go up to lunch with Bella tomorrow. And whats the private position? So black I cant gather together. Work I suppose. If it is war, then every country joins in: chaos. To oppose this with Roger my only private position. Well thats an absurd little match to strike. But its a hopeless war this—when we know winning means nothing. So we're committed, for the rest of our lives, to public misery. This will be slashed with private too. Quentin: all the young married people. Ann &c. We—L. & I—can make out I suppose down here: vegetables & fruit. And I've made some money. Needn't cringe. Thats about all. I feel I said what I wanted in 3 Gs. & am not to care if its 1: made my own friends hostile; laid me open to abuse & ridicule; also praise where I dont want it; & paying bills for Wms. Societies: £3.9 for a ridiculous leaflet— Thats my debt to civilisation. Then suppose John called up! The Press? But all wallows & wavers in complete chaos. Odd that this should be a stimulus to the complete artist. One will have to sit at home & write. I suppose air raids may toss a bomb through the skylight. Growls go on overhead. Louie says the carpenter is on the reserve. They chaff him as he's a socialist. 1914 but without even the illusion of 1914. All slipping consciously into a pit.

But John lunches. Q. & A. to tea. Dine tomorrow at Charleston. Fine summer day.

Friday 16 September

Chamberlain has flown to see Hitler. Universal relief & approval. No news yet. They say this means Peace. Peace was written large on the Evening Standard placard yesterday in London. There'll be no war, the shopkeeper in Long Acre said when I bought cardboard for Eddie's book. Rosinsky says they will give way. Hitler will save his prestige: the C[zecho] S[lovak]s will be sacrificed. War staved off for one year. But

---

10. Hitler's Nuremberg speech gave the signal for demonstrations and counter-demonstrations in Czechoslovakia, and the consequent imposition of martial law in some districts; its immediate revocation was demanded by the Sudeten Germans.

until the wireless announces the result of the visit—& there's to be another—tonight we once again mark time.[11] Nessa Duncan Angelica & Q. start for Cassis tonight, driving across France. We settle in for 10 days alone—that is, Clive & Janice come on Sunday; but I mean to make these 3 weeks serve me to finish, sketch out rather, the last chapters.

Dined at Charleston. All seem agreed that a country life is best. Clive is giving notice to Gordon Square. We hear or rather the Garden Comttee heard, that T. Sqre will be pulled down in 3 years. Shall we not all provide ourselves with single rooms in London & live here? Never make any fixed plans for life—thats my motto. Really, for the 10 years that remain, be free of the world. But I'm kicking my heels with P.H. after Roger this morning, & the relief of fiction after all that fact, lightens the load of both worlds inconceivably. And I feel so free from any criticism; own no authority.

HAL Fisher asks me to go & see him. After my remarks on OM's this is conciliatory. He wants me to send a signed copy. And his time is drawing out: resignation impending.[12] Very fine clear weather. I saw a kingfisher. The lunch [*with Mrs Woolf and Bella*] was very heavy, stodgy, full of meat & wine. Walked down the Strand all a buzzing, full season feeling, in the afternoon.

Saturday 17 September

Chamberlain back. In a hard business man's voice told us, as he stepped out of the plane at Croydon, that he was to meet Hitler again: that Hitler was coming to meet an old man half way (is this symbolical?) & we meanwhile not to believe rumour. No statement today. Cabinet meeting. Just as in violent personal anxiety, the public lapses, into complete indifference. One can feel no more at the moment. And its the essence of an English September. Saw the yearling sale at Northease yesterday. Mrs Mounsey writes to ask me to head an Outsiders' movement. Clive & Janice tomorrow. Nessa &c lunching now at Auppegard—

11. On his own initiative, Chamberlain flew to Germany and met Hitler at Berchtesgaden on 15 September. The Sudetenland Nazis were now demanding incorporation into the Reich, and Hitler's army was poised to put this into effect should the Czechoslovak Government stand firm. Herbert Rosinski had been an instructor at a German Staff College and was now a refugee; he came to meet the Woolfs at Tavistock Square on 15 September; his book, *The German Army*, was published by the Hogarth Press in November 1939.

12. VW's cousin the historian H. A. L. Fisher (1865-1940), Warden of New College, Oxford, since 1925, was awarded the Order of Merit in 1937; for VW's remarks, see *Three Guineas*, pp. 38, 53.

& thats all for the moment.[13] I thought yesterday, enjoying my valley walk, that Julian wd entirely have approved of that. And, oddly enough, I never said that the whole summer here was set on its feet the first day by L. visiting the Lewes Dr who pronounced him absolutely normal. Yet I suppose it was the most important feeling of all. We met on the towing path the very day after we came here.

Dreamt of Julian one night: how he came back: I implored him not to go to Spain. He promised. Then I saw his wounds. Dreamt of Roger last night. How he had not died. I praised Cezanne. And told him how I admired his writing. Exactly the old relationship. Perhaps easier to get this in dreams, because one has dreamt away the fact of his death, to which I woke as L. came in.

Tuesday 20 September

Since I'm too stale to work—rather headachy—I may as well write a sketch roughly of the next chapter.[14] (I've been rather absorbed in P.H. hence headache. Note: fiction is far more a strain than biography—thats the excitement.)

Suppose I make a break after H[elen']s death (madness). A separate paragraph quoting what R. himself said. Then a break. Then begin definitely with the first meeting. That is the first impression: a man of the world not professor or Bohemian. Then give facts in his letters to his mother. Then back to the second meeting.

Pictures. Talk, about art. I look out of window. His persuasiveness—a certain density—wished to persuade you to like what he liked. Eagerness—absorption—stir—a kind of vibration like a hawkmoth round him. Or shall I make a scene here—at Otts?

Then C[onstantino]ple. Driving out—getting things in—his deftness in combining. Then quote the letters to R.

The first 1910 show.

The ridicule. Quote W[ilfred] Blunt.

Effect on R. Another close up.

The letter to MacColl. His own personal liberation. Excitement. Found his method (but this wasn't lasting. his letters to V[anessa]. show that he was swayed too much by her.)

13. Mrs Mounsey wrote from Cold Ashton, near Bath, on 14 September: 'at a time like this there is not a moment to be lost and there are so many of us who want a lead . . .' (see MHP, Sussex (LVP)). She wrote again on 22 September from 15 The Vale, Chelsea, the house she had bought the previous year from Ethel Sands—with whom Vanessa &c were lunching at Auppegard in Normandy.

14. Cf.: *Roger Fry*, Chapter 7: 'The Post-Impressionists'. For Fry's letters to MacColl and Bridges (below), from which VW proposes to (and does) quote, see *Letters of Roger Fry*, edited by Denys Sutton, 1972, vol. II, nos. 319 and 541.

Love. How to say that he now was in love?
Give the pre-war atmosphere. Ott. Duncan. France. Letter to Bridges about beauty & sensuality. His exactingness. Logic.

Thursday 22 September

By mistake I wrote some pages of Roger here; a proof, if proof is needed, as I'm in the habit of saying, that my books are in a muddle. Yes, at this moment, there are packets of letters to V.B. 1910-1916—packets of testimonials for the Oxford Slade—endless folders, each containing different letters, Press Cuttings, & extracts from books.[15] In between come my own, now numerous, semi-official 3 Gs letters (now sold 7,017. .) I never get a disinterested letter: always demands. But all the same we get asked to have Noel & Virginia, Judith, & go to Sissing-hurst in order that L. may discuss politics with Harold. No sober silent weeks of work alone all day as we'd planned, when the Bells went. I suppose one enjoys it. Yet I was just getting into the old, very old, rhythm of regular reading, first this book then that; Roger all the morning; walk from 2 to 4; bowls 5 to 6.30: then Madame de Sevigné; get dinner 7.30; read Roger; listen to music; bind Eddie's Candide; read Siegfried Sassoon; & so bed at 11.30 or so.[16] A very good rhythm; but I can only manage it for a few days it seems. Next week all broken. A minor treat today: solicitor in Lewes; then walk. . .

The public fluctuates. Chamberlain flying today to Gotesberg (?). A strong opposition has risen. Eden, Churchill & the L[abour] P[arty] all denounce serving C.S. on the altar & bidding it commit suicide. CS. very dignified & tragic. Everyone calling everyone else a pick pocket. The prospect of another glissade after a minor stop into abyss. All Europe in Hitler's keeping. What'll he gobble next? Thats the summary of us in Sussex.[17]

15. The 'pages of Roger', being on loose-leaf paper, were presumably transferred elsewhere. Fry applied for the Slade Professorship of Fine Art at Oxford in 1910 (and in 1927), but was rejected.
16. VW bound *Candide*, 'very clumsily too', for E. W. Playfair. Siegfried Sassoon: *The Old Century* (1938).
17. The British and French Prime Ministers, convinced that only the cession of the Sudetenland to Germany would dissuade Hitler from carrying out his threat to invade Czechoslovakia and thereby involve France and Britain in a European war, gave the Czech government less than forty-eight hours to agree to their plan to cede to Germany those areas where the population was over 50% of German origin. Under pressure the Czechs yielded, and Chamberlain flew to Godesberg on the Rhine to inform Hitler—who then rejected the Anglo-French proposals as being too dilatory, and insisted that German troops must occupy the Sudetenland by 1 October. (Harold Nicolson's *Diaries 1930-39* give a vivid and informed account of the politics of this period, and of Eden's and Churchill's attitudes.)

Wednesday 28 September

This may be the last day of peace; so why not record it, as I've 20 minutes & nothing to do? Why record it? But this "why?" has to be battened down.

A tumultuous week end—Judith, Noel & Virginia; Charleston: Clive Janice Raymond. Pouring wet Monday. L. came out to say Kingsley Martin begged him to come up, in order to act as liaison between the LP & the Liberals. He was the only person &c. So we decided to go at once & spend the night. Drove up in the rain. Men digging trenches at Turnham Green. London crowded. Dropped Judith. L. went to see K.M. I to buy coffee &c. "Its a miserable day & our thoughts are miserable" the woman at de Bry [*Coffee Merchants, New Oxford Street*] said. She said we should win; & that it would not be a long war. "But whats the point of winning?" I said, at which she exclaimed & shrugged her shoulders in agreement. Then KM to dinner; charcoal black round the eyes; as usual something histrionic. All about his article in the NS: had he been wrong? We've all been wrong. A desire to confess. But also very wretched.[18] Hopelessly restless. Melodramatic in his gestures, swaying as he walked to the telephone; perpetually looking at the time & ringing people up. Got the BBC. "Well A.C. Whats Hitler said? Ah hah—" Then Phil Baker. Do you agree with what I wrote? No word of any possible plan or reason for summoning L. Stayed on, drinking, smoking. Then said he was going to walk the streets. Couldnt sleep. Still thought it possible we should rat. Also Phil said Hitler would cry off. So to bed. Telephones all the morning. I went to the London Library. Sat in the basement & looked up The Times on PIP [*Post-Impressionism*] in 1910. Old sweeper gently dusting. Came & said, Theyre telling us to try on our masks. Have you got yours I asked. No not yet. And shall we have war? I fear so, but I still hope not. I live out in Putney. Oh theyve laid in sand bags; the books will be moved; but if a bomb strikes the house . . . . May I dust under your chair? I looked in at the Nat Gall. being warned by a sober loud speaker to get my gas mask as I walked down Pall Mall. A man repeats this warning through a megaphone as he drives. A lecture being given by a red faced elderly man on Watteau & French painting. A largish crowd following. I looked at Renoir, Cezanne &c: tried to see through Roger's eyes: tried

18. In the *NS&N* of 27 August 1938, in a burst of editorial candour, Kingsley Martin had expressed the view that since, in the event of a German attack, 'Nothing we or anyone else could do would save Czechoslovakia', the question of frontier revision ought to be tackled: 'The strategical value of the Bohemian frontier should not be made the occasion of a world war.' Bitterly criticised by left-wing colleagues and readers for giving what seemed a pro-Nazi appraisal of the situation, he suffered agonies of self-reproach, and in subsequent issues of the *NS&N* maintained a staunchly anti-appeasement stance.

SEPTEMBER 1938

to get some solidity into my mind. So to lunch. Question what to do
about the Press. The girls sensible but of course apprehensive. Plans
can only be sketched. Possibly John will transport the whole Press to
Fieldhead.[19] Nothing can be done till Saturday. House meets today. We
arranged for Mabel to go to Bristol. We shall stay here, provisionally.
I went to Lewis & bought folders.* We must settle into
work at any rate. We must drive our pens & keep the
Press going that way. Rain settled in. Miss Moir of the
Forum arrived at 3.15—& John & Rosinsky for L. She
was a painted battered professional journalist. Wants
controversial articles: £20 only: but can say what I like.
I gave her vermouth. Stayed talking. Sister of a Suffolk
clergyman. The Govt. is evacuating the East End to
Suffolk. All cottages prepared to billet.[20]

* The boy
there the only
person I saw
obviously
frightened &
therefore
snappy &
rude—poor
little wretch.

So it goes on. We had a rather unpleasant farewell with
the Press—they staying, we going. Its reasonable of course. But one
doesnt like leaving them there: & yet they want to stay, for the money.
We may have to pay them, or let them go, & try to keep on paying. But
as L. & I say, we cant now decide, or think. A violent rain storm; a
great crowd in the streets. The worst—longest drive in half lights under
trees, rain splashed; & so late that we only got here at 8.15. Poor Louie
missed the PM's broadcast. He said nothing—except that we cd not
fight for the small C.S. matter *only*—a possible hint.[21] But we've given
up stressing the importance of hints. Hitler seems as they say "for it."
These futile notes are now ended by lunch. It was oddly peaceful &
sane, getting out here after London. Mr Perkins brought gas masks
about 10.30. & so at last we went to bed.[22]

Thursday 29 September

We listened in yesterday at 5 expecting to hear that War was declared.
Instead "Mr Chamberlain made a sensational announcement. He has

19. Fieldhead, on the Thames at Bourne End, was Lehmann's family home; the Woolfs
    had lunched there with his mother in July.
20. Phyllis Moir of the New York *Forum*, which had published four contributions by
    VW in the late 'twenties, wrote after the outbreak of war to remind her of this
    meeting, and to solicit an article: see below, 8 December 1939, n. 4.
21. In his broadcast 'to the Nation and Empire' on 27 September, Mr Chamberlain
    referred to 'a quarrel in a far-away country between people of whom we know
    nothing' and said: 'However much we may sympathise with a small nation
    confronted by a big and powerful neighbour, we cannot in all circumstances
    undertake to involve the whole British Empire in war simply on her account. If
    we have to fight it must be on larger issues than that.'
22. Mr A. F. Perkins was Clerk to Chailey Rural District Council which was respon-
    sible for civil defence organisation at Rodmell.

175

been invited by Herr Hitler to meet him tomorrow at Munich. Signor Mussolini & Daladier will be present. Mobilisation is postponed for 24 hours."[23] It was like coming out of a dark room. Now we are waiting. Some compromise? The selling of the C.S? What? Anyhow war for the moment is postponed. Perkins & Janson called last night to say 50 children arrive in Rodmell today & to note numbers of our rooms. Off to Sissinghurst this afternoon to see Harold.

Friday 30 September

L. has just come in, it being 11.15. to say that he overheard a Broadcast when he was in the W.C.: dashed out: turned on our wireless; & heard that terms are being made at Munich. I cant go into them. But it means peace. That was the upshot of the stop press in The Times this morning. They are agreeing to let some Germans into C.S. today: then English Italian & French are to enter & guarantee: then a 3 months pause.[24] Three months in which to settle the question, instead of bombs on London & Paris today! Well, Chamberlain must be looking on the bright sunshine this morning with a good deal of relief. He went off yesterday quoting Hotspur "Out of this nettle danger we pluck the flower safety"—words that Katherine Mansfield has on her tomb.[25] Such a reversal was never known: save that there was always a huger nightmare unreality that clouded all distinct feeling. I'm doing Roger & PIP [Post-Impressionism] & must break off this historical note to go back to that.

Harold kept in London caballing with Winston & Eden to keep the PM from giving away too much. Certainty of peace not quite certain

23. On 26 September Hitler repeated his ultimatum to the Czechs: he would march into the Sudetenland on 1 October unless they acquiesced in his demands by 2 p.m. on 28 September. On the morning of that day, the mobilisation of the British Fleet was announced; and during the afternoon, towards the end of his grim report to the House of Commons, Chamberlain received Hitler's message agreeing to a four-power meeting the following day at Munich.

24. The Munich agreement was signed by Chamberlain, Daladier, Mussolini and Hitler at 1.30 a.m. on 29 September; neither the Czechs, nor the Russians, were invited to be present. The terms decreed the cession of the Sudetenland and its occupation by German troops within ten days from 1 October; the surrender intact of all Czech military and civil installations; and the guarantee by the four signatories of new frontiers to be determined by an International Commission. Chamberlain then secured Hitler's personal signature to a Note expressing 'the desire of our two peoples never to go to war with one another again'.

25. The inscription on Katherine Mansfield's grave in the cemetery at Avon near Fontainebleau reads: 'Katherine Mansfield, wife of John Middleton Murry, 1888-1923. *But I tell you, my Lord fool, Out of this nettle, danger, we pluck this flower, safety.*' (*Henry IV*, Part I, II iii).

yesterday; but the 9,000 children who were to have come to Sussex held up. The obvious feeling everywhere was We dont want this war. No glorification, as Mrs Dean [*the smith's wife*] remarked: the mouthpiece of the nation, as much as Chamberlain. Oh & the K. of Italy is said to have stiffened Musso: who stiffened Ch[amberlai]n., & thus weakened Hitler, by threatening abdication. So Vita reported from Harold.

I will continue, as I have 10 minutes before lunch: continue that is to try & describe the reversal; which is soberly & truly life after death. For we, even if we escaped, should have had our noses rubbed in death; ruin; perhaps the end finally of all order, so L. admitted was his background. It would have meant our last 15 years of life spent in battling for a thread of liberty; keeping the Press going among the deaths of the young. And now suddenly we can travel & move & use our normal faculties. No slaughter of the young beneath us. I wonder if we could have faced it even here—entertaining East end children in the hall; writing; getting all the dismal fag ends of things thrown us; & reading Casualty Lists. Now of course one makes not new resolutions, but attacks the old with some fervour. They seem to have blood in them. I wonder how far we cd. really get a move on; make a difference, if we tried? Possibly— sanguinely—a new view will dominate. Hitler will sink instead of swell. But what a shave! Northease Barn already turned into a hospital; Gwen's daughter "evacuated" to school at Stanmer Park; 60 children laid on mattresses in the gallery; marvels of organisation recited on the BBC last night. All who wish to leave London to go to certain tube stations, with a thick coat & enough food for the day: children to bring no [?] glass bottles: parents not to come. Public will then be taken free of charge to towns & villages 50 miles out of London. Each will be given a stamped card on wh. to write to friends. No choice of destination. &c. Eddy Sackville volunteered to drive an ambulance in London. Food all arranged for. The net result is that we are presented with 2 gas masks by the Govt: & have bought 4 candlesticks at Woolworths, & ordered an extra supply of coals.

A very fine day.

[*Saturday 1 October*]

A violent storm—purple ink clouds—dissolving like blots of ink in water—strong enough to drive us in here in the middle of our game. L. is storing apples—finest harvest for perhaps some years. No longer a matter of concern. We were to live on apples honey & cabbage. Postman delivered an oration—"just my own thoughts" on War & Dictators. How all will worship C[hamberlai]n. now: but in 5 years time we may be saying we ought to have put him, Hitler, down now. These dictators & their lust for power—they cant stop. He'll get stronger & stronger.

Then . . . But now we cant help being glad of peace. Its human nature. We're made that way. A solid clear spoken if repetitive private thinker who kept our letters waiting 10 minutes. Only the N. Statesman &c. Soon looked through & tossed aside. Peace when they went to Press hung on a straw. Now grown (we suppose) to a rope—unless this storm is symbolical; its odd how susceptible the mind becomes to weather symbols—roping everything in—in crises like this is, or was. Of course there's bound to be a turn against relief—but I'm watching the storm— as in violent illness. One turns peevish & has a sense of emptiness. I should fill this now either by letter writing or sketching R. wh last as the least burdensome, I will do.

Sunday 2 October

Yesterday would have been the first day of the proclamation of war. It might be amusing to scribble down pall mall some higgledy piggledy of incidents: as they remain over; & will soon be forgotten.

The BBC in a measured trained voice: how the public was to go with warm clothing: no glasses: post cards: this interrupted by the ArchB's prayers: then cold menace: a spaced dictated message from the Admiralty to ships. Obviously we'd sunk mines. Then the afternoon (Wednesday) when all foreign stations were jammed. War broken out already L. thought. Then the statement that all poisonous snakes at the Zoo would be killed, & dangerous animals shot— Vision of London ravaged by cobras & tigers. Sense of preparation to the last hair. Some complacency on the part of organisers. How Mrs Nicholls was refused the key of the Square: trenches only available to residents. All this mixture of minute detail; with invocations to God; with Hitler baying & the Germans howling; then the composed & cultured voice breaking in, say about not taking pets. Then over all a feeling of the senselessness, futility, so that there was a dilution of emotion. A childs game. Yet extreme physical relief when peace seemed 24 hours longer. Some instinctive self preservation. I felt this most when we drove away from 52, a selfish gladness that we should be quietly in the country. Some remorse at leaving the clerks exposed. Now rapidly other emotions chase each other; that peace seems dull, solid. Then that we must have a bone to gnaw. The opposition already marshalling & we shall be attacked. Some obliquity: after all we admired Chn. in the crisis. Is it fair to abuse him now? Duff Cooper has resigned.[1] A wet day. Keynes come to tea.

1. Duff Cooper, First Lord of the Admiralty, resigned from the government on 1 October to signalize his profound mistrust of and disagreement with Chamberlain's conduct of foreign policy which had led to the ill-judged and dishonourable sacrifice of Czechoslovakia.

[Monday 3 October]

The Keynes to tea yesterday. All a put up job between Chamberlain & Hitler, Maynard said. Never had been any chance of war. But I've written this to Nessa & cant repeat.[2] I wish I could get the ripples of all these complexities to land. I'm incapable still of sinking into R[oger]. Rain. Wind. Apples falling. M. & Lydia very congenial—dear old M. so sanguine, so powerful, somehow lovable too, & Lord how brilliant. I kissed him. Hope all is forgotten & forgiven. A life time—what remains—of peace now. Auden & I.'s play to be suppressed. Out of date.[3] And I hope they will no longer pose as the young men to be sacrificed. All orientations must now change. Duff Cooper resigned. Reaction of shame beginning. D.T. decent, & starts a pro Czech movement. Times disgraceful. Harold censured &c.[4]

Thursday 6 October

Another 10 minutes. I'm taking a frisk at P.H. at wh. I can only write for one hour. Like the Waves, I enjoy it intensely: head screwed up over Roger. A violent storm two days ago. No walking. Apples down. Electric light cut off. We used the 4 6d candlesticks bought at Woolworths. Dinner cooked, & smoked, on dining room fire. Men now staining boards. The room will be done actually this week. Politics now a mere "I told you so . . . You did—I didnt". I shall cease to read the papers. Sink at last into contemplation. Peace for our life time: why not try to believe it? Cant make a push & go to S. Remy. Want to—dont want to. Long for change; love reading Sevigné even by candlelight. Long for London & lights; long for vintage; long for complete solitude. All this discussed with L. walking to Piddinghoe yesterday.

E. Bowen has sent her book; also Marie Mauron.[5]

2. See *VI VW Letters*, no. 3449; also Keynes's article, 'Mr Chamberlain's Foreign Policy', *NS&N*, 8 October 1938: 'The actual course of events has been dictated by the fact that the objectives of Herr Hitler and Mr Chamberlain were not different, but the same . . .'

3. Keynes had undertaken to finance a Group Theatre production of Auden and Isherwood's melodrama *On The Frontier* at the Cambridge Arts Theatre; in the event it was postponed until November 1938. It was given a single performance in London on Sunday 12 February 1939 at the Globe Theatre, where the Woolfs saw it.

4. On both 1 and 3 October the *Daily Telegraph* carried leaders stressing the great sacrifice made by the Czechs for peace. The *Times* leader on 3 October 1938 pontifically rebuked Harold Nicolson for criticising defenceless civil servants in a speech attacking the Munich settlement; but for the hidden irony of the situation, see his *Diaries 1930-39*, pp. 373-4.

5. *The Death of the Heart* (1938) by Elizabeth Bowen; *Le Quartier Mortisson* (1938) by Marie Mauron.

Thursday 13 October

I should be well advised to take a holiday from writing, & maunder off into the vineyards at Cassis. But I cant: too weak minded; dependent upon L.: & life's too fixed. So I must dandle my brain, & find a substitute. Tired after London yesterday. Cant screw either to PH or Roger. Elizabeth Bowen now? A walk? Pick apples? only 11.30—a familiar, but not hopeless, situation. In fact I'm like a teetotum, that's so weighted it always spins, wherever dropped. Only too sleepy today to spin. Finish after a devilish week end. Richard & Ann here. Talk for 48 hours. A nice couple: I like him. Some body & some brain. Charm & integrity. She helter skelter, adolescent, vigour, but I daresay neurotic. Much younger, more uneven than he. Oh & we went to Tilton & read L.'s play [*The Hotel*] to the K.s. They gravely approved. M. as intent as a terrier. Very interesting. We like it very much. Suggest the Group Theatre. Off to Cambridge. End of the season. Clive gone already.

Sandbags still in position in B[loomsbur]y. Southampton Row being pulled down. Clerks had bought spade & first aid outfit. John reasonable. Nice to come home to duck. Today the first time without workmen. L. arranging books in the gallery.

Friday 14 October

Two things I mean to do when the long dark evenings come: to write, on the spur of the moment, as now, lots of little poems to go into P.H.: as they may come in handy: to collect, even bind together, my innumerable T.L.S. notes: to consider them as material for some kind of critical book: quotations? comments? ranging all through English lit: as I've read it & noted it during the past 20 years.[6]

Now, having made this note, I must in sober earnest write letters; to Ray [Strachey]: to Joan Easdale, who's marrying Jim Rendel; to Suh about her autobiography.[7] In fact I must clear my table, as L. calls it &

6. This is VW's first reference to her nascent idea (also adverted to below, 17 February and 16 March 1939, and 12 September 1940) for a survey of English literature which was to occupy her during the last six months of her life when *Pointz Hall/ Between the Acts* was finishing or finished. See Brenda Silver, ' "Anon" and "The Reader" ' in the Virginia Woolf issue of *Twentieth Century Literature*, New York, Volume 25, Fall/Winter 1979.

7. On 13 October the poet Joan Adeney Easdale (see above 22 October 1937, n. 6) announced her engagement to James Meadows Rendel, grandson of Lytton Strachey's eldest sister and nephew of VW's doctor Elinor (Elly) Rendel. Ling Su-Hua was the wife of a professor at Wuhan University and had been a close friend of Julian Bell while he was in China; greatly distressed by his death, she had written both to Vanessa and to VW, who in replying had recommended her usual specific; see *VI VW Letters*, nos. 3377, 3379, 3457.

does it—before we go on Sunday. No more then here. But at last its a fine day: & head better.

The Woolfs returned to Tavistock Square from Rodmell on Sunday afternoon, 16 October.

Thursday 20 October

52 Tavistock Square.

Only Thursday! It seems 14 days since we left MH. I knew the break would be a jangle; but not that I should feel the mixture of humiliation & dissolution wh. I feel today, after a sleeping draught. And the curious fact is all this is the result of offering to pay Helen Anrep's overdraught. I thought it wd be 50 it is 150 or 200. So I've committed myself again, on the impulse of the moment: just as I'd sworn not to. Cant spend freely. Must write an article. And is it worth it? L. at once says he will go shares. No. But why do I hesitate over this? 1. She disliked 3 Gs. I know its the right thing to do. I dont like talking emotionally (about Roger chiefly [?]). Then I was jangled by the temptation of a week at Cassis. L. very divine—walked in the Sq. I dont think I come altogether badly out of it. I've forced myself to work at R. this morning. Theres some taste about it that I dislike. And worrying L. And the sleeping draught heavy on me, like a hand. Yet it is right to give her the money, as she's doing without a servant. I mean if one cared for R. this is a way to show it—better than buying clothes or another room. So don't let me vacillate. Only be more careful in future.[8]

Saturday 22 October

Decidedly less jangled; though my promise to pay H.'s overdraught still remains: she has not sent me any word tho', & thus cowardlike I hope I may keep my hoard intact. Yet I'm glad not to have to buy expensive clothes. An odd little kink in my mind, which I cant untwist. I daresay this will make interesting reading to me one of these days, should I write a true memoir. Anyhow, it did slightly bear fruit when Colefax came to see me yesterday. I said I will only dine with you if I may walk. Dressing & driving in a cab destroy my sentence—jerk me fr one consciousness to another. I'll dine with you to meet the D. of Devonshire as I am. Now this was logical & sensible: making the best of modern conditions as R. has it. She asserts that her ambition is to

8. Helen Anrep, who dined alone with VW on 19 October, distracted by money troubles caused by her own financial ineptitude and the wants of her children Anastasia and Igor, both students, was trying to economise by managing without a servant. VW's impulsive generosity (she lent Helen £150) was to prove a source of disproportionate vexation to her.

preserve civilisation. So is my ambition. It boils down to dining with S[ibyl]. in day clothes. Also to bring Isherwood & Auden to dine there. That I dont promise: but why not explore this possibility of seeing the great world from a new angle? I think it fits in with my general scheme at present. Then I can pay Helen: keep my self respect &c. And we're lunching early to go to Hampton Court, after a long grind—not quite fruitless—at R.—the Broussa scene.[9] I'm interested, though the drudgery is intense—quotes & general outline. But I see it: its the doing the detail in words thats the worry.

Sunday 30 October

Words, words, words, so many & so many—That I think is the vocalisation of my little sensation this morning.[10] I am tired of writing. At least its a bad life when for some reason one has an intermittence of feeling. Perhaps this is due to the jerk of 2 days at MH: & then straight back, yesterday, from perfect warmth & summer blue to London, dinner with all the W[oolf]'s at Freda's Club. This was Lord Spencer's house. I sat next Martin [Abrahamson] & Harold & said almost exactly what I said a year ago. These reunions are rather like shows of old clothes. Freda & Alice & Sylvia all stouter; & so on. Mrs W. shrivelled, upheld by a new belt.[11]

"Words" refers partly to Vita's new poem, Solitude. Does it jab on the nerve? Is it only sleek eloquence? The words I found on my lips were "suave & sumptuous". I suspect there's a good deal more. But no doubt I'm at an angle, as I say. I dont want reflections on God: nor do I altogether forget her superficial view of 3 Gs: that she never troubled to think out what I meant. This is partly personal; partly not.

Miss Gardiner hauled me out of the Lodge yesterday. The young are reading 3 Gs: it is a revelation. I let her explain. It seemed to explain to us what we're doing. She gave me Thomas Mann. who does the same. Now Vita never contemplated that quality in 3 Gs.[12]

9. It was at Broussa (Turkey) in 1911, in an emergency caused by Vanessa Bell's illness, that Roger Fry's remarkable practical capability, sympathy, and intelligence were first impressed upon VW, who was present. See *Roger Fry*, chapter 7.

10. Cf. *Roger Fry* (*Penguin* edition, 1979), p. 151: 'Underneath all these theories, fertilizing them, there was his own "petite sensation".' The expression was Cézanne's.

11. Mrs Woolf's 88th birthday dinner was held at the Ladies Army & Navy Club, then housed in Earl Spencer's magnificent eighteenth-century town house in St James's Place.

12. The Woolfs' young village neighbour and Labour Party supporter Diana Gardner was an aspiring writer herself; she gave VW *The Coming Victory of Democracy*, the text of a lecture by Thomas Mann, recently published in an English translation by A. E. Meyer.

Nessa away slightly rasps me. I have no circumference; only my inviolable centre: L. to wit. He has been offered £500 by Gollancz for a book on Civn. His play will be tried by the Group. Stephen S. thinks it a roaring comedy & very original.[13]

I should like to be quit of all this: am more & more dissatisfied with modern lit: & the criticism thereof; envy painters; yet suspect that I must grate myself upon people to get my sense of "words" dried up. So dine tomorrow to meet Max [Beerbohm] &c: & C. Isherwood comes too. I think I shall read Chaucer: & En[glis]h poetry concurrently with French prose. But I'm word haunted. The ugliness of the W.s in middle life last night rasped me: & their complete lack of—what? Something I shall find at Sybil's? I wonder. Fire at Marseilles; Parliament meeting; To the L. out in Dents. CR in Pelican. Asked to write a story for Harpers. Also to give a book to the Ox. Univ. Press. Hugh writes. A great deal on foot. Words words & now roast beef & apple tart. An evening alone.[14]

Tuesday 1 November

Max like a Cheshire cat. Orbicular. Jowld. Blue eyed. Eyes grow vague. Something like Bruce Richmond—all curves. What he said was, Ive never been in a group. No, not even as a young man. It was a serious fault. When you're a young man you ought to think Theres only one right way. And I thought—this is very profound, but you maynt realise it—"It takes all sorts to make a world." I was outside all the groups. Now dear Roger Fry who liked me, was a born leader. No one so "illuminated". He looked it. Never saw anyone look it so much. I heard him lecture, on the Aesthetics of Art. I was disappointed. He kept on turning the page—turning the page . . . . Hampstead hasnt yet been spoilt. I stayed at Jack Straw's Castle some years ago. My wife had been having influenza. And the barmaid, looking over her shoulder said—my wife had had influenza twice—"Quite a greedy one arent you?" Now thats immortal. There's all the race of barmaids in that. I suppose I've been ten times into public houses. George Moore never used his eyes. He never knew what men & women think. He got it all out of books. Ah I was afraid you would remind me of Ave atque Vale. Yes. Thats

13. LW wrote *Barbarians at the Gate* for Gollancz's Left Book Club; it was published late in 1939 (see *V LW*, pp. 11-13). His play *The Hotel* was not performed.

14. A disastrous fire broke out in the Canebière district of Marseilles on 28 October, destroying an hotel and a department store and causing over seventy deaths. Parliament reassembled on 1 November. *To the Lighthouse* was published in Dent's 'Everyman's Library' on 27 October (Kp A10d); on 8 October Penguin Books published *The Common Reader* as a Pelican Book (Kp A8d). Hugh Walpole's letter does not survive; for VW's reply, see *VI VW Letters*, no. 3463.

beautiful. Yes, its true he used his eyes then. Otherwise its like a lovely lake, with no fish in it. The Brook Kerith . . .[1]

Coulson Kernahan? (I told how CK. stopped me in Hastings. Are you Edith Sitwell? No, Mrs W. And you? Coulson Kernahan.) At this Max gobbled. Instantly said he had known him in Yellow Book days. He wrote God & the Ant. Sold 12 million copies. And a book of reminiscences—How I visited Lord Roberts . . . The great man rose from his chair. His eyes—were they hazel? were they blue? were they brown?— no they were just soldier's eyes . . . And he wrote, Celebrities I have not met—Max Beerbohm.[2] I gave him Ottoline's ring. "I only knew her superficially—Was she happy. She quarrelled— Eleanor (or whatever Mrs B.'s name is [Florence]: she is drooping; washed out; loose lipped; sympathetic; one finger plastered) & Ottoline quarrelled. Your obituary was lovely. Did he indeed ring you up? Well, how strange people are. And they write, Lady Eglantyne . . . has raised the standard of heaven . . .

About his own writing: dear Lytton Strachey said to me: first I write one sentence; then I write another. Thats how I write. And so I go on. But I have a feeling writing ought to be like running through a field. Thats your way. Now how do you go down to your room, after breakfast—what do you feel? I used to look at the clock, & say Oh dear me, its time I began my article . . . No, I'll read the paper first. I never wanted to write. But I used to come home from a dinner party & take my brush & draw caricature after caricature. They seemed to bubble up from here . . . he pressed his stomach. That was a kind of inspiration, I suppose. What you said in your beautiful essay about me & Charles Lamb was quite true.[3] He was crazy. he had the gift . . . genius. I'm too like Jack Horner. I pull out my plum. Its too rounded, too perfect . . . I have a public of about 1500—Oh I'm famous, largely thanks to you, & people of importance at the top like you. I often read over my own work. And I have a habit of reading it through the eyes of people I respect. I often read it as Virginia Woolf would read it—picking out the kind of things you would like. You never do that? Oh you should try it.

Willie Maugham came in: like a dead man whose beard or moustache has grown a little grisly bristle after death. And his lips are drawn back

---

1. *Ave* (1911); *Salve* (1912); *Vale* (1914)—George Moore's autobiographical trilogy, collectively entitled '*Hail and Farewell*'. *The Brook Kerith*, 1916.

2. Coulson Kernahan (1858-1943), prolific author, lived near Hastings, where the Woolfs met him on 28 October when travelling Hogarth Press books there. His books include *An Author in the Territorials* (1908), with a foreword by the military hero Field-Marshal Lord Roberts of Kandahar (1832-1914), and *Celebrities: Little Stories about Famous Folk* (1923). *God and the Ant* was published in 1895.

3. In her article 'Modern Essays' (Kp C229), written in 1922 and reprinted in *The Common Reader*, VW saluted Max Beerbohm as 'without doubt the prince of his profession'.

like a dead mans. He has small ferret eyes. A look of suffering & malignity & meanness & suspicion. A mechanical voice as if he had to raise a lever at each word—stiffens talk into something hard cut measured. Talked of Aldous—his conversion. He thinks his soul & Gerald Heard's soul are one soul. Max said he had been taught by Leonard Huxley at Charterhouse. Poor fellow, so distinguished, so cultivated . . . they ragged him. And I could picture the interview with the headmaster. I am so glad that you are finding a larger scope for your abilities—getting rid of him. And I could imagine this charming fellow, newly married to a delightful young lady &c &c.[4] Willie M. never imagined in this way. Sat like an animal in a trap: or like a steel trap. And I could not say anything that loosed his dead man's jaw. He wanted searching analytical statement about Gerald Heard's character. GH has been very kind to me, he said, as if he needed kindness. But I want to know: do you think he has—I think he wanted to know if he were a genuine person; but I couldn't fit my mind to his. Then the B[eerbohm]s went; & MB reappeared, in a smart overcoat (he wore double breasted blue suit) carrying a black cane with a white billiard ball on top. "Do you see how careful I was to say Sybil? before I came in, to warn her, lest she might be saying, What an old bore Max has become!"

Isherwood & I met on the doorstep. He is a slip of a wild boy: with quicksilver eyes. Nipped. Jockey like. That young man, said W. Maugham "holds the future of the English novel in his hands." Very enthusiastic. In spite of Max's brilliance, & idiosyncrasy, which he completely realises, & does not overstep, this was a surface evening: as I proved, because I found I could not smoke the cigar which I had brought. That was on the deeper level. All kept to the same surface level by Sybil's hostesscraft. Stories. Compliments. The house: its shell like whites & silvers & greens; its panelling; its old furniture. And Lord Ivor: & Lord de la Warr.[5]

We are going to look at 6 Endsleigh St after lunch, a freehold house, costing £7,500.

[?*Monday 14 November*]

So many pages, I see about the Colefax party, & none about the incessant stream here. I use my old image. Trying to drink a cup of tea, & having it knocked out of ones hand. Spenders & Joan [Easedale];

4. Leonard Huxley (1860-1933), father of Aldous, became a schoolmaster in 1884 to enable him to marry Julia Arnold; he perforce remained one until the success of his biography of his father T. H. Huxley, published in 1900, released him to follow a literary life.
5. Earl De La Warr (1900-76), a cousin of Vita Sackville-West, was a minister in Chamberlain's cabinet. VW met him at Garsington in 1919.

then Hugh [Walpole], Spenders, Elizabeth [Bowen] & Sybil. Then
Helen (on Saturday, my only day's solitude) followed by Adrian. . .

I am a little ruffled: spending my morning writing Biography for
America in order to pay off Baba's debts. So it seems.[6] My £150 has
been lent; given I suppose; & I must replace it. I feel I maynt have the
chance in a year or two. We never reach the pinnacle where I needn't
make owing to my—shall I say generosity? or impulsiveness? Helen
came—oh yes—no doubt she wants the money—was desperate, evidently,
if I decided not to give it. So I gave it. Voila qui est fait, as Mme de
Sevigne says. To school myself against silly puritanism, I instantly spent
£5.10 on a very charming bookcase. And shall buy a dresser this afternoon. But my brain racked by biography wont describe life; or analyse
the lending emotions. Some were very happy. I mean, paying the debt
to Roger. Then the reaction. Irritation. Then the refugees—They
clamour. So I dig my toes in: & on the one hand buy furniture; on the
other make money.

A letter from Duncan. Complete bliss at Cassis. has a country life in
view, Angelica perfect.[7] So's the weather today. Jews persecuted, only
just over the Channel. Here we feel a faint heat under us, like potatoes
frying. But no more than that. I here vow to see no one till Vita on
Thursday.

Tuesday 15 November

I did not buy the dresser. We cannoned into Rose Macaulay, an
incredibly shrunk, hair twisted figure, dealing with her car at a garage.
She never saw us. I like these unseen visions. Then I walked to Selfridge:
so across all the Parks, following two perfect Guardsmen. A soft &
remote blue ceiling of sky over the Park. My one quiet evening since
Thursday. Read Chaucer: began Lytton Q.E. & Essex [Strachey's
Elizabeth and Essex, 1928] for my article. Ideas popped up, but I want to
write fiction, my weeks off, not more hard highroad prose.

Tonight we dine with Clive. Ethel Sands pesters. Fixed for Tuesday
fortnight I should say. I am determined not to be a means provider: to
have & enjoy things as ends. Otherwise I could go on lending money;
earning money in order to lend money; writing books in order to please
Nessa & Ha [Margery Fry] & Helen; no I must dig my feet in & do the
things I think my own ends. And so left L. & walked across the park:
this was an end, not a passage way to this that & the other. What end

6. Published as 'The Art of Biography', *Atlantic Monthly*, April 1939 (Kp C359).
7. Duncan Grant's letter of 12 November—'to thank you for all the pleasure your
   letters have given . . . they have been the salt of our life' is in MHP, Sussex; for
   VW's reply, see *VI VW Letters*, no. 3467.

shall I make this afternoon? Very foggy which obscures the end. Might have gone to Cockfosters.

I shall read Sevigné & Chaucer & 50 Years of a Drs life if it comes from the Library.[8] Many publicity letters. The Cigar quarrel. In[tellectua]l. Liberty appeals & Mrs Moggridge [*unidentified*].

Wednesday 16 November

There are very few mountain summit moments. I mean, looking out at peace from a height. I made this reflection going upstairs. That is symbolical I'm "going upstairs" now, when I write Biography. Shall I have a moment on top? Or when I've done Roger? or tonight, in bed, between 2 & 3? They come spasmodically. Often when I was so miserable about The Years.

Viola Tree died last night, of pleurisy: 2 years younger than I am.

I remember the quality of her skin: like an apricot; a few amber coloured hairs. Eyes blistered with paint underneath. A huge Goddess woman, who was also an old drudge; a big boned striding figure; much got up, of late. Last time I saw her at the Gargoyle [Club] Cocktail; when she was in her abundant expansive mood. I never reached any other; yet always liked her. Met her perhaps once a year, about her books. She dined here the night her Castles in Spain came out. And I went to tea in Woburn Sq. & the butter was wrapped in a newspaper. And there was an Italian double bed in the drawing room. She was instinctive; & had the charm of good actress manners; & their Bohemianism, & sentimentality. But I think was a sterling spontaneous mother & daughter; not ambitious; a great hand at life; I suppose harassed for money; & extravagant; & very bold; & courageous—a maker of picturesque surroundings. So strong & large, that she shd. have lived to be 80: yet no doubt undermined that castle, with late hours; drink? I dont know. She could transmit something into words. Her daughter Virginia to be married this week. And think of Viola lying dead— How out of place— unnecessary.[9]

Dinner at Clive's. Janice lashing out, like a bird that begins to flutter & peck. Wants to be off? Anyhow we all talked: about Jews: about Clive's lunch party with Willy Maugham & de la Mare: which are the best books for the illiterate: then about being Jews: then about technique: the word broken in the Bible; L. read passages. A confused argument

8. W. M. Macartney, *Fifty Years a Country Doctor*, 1938.
9. Viola Tree—Mrs Alan Parsons (1884-1938), eldest daughter of the actor-manager Sir Herbert Beerbohm Tree, died in hospital on 15 November. She had been a singer and an actress; two books by her were published by the Hogarth Press (*HP Checklist* 111 and 422)—*Castles in the Air* in 1926. Her daughter Virginia Parsons married the Hon. David Tennant on 23 November.

about technique; wh. Janice sided I dont know. Anyhow she spoke up. A symptom of revolt from the elderly? She left when we did. Clive looking down from his dining room window. He leaves Gordon Square in January.

Friday 18 November

Leonard has a rash on his back; decided it was the result of the prostate; sent for Rau; who says no its your new pyjamas; takes a sample; dismisses idea of prostate about wh. he was so positive—& the result of all this is, I was all on edge with Vita yesterday: & still think, if the telephone rings, Oh thats Rau to say the specimen is impure. But there is no message— 12.45. And yet my morning has been spoilt. I cant settle to Biography yet intend to finish it by Monday. The old wound of last Januarys anxiety has made me irrational. We are off to MH. on a milky blue day, for this autumn is unparalelled—a summer heat. Vita sensitive about Solitude.

Tuesday 22 November

I meant to write Reflections on my position as a writer. I dont want to read Dante; have 10 minutes over from rehashing Lappin & Lapinova, a story written I think at Asheham 20 years ago or more: when I was writing Night & Day perhaps.[10]

Thats a long stretch. And apparently I've been exalted to a very high position, say about 10 years ago: then was decapitated by W[yndham] Lewis & Miss Stein; am now I think—let me see—out of date, of course; not a patch, with the young, on Morgan; yet wrote The Waves; yet am unlikely to write anything good again; am a secondrate, & likely, I think, to be discarded altogether. I think thats my public reputation at the moment. It is based largely on C. Connolly's Cocktail criticism: a sheaf of feathers in the wind.[11] How much do I mind? Less than I expected. But then of course, its all less than I realised. I mean, I never thought I was so famous; so dont feel the decapitation. Yet its true that after The Waves, or Flush, Scrutiny I think found me out. W.L. attacked me. I was aware of an active opposition. Yes I used to be praised by the young & attacked by the elderly. 3 Gs. has queered the pitch. For the G.M. Youngs & the Scrutineers both attack that. And my own friends have

10. 'Lappin and Lapinova' was published in *Harper's Bazaar*, New York, in April 1939 (Kp C360).
11. See Cyril Connolly, *Enemies of Promise, or How to live Another Ten Years*, published in October 1938, which surveyed the literature of the last twenty years, and gave an analysis of the conflict between the practitioners of the mandarin style (including VW) and the writers in the vernacular.

sent me to Coventry over it. So my position is ambiguous. Undoubtedly Morgan's reputation is much higher than my own. So is Tom's. Well? In a way it is a relief. I'm fundamentally, I think, an outsider. I do my best work & feel most braced with my back to the wall. Its an odd feeling though, writing against the current: difficult entirely to disregard the current. Yet of course I shall. And it remains to be seen if there's anything in P.H. In any case I have my critical brain to fall back on. But how widely I feel outside it all: untrapped by the Morgan communist group. And I know, I think, my faults. This is not the measured criticism of my position I meant to write. I'm not able to go deeply. For heres the usual stir & bother—Nessa back tomorrow, Flossie ill: am I to go Hunting? & so on.[12] A wild wet Sunday [*at Rodmell*]; a walk to Muggery; no Quentin; alone; & thank heaven, no message whatever from Rau; so all that strain was gratuitous. An odd reflection: how much anguish I wasted last January. Had I only known then that it would be dispersed thus—

Thursday 24 November

Yes & when Nessa came back, whom I so much wanted to see, the old irritation about Helen bubbled up, & I walked all through Finsbury Park this afternoon, telling over & over the story of my loan. I wonder why. Why life suddenly seems empty & endless: & I seem for ever climbing the endless stair, forced; unhelped; unthanked; a mere slave to some harsh—shall I say destiny—or is the word too big for what is probably some superficial reaction; part the old jealousy of Nessa's children is it? And then oh the bore of writing out a story to make money!

Friday 25 November

L.'s birthday—58? But I open this, to note, at the foot of the last pessimistic page, in 2 minutes, the fact that pessimism can be routed by getting into the flow: creative writing. A passage in Bio[graph]y. came right. After an incredible empty churning & grinding. Cold tears standing behind my eyes. It came right & I'm floated. So why not, when pessimistic, dandle the brain a little, until it gets into its circuit?

A fine cold day: L.'s birthday.

Monday 28 November

More brain churning to add a passage to L[appin] & L[apinova]. & all my courage needed. Then R.'s letters to his father. I can work my brain. So thats all right. And one of these days I shall be off writing what I like. To Harrow yesterday: sudden fog: shouts; terror; never was so

12. An allusion to Mrs Hunt's Domestic Employment Agency.

suddenly obliterated. Turned & walked at Hampstead. Dinner at Clive's. An English Turkey. Duncan flown; argumentative, persistent; chattering against T. E. Lawrence &c. amusing.[13]

[*Thursday 1 December*][1]

I think it would be a relief to write a free sentence here, after so much churning. And so much fitting in. Let me count the people only: Angelica, silent & reserved took my free Monday evening. On Tuesday, I went to Ethel Sands. Did my tricks in front of Guy Ridley, little Sinclair & Shaw Taylor: ashen coloured heap of ashes, that house. Fine, silver, suffocating. Sally, a smudge, talked of Baba; then Ann & Richard: Sally stayed till 12.30.[2] On Wednesday, Mary at 4, Richard Hughes at 5: Colefax at 6: went to see the moon at Elizabeth Williamson's observatory, & did not see it. Tonight Vita. Tomorrow MH. Is it wonderful that I break in upon L. & exclaim we will sell the Press & live in the country? John is making scenes. This adds to the strain. Turns red & gobbles. So whats the point of hoping for a balmy & fruitful future? A very bad season. No sales. Can I afford D[uncan']s £40 carpet?[3] Regret Helen's £150: but I'm a little proud that I made myself write the story & the article in two weeks; & started Roger again. But I have lost the scent. Dont feel him real any more. Chafing & drudgery necessary. Shall work at that till April now. And then rest my head.

Sunday 11 December

A few scattered notes.

We walked back from 12th Night (disappointing) on a clear cold night. Talked of death in Russell Sqre. L. said he had taught himself not to think about it. 2 or 3 years ago fear of death became an obsession. I said I should not wish to live if he died. But until then found life what? exciting? Yes I think so. He agreed. So we dont think of death. This came from David Cecil's account of Desmond: who has an idee fixe: his old mothers death; & then cant rouse himself from accusations; how he is war guilty or "we" are: the English presumably.[4]

13. *The Letters of T. E. Lawrence*, edited by David Garnett, had just been published.
1. VW has misdated this entry *30th Nov.*
2. The tea-party, at Ethel Sands' new house at 51 Chelsea Square, included Jasper ('Bubbles') Ridley (1913-43)—VW mistook the name—, Ethel's great-niece Catherine Sinclair, then an art student, and the critic Desmond Shawe-Taylor. Sally Chilver dined with the Woolfs.
3. She did: see *VI VW Letters*, no. 3473.
4. After giving tea to David Cecil on 8 December, the Woolfs went in the evening to Michel St Denis's production of *Twelfth Night*, with Peggy Ashcroft and Michael Redgrave, at the Phoenix Theatre. Desmond MacCarthy's long-widowed mother was German by birth; she had died, aged 85, in October 1938.

Very long hours of semi-drudgery on R. The war years. I want to sum up my 3 G. conclusions, had I time or brain before the end of the year.

How horribly the year began! As a detail, I chose a gay cover [*for her diary*] to counteract what I suspected—L.'s serious illness. All that blown away. The rash is caused possibly by Sally's hair. Mrs W. has had a heart attack. But her vitality may again pull her over. The Jews obsess her. My private naggery to coin a word for the bone one gnaws at odd moments is Helen taking £150 off me with which to supply sympathy to sympathy addicts. But thats unfair. But then one is unfair at 2 in the morning. This autumn reveals plainly our 'celebrity': that is, that we never get a day to ourselves; & attract a constant stream, from all quarters. Political, social, literary. I suppose this is secretly pleasing. I wonder. A month in winter fields will cool me down. Biography writing not much tax on the higher faculties as I perhaps shd. not call my rather doubtful gifts in that line. The young all swarm, even if they criticise. And I'm working in Rose Macaulay, Tom Eliot, Martin Freud, the Robsons & Ethel Smyth—all this week: a hint that I shd. use the morning then for Roger & not scribble, in a hand so worn with writing it hardly writes, any longer.

Monday 12 December

Rather a debauched Sunday evening at Clive's last night. Was he drunk? He was so quarrelsome & peevish, after dinner. A long tirade against motorists. Suddenly Nessa got quite red & said "This conversation is so foolish we'd better change it". But Clive wdn't change it. Every change had its head snapped off. David Cecil derided; Lytton's books dismissed. I thought of Roger & Lytton & how we used to talk of a Sunday evening. Now all personal gossip & these tedious bickerings.

L. lacerated with his rash. Injections only painful & do no good. He limped round St James Park. Very gloomy today. Fine weather—thats all that can be said in favour of the world & my grind at R. joyless & unprogressive. 2 days rewriting the transition page after 1918.

Thursday 15 December

This is hells Black Calcutta hole week.

Monday Angelica. Tuesday Rose. Wednesday lunch Vita to meet Stark: after dinner to William's to meet von Schuberts; Freud & E. Williamson to dine tonight. Tomorrow E. Bowen & Robson: Cal[edonian]. Market: Ethel Smyth; Saturday Robsons: Sunday Tom— & why?[5]

5. Freya Stark (b. 1893), the Arabist, traveller, and writer. von Schuberts, unidentified.

But I have invented a very good scheme: putting weight on enjoyment not duty. I think it works. I am going to make out a private budget for the New Year. Clothes; presents; &c: & see if this will give me more money to spend lawfully on myself. Last year I gave away £20 to Nessa; £8 for her chair; £100 to Angelica; bought D.'s picture £30: Q.'s table 5: tiles £10: mirror £15: lent H. 150. Sophie [Farrell] £10. That (roughly counted) makes £348 given or lent, with a philanthropic element; as in the art objects. This I must control. I must continue A.'s 100 & Sophie's £10. but draw in the other miscellaneous givings. No verbal commissions any more. But how much on dress & pocket money & house furnishing? Charity? And I will forecast my income. H[arper's]. B[azaar]. (London) "likes" L[appin and]. L[apinova]. but wont commit themselves till they hear from Davis. I suspect they wont take it.

```
 20
  8
100
 30
  5
 10
 15
150
 10
——
348
```

Monday 19 December

I will spend the last morning—for tomorrow will be an odious scramble—in summing up the year. True, there are 10 days or so to run; but the liberty of this book allows these—I was going to say liberties, but my meticulous conscience bids me look for another word. That raises some questions; but I leave them; questions about my concern with the art of writing. On the whole the art becomes absorbing—more? no, I think its been absorbing ever since I was a little creature, scribbling a story in the manner of Hawthorne on the green plush sofa in the drawing room at St Ives while the grown ups dined.

The last dinner of the year was to Tom Eliot last night. Physically he is a little muffin faced; sallow & shadowed; but intent (as I am) on the art of writing. His play—Family Reunion?—was the staple of the very bitter cold evening. (The snow is now falling: flakes come through my skylight: I am huddled in my red rain jacket, opportunely given by L.) It has taken him off & on 2 years to write, is an advance upon Murder; in poetry; a new line, with 3 stresses; "I dont seem popular this evening": "What for do we talk of cancer again" (no: this is not accurate). When the crisis came, his only thought was annoyance that now his play would not be acted. And he hurried up the revision (so David Cecil came to town & divided Melbourne into 2 vols.: so that at least one should be printed).[6]

Tom said the young don't take art or politics seriously enough. Disappointed in the Auden-Ish[erwoo]d. He has his grandeur. He said that there are flaws in the new play that are congenital, inalterable. I

6. Eliot's play *The Family Reunion* was first performed on 21 March 1939 at the Westminster Theatre, where it ran for five weeks. Lord David Cecil's *The Young Melbourne* was published in 1939; the second part, *Lord M.*, not until 1954.

suspect in the department of humour. He defined the different kinds of influence: a subtle, splitting mind: a man of simple integrity, & the artists ingenuous egotism. Dines out & goes to musical teas; reads poems at Londonderry house; has a humorous sardonic gift which mitigates his egotism; & is on the side of authority. A nice old friends evening. And we did not go to Judith's party.

This year I have worked at 3 Gs; & began, about April 1st, Roger: whom I have brought to the year 1919. I have also written Walpole; Lappin & Lapinova, & the Art of Biography. John says that 2 cabinet ministers are in favour of giving me the OM. The other candidates are Clemence Dane & Dame—the painter who does circuses. So the compliment is not as high as I should like: though its true I was the chosen . . . I mean, preferred; but its only lunch party gossip at Kenneth Clarks.[7]

The reception of 3 Gs. has been interesting, unexpected—only I'm not sure what I expected. 8,000 sold. Not one of my friends has mentioned it. My wide circle has widened—but I'm altogether in the dark as to the true merits of the book. Is it . . ? No, I wont even formulate qualities; for, its true, no one has yet summed it up. Much less unanimity than about Room of Ones Own. A suspended judgment upon that work then seems fittest. I've written too 120 pages of Pointz Hall. I think of making it a 220 page book. A medley. I rush to it for relief after a long pressure of Fry facts. But I think I see a whole somewhere—it was simply seized, one day, about April, as a dangling thread: no notion what page came next. And then they came. To be written for pleasure.

Money I've summed up: & good resolutions. We shall find the new window in at MH. And its the coldest day for 5 years. Snow steadily falling. John temperamental. Another boil over on Saturday. A very bad season. Probable loss.

Reading Chaucer & Sevigne & the usual trash books. 2 years more of 52. The new flats going up in Southampton Row. Clive leaving 50. A last message from Ottoline this morning [*unexplained*]. Deaths this year: Ottoline, Ka. Mrs W. recovering.

In snowstorms and freezing temperatures—which persisted until Boxing Day—the Woolfs drove to Monks House on 20 December for a stay of almost four weeks. On Christmas Day they had the now traditional reunion—this year tea at Tilton—with Lydia and Maynard Keynes, and then dined at Charleston.

7. Lunch party gossip at the Kenneth Clarks—he was then the brilliant young director of the National Gallery—was wide of the mark: neither the author Clemence Dane (1888-1970) nor the painter Dame Laura Knight, R.A. (1877-1970), nor VW herself, received the Order of Merit.

— 1939 —

1939

VW here begins DIARY XXVIII—a red-covered loose-leaf book—at Rodmell.

[*Thursday 5 January*]

So I take a new nib, after bringing Roger to the verge of Josette with the old one, & spend my last 5 minutes, this very fine January morning, in writing the first page of the new Year. Last 5 minutes before lunch—how inaugurate this important volume in that time, with this brain? A brain still running in the rut of the last sentence, which last sentence will be re-written a dozen times, too. So the dominant theme is work: Roger: the others the usual Rodmell themes. That is, I've let the frost go too far away. We came down 14 or 15 days ago & found all pipes frozen. There was snow for 5 days—bitter cold; wind. We staggered for one hour through the blizzard. Chains were on our wheels. We ground over to Charleston & Tilton on Christmas day. Then, 2 days later, woke to find green grass everywhere. The long spikes of ice that hung down the kitchen window had drops on their noses. They melted. The pipes thawed. Now its a June morning with an east wind. And times up. But the book's begun anyhow. And perhaps I shall get a clearer head & say 10 minutes tomorrow. To Alciston yesterday, & envied the view & the farmhouse. But L. says "I prefer Monks House" Walked in Firle Park. At sight of that great yellow white mansion, L. said, "I prefer Monks House."[1] So to lunch.

Monday 9 January

Now that I have brought my brain to the state of an old washerwomans flannel over Roger—Lord the Josette chapter—& its all too detailed, too tied down—I must expand, first on this irresponsible page, & then, for 4 days I swear, before we go back on Sunday, in fiction. Though I've ground out most wish to write, even fiction. Rodmell is a grind on the brain: in winter especially. I write 3 solid hours: walk 2: then we read, with intervals for cooking dinner, music, news, till 11.30. I've thus read L.'s second volume: very good; full; moulded; subtle; & ever so many packets of R.'s letters; & some Sevigné, Chaucer—&

---

1. Firle Place, externally a largely 18th century great house, has been the seat of the Gage family since Tudor times. Henry Rainald, 6th Viscount Gage (1895-1982), great landowner and local magnate, was Vanessa's landlord.

some nonsense books. Weather now broken. Floods & gales; marsh under water. Charleston broken up. Maynard's father dying.[2]

And that reminds me of 2 obituaries I should have written, had I not been immersed: Jack Hills & Mitz. Mitz was found dead on Boxing day I think: her white old womans face puckered; eyes shut; tail wrapped round her neck. L. buried her in the snow under the wall. Jack died the same day about—no Xmas Eve: & if I had a brain (but havent) I could retell his life; as it affected ours, 30 years ago. The last time I saw him was in the London Library a year ago: grown stout & rosy; I heard his odd stammer: was too shy to speak. He was talking to a lady about a visit they had paid together—a sign of his unknown life. For who he saw, where he lived even had long been lost to me. Yet of all our youthful directors he was the most open minded, least repressive, could best have fitted in with later developments, had we not gone our ways—he to politics & sport, we to Bloomsbury. I remember his address to me in Fitzroy Square after V[anessa]'s marriage on the sexual life of young men. Can they be honourable? I asked—when he said how all male talk was about women; how every young man had his whore. He was amused. I remember the moonlight night at Hindhead: the tramp: the shadows in the garden; Stella & he in the summer house; Thoby shouting at the tramp. Sophie confirms this: the tramp looked in at the kitchen window, where she sat getting a meal for Mr George. And then Stella's death, one year later, & how he came round & sat with me, & talked in his natural voice. And then those appalling evenings at Painswick, sitting with him in a summer house, after dinner; he grasping my hand in agony: torn asunder—you cant understand—& I fixing a small bush & making it a symbol of agony. Then the long interviews with Nessa: her love; the row with George. "Are they going to get married?"—how he burst in on me & rather brutally told me his suspicion; asked me to speak to her—to warn her. I remember her dignified reproach—"You too?". And father's sense. "If she wants to I wont interfere." Then he fell in love, with Elena; with Imogen. A letter from Italy: "Never think that I've forgotten Stella, tho' I've loved other women"—& so the dispersal, the very casual meetings; his marriage; & the end. This sketch must serve, since I'm too jaded to write.[3]

2. LW's *After the Deluge. A Study of Communal Psychology*, volume II, was published by the Hogarth Press on 25 September 1939; volume I had appeared in 1931. John Neville Keynes (b. 1852), Registrary of the University of Cambridge from 1910-25, did not die until 1949—three years after his son Maynard.

3. VW gives a more extended account than the above sketch of her half-sister Stella Duckworth's widower Jack Hills and the part he played in her family's life at Hyde Park Gate in the 1890's in two memoirs: 'Reminiscences', written in 1907-08; and 'A Sketch of the Past', 1939-40, both published in *Moments of Being* (Kp A45). Elena Rathbone (later the wife of Sir Bruce Richmond) and Imogen Booth (later

Tuesday 17 January

[52 Tavistock Square]
London on Sunday. Five minutes left of the morning. Yesterday I went to the London Library; thought I'd been there for 40 years; read Tom's swan song in the Criterion, or rather slipped his condensed meanings over my fluid mind;[4] home & read Delacroix journals; about which I could write: I mean the idea that its among the painters not the writers one finds stability, consolation. This refers to a sentence of his about the profundity of the painter's meaning; & how a writer always superficialises.[5]

I wish I could distill some of my thoughts about "the situation" into nuggets. The Spanish war is being won yesterday today tomorrow by Franco. I dreamt of Julian. A sniping [?] article on him "The limitations of Bloomsbury" by Janet Adam Smith. She advises life in a mining village as a remedy: what is her practice? This represents a vein of thought that I may work out.[6] Igor [Anrep, *Helen's son*] has bought a motor car—out of my £150? Another vein of thought with which I struggle. The purification of the soul. This is a fact, however: my struggle. Today—dreary wet—I may go to Mathew Smith's pictures; or may not.[7] John comes. Question of our relations with John.

At Clive's on Sunday. A good discussion of painting & music. Janice gave tongue. Angelica sang a song. L. talked. So did Nessa.

I'm taking 4 days holiday from Roger, writing P[ointz] H[all], the Barn scene. I've learnt something from The Years—just translated into French.[8]

Now the clock strikes one.

Gore-Browne) were of the Duckworth–Stephen social circle of VW's Kensington youth. In 1931 John Waller Hills, then a 64-year-old MP, married for the second time.

4. See *The Criterion*, January 1939: 'Last Words'; 'With this number I terminate my editorship . . . I have been considering this decision for about two years: but I did not wish to come to a conclusion precipitately, because I knew my retirement would bring *The Criterion* to an end.'—(which it did). T. S. Eliot had been editor since 1922.

5. *Journal de Eugène Delacroix*, edited by André Joubin, 3 vols. Paris 1932. VW possibly refers to a passage in the entry for 8 October 1822.

6. See Janet Adam Smith in *The London Mercury*, January 1939, on *Julian Bell, Essays, Poems and Letters* (published by the Hogarth Press on 7 November 1938), a highly disparaging analysis of the equivocal nature of Bell's views on war, socialism, and the 'whole set of ideas and values that are commonly called Bloomsbury.'

7. 'Jacob Epstein's Collection of 28 Paintings by Matthew Smith' at the Leicester Galleries, Leicester Square.

8. *Années*. Traduit de l'Anglais par Germaine Delamain, Paris, 1938 (Kp D28).

JANUARY 1939

Wednesday 18 January

It is undoubtedly a great freshener to have my story [*Lappin and Lapinova*] taken by Harper's. I heard this morning. A beautiful story, enchanted to have it. 600 dollars made then. Therefore I am paying off Helen's money, as I said I would. But the encouragement, I must note, by way of ruffling my theories that one should do without encouragement, is a warmer, a reviver. I cant deny it. I was, perhaps partly on that account, in full flood this morning with P.H. I think I have got at a more direct method of summarising relations; & then the poems (in metre) run off the prose lyric vein, which, as I agree with Roger, I overdo. That was by the way the best criticism I've had for a long time: that I poetise my inanimate scenes, stress my personality; dont let the meaning emerge from the matière—Certainly I owed Roger £150.

I went to Her[t]ford House in the yellow rain yesterday & saw Bodington and Bumalfacco—no thats not the name—a little bit of verification for the book to which I must turn tomorrow.⁹ Next pages are about R.'s politics. Now dont, because [Janet] Adam Smith gibes, apologise, for she's not worth a nail on Roger's toe.

John to tea—depressed. He & L. never alluded to their exchange of abuse. But I thought him rather worn down. I am not yet up in London politics. One of our lulls. We are still away to our friends; but I must see Mela Spira the refugee Austrian Jewess; & today Mrs Woolf—the blanks will fill.¹⁰ I am going walking & adventuring going to see pictures of an afternoon; & often come face to face, after tea, at odd moments, with the idea of death & age. Why not change the idea of death into an exciting experience?—as one did marriage in youth? Age is baffled today by my creative gift—still a bubble. And then the steady passion with which I now read . . . A rainy day. Rain real wet drops: white splashing from the road. I must somehow ease my way back into Roger—shut PH firmly; my mind full of figures—Isa in the greenhouse—to be put in their boxes.

9. Hertford House in Manchester Square is the home of the Wallace Collection, which contains a number of paintings by Bonington. Buonamico Buffalmacco was a 14th century Florentine; Roger Fry made a painting from a photograph of one of his frescoes for an exhibition of 'Copies and Translations' which he organised for the Omega Workshops in 1917; see *Letters of Roger Fry*, edited by Denys Sutton, 1972, vol. II, no. 387—from which VW quotes in her *Roger Fry* (Penguin edition), p. 179.

10. Robert Spira (b. 1888), an Austrian lawyer, and his wife Mela came to England as refugees in 1938, when he registered as a student at the Courtauld Institute of Art, and obtained a BA degree in 1940. Who introduced them to VW has not been discovered.

Sunday 22 January

And my article on Biography has been taken by the Atlantic. Thus in a little over 2 weeks I made something ⟨over⟩ round about £160. Helen paid off. At the same time, the Spiras, a battered couple lodging in Hampstead, came to tea [*on 20 January*]; implore us to get her a permit to teach German; both in the depths of a kind of shifty unformulated despair: driven from Gratz with a bundle of old pictures only which no one will buy. Also, war is coming close again, just as in September. L. thinks the next screw will be in March. PM to broadcast today on National service.[11] We are warned to buy extra food & see to our supply of water. Desmond came to lunch, outstayed the Spiras, left at 8. Suddenly his face falls into the fixity of a tragic old man's despair. Then twinkles. Always thinking. "My chief delight is in the uprush of thought to the brain. No I dont care whether Rachel has a child or not. I live in ideas. And what a world to bring children into" (another fixed moment). A discussion about readers & writers criticism. How to uphold the standard; & yet have a sense of direction. That is to encourage St Denis even if the particular play is bad. How the cultivated always kill their own offspring i.e. the Omega, or the Life & Letters: partly snobbery. "I've too high a standard." He is off to America to net £200 by lecturing. I look at my letters from editors. Its odd [*text ends*][12]

Tuesday 24 January[13]

On the placards this afternoon: Franco at the gate of Barcelona: Measures for defence. This refers to our new voluntary service. The one is the cause of the other. Yesterday 300 bullets were found thrown into the bushes the other side of Tavistock Square. A reporter came to ask if Mr Woolf could give any information. One of the Irish rebels lodges in Tavistock Place or Court.[14] These are notes I scribble hastily, while L. (exacerbated by the itch again) goes to the Cocktail at the BBC. I to read over Helen's letters, on a fine spring day, the eve of my 57th

11. Mr Chamberlain's call to service—'every man's duty to ensure the security of the country'—was in fact broadcast on Monday 23 January.
12. The Omega Workshops, 'Artist Decorators', were started by Roger Fry in 1913 and closed in 1919 owing to lack of support. *Life and Letters* was first issued as a monthly in June 1928; in Desmond MacCarthy's five years as editor, it dwindled to a quarterly. This may have been due as much to his inefficiency as to his high standards.
13. VW has misdated this *Wednesday Jan 24th*.
14. In the previous week there had been a series of synchronised explosions in London and elsewhere, attributed to IRA extremists; the retrieval by police of 340 rounds of ammunition in Tavistock Square gardens on 23 January was assumed to be further evidence of the activity of Irish terrorists on the British mainland.

birthday. And on the bus coming back from the Flower Show I described my new 'novel': & we planned the books we shd. write, if we could live another 30 years.[15]

Sunday 29 January

Yes, Barcelona has fallen: Hitler speaks tomorrow; the next dress rehearsal begins: I have seen Marie Stopes, Princesse de Polignac, Philip & Pippin, & Dr Freud in the last 3 days. also had Tom to dinner & to the Stephens' party.[16]

Dr Freud gave me a narcissus. Was sitting in a great library with little statues at a large scrupulously tidy shiny table. We like patients on chairs. A screwed up shrunk very old man: with a monkeys light eyes, paralysed spasmodic movements, inarticulate: but alert. On Hitler. Generation before the poison will be worked out. About his books. Fame? I was infamous rather than famous. didnt make £50 by his first book. Difficult talk. An interview. Daughter & Martin helped. Immense potential, I mean an old fire now flickering. When we left he took up the stand What are *you* going to do? The English—war.

Monday 30 January[17]

Freud said It would have been worse if you had *not* won the war. I said we often felt guilty—if we had failed, perhaps Hitler would have not been. No, he said, with great emphasis; he would have been infinitely worse. They considered leaving for 3 months; made up their minds in 24 hours. Very alert at L.'s mention of the case when the Judge decreed that the criminal should read 20 of Freud's books. Adrian says the Pss Bonaparte gave him this great silent solid Hampstead mansion. "But we dont like it as well as our flat in Vienna" said Anna. A certain strain: all refugees are like gulls with their beaks out for possible crumbs. Martin & his novel; she on her book. The strain on us too of being benefactors.[18]

15. Cf. LW's diary, 24 January 1939: 'Picture Gallery & Flower Show. BBC Listener party.' The Royal Horticultural Society's fortnightly show was of greenhouse and hardy spring plants.

16. The writer and sex-educationist Dr Marie Stopes (1880-1958) saw VW on 25 January, probably to secure her support for an appeal to the Royal Literary Fund on behalf of the indigent Lord Alfred Douglas. The Princesse de Polignac had tea with VW on 27 January. Philip Woolf and a daughter lunched on 28 January; that afternoon VW and LW went to visit Freud in Hampstead; and after dinner went with T. S. Eliot to Adrian Stephen's fancy dress party at York Terrace, Regent's Park.

17. VW has misdated this *23rd January*—the previous Monday.

18. With the help of his rich, influential, and devoted pupil Princess Marie Bonaparte (1882-1962), wife of HRH Prince George of Greece, the 82-year-old Sigmund

A[drian]'s party varied & no doubt successful. The young danced till 3. Bobo in crimson velvet, Tom in Lytton's beard with a brown pop eye: Janice in a great nose; Clive ebullient, dancing with Bobo; repairing that old breach. Duncan a blond French prince: Ann almost naked, very distinguished, lovely; aloof; fierce; Richard urbane & inscrutable: always the same, Angelica said; Molly oldish; Rachel in a red shawl, about to bear a Cecil; David chirping about his book [*The Young Melbourne*], out on Thursday; attacked, liked, disliked; refused by USA & Book Society &c. And the usual bobbing corks on the waves—dullards hoping to get into touch with someone or thing & approaching & driven off & then attaching themselves: Portia Holman, the Enfields. A kind of liberation caused by wearing a mask, tipsiness & abandonment at not being one's usual self. Tom expanding in the lights & stir, much as I do.[19]

Last night Yeats' death announced. That great thick long jowled poet, whom I met last at Ottoline's. Dotty will fall from her high estate; but I try to cultivate sympathy rather than satire.[20] And we are all on tiptoe, waiting Hitler's speech tonight.

Tuesday 31 January[21]

A very sensible day yesterday. Saw no one. Took the bus to Southwark Bridge. Walked along Thames Street; saw a flight of steps down to the river. I climbed down—a rope at the bottom. Found the strand of the Thames, under the warehouses—strewn with stones, bits of wire, slippery; ships lying off [?] the Bridge (Southwark?—no, the one next to Tower Bridge [London Bridge]). Very slippery; warehouse walls crusted, weedy, worn. The river must cover them at high tide. It was now low. People on the Bridge stared. Difficult walking. A rat haunted, riverine place, great chains, wooden pillars, green slime, bricks corroded, a button hook thrown up by the tide. A bitter cold wind. Thought of the refugees from Barcelona walking 40 miles, one with a baby in a parcel. So to Tower. Made a circuit: discovered St Olave's Hart Street: Pepys

---

Freud was able to leave Nazi-controlled Vienna the previous summer, and since September had been installed at 20 Maresfield Gardens with his youngest daughter the child psychologist Anna Freud (1895-1982). Martin Freud's picaresque novel *Parole d'Honneur* was published in England later this year.

19. The Enfields were Bloomsbury residents; she was a literary lady (published by the Hogarth Press) whom VW knew by her maiden name of Hussey before her marriage to Ralph Enfield, a civil servant, in 1921.

20. W. B. Yeats died at Roquebrune-Cap-Martin on 28 January 1939; in the weeks up to his death his friend Lady Dorothy Wellesley, who had a villa at nearby La Bastide, saw him constantly. For VW's last meeting with him, see *IV VW Diary*, 26 October 1934.

21. VW has misdated this entry *January 30th*.

Church; too cold to explore;[22] wandered about Fenchurch alleys, Billingsgate; walked through Leadenhall Market; thought of Thoby buying the wild geese; saw a golden pheasant; so back by omnibus; the street & shops the product of this factory world; tried to buy Wells (Country of the Blind) praised by Tom t'other night; failed; so home; left the kettle on; it blew out its connection; read Michelet; wrote to Desmond about his poetess; L. out at Fabians; played gramophone; listened to Our Masters Voice, Hitler less truculent than expected; read MSS; read The Magnificent Rothschilds; & so to bed.[23]

My head has now protested once more against Roger & facts; so to humour it, I wrote the old Henry Taylor telescope story thats been humming in my mind these 10 years; & have a feeling of life & activity again. Put off Eth Bowen & Sean O'Faolain this afternoon, we go to Mrs Woolf instead: & now, as usual, lunch.[24]

[Thursday 9 February]

Too tired even to fold up Nessa's Berlin letters [*to Roger Fry, 1929*]. This tiredness was bred of 8 hours incessant talk after four days incessant sun. That was our 4 days at MH. So people accumulate. Eth Bowen, Sean O'Faolain, Busch concert.[1]

Looking at my old Greek diary I was led to speculate. I extract only this: that I won't budge from the scheme there (1932) laid down for treating decline of fame. To accept; then ignore; & always venture

22. Pepys lived in Seething Lane, which runs south from St Olave's at which church he regularly worshipped; it was largely destroyed in the blitz, but has been rebuilt, and contains the bust of his wife Elizabeth.

23. H. G. Wells, *The Country of the Blind and Other Stories*, 1911; VW later succeeded in buying a copy from the bookseller David Nutt in Shaftesbury Avenue, as well as two volumes of Michelet's *Histoire de France*: see below, 17 February 1939 (also *Holleyman*, MH V, p. 9; VS VII, p. 5). *The Magnificent Rothschilds* (1939) by Cecil Roth.

24. Sir Henry Taylor (1800-86), author of the verse-play *Philip van Artevelde* (1834), held a post in the Colonial Office under VW's grandfather Sir James Stephen, who became a friend; her father Leslie Stephen wrote the account of his life for the *DNB*. As a young man Taylor spent some years in a remote border tower in his native County Durham; a tower is the setting of VW's 'telescope story' (see holograph dated *31 Jan. 1939* in the Berg Collection, and earlier versions in MHP, Sussex: B 9k (1930) and B 10f). A variant (see MHP, Sussex, B 19) was posthumously published as 'The Searchlight' in *A Haunted House* (Kp A28).

The Irish writer Sean O'Faolain (b. 1900) was a friend of Elizabeth Bowen; VW put them off until 8 February.

1. On 8 February the Woolfs went to the second of a series of recitals by the Busch Quartet at the Wigmore Hall; they heard Beethoven's Quartet in C sharp minor; Schubert's in B flat major (D 112); and Mozart's Quintet in G minor.

further. Obviously there are no limits unless one submits. Always shave off the expected, dictated attitude; & find whats under it. But I cant even write this plain.[2] And Molly . . . But we go to Crufts dog show: fine again.[3]

Friday 17 February

Jangled with talk—talk to David [Cecil] from 4 to 5; then to Katie Lewis; the Hambourgs, talk;[4] home, & Raymond, Anna Freud, the Chilvers talk till 12.30—9 hours solid, frothy, talk, varied by buying Michelet at Nutts, & the Country of the Blind. A hammer & a drill this morning exacerbate still further: they're pulling down T[avistock]. S[quare]. & building offices. So out in the brisk cold to buy note books. I'm starting my grand tour of literature. That is I'm going to write a book of discovery, reading as one pulls a string out; & must follow my trail through Sevigne Michelet Somerset Maugham &c. Thats the idea; encouraged by that vast marsupial Margery Strachey, who implored me to do criticism: as indeed I've long wanted. David grows friendlier: Raymond—oh what a little bank clerk, snub, common, he's grown; hard as nails, & smug, with a new sawing motion with his hands, & none of the old flutter & sweetness. Severe is your toll, oh age. And I too shrivelled, & was very very old. Rachel waiting her child.

Tuesday 28 February

It is unfortunate, for truths sake, that I never write here except when jangled with talk. I only record the dumps & the dismals, & them very barely. A holiday from Roger. And one day's happiness with P.H. Then too many parcels; books coming out; & a head numb at the back. As usual, when I'm prone, all the gnats settle. The usual ones: I neednt specify. I have to 'speak' to polytechnics; & engagements multiply. Innumerable refugees to add to the tangle. There—I've recorded them when I said I wouldnt. Harold [Woolf] upstairs talking, about refugees, to L. I go in, out of courtesy. He is doing a job for me.

Morgan to lunch yesterday. Much argument: communism defined, also his duties on the Libel Commission:[5] also gossip about Peter & Prudence [Lucas]; she mad. Nessa after dinner. My old thorn about

2. See *IV VW Diary*, 17 May 1932: 'What is the right attitude towards criticism?'

3. Cruft's Dog Show was at the Royal Agricultural Hall, Islington; Molly MacCarthy came to tea on the Woolfs' return thence.

4. The Russian-born virtuoso pianist Mark Hambourg (1879-1960) and his English wife were friends of Miss Lewis, whose family were notable patrons of music and musicians.

5. E. M. Forster has been invited by the Lord Chancellor to serve on a Committee of Inquiry being set up to consider and report on the law of defamation.

Helen rankles. Oh she'll never repay you. Lives as usual. Saxon 20 minutes on the phone. Will I lunch with Graham Harris.[6] Odd change into a deliberate old man's voice. Add to this my petty jealousies. All the same I think I can stamp it out, literally, by walking this afternoon. Plenty of things to see; neednt buy clothes; & sleep over a book. So shall be sane tomorrow. If it were not 12.15 I would walk now. Only it pours. So I will read poetry quietly, I think—having Shelley down here with me.

I have just read [Shelley's] Mont Blanc, but cant make it "compose": clouds perpetually over lapping. If a new poem, what should I say? I think a great idea somewhere; but the language so nebulous, or rather words overlapping, like ripples, each effacing the other, partly: & a general confusion results.

Yesterday, Franco was recognised. And Julian killed for this. Nessa though I suppose making herself live: succeeding: very busy.[7]

Friday 3 March

Whats the origin of the expression A flea in his ear?—thats what I've just written:[1] & must—(12.15) switch from that to describe yesterday, Thursday: a very long day, but on the whole successfully accomplished. Not at all a nice morning, & worried by my speech, so I walked. And bought some frilling; & then off we went to the Polytechnic; & met a little brown faced supple man in corduroys; inspected a wall of illustrations to O[rlando]. & then in came, say 50 art students: blouses, shirts; nimble, young, inquisitive; stood up, & not very nervously spoke, improving, colloquially. Then L. gave his views; as a publisher. And that was a great success—very valuable indeed, said the professor: & asked him to start again, which he did.[2] No it wasnt formidable. It was rather cheerful. And free & easy. Better much than Oxford & Cambridge: which reminds me that Liverpool today offered me a Doctor's Degree; which I refused. Then they gave us a specimen book of rather too artistic

6. Francis Graham-Harrison (b. 1914), Eton and Oxford and a recent recruit to the Civil Service (Home Office), was the son of an ex-Treasury colleague of Sydney-Turner's.

7. On 27 February Mr Chamberlain announced in the House of Commons the decision of the British Government to recognise that of General Franco—now in control of the greater part of Spanish territory.

1. See *Pointz Hall...*, edited by Mitchell Leaska, 1938, p. 126 ('The Earlier Typescript, p. 155' and his note, p. 225). The origin of the phrase, which dates at least from the 15th century in English and earlier in French, is not identified by Brewer, *Dictionary of Phrase and Fable*.

2. The Woolfs spoke to a class of book-production students given the exercise of designing a dust-jacket for *Orlando*; but I cannot discover *where*.

printing; & then we got off. And I cooled myself with Chaucer. Then to dine at the studio, & a long, but on the whole, admirable & agreeable, Thursday evening. Rogers: 2 fat beavers, identical; artists; Spenders; Inez improving, independent sharp; Tangye Lean, the man with the absurd name who writes in the N. Chronicle; & Dermod MacCarthy; & L. in from The Cranium.[3] I was pleased, vanitously, to find that Inez thinks me a poet-novelist, not a fraud; & T.L. also liked something or other. So we talked shop. The novel. They both incubate novels. He tears up. She has her's in a drawer. And my jadedness thawed. So that I've written several pages of P.H. although Miss Compton Burnett is praised.[4]

Must face the end of Roger. perhaps at MH. this week end. A very fine June blue day at top of the skylight. But I meant to say that Nessa's conduct of these parties seemed to me admirable; & once she laughed, & laughed & laughed; trying to describe the prevalence of 'stuff'". I laughed too. Then we discussed tin: iron; & D[ermod]. who has his vein of queer humour, told us how Raymond Abbott said that organ pipes are pure tin. Mrs Rogers described the making of felt: & so on. Very easy, & sensible, & sympathetic. A great many parties in the offing. We have the materials for happiness again. A new Pope elected. A lull in the shindy. Poor Spira's pictures all frauds. & a Labour P. meeting tonight.[5]

Saturday 11 March

Yesterday, that is Friday 10th, I set the last word to the first sketch of Roger. And now I have to begin—well not even to begin, but to revise & revise. A terrible grind to come: & innumerable doubts, of myself as biographer: of the possibility of doing it at all: all the same I've carried through to the end; & may allow myself one moments mild gratification. There are the facts more or less extracted. And I've no time to go into

3. Claude Rogers (1907-79) and his wife Elsie, *née* Few (1909-80) were both painters trained at the Slade; he was one of the founders of the 'School of Drawing and Painting' (later known as 'The Euston Road School') with which Duncan and Vanessa were associated and of which VW was one of the guarantors (see *VI VW Letters*, no. 3464). (Edward) Tangye Lean (b. 1911), author and journalist, had been at Leighton Park School with both Julian and Quentin Bell. Dermod (b. 1911), the youngest of Desmond and Molly MacCarthy's three children, was now a doctor. The Cranium was a dining club.

4. Ivy Compton Burnett's latest novel, *A Family and a Fortune*, received prominent and laudatory reviews both in the *TLS* and the *NS&N* this week.

5. Raymond Abbott was an old crony of Desmond MacCarthy's. On 2 March, with 'almost unexampled rapidity' (*Times*), Cardinal Pacelli (Pius XII) was elected to succeed Pope Pius XI who died on 10 February. The Woolfs went to Monks House this (Friday) afternoon until Tuesday.

all the innumerable horrors. There may be a flick of life in it—or is it all dust & ashes?

A day in bed at MH: such a rush with the meeting, & dining at C[harleston]. & then back to the burglary. I heard the burglar laugh as he slammed the door taking our £6 in a cashbox. We thought it was John. Then the Great Psycho Analysts dinner on a wild wet night: Adrian late: dinner at 9 till 12.30. Speeches of a vacancy & verbosity incredible. Lord de la Warr rambling jocosely. And gossip with Duncan & Adrian; the rest of our table sit in unmitigable gloom. Poor Mrs so & so—Meynell & Money Kyrle dead silent: food profuse, snatched, uncharacteristic. Mary Hutch: Rebecca West: & set upon & committed to ask to dinner Mrs Klein.[6]

Then a cocktail at John's; Rosamond & her new fancy, little self conscious G. Rees, underbred, intelligent; & our German von— something. I shall call you Renny said L.[7] And I dont know why I agreed to lunch with Diana Cooper to meet Ethel Smyth on the spur of the moment—why am I so impulsive? Why am I so old, so ugly, so— & cant write. And the Spender grandmother on Sunday; but alone today.[8]

Thursday 16 March

Jack [Hills] I see in this mornings paper left £3,000 only. I see too that Hitler has marched into Prague. This, says the PM. "is not in the spirit of the Munich meeting". My comment anyhow is superfluous. We sit & watch.[9] Yesterday in Bond Street where I finally did lay out £10 on

6. The 25th Anniversary Dinner of the British Psycho-Analytical Society took place at the Savoy Hotel on 8 March; Lord de la Warr, now President of the Board of Education, was among the half-dozen speakers. Vera Meynell was the second wife of the book-designer and bibliophile Francis Meynell; R. E. Money-Kyrle (1898-1980), psycho-analyst and writer: his short book *Superstition and Society* had just been published by the Hogarth Press. Melanie Klein (1882-1960) was a child psychologist of Viennese origin, whose books were also published by the Press.

7. On 9 March the Woolfs had 'an unknown German' visitor, René Podbieski, whom they took with them to John Lehmann's in Mecklenburgh Square. Goronwy Rees (1909-80), Fellow of All Souls, was assistant editor of *The Spectator*.

8. Stephen Spender's widowed grandmother Hilda Schuster lived in a vast and gloomy mansion flat near the Albert Hall, from which she exercised a diligent and benevolent supervision over the lives of her four orphaned grand-children. The Woolfs, after a walk in Hyde Park, had tea with her on 12 March.

9. Incited by Hitler, Slovakia declared its independence from the already truncated Czechoslovak state on 14 March; during that night the ailing Czech President Hácha was forced under duress to agree to German 'protection' of Bohemia and Moravia; and on 15 March Hitler entered Prague with German troops and asserted 'Czecko-Slovakia has ceased to exist.' In the House of Commons that day Mr

clothes, I saw a crowd round a car, & on the back seat was a Cheetah with a chain round his loins. I also found a presentation copy of Tom's *Family Reunion;* & sucked no pleasure from the first pages. Yet I enjoyed Chaucer, Michelet & Me. de Sevigné. I reserve judgment.[10] The night before Mrs Klein dined—the backwash of my P[sycho]. A[nalysts']. party—unrecorded? A woman of character & force & some submerged— how shall I say—not craft, but subtlety: something working underground. A pull, a twist, like an undertow: menacing. A bluff grey haired lady, with large bright imaginative eyes.

It was on the tip of my pen—only I had to write—to re-write Roger— to record, in brief form, Lunch with Lady Diana Cooper costs 3/6. Yes, for some impulse of my own, I said I would lunch to meet old Ethel. Old Ethel very deaf. So as to impress the aristocracy who aren't ever impressed, I took a 1/- cab from Hyde Pk Corner: & Chapel Street was only one step down the road.[11] Curious, the feebleness of the aristocracy in the eye line. Diana has inherited a vast house—sat in a drawing room like the floor of a shop: was furnishing—Chin[t]zes piled up. A glass room, looking on to the D. of Westminster's great wall—he has a private tennis court. Dishevelled creepers hang down. This great house is so timidly faced. The tinted mask of the late Duchess in a glass case. Rex Whistler discreet amusing fakes of 18th Century decoration—all diluted, reminiscent. And then Duff's great library, that might have done for Lord Acton or Lord Macaulay—here Rex again at work, fabricating 18th Century. Praise of Sargent. Praise of the late Duchesses tomb at the Tate.[12] The usual space & simplicity. Many little dishes. Many concoctions. But empty & full of unsaturated possessions. "I dont like possessions" said D. She has a bedroom like a shop again. On the table a 6d Penguin. Rooms for Madame de Maintenon, Montespan &c. Only Diana, all niceness, goodness, with that free sweep that I like in the aristocracy: putting on Ethel's 3 cornered hat (wh. became her) as if

Chamberlain announced that since the extinction of Czechoslovakia was caused by internal disruption, the British Government was no longer bound by the guarantees given to her under the Munich Agreement.

10. VW's inscribed copy of T. S. Eliot's play *The Family Reunion* was sold at Sotheby's on 27 April 1970, lot 43.

11. VW lunched with Lady Diana Cooper on 13 March at the house—two adjacent houses—near Belgrave Square left her by her mother Violet, Duchess of Rutland (1856-1937); she had moved there from Admiralty House following Duff Cooper's resignation from the Government in October 1938.

12. Owing to the war, Rex Whistler's decorations for the library were never completed; the fake 18th century decorations have vanished. The Duchess of Rutland was an artist; the plaster model (recumbent figure on a decorated base) of her monument to her eldest son Lord Haddon, who died at the age of nine in 1894, was presented to the Tate Gallery by her family in 1938.

they were free, but had nowhere to go. Talk trumpeted, emphatic, difficult, about Maurice Baring. Little rough haired boy came in.[13] So I drove Ethel to Waterloo & paid 2/6 & was then too cold in my finery to walk, so home. Refused lunch with Harry [Stephen] at the Athenaeum.

I'm thinking of a critical book. Suppose I used the diary form? Would this make one free to go from book to book—or wd it be too personal? I might take some fribble, like Peter Opie: so to Sevigne &c. But I must let it simmer.[14]

A blessed space of quiet today—tea with Nessa; then alone tonight; MH. this weekend, & my new green linen waterproof. L.'s back improving. Rau talks of an allergic doctor, who discovers sensibilities; but Rau does not ring up.

Wednesday 22 March

Tom sent me his play, Family Reunion. No, it dont do. I read it over the week end. It starts theories. But no . . . You see the experiment with stylised chatter isnt successful. He's a lyric not a dramatic. But here theres no free lyricism. is caught back by the character: has no power to embody: as stiff as pokers. And the chief poker is Tom: but cant speak out. A cold upright poker. And the Fates behind the drawing room curtain. A clever beginning, & some ideas; but they spin out: & nothing grips: all mist—a failure: a proof hes not a dramatist. A monologist. This is stated very politely by the papers this morning. The News not so politely.[15] We go on Thursday. I'm of course for reasons I can't go into selfishly relieved: why? Had it been a success would it have somehow sealed—my ideas? does this failure confirm a new idea of mine—that I'm evolving in PH about the drama? Or is it jealousy? & then theres L.'s play. A mixture of motives . . .

Very fine at the moment; & alone; & confronted with a dress maker; & L. all rash. Rau says it will go in time. Reading Eddie Marsh. Finished the 18th cent scene in PH. Odd how freely & happily I dash that off. Roger put aside. No, I cant write here. Politics lulled: but Kingsley vocal on the phone. An account of Ly Astor's lunch party.[16]

13. The Coopers' nine-year-old son John Julius (now Lord Norwich).
14. *I Want to be a Success* (1939) by Peter Opie, an 18-year-old who had only recently left Eton.
15. *The Family Reunion* was put on for a limited run from 21 March at the Westminster Theatre. The *News Chronicle* critic Lionel Hale wrote of it: 'There is no continuous theatrical impulse in the play; it is an un-signposted, barren, arid, gritty wasteland . . .'.
16. Sir Edward Marsh's reminiscences *A Number of People* had just been published. The American-born Lady Astor (1879-1964), MP, the first woman to enter Parliament, was a conspicuous partisan of the policy of appeasement.

Wednesday 29 March

There can be no doubt that Tom knew that his play was a failure. He was very yellow & heavy lidded. We talked about his cold, & I noted that he said his lectures, on Church & State, were "very bad", a proof, I think, that all his work now seems so.[17] But the evening was oddly successful. Kingsley Martin invited himself, & gave Ann & Sally their modicum of politics; otherwise literature wd have been too ascendant. Then Mr Ellis St Joseph, also self-invited, came. And paid out elaborate, yet oddly interesting, stories: about smoking hashish—how he was given for 10/- amber cigarettes wh. he supposed to be drugged; & puffed in & out, with Oliver Bell on the next bed. And they were only scented. An intricate, pompous, yet interesting young man. And they stayed till 12.30.[18] Hence I'm tired in the head, & cant tackle anything. Think of walking, to prepare for Hugh. A silly idea, having him alone; but I must brisk up something, not sit dreaming here, or my head will ache. KM. privately told L. that German aeroplanes have been flying over London.

Madrid surrendered. KM. says war is inevitable.[19]

Thursday 30 March

No, it was a good idea having Hugh alone. He gave me a full account of his sexual life, of which I retain these facts. He only loves men who dont love men. Tried to drown himself once over Melchior. Jumped into a river; stuck in mud; seized a carving knife; saw himself in the glass; all became absurd. reconciliation. Told me too of the Baths at the Elephant & Castle. How the men go there: saw Ld C[*name omitted*] naked: saw Ld B[*name omitted*] in the act with a boy; later at the Beefsteak all medals. Has had a married life with Harold for 15 years without intercourse.[20] All this piles up a rich life of wh. I have no knowledge: & he cant use it in his novels. They are therefore about lives he hasnt lived wh. explains their badness. Hasnt the courage to write about his real life. Would

---

17. The Woolfs saw T. S. Eliot's play *The Family Reunion* on 23 March; he dined with them on 28 March. In February and March he had given the three Boutwood lectures at Corpus Christi College, Cambridge, which were published later in the year as *The Idea of a Christian Society*.

18. Ellis St Joseph was a friend of Oliver Bell, an Oxford contemporary of Sally Chilver who introduced him to VW; both men emigrated to America in 1939.

19. On 28 March, virtually unresisted by its starving and disunited defenders, Franco's forces occupied Madrid, bringing the Spanish Civil War to its end.

20. Lauritz Melchior (1890-1973), the Danish *Heldentenor*, was for many years the personification of Hugh Walpole's 'ideal friend'; in about 1926 his pre-eminence in this role gave way to Harold Cheevers (1893-1971), a policeman who became, and remained until Walpole's death, his chauffeur-secretary-companion.

shock people he likes. Told me how he had had a father & son simultaneously. Copulation removes barriers. Class barriers fade. Lives at Hampstead with Harold's family & friends completely naturally. All this is a great deal better than his literary talk. It led me to compare experience with thought. Apostles with phenomenons. He's been at Rome writing daily articles for Hearst papers. We couldn't do this.[21] Started making 2 or 3000 a year in 1912. Has supported Melchior & others. Saw, at any rate, another Hugh. Odd that he's never felt any feeling for women; but his sister is a suppressed Lesbian; & his brother entirely without sex—a schoolmaster. This lasted from 4.30 to 7.30; without a break. And I liked him & enjoyed it, tho' crushed in the head.

I went to Highgate in the morning; saw the Whittington Stone,[22] & met 2 old women on Parliament Hill: each wore a cap of Turkish embroidery on her white straggly hair: very poor unkempt; big boots; black wrinkled stockings & a dog. One said Now if you dont come Peter I shall run away . . . they were hobbling. Curious vision of their extreme poverty, decrepitude, & the place played in their lives by Peter. How they fed him; & were identical—. . Still brain compressed: Memoir tonight. Molly's operation over, apparently successful. Desmond with a bad cold; Clive to read. So thats all, & I'm fiddling again with Roger.

Friday 31 March

Yes I made a phrase last night about bearing the panoply of life, & being glad to lay it down.[23] I wonder if its true. After a worried domestic day; then L. had a temperature & went to bed; the Memoir Club was imminent. I felt I was bearing up the panoply of life & wd be glad to let it sink. I said to myself, Remember, this is the description of age coming. I'm on the qui vive to describe age: to note it. I often think of things in this way, but forget them. And as L. is normal & up & as its a fine morning, I'm not conscious of holding up my panoply, only distracted rather & cant settle in but must do R.'s Cambridge letters.

Clive read, truculently, with some motive I guess at the back of him,

21. In Apostolic parlance, the world outside the Society, the world of appearances, is 'phenomenal' and those belonging to it 'phenomena'; only the Society is 'real'. Commissioned by the Hearst Press, Walpole had been in Rome for a month to cover the funeral of Pope Pius XI and the election and coronation on 12 March of his successor Pius XII.

22. The stone, erected in 1821 on Highgate Hill, marks the approximate spot where Dick Whittington (and his cat) rested and, hearing Bow bells, turned again.

23. VW uses this phrase some weeks later in writing of her mother (see *Moments of Being*, p. 83): 'She was keeping what I call in my shorthand the panoply of life . . . in being.'

about R., amusing stories—"The old creature was lying on a camp bed reading with a candle beside him" this is the only touch I need to remember, at Charleston, at 1.30 in the morning. Said R. grew less magnanimous with age: reference to the NS. review, I expect. Nessa silent, disagreeing.[24] Desmond did not come. Rang up. A rather scattered meeting.

The Woolfs were at Monks House from 6-24 April; they had tea at Charleston on Easter Sunday (9 April) and at Tilton the following day.

Tuesday 11 April

How much identity, to use my own private slang, is needed to surmount a little hillock: for instance, Lydia on Lappin & Lapinova yesterday at Tilton; & Tilton's comfort, & quiet; all seem to make it harder for me to get on with revising Roger. Revising Roger at the rate of 2 weeks to a chapter will take me 3 months. Then there's the war. The finest Easter possible has this purple background. We wait like obedient children to hear what we shall be told when Parliament meets on Thursday. At Tilton we talked first medicine; Maynard's drastic cure by Plesch; then politics; five minutes left for Tom's play. Every day, save 2, something's turned up. Private peace is not accessible. Miss Robins tomorrow. Then Charleston. Then L.P. here. Maynard, even Maynard, cant find much that's hopeful now that Italy has nipped off Albania save that theres a unity of hatred. The men women children dogs &c. are solid for war if war comes.[1] But privately—how one rockets between private & public—his eyes are bluer, his skin pinker, & he can walk without pain. Lydia has devoted herself to the treatment. They think Nessa suppresses Clive—wont have things out. Never will have anything out. But the[n] L[ydia]. is always on husbands side—a

24. Fry grumbled at times that Bell cribbed his ideas: specifically, the latter's article 'Dr Freud on Art' in the *Nation & Athenaeum* of 6 September 1924 he felt (justifiably) had been 'bagged' from a lecture he gave to the British Psychological Society on *The Artist and Psycho-Analysis* (later published in November 1924 as a 'Hogarth Essay', *HP Checklist* 45).

1. Alive at last to the dangers of Hitler's military and territorial ambitions in Eastern Europe, a disillusioned Mr Chamberlain announced on 31 March that Britain and France would guarantee support to Poland should her independence be threatened (which it was); when Parliament reassembled on 13 April—after the invasion and annexation of Albania by Mussolini's troops on Good Friday (7 April)—this guarantee was extended to Greece and Roumania. The Hungarian-born Dr János Plesch (1879-1957) gave up his practice in Germany when the Nazis came to power, and settled in England; he had treated Keynes since 1937 and became a friend as well as his doctor.

serf like spirit, natural in the circumstances. My allegiance is to N. & D. as usual: but I like all my friends—though not the taste of Tilton.

Roasting hot: birds a chirp: butterflies.

I am reading Dickens; by way of a refresher. How he lives; not writes: both a virtue & a fault. Like seeing something emerge; without containing mind. Yet the accuracy & even sometimes the penetration—into Miss Squeers & Miss Price & the farmer [in *Nicholas Nickleby*] for example—remarkable. I cant dip my critical mind, even if I try to. Then I'm reading Sevigné, professionally for that quick amalgamation of books that I intend. In future, I'm to write quick, intense, short books, & never be tied down. This is the way to keep off the settling down & refrigeration of old age. And to flout all preconceived theories—For more & more I doubt if enough is known to sketch even probable lines, all too emphatic & conventional.

Maurice, the last of the Ll. Davies brothers is dead; & Margaret lives—lives too carefully of life, I used to feel. Why drag on, always measuring & testing one's little bit of strength & setting it easy tasks so as to accumulate years?[2]

Also I'm reading Rochefoucauld. Thats the real point of my little Brown book—that it makes me read—with a pen—following the scent: & read the good books; not the slither of MSS & the stridency of the young chawking—the word expresses callow bills agape & chattering—for sympathy. Chaucer I take at need. So if I had any time—but perhaps next week will be more solitudinous—I should, if it weren't for the war—glide my way up & up in to that exciting layer so rarely lived in: where my mind works so quick it seems asleep; like the aeroplane propellers. But I must retype the last Clifton passage; & so be quit for tomorrow & clear the decks for Cambridge. Rather good, I expect it is: condensed & moulded.

Thursday 13 April

Two days of influenza after that, mild but sucking one's head as usual, so I'm out here this morning only to drone my way through a few Roger letters.

I finished my first 40 pages—childhood &c—well under the week; but then they were largely autobiography. Now politics impend. Cham[berlai]n's statement in the House today. War I suppose not tomorrow, but nearer. Charleston to tea today. L. went to Brighton yesterday, & had a long talk with Miss Robins in bed, which was interesting, so I'm sorry I missed it, yet glad of solitude, such as it is here. If I could only embed myself for 10 days . . . I read about 100 pages

2. Margaret Llewelyn Davies, now seventy-eight, had six brothers; Maurice (1865-1939) was the third.

of Dickens yesterday, & see something vague about the drama & fiction: how the emphasis, the caricature of these innumerable scenes, forever forming character, descend from the stage. Literature—that is the shading, suggesting, as of Henry James, hardly used. All bold & coloured. Rather monotonous, yet so abundant, so creative: yes: but not *highly* creative: not suggestive. Everything laid on the table. Nothing to engender in solitude. Thats why its so rapid & attractive: nothing to make one put the book down & think. But these are influenza musings; & I'm so muddled I shall take Sir Edward [Fry's letters] into the house & extract him over the fire. Weather now blackening a little, after 4 days full summer heat—over 70. A Comma butterfly, sunning on the wall. L.'s rash improving. We live on macaroni.

Note: Lydia's hostility to all married women.

Saturday 15 April

Its odd what extreme depression a little influenza & a cold in head produces. Happily I'm interested in depression; & make myself play a game of assembling the fractured pieces—I mean I light a fire, & somehow dandle myself over it. Cooking is helpful. Oh but I was very down & dismal yesterday. And then noises & houses abuilding oppress: & there's always our dear old war—now postponed for a month. Sneezing & blowing is better than incubating germs.

I've done rather well at Roger considering: I dont think I shall take 2 weeks over each chapter. And its rather amusing—dealing drastically with this years drudgery. I think I see how it shapes: & my compiling method was a good one. Perhaps its too like a novel. I dont bother. No letters; no news; & my head too stupid for reading. L. galloping through his book [*Barbarians at the Gate*]. I should like a holiday—a few days in France—or a run through the Cotswolds.

But considering how many things I have that I like—whats odd— (I'm always beginning like this) is the severance that war seems to bring: everything becomes meaningless: cant plan: then there comes too the community feeling: all England thinking the same thing—this horror of war—at the same moment. Never felt it so strong before. Then the lull & one lapses again into private separation—

But I must order macaroni from London.

Wednesday 26 April

[*52 Tavistock Square*]

I've done a $\frac{1}{4}$—100 pages of Roger—well I shall have by tomorrow. As there are 400 pages, & one hundred takes 3 weeks (oh but I was interrupted)—it will take 9 weeks to finish. Yes, I ought to have finished it by the end of July—only we may go away. Say August. And have it all typed in September. . . . Well—then it will be out this time next year. And I shall be free in August—What a grind it is; & I suppose of little interest except to six or seven people. And I shall be abused.

Friday 28 April

Very much screwed in the brain by trying to get Roger's marriage chapter into shape; & also warmed by L. saying last night that he was fonder of me than I of him. A discussion as to which would mind the other's death most. He said he depended more upon our common life than I did. He gave the garden as an instance. He said I lived more in a world of my own. I go for long walks alone. So we argued. I was very happy to think I was so much needed. Its strange how seldom one feels this: yet 'life in common' is an immense reality. For instance, I cant go to The Wreckers tonight with Ethel Smyth because: 1. I have a little temperature: 2: (& more serious) I'd rather stay at home with L. Its no use fighting against this. Its one of the facts.[3]

Oh such a dismal tea with Mrs W. yesterday. She is completely lifeless—like an old weed on a rock. And always recurring to the complaints. That was how, by the way, we came to discuss our deaths. L. said he hoped he would predecease me. Her lonely old age is so intolerable. But its lonely, he said, because she has adopted an unreal attitude. Lived in a sentim[ent]al make believe. Sees herself as the adored matriarch, & forces the children to adopt her attitude. Hence the unreality of all relations. This obsession of hers has also shut her off from all other interests: doesn't care for any impersonal thing—art, music, books. Wont have a companion or reader; must depend on her sons. Constant innuendoes therefore about the goodness of Herbert & Harold; inference that L. neglects her; hints that I have taken him away from his family; absorbed him in mine. So in that crowded pink hot room we sat for 2 hours trying to beat up subjects for conversation. And there were awful silences, & our heads filled with wool; & all was dusty, dreary, old, & hopeless. Yet she followed us out on to the stair & made L. swear that she looks better—"Sure Len? Sure I look better?" as if she still clings hard to life & cant be removed. So to walk in the hail in Ken. Gardens; & see the cherry trees livid & lurid in the yellow storm haze. Very cold winter spring.

Saturday 29 April

But what are the interesting things? I'm thinking of what I should like to read here in 10 years time. And I'm all at sea. Perhaps literal facts. The

3. Ethel Smyth's opera *The Wreckers* was given its last performance of the season at Sadler's Wells this evening.

annal, not the novel. Yesterday I went out in a fur coat, for it was bitter cold, to walk in London. I stopped by the Savoy Church: there were photographers. Soon the Bride arrived. The car glided on[;] there were too many cars behind. Mother & small page arrived: 2 girls in absurd little boat hats. They helped the Bride with her veil. "Can you get it over my bouquet?" she asked—very gay; rather red; very slim. Husband & best man waiting in grey trousers & cutaway coats. Old sitters in the sun watching. Camera men. A little procession—rather skimpy & cold & not very rich I thought. The old man—my age—had shabby boots. Shaven, brushed, red, thin. They are Mr Sholto Douglas Barnes, & Miss Marjorie Berkeley, daughter of a deceased ICS Colonel—so I learn today.[4] Then I walked along the Embankment, up into the fur quarter behind Blackfriars. Men in white coats aparelled in silver fur skins. A smell of fur. Found some old City Company houses. One the Inn Keepers Company.[5] Also a green plant bursting out of a factory. Also one of the usual 18th Century mansions tucked away. So into Cannon St. Bought a paper with Hitler's speech. Read it on top of Bus. Inconclusive—cut up in Stop Press. Everyone reading it—even newspaper sellers, a great proof of interest.[6] So to Kingsway. Bought some folders. Failed to buy a guide to Cotswolds. L. had 4 gents to discuss Sir John Maynard's memo.[7] Read Chaucer. Enjoyed it. Was warm & happy not to go to Sadlers Wells. Nessa rang up. Bed.

Monday 1 May

A bad morning, because I'm dried up about Roger. I'm determined tho' to plod through & make a good job, not a work of art. Thats the only way. To force myself on—& yes to relax with a [*indecipherable*] fiction: & then a few days in the Cotswolds. But there's no blinking the fact that it is drudgery & must be; & I must go through with it. My hand, as I see, wont write.

Sunday 14 May

That last sentence might be repeated. Its a fortnight I see since I had my few minutes margin between Roger & lunch. And thus I need not

4. This society wedding, reported in *The Times* of 29 April, took place in the Savoy Chapel, off the Strand.
5. VW walked from Blackfriars Bridge by way of Upper Thames Street towards Cannon Street; Innholders Hall is in College Street.
6. In his Reichstag speech on 28 April, Hitler denounced the Anglo-German Naval Agreement signed in 1935; the German-Polish Non-Agression Pact of 1934; and demanded the return to the *Reich* of the Free City of Danzig.
7. Sir John Maynard (1865-1943) was the chairman of the Labour Party Advisory Committee on Imperial Affairs, of which LW had been secretary for over twenty years.

repeat the fact that my head is a tight wound ball of string. To unwind it, I lie on my Heal chair bed & doze of an evening. But the noise worries me. The 2 houses next door are down; we are shored up. There are patches of wall paper where there used to be hotel bedrooms. Thus the Southampton Row traffic gets at me; & I long for 37 Mecklenburgh Sq: but doubt if we shall get it. Pritchard is negotiating with the Bedfords.[1] A talk about the future with John. He is harassed by the lean year. Cant live in London on £500 minus his mothers interest &c. 37 is a large seeming & oh so quiet house, where I could sleep anywhere. But it dont do to dwell on it. & there would be the horror of the move in August.

Day Lewis came one day; thrust in on the wake of Elizabeth. A stocky sturdy man. truculent. a little like Muggins 40 yrs ago, as I think George called Malcolm Macnaghten. "Priestley lolling on the beach" was discussed.[2] I made him laugh by repeating that word. I wish I could repeat more words. Boswell did it. Could I turn B. at my age? "I'm doing films for the gas people . . . I live a purely country life. A rather too arty home. Devonshire." I infer some rupture with the Bugger Boys.

should it be lõl ling or lolling?

Boswell at Sissinghurst. Gwen walking through the Bluebell woods, speaking of her youth—a little to justify herself. Had been advertiser to a scent shop. had done welfare work. Her daughter Jiccy meets a prostitute outside the Berkeley whom she has deliv[er]ed. "Must just speak to Bessy" she says to the youth who's treating her—"Its her beat." G. a little shocked.[3] And I liked the soft cream & yellow flowers on the sunny grass & the bend stooping like a picture. And the thread of bright blue bells: & Vita in her breeches.

We are going to Brittany by the way after Whitsun. A whole 2 weeks rambling. Now that'll fill my dry cistern of a head. But this is nothing

1. Although the Woolfs' lease of 52 Tavistock Square ran until 1941, the din and disturbance caused by the adjacent demolitions compelled them to move. On 9 May they saw over and resolved upon 37 Mecklenburgh Square, and their solicitor-tenant Mr Pritchard—who agreed to move with them—attempted (unsuccessfully in the event) to persuade their landlords, the Duke of Bedford Estates, to accept the early surrender of their current lease.

2. Elizabeth Bowen came to tea with VW on 3 May; they were joined by the poet Cecil Day Lewis (1904-72), who was currently writing the script for a projected documentary film on colliers for the British Commercial Gas Association. The High Court judge Sir Malcolm MacNaghten (1869-1955) had been at Eton and Cambridge with George Duckworth. The Woolfs saw J. B. Priestley's play *Johnson Over Jordan* at the Saville Theatre on 4 May.

3. The Woolfs had gone to Sissinghurst on 8 May *en route* from Rodmell to London. Gwen St Aubyn's daughter Jessica (b. 1918) is (1983) mystified by this story.

like so bad as The Years. A nun writes to invite me to stage a meeting of Outsiders in Hyde Park. I stop to answer her. Gertler tonight.[4]

Thursday 25 May

A queer little note to run off in a hurry: L. is bargaining for 37 M. Sq upstairs: I'm packing. We're off: & very likely I shant write much more in this now so tidy studio. Tidied for Ben to work in. I must pack upstairs. Brittany & Rodmell for 3 weeks.

Party last night. G. Keyneses: Eth Wn & her underworld friend. Ben Nicolson.[5]

Interrupted by parties come to see the house. The first day its in the agents hands. Shall we end our lives looking in that great peaceful garden; in the sun? I hope so.

On the afternoon of 25 May the Woolfs drove to Rodmell for Whitsuntide, and on 5 June crossed the Channel to Dieppe for a motor tour of Normandy and Brittany. They visited Les Rochers, *Mme de Sévigné's château near Vitré, and continued to Vannes and round the Brittany peninsula to Dinan and Bayeux. (Their itinerary is briefly recorded by LW (Diary, LWP, Sussex); the notebook to which VW refers does not survive). They returned to Monks House on 19 June and to Tavistock Square on Thursday 22 June.*

Friday 23 June

Back to London again after 4 weeks. Two spent driving about Brittany. I kept notes in a little square ruled pocketbook in my bag; a good method perhaps, if carried out in London; but I doubt if its worth sticking them here. Perhaps a few, for like pressed leaves they somehow bring back the whole forgotten hedge. So soon forgotten in bulk. The London uproar at once rushes in. Okampo today; John; then I must go to Penman. We have 37 M[ecklenburgh] S[quare]: & this is still unlet.[6]

4. For the nun's letter, see MHP, Sussex, LVP (Books). VW had asked Gertler to dine as she 'was anxious to get your account of the way [Roger Fry] struck younger painters.' (*VI VW Letters*, no. 3501.) See also *Moments of Being*, p. 85: 'May 15th 1939. . . . Last night Mark Gertler dined here and denounced the vulgarity, the inferiority of what he called "literature"; compared with the integrity of painting.'

5. The Woolfs' dinner guests were Maynard Keynes's younger brother the surgeon and bibliophile Geoffrey Langdon Keynes (1887-1982) and his wife Margaret, *née* Darwin. Elizabeth Williamson, her friend Leonie Leontineff (?), and Benedict Nicolson—to whom VW was to lend her 'studio' while she was away—came in afterwards.

6. Victoria Ocampo (1880-1979), the wealthy Argentine founder and publisher of the literary review *Sur*, was an extravagant admirer of VW, whom she met in 1934 (see

JUNE 1939

Ben Nicolson has spread my studio with MSS all laid on the floor. This
scarcely helps my attack on R[oger Fry]. begun this morning. The
appallingly difficult PIP [Post-Impressionist] chapter. How to get the
right proportions &c. I have now 5 weeks before August. And 200 pages
to do. Difficulties with Gollancz about L.'s book not yet stated.[7] And
people abound. But I must do my job like a navvy & let society rip &
clothes &c. Here's lunch.

Saturday 24 June

Yes, London broke in fairly vigorously yesterday. Ocampo bringing
Giselle Freund & all her apparatus, which was set up in the drawing
room, & all the lit. gents & ladies shown on a sheet. On top of them
house seers—an old lady who was born at 52, & whose father had built
this studio. And the upshot is, a sitting—oh curse this petty vulgar
photography-advertising stunt—at 3. No getting out of it, with Okampo
on the sofa, & Freund there in the flesh. So my afternoon is gone in the
way to me most detestable & upsetting of all. A life sized life coloured
animated photograph—however L. is drawn in.[8] Also, on top of this,
sheets of evasion & dishonesty from Gollancz; & John; & Nessa about
Angelica. She is in a nursing home with an infected kidney. All the old
anxieties rampant—for Nessa again. And old Mrs W. this afternoon.
And Tom & a friend—& Sarton. I suppose there's stir in it; & stimulus;
but I'm bothered about the PIPs—cant get into the right mood; & its
so laboured, & I cant, without a mood, toss it & lighten it: yet must
somehow drive thro' to the end.

Now to prepare for photography. Such are one's friends—& their
deformities.

IV VW Diary, 26 November 1934) and sought out on her subsequent visits to
Europe. Penman & Co of Guilford Street were the agents for 37 Mecklenburgh
Square, for which the Woolfs had obtained a 9½-year lease; they were trying to find
a tenant to take over the unexpired portion of their lease of 52 Tavistock Square (see
above, 14 May 1939, n. 1).

7. Victor Gollancz had invited LW to write a book for the Left Book Club (see above,
30 October 1938); now he wrote to say that, having read the manuscript, he and his
fellow-editors felt misgivings about *Barbarians at the Gate*, and proposed delaying
its publication: see correspondence in LWP, Sussex, I L3, and *V LW*, pp.
11-13.

8. Gisèle Freund (b. 1913), a young Parisian photographer championed by Victoria
Ocampo, specialised in portrait-photographs of writers and artists. VW had already
rebuffed her request for a sitting, and was incensed that Ocampo should appear to
act as a Trojan horse for her protégée's benefit. (Nonetheless, posterity can be
grateful for the results of this *ruse de guerre*—or treachery.)

Monday 26 June[9]

Talk at Nessa's last night. Much about Gertler's suicide. He gassed himself 2 nights ago in his studio. We had talked with him about his other attempt the night he dined with us. It was because of some hitch in his work he said then, & he had completely recovered. He had got through into a new stage as a painter. This was true, Nessa & Duncan said; his last show, just over, was a great advance & very remarkable. So why did he turn on the gas, when his model left him? She found him, when [she] came back, still alive, but unconscious. A most resolute serious man: intellectual; fanatical about painting, even if a fanatical egotist. And he seemed established; with his own friends; dining out with Priestleys & Lynds. Poor of course, & forced to teach; & fundamentally perhaps too rigid, too self centred, too honest & narrow, like Kot in his uncompromising severity, to be content or happy. But with his intellect & interest, why did the personal life become too painful? His wife? We know no more.[10]

Angelica better; & no time to describe our lunch with Flora, & her analysis, clear & unflinching, of the old tyrant, the matriarch manqueé.[11]

Tuesday 27 June[12]

Talk of Gertler at Clive's. Old Cory rather deflated (in spirit, not body). Frothy talk, succeeding 2½ hours interview with Philip [Woolf] & his milky eyed little boy who wants to be a sailor. But doesnt want it very much. No, they dont want anything, said Phil, who doesnt want to go to Brittany, about which he consulted us.

Eliot & Morley today. So the days are rushed through.[13]

Gollancz prevaricating.

9. VW has misdated this entry *June 25th*: she and LW went to Vanessa's studio after dinner that (Sunday) evening.

10. An intermixture of persistent ill-health and money problems, the disintegration of his marriage, the menace of another war, and loss of faith in his own creative powers, induced Mark Gertler to end his life on 23 June; he was forty-seven. (See *Mark Gertler* by John Woodeson, 1972.) He had dined with the Woolfs on 14 May.

11. LW's sister Flora (1886-1975) was the seventh of old Mrs Woolf's nine children; she married George Sturgeon in 1918, and had one child, Molly Bella.

12. VW has mistakenly dated this entry *June 26th*: that evening the Woolfs dined with Clive Bell and his elder brother Lt.-Col. (retired) Cory Bell (1875-1964), one-time Tory MP.

13. Eliot's friend Frank V. Morley (1898-1980), like him an Oxford-educated American expatriate, was a fellow-director of the publishing house Faber & Faber.

JUNE 1939

Wednesday 28 June

Vita came to a late lunch; Mrs Woolf fell down & broke 2 ribs; Tom brought Mr Morley to tea. . . These are the elements upon which yesterday was founded. [*illegible*] with Vita. Home. Change. Talk. Telephone. L. to the nursing home after dinner. She will not die, so I assume. There is a terrible passive resistance to death in these old women. They have the immortality of the vampire. Poor Flora will be sucked drop by drop for years to come. This is I suppose a cruel remark to make. But honestly, everyone would be relieved if she could make an end of it. Its so exhausting, & as Flora said, she has contrived to falsify all emotions, till the end is the only thing the family who are forced to be so devoted by her fantasy honestly wish for. And now John to lunch. After wh. can I escape to buy some shoes, & ought I to buy shoes with the flat still to let? I've said I'll write an article on Royalty for PP. for £25 by way of a sop to our income & our liabilities.[14]

Thursday 29 June

The grind of doing Roger & PIP makes my head spin, & I let it reel itself off for 10 minutes here. I wonder why; & if I shall ever read this again. Perhaps if I go on with my memoirs, also a relief from R., I shall make use of it.[15]

A dismal day yesterday; shoe hunting in that Hall of humbug, Fortnums. A Sale; but only of the unsaleable. And the atmosphere, British upper classes: all tight & red nailed; myself a figure of fun—whips my skin: I fidget: but recoup myself walking in the rain through the Parks. Come home & try to concentrate on Pascal—I cant; still, its the only way of tuning up, & I get a calm if not understanding. These pin points of theology need a grasp beyond me. Still I see Lytton's point—my dear old serpent.[16] What a dream life is to be sure—that he should be dead, & I reading him; & trying to make out that we indented ourselves on the world; whereas I sometimes feel its been an illusion—

---

14. VW's article 'Royalty', commissioned but not published by the illustrated weekly *Picture Post*, is one of two with this title included in the posthumous collection *The Moment* (Kp A29); the other is a review written in 1934 (Kp C345).

15. On 18 April 1939, at Rodmell, VW began writing what she called 'a sketch' for her memoirs, a theme to which she returned intermittently during the following nineteen months: see 'A Sketch of the Past' in *Moments of Being*.

16. See Lytton Strachey, *Landmarks in French Literature* (1912): 'In sheer genius Pascal ranks among the very greatest writers who have lived upon this earth.' 'In the *Lettres Provinciales* Pascal created French prose . . . their actual subject matter—the ethical system of the Jesuits of the time—is remote from modern interests; yet such is the brilliance of Pascal's art that every page of them is fascinating today.'

gone so fast, lived so quickly; & nothing to show for it, save these little books. But that makes me dig my feet in, & squeeze the moment. So after dinner I walked to the Clinic with L.: waited outside with Sally tugging; watched the evening sight: oh & the purple grey clouds above Regents Park with the violet & yellow sky signs made me leap with pleasure.[17]

Noise here very great. Even if we lose our rent, no doubt its worth it—37 will be heavenly quiet. The letter war with Gollancz continues—more time frittered, wasted. L. very calm; & how sane, compared with me.

Monday 3 July

L.'s mother died last night. And its been jading & somehow very depressing—watching her die. She gradually ceased to breathe. There were 3 days though of going there—sitting in the alcove in that long corridor. Flora sat with her. Sometimes she talked. L. found her cheerful one night. Virginia must write a book called "The fallen woman." I remember that; out of a litter of odds & ends, because it was the last time she spoke of me. It was like watching an animal die, L. said. Rau burst into tears. She wanted to live, asked the matron if she had known an old woman recover, asked Rau. Both of course said Yes. Last night, as Flora, Edgar & Harold were dining here off cold chicken, Herbert rang up to say it was critical; & she had just died when they got there. Her breathing, as Rau said it would, stopped. And then they decided that her wish—to be taken to a private home, not left in the mortuary, must be gratified: so the body is taken to Laleham [*Harold Woolf's home*] today: then will go to the Jewish Cemetery. A watcher came from the Synagogue. It was a bright, showery day. We walked in Regents Park, after giving Kingsley Martin lunch. I always notice the weather in which people die, as if the soul would notice if its wet or windy. Then, when L. had come back, we went round to Clive's: found Nessa interviewing Lottie; & talked about doctors & skin diseases with Clive & Duncan.[1]

But I cannot do my Royalty article, & have a regret for that spirited old lady, whom it was such a bore to visit. Still she was somebody: sitting on her high backed chair with the pink cushion, all the flowers round her, a cigar always for Leonard, & plates of cakes which she pressed us to eat. Last time—Saturday week—she was peevish & querulous. It was about not seeing Herbert as usual. Children no longer

17. After her fall, Mrs Woolf was taken to the London Clinic, the large private nursing home facing Marylebone Road.
1. Lottie Hope, who had been the Woolfs' housemaid when they lived at Richmond, later became Clive Bell's cook at 50 Gordon Square; he was now giving up his rooms there, and Lottie was to go as cook to Charleston.

respected their parents. And she got up & fell back. But these feelings are mixed, scrappy, & I'm in the scraped state when writing, dont work.

Thursday 6 July

"Lady" to call her by the name she liked to explain—she always talked about the past best—was buried yesterday; & there was a service in the Synagogue. Women admitted, so I went. But its a compromise; & had nothing whatever to do with "Lady".[2] What was she like then? Let me see— She was small, narrow shouldered—things slipped off— she wore a low blouse with a pearl necklace—& rather heavy. Her head nodded. She had stiff curled grey black hair. She would say as we came in "And Virginia?" My joke was, Conceal your disappointment at sight of me. Then she would laugh, kiss me, & give me a little pat. We were on friendly laughing terms, always at the same stock joke, which carried us through those 2 hour teas. "And tell me what you have been doing?" I would have some story ready. She liked hearing about Ann & Judith: not much interested in any other relations of mine. For many years we never reached even this intimacy. I think she suspected me of not being family. She came over to see us of course. And how often we drove to Worthing! It was trumped up mostly. Yet there was something spontaneous about her. A great joy in family; in society; she could make friends out of anyone: was very popular with elderly gentlemen. One at Worthing stood her dinners, took her to the theatre. She liked telling the story of plays. She would tell the whole plot of Gone with the Wind for example; talking as if they were real: a trait odd to me in so shrewd a woman; for she had as she was often boasting, brought up 9 children. Never went to bed, she said, without a basket of socks by her side. All was personal. And the ruts of course became deeper; one knew what would come next. Sometimes tho' she made me feel the daughter emotion—when I kissed her when Clara died.[3] She attaches to nothing in my own life: except the comment she made; that she was the 'elder generation': & I (now the elder, to most people) was the younger. I never saw her save in her own surroundings. These were fussy, yes, but full of stir: always presents of flowers: children's letters: What news of Bella & Tom? Where is Phil going for his holiday? She was the centre of that net work & until Edgar & Flora disabused me, I thought they depended on it. Perhaps, when the freedom is over, they will miss it. "Bel"—the day of whose retirement in March—poor old lady—was the "day I count the days to it . . ." so she said last Saturday week—Bel cabled a silly effusion wh. makes their

2. The funeral of Mrs Sidney Woolf, LW's mother, took place at Balls Pond Road Cemetery on the morning of 5 July; the memorial service was at the West London Synagogue, Upper Berkeley Street, at 5 pm that day.
3. See *IV VW Diary*, 6 January 1934; Clara was the sixth of Mrs Woolf's children.

relation look artificial. The truth was, age had taken everything away that was real, I think: only age left the pathetic animal, which was very real; the body that wanted to live. I know nothing of any interest about her, now that I come to write, only little anecdotes, about Holland: nothing that makes her a real person—save Is Virginia coming? which touches me.

Tuesday 11 July

Interrupted by a man to look over the Studio. Would take the place at once, if he could have it for 6 years. Thats the end of all these visits. Back from MH. & cross—to use the nurses word. Cross at my waste of time over PIPs, doubtful about the book—angry at the immense drudgery. Still I must get on. Q. for the weekend—oh that we could ever be wholly alone: & yet I dont want to be wholly alone. The usual fight between solitude & society, scarcely worth noting, let alone dissecting. Very fine July weather. And is Charles [Mauron] blind? And am I to buy a new dress? And what about— I think the true proportions are better in the country. Over all hangs war of course. A kind of perceptible but anonymous friction. Dantzig. The Poles vibrating in my room. Everything uncertain. We have got into the habit however. Work, work, I tell myself.[4]

Wednesday 12 July

For the first time for weeks, after being so damnably down in the mouth yesterday, I've worked with some pleasure at R. The new Omega chapter. I might still pull it through. Yet how dumpish we were—starting off to the Movies, after dinner—L. asking me what I wanted to see, I not wanting to see anything—the crowds of deformed & stunted & vicious & sweating & ugly hooligans & harridans in the Tott. Ct. Road—the sticky heat—all this brooded, till I was saying, step out, on, on, in my usual desperate way. Then instead we went to Nessa's. A[ngelica]. in bed. Clive there: Duncan bubbling. I read Philip's letter about L.'s Latin epitaph & we had a good laugh & gossip. P. has denounced Duncan's portrait. I think a fine one. Wants a jolly girl; instead of this black frump. Mrs Gertler had been round to Pip at midnight with her guitar. P. looked out of the window & refused it. This is in the old B[loomsbur]y manner. P. in his nightcap, vagrant & vagulous.

---

4. Since 1933 the government of the Free City of Danzig, the majority of whose citizens were German, had been Nazi-dominated; in July 1939, ostensibly as a defensive measure but in reality in furtherance of Hitler's intention to re-incorporate Danzig in the *Reich* and conquer Poland, the city was militarized.

Duncan pobbling his words.[5] Couldn't remember Lady David Cecil, who has been arrested—no threatened. Burbling on about a book by a clergyman bought in Berwick Church. V. very silent, worried I suppose: yet 'cheerful' too. She will laugh & take part, even if she sinks again. Queer horror of seeing her exert herself. Perhaps I exaggerate. Julian in the background. Oh dear—why waste all that? But a jovial sunny evening that rolled off my glooms effectively; perhaps L.'s. Its not a nice season in London. To 37 this afternoon.

Now my mind is running on R. a good sign. at p. 230, so that's more than half.

Thursday 13 July

A bad morning. All fiddling again. Because I woke worried—about what? L.'s gloom: not lifting this; I dont know what; & lit up & read MacColl & started the machine running. And so am numb headed.[6] What a head to work with—never again a long book. And no walk. 2 hours at M[ecklenburgh]S[quare]. planning, electric light kitchen &c. The practical difficulty appals—all our books carpets furniture & L. gloomy. This is all surface gloom though. A grim thought struck me: wh. of these rooms shall I die in? Which is going to be the scene of some—oh no, I wont write out the tragedy that has to be acted there. A free man thinks of nothing &c.[7] So I read Pascal & Pater & wrote letters & cooked dinner & did my embroidery. But couldnt sleep sound.

Tuesday 25 July

On this page I should sum up reflections on leaving 52 Tavistock Square. But—
Interruption. This must wait till M.H.

In the ten days before leaving London on 25 July for their summer sojourn at Rodmell, VW had a very busy and social time, seeing a great number of

5. Philip Morrell had appealed for suggestions for an epitaph for his wife's gravestone. Grant's portrait of Lady Ottoline, painted *ca.* 1913 and now in a private collection, is reproduced in the Catalogue of *Duncan Grant and his World*, Wildenstein, London, 1964. The Morrells had been generous supporters of Mark Gertler; his widow probably wished to maintain the connection by giving (or selling) a still life painting to Philip Morrell.

6. In his *Confessions of a Keeper and Other Papers* (1931) D. S. MacColl (1859-1948) reprinted three articles relating to Roger Fry: 'A Year of Post-Impressionism' (1912); 'Drawing, New and Old' (1919); and 'Cézanne as a Deity' (1928).

7. 'A free man thinks of death least of all things; and his wisdom is a meditation not of death but of life.'—with these words of Spinoza, which were read at his Cremation on 13 September 1934, VW ends her biography of Roger Fry.

people both at home and abroad: May Sarton, Dorothy Bussy, E. Sackville-West separately to tea; Margery Fry and others to dinner; a party at Benedict Nicolson's; dinners with Vanessa and with Helen Anrep; expeditions to Osterley and to Herbert Woolf's at Cookham Dean—all against a background of preparations for moving to Mecklenburgh Square. At Monks House, on LW's instructions, foundations for a greenhouse were being laid.

Friday 28 July

The use of this book is to write things out, hence: the Greenhouse. I'm so unhappy. A portmanteau word. Analysed: headache; guilt; remorse . . . The house, L.'s house, . . . oh dear, his hobby—his ⟨pear tree⟩ peach tree—to be pulled down because of me. How can I get sensible? I mind so much. Oh dear—the conflict—the ugliness: v: L.'s wish. And is it worth this misery?—oughtn't I to have said go ahead, when he came to me in the Bath this morning? The men had come—Shd. they put it up? I said you must decide. So he sent them away & its to be pulled down. How to live it over? Forget he says: but I shant . . . & cant read or write—. . .

I have composed myself, momentarily, by reading through this years diary. Thats a use for it then. It composes. Why? I think shows one a stretch, when one's grubbing in an inch. Head relieved anyhow by reading. Odd that I can read here without repulsion. Why? My own mind I suppose claws me when others slip.

I forget that we came down; & its been fine, rather; lovely on the marsh. Hay cutting. Figures spaced on the marsh. Old Bob thanks me for my letter. Much hurt by Stephen's review. A letter from Susie Tweedsmuir—deadly dull at Quebec. Reading Gide's diaries, recommended by poor death mask Eddie [Sackville-West]. An interesting knotted book. Its queer that diaries now pullulate. No one can settle to a work of art. Comment only. That explains but scarcely excuses Peter Lucas; & his exhibition of Prudence.[8] Shd. one judge people by what they write? Shd. people show their naked skins? Eddie shows his death mask—Dear, I forgot my shudder at Helen's son [omission]; nor can dissect my mix up of the debt, the dislike of Igor's great fleshy mouth. (I'm whistling to keep up my spirits this very strained grey day—the

---

8. VW had written to R. C. Trevelyan (*VI VW Letters*, no. 3538) to thank him for his *Collected Works, Volume I: Poems* (1939) which had been disparagingly reviewed by Stephen Spender in the *NS&N* of 22 July 1939. Lady Tweedsmuir's letter of 14 July from The Citadel, the Governor-General's Quebec residence, is in MHP, Sussex. *André Gide's Journal 1885-1939* (1939). With the title *Journal under the Terror*, F. L. Lucas in 1938 published what he called 'the unedited truth of . . . day-to-day impressions of a year [1937] in modern Europe.' From November onwards it contains references to his wife Prudence's nervous breakdown.

Greenhouse morning.) I must now carry off lunch. What annoys me is
L.'s adroitness in fathering the guilt on me. His highhandedness. I see
the temptation. "Oh you dont want it—so I submit." This spoilt bowls
last night. We shied them at the Jack. Yet so happy in our reconciliation.
"Do you ever think me beautiful now?" "The most beautiful of women"—

Sunday 30 July

The great affair of the GH. has been settled; amicably: a cold house
at the back. So its over; what a waste of emotion. Is it that I lack will?
For now Nessa bothers me about mantelpieces. Human voices wake us
& we drown.[9] Never been so free & happy; but human voices do wake
one. Its fine; & our day's varied with what we enjoy. Such an expansion
after the London pressure. I take my brain out, & fill it with books, as a
sponge with water. Miss Robins—Kilvert—Gide—cdn't read a word in
London. Taking a day or two with PH. to rest myself from Roger. And
have spun off a speech for Flavinda. Whether this book will ever compose,
written thus at 3 month intervals, I doubt. But I'm all in favour of the
wild, the experimental.[10]

Sunday 31 July[11]

Human voices wake us & we drown—quotations on hearing the
telephone yesterday asking us to Charleston. Bunny there; Angelica
moody; conversation however well beaten up—Duncan's 480 canvases;
new studio: N.'s bedroom on the garden; Q.'s potting shed.[12] Talk
about Rumours of war. Bunny described K[ingsley] M[artin]'s ague, or
malaria: fever high on Monday; sub-normal on Wednesday when paper
gone to press. L. caps with anecdotes. N. gives an account of McDougall's
methods of selling pictures. How he wheedled Mr Schiff.[13] Next Memoir
meeting discussed. So home. Very cold & cloudy—yet the downs aglow

9. 'We have lingered in the chambers of the sea
   By sea-girls wreathed with seaweed red and brown
   Till human voices wake us, and we drown.'
   T. S. Eliot, *The Love Song of J. Alfred Prufrock* (1917).
10. VW was reading the manuscript of Elizabeth Robins's memoirs, later published
    (by Heinemann, 1940) as *Both Sides of the Curtain*; and *Kilvert's Diary* edited by
    William Plomer in 3 volumes, 1938-40. Flavinda is a character in the play 'Where
    there's a Will there's a Way' in *Pointz Hall* (*Between the Acts*).
11. VW has misdated this entry *July 30th*.
12. Anticipating that Charleston would become the regular family home in case of
    war, Vanessa had initiated various alterations and improvements to the house.
13. McDougall is probably a mistake for Duncan MacDonald, a partner in the picture
    dealers Reid & Lefevre; Sydney Schiff (c. 1869-1944) was a patron and collector
    (and, under the pen-name Stephen Hudson, an author).

with corn much to my liking .Today theyve chipped off the pink brick & removed the greenhouse shed. Really a load off my eye—queer what a relief—to see the shape of the wall & the pink Jackmanna again. How my eye feels rested. Now for the mantelpiece question. Then lunch. My poor old head very feeble—tho' why? Trying it on PH. Age is it? or Roger? Walk this afternoon, & so lull oneself asleep.

[*Wednesday 2 August*]

I am trying to kid myself into believing that a penholder is a cigarette. So far I'm taken in. This by way of a solution of the old age problem, & improving my bowls.

London tomorrow. Katherine Furse to tackle . . . Certainly no cigarettes clears the brain—certainly the tongue. Must copy out Roger on J.A.S. Oh these old bits of bones . . . Begin R. again on Friday I suppose.[1]

Monday 7 August [*Bank Holiday*]

I am now going to make the rash & bold experiment of breaking off, from condensing Vision & Design,[2] to write here for 10 minutes instead of revising, as I ought, my mornings grind.

Oh yes. I thought of several things to write about. Not exactly diary. Reflections. Thats the fashionable dodge. Peter Lucas & Gide both at it. Neither can settle to creative art (I think, sans Roger, I could). Its the comment—the daily interjection—that comes handy in times like these. I too feel it. But what was I thinking?

I have been thinking about Censors. How visionary figures admonish us. Thats clear in an MS I'm reading. If I say this So & So will think me sentimental. If that . . . will think me Bourgeois. All books now seem to me surrounded by a circle of invisible censors. Hence their selfconsciousness, their restlessness. It wd. be worth while trying to discover what they are at the moment. Did Wordsworth have them? I doubt it. I read Ruth before breakfast. Its stillness, its unconsciousness, its lack of distraction, its concentration & the resulting "beauty" struck me. As if the mind must be allowed to settle undisturbed over the object in order to secrete the pearl.

Thats an idea for an article.

1. Dame Katherine Furse (1875-1952) was the youngest and only surviving daughter of the writer John Addington Symonds (1840-93), whose company and conversation had proved a stimulus and education to the young Roger Fry in Venice in 1891. Katherine Furse's letters to VW on this subject are in MHP, Sussex; VW's letters to her do not survive.
2. i.e.: VW's heading to Chapter 10 of *Roger Fry*, which deals with his book of this title.

The figurative expression is that all the surroundings of the mind have come much closer. A child crying in the field brings poverty: my comfort: to mind. Ought I to go to the village sports? Ought thus breaks in to my contemplation.

Oh & I thought, as I was dressing, how interesting it would be to describe the approach of age, & the gradual coming of death. As people describe love. To note every symptom of failure: but why failure? To treat age as an experience that is different from the others; & to detect every one of the gradual stages towards death which is a tremendous experience, & not as unconscious at least in its approaches, as birth is.

I must now return to my grind. I think rather refreshed.

Clive at Cn yesterday, with an enormous white jersey which he patted & prodded from time to time. A little testy about his room.

I needn't say I've been palmed off with the worst in [the] house. Desiring sympathy, Duncan said, & admiration. All his books were put in order by the others. Rather an elderly tea party. Q. away.[3]

Wednesday 9 August

My grind has left me dazed & depressed. How on earth to bring off this chapter? God knows.

Percy gave notice yesterday. Something about leaving lilies in the shed did the trick. You dont like what I do—&c . . . Whether final or not, God knows, & we dont much care. These things always blow up once every other year. To Miss Robins today. A yeasty frowsty August in weather. I'm beaten nightly at bowls. Must air my head before lunch.

The Woolfs drove to London and back on Thursday 17 August to superintend the removal of the Hogarth Press from 52 Tavistock Square to 37 Mecklenburgh Square; they went up again the following Thursday (24 August) when their own furniture and possessions were moved; they lunched with John Lehmann.

[Friday 25 August][4]

Perhaps it is more interesting, to describe 'The Crisis' than R.'s love affairs. Yes we are in the very thick of it. Are we at war? At one I'm going to listen in. Its very different, emotionally, from last September. In London yesterday there was indifference almost. No crowd in the train—we went by train. No stir in the streets. One of the removers called up. Its fate, as the foreman said. What can you do against fate? Complete chaos at 37. Ann met in graveyard [St. George's Fields]. No war, of course not, she said. John said Well I dont know what to think.

3. Clive in fact had three of the best rooms in Charleston, and a private bathroom.
4. VW has misdated this entry *24th August.*

But as a dress rehearsal its complete. Museums shut. Search light on Rodmell Hill. Ch[amberlai]n says danger imminent. The Russian pact a disagreeable & unforeseen surprise.[5] Rather like a herd of sheep we are. No enthusiasm. Patient bewilderment. I suspect some desire "to get on with it". Order double supplies & some coal. [Duncan Grant's] Aunt Violet in refuge at Charleston. Unreal. Whiffs of despair. Difficult to work. Offer of £200 from Chambrun for a story. Haze over the marsh. Aeroplanes. One touch on the switch & we shall be at war. Dantzig not yet taken. Clerks cheerful. I add one little straw to another, waiting to go in, palsied with writing. There's no cause now to fight for, said Ann. Communists baffled. Railway strike off. Ld. Halifax broadcasts in his country gentlemans voice. Louie says will clothes be dear? Underneath of course wells of pessimism. Young men torn to bits: mothers like Nessa 2 years ago. But again, some swerve to the right may come at any moment. The common feeling covers the private, then recedes. Discomfort & distraction. And all mixed with the mess at 37.

Monday 28 August

I stay out here, after bowls, to say—what? on this possibly last night of peace. Will the 9 o'clock bulletin end it all?—our lives, oh yes, & everything for the next 50 years? Everyone's writing I suppose about this last day. I walked on the downs; lay under a cornstack & looked at the empty land & the pinkish clouds in a perfect blue summer afternoon sky. Not a sound. Workmen discussing war on the road—one for it, one against. So to bowls. I bowling am happy: I outside the garden what? Numb I think. Vita says she feels terror & horror early—revives then sinks. For us its like being on a small island. Neither of us has any physical fear. Why should we? But theres a vast calm cold gloom. And the strain. Like waiting a doctors verdict. And the young—young men smashed up. But the point is one is too numbed to think. London seemed cheery. Most people are numb & have a surface optimism. Hugh Slater yesterday, has an instinct that there wont be war.[6] Old Clive sitting on the terrace, says "I dont want to live through it." Explains that his life recedes. Has had the best. We privately are so content. Bliss day after day. So happy cooking dinner, reading, playing bowls. No feeling of patriotism. How to go on, through war?—thats the question.

5. During the night of 23 August, the German–Soviet Non-Aggression Pact was signed in Moscow. In England, Mr Chamberlain and the Foreign Secretary Lord Halifax confirmed the guarantees already given to Poland; Parliament was recalled on 24 August to receive the Emergency Powers Bill and precautionary measures for defence were accelerated.
6. Humphrey Richard Hugh Slater (1906-58), painter and writer, a veteran of the Spanish Civil War, was brought by the Bells to tea at Monks House.

Of course I have my old spurs & my old flanks. No I cant get at it—so whats the use of staying out? One wanders in; dines; then listens. Sense tells me there'll be no news till tomorrow. Yes, its a lovely still summer evening; not a sound. A swallow came into the sitting room. I talked to the girl who keeps elk hounds on the hill, by the ivy bloom tree. May flies buzz. I'm sleeveless in the heat. No word from Vita who was coming. How difficult, unexpectedly to write.

Wednesday 30 August

Not at war yet. Par[liamen]t met: yesterday. Negotiations. We are firm. A pause. L. & I discussing the Broadcast are up & down. Very black—then less so. L. pessimistic more than I am this morning. He thinks that H[itler]. is making up his mind to spring. Raging voices began again last night in German. Last years mad voice heard again, as if he were lashing himself up. At the same time, a reply of 8 pages has been sent last night to the Cabinet. The French are out of it this time.[7]

I'm dull headed. Spreading my mind out to synthesise the last chapter. Well, its a good thing as a distraction. Also wrote a synopsis of a story for Chabrun [Chambrun]. Will they really order 3,000 words on that flimsy sketch for £200? Seems impossible. Nobody keeps engagements or answers letters. A kind of block & suspension. No furniture unpacked. We go up tomorrow.

Brilliant—yes, the light is very evanescent—shining—weather. Very hot. To Lewes about shoes &c. All the tradespeople one wd say indifferent. Question of buying bicycles. Lots of bicycles. But why? Oh d'you think there'll be a war?

Now I must listen to the one 'clock.

Red faced boys in khaki guarding Rodmell Hill. The soldiers in the village. Otherwise quiet & usual eno' . . .

Friday 1 September

War is on us this morning. Hitler has taken Dantzig: has attacked—or is attacking—Poland. Our P[arliamen]t meets at 6 tonight. This after a day in London, submerged doubts & hopes. Last night we heard terms to Poland read. We then had some hope. Now at 1 I go in to listen I suppose to the declaration of war.[1]

7. Since the signing of the German–Soviet Pact there had been intense diplomatic activity in an attempt to avert Hitler's intended attack on Poland and, on his part, to prevent Britain and France fulfilling their obligations towards her.

1. Germany attacked Poland at dawn on 1 September, and announced the incorporation of Danzig into the *Reich*. The previous evening the Germans had broadcast their 16-point plan for a settlement with Poland—in effect an ultimatum, which there had been no conceivable possibility of the Poles accepting.

A dull hot day. I dont know why I write this. or what I feel. or shall feel. Children may come at 2—have told Mabel to come. All is hovering over us. And a grouse bought for John at Wimbledon for lunch & L. putting bags on fruit trees, & the man putting up our columns; & complete silence everywhere. 5 to 1 . .[2]

Sunday 3 September

This is I suppose certainly the last hour of peace. The time limit is out at 11. PM to broadcast at 11.15. L. & I "stood by" 10 minutes ago. Why repeat what'll be in all the papers? We argued. L. said Greenwood was right—forcing the PM in the House last night.[3] I argued its "they" as usual who do this. We as usual remain outside. If we win,—then what? L. said its better to win; because the Germans, vanquished, are what they are. Mus[solini']s last try, a try on. All the formulae are now a mere surface for gangsters. So we chopped words. I suppose the bombs are falling on rooms like this in Warsaw. A fine sunny morning here; apples shining. Mabel came to my regret last night. Atmosphere at once stiff & prickly. Mustn't mind, says L. No children yet come. Nessa & Angelica over as I took up the book yesterday. 14 in house: 3 children dumped. Maynard has given Q. a job as tractor driver.[4] This is a relief. No one knows how we're to fight. Rumours beginning. A flurry of people shopping in Lewes yesterday: the flight of cars with beds fairly thick. Shops rather empty. People buying stuff for windows. Little girl says If we have a chink they'll spy us out. Flint [*grocer*] cross. Many of them that—as if half unhappy half resentful. No excitement visible. M[abel]. said train very empty. I believe little exact notes are more interesting than reflections—the only reflection is that this is bosh & stuffing compared with the reality of reading say Tawney; writing, & re-writing one sentence of Roger.[5] So this experiment proves the reality of the mind. Two hours sewing [*black-out*] curtains. An anodyne. pleasant to do

---

2. Mothers and children from South London were evacuated to Rodmell, but none were billeted at Monks House. The pair of fluted wooden columns form a decorative feature of the dining room there.

3. The House of Commons met on Saturday 2 September; Chamberlain, still hoping to avoid a European war, reported that Mussolini had proposed an immediate cessation of hostilities and a conference ... Arthur Greenwood (1880-1954), Deputy Leader of the Labour Party, urged to 'speak for England', insisted that the time for compromise was past and that England's duty was to honour her guarantee of aid to Poland.

4. Quentin Bell had been rejected for military service because of his history of tuberculosis.

5. R. H. Tawney (1880-1962), economic historian and social critic; his most influential book was *Religion and the Rise of Capitalism* (1926).

something: but so tepid & insipid. One's too tired, emotionally, to read a page. I tried Tawney last night—cdn't concentrate. Church bells ringing. Mrs Ebbs carrying a sheaf of gladioli. Where from? Breaky Bottom. They hardly ever come to church, but now & then send lovely flowers for the church.[6] Question: if we had a church? The relief of having some common outside interest or belief. If it were a belief . . . Q. & A. to eat John's grouse.

Its the unreality of force that muffles every thing. Its now about 10.33. Not to attitudinise is one reflection. Nice to be entirely genuine & obscure. Then of course I shall have to work to make money. Thats a comfort. Write articles for America. I suppose take on some writing for some society. Keep the Press going. Of course no beds or heat on at 37. So far plenty of petrol. Sugar rationed. So I shall now go in. Nothing in the garden or meadows that strikes me out of the way—& certainly I cant write.[7]

Wednesday 6 September

Our first air raid warning at 8.30 this morning. A warbling that gradually insinuates itself as I lay in bed. So dressed & walked on the terrace with L. Sky clear. All cottages shut. Breakfast. All clear. During the interval a raid on Southwark. No news.

The Hepworths came on Monday.[8] Rather like a sea voyage. Forced conversation. Boredom. All meaning has run out of everything. Scarcely worth reading papers. The BBC gives any news the day before. Emptiness. Inefficiency. I may as well record these things. My plan is to force my brain to work on Roger. But Lord this is the worst of all my life's experiences. I note that force is the dullest of experiences. It means feeling only bodily feelings: one gets cold & torpid. Endless interruptions. We have done the curtains. We have carried coals &c into the cottage for the 8 Battersea women & children. The expectant mothers are all quarrelling. Some went back yesterday. We took the car to be hooded, met Nessa, were driven to tea at Charleston. Yes, its an empty meaningless world now. Am I a coward? Physically I expect I am. Going to London tomorrow I expect frightens me. At a pinch eno' adrenalin is secreted to keep one calm. But my brain stops. I took up my watch this morning & then put it down. Lost. That kind of thing annoys me. No

6. Breaky Bottom is an isolated farm in a fold of the downs west of Rodmell.

7. The Prime Minister broadcast to the nation at 11.15 a.m. on Sunday 3 September: as Germany had not replied to his Government's ultimatum that their forces be withdrawn from Poland by 11 a.m. that day, he announced that Great Britain was already at war with Germany.

8. Barbara Hepworth from the Hogarth Press and her sister stayed at Monks House from 4-7 September.

doubt one can conquer this. But my mind seems to curl up & become undecided. To cure this one had better read a solid book like Tawney, an exercise of the muscles. The Hepworths are travelling books in Brighton. Shall I walk? Yes. Its the gnats & flies that settle on non-combatants. This war has begun in cold blood. One merely feels that the killing machine has to be set in action. So far, The Athena has been sunk.[9] It seems entirely meaningless—a perfunctory slaughter, like taking a jar in one hand, a hammer in the other. Why must this be smashed? Nobody knows. This feeling is different from any before. And all the blood has been let out of common life. No movies or theatres allowed. No letters, except strays from America. "Reviewing" rejected by Atlantic.[10] No friends write or ring up. Yes, a long sea voyage, with strangers making conversation, & lots of small bothers & arrangements seems the closest I can get. Of course all creative power is cut off.

Perfect summer weather.

[*Later.*] Its like an invalid who can look up & take a cup of tea—Suddenly one can take to the pen with relish. Result of a walk in the heat, clearing the fug & setting the blood working. This book will serve to accumulate notes, the fruit of such quickenings. And for the 100th time I repeat—any idea is more real than any amount of war misery. And what one's made for. And the only contribution one can make—This little pitter patter of ideas is my whiff of shot in the cause of freedom —so I tell myself, thus bolstering up a figment—a phantom: recovering that sense of something pressing from outside which consolidates the mist, the non-existent.

I see Priestley consolidating his idea of himself too. Begins his article, Helping to receive refugees &c. . . . thus bringing before himself P. the active, the helper in the cause of common life: & so doubtless releasing his rush of ideas. But I dont like P.'s figment, necessary as it may be.[11] I conceived the idea, walking in the sun baked marsh where I saw one clouded yellow, of making an article out of these 15 odd diaries. This will be an easy slope of work: not the steep grind of Roger. But shall I ever have a few hours to read in? I must. Tonight the Raid has diminished

9. On 3 September the liner *Athenia*, bound for Canada with 1400 passengers and crew, was torpedoed by a German submarine and sunk 250 miles west of the Hebrides; 112 lives were lost.

10. VW finished writing her essay 'Reviewing' in June 1939 (see *VI VW Letters*, no. 3519); it was published, with a dissenting note by LW, as a Hogarth Sixpenny Pamphlet on 2 November 1939 (Kp A24), but did not appear in America. See below, 9 November 1939.

11. See J. B. Priestley in the *News Chronicle*, 4 September 1939: 'Two-Ton Annie': 'We had been asked to lend a hand at receiving and distributing the patients, who had been evacuated from Portsmouth hospitals. So there I was, at the end of Ryde Pier, watching the sick folk arrive . . .'

from a raid on Southwark; on Portsmouth; on Scarborough, to an attempt on the E. Coast without damage. Tomorrow we go up.

Monday 11 September

I have just read 3 or 4 Characters of Theophrastus, stumbling from Greek to English, & may as well make a note of it.[12] Trying to anchor my mind on Greek. Rather successful. As usual, how Greek sticks, darts, eels in & out! No Latin wd have noted that a boor remembers his loans in the middle of the night. The Greek has his eye on the object. But its a long distance one has to roll away to get at Theophrastus & Plato. But worth the effort.

Mrs Nicholls a great frost. A painted metallic shrill nagging woman; with a mind that pecks the same rotten apple again—this side, that side. Her daughter: & her future: & Tigger the Dalmatian: full of her shoddy contacts; her cocktails: shall I buy a housecoat for raids or trousers? At last, at 8 am, she left us; but depressed, for one doesnt like coins to turn out false. Of course she ruined Sunday tea: Charleston over. Much grumbling from Clive at their inmates. Nessa who is making a chicken house is philosophic. But she compares the Grants & Breretons.[13]

To London on Thursday. Pitiless fine weather. Over London a light spotted veil—the balloons. Very empty streets. A curious strained silence. At the Press, Miss P[erkins, *clerk*]. listening for Sirens. So I listened. Sat in the sunny window. Cases all empty but piled up. Mabel & I laid carpets. Sandwiches with John. Stephen came in. His great joints seemed to crack. Eyes stared. Is writing reams about himself. Can't settle to poetry. London after sunset a mediaevel city of darkness & brigandage. Mrs [Cyril] Connolly told by a taxi man he had just been robbed & knocked over the head. The darkness they say is the worst of it. The air raid had been very trying—at 2.30. John had drunk a glass of water & sat in the cellar. No one can control their nerves. So I was glad to be on the road home. No raids yet. Poland being conquered, & then—we shall be attended to.

I've offered to write for the NS. I dont know if wisely: but it's best to have a job, & I dont think I can stand aloof with comfort at the moment. So my reasons are half in half. Intolerable tedium.—no papers: no letters; & all this made up talk with Nicholls.

Cooler now.

12. Theophrastus, a pupil of Plato and of Aristotle; his 'Characters' consist of brief delineations of moral types.

13. Norah Nicholls of the Hogarth Press office staff stayed at Monks House from Saturday to Monday morning. Julian and Quentin's governess Mrs Brereton and her daughter formed part of Vanessa's household at Charleston towards the end of the 1914-18 war; now it was a refuge from the expected dangers of war for Duncan Grant's mother and her sister Violet McNeil.

Saturday 23 September

Meanwhile Poland has been gobbled up. Russia & Germany divide it. An aircraft carrier has been sunk. But there have been no raids.[14] And I—having said impulsively that I would write for the NS by way of using my faculties patriotically—have written 2 & used up every morning to the margin. Also people have been staying here . . . oh such a fritter & agitation—solid weekends with Mrs Nicholls, Miss Perkins, Miss Woodward—both very good samples: public house life & green-grocers. So distracted I've scudded over the surface of the days. And now Stephen is on us alone; & so we shall be lip sore & addle headed. Then theres John on Monday.

Civilisation has shrunk. The Amenities are wilting. Theres no petrol today: so we are back again with our bicycles at Asheham 1915. And once more L. & I calculate our income. Can I give A. her allowance? How much must we both earn? Once more we are journalists. I've offered to do an article, required by The Times, on artists & the crisis; offered others. My old age of independence is thus in danger. But in fact its hard to keep aloof & do my books. Theres a pressure about an article—even White & Bewick—that keeps one absorbed. But how sick of 1500 words by Wednesday I shall get![15]

Then one begins stinting paper, sugar, butter, buying little hoards of matches. The elm tree that fell has been cut up. This will see us through 2 winters. They say the war will last 3 years. We had an SOS from Kingsley. He came for the night. What was it he cdn't say on the telephone? Nothing. Should he come out in favour of peace? Cha[mberlai]n has the terms in his pocket. All in the know say we are beaten. Troops guard the East end. A bomb—& he means to bomb the docks—will lead to revolution. He was happy—but chuckling, quick & low, like a delirious bird. Always seeing himself, & pleased to see himself a martyr. Nothing of the least importance is said though in his article. A sensationalist—his mind rotted with hot coterie talk—all pitted & soft as a

14. Invading German forces from the West and Russian from the East overran Poland and met at Brest-Litovsk on 18 September; by the end of the month the partition of the country secretly agreed in the German–Soviet Pact was effective and ratified. *HMS Courageous* was torpedoed and sunk in the Bristol Channel on 17 September with a loss of over 500 men.

15. Nothing came of the proposed *Times* article; that on 'White's Selborne' was published in the *NS&N* on 30 September 1939 (Kp C361); that on the artist William Bewick (1795-1866), based on his *Life and Letters . . .* (1871) edited by Thomas Landseer, and J. G. Tait's 1939 edition of the first volume of Sir Walter Scott's *Journal* (1825-26), appeared under the title 'Gas at Abbotsford' in the *NS&N* on 27 January 1940 (Kp C364).

hot dis[h]cloth—steaming, unwholesome, unreal. Yet I rather liked him—a Celt.[16]

I forget who else has been. Nessa painting L.[17] Drove to Newhaven yesterday to buy plaster of Paris for Q. & we saw the 2 hospital ships painted green & white in the harbour. Many games of bowls. No reading. No Theophrastus—only article reading. But this must be stopped, as I'm now up to time with my little flutterers; & thank God old Mabel who is like one of the clammy kitchen flies, goes back on Tuesday. London no worse, she says than anywhere. An opinion I encourage.

Sunday 24 September

Stephen scribbling diary—no, reading Proust in English in the drawing room. Doubts thrown upon Gilbert White out here. Odd how the diffuse, expostulating, exaggerating young disturb my atmosphere. Yet I shall get back. I've talked miles since last night, in spite of Stephen's colic. A loose jointed mind—misty, clouded, suffusive. Nothing has outline. Very sensitive, tremulous, receptive & striding. So we've rambled over Inez: can she forgive herself. She has taken his money. Can she still be generous & large minded? over religion, at breakfast; over justice; & walking the terrace, we plunged & skimmed & hopped—from sodomy & women & writing & anonymity &—I forget. At last I said I must write—tho' my little bowl was clouded & troubled by all this talk—& he must write; & so ordered boiled potatoes for his lunch; & sit in semi-retreat out here, re-typing without much conviction, G[ilbert] W[hite]. for the N.S. My own flurry & responsiveness is an awful bore—I can catch so many rumours & reverberate so instantaneously.

Freud is dead, the stop press says.[18] Only these little facts interrupt the monotonous boom of the war. I get restless now & then & wd. like to be rubbing my back against London. And so must take a turn on the terrace, throw away my cigarette & go in to more rambling & discursive sauntering over all the countries of the mind. Yet, he says, I like the finished the definite: Bach & Gluck: then why sprawl so? But a very

16. Kingsley Martin came to Monks House for the night on 19 September; his leading article in the *NS&N* of 23 September, 'Brest-Litovsk Revenged', makes no allusion to the alleged peace terms proposed to the Allies by Hitler following the 'collapse' of Poland—which were not made public until the end of the month.

17. Vanessa Bell's finished portrait of LW hung at Monks House until his death, when it was given to the National Portrait Gallery by Mrs Ian Parsons; the preliminary study is in a private collection in Chicago.

18. Sigmund Freud died at his Hampstead home early on 23 September 1939; he was eighty-three.

sensitive considerate man—not condensed into anything. And tremulous. And fertile. & I suppose poetical. Yet discriminating. John a bit coarse, obtuse. He has bought for £5 in the Ladbroke Road a press & type. Talk of starting a magazine. I read his MSS poems—all repetitions & gradual beatings out, mostly unintelligible. When I say we must discuss our works, without caring for praise, am I sincere? Could I do it? Never mind. Forge ahead, in my own little way.

Monday 25 September

The week end was sheer drudgery & has left me out of temper out of mood. Roger seems hopeless. Yet if one cant write, as Duncan said yesterday, one may as well kill oneself. Such despair comes over me— waking early. And we're fretted & tormented with people—Portia Holman today, John—Vita. Then Q. & perhaps Judith—How can I cool & smooth my head? But I intend to work.

L.'s book [*After the Deluge, vol. II*] out today.

[*Wednesday 27 September*][19]

No I'm not sure of the date. And Vita is lunching here. I'm going to stop R[oger] at 12. Then read something real. I'm not going to let my brain addle. Little sharp notes. For somehow my brain is not very vigorous at the end of a book tho' I cd. dash off fiction or an article merrily eno'. Why not relieve it then? Wasnt it my conscientious grind at The Years that killed it. So I whizz off to Stevenson—Jekyll & Hyde— not much to my liking. Very fine clear Sept weather windy but lovely light. And I cant form letters.

Sunday 1 October

This last week a mere scramble of people. Q. & Bradfield;[1] then Judith; asked if she might stay. Then Leslie . . . talk talk—bowls in a blizzard. Proof correcting. Then the divine relief last night of silence alone with L. Rain today. But peace—my private peace—restored. London tomorrow. Sunday clearing up. Oh how torturing life in common is! like trying to drink a cup of tea & always its dashed from one. Judith has her jocose school girl garrulity increased by the rather commonplace Leslie. A pity she shd. marry him—porous, stupid, good humoured, Tunbridge Wells to the backbone.

19. This entry is dated simply: *28th.*
1. John Bradfield was the Workers' Educational Association (WEA) organiser for East Sussex from 1933-40.

OCTOBER 1939

Friday 6 October

Well, I have succeeded in despite of distractions to belong to other nations in copying out again the whole of Roger. Needless to say, its still to be revised, compacted, vitalised. And can I ever do it? The distractions are so incessant. Today I'm asked to take on Bunny's job on the N.S. Yes I've been slipping into the frying pan of journalism—letting myself in for a monthly article, making, or attempting to make, £15.15 terms. All this is very frittering, exciting, degrading. And shivers my detachment. Also theres the war: or rather the non-war. Nothing happens. All is held up. Nightly we're served out with a few facts, or a childstory of the adventures of a submarine. Hitler is said to make peace terms today. London is all agog; & also all a quiver. Raymond wrote me an SOS letter; describing the whirlpool—round round round—twigs, old curling paper & bits of straw—at the NS Office. Shaw writes an article; Maynard has a heart attack over it; KM. an attack of hysteria. Stonier is stony. Poor RM. prays for help from Leonard, even from me.[2] Here its distracted weather—hailstorms & gales & sun; Nessa is painting L.: & theres a centre of rustic simplicity—old Botten picking up the walnuts & burbling on & I sitting on Kingston Hill & watching the destroying clouds point like a great feathered grey blue wing over the channel. Suddenly rain bursts & I dash home: a great evening, & bowls with L. I'm beaten. I compose articles on Lewis Carroll & read a great variety of books—Flaubert's life, R.'s lectures, out at last, a life of Erasmus & Jacques Blanche.[3] We are asked to lunch with Mrs Webb, who so often talks of us. And my hand seems as tremulous as an aspen. I have composed myself by tidying my room.

2. Raymond Mortimer, literary editor of the *NS&N*, wrote to VW on 4 October 'describing the whirlpool'; the following day he wrote again: 'Since writing to you yesterday, Bunny has announced that he is too busy in the Air Ministry to write his weekly page ['Books in General']. I suppose it is useless to beg you to send us 1200 words every week—any subject? Failing this, could you manage every other week?' (MHP, Sussex). Shaw's article, 'Uncommon Sense about the War' (*NS&N*, 7 October 1939), argued with Shavian vigour that England should make peace with Hitler as quickly as possible. G. W. Stonier (b. 1903) was an assistant-editor of the *NS&N* from 1928-45.

3. VW's article on Lewis Carroll, prompted by the publication in 1939 of his *Complete Works* by the Nonesuch Press, appeared in the Christmas Books Supplement of the *NS&N*, 9 December 1939. The 'lives' she read were probably *Flaubert and Mme Bovary. A Double Portrait* by Francis Steegmuller, and *More Portraits of a Life-time, 1918-38* by Jacques Emile Blanche, both recently published. (Life of Erasmus unidentified.) Blanche met VW at Auppegard in 1927, and his portrait sketch of her forms the frontispiece to his book, which includes liberal quotation from her writings of which he was a great admirer. Roger Fry's *Last Lectures*, introduced by Kenneth Clark, was published by the Cambridge University Press.

Cant quite see my way now as to the next step in composition. Tom this week end.

I meant to record a Third Class Railway carriage conversation. The talk of business men. Their male detached lives. All politics. Deliberate, well set up, contemptuous & indifferent to the feminine. For example: one man hands the E. Standard, points to a womans photograph. "Women? Let her go home & bowl her hoop" said the man in blue serge with one smashed eye. "She's a drag on him" another fragment. The son is going to lectures every night. Odd to look into this cool man's world: so weather tight: insurance clerks all on top of their work; sealed up; self sufficient; admirable; caustic; laconic; objective; & completely provided for. Yet thin, sensitive: yet schoolboys: yet men who earn their livings. In the early train they said, "Cant think how people have time to go to war. It must be that the blokes haven't got jobs." "I prefer a fools paradise to a real hell." "War's lunacy. Mr Hitler & his set are gangsters. Like Al Capone". Not a chink through which one can see art, or books. They play cross words when insurance shop fails.

Saturday 7 October

Its odd how those first days of complete nullity when war broke out— have given place to such a pressure of ideas & work that I feel the old throb & spin in my head more of a drain than ever. The result partly of taking up journalism. A good move, I daresay; for it compacts; & forces me to organise. I'm masterfully pulling together those diffuse chapters of R. because I know I must stop & do an article. Ideas for articles obsess me. Why not try the one for The Times? No sooner said than I'm ravaged by ideas. Have to hold the Roger fort—for I will have the whole book typed & in Nessa's hands by Xmas—by force. Cha[m]brun now demands a dog story: the other too sophisticated. So I have that floating about.[4] In short I'm more on the buzz than when I was contemplating books only. And it keeps me feverishly skating over the thin ice.

We have a fortnight its said to consider Hitler's terms. If rejected, all the guns boom.[5] So we may get a last safe week in London. And I dont

4. The story requested and rejected by Chambrun as 'too sophisticated' has not been identified. The 'dog story' was definitely commissioned for $1000 on the basis of a synopsis VW sent him in November, and the story itself, 'Gipsy, the Mongrel' was despatched in January and paid for in February 1940; but appears not to have been published. The typescript (B 9h) is in MHP, Sussex; see also correspondence with Chambrun in LWP, Sussex.

5. Hitler, still convinced that Britain and France were fundamentally reluctant to fight Germany, on 6 October announced his 'last offer' to the Allies—a vague Peace Plan; his proposals were rejected—though it was to be six months yet before his guns really 'boomed'.

much want to go. Once settled here, it seems congenial to stop. The war has at least made the country question easy to solve. Tom sent me his Cat poems today.[6] A very wet day.

Ch[arlesto]n. yesterday. Gages heard booming. Nessa exposed to show the house. A. & Q. in hiding A. says she will cry if I call her, compared with the public spirited Judith a butterfly. One review of L.'s book: good; but merely expositional.

Clive says everyone wants peace.

The Woolfs drove up to Mecklenburgh Square on Friday 13 October, and returned to Rodmell the following Friday.

Sunday 22 October

Oh let me fly from Roger to a page of a very different sort. We have spent a week in London. The poster read, at Wimbledon: "The War begins . . . Hitler says, Now its on". So as we drove to M.S. I said "Its foolish to come to London the first day of war." It seemed as if we were driving open eyed into a trap. The trap feeling was strong those first days. I kept one ear pricked. The flat was oh in such a mess—very small, very crowded. Whistles sounded. The dark was as thick as Hell. One seemed cut off. No wireless. There we sat. And people came running in & out. The Arnold Fosters: Tom: Stephen: John: we lunched with the Webbs.[7] I recover; old age means an accumulation of the past. Like Wells one's obsessed; or like Shaw scatter brained. The old woman, wearing a white spotted headdress, was as alive as a leaf on an autumn bonfire: burning, skeletonised. I was, & am, no not so much now, so harassed & distracted, with the trap on me, that I could not expand my mind to receive impressions.

You never escape the war in London. People are all thinking the same thing. All set on getting the day's work done. Hitches & difficulties hold one up. Very few buses. Tubes closed. No children. No loitering. Everyone humped with a gas mask. Strain & grimness. At night its so verdurous & gloomy that one expects a badger or a fox to prowl along the pavement. A reversion to the middle ages with all the space & the silence of the country set in this forest of black houses. A torch blinks. An old gentleman revealed. He vanishes. That red light may be a taxi

6. This inscribed copy of Eliot's *Old Possum's Book of Practical Cats* (1939) was sold at Sotheby's, 27 April 1970, lot 44.
7. Will Arnold-Forster, who had remarried since Ka's death, brought her legacy to VW (see *VI VW Letters*, no. 3559) on 19 October. On 16 October the Woolfs had lunched with Beatrice Webb at the Kensington home of her neice Barbara Drake. Mrs Webb was now over eighty.

or a lampost. People grope their way to each others lairs. We were talking in our lair about 6 hours daily. Great caterpillars dug up the square. Gradually the sense of siege being normal replaced the fear— the individual fear. My ears were not pricked. It was irritating & one's temper was rubbed. This was increased by the sheer discomfort & perpetual need for clearing drawers, arranging furniture. The kitchen very small. Everything too large. Stairs bad. No carpets. The clerks scream like parrots. Miss Woodward left in torrents of tears. Rain poured —profuse unbridled mediaeval rain. I wrote & rewrote in barren horror Lewis Carroll—my hands & feet cold. Did nothing—was indeed in fretful useless distraction. Sally was paralysed. L. had her rib plastered. So we came down & the world rises out of dark squalor into this divine natural peace. My brain is smoothing already, in spite of A. & Q. yesterday. Alone today & for many days. It was an odd morbid week of many disagreeable sensations.

Wednesday 25 October

About the 24th anyhow. And "the war begins today." So Ribbenthrop said or rather howled last night.[8] For so far its sporadic & halfhearted. How then can I say anything about it here? Here it peters out. I rode my cycle to Lewes yesterday. Now Nessa's come & is painting L. & Sally is recovering. And its a blowy but sunny autumn day. And I'm screwed like a vice to the re composing of the last chapter wh. I'm running into one, called Transformations. Its a question of arrangement. Then a new quote comes & alters all the proportions. But I think if I can see steadily for a fortnight I shall have grasped it. Temptations to write other things fret me. R.M[ortimer]. sends books. A dog story wd. bring in £200. & Freud's papers.[9] As a journalist I'm in demand (not with the TLS though). To relax I read Little Dorrit & think of going on with my Au[tobiograph]y. Never have I been so set on my own spinning. Gerald Heard's book spun me to distraction last night. So good & suggestive & firm for 200 pages: then a mere bleat bitter repetition contorsion & inversion. Like a dog going after its tail; & there is no tail. No, he's nothing to offer, once he's done historical accounting. A mere tangle. And his fanatical starved or as he would say strangulated

---

8. VW has dated this entry *Wednesday 24?* *October*; on the night of the 24th, in Danzig, the German Foreign Minister von Ribbentrop delivered an abusive and demagogic diatribe against Britain.

9. Following Freud's death, the Hogarth Press, in an advertisement in the *NS&N* of 30 September 1939, reminded the public that they were the publishers of his works (which were listed) in England; probably VW had brought copies to Monks House, including the 4-volume, *Collected Papers* 1924-5. There is no evidence that VW had seriously read Freud before this year.

individuality presides. A scream, a distracted scream issues, instead of the soaring spirit. So I shant read Aldous. wh. develops GH in fiction.[10] So to lunch. And a [WEA] meeting tonight.

Wednesday 1 November

Oh how gladly I reach for this free page for a 10 minutes scamper after copying & re-copying, digging in those old extract books for quotes all the morning! And how ⟨compose⟩ adapt oneself to the sense of freedom? How compete with the compression & lucidity & logic of Gide writing his Journal? Well, the plain truth is I cant. Yet ideas shoot into my head perpetually. Only as my head is always on the anvil—for I will finish this week—they skim away uncaught. It strikes me that Morgan probably keeps an admirable diary. I'd like to ask Morgan down. Our week ends are now taking the place of our dinners. Rather a laborious extension. But here we are settling in, very steadily, to a country life, & there's much to be said for it. The space, the concentration, the freedom. Every day on my walk I get a colour bath: the greens dying, the winter colours burnishing. Society too is fairly brisk. There was Raymond (green trousers) Dora Morris (yellow jersey) at C[harlesto]n. last Sunday. Clive with his hair cut abrupt & truculent. Janice's car has come. We are as free as before almost with our double ration. The car bucks & is draughty.[1] We went to Tun. Wells [*on 30 October*]. Here am I evading ideas. One of these days I shall be free to write them. Tonight L. lectures to the new village group on Democracy. The village is hungry for lectures. Tom comes for the week end. Eddy Sackville invites himself for next week. London & 37 recede. Dim voices reach us. No war news. An admirable naval man broadcast about a convoy. And its grey & misty.[2]

10. Gerald Heard's book was *Pain, Sex and Time*, published 5 October 1939. Reviewing *After Many a Summer* by Aldous Huxley—'the Evangelist of Mr Gerald Heard's Neo-Brahminism'—in the *NS&N* of 14 October 1939, Anthony West describes the novel as one 'in which the principles of the faith are displayed functioning in the everyday world, and the result is as depressing as [Heard's] cloudy expository work led one to expect.'

1. Dora Morris (later Lady Romilly) was the sister of the painter Peter Morris, a great friend of Duncan and Vanessa. On returning to the USA Janice Loeb arranged to garage her car at Monks House, giving the Woolfs the use of it and its allotted petrol coupons (petrol rationing was introduced on 23 September).

2. Between 1 November and 10 April 1940, LW gave twelve Wednesday evening lectures to the WEA on 'Causes and Issues of the War'. 'In Convoy' by A Naval Eye Witness was broadcast on 31 October; it was published in *The Listener* of 9 November 1939.

Thursday 9 November

How glad I am to escape to my free page. But I think I'm nearing the end of my trouble with Roger, doing once more, the last pages: & I think I like it better than before. I think the idea of breaking up the last chapter into sections was a good one. If only I can bring that end off. The worst of journalism is that it distracts. Like a shower on the top of the sea. Rev[iewin]g. came out last week; & was not let slip into obscurity as I expected. Lit Sup had a tart & peevish leader: the old tone of voice I know so well—rasped & injured. Then YY polite but aghast in the NS. And then my answer—Why an answer should always make me dance like a monkey at the Zoo, gibbering it over as I walk, & then re-writing, I dont know. It wasted a day. I suppose its all pure waste: yet if one's an outsider, be an outsider—only dont for God's sake attitudinise & take up the striking the becoming attitude.[3]

We had a day in London [*on 6 November*]. Oh, yes, Tom for the week end: more supple, less caked & rigid than of old. His teaching he told me, is that one improves with age. I suppose the working of the divine spirit which as usual he adored at 8 on Sunday morning, receiving communion from Mr Ebbs—who did not impress him. The flat improved; a great thunderstorm; L. caught Louie's cold: had to stand about; a feverish cold: better now; but now its pouring; & owing to my impulsive idiocy—saying I hoped to see him—Eddy Sackville has imposed his petulance upon us for this week end. Shall I tell him so? or must impulsiveness be punished? But remember another time how people grasp at straws. And how I hate being a straw. Two days will be ruined, just at the climax. And we've seen so many people; & these solitary days are so completely satisfactory. And if duty calls, its not to amuse young men with large country houses. Duty did not call me to listen to Mr Bradfield last night. Instead we listened to the ravings, the strangled hysterical sobbing swearing ranting of Hitler at the Beer Hall. The offer of mediation—Holland & Belgium—is the fat on the fire. Today they say there was an explosion after he'd left. Is it true?[4] Theres no getting at truth now all the loud speakers are contradicting each other. Its a crosseyed

3. *Reviewing* by Virginia Woolf. With a note by Leonard Woolf, was published on 2 November 1939 as Hogarth Sixpenny Pamphlet No. 4 (Kp A24). The 'tart and peevish' leader entitled 'Reviewer or Gutter?' appeared in the *TLS* of 4 November. YY (Robert Lynd), in the *NS&N* of the same date, maintained that 'the reviewer's is a reputable, essential, and vital craft—with a future'. For VW's reply to Lynd, *NS&N*, 11 November, see *VI VW Letters*, no. 3566.

4. On 7 November the Sovereigns of the Low Countries, appealing for peace, offered to mediate between the belligerents, but to no avail. After Hitler's rancorous speech in the Munich *Bürgenbraukeller* on 8 November—the anniversary of the abortive Nazi *putsch* of 1923—an explosion wrecked the hall, killing six and injuring over sixty people; but the Fuehrer had already left.

squint, like the beams that make a tent over the church at night—the searchlights meet there.

Mabel is here: pathetic to me in her dumb acceptance of snubs & all life is a snub to her. And now she's ringing for lunch.

Monday 12 November

Monday morning after a week end is a wash out. I cannot re write R.'s last page. Thats laid to the account of Eddy. He was on guard against egotism, & was spry & bonny[?] eno'; but I walked 7 miles alone to Charleston & suffer for it (as Nurse Lugton used to say).[5] Today restless & unidead. Its a good shake up no doubt; but I wanted peace. I must devise a plan for evading the after book gloom. My flutter in the NS was a fritter. I had a letter of abuse in the TLS so I must dig myself in.[6] Indeed I dont see why I should poke my head out again for a very long time. I've done my duty as an outsider for some months. And I suppose have only made myself more unpopular: ah yes: but freer. Thats the point. Never again shall I be asked to write for the TLS: thats a gain.

Mabel goes back on Wednesday; & we revert to the old happy obscurity with Louie. Save for Robson & A. & Q. . . . but they dont count.

Monday 27 November

Since I wrote here, we have been in London, had a party, A. & K. & Rose Mac; seen Colefax; & come back.[7] It is all storm & rain now. Many ships sunk. Men out in boats. The magnetic mine active. Ch[amberlai]n. speaking like a military shopwalker. Ive been drudging at 2 articles, one Bewick; done & sent off R.'s first chapters. Feel rather free now I'm thoroughly snubbed & put in my place for Reviewing. L. was praised by Desmond in the Sunday Times[8]—& Lord what a day! What a storm to rush through back to the house.

5. LW drove their guest Edward Sackville-West to Charleston for lunch on Sunday; VW—perhaps to avoid his company—walked. It appears from VW's recollection of this authentically nannyish saying that Nurse Lugton—the protagonist of her posthumously published children's story, *Nurse Lugton's Golden Thimble* (Kp A38) —may have had a real existence in the Stephen household.
6. See letter from Malcolm Elwin, *TLS*, 11 November 1939, on the subject of VW's pamphlet *Reviewing*, 'which I have not read . . .'
7. On 20 November the Woolfs drove to Mecklenburgh Square for three days. Their 'party' on 22 November was a dinner for Adrian and Karin Stephen and Rose Macaulay, with Sally Chilver and Raymond Mortimer joining them later.
8. LW's *After the Deluge*, Volume II was discussed, together with other books, by Desmond MacCarthy in two consecutive issues of the *Sunday Times*: 19 and 26 November 1939; on the former date, VW's pamphlet *Reviewing* was also considered.

Lunch Charleston yesterday. Judith Bagenal; sharp; obvious; but assured & I should say a good worker. not a drone. will marry her clergyman I should say. Clive away. D. has sold a picture to the Queen.[9] I forgot about our legacy. Nor do we know how much. Stella's settlement money. This was a surprise. Henry wrote & told me. Perhaps 4 or 500 each? This will serve at anyrate to gild our pill—the 7/6 income tax.[10] A long war its to be, Sybil said. The Empire to be destroyed in May. This is only the prelude to the operation. Now for the wet.

Wednesday 29 November

A nice dine & sleep visit from John, who pans out well under familiar scrutiny—dining in the kitchen &c—& things aren't doing badly: in fact stirring under the blanket of war. Rosinski sells: L. slowly. Ideas sprout. For a Bloomsbury Book Club . . . for 'our' new magazine; I mean a revival of N[ew].W[riting].: to which Rosamund has sent a long story. Yes, the young do manage to pull along. I'm never to have a good review again. The Spec vicious, John says. And a long gossip . . . bed wetting at Eton; its disastrous consequences. Repressions—homosexuality: this explains, I suppose, John's dash. One odd thing about the war is the failure of the post. No letters. John gets garrulous after wine. He cant make it up with Stephen. Stephen half lies about Horizon & his part in it mostly. Offers to bring it to the Hog. Steals young writers &c. I think its an emotional crux.[11]

Wind & rain. Again, after a screw at articles, screwing at R. Withers says do I want stock or cash? L. says cash. How much? I have only 2 minutes left. I think I shall write a Monday Tuesday for N.W. No more long laboured articles at the moment. J. enthusiastic about [LW's] Bs at Gate, which is out tomorrow. So I take a back place. Now I dont mind that. Should I, 20 years ago? J. says my R[eviewing]. p[amphle]t. very

9. Duncan Grant's painting 'St Paul's' was bought by the Queen from an exhibition of Contemporary English Painting at Agnews.

10. By his will J. W. Hills restored to Vanessa, Adrian, and VW the capital from Stella Duckworth's marriage settlement which he had reclaimed at the time of his second marriage (see *IV VW Diary*, 1 July 1931, n. 2). Henry Duckworth—VW's half-brother Sir George's eldest son—was a partner in Withers & Son, the firm of solicitors which drew up the marriage settlement in the first place. In the event VW received some £1300 in securities; see LWP, Sussex.

11. John Lehmann's twice-yearly miscellany *New Writing* was to continue in a leaner wartime form as *Folios of New Writing*; the first issue, in Spring 1940, contained Rosamond Lehmann's story 'The Red-Haired Miss Daintreys'. Lehmann's quarrel with Spender arose out of what appeared to be the latter's defection to the editorial board of the emergent review *Horizon*; see John Lehmann, *I Am My Brother* (1960), pp. 42-4.

interesting: couldnt be said by the young. Part of my Outsider Campaign. A letter from Shena Simon referring to 3 Gs.

Thursday 30 November

Very jaded & tired & depressed & cross, & so take the liberty of expressing my feelings here. R. a failure—& what a grind . . . no more of that. I'm brain fagged & must resist the desire to tear up & cross out— must fill my mind with air & light, & walk & blanket it in fog. Rubber boots help—I can flounder over the marsh. No I will write a little memoir.

Saturday 2 December

Tiredness & dejection give way if one day off is taken instantly. I went in & did my cushion. In the evening my pain in my head calmed. Ideas came back. This is a hint to be remembered. Always turn the pillow. Then I become a swarm of ideas. Only I must hive them till R. is done. It was annoying to get on to the surface & be so stung with my pamphlet [*Reviewing*]. No more controversy for a year, I vow. Ideas: about writers duty. No, I'll shelve that. Began reading Freud last night; to enlarge the circumference. to give my brain a wider scope: to make it objective; to get outside. Thus defeat the shrinkage of age. Always take on new things. Break the rhythm &c. Use this page, now & then, for notes. Only they escape after the mornings grind.

L.'s book [*Barbarians at the Gate*] out and noticed at length. I forgot to note our very interesting talk about detachment at 37 t'other night. L. has trained himself to cut adrift completely from personal feelings: its common sense, because one has no real identity there: & losing it gives one the only happiness thats secure. Yes. to learn to discuss say ones work eliminating oneself. This is quite true—one gets it now & again— an astonishing freedom & expansion. L. very subtle & wise: & down here its made easier, owing to the open country. I saw a Kingfisher & a cormorant the other days walk in rubber boots. Planes very active. Russia attacking Finland.[1] Nothing happens in England. Theres no reason anywhere. Brutes merely rampant. This suspends one's judgment: makes it foolish even to discuss. Its like being in a temporary shelter with a violent storm raging outside. We wait. L.P. meeting here. Great diversity & freedom among the villagers.

Oh & my memoir will have to be compacted. And no letters. And the

---

1. Soviet forces attacked Finland on 30 November after the latter's refusal to agree to make certain territorial concessions to their powerful neighbour; it was not until March 1940 that the stubbornly resisting Finns were forced to accept terms.

legacy may be £7 or 800. We go to 37 for 2 nights next week, & I see Ethel & Shena Simon. This life here has now become the rule; t'other the exception.

Friday 8 December

Two days in London: a great distraction; leaving my mind in a torn state, which I record, being all of a muzz. Lady Simon; a 3 talk, so a little disappointing. A nice woman. Did I wish to expose some egotism? I suppose so. Its breaking into new levels after concentrating here thats so distracting, & I daresay salutary. Shopping—tempted to buy jerseys & so on. I dislike this excitement. yet enjoy it. Ambivalence as Freud calls it. (I'm gulping up Freud). Then Ethel & Gillies.[2] That upset me— Ethel's wig—5 incongruous curls, that made her look babyish & foolish. Also she has gone downhill. She is now shut up quite alone in her old age—talks to herself, about herself. I felt this pathetic: also somehow ugly; humiliating; watching the old baby sucking its corals; compliments; the old story of her genius & its non-recognition. How hideous to be reduced to that kind of feeblemindedness—at 84. Something pitiable, unvenerable; not imbecile, but near it. Or was it partly her curls that were so distasteful? Gillies chattering about war secrets: Ethel mumbling on about what Bruno Walter said to—no I didnt listen after a time. And HB's death; & what he said in 1890 about The Wreckers.[3] I think it was pity more than anything that I felt; & all her clothes were undone; shaggy; untidy—like King Lear only without any tragedy or poetry. And the old charm in abeyance. Off she went to Plesh [Dr Plesch]. Then off I went to the Galeries Lafayette [*Regent Street*]. Out of that brilliancy I stepped into dead darkness—had no torch. A curious wild beauty— medieval, furtive—figures shuffling & darting Then Willie Robson. To stir the brew still further, into a race & whirlpool, a letter from The Forum asking me to write about women & peace. All the old, & a few new, ideas at once rise to the surface. I lay awake writing articles. It might be an outlet. But didn't I swear I would abjure controversy for a year? Isnt R.F. a finer piece of work? But for America?—then the money —then the desire to let fly: also, I suppose, to justify myself? Cant form letters. Raining hard.[4]

2. William Gillies was Secretary of the International Department of the Labour Party; he and Ethel Smyth lunched at 37 Mecklenburgh Square on 6 December.

3. The German conductor Bruno Walter (1876-1962) and the Anglo-American poet-philosopher Henry Brewster (1859-1908), who wrote the libretto for her opera *The Wreckers*, were both stars in Ethel Smyth's firmament.

4. Phyllis Moir, of the New York review *The Forum*, wrote to VW on 17 November 1939 reminding her that she had told her she would be glad 'to boil over some time', and asking her if the moment had come. See MHP, Sussex, LVP.

DECEMBER 1939

Saturday 9 December

I suppose that is the date. It is a Saturday morning, & looks fine & still, after the broken whirlpool of weather yesterday. We took Louie to Lewes to have teeth out, & it was blackout driving for the first time. Like fog driving, one cant see people. All the cars have small red eyes. The margins of the road are lost. But I'm thinking of a dozen things as usual. Should I begin my Forum article with a definition of angle, to explain my angularity? Ideas pullulate, but escape when I try to catch them here. Freud is upsetting: reducing one to whirlpool; & I daresay truly. If we're all instinct, the unconscious, whats all this about civilisation, the whole man, freedom &c? His savagery against God good. The falseness of loving one's neighbours. The conscience as censor. Hate . . . But I'm too mixed.[5] I'm going to begin Mill on Liberty [1859]. I'm making up for the hurried London years; spreading my mind, calmly to take in things wholly. Only thats Louie ringing for lunch. And L. is irritated with Percy—all the bulbs dug up when we were in London. And then Raymond wants me to write. And Shena is writing something for me—took that random shot to heart.[6] I'm driving so many horses in my team. Probably we get 1100 (gross) from Stella. A great hare is hung in the kitchen. odd that we shall eat it. So, these are the little wild ponies that tug me so many ways at once. And I shall walk myself calm this afternoon.

Saturday 16 December[7]

The litter in this room is so appalling that it takes me 5 minutes to find my pen. R. all unsewn in bits. And I must take 50 pages, should be 100, up on Monday. Cant get the marriage chapter right. Proportion all wrong. Alteration, quotation, makes it worse. But its true I dont fuss quite so much as over a novel. I learned a lesson in re-writing The Years wh. I shall never forget. Always I say to myself Remember the horror of that. Yesterday I was, I suppose unnecessarily[?], cheerful. 2 letters from admirers of 3 Gs; both genuine: one a soldier in the trenches; the other a distracted middle-class woman at Yeovil. And a letter which I must now answer from Stephen, asking me to contribute "On the

---

5. VW appears to have been reading Freud's *The Future of an Illusion* and *Civilisation and its Discontents*.

6. In preparation for the article requested by *The Forum* (see above, 8 December 1939), VW enlisted the help of Lady Simon; see *VI VW Letters*, no. 3574, and Shena Simon's 11-page response, dated 8 January 1940 (MHP, Sussex). In the event VW did not write the article, possibly because *The Forum* was only able to offer a fee of $100—then only about £20.

7. VW has dated this entry *Saturday 18th Dec?*

Young" or anything to Horizon. No no. Still at war, he says, with John. If I write for glory its to be in our own paper.[8]

Bought rubber boots yesterday. Met Lydia. Slapped her shoes on counter "Hugh Walpole—Priestly—tell Leonard—gossip—catching bus—off ". Roars of laughter in the shop. I explained her celebrity. L. bought a new mackintosh.

Horizon out; small; trivial, dull. So I think from not reading it. And now—oh now must I tidy up? London, the Hutchinsons &c looms. And I've promised to lecture the WEA at Brighton. And to write for the Forum.

Sunday 17 December[9]

Once more, as so often, I hunt for my dear old red-covered book, with what an instinct I'm not quite sure. For what the point of making these notes is I dont know; save that it becomes a necessity to uncramp, & some of it may interest me later. But what? For I never reach the depths; I'm too surface blown. And always scribble before going in— look quickly at my watch. Yes. 10 minutes left—what can I say. Nothing that needs thought: which is provoking; for I often think. And think the very thought I could write here. About being an outsider. About my defiance of professional decency. Another allusion of a tart kind to Mrs W. & her desire to kill reviewers in the Lit Sup. yesterday. Frank Swinnerton is the good boy, & I'm the bad little girl.[10] And this is trivial. Compared with what? Oh the Graf Spee is going to steam out of Monte Video today into the jaws of death. And journalists & rich people are hiring aeroplanes from which to see the sight. This seems to me to bring war into a new angle; & our psychology. No time to work out. Anyhow the eyes of the whole world (BBC) are on the game; & several people will lie dead tonight, or in agony. And we shall have it served up for us as we sit over our logs this bitter winter night. And the British Captain has been given a KCB.[11] & Horizon is out; & Louie has had her

8. The admiring soldier, Sapper Ronald Heffer, was in Hampshire, not the trenches; see MHP, Sussex, LVP. For VW's answer to Stephen Spender, see *VI VW Letters*, no. 3573.

9. VW has dated this entry *Dec. 18th*; but that Monday morning the Woolfs drove to London for three days.

10. 'Advice to Reviewers', the second leader in the *TLS* of 16 December 1939, adverted to 'Mrs Woolf's recent assault upon the *Lebensraum* of the book reviewer' and found reassurance in Frank Swinnerton's recently published Dent Memorial Lecture, *The Reviewing and Criticism of Books*.

11. On 14 December, after an engagement with British warships in the South Atlantic, the German pocket battleship *Graf Spee* took refuge in the harbour of Montevideo; given a time-limit of seventy-two hours by the Uruguayan Government, she had

teeth out; & we ate too much hare pie last night; & I read Freud on
Groups; & I've been titivating Roger: & this is the last page; & the
year draws to an end; & we've asked Plomer for Xmas; &—now times
up as usual. I'm reading Ricketts diary—all about the war the last war;
& the Herbert diaries & . . . yes, Dadie's Shakespeare, & notes overflow
into my 2 books.[12]

*From 18-21 December the Woolfs were in London, where they gave dinner
to the Hutchinsons and saw a good many people. William Plomer could not
come for Christmas; on Christmas Day the Woolfs bicycled to Charleston in
a fog for dinner; and on 23 and 27 December exchanged visits with the
Keyneses. On the 28th there was snow, followed by a hard frost which
enabled LW to skate on the last day of the year.*

---

either to submit to internment, to run the gauntlet of the waiting British cruisers,
or to scuttle. On 17 December, after off-loading her crew and supplies, she steamed
out into the sunset and blew herself up. Commodore Harwood, R.N., was
promoted Rear-Admiral and knighted.

12. VW was reading Freud's *Group Psychology* (1922); *Self-Portrait, Taken from the
Letters & Journals of Charles Ricketts, RA*, compiled by T. Sturge Moore (1939);
Letters and Diaries of Henry, Tenth Earl of Pembroke and his Circle, 1734-80,
edited by Lord Herbert (1939); and *The Ages of Man: Shakespeare's Image of Man
and Nature*, an anthology selected by George Rylands (1939).

— 1940 —

1940

DIARY XXIX for 1940 which follows is written on loose-leaf paper.

Wednesday 3 January

Monks House, Rodmell

This very large sheet which I bought at Baxter's [*Lewes stationers*] two days ago begins a new year, on a new system. Evening over the fire writing, instead of end of the morning scrambling. Thus I hope to write a better hand, &, if it weren't that I've just heated my head over Roger, the PIP [*Post-Impressionists*] (a bad chapter) more solidly. For unless I can put a little weight into this book, it'll have no interest, even for an old woman, turning the pages. I have just put down Mill's autobiography, after copying certain sentences in the volume I call, deceptively, the Albatross.[1] We have been out in Janice's car, looking for skating. Its a long bitter winter frost—I forget how many degrees of a night—I think 22 below freezing. Figure an Italian sun yesterday; & hard white snow; & the street like glass; the village treat to Brighton; chains round the wheels; the butcher saying he'd had enough of it, which, as he has to be in the shop cutting joints at 6, I can follow.

I am oppressed & distracted with all my ideas. All the little cuckoos shoving the old bird—Roger—out of the nest. A book on W[ome]n & peace—& here's L. down from his book.

Saturday 6 January

Which of our friends will interest posterity most? Maynard? So that if I had any regard for the future I would use this hour to record what he said. About his parents. Lying extended on the sofa the other night with the two fog lamps burning, & Lydia a sort of fairy tale elf in her fur cap. We were talking of my legacy; of Leonard's mother. And L. said how she had lived in a dream world. So that he made her cry. Upon which M. said his parents had always let him alone: now they reaped the benefit. The old Dr plays Bridge; Mrs, his mother has M.'s temperament. "But not ruthless as you can be" said Lydia. M. hesitates, gulps & all his

---

1. See MHP, Sussex, B2a: a loose-leaf notebook, labelled by VW on the spine *The/ Albatross/Letters &/Memoir*, in which she has copied from her father's first (1873) edition of J. S. Mill's *Autobiography*: 'This lesson of keeping my thoughts to myself, at that early age, was attended with some moral disadvantages' on p. 44, to the first line of p. 45.

words come out in a rush. He is now supreme, mounted on his sick throne, a successful man—farmer, bursar, a man of business, he called himself, applying for petrol. A heavy man with a thick moustache. A moralist. As interested in Patsy the black dog with the bald patch as in Europe. He was saying—odd how hard it is to remember—he was telling us about salt; water; heat & cold & their effect on the urine. About Roger. "Can I mention erection?" I asked. Lydia "What?" M. "Stiff" (their private word). No you cant. I should mind your saying it. Such revelations have to be in key with their time. The time not come yet. Sodomy & the WC disinfected. Is he right, or only public school? All is now so ordered, so royally arrayed, that we had to go that Wednesday [27 December], because otherwise—"No Maynard says it is not convenient" L[ydia]. on the telephone. But words are soon lost. I am writing this, the d—d party, the dark drive in prospect & L. glooming, in order to have a free fling.

So tight & tortured of a morning, but enough of that. Can I descend to the spontaneous populous strata . . . after living so long above ground? An obituary: Humbert Wolfe. Once I shared a packet of choc. creams with him, at Eileen Power's. An admirer sent them. This was a fitting tribute. A theatrical looking glib man. Told me he was often asked if I were his wife. Volunteered that he was happily married, though his wife lived—Geneva? I forget; remember thinking, why protest? whats worrying you? Oh it was the night Arnold Bennett attacked me in the En Standard. Orlando? I was going to meet him at Sybil's next day. There was a queer histrionic look in him, perhaps strain in him. Very self assured, outwardly. Inwardly lacerated by the taunt that he wrote too easily; & deified satire; thats my salvage from an autobiography of him—one of many, as if he were dissatisfied & must always draw & redraw his own picture. I suppose the origin of many of the new middle-aged autos. A kind of self psychoanalysis; oh & Viola Garvin—a fume rises from the old cabbage pail of literary gossip—was in love with him; a fact she expressed in a review of Requiem that positively split its sides, ripped open like a balloon—the pressure of praise in it was so terrific. Requiem Vita had with her at Oxford when I lectured once. How rotten, I said, looking at it, as it lay on the dressing table in the Inn. And she was glad she said, owning with her usual simplicity what I, should I?—have hidden. So the inspirer of these vague winter night memories—he who sends for the last time a faint film across my tired head—lies with those blackberry eyes shut in that sulphurous cavernous face.[2] (If I were

2. Humbert Wolfe (b. 1886), poet and civil servant, died on 5 January 1940; born Umberto Wolff in Milan, he was brought up and educated in England. His large literary output includes reminiscence, essays, translations, plays and poetry. Arnold Bennett's attack on *Orlando* appeared in the *Evening Standard* of 8

writing I should have to remove either lies or eyes. Is this right? Yes, I think for me; nor need it spoil the run. Only one must always practise every style: its the only way to keep on the boil: I mean the only way to avoid crust is to set a faggot of words in a blaze. That phrase flags. Well, let it. These pages only cost a fraction of a farthing, so that my exchequer isnt imperilled.)

Mill I should be reading. Or Little Dorrit, but both are gone stale, like a cheese thats been cut in & left. The first slice is always the best. Mr Gwynn[e] caught me at Piddinghoe on the down yesterday—a nobleman: lean, sporting, dried, with little wet pebble eyes; a severe man. I smiled. He I think apprehended some incongruity: I was scrambling under the barbed wire in my wool helmet. "Where d'you come from?" "Only taking a walk". "This is private." "Hope I'm not spoiling your sport?" "Not at all. You can go on . . ." He'll ask his wife, what odd looking woman lives at Rodmell. She'll guess, Mrs Woolf. He'll say . . . Louie says he'll say he dont hold with the Labour Party. He had a row with Paul about the wood on his down. The villagers mustn't steal it. Paul said they had a right. Story dwindles off. The idiot boy has pneumonia, should die but of course, wont.[3]

Friday 19 January

I cant say that this after tea system has been good for this large page. But Sussex has been sociable. A[ngelica]'s 21st birthday party, & its legacy of Lewises; then Flora; then Morgan; then London, from which we came back this afternoon to frozen pipes. Dean is flaring away at the spare room at this instant, & this gives me an excuse for not nailing my brain to some solid book—an essay of Bertie [Russell]'s say.[4] My London technique is improving. A concert at Nat Gal; Hugh [Walpole]

November 1928, but VW made no record of meeting Wolfe with the mediaeval historian Eileen Power (1889-1940) at that time. Wolfe's poetic sequence *Requiem* (1927)—which VW looked at with V. Sackville-West at Oxford in May 1927 (see *III VW Diary*, p. 136, n. 1)—was extolled in *The Observer* by the literary editor Viola Garvin (1898-1969), daughter of the paper's famous editor J. L. Garvin.

3. E. W. Paul was the tenant farmer at Southease, whose land adjoined Mr Gwynne's. The 'idiot boy' (see below, 30 May 1940, n. 17) was Louie's youngest brother Tony, devotedly cared for by her mother, Mrs West.

4. The 'd—d party' anticipated in the foregoing entry—'one last Bloomsbury celebration' (*II QB*, p. 213)—took place at Charleston on 6 January; E. D. Lewis and his (then) wife the pianist Michal Hambourg were among Angelica's guests. LW's sister Flora Sturgeon and her daughter Molly came to Monks House for lunch, and E. M. Forster for the night, on 12 January. On 15 January the Woolfs went to London for four days. Mr Dean, of The Forge, Rodmell, was the local builder and smith.

& Wm Plomer to dinner, Sybil to tea—all accomplished. And last night The Importance of Being Earnest, a thinnish play, but a work of art; I mean, its bubble dont break. And I took about 60 pages to be typed.[5]

By way of a brain graph, I record that for 5 days I could do nothing but improvise my WEA lecture—syllabled it in the bath, on walks; wrote a sketch nefariously. Now its spent, that fever, & I shall attack the Omega with appetite tomorrow. Why this sudden pressure on the brain? Its uncontrollable.[6]

Hugh is rather like the winter sun—his ruddy edges slightly blurred. He wore a red flower. Wm. in a buff waistcoat, but sharpened, disappointed,—life unsatisfactory; embittered—no blur, rather a chopping block. I diagnose some sense of defeat & strain, part private, part war. A man in pain—on the stretch; so that some string gives a discord. No, thats not quite it. Looks dissipated, with work, with dull & dreary work; & no creativeness; but a standard, which dear old Hugh (he wrote to thank "Dearest Virginia" this morning) has forced down. I suppose a little second rate. At dinner when I told him that Maynard had read Sea Tower [1939], he looked like a small boy tipped—an endearing bashfulness. We talked—if I could face the labour of inverted commas—about Horizon: Stephen condemned; & about Humbert Wolfe; dead of overwork; about Frankau (his memoirs as chirpy as a robin—honest, edited of course, rasping, & with the real life profusion which only the shelly & tough skinned can stand)[7] & then Hugh told us the story of the Conrads, told it very well: about C. sizing up the sod. masseur at tea; withdrawing, shrieking; & Miss Hallows & Jessie, who wouldnt ask Miss Hallows for the salt; & C. shut up alone with her; & Jessie growing fat on the sofa with her bad leg; about Boris & his forgery;[8] so to diaries, his own left to Rupert Hart Davis;[9] [omission] & so to Dickens; & the Vn hypocrisy, Thackeray haling a prostitute in the

5. The National Gallery, emptied of its pictures for the duration of the war, offered daily lunch-time concerts for a shilling; VW went on 16 January. The production of Wilde's play at the Globe Theatre was notable for Edith Evans's immortal Lady Bracknell.

6. VW's lecture, originally intended to be read to the Brighton branch of the WEA on 2 March, had to be postponed until 27 April 1940 because of her illness; it was later published as 'The Leaning Tower' in Folios of New Writing, Autumn 1940 (Kp C372). 'The Omega' was Chapter 8 of Roger Fry.

7. Gilbert Frankau's Self-Portrait. A Novel of his Own Life (1940).

8. Walpole revered Joseph Conrad (1857-1924), visited him frequently during his later years, and was familiar with his domestic circumstances and afflictions: his over-weight and constantly suffering wife Jessie, his improvident elder son Borys, his ever-present secretary-nurse Miss Hallowes.

9. Rupert Hart-Davis (b. 1907), publisher, was to become Walpole's biographer (1952).

street opposite the Garrick; Dickens & his mistress; (all spoken as if they were old friends—so they are—if youre in the Hugh tradition, but Wm. & I arent)—so to Trollope; & defamation of Wells; a mere scribbler; compare him with Conrad. What then is an artist? A question I'd like to solve. A bitter cold night & they stayed till 12.30: then went into the moonlight, & left the door open.

Here I change pens: my hands are so cold; & my brains cold, yes, very like Janice's cheap car, which wont start. One should have a piece of porous paper to press on the brain when its hot, instead of chafing it to work, as I do now, from idleness, from distraction. Oh I made up a little of P.H. at 37, & think I've tapped something perhaps—a new combination of the raw & the lyrical; how to slide over. I think 2 years at Roger may have filled the cistern.

Then Sybil. I was touched. Her cheeks were so cold when she came in. Why did she think it worth coming? Vanity was flattered. After working off all our graces & paces—Hugh to dine—oh Hugh wrote to me this morning—we got warmer about the past. She never liked George. Used to meet him at the Wards. He patronised her. He broke hearts. Dorothy Ward was in love—passionately. G. didn't care. An arch snob. Old Gerald, the greedy, the vulgar, far more to him. The young intellectuals at the Savile liked him; disliked George. So I sketched our family life. She was more human—asked me to dine at the Ordinary. & went out into the bitter black & white square.[10]

Saturday 20 January

I think it would be better to read quietly some severe classic, & not make up some ranting rhymes, this bitter cold night. Smoking cigarettes over the fire & feeling—just because the rent of 37 is so high [£250 p.a.] —that we were, for once, foolish. Then L. went & skated & I walked on the bank & home over the marsh. The beauty was etherial, unreal, empty. A June day. 10 degrees of frost. All silent, as if offered from another world. No birds, no carts, men shooting. This specimen against the war. This heartless & perfect beauty. The willows ruby red, no rust red; plumed; soft; & all the roofs orange & red; & the hills white. But some emptiness in me—in my life—because L. said the rent was so high. And then the silence, the pure disembodied silence, in which the perfect specimen was presented; seemed to correspond to my own vacancy,

10. Lady Colefax had tea with VW on 18 January. The Wards—Mrs Humphry Ward and her family—lived from 1891 at 25 Grosvenor Place, SW1, and their social connections embraced VW's half-brothers George and Gerald Duckworth. Dorothy Ward (1874-1964), the eldest child, was her mother's companion and helpmeet until the latter's death in 1920. An 'Ordinary' was a fixed price restaurant meal.

walking muffled with the sun in my eyes, & nothing pressing urging only this iron hard, ground, all painted. The men were waiting for widgeon—the quickest birds. Come down like an express. We sat in the sun on the bank. All looked very distant, & picked out—the little stems of smoke—the wild duck—the horses huddled & still. No thoughts populated; I was somehow held in a pair of pincers, & came home to cook crumpets to revise my article; & all the words seem bodiless too. So what about a severe classic?

A fire at Charleston. Fire Engines called out on Wednesday night.[11] No letters. Reaction after London? And Roger reeling off my fingers. And the future. I must tuck myself in with work. A child crying in the school. What do I do to help? But in fact, these are the moments for compacting; for living: unless one's to blow out; which I entirely refuse to do.

Friday 26 January

These moments of despair—I mean glacial suspense—a painted fly in a glass case—have given way as they so often do to ecstasy. Is it that I have thrown off those two dead pigeons—my story, my Gas at Abbotsford (printed today).[12] And so ideas rush in. I began one night, absolutely submerged, throttled, held in a vice with my nose rubbed against Roger—no way out—all hard as iron—to read Julian. And off winged my mind along those wild uplands. A hint for the future. Always relieve pressure by a flight. Always violently turn the pillow: hack an outlet. Often a trifle does. A review offered of Marie Corelli by the Listener.[13] These are travellers notes which I offer myself shd I again be lost.

I think the last chapter must be sweated from 20 to 10 thousand. This is an attempt at the first words:—

"Transformations is the title that Roger Fry ~~chose for his~~ gave to [his]
last book of essays. And it seems natural enough,
But transformations   looking back at the last ten years of his life, ~~so full~~
must express not   to choose it by way of title for them too ~~so~~ full
only change, but   were they of change, ~~so little & also of achieve-~~
achievement   ~~ment. For~~ They were also full of achievement.
His position as a critic ~~was~~ became established

11. The fire at Charleston was confined to a smouldering timber behind the kitchen chimneypiece.

12. VW's 'Dog Story' was sent to Chambrun in New York by LW on 22 January 1940 (see LWP, Sussex, II D 1a); 'Gas at Abbotsford' appeared in the *NS&N*.

13. 'The Dream', VW's review of *Marie Corelli: The Life and Death of a Best Seller* by George Bullock, appeared in *The Listener* of 15 February 1940 (Kp C365).

to choose a title wh. expresses change; they were full of experiment & experience Those changes, it was because they were he acquired a position

They were ~~years not~~ years not of repose & stagnation. ~~They were years of change.~~ but of perpetual experiment & new experience. ~~In the course of them~~ His position as a critic became established. "At the time of his death" writes Howard Hannay, "Roger Fry's position in the English art world was unique, & the only parallel to it is that of Ruskin at the height of his reputation." ~~And the perpetual~~ ~~This was achieved Perpetual speculation, But that position was only his because a room So he~~ But it was a position that ~~transfor~~ The transformations then, ~~the perpetual revisions of the his left threw out~~ left behind them ~~something that his thought that~~ This perpetual revision of thought in the light of experience, resulted in something But this ~~reputation~~ position ~~depended upon~~ was the result of the freedom ~~of his~~ which ~~he had~~ the ~~energy & the~~ & the vigour with which he carried on his intellectual life; & so closely connected ~~that it [is] impossible to separate them, went the other adventure~~ with which he extended & enlarged his view. ~~And it~~ Nor was he less adventurous in ~~his~~ the other life ~~which after all~~ with ~~which the oth nor is it possible to separate the two.~~ And there too, transformations ~~left~~ resulted in ~~what was~~ something permanent. as Sir K Clark says: Although he was remarkably consistent in the main outlines of his beliefs, his mind was invincibly experimental & ready for any adventure, however far it might lead him beyond the boundaries of ~~aesthetic~~ academic tradition.

~~And~~ Physically, the strain was very great. His health had suffered from the long years at the Omega

No I cannot reel it off at all. How queer the change is from private writing to public writing. And how exhausting. My little fund of gossip & comment is dried up. What was I going to say? Oh that the lyric mood of the winter—its intense spiritual exaltation—is over. The thaw has set in, & rain & wind, & the marsh is soggy, & patched with white, & two very small lambs were staggering in the east wind. One old ewe was being carted off; & shirking the horror I crept back by the hanger. Nor have I spent a virtuous evening, hacking at these phrases. I'm enjoying Burke though, & shall tune up on the French Revolution.

Q. last night. Miss Gardner on Federation. She writes short stories; her brother [Paul], a slip of a blue bell stalk beside Q.'s rosy sun, writes poetry, & is in touch with "our group". We plan printing; indeed L. set up an address this afternoon. Then we hung Nessa's picture, & it being now 6 o'clock, I shall take a plunge into some current. We go up next week, shall have Tom to dine & go to the new O'Neil play. No, its useless writing biography between tea & dinner. Better dream.

FEBRUARY 1940

Tuesday 30 January

Unable to go to London because of the worst of all frosts. A sudden return. Everything glass glazed. Each blade is coated, has a rim of pure glass. Walking is like treading on stubble. The stiles & gates have a shiny green varnish of ice. Percy has to dig paths. Ink frozen. On Sunday no cars cd. move. Nessa said the Lewises had to give up. Thats the last I heard from Charleston. On Monday the electric light failed. Cooked breakfast on dining room fire. Came on at 12.30. Today all idea of travel impossible. Trains hours late or lost. No buses running. Walked to Lewes & back. Met snow plough; 2 or 3 cars; no walkers. Lewes very empty. Home by the short cut; which was painful. A great flight of wild geese. The grass is brittle, all the twigs are cased in clear brown cases, & look thick, but slippery, crystallised, as if they were twigs of fruit at dessert. Now & then the wireless reports a ship sunk in the North Sea. Almost out of meat, but at last the Coop sent. Very still tonight. More snow? No papers till the afternoon.

[? *Wednesday 31 January*]

To that rapid note—how odd that I still feel I cant leave a new sight undescribed—there is nothing much to add today. It is thawing. Theres a rush, like a mattress falling, as the snow slides off the roof. We walked on the marsh, & saw a half devoured hare. Dabs of blood on the snow, & such a scrape of a wind, & such hobbling & tumbling over frozen tussocks into the snow that I cut the walk, & came home to type out my ten guinea Corelli. Vita is offered £1,850 for a 25,000 word story. My righteous backbone stiffens. Then what about my £200 dog story? Ah, but I wouldn't for any money write 25,000 words. I think I've proved that to be true in this way: the humiliation, that is the obstinate refusal of the brain to comply & one's drubbings, & re-writings, & general despondency, even for 2,000 words, make it not so much morally, as physically, intellectually a torture. But its interesting to take the moral temperature now & then. A little quick article I enjoy.

Settled in for another 2 weeks, & only village meetings & books; which however are very 'real'—I like Burke. I think with luck I may concentrate & sweat out R.'s last Transformations. True, I should have enjoyed a wander, but old Mabel reports streets all ice & so on. And I cling to my tiny philosophy: to hug the present moment (in which the fire is going out).

Friday 2 February

Met Nessa outside Uridges today so the frost of isolation is over. It was broken by a meeting though, at which I gossiped with Mrs Funnell

& said I'd find her a dachshund. "Dasshund" she called it, being lower class.[1]

I wish I could conglobulate reflections like Gide. Half of his are daily jottings. Then something solid forms. And they occur at breakfast, or when I'm up to my knees in mud. The lost thoughts—a fine covey they'd make if ever hived—the thoughts I've lost on Asheham down, & walking the river bank. Yesterday a smart car stopped: a glowing lady gave me a lift; burnished & aquiline like Bobo; said to [be] Mrs Drawbell of the hated house.[2] The snow remains, slightly pocked, but the road is clear. The cream woman slipped another ½lb of butter into my bag; the Coops. inserted a lb. of sugar instead of sago into our groceries. And I'm asked not only to write, combatively on peace, for The Forum, but they want to reprint Reviewing. So, what with the Statesman & The Listener, no doubt I could grind out a good many Guineas: & I enjoy the friction: keeps my mind warm, thinking lost thoughts.

Mabel coming (alas) tomorrow. Then London.

I forget to make extracts from the papers, which boom, echoing, emptily, the BBC. Hitler's speech—Churchill's—a ship sunk—no survivors—a raft capsized—men rowing for 10 or 12 or 30 hours. How little one can explode now, as perhaps one would have done, had it been a single death. But the Black Out is far more murderous than the war. Prices rise by 2d then 3d. So the screw tightens gradually; & I cant even imagine London in peace—the lit nights, the buses roaring past Tavistock Square, the telephone ringing, & I scooping together with the utmost difficulty one night or afternoon alone. A reminder to use the present astonishing space for Burke &c. Only the fire sets me dreaming—of all the things I mean to write: the break in our lives from London to country is a far more complete one than any change of house. Yes, but I havent got the hang of it altogether. The immense space suddenly becomes vacant; then illuminated. And London, in nips, is cramped & creased. Odd how often I think with what is love I suppose of the City: of the walk to the Tower: that is my England; I mean, if a bomb destroyed one of those little alleys with the brass bound curtains & the river smell & the old woman reading I should feel—well, what the patriots feel—L. & Sally arrive.

Wednesday 7 February

(Mother's birthday: Nessa's wedding day.) Oh I had such a profound reflection on the tip of my tongue, L. being downstairs, chiming in with Bradfield's lecture. It was to the effect that now, no longer in the move-

1. Uridge was a grocer's in Lansdown Place, Lewes. The meeting was of the WEA on 31 January; Funnell is a common Sussex name.
2. See above, 25 October 1937, n. 8.

ment, & remote in this water sogged country, now's the time to see if the art, or life, creed, the belief in something existing independently of myself, will ⟨weather the/stand the⟩ hold good. These hesitations signify that I've been titivating R.: how spell Fr Bartolomeo?

Well, if it dont stand like a flagstaff, then its been a washout. (word chosen in deference to the new movement.) John for the night; & he plunges us in new this & that. Very nice—so eager & 'boyish' as the old women say: pulling up his shirt to show his rash. We had the Gardners to tea. The old wispy red veined blue eyed pussy purring Major. Very courteous, rather rambling, & inclined to dodder off into moralities about the Crab. That is why the crab is so small, & walks sideways— an old Indian story. The children bolt eyed & transfixed, partly in fear of what Papa might say. And John rather Prince Consort. So a fair beat up talk about poetry, about communism. John obviously bored, but chivalrous. And then out with his documents, & his plans. Radiant hope for the New Writing; for the young. Clearly his metier to go ringing his cowbell in advance. Inclined to write about Wm Morris. Oh & all the doings of the boys. Peter Watson sponged upon by Connolly, Guardsmen & Hamilton.[3] The sink of buggery. Berkeley Square houses the whole hive. Stephen fallen into vice again; sentimentalising with Freud & another. Bleeding his heart all over the place; & J. half hurt, half scornful. Its a queer little eddy, just below the surface;—& familiar of old, tho' not so highly organised. So I drivel longing for the meeting to be over. I will copy the days headlines—Towards a Settlement with Japan. The next phase in India; Red rout in Finland. 5,000 killed & no room for the rest.

Thursday 8 February

⟨Frau⟩ Dr—yes, she wasn't Frau though she looked it—& her name? Hinder? Hinckel?—I never caught it so to speak firmly,—has just gone.[4] This murky February day in which is concealed some flower, some little gesture, of spring—how does one feel that? how say it. The light that comes in a London street—more widely here; she has gone, back to London, to her house with its lounge & its modern Swedish furniture, in Hampstead Garden suburb. She saw her two babies off to Liverpool this morning to stay with their grandmother. And her husband is a doctor, & they are about to spend two weeks in Bath,—Oh to have a

---

3. Victor William ('Peter') Watson (1908-56) inherited a fortune made from margarine in the first World War; a collector of modern painting, he acted as art editor to Cyril Connolly's magazine *Horizon*, to which he gave financial support. Gerald Hamilton (1890-1970) was the prototype of Isherwood's Mr Norris.

4. Dr Rita Hinden, *née* Rebecca Gesundheit (1909-71), graduate of the London School of Economics, became the secretary of the Fabian Colonial Bureau when it first started in 1939; she wrote extensively on Colonial affairs.

knapsack & go tramping! she said, being a swarthy hooknosed red cheeked racy Jewess. At least that phase lasted out lunch— We discussed races; she was born in South Africa. Natives smell she said. Native servants rooms smell very strong. We discussed how nice ordinary people are. Then why are they so repulsive in the mass? A question not solved, partly because the landslip at Redhill had made her so late that lunch (roast chicken; apple amber;) lasted till 2.30. After that she & L. retired to the library to discuss a Fabian treatise on South Africa, wh. she is to undertake, & he to supervise;[5] & I in rubbers & great coat plunged into the marsh, which was, as I've said, veiling, oh very effectively, for the wind blew, our unopened Spring. Here I stop to insert a remark often occurring: how we're being led to the altar this spring: its flowers will I suppose nod & yellow & redden the garden with the bombs falling—oh, its a queer sense of suspense, being led up to the spring of 1940— So I came back, & had to offer tea. Now at tea she shrivelled in a hard high hat into the common, the lemon on steel acid vulgarity of the obvious, the cheap hard Jewess, which at lunch I hadn't seen. Confronted with Nessa's carpet Duncan's table she could only remember her Hampstead lounge; a transition which made me think of the future: & what'll it be, ruled & guided by these active & ambitious & after all competent, & I suppose able, Fabians—oh why dont they any of them embrace something—but what? Poetry, I suppose, the sensuous, the musical? Why must they always stress the ugliness of life; & yet be themselves so vital? And feeling chilled & put in my little compartment, I posted my letters & met poor dying Botten, & stopped L. on the high road & so have arrived here.

Friday 9 February[6]

For some reason hope has revived. Now what served as bait? A letter from Joe Ackerley approving my Corelli? Not much. Tom dining with us? No. I think it was largely reading Stephen's autobiography: tho' it gave me a pang of envy, by its youth & its vigour, & some good novelists touches—I cd. pick holes though. But its odd—reading that & South Riding both mint new, give me a fillip after all the evenings I grind at Burke & Mill. A good thing to read one's contemporaries, even rapid twinkling slice of life novels like poor W. H.'s.[7] And then, I've polished

---

5. This was probably *Plan for Africa*, a report prepared for the Colonial Bureau of the Fabian Society by Rita Hinden, published by Allen & Unwin in 1941.

6. VW has misdated this entry *Friday 10th February.*

7. Stephen Spender's novel *The Backward Son*, a thinly-veiled account of a year in his own childhood, was to be published by the Hogarth Press in the Spring of 1940. Winifred Holtby's *South Riding* (1935) was lent to VW by Ethel Smyth; see *VI VW Letters*, no. 3584 of 7 February 1940.

off, to the last gaiter button, the 3 d—d chapters for London on Monday;
& got my teeth I think firm into the last Transformations; & though of
course I shall get the black shivers when I reread let alone submit to
Nessa & Margery, I cant help thinking I've caught a good deal of that
iridescent man in my oh so laborious butterfly net. I daresay I've written
every page—certainly the last—10 or 15 times over. And I dont think
I've killed: I think I've brisked. Hence an evening glow Yet the wind
cuts like a scythe: the dining room carpet is turning to mould; & John
Buchan has fallen on his head & is, apparently, dying. I have already
composed a letter to Susie, who, poor goose, will be crying her eyes
out, over there in the great carpeted Palace that she hated so. I think she
"adored" him: that is being a goose, believed poor prolific John to be a
kind of Providence. I remember all the MSS bound in blue morocco—
scarcely corrected—a kind of genius, she said—wistfully looking for
some corroboration. Indeed, she flattened me out with John's biographies,
inscribed by John. Monty Shearman is also dead; & Campbell, L.'s
absurd nice old Parson friend—his bachelor Buffy friend.[8]

Now the wind rises; something rattles, & thank God I'm not on the
North Sea, nor taking off to raid Heligoland. Now I'm going to read
Freud. Yes, Stephen gave me 3 hours of continuous illusion—& if one
can get that still, there's a world—whats the quotation—There's a
world outside? No. From Coriolanus?[9]

Sunday 11 February

By way of postponing the writing of cheques—the war, by the way,
has tied up my purse strings again, as in the old days of 11/- a week
pocket money—I write here: & note that the authentic glow of finishing
a book is on me. Does this mean its good; or only that I have delivered
my mind successfully? Anyhow, after shivering yesterday, today I made
a stride, & shall I think finish this week at 37. Its tight & conscientious
anyhow. So, walking this mildish day, up to Telscombe I invented
pages & pages of my lecture: which is to be full & fertile. The idea
struck me that the Leaning Tower school is the school of auto-analysis

---

8. John Buchan, 1st Baron Tweedsmuir, Governor-General of Canada, fell whilst on
a visit to Montreal on 7 February and sustained a concussion from which he died
four days later, in his sixty-fifth year. Montague Shearman (1885-1940) barrister
and picture collector, died on 4 February. The Rev. Leopold Colin Henry Douglas
Campbell-Douglas, 6th Baron Blythswood (b. 1881), a friend and contemporary
of LW's at Trinity College, Cambridge, died on 7 February 1940.

9.   'Despising,
  For you, the city, thus I turn my back:
  There is a world elsewhere.'

                    Coriolanus, III. iii. 131

after the suppression of the 19th Century. Quote Stevenson. This explains Stephen's auto[biograph]y; Louis MacNeice &c.[10] Also I get the idea of cerebration: poetry that is not unconscious, but stirred by surface irritation, to which the alien matter of politics, that cant be fused, contributes. Hence the lack of suggestive power. Is the best poetry that which is most suggestive—is it made of the fusion of many different ideas, so that it says more than is explicable? Well thats the line; & it leads to Public Libraries: & the supersession of aristocratic culture by common readers. Also to the end of class literature: the beginning of character literature; new words from new blood; & the comparison with the Elizabethans. I think there's something in the psycho-analy[s]is idea: that the L.Tower writer couldn't describe society; had therefore to describe himself, as the product, or victim: a necessary step towards freeing the next generation of repressions. A new conception of the writer needed: & they have demolished the romance of 'genius' of the great man, by diminishing themselves. They haven't explored, like H. James, the individual: they havent deepened; theyve cut the outline sharper. And so on.

L. saw a grey heraldic bird: I only saw my thoughts. No news from Charleston, but so absorbed in all this, I'm indifferent.

Friday 16 February

This diary might be divided into London diary & Country. I think there is a division. Just back from the London chapter. Bitter cold. This shortened my walk, which I meant to be through crowded streets. Then the dark—no lighted windows, depressed me. Standing in Whitehall, I said to my horses "Home John", & drove back in the grey dawn light, the cheerless spectral light of fading evening on houses—so much more cheerless than the country evening—to Holborn, & so to the bright cave, wh. I liked better, having shifted the chairs. How silent it is there —& London silent; a great dumb ox lying couchant. The people I saw were, Margery Fry: 2 or 3 hours: a touching soft furred bundle; red nosed, or cheeked, with so many thorns in her softness. I remember: "People are divided into lovers & friends"—to justify her lack of love. So we rummaged in old memories, & revived whats been said so often about Roger's loves & character. She is off to France, & pricked my apathy by suggesting that I should come—& made me deplore my spineless acquiescence; she so mobile.

Dinner party: Tom & Saxon: Clive in afterwards. Saxon a pink plump hoarse oldish man: in his raucous sudden mood: complete silence;

10. Cf. 'The Leaning Tower' in *The Moment*, pp. 116-19, where VW quotes freely from Louis MacNeice's lyric retrospection, *Autumn Journal* (1939): and on p. 121, from R. L. Stevenson.

then raps out some statement, as hard as a walnut—no sequence, no suggestiveness. Tom's great yellow bronze mask all draped upon an iron framework. An inhibited, nerve drawn; dropped face—as if hung on a scaffold of heavy private brooding; & thought. A very serious face. & broken by the flicker of relief, when other people interrupt. But our talk?—it was about Civilization. All the gents. against me. Said very likely, more likely than not, this war means that the barbarian will gradually freeze out culture. Nor have we improved. Tom & Saxon said the Greeks were more thoroughly civilised. The slave was not so much a slave as ours are. Clive also pessimised—saw the light going out gradually. So I flung some rather crazy theories into the air. Then to Humbert Wolfe, striking odd little sparks from Tom's 'genius' vanity. Thats refreshing, his innocent seriousness about himself as a writer. About H.W. Clive told a story—how at the Ivy [Restaurant] he received his death blow from E. Bibesco, who read him 30 pages: so he went home & died.[11] That led to Tom's saying he used commas at the beginning of a line; so I added, & no capitals. Then we searched for an old book to trace capital letters. Saxon emitted some scholars facts. What else? It lasted till 12, so there must have been other sayings: John Buchan, I suppose. Yes, he died, & I haven't yet written to poor black Susie, who's unhappy I suspect, clinging to her John as lightning conductor. Tom talked about Stephen's diary. Pages of S.'s conversation "for I cant remember what T.S.E. said"—were sent to T.S.E. He's benevolent & tolerant of the young. Oh & Yeats. Tom said Turner had made up to Yeats; who was an ill read man; & Dotty successfully imitated him— hence her trumpeting.[12] A good deal of cold weather talk—Tom's landlady providing one jug of water, & Tom bathing at Fabers. Oh & Sydney Waterlow. "I never knew them (S. & Dawks) in the moment of e[c]stasy"—Tom said with his sly smile. & I thought the same of Tom & Vivienne.[13] S. says Saxon feels himself on the shelf, & so digs hard. This is more or less an accurate specimen of talk in the winter preceding the Spring of 1940.

I had Cilla's Finnish letter. People suddenly become grave: forget

---

11. Elizabeth Bibesco (1897-1945), née Asquith, daughter of the late Liberal Prime Minister and wife of the Roumanian diplomatist Prince Antoine Bibesco, was a writer.

12. Stephen Spender's 'September Journal' was published in the February, March, and May issues of *Horizon*, 1940. Poems by W. J. Turner (1889-1946) and Dorothy Wellesley were included in W. B. Yeats's idiosyncratic anthology, *The Oxford Book of Modern Verse* (1936).

13. The diplomatist Sir Sydney Waterlow (1878-1944) and his wife Margery ('Dawks') had been quasi-friends of VW's since before the first World War. Eliot's own disastrous marriage in 1915 to Vivienne Haigh-Wood ended in 1933 (see *IV VW Diary*, 10, 20 July 1933).

gossip; remember what at least they ought to be feeling. She [*unidentified*] wrote to me, out of the blue, about the death, or immortality of Finland. How little that means, at 37 . . . no: it means something, but what?— Then I suffered from my clothes complex acutely buying 2 new sets of clothes, & being persuaded into a blue striped coat by an astute & human woman at Lewises. "But I want you to have this—I dont want you just because you're in the country, to fling on anything. You've got to think of others" . . as if she guessed all my private life—queer: she seemed genuine. Of course I looked a shaggy dowdy old woman. Then to Desire under the Elms: disappointing; flat; elemental situation bare of words; like a scaffold. And B.L. not exciting: & the streets tunnels of gloom.[14]

Monday 19 February

I may as well make a note I say to myself; thinking sometimes who's going to read all this scribble? I think one day I may brew a tiny ingot out of it—in my memoirs. Lytton is hinted as my next task by the way. And 3 Gs a dead failure in USA: but enough. I was going to write about Sally [Chilver].

The snow came down on Saturday: thick white cake sugar all over the garden, blowing into my room in the night: door hinge frozen. She arrived battered, carrying her case, how unlike John, up from Southease; left this morning. And oh to be alone—after 5 nights talk— A very nice young woman, with a brain; a magpie I called her: has picked up so many facts: & adds objective facts: about cars, pumps, politics. Thats her line. Not art: tho' she struck me by her dispraise of the neo Coms; & her respect for the artist—Sitwells for instance. A lunch & tea at Charleston. "Blow your nose" said Clive. Snow falling. Talk—gossip: Robert Graves has left Laura;[15] Anreps; An[astasi]a left debts to be paid by Sally; Nessa feeding hens; gave us 6 new eggs. Duncan asked us to buy cigarettes, wh. I did standing in the snow. Political argument about USA & Ireland between Q., Clive, & Sally. Her real name's Elizabeth. Angelica silent, not disapproving. Sally (dog) kissed Leonard. L. smiled at me. Talk about Hugh W. about Eddy Devonshire—about—I suppose mostly gossip, with some extravagance, about Frys, & poor Helen's autopsy—brain pressed by a bone—contributed by me. London

14. On 15 February the Woolfs saw Eugene O'Neill's play *Desire Under the Elms* at the Westminster Theatre, with John Lehmann's youngest sister Beatrix (1903-79) in the principal part of Abbie.

15. The close emotional and intellectual association between Sally Chilver's uncle the poet Robert Graves and Laura Riding, which began on the latter's first arrival from America in 1926, finally disintegrated during a visit to Pennsylvania in the summer of 1939. He returned to England; she remained.

adventures. Saxon by the way wrote to thank me. Home to cook turkey—tough.[16]

Now the thaw has come: L. has his barometer: explains it to me. Walk over Mount Misery. Snow still thick, but the cart tracks run with rivulets. Snow cleared half way to Knotts Bushes. A dim wet ordinary spring winter day. Snowdrops on the graves. L. lent Connolly [Frederick Conolley, *a farm hand*] a pound. Turned in to the Army by Botten.

So Sally went, & kissed me, being a warm hearted woman, rather valiant, & free minded. What'll become of her? Oh & my new coat, the blue striped one, came, & its not too loud: I'm pleased. And so the week starts again; & I must send off—oh I cant defer it—Roger to M[argery Fry].

On 23 February VW noted in her pocket engagement book: 'Sent MS to M.F.' (Margery Fry). The following day she felt unwell, and spent the next day in bed, but on Monday 26 February drove with LW to Mecklenburgh Square and again took to her bed, returning to Rodmell and bed on 2 March.

Thursday 7 March

A fortnight—well on Saturday it will be a fortnight—with influenza. Up today for the first time. So it shows my inveterate—whats the word for love of writing?—that I open this. Head a white vapour: legs bent candles. All hope abandoned. I think *that* was the main current, lying in bed. Too feverish in London to abandon hope. Had to scribble down my Lecture, until that was abandoned; & correct the last script of R. Then back on Saturday to bed: with a throat like plates of rough iron, which cracked when I swallowed. Oh & before getting into bed that bitter afternoon I read my epitaph—Mrs W. died so soon, in the N.S. & was pleased to support that dismissal very tolerably.[1] A firm conviction somewhere in my survival power. Yet there I lay abandoned. And read all Havelock Ellis, a cautious cumulative, teased & tired book; too pressed down with that very common woman, Edith: so I judged her;

16. The information on the cause of Helen Fry's illness, which VW used in her biography of Roger, was obtained from Margery Fry whom she had seen twice the previous week in London. Recent enquiries by Frances Spalding at The Retreat, York, where Helen was confined from 1910 until her death in 1937, reveal that it was more acceptable than accurate: she in fact suffered from chronic paranoid schizophrenia. No *post-mortem* examination was carried out. The 10th Duke of Devonshire (1895-1950) had become rather a crony of Clive's at the Beefsteak Club.

1. See Result of Competition No. 523, *NS&N*, 2 March 1940: 'Mrs Woolf has passed away;/Rather early, one might say/Considering Orlando's prime/Took such a devil of a time.'

but she was life to him: he lacked life; lacked all quick response: & she was stirring; farmed; preached; at last leapt out of [a] window. And loved women. He's honest & clear but thick [*illegible*] & too like the slow graceful Kangaroo with its cautious soft leaps.[2] But thats much due to influenza. Nessa yesterday. Out on terrace today. Spring smells—clean, sharp, varied. Crocuses out & snowdrops. L. making rock garden. All sounds of human life stilled. Robins & Smyth bag unattended. Some nice person, wanting to hear me lecture, sent me violets. A calm convalesence. But how now can we bring out R.? And does it matter? Anyhow finished. And my brain neednt run on. The lecture can run itself. And . . . & . . . I forget. Oh its the spring thats come while I was ill—birds chirping. P[ercy]. spraying apple trees; blue crocuses with snowdrops. Yes: eno' to try my hand on is done.

Wednesday 20 March

Yes, another attack—in fact 2 other attacks: one Sunday week [*10 March*]—101 with Angelica there to put me to bed; tother last Friday, 102 after lunch. So to bed up here in L.'s room, & Dr Tooth, who keeps me in bed (where I sit up with L. reading proofs) till tomorrow.[3] Thats the boring history. What they call recurring with slight bronchitis. Yes. And the Book's read [*Roger Fry*]. & cd. I write out my chart, it wd. be interesting. One Sunday (the 101 Sunday) L. gave me a very severe lecture on the first half. We walked in the meadows. It was like being pecked by a very hard strong beak. The more he pecked the deeper, as always happens. At last he was almost angry that I'd chosen "what seems to me the wrong method. Its merely anal[ysis], not history.[4] Austere repression. In fact dull to the outsider. All those dead quotations." His theme was that you cant treat a life like that: must be seen from the writers angle, unless the liver is himself a seer, wh. R. wasnt. It was a curious example of L. at his most rational & impersonal: rather impressive; yet so definite, so emphatic, that I felt convinced: I mean of failure; save for one odd gleam, that he was himself on the wrong tack, & persisting for some deep reason—dissympathy with R.? lack of interest in personality? Lord knows. I note this plaited strand in my mind; & even while we walked & the beak struck deeper deeper had this completely detached interest in L. character. Then Nessa came; disagreed: Margery's letter "very alive & interesting"; then L. read the 2nd half thought it ended on the doorstep at Bernard St.; then N.'s note "I'm crying cant

---

2. *My Life* (1940) by Henry Havelock Ellis (1859-1939); in 1891 he married Edith Lees (d. 1916); their unusual marriage relations are fully described in the book.

3. Dr R. S. Tooth, of High Street, Southover, Lewes.

4. The word which appears in the ms as 'anal', *tout court*, is spelled out as 'analysis' in LW's edition of *A Writer's Diary* (1953), p. 328.

thank you"—then N. & D. to tea up here; forbid me to alter anything; then Margery's final letter—"Its *him* . . . unbounded admiration". There I pause.[5] Well, I think I re-write certain passages, have even in bed sketched them, but how in time for this spring? That I shelve till tomorrow. Great relief all the same. Its a slippery floor this: great flower pots; L. walking on his rubber soles; a plan to make this my bedroom: have a bath in cupboard. Yes, its a great relief. Suppose all the first half were to do again—as I'd decided—3 months grind . . And Lord to be quit of it & free—& Lord to have given Nessa back her Roger, lost since Julian died. Also I'm rather proud of my tenacity & conscience in that book: & want to—I suppose to increase my reputation, as biographer, when its sunk as novelist: want to be winging off on small articles & stories. Dog story brought in £170 today; a translation £20; & then Cha[m]brun says Harpers wants an essay on Ly Hester Stanhope: the book I read that Christmas at Lelant, & finished too soon, & put Lytton on the scent of.[6] Yes; so I'm set up: & had a letter from Vita, who says we're out of touch, & she minds. Not on my side I reply. She dont answer. I write to say why dont you answer . . . I think thats a fair though fuggy & frowsty annal (hows it spelt?) of the past 2 weeks. Cold blue & white weather from my window. Mabel here. Suavity & capacity itself, tho' the usual strain with L. & Louie. War thought to be beginning. Peace with Finns. The G.'s raid Scapa. A disgrace. So we raid them. This may prelude a general attack.[7] But why waste even this half inch upon these blaring & boring politics? Even Tooth, the red haired Dr whose name shd. be Hector told me he had no kind or sort of enthusiasm for this war—yet had craved for the last. Yet we must stick it out he said. An average decent opinion.

Thursday 21 March

Here is the Good Friday festival beginning. How one can sense that in a garden, with flowers & birds only, I cant say. Now for me begins

5. Margery Fry's letters do not survive; that from Vanessa Bell, dated 'Charleston—Wednesday—midnight' is in the Berg, and is published as a footnote to *VI VW Letters*, no. 3589.

6. See Jacques Chambrun to LW, 24 February 1940 (LWP, Sussex, II D 1a) enclosing cheque and transmitting the request from *Harper's Bazaar* in New York. VW spent the Christmas of 1909 alone at Lelant in Cornwall, reading with delight *The Memoirs and Travels of Lady Hester Stanhope* by her physician Dr C. L. Meryon, in order to review a dull biography of her by Mrs Charles Roundell (see Kp C42).

7. On 12 March Finland signed a harsh treaty of peace with the USSR, ceding territory and with it her strategic independence. The British naval base of Scapa Flow in the Orkneys was a prime target for German attacks by sea and air; on 19 March the RAF raided the German air-base on the Isle of Sylt as a reprisal for one such attack.

the twilight hour, the emerging hour, of disagreeable compromise. Up to lunch. In the sitting room for tea. You know the dreary, messy, uncomfortable paper strewn, picking at this & that frame of mind. And with R. hanging over me. Walk out as soon as possible, & keep on reading Hervey's memoirs. And so come to the top slowly. I'm thinking of some articles. Sidney Smith. Madame de Stael. Virgil. Tolstoy, or perhaps Gogol. Now I'll get L. to find a life of Smith in the Lewes Library. A good idea.[8] Poor L.—who looks like an Elizabethan, the picture of Charles Lamb, with his green velvet collar standing round his neck—& so bothered with fetching & carrying, & so serious, & with the old roadmenders bucket of red coal smouldering in him.[9] I'll ring up Nessa about sending Helen that chapter, & establish an engagement.

I read Tolstoy at Breakfast—Goldenweiser, that I translated with Kot in 1923 & have almost forgotten.[10] Always the same reality—like touching an exposed electric wire. Even so imperfectly conveyed—his rugged short cut mind—to me the most, not sympathetic, but inspiring, rousing; genius in the raw. Thus more disturbing, more 'shocking' more of a thunderclap, even on art, even on lit.re than any other writer. I remember that was my feeling about W. & Peace, read in bed at Twickenham. Old Savage picked it up. "Splendid stuff!" & Jean tried to admire what was a revelation to me. Its directness, its reality. Yet he's against photographic realism.[11]

Sally is lame & has to go to the vet. Sun coming out. One bird pierces like a needle. All crocuses & squills out. No leaves, or buds on trees.

I'm quoted, about Russian, in Lit sup leader oddly enough.[12]

Easter Sunday 24 March

A curious sub-life has set in, rather spacious, rather leisured, & secluded & content. Still sleep in L.'s room; then I slowly bath & dress

8. *Memoirs of the Reign of George II* by Lord Hervey, edited by J. W. Croker, 1848 (for VW's copy, see *Holleyman*, VSI, p. 55). VW did not pursue her idea of writing on any of the subjects she lists.

9. LW bore a distinct resemblance to Hazlitt's 1804 portrait of Charles Lamb in the dress of a Venetian Senator, now in the National Portrait Gallery (n. 507).

10. *Talks with Tolstoi* by A. B. Goldenveiser, translated by S. S. Koteliansky and Virginia Woolf, The Hogarth Press, 1923 (*HP Checklist* 32).

11. On the advice of Sir George Savage (1842-1921), friend and physician to the Stephen family and a specialist in mental illness, VW in 1910 spent some six weeks in the private nursing home at Twickenham of Miss Jean Thomas, who became devoted to her.

12. *TLS*, 23 March 1940, leader entitled ' "WAR AND PEACE" TODAY': 'Mrs Woolf somewhere remarks the preoccupation of the Russian novelists with "the soul" '. (See 'The Russian Point of View' in *The Common Reader* (1925): 'Indeed, it is the soul that is the chief character in Russian fiction.')

& sit in the sitting room, quietly, entering M[argery']s corrections. Not much bothered really, though I've so short a time. I cant help thinking, in spite of L., that its interesting: & I can I think liven & improve. And I'm buoyed up by M. & N. & D. And feel in one fortnight I shall be quit (oh no, there'll be proofs). This is an egg shell life—so gingerly do I step to avoid rousing my temp: which was 99 pt 4 & is again a little up: but if I dont walk in the wind I think I can refrigerate, & yet keep my brain calm for the morning. Wobbly like one of the spring lambs in my legs. Mabel increases comfort 100 fold. And its refreshing & rejuvenating to see the gold thick clumps of crocuses, & the unopened green daffodils, & to hear my Asheham rooks dropping their husky caws through the gummy air. Birds are having a trial. L. works all the afternoon in his blue shirt making the rock garden. Old Botten is dying. Mabel & Louie have gone to church at Southease, & the Lambs bleat.

I'm beginning Sense & Sensibility—& reading about Apes. That reminds me—to do a C[ommon]. R[eader]. on Darwin. V. of the Beagle one section: Downe the other.[13] So when I'm quit of R. & of the WEA I shall do little articles—& oh the relief of not having the whole building of a book on my shoulders! Of course there'll be the wave splash in June, if we bring it out; but I'm fortified beforehand—thats odd. The first book thats been read first by others. Dear me, tho', I've many paragraphs to rewrite, & there's the end, & Helen still to comment. All the birds are sitting up in L. & V.[14] The twig carrying has begun, & this goes on while all the guns are pointed & charged & no one dares pull the trigger. Not a sound this evening to bring in the human tears. I remember the sudden profuse shower one night just before war wh. made me think of all men & women weeping.

Tuesday 26 March

A curious letter from Hugh this afternoon, part of which I will copy, for I like reading old letters.

"As to my book (I wrote about Roman Fountain) of course I knew that you would dislike some of it very much, but hoped you wd like some which apparently you do. MacCarthy speaks to me as to a child, so does Harold N. talking of my babyish love of my toys in the D.T. . . .

13. Charles Darwin settled with his family at Downe (then Down), Bromley, Kent, in 1842, and died there forty years later; his account of his voyage in HMS Beagle was published in various versions under different titles: VW had a copy of *A Naturalist's Voyage Round the World* given to her father by the author (see *Holleyman*, VSI p. 5).

14. i.e.: 'Leonard and Virginia', the pair of great elms on the far side of the bowling lawn from VW's writing lodge in Monks House garden.

But do you care to hear the truth? Half of me is very mature, half has never grown up at all. I cant help my excitement which irritates you all. I never had anything when I was young (cant read). As to my writing you & I are the opposite ends of the bloody *stick*? You are the supreme example of the aesthetic-conscience—there has never been such another in English fiction. But you *dont* write novels. What you write needs a new name. I am the *true* novelist—a minor one but a true one. I know a lot about the novel & a lot about life seen from my very twisted child-haunted angle. Had I been normal I might have been a major novelist. As it is I am a Siamese twin . . ."

No I cant be bothered to copy any more. It rushes up into a Bengal light spirit of self-glorification—crocuses, sausages, Harold & chess—at the end, & skirts all the thorns & all the truth as usual. What Desmond said was he hasnt a "rare" mind . . . Dear dear, I've no mind to add my own comment.[15]

John rings up to ask if he may bring a friend—a London friend—to lunch tomorrow. Then shall we ask Nessa to bring Helen to meet Margery? And there's London on Monday . . . And I'm half inclined to kick my heels & despatch R. to the printer; & get rid of my artistic conscience. Ignorance was the begetter of that conscience. When I wrote TLS articles & knew nothing I slaved to make every sentence do instead of accuracy. How one's mind interests one! A mercy, seeing its a wild tempest of a day: no outing; rain lashing & streaking the windows. Lottie & Grace over. A great flirt with Percy & presents of tomatoes & plants.[16] And yesterday old Botten faded out under the eyes of Mrs West who's layer out & night watcher to the village. A frail old man; the last of the old villagers—save Dedman—talking the melodious Sussex, sprinkled with words like 'nard' for shoulder, wily & sly & grasping; yet poetic too. And a bore. Bringing the milk he'd stay talking, so we always cut at the sight of him. Like a pollard willow grey greaved moss grown to look at—a tree I mean with very small shrivelled grey leaves.

And what else to fill the page! Such a batter at the window. The effect of the war on weather. Shall I listen in, & rake some music my way instead of raking my mind? No, I will *not* look at R. again.

15. Hugh Walpole had sent VW a copy of his quasi-autobiographical *Roman Fountain*, published on 15 March 1940, which she acknowledged on 19 March (*VI VW Letters*, no. 3592). His response of 23 March, here partly copied by VW, is in MHP, Sussex (copy); in it he refers to reviews by Desmond MacCarthy and Harold Nicolson in the *Sunday Times* of 17 March and the *Daily Telegraph* of 23 March respectively.

16. Grace Higgens, *née* Germany (1904-83) came from her native Norfolk as a girl of sixteen to work for Vanessa Bell; in 1934 she married a local Sussex man, and continued to live and work at Charleston until her retirement in 1970.

Friday 29 March

What shall I think of that[s] liberating & freshening? I'm in the mood when I open my window at night & look at the stars. Unfortunately its 12.15 on a grey dull day, the aeroplanes are active, Botten is to be buried at 3: & I'm brain creased after Margery, after John & his John after Q.[17]. But its the little antlike nibblings of M. that infest me—ants run in my brain—emendations, tributes, feelings, dates—& all the detail that seems to the non-writer so easy ("just to add this about Joan &c") & to me is torture. Thumbing those old pages—& copying onto the carbon. Lord lord! And influenza damped. Well I recur what shall I think of? The river. Say the Thames at London bridge; & buying a notebook; & then walking along the Strand & letting each face give me a buffet; & each shop; & perhaps a Penguin. For we're up in London on Monday. Then I think I'll read an Elizabethan—like swinging from bough to bough. Then back here I'll saunter . . . oh yes & we'll travel our books round the Coast—& have tea in a shop— & look at antiques, & there'll be a lovely farmhouse—or a new lane—& flowers—& bowls with L. & reading very calmly for C.Rs. but no pressure. & May coming & asparagus, & butterflies. Perhaps I'll garden a little oh & print, & change my bedroom furniture. Is it age, or what that makes life here alone, no London no visitors seem a long trance of pleasure—or might be, could I be quit of Helen A. & R.

I'm inducing a state of peace & sensation feeling—not idea feeling. The truth is we've not seen spring in the country since I was ill at Asheham—1914—& that had its holiness in spite of the depression. I think I'll also dream a poet-prose book, perhaps make a cake now & then. Now, now—never any more future skirmishing or past regretting— relish the Monday & the Tuesday & dont take on the guilt of selfishness feeling: for in Gods name I've done my share, with pen & talk, for the human race. I mean young writers can stand on their own feet. Yes, I deserve a spring—I owe nobody nothing. Not a letter need I write (there are the poems in MS all waiting) nor need I have week-enders— For others can do that as well as I can, this spring. Now being drowned by the flow of running water, I will read Whymper till lunch time.[18]

Sunday 31 March

I would like to tell myself a nice little wild improbable story to spread my wings after this cramped ant-like morning—which I will not detail—

17. John Lehmann and his young friend John Irwin lunched on 27 March, and Margery Fry came for that night; after she had gone on 28th, Quentin dined at Monks House before the meeting there of the Rodmell Labour Party.

18. Probably the recently published biography of the alpine climber Edward Whymper (1840-1911) by Frank S. Smythe.

for details are the death of me. Thank God, this time next week I shall be free—free of entering M[argery']s corrections & my own into margins. The story?—oh about the life of a bird, its cheep cheep—its brandishing of a twig by my window—its sensations. Or about Botten becoming one with the mud—the glory fading—the million tinted flowers sent by the doleful mourners. All black like a moving pillar box the woman was—& the man in a black cardboard casing. A story dont come—no but I may unfurl a metaphor—No. The windows very dove grey & dim blue islands—a rust red on L. & V. & the marsh green & dark like the floor of the sea. At the back of my head the string is still wound tight. I will unwind it playing bowls. Then Bobo. And still waxen legs. To carry the virtues of the sketch—its random reaches its happy finds—into the finished work is probably beyond me. Sydney Smith did in talk. Note. To Read P. Plymley.[19] Yes, bare wood spring painted is very fine—flesh pink & elephant grey. Knitting is also a help. Margery says its useless.

Butter all eaten by guests. Asked to meet Tom & Desmond at Hutchinsons. Excitement. Wine. Good food. Old Desmond—shall we go? I wd like to write short book stories. I would like to recapture my own fling.

S[ense]. & S[ensibility]. all scenes. very sharp. Surprises. masterly. Some pedestrian stylised pages. wh. she ends brusquely. The door opened. In came . . . . Willoughby . . or, Edward. Very dramatic. Plot from the 18th Century. Mistressly in her winding up. No flagging. Rather heres an end. And the love so intense, so poignant. And marriage ends all. Sisters love sympathetic. Old Mrs Dashwood the image of— Mrs Curtis? Mrs Easdale?— Elinor I suppose Cassandra: Marianne Jane, edited. Well now for my blue knitting.

Saturday 6 April

Whom did we meet in London this week? Bonamy Dobrée the very moment we arrived. Spick & span, clipped, grey, with a rainbow of medal ribbons across his breast. Training cadets at Filey.[1] Keen unconscious young men, very good at their jobs: instinctively patriotic; the rest 'Bolshies'—I mean the intellectuals. Asked his professional opinion about the war, B. said it might last years. No one can afford to

19. *Letters of Peter Plymley*, by Sydney Smith, published 1807-8. Beatrice Mayor (Bobo), Helen Anrep, Quentin and Angelica Bell, were to come to tea in the afternoon.

1. The Woolfs drove to London on 1 April. Bonamy Dobrée (1891-1974), Professor of English Literature at the University of Leeds from 1936-55, was initially trained for the army, served in the first World War, and had now rejoined as an officer. The Woolfs had known him (and his wife Valentine) since the 'twenties, and had published three of his books.

attack. So, unless driven by some goad, there we shall sit: until perhaps food or other shortage drives Hitler to sting. No sign of it so far. All quiet save for spasmodic raids. So, having little to add, we planed down on to civilisation talk: about books, the young, the growth of classes, the origin of biography; Tom's last poem "didactic", & he left thanking us for civilisation.[2] Also he mentioned Valentine, & her house keeping; & how her child is in America; & how we all descend the rungs of lady & gentlemanhood. Has inherited from his odd Pawnbroking banking forefathers a great chest of V[ictoria]n Silver.

Then a day in bed with headache. Then to my task again—*Thurs*; lunch with John: met Worsley; a round mild spectacled brown young man, rubbed, smoothed. No relation of GT's: now at the N.S: where he tidies Raymond's table.[3] As we talked we hacked thick steak; Oh said John my woman has a dodge for getting rations. No wonder. Some Bloomsbury cabhorse; & for the first time in my lunching out, I had to exchange for a steak that I could cut—And that with difficulty. Then L. was riddled & needled by Miss Robins for 2 hours. A French clock left by Sir Hugh Bell went on striking. She uncovered her secret after the man from Frodsham had mended it—to leave us the MS of Raymond in her will.[4] I spent one afternoon at the L[ondon] L[ibrary]. looking up quotes. Another buying silk for vests. & we did not dine with the Hutchinsons to meet Tom & Desmond, & how glad I was of the drowsy evening. And so, at 12.45 yesterday handed L. the 2 MSS & we drove off as happy as Bank holiday clerks—Thats off my shoulders! Good or bad—done. So I felt wings on my shoulders: & brooded quietly, till the tire punctured: we had to jackal in mid road; & I was like a stalk, all crumpled, when we got here. And its a keen spring day; infinitely [?] lit & tinted & cold & soft: all the groups of daffodils yellow along the bank; lost my 3 games, & want nothing but sleep. Still, other ideas prick; & Watkins offers £400 (about) for an essay on a character. Brace shies at Roger though "no interest in him in the USA".

2. T. S. Eliot's *East Coker* was first published in the Easter number of the *New English Weekly*, 1940.

3. T. C. (Cuthbert) Worsley (1907-77) had been a Public School master, had driven an ambulance for the Republicans in Spain, and in 1939 joined the staff of the *NS&N* under Raymond Mortimer, who for a while he succeeded as literary editor after several intervening years in the RAF. G. T. Worsley (d. 1920) was the headmaster of the prep-school, Evelyns, attended by VW's brothers.

4. After he and VW had lunched with John Lehmann on 4 April, LW went to see Elizabeth Robins in her London flat at Palace Gate, W.8. For the 'MS of Raymond', see above, 10 January 1937, n. 6. Dame Florence (d. 1930), the wife of Sir Hugh Bell, Bt (1844-1931), had been Miss Robins's closest friend. Charles Frodsham & Co., then of South Molton Street, was a celebrated firm of clock-makers and -restorers.

Two days holiday before I begin my lecture. Knitting ties. Reading Sydney Smith. Odd feeling to have done (temporarily) a book. And is it good or dull? And what'll the old friends say? Never mind that for 3 weeks.

Saturday 13 April

"The first crunch of the war"—thats how Winston puts it. The Gs. have invaded Norway.[5] Battles are going on. News leaks out. Some say this is Hitler's downfall. I must make this record, for in fact it gives the old odd stretch to the back curtain of the mind. A fine spring day in front; daffodils luminous groups along the terrace. Aeroplanes overhead. Mine fields laid, apparently to let us land our army. I write, because it is a crunch; after the long lapse; also that I'm maggoty with lecture writing. Must ease my head. These are my motives. And Nessa rings up about the Roger pictures. Herbert Fisher was knocked senseless, had arm & ribs & skull fractured 2 days ago by a lorry.[6] On Tuesday, London: perhaps Sybil Tom & Desmond. No letters. Mrs Chavasse to tea about the play on Monday.[7] Walking up the violet bank this afternoon. Reading Sydney Smith. Damn this running in the head that comes of lecture writing—cant think why I bother: why I let myself run on—is it suppressed jealousy? partly. Also I'm interested. But surely its excessive to go on making up, when its only 20 old ladies in black bonnets I shall make up for. Dinner in the oven. Meat bad & scarce. Eggs for dinner. Fish for L. maccaroni. And its time

Saturday 20 April

Desmond to dinner [on 18 April]. London week. Talk went like this: "Youre the spit of Sydney Smith—" He said he wanted streets not country. "Must have the muddy London streets—So S.S. said. Oh & there's so much to talk about. And let me see your fathers shabby old books— Now (at dinner) a few leading questions . . . about the war. I have a plan for giving G[ermany]. everything, everything: but no arms. We must see to that. And is it impossible? . . . Then, I must tell you— I've told several people—of my revelation. I was reading the Hesperides

5. 'We have probably arrived now at the first main clinch of the war'—Churchill in the House of Commons on 11 April, relating the events leading up to and following the German invasion of Denmark and Norway which began during the night of 8/9 April, and in which British naval forces were heavily engaged.
6. VW's eminent cousin H. A. L. Fisher was knocked down on the Embankment on 11 April and was taken to St Thomas's Hospital, where he died early on 18 April.
7. Mrs Chavasse, the doctor's widow, was President of the Rodmell Women's Institute and as such, in wartime, played a prominent part in village life, into which VW was inevitably drawn.

—the smutty bits—when a voice said August 16th Armistice day . . . But which August? And I wasnt excited. It was an outer voice. I was thinking of Herrick. . . ."⁸ After dinner,—"Michael in an unhappy state. No sense of comfort. Cant love a silly cocktail woman, nor live with a rough woman . . . The women I've loved never cared for clothes. I like quizzy cats. Why all this larding? Even Rachel has a silly row of curls. You wdnt dream of painting your face. Diana [Cooper], after a time, I found in spite of her esquimaux trousers & pearls—oh how ridiculous she looked meeting me at the station—she's humble. Roger . . . a very dull letter writer. I'm very curious to read yr book. It'll be such an odd book. I saw him in Trinity Great Court. Thats R.F. said Eddy Marsh. A gigantic intellect. Its too hot to talk to a man with that intellect . . . Molly is a lady. Desmond says all the same she enjoys my coarse stories. I'm writing Desmond M[acCarthy']s Dictionary. Its my autobiography. Under M. marriage, money—easier for a short winded writer than a book. . . One loses the power of sequence with age. Cant prolong an emotion. The senile forget at once. My daughter dead? (weeps) but why d'you give me marmalade for tea? I only like it at breakfast. . . I'm noting every stage of old age. Its this lack of intensity the young mind in us. Certain gifts are sucked by age . . . The Sunday Times has cut me down £250. And my mother only left 11,000. I gave D[ermod]. & M[ichael]. each £1000. So I'm about square. But cd I afford to buy a house in Lewes? Molly wants to have a very nice tidy home. I dont mind squalor. Then I shd have a room in London—a cup of tea sent up, like Morgan . . . The young can describe passing things—a bridge seen from the train. No. One doesnt remember them. We read Tolstoy. I kept Dos[toevs]ky to myself in my selfish way. They read Jane Austen—Eddie cd say what Mr Woodhouse did on Wednesday. Thats odd about Hugh Walpole— Spender ought to tell us more about Inez—everything or nothing. The idea of being perfectly frank with the public— When is Moore coming? Ask him to stay an extra day. I'll mark that week end—May 18th in my book. Juliet Duff gave it me—gives me one every year. Oh I've stayed so late—¼ to 1 . . ."⁹

And we had Sybil [Colefax] & Herbert Woolf [*to tea*]. And came back yesterday. I remember Clive saying how he was the only person who felt uncomfortable when a singer had a flybutton undone. I had meant to note some such fragments; but the talk has rattled me.

A stuffy evening. News suspended. Herbert Fisher dead. Sybil saw him the day before—of course.

---

8. The second world war ended in fact on 14 August 1945, with the surrender of Japan. Robert Herrick's collection of poems, *Hesperides*, was first published in 1648.
9. Lady Juliet Duff (1881-1965), only child of the 4th Earl of Lonsdale; widowed, divorced, she was a liberal and constant friend.

Thursday 25 April

My mother, I was thinking had 2 characters.

I was thinking of my memoirs. The platform of time. How I see
father from the 2 angles. As a child condemning; as a woman of 58
understanding—I shd say tolerating. Both views true? Herbert's death
recalls him. The groan. That man will kill me! H. going up to talk in the
study. Hearing his wheeze of a laugh on the stairs at night. Essence of a
prig—a don, I thought. He came into the day nursery. Advised us to
read some shilling shocker. Uneasy condescension. A more friendly
memory of a walk at Brighton. I had to choose the way. Chose against
his wish. His frock coat. The King coming to Oxford. Uncle H. advising.
Cd be pressed. H.'s shyness. How he told Emmy "dont be a fool!"
crossing the road, when she screamed. At Oxford when a don. Walking
to Bores Hill. He asked me about Trevy's book. I praised it. He demurred.
The same question next year. I denigrated it. He defended—but pleased.
His vanity. His advice at the Ilberts' house. History required special
training. I was left alone to consult him. Did I suggest history? or
fiction? a serious depressing interview. "H. posts his letters on the school
room table."[10] Then the Cabinet—coming to Hogarth House, discussing
action v. contemplation. "I'm not a great hand at writing . . ." Some
uneasy self-consciousness. The Magnolias at Kew. H. looking. And the
lunch—the Dutch sweets. "Mr F. at a Cabinet meeting." A long talk
alone about Armistice day. Olive brought him. He stayed. Told me
about Milner. The war won today.[11] So to the last social meeting at New
College. The party. His light cats tread. His hollow benevolence. His
shell. His affection. His considerateness. His enthusiasm. Father & Fred.
His stories. Warmer & mellower—asking me to come again. Gave me
Homer, gave me his books. But the distance too great. & so—I shant
give him the pleasure—never went there. And thats over.[12]

Herbert Fisher as a young man was almost ungainly: with his prominent cheekbones & adams apple. He had innocent blue eyes: a wisp of

10. H. A. L. Fisher was the eldest son of Herbert Fisher (1825-1903), tutor and then
secretary to the Prince of Wales, and VW's Aunt Mary; Emmeline (1868-1941)
was the second of his four sisters. He was elected a fellow of New College, Oxford,
in 1888 and taught modern history there; in 1899 he married Lettice, the eldest
daughter of Sir Courteney Ilbert, Clerk to the House of Commons 1901-21, and
as a young woman VW several times stayed with them in Oxford. 'Trevy's book'
was probably G. M. Trevelyan's *England under the Stuarts* (1904).

11. For Fisher and the Magnolias, and the Armistice, see *I VW Diary* 17 April 1919
and 15 October 1918 respectively. Olive Heseltine, *née* Ilbert, was Fisher's
sister-in-law.

12. For VW's last visit to the Fishers at New College, see *IV VW Diary*, 4 December 1933. Fred—the historian F. W. Maitland (1850-1906), Leslie Stephen's biographer, had also been Fisher's brother-in-law.

hair. Much improved in dignity & distinction as he aged. Finally the very type of culture & distinction—light in a pea jacket. Composed, ben[ev]olent, wary. A crane like man. Much like Adrian.

Butterflies ball day 3 days ago. Cuckoo heard. Swallows come.

Advertisements: For 16 years housekeeper & faithful friend . . . *Note* the doglike attribute.

There is nothing in the world so much admired as a man who knows how to bear unhappiness with courage. Seneca.

Lady, formerly supported by brother, Army Colonel . . . in urgent need as only income gifts from former servant.

VW gave her postponed lecture—'The Leaning Tower'—to the WEA in Brighton on Saturday 27 April; on Monday 29th she and LW drove to Mecklenburgh Square, dining that evening with Raymond Mortimer; on Tuesday 30th May she had tea with Hugh Walpole in his Piccadilly flat overlooking Green Park, and dined with Clive Bell. The following day she saw Desmond MacCarthy and Lady Simon; and on Thursday Stephen Spender and Wogan Philipps dined with the Woolfs, who returned to Monks House on 3 May.

Monday 6 May

Nessa has just been & told us a 'very tiresome piece of family news'—A.'s affair with B. (I keep to the discretion of initials).[1] A most astonishing piece of news. Today they set off for 2 months alone in Yorkshire. Pray God she may tire of that rusty surly slow old dog with his amorous ways & his primitive mind. It makes one feel oddly old: even to me comes the emptiness that Nessa feels, as I can guess. A. off alone in love, passionately, with someone old eno' to be her father. How curiously without youth & laughter; Julian's death renewed— And what can she be feeling, in the train to Yorkshire this sullen May night? All the nightingales singing from that rusty canine jaw? And the future? I prognosticate an excuse to return in 5 weeks from now. A scene with B.: then a happy summer here, half repentant, as when she gave up the stage.

This blocks the way to my crowded London diary, & reduces it to fribble & patter. Clive's night: the police; & Mary's visit; the Duke of Devonshire & his midnight daffodils; Clive's unshaven cheeks; Desmond next day—all this I leave like torn scraps in a wastepaper basket. Item my tea with Hugh; the fall of Fatty [Claude] Rogers' picture; Hart Davis fresh from Peter Fleming [1907-71, *travel writer*]; the sulphurous vista of the Green Park; the traffic; Hugh's sodomitic confession of affection; our intimacy interrupted; then Raymond; & little soft round Worsley's

1. A. = Angelica Bell; B. = Bunny Garnett.

discourse on the young [?]—which should bring in my lecture; 200 about there; Robins' carnations; no fear on my part—& so home, last Friday, jaded & jangled, with my proofs—& this evenings work blown up, by this explosion of love; & the dream of the Yorkshire moors, & those two setting the supper in order, & retiring to the couch. Nothing will induce her to marry. So the land recedes from my ship which draws out into the sea of old age. The land with its children.

And we have withdrawn from Norway. The first defeat of the war. Hawhaw has it all his own way.[2] Nessa advises us to prognosticate about that. Compare Maynard's optimism 3 weeks ago. War practically over . . . Kingsley of course croaks in triumph. Another lull.

In London we had Wogan & Stephen: then Stephen again with his last poems at 12 am. His book [*The Backward Son*] sneered at; I praised it. John—well, Mrs L[ehmann]. has broken her thigh. The cold is such I shall have my wood fire. Wrote to GBS this evening.[3]

The worst year we've ever had in the Press, I gather.

An old tramp comes to grind scissors. I give him 2, & then reflect—should I spend 1/8 on scissors? This money anxiety contracts & loosens. Oh & I've forgotten I think Vita's visit [*on 23 April*], & can only assure whoever may read this page that we've seen & talked a great deal, & I've laboured over my wretched book, unable to strangle my conscience or to write one line as I write here—for the 2 weeks that have passed since I described Herbert's death—about which Mary, by the way, was highly philosophic. But there's no Angelica to hoard gossip for.

Its odd how much I thought of that lecture, & now its all forgotten—the agony & the sweat & the old man praising me, & the tea at Fullers, & the man in tweed with the whore, so L. called her.

Monday 13 May

I admit to some content, some closing of a chapter, & peace that comes with it, from posting my proofs today: I admit—because we're in

2. Since the German seizure of vital Norwegian ports on 9 April, Allied help for oppressed Norway had been directed towards the recovery of Narvik and Trondheim. Troops landed in mid-April to effect a pincer attack on the latter were withdrawn in the face of superior German force during the first days of May. (Narvik was in fact captured on 28 May but evacuated some ten days later, with heavy naval losses.) William Joyce, known as Lord Haw-Haw for his supercilious voice, gave regular pro-Nazi propaganda broadcasts from Germany during the war; he was convicted of High Treason and executed by the British in January 1946.

3. A copy of Shaw's long reply, dated 10 May 1940, to this letter (which does not survive) is in MHP, Sussex; in it he describes an encounter between Sir Edward Elgar and Roger Fry from which VW quotes in *Roger Fry: A Biography*, the proofs of which she was still correcting. Shaw's letter ends on a note of gallantry: '. . . first met you and, of course, fell in love with you. I suppose every man did.'

the 3rd day of "the greatest battle in history." It began (here) with the 8 oclock wireless announcing, as I lay half asleep, the invasion of Holland & Belgium. The third day of the Battle of Waterloo. Apple blossom snowing the garden. A bowl lost in the pond. Churchill exhorting all men to stand together. "I have nothing to offer but blood & tears & sweat".[4] These vast formless shapes further circulate. They aren't substances; but they make everything else minute. Duncan saw an air battle over Charleston—a silver pencil & a puff of smoke. Percy has seen the wounded arriving in their boots. So my little moment of peace comes in a yawning hollow. But though L. says he has petrol in the garage for suicide shd. Hitler win, we go on. Its the vastness, & the smallness, that make this possible. So intense are my feelings (about Roger): yet the circumference (the war) seems to make a hoop round them. No, I cant get the odd incongruity of feeling intensely & at the same time knowing that there's no importance in that feeling. Or is there, as I sometimes think, more importance than ever?

Basket given us by the WEA—then G. & Annie[?]. A horrid little scrub called Lee wastes a morning, about Curtis. Q. & Eth Watson dine. And we have Desmond & Moore this week end. I made buns for tea today—a sign my thralldom to proofs (galleys) is over.

Tuesday 14 May

Yes, we are being led up garlanded to the altar. A soldier with his rifle. The Dutch Govt & Court here. Warned of clergymen in parachutes. War war—a great battle—this hot day, with the blossom on the grass. A plane goes over—

Wednesday 15 May

An appeal last night for home defence—against parachutists. L. says he'll join.[5] An acid conversation. Our nerves are harassed—mine at least: L. evidently relieved by the chance of doing something. Gun & uniform to me slightly ridiculous. Behind that the strain: this morning we discussed suicide if Hitler lands. Jews beaten up. What point in waiting? Better shut the garage doors. This a sensible, rather matter of

4. Without pretext or warning, German air and land forces assaulted and invaded neutral Holland, Belgium and Luxembourg early on 10 May. On that day Mr Chamberlain, having lost the confidence of the country, resigned as Prime Minister and Winston Churchill was called upon to lead a national coalition. In seeking a vote of confidence in his new administration on 13 May, his actual words were: 'I have nothing to offer but blood, toil, tears and sweat.'

5. The Local Defence Volunteers—soon to be re-named the 'Home Guard'. LW did not join, but undertook Fire Watching and Air Raid Precautions duties in the village.

fact talk. Then he wrote letters, & I too: thanked Bernard Shaw for his love letter. Copied my lecture contentedly. A thunderous hot day. Dutch laid down arms last night. The great battle now raging. Ten days, we say, will settle it. I guess we hold: then dig in; about Nov. the USA comes in as arbitrator. On the other hand—

Mabel just come. She says theyre building wooden bridges beside the others on the Thames. Pop-pop-pop, as we play bowls. Probably a raider over Eastbourne way. Now thunder rain sets in. L. & P[ercy] discussing Miss Emery's fruit. John wishes we'd come up. Mr Pritchard (the old one) dead at last. No, I dont want the garage to see the end of me. I've a wish for 10 years more, & to write my book wh. as usual darts into my brain. L. finished his yesterday.[6] So we've cleared up our book accounts—tho' its doubtful if we shall publish this June. Why am I optimistic? Or rather not either way? because its all bombast, this war. One old lady pinning on her cap has more reality. So if one dies, it'll be a common sense, dull end—not comparable to a days walk, & then an evening reading over the fire. Hospital trains go by. A hot day to be wounded. Anyhow, it cant last, this intensity—so we think— more than 10 days. A fateful book this. Still some blank pages—& what shall I write on the next 10?

This idea struck me: the army is the body: I am the brain. Thinking is my fighting.

Monday 20 May

This idea was meant to be more impressive. It bobbed up I suppose in one of the sentient moments. The war is like desperate illness. For a day it entirely obsesses; then the feeling faculty gives out; next day one is disembodied, in the air. Then the battery is re-charged, & again— what? Well, the bomb terror. Going to London to be bombed. And the catastrophe—if they break through: Channel this morning said to be their objective. Last night Churchill asked us to reflect, when being bombed, that we were at least drawing fire from the soldiers for once.[7]

6. W. B. Pritchard, who was admitted in 1876, had been the senior partner in Dollman & Pritchard, the firm of solicitors who became the Woolfs' tenants in Tavistock Square in 1924, and moved with them to Mecklenburgh Square; his son George had succeeded him. LW's book was *The War for Peace*, a short book written for the Labour Book Club and published by Routledge in September 1940.

7. Overpowering German forces had broken through the French frontier defences near Sedan on 15 May, and were rapidly advancing towards the Channel, cutting communications between the Allied Northern Armies (including the British) which had advanced into Belgium, and the main French forces and overall Supreme Command.

Desmond & Moor[e] are at this moment reading—i.e. talking under the apple trees. A fine windy morning. Moor[e] has a thatch of soft unattached hair: red rimmed eyes, very steady; but less force & mass to him than I remembered. Less drive behind his integrity which is un-alloyed, but a little weakened in thrust by the sense of age (65) & not quite such a solid philosophic frame as I suppose when we were all young we anticipated. So that our reverence—how mute I was at the Sangers—how timidly I ventured my little compliment—is now what one might call retrospective. At tea yesterday with Nessa & Quentin we *remembered* his great influence: his silences. "I didnt want to be silent. I couldnt think of anything to say" he said, rebutting, I think with some feeling that he'd carried this influence too far—our charge that he had silenced his generation. Hence his dependence on Desmond; who started talking, to the towel horse, to the cat, when he was a baby, & was sent to school to silence him. Many old memories. These spin a kind of gauze over the war: wh. is broken by papers: & at listening in time. The war then is waged vigorously till I throw Coleridge into the fire: & it takes another leap. D. & I discussed Irene; & some of the old anecdotes of course appear intact.[8] A good talker makes his toilet of a morning much as a Mary Hutchinson makes up. Word for word we had the definition of age; wh. I think I recorded after our dinner. What is impressive however, are the improvisations. I like hearing Desmond give his first version—say of—I forget—on the spur of the moment. Nessa & I sat & talked here (the Lodge) while they bowld. Politics—the peace terms—how the young havent had a chance—Even we. She knitting Q.'s grey stockings: will have a show at the Leicester Galleries. Then to London the whole lot of us tomorrow; & on Friday here again. Roger & the proofs have entirely receded; nor can I tackle Walpole—havent even read the book;[9] & its $\frac{1}{4}$ to 12: then lunch: extravagant guinea fowl; Moor[e] munches like a chaff cutter; I guess has not a liberal table at home; takes a logical view of food; eats philosophically to the end: while Desmond sprinkles sugar & cream, also liberally but erratically. So the housekeeper in me rises into being, in this miserable life of detail & bombast.

Saturday 25 May

Then we went up to what has been so far the worst week in the war. And so remains. On Tuesday evening, after my freshener, before Tom & Wm. P. came, the BBC announced the taking of Amiens & Arras.

8. See *I VW Diary*, 27 January 1918 for Irene Noel-Baker (1889-1956) and Desmond MacCarthy's 'Ireniad'.

9. R. W. Ketton-Cremer, *Horace Walpole*, 1940, which VW wrote about in 'The Humane Art', *NS&N*, 8 June 1940 (Kp C366).

The French PM told the truth & knocked all our "holding" to atoms. On Monday they broke through.[10] Its tedious picking up details. It seems they raid with tanks & parachutists: roads crammed with refugees cant be bombed. They crash on. Now are at Boulogne. But it also seems these occupations arent altogether solid. What are the great armies doing to let this 25 mile hole stay open? The feeling is we're outwitted. Theyre agile & fearless & up to any new dodge. The French forgot to blow up Bridges. The G.s seem youthful, fresh, inventive. We plod behind. This went on the 3 London days. The party (Tuesday) agreed to ignore. William told a story about Mrs Hyde Colville's camellia hat being burnt as a wreath at a cremation.[11] Tom, I thought, is ossifying (after Desmond's geniality) into that curious writers egotism. "Coleridge & I . . . people read only our best poems. They ignore all the rest of me. It is difficult, when lecturing, to leave out oneself . ." Yet poor man if this complacency gives him a shell, no doubt it protects him from suffering. A very self centred, self torturing & self examining man, seen against Desmond's broad beam, & Moore's candid childs eyes.

Then I had Sybil: & noted her—what in another would be heroism: her son at Arras: she working all day: yet has so much fluid worldliness, & something hard at bottom that one doesnt credit her with enough of her courage. "We're all in it" she said; simply; yet then curled & shrivelled, because we had had D. & M. & she had been talking to the respectable Cynthia Asquith. Envy writhes at once.[12] Then there was the mad Kot: all his hair brushed up; heavy, yellow, bloodshot. To begin with he told us the story of a Tolstoy. It struck me he lives in what he reads: makes it do instead of living. Then fabricates what he calls a theology. From that he turned to Gertler: his suicide. Has become opinionated & violent. But his madness was about the war. He seemed raving. He seemed almost drunk. All the old rage with Murry is now with Fascists. All Germans are devils. We must kill every one. Then some hare brained scheme. Smoking his expensive cigarettes. And his handshake as crushing as ever—as positive. But something gone queer—a screw loose. He gets up at 6 to listen to the BBC at 7. is obsessed—brooding alone at Acacia Road. Does his own housework, & denounces, lays down the law. Had lectured Gertler about his son.

10. The so-called Weygand plan to halt the German thrust to the Channel by a British attack southwards in the Arras area to join up with French forces pushing northwards across the Somme, was put into operation on 21 May, but by the following night the British were forced to retreat. In the confusion of the times, this news first reached the British Government in a reproachful telegram from the French Prime Minister Paul Reynaud.
11. Mary Colville-Hyde was the mother of Plomer's friend Anthony Butts.
12. Lady Cynthia Asquith (1887-1960) was the wife of the Liberal Prime Minister's second son, Herbert Asquith.

Rodmell burns with rumours. Are we to be bombed, evacuated? Guns that shake the windows. Hospital ships sunk. So it comes our way.

Todays rumour is the Nun in the bus who pays her fare with a mans hand.

Tuesday 28 May

And today at 8, the French P.M. Broadcast the treachery of the Belgian King. The Belgians have capitulated. The Government is not capitulating. Churchill to broadcast at 4. A wet dull day.[13]

Wednesday 29 May

But hope revives—I dont know why. A desperate battle. The allies holding. How sick one gets of the phrase—how easy to make a Duff Cooper speech, about valour, & history, where one knows the end of the sentence. Still it cheers, somehow.[14] Poetry as Tom said is easier to write than prose. I cd reel off patriotic speeches, by the dozen. L. has been in London. A great thunderstorm. I was walking on the marsh & thought it was the guns on the channel ports. Then, as they swerved, I conceived a raid on London; turned on the wireless; heard some prattler; & then the guns began to lighten: then it rained. Mrs Dedman off north for the duration. We had our First Aid meeting. Miss Emery English country spinsterhood at its best: sturdy, yet conciliatory, lucid, humorous, with a bar of medal tabs. Everything spaced, brief & clear. L. said the English genius for unofficial organisation. All about the Water Co. & the tap & the Rectory scullery—very tactful too. Mrs Hubbard, like a great turkey cock, head of the committee. Hubbard limping outside.[15] Then the [W.I.] plays rehearsed here yesterday. My contribution to the war is the sacrifice of pleasure: I'm bored: bored & appalled by the readymade commonplaceness of these plays: which they cant act unless we help. I mean, the minds so cheap, compared with ours, like a bad novel—thats my contribution—to have my mind smeared by the village & WEA mind; & to endure it, & the simper. But this is to be qualified—only theres Miss Griffiths [*Hogarth Press clerk*] coming for the weekend—

13. In the early hours of 28 May, on the orders of King Leopold and without prior warning to the Allies, the Belgian army surrendered to the Germans, exposing the flank of the British and French, already retreating on Dunkirk. The news was first broadcast from Paris in terms of bitter scorn; Mr Churchill, having foreseen the probable collapse of the Belgians—whose Government dissociated itself from the King's action—was less condemnatory.

14. Duff Cooper was appointed Minister of Information by Churchill in May—a post he held until July 1941.

15. Audrey Hubbard (who had refused to divorce her husband to enable him to marry Doris Thomsett—see above, 7 February 1938) was born a Dedman.

all simper & qualification. So, if Margaret Ll. Davies says, how insolent we middleclass women are, I argue, why cant the workers then reject us? Whats wrong is the conventionality—not the coarseness. So that its all lulled & dulled. The very opposite of "common" or working class.

Began P.H again today, & threshed & threshed till perhaps a little grain can be collected. I sent off my Walpole too. After dinner I began Sidney Smith; plan being to keep short flights going: P.H. in between. Oh yes—one cant plan, any more, a long book. H. Brace cable that they accept Roger—whom, which, I'd almost forgotten. So thats a success; where I'd been expecting failure. It cant be so bad as all that. 250 advance. But we shall I suppose certainly postpone. Reading masses of Coleridge & Wordsworth letters of a night—curiously untwisting & burrowing into that plaited nest. Withers Green cant sleep for thinking of raids. No news of Louie's brother [Harry West]. Rumours about Gwyn's wounds & Col. Westmacott.[16] They're fully furbished in 5 minutes. Rain—& purple & now its over—clear over Caburn & the birds shouting. A rill of sound—a flutter of ribands—no continuity or connection with each other. Reading Thomas A'Quinas [1933] by Chesterton. His skittish over ingenious mind makes one shy (like a horse). Not straightforward, but has a good engine in his head. I want to send out parachutes into these remote places—I cant find the word I want.—prospectors, perhaps?

Thursday 30 May

Walking today (Nessa's birthday) by Kingfisher pool saw my first hospital train—laden, not funereal, but weighty, as if not to shake bones. Something what is the word I want: grieving & tender & heavy laden & private—bringing our wounded back carefully through the green fields at which I suppose some looked. Not that I could see them. And the faculty for seeing in imagination always leaves me so suffused with something partly visual partly emotional, I can't though its very pervasive, catch it when I come home—the slowness, cadaverousness, grief of the long heavy train, taking its burden through the fields. Very quietly it slid into the cutting at Lewes. Instantly wild duck flights of aeroplanes came over head; manoeuvred; took up positions & passed over Caburn. Percy has seen Westmacot[t]'s man, home on leave, very thin, drawn & aged; says its a hell: was at Arras: all had to fight. And the same stories as the papers about the brutality to refugees. Mrs Dedman is off north. Louie worried & sad. Her mother cant stand the strain now the boys are

16. The Rev. Samuel Withers-Green, of Midease, was elected Hon. Secretary of the newly-founded Rodmell Voluntary First Aid Post; he and his wife left the village later in the year. Major Guy Randolph Westmacott of Old Farm House, Rodmell, with a D.S.O. from the first war, had rejoined his regiment and was decorated by the French in 1940.

gone, alone with the chattering idiot. A Mrs Ayres, who loves my books, called, to suggest a mental home. Mrs West has made up her mind to become a nurse & let him go. So whats to become of father, Louie asks, whose nerves are bad?[17] This is a pinch of Hitler in the cottages of Rodmell too. No news today. Holding the line—heroism—all the usual perorations, in the usual highflown tense voice. Oh for a speaking voice, once in a way—not Harold's though, which disgusted me as well as Mr McLaren.[18] "Does Mr Nicolson speak before or after dinner?—" Like the imposition of personality in writing—say Meredith's style, or Carlyle's, when one wants facts. And being beaten at bowls irritates me; & I'm strained writing PH—so much more of a strain than Roger. And no meat today. And weeded this morning. And was very happy —the moment can be that: only theres no support in the fabric—if you see what I mean, as Charlie Sanger used to say—theres no healthy tissue round the moment. It's blown out. But for a moment, on the terrace, no one coming, alone with L., ones certainly happy. And I like the wind-blown state of ones body in the open air—wind, warm wind washing all the crevices, a feeling one doesnt have in London. an air cleanliness, not a soap & water one.

Marginal note: Armies retreating unbroken in spite of uncovered left wing

Friday 31 May

Scraps, orts & fragments, as I said in PH. which is now bubbling— I'm playing with words; & think I owe some dexterity to finger exercises here—but the scraps: Louie has seen Mr Westmacot's man: "Its an eyesore"—his description of fighting near Boulogne. Percy weeding: "I shall conquer 'em in the end. If I was sure of our winning the other battle . . ." Raid, said to be warned, last night. All the searchlights in extreme antennal vibration. They have blots of light, like beads of dew on a stalk. Mr Hanna 'stood by' half the night.[19] Rumour, very likely: rumour wh. has transported the English in Belgium who, with their golf sticks ball & some nets in a car coming from Flanders, were taken for parachutists: condemned to death, released; & returned to Seaford. Rumour, via Percy, transplanted them to "somewhere near Eastbourne" —& the villagers armed with rifles, pitchforks etc. Shows what a surplus

17. Mrs West's youngest child Anthony, aged about ten, was an incapable mental defective, to whose care she devoted herself; her family sought LW's help in relieving her of this gruelling burden, and he got in touch with the East Sussex Association for Mental Welfare, of which Mrs Ayshford-Ayre was the Secretary. See *V LW*, pp. 49-51, and LWP, Sussex, II E 2k.

18. Jack McLaren (1887-1954), Australian writer and broadcaster, on the staff of the Ministry of Information.

19. B. J. Hanna of Rodmell was captain of the Local Defence Volunteers.

of unused imagination we possess. We—the educated—check it: as I checked my cavalry on the down at Telscombe & transformed them into cows drinking. Making up again. So that I couldnt remember, coming home, if I'd come by the mushroom path or the field. How amazing that I can tap that old river again; & how satisfying. But will it last? I made out the whole of the end; & need only fill in; the faculty, dormant under the weight of Roger, springs up. And to me its the voice on the scent again. "Any waste paper?" here I was interrupted by the jangling bell. Small boy in white sweater come, I suppose, for Scouts, & Mabel says they pester us daily at 37, & make off with the spoils. Desperate fighting. The same perorations. Coming through Southease I saw Mrs Cockell in old garden hat weeding. Out comes a maid in muslin apron & cap tied with blue ribband. Why? To keep up standards of civilisation? I also heard a pick-pick as I passed Mount Misery, & crouched low under the thick hedge of cow parsley & saw the scrub—Lee—risked rudeness, & marched on. Land girls weeding in the field by the river. One elegant in blue trousers & green head band; the other a dumpy elderly spinster, with a vast bottom in knickerbockers. Two more, with hairdressed hair, among the Dedman, Wests & Thompsett men. Began Balzac, Vautrin.[20]

[*Monday 3 June*]

Leonard said, after Miss Griffiths went, "If it gives them so much happiness, we ought to put up with it from time to time". I said, But how, seeing she never spoke & was as unresponsive as a fish, could it have given her pleasure? "She leads such an awful life in Acton. She likes the food & sitting in a garden." This fairly sums up a very laboured week end; when we drew bucket up after bucket & nothing happened. Acton is noisy. She lives with an Aunt and a grandmother who forgets things, & they have gas. But we made her sing, Monteverdi: & she sang quite simply. Will she marry? or fade? Again I'm struck with the helplessness of the lower orders. All of us on top. What can they get at—? Louie said this morning "The Duke of Northumberland has been killed". I had a sense of a very heavy tree fallen. A young man so loaded with everything to be lopped. A kind of crash it seemed, for a duke to fall, compared with a Harry West.[1] I was woken by a great boom rattling my windows. Listened for another; none came. But 2 bombs were dropped "in Sussex". Buttercups & sorrel week end—the very flush of the first summer. May still in but bruised: a tossing wind today; none yesterday. Poor little Griffiths looking at the evening. So quiet after Acton.

20. Vautrin was the master-criminal who figures in several novels of Balzac's *La Comédie humaine*.
 1. The 9th Duke of Northumberland, a lieutenant in the Grenadier Guards, was killed in action, aged twenty-seven, on 21 May.

Nessa & Duncan & Q. over on Saturday. We discussed Helen. D. said, She's not intimate eno' with you to be honest about money. Then A. & B.—how discreet! D. can only say to him Pass the salt— He would not begin upon his anger, as I expressed mine. Nessa said, One must look on the good side. She might have loved an airman. She has an odd streak of luck. Then the weekend descended. I've *just* only just been beaten at bowls. Breakfast was at 7.30. And this time tomorrow shall I or not be having cocktails with Colefax? I think so yes: in order to discipline myself. Only clothes? gloves? stockings? 4 5ths of the army over here now.[2] A respite, a pause, perhaps. Perhaps Italy comes in . . . Then what about Roger? No proofs. We have now been hard at it hero-making. The laughing, heroic, Tommy—how can we be worthy of such men?— every paper, every BBC rises to that dreary false cheery hero-making strain. Will they be grinding organs in the street in 6 months? Its the emotional falsity; not all false; yet inspired with some eye to the main chance. So the politicians mate guns & tanks. No. Its the myth making stage of the war we're in. "Please, no letters" I read this twice in the Times Deaths column from parents of dead officers.

Friday 7 June

Just back this roasting hot evening. The great battle which decides our life or death goes on.[3] Last night an air raid here. Today brittle [?] hard sparks. Up till 1.30 this morning, Kingsley diffusing his soft charcoal gloom. Question of suicide seriously debated among the 4 of us— R. Macaulay the other—in the gradually darkening room. At last no light at all. This was symbolic. French are to be beaten; invasion here; 5th Coln active; a German pro-Consul; Engsh Govt in Canada; we in concentration camps, or taking sleeping draughts. The menace now is Ireland. K.M. gives us about 5 weeks before the great attack on Engld begins. I will continue tomorrow when less sleepy. Saw Stephen, Sybil, John, Morgan, Judith, Raymond, K.M. Rose Macaulay, finally W. Robson—but cant discriminate

Sunday 9 June

I will continue—but can I? The pressure of this battle wipes out London pretty quick. A gritting day. As sample of my present mood, I reflect: capitulation will mean all Jews to be given up. Concentration

---

2. The evacuation of British and French troops from Dunkirk and the nearby open beaches began on 26 May and continued until 4 June; nearly 340,000 men were brought over to England.

3. The Woolfs drove to London on the afternoon of 4 June; on 5 June the final phase of the Battle of France began, when the Germans launched their offensive on a 70-mile front across the Somme towards Paris.

camps. So to our garage. Thats behind correcting Roger, playing bowls. One taps any source of comfort—Leigh Ashton at Ch[arlesto]n yesterday for instance.[4] But today the line is bulging. Last night aeroplanes (G?) over: shafts of light following. I papered my windows.

Another reflection: I dont want to go to bed at midday: this refers to the garage. What we dread (its no exaggeration) is the news that the French Govt. have left Paris. A kind of growl behind the cuckoo & t'other birds: a furnace behind the sky. It struck me that one curious feeling is, that the writing 'I', has vanished. No audience. No echo. Thats part of one's death. Not altogether serious, for I correct Roger: send finally I hope tomorrow: & could finish P.H. But it is a fact—this disparition of an echo.

Monday 10 June

A day off. I mean one of those odd lapses of anxiety which may be false. Anyhow they said this morning that the line is unbroken—save at certain points. And our army has left Norway & is going to their help.[5] Anyhow—its a day off—a coal gritty day. L. breakfasted by electric light. And cool mercifully after the furnace. Today, too, I sent off my page proofs, & thus have read my Roger for the last time. The Index remains. And I'm in the doldrums; a little sunk, & open to the suggestion, conveyed by the memory of Leonard's coolness, enforced by John's silence, that its one of my failures. Reading it as closely as I did, I couldn't generalise the whole. I think it has a certain completeness; but I also think there are patches of anal; too much quotation; sometimes its cramped & poky. Thats about all I can lay hands on at the moment. The after book stage is on me.

Now to record a funny little—what shall I call it?—snag in my Elizabeth Bowen relationship. I decided, as my October letter went unanswered, & as Rose said she'd seen her, to take that little bull by the horns & telephone; she was out. So I sent a card, asking if we could meet. No answer today. If there's no answer at all, then that friendships over. But why? Cant conceive. But as I cant go on writing, over it must be. And indeed, its not so petty a snag; for I was fond of her; & I think she of me. And we could talk seriously. And she's the only one of the younger generation of women. . . But whats the use of asking what can have happened? Some gossip? Some mischief making? But as I never

4. Leigh Ashton (1897-1983), was seconded to the Ministry of Information by the Victoria and Albert Museum, of which he became Director in 1945. He was a friend of Clive Bell.

5. The French units evacuated from Narvik and those rescued from Dunkirk were returned to France, and a British and a Canadian Division were sent to augment the British contingent still trying to hold the line of the Somme in Normandy.

said a word, or saw any go between,—again, whats the use? If she's dumb, one of these days I'll ask David Cecil. Thats my little snag.

Now I must at once forage, & busy myself. Raymond, who is leaving the NS for the M. of Information, sends me Haryo.[6] I'm not in the mood for memoirs. What next? Darwin? Mme de Stael? It must be solid, yet short. I must put my head to the gallop, so as to cover these weeks. PH can be finished. And my Sketch of the Past continued.[7] Some experiment I think. The old book of critical excursion, perhaps . . . Yes, an experiment not a drudge.

Tuesday 11 June

Today or yesterday Italy came in:[8] French said to be holding most lines; Govt offices leaving Paris; no letter from Eth Bowen; plays rehearsed, working till eyes blind at Index.

A slaty queasy feeling about E.B. discussed it with L. What a time to quarrel with friends. Wound to vanity & affection.

Wednesday 12 June

Black news. French apparently withdrawing but only guarded news. Maurois begging for help last night.[9] Percy says the little boats all summoned again, as if to fetch off more troops. Mrs Richardson (Lady Reading's gardeners wife [*of Southease*]) told me of a friend of her husbands dead on the beach at Dunkirk—not a wound—shock. The West boy [Harry] writes he's hunting his battalion—no clothes—won't go back he says; but gives no word of his wounds. Some say hes the only survivor of his regiment. Landed in a sailing boat at Ramsgate. Twined in with all this—& the fine weather—& the drill & drone of the planes at night—& Mabel here—& my long long Index making—twined in is E. Bowen: who dont answer, & is I suspect to be written off henceforth. Why? Is she a touchy? Is she a lover of rows? Really I dont know her well enough to diagnose. And how soon anger & sternness & complete disregard for this sort of twittering triviality come to one's help. I'm not

6. Mortimer was put in charge of French broadcasting in the European Service of the BBC at Bush House, but returned to the *NS&N* after some nine months there. VW wrote a 'Books in General' page on *Hary-O: The Letters of Lady Harriet Cavendish*, edited by Sir George Leveson-Gower, which appeared in the *NS&N* on 6 July 1940 (Kp C367).

7. See *Moments of Being*, p. 100: 'June 8th 1940. I have just found this sheaf of notes, thrown away into my waste-paper basket.'

8. Mussolini declared war on Britain and France on 10 June.

9. The Anglophile man of letters André Maurois (1885-1967) had been attached as an observer to the British GQH in France; he reached London from Paris on 11 June, and broadcast on the BBC.

wounded in my vanity, for I cant play those games. So have drafted a letter, & shall send it on Friday—for I'm almost sure, in my bones, as L. wd say, that she's set on a break. If the Index is finished tomorrow, thats the very last load home. Whether we publish or not, I'm quit.

No letters of any sort: & no Times book: but all the same I feel decks cleared & scrubbed, & can set to, in a jiffy—oh dear, I've not thanked Shaw—yes, I'll write all my letters tomorrow. I was asked to write a life of Margaret Bondfield—I forgot to say: also to contribute to some Womens Symposium in USA; and Judith is the only one to get a First.[10]

[Thursday 13 June]

I should *love* to see you—would you be in &c—Elizabeth. Let that abstract of this mornings postcard be a reminder & a warning about mares nests & jumping to conclusions & feeling in ones bones—not but what I had some justification. If it werent for—oh dear the retreat— Paris now almost besieged—20,000 of our men cut off—still the Fr. have gained 5 miles somewhere—if it werent for this—today wd have been a happy day. Elizabeth to begin with, which warmed & consoled, for if one's friends are to die in the flesh now, whats left?—Then Dotty's Yeats book with her praise of Virginia; then the milkman with 400 eggs for sale. We have bought two great crocks & glass water, or whats it called.[11] My Index sent off—so thats the very final full stop to all that drudgery. John rang up yesterday to say he's been offered a job at India Office, wh., foreboding as it does Mrs N. & Miss H. here, if evacuated, greatly increased my private gloom. Indeed, after we'd heard Haw-Haw, objectively announcing defeat—victory on his side of the line that is—again & again, left us about as down as we've yet been. We sat silent in the 9 o'clock dusk; & L. could only with difficulty read Austen Chamberlain.[12] I found the Wordsworth letters my only drug. Yet today we're again publicly more cheerful. Why? Up & down—up

10. Shaw had given VW a landscape by Roger Fry; for her thanks, see *VI VW Letters*, no. 3613. The trade unionist and labour leader Margaret Bondfield (1873-1953) wrote her own life: *A Life's Work* (1949). VW's contribution to the American symposium finally took shape as 'Thoughts on Peace in an Air Raid' (Kp C369), after pressure from 'the American lady' (25 July, 6 August); see below 31 August 1940: 'that infernal bomb article'. Judith Stephen was placed in Class I in the Cambridge Archaeology and Anthropology Tripos, 1940.

11. *Letters on Poetry from W. B. Yeats to Dorothy Wellesley* was published in April 1940 by the Oxford University Press; it includes letters from her to him referring to VW's 'genius'. Water-glass (sodium silicate) was used for preserving eggs.

12. i.e.: volume II (1914-37) of the official biography of Sir Austen Chamberlain by Sir Charles Petrie, just published. LW reviewed it in *The Political Quarterly*, Vol. XI, no. 4, together with four other books.

& down. No petrol at the pumps—providing for Invasion, only served a dribble, the man said.

Friday 14 June

Paris is in the hands of the Germans. Battle continues. We spent the day seeing Penshurst with Vita—picnicked in the park.[13] Gwen in military dress—V. in trousers. Very fine & hot. The house of yellowish Oxford stone. Banqueting hall: disappointing furniture, like heavy & over ornamental Tot Court Rd. only made 1314—Q. Elizth dancing— tilted up by Essex? Ladies & gents all sitting on the benches laughing. Elizabeth herself in another picture, delicate skinned red haired, aquiline. Then the shell of Lady Pembroke's lute—like half a fig. Then Sidney's shaving glass. Then some very ugly tables . . . a long panelled room with soft veined panels. Out into the garden, which has certain trim lawns, & long grass walks, then lapses into wilderness. Sidneys very poor—given up weeding. A great lily pond; the goldfish making an odd subacqueous tapping as they moved among reeds. Then through old pink courtyards, with the Boar & the broad arrow to the car:[14] but the butler came & said his Lordship wanted to see us. Vita went—we stayed. Then were summoned. Ld. de Lisle & Dudley is like a very old liver & white Sussex spaniel—heavy pouched, both eyes with cataract, 87 but looks younger, waistcoat undone. Glad of company. Easy going at his ease, loose limbed, twinkling. "Do you mind if I say it—but the statue of the Q. outside Buck Palace is like a lady on a close stool— Showed that (Q. Charlotte) to Queen Mary. She didnt like it when I said it was like her." Padded us into a small room; made us look at pictures said to be good— one, skied, of A. Sidney. Then a reputed Rembrandt. Can only keep a few rooms open. And those like seaside lodging rooms—There we left him alone, blind, with his shilling box of cork tipped cigarettes, some patience or other game, a few novels, & the photographs of his nephew "—a very nice boy" & his grey lady the only signs of youth, on a side table.[15] Vita said he'd told her he was so poor he couldnt have people to stay: whole place run by 2 maids & a boy & butler; is alone—but d'you mind being alone? she asked. "Hate it" he said. Twice a week he goes to Tonbridge & plays Bridge. There this old snail sits in the corner of his

13. The mainly Elizabethan great house, Penshurst Place, near Tonbridge in Kent, originated in the 14th century; it came into the Sidney family in 1552. Its present owner was Algernon Sidney, 4th Baron De L'Isle and Dudley (1854-1945).

14. Bears, porcupines and broad arrows (pheons), components of the Sidney arms, are conspicuous at Penshurst; but not boars.

15. Lord De L'Isle's nephew William Philip Sidney (b. 1909) succeeded as 6th Baron in 1945 after the death of his father, who only survived his brother for a few months. His 'grey lady': unexplained.

tremendous shell. The taste of the present Sidneys is all for carved tables & yellow varnish. He had hardly any fingers when we shook hands, each thanking him, & he was anxious to give us tea. But I must get back for my fire practice Gwen said. Whats the use? he remarked. Odd to have seen this Elizabethan great house the first day that invasion becomes serious. But I like MH better.

Thursday 20 June

London diary: just back; & dinner so close & events so crowded that I must abstract. Monday lunch: John. The French stopped fighting: whats to become of me? Offered a Roumanian bookshop. Then what about Press? KM. after dinner. Now we suffer what the Poles suffered. Fight in our fortress: are conquered: I have my morphia in pocket. Tuesday, dine with Adrian. They both off to air raid rehearsal at Middlesex hospl. Adrian promises us a prescription. Ch[urchi]ll broadcasts. Reassuring about defence of England; not all claptrap. Now we're fighting alone with our back to the wall. Bombs first, then invasion.[16] Ethel Smyth tea. Oh of *course* we shall fight and win. Then Wednesday. Mrs N[icholls]. & daughter fled from air raid at Thetford. Tea with her & Eth Bowen. In comes L.: air raid practice at H. of C. Those are the skeleton facts of our 3 London days. Monday ended in charcoal gloom. KM. says we must & shall be beaten. He says perhaps 4 more numbers of NS will come out.

Here, as soon as we begin bowls, Louie comes agog. Harry came back on Monday. It pours out—how he hadnt boots off for 3 days; the beach at Dunkirk—the bombers as low as trees—the bullets like moth holes in his coat—how no English aeroplanes fought; how the officer told them to take their shoes off & go past a pill box on all fours. Then went himself with a grenade & blasted it. At Dunkirk many men shot themselves as the planes swooped. Harry swam off, a boat neared. Say Chum Can you row? Yes, he said, hauled in, rowed for 5 hours, saw England, landed—didnt know if it were day or night or what town—didnt ask—couldn't write to his mother—so was despatched to his regiment. He looted a Belgian shop & stuffed his pockets with rings, which fell out in the sea; but 2 watches pinned to his coat survived: one is chased, & chimes. Mrs Everest has them. He saw his cousin dead on the beach; &

16. The Woolfs drove to London on Monday 17 June. On the day Paris fell, 14 June, the French Government which had moved to Tours, withdrew to Bordeaux; and on 16 June the Prime Minister Paul Reynaud, overborne by his defeatist ministers, resigned, and the aged Marshal Pétain formed a government with the immediate purpose of concluding an armistice with the all-conquering Germans; it was signed on 22 June. On 17 June Churchill broadcast a threnody for the French and a rallying call to the British.

another man from the street. He was talking to a chap, who showed him a silk handkerchief bought for his joy lady. That moment a bomb killed him. Harry took the handkerchief. Harry has had eno' war, & is certain of our defeat—got no arms & no aeroplanes—how can we do anything?

Saturday 22 June

Is Harry the real animal behind the brave, laughing heroic boy panoply which the BBC spreads before us nightly?—[*omission*] a natural human being, not made for shooting men, but for planting potatoes. [*omission*] And is he, as I suspect, the average sample? I gather he'd shoot himself rather than go to France again. And he hates the French, who gabble & become hysterical & run mad; & yet dont give him little loaves for nothing like the nice Belgian woman. So it was at Waterloo I suppose.[17] And the fighting goes on in France; & the terms aren't yet public; & its a heavy grey day, & I've been beaten at bowls, feel depressed & irritated, & vow I'll play no more, but read my book.

My book is Coleridge; Rose Macaulay; the Bessborough letters— Lord Moynihan's life; rather a foolish flight inspired by Hary-o; I would like to find one book & stick to it. But cant.[18] I feel, if this is my last lap, oughtn't I to read Shakespeare? But cant. I feel oughtn't I to finish off P.H.: oughtn't I to finish something by way of an end? The end gives its vividness, even its gaiety & recklessness to the random daily life. This, I thought yesterday, may be my last walk. On the down above Bugdean I found some green glass tubes. The corn was flowing with poppies in it. And I read my Shelley at night. How delicate & pure & musical & uncorrupt he & Coleridge read, after the left wing group. How lightly & firmly they put down their feet, & how they sing; & how they compact; & fuse, & deepen. I wish I cd invent a new critical method—something swifter & lighter & more colloquial & yet intense: more to the point & less composed; more fluid & following the flight, than my C.R. essays. The old problem: how to keep the flight of the mind, yet be exact. All the difference between the sketch & the finished work. And now dinner to cook. A role.

Nightly raids on the east & south coast. 6, 3, 12 people killed nightly.

---

17. Harry West rejoined his regiment and fought with it overseas until the end of the war.

18. VW bought the 3-volume Pickering edition (1835) of *The Poetical Works of S. T. Coleridge* in Tunbridge Wells when she and LW went to travel Hogarth Press books there on 22 April 1940 (*Holleyman*, MH II, p. 7); her other books were (probably) Rose Macaulay's latest novel *And No Man's Wit* (1940); *Lady Bessborough and her Family Circle*, edited by the Earl of Bessborough with A. Aspinall, 1940; and *Berkeley Moynihan: Surgeon* by Donald Bateman, 1940.

[*Thursday 27 June*]

How difficult to make oneself a centre after all the rings a visitor stirs in one—in this case E. Bowen.[19] How difficult to draw in from all those wide ripples & be at home, central. I tried to center by reading Freud. These rough rapid twinkling ripples spread out & out—for some hours after EB is in the train. It is a disagreeable after-visit feeling. It has its connection too with too many cigarettes, with incessant knitting. A high wind was blowing; Mabel & Louie picking currants & gooseberries. Then a visit to Charleston. Threw another stone into the pond. And at the moment, with PH only to fix upon, I'm loosely anchored. Further, the war—our waiting while the knives sharpen for the operation—has taken away the outer wall of security. No echo comes back. I have no surroundings. I have so little sense of a public that I forget about Roger coming or not coming out. Those familiar circumvolutions—those standards—which have for so many years given back an echo & so thickened my identity are all wide & wild as the desert now. I mean, there is no 'autumn' no winter. We pour to the edge of a precipice . . . & then? I cant conceive that there will be a 27th June 1941. This cuts away something even at tea at Charleston. We drop another afternoon into the millrace. Clive sullen, & effort ridden. Duncan patched & peeled like an onion. He fell down stairs. Then Bunny as bluff & burly & beefy as a Farmer lurches in with Angelica. A clock ticks somewhere. Nothing said.

And so, in this high wind, we reach the present moment; & I find it difficult to centre. I think I must force a C.R. essay into being. E.'s stammer also had a disintegrating effect: like a moth buzzing round a flower—her whirr of voice as she cant alight on a word—a whirr of sound that makes the word quiver & seem blurred. We talked however— & very on the whole congenially. But having spent my words on analysing the central, & being apprehensive that Judith will come & smash [?] me again, I do not record what we said. A very honourable horse faced, upper class hard [?] constricted mind.

The Woolfs, leaving Judith Stephen in Lewes, drove to London on Monday 1 July, returning to Rodmell on Thursday evening; the Hutchinsons dined with them on Tuesday; and Wednesday afternoon VW spent wandering through the City with Elizabeth Bowen.

Thursday 4 July

Again, back from London. But its here that the events take place. Louie, toothless, but all agog: yesterday at 5 pm. pop, pop pop out over

19. Elizabeth Bowen came to stay at Monks House for two nights—25 and 26 June.

the marshes. She was picking fruit. Backfiring she thought. Told by someone it was a raid. So she went in. They bombed the train at Newhaven: the driver died this morning. Passengers lay under seats. Rails wrecked. Today a plane—ours—crashed at Southease. So, the Germans are nibbling at my afternoon walks. The French fleet has been seized & sunk. All Lewes listening to the wireless. Mr Uridge, of whom I bought butter, says the PM "made a strong speech. Now we're getting to business". Indeed the fleet capture is the first good news since—Narvik?[1] In London K.M. decreed that Tuesday, or today, Thursday, was fixed for invasion. London very safe & solid in feeling. Pink brick fortresses—for ammunition?—in main streets. Wire mazes in Whitehall &c. We passed strings of ambulances coming down tagged with boughs. Canadians swarm—want to see Buck Palace. Theres dinner: so private life must be postponed.

Friday 5 July

Why should I be bothering myself with Coleridge I wonder—Biog. Lit. & then with father's essay on Coleridge, this fine evening, when the flies are printing their cold little feet on my hands?[2] It was in order to give up thinking about economy; whether to give up Mable. I wanted to think myself up into calmness. Economy, means that I must make money: thus when Dotty offers me £50 for an essay upon fiction, 10,000 words, I cut it up into articles, & reckon; no: thats poor pay. I'd better finish Pointz Hall.

I took my Times [Book Club] order to the post & there met Mrs Ebbs. "So Mr Woolf has seen Monks House again!" she said. I of course said, "but you've been having fighting here." Then she told me how the cups rattled in her hand, at tea, at Seaford, when the raider was fired at, & brought down at sea. "The poor fellow, the engine driver was killed between Newhaven & Seaford" she said. Also that the silly fellow who crashed his plane on the marsh, tipped its nose over the brook. He didnt know about the brooks. So I walked down & saw it—a little gnat, with red & white & blue bars; a tent keeping guard. Louie said that Audrey Hubbard who was in the pea field ran to give first aid. The man had a face like two faces. She made him write his name on a cigarette card: he was taken to Lewes, & has lockjaw. But this is rumour—rumour, via

---

1. To prevent the French fleet falling under the control of the Germans the British Navy, after due warning, took measures on 3 July for the seizure, disablement, or destruction of all accessible French naval vessels in British, Mediterranean, or Atlantic ports. On 4 July Churchill reported on the success of the measures reluctantly though necessarily taken.

2. *Biographia Literaria* (1817) by S. T. Coleridge. Leslie Stephen's essay on Coleridge appears in his *Hours in a Library* (1892); he also wrote the *DNB* entry on him.

Percy, has it that the streets of Newhaven were machine gunned. L. gets annoyed with Percy. I see the imagination—that should have turned a wheel, running to waste & foam instead. L. back from the Library with a great volume of Gifford's Laws.[3] So to bowls. The French Fleet fought: Petain cuts off diplomatic relations. So shall we be at war with our ally? Last month indissolubly determined to fight to the end.

If someone comes in one writes differently: now, having been beaten at bowls, in a high wind, hearing planes above,—I note: to remember: the circular walk at the Tower with the hollyhocks; & the little 1870 girl in white with bands of black looking out of the window in its deep wall, as Eth Bowen & I sat talking. We walked from 37 through Temple, along river, up Thames Street, to the Tower, talking talking about what? her going to Ireland on a Govt mission; leaving Clarence Terrace; writing, it was my 'greatness' as we circled the town. No, I dont think it was only flattery I wanted. Something warmer. On top of bus, we talked again—a good idea; talking in many changing scenes: it changes topics & moods, battling among the Billingsgate porters with their shelly fishy hats; then stopping: crossing: running up bus steps.

I forgot to record my idiotic anguish, the night the Hutches—J., M. & Jeremy dined, about my dress. How queer that wave of agony: about 2 in the morning: so overpowering & irrational. Next day I found Jeanne in Judd Street to alter it & recovered serenity, & even had, once more, the bright inspiration that Jeanne of Judd Street—a small brown moth of a woman—who succeeded the old improper Frenchwoman—shall make all my clothes in future, beautifully, & for nothing.

Friday 12 July

How odd that I should have had 3 letters in praise of Trimmer—Lady Oxford, Pipsey & a Helen Browne—when I was going to tear the proof up![4] How silly I was to be enraged yesterday (1) by Miss Gardner (2) by being beaten at bowls. Yet how the grass shone pale emerald green when I walked off my temper on the marsh after dinner. The passages of colour, over Asheham, like the green backgrounds in Vermeer & then the little rusty grey church, & the cows, sun beaded, fringed with sun. We quarrelled about our communal feeling: I said I simper when I cohort with Gardner. L. said . . . but we made it up.

3. *The Laws of England* (1905-16), known as Giffard's (or, more often, Halsbury's) Laws after H. S. Giffard, 1st Earl of Halsbury (1823-1921), three times Lord Chancellor, who presided over the production of the 31 volumes of the first edition (1907-17).
4. 'Selina Trimmer' was VW's title for her 'Books in General' essay on *Hary-O* (Kp C367; see above, 10 June 1940, n. 6), which appeared in the *NS&N* on 6 July 1940.

We were shown how charcoal absorbs gas in the Hall. And then, after a dull necessary lecture, old Miss Green, shedding her officers cloak, appeared in blue trousers & let herself down from the Rectory window, hanging by her toenails & descending with a jump. Captain Hanna said his bones were like glass. If he jumped, even from a bus, they would break. A red lipped woman asked me if Aga saucepans were made of aluminium; & L. has given all our saucepans to Mrs Ebbs to make aeroplanes with. I dont like any of the feelings war breeds: patriotism; communal &c, all sentimental & emotional parodies of our real feelings. But then, we're in for it. Every day we have our raids: at night the bloodhounds are out. I open my window when I hear the Germans, & the broad stalks of light rise all over the meadow feeling for them—a strange early morning spectacle. One sees nothing but the feelers of light. Then the drone buzz booms away, rather like a dentists drill. No invasion so far.

I refused Dotty & Hilda, rather tartly; for Hilda's hand on the reins is a heavy one—why not write the same article, she suggests, twice in different words? Why not indeed. The idea of their book is one of those meritorious meretricious tidy-minded ideas, that are the most detestable & the least pinned downable. Money patriotism, literature & some organising [?] arranging [?] motive, all embracing & intertwining.[5]

The Woolfs drove to London on Tuesday afternoon, 16 July and spent three nights at 37 Mecklenburgh Square.

Saturday 20 July

Things to write about when I'm less sleepy (back an hour ago from London). 1. Ray's death; 2. Talk with Rose Macaulay; 3. Book to come out on 25th; 4. Madame Spira; 5. Lady Oxford: 6. Bella & Tom. I daresay theres a 7th & an 8th. But these headings will remind me, when I've walked & slept off the extreme jadedness of London. 7 might be Jack & Jeremy Hutch to stay the night. 8 the photographs of the womans body in the abortionists cupboard: her dead face: long hair: legs trussed up. 9. Must be Hitler's speech yesterday: lets talk common sense & end the war—if not: & instead of any more headings I shall now cool & expand on the marsh. Oh 10 might be my new resolve of tidiness. Desk & table both clear.[6]

5. Hilda Matheson (1888-1940), one-time Director of Talks at the BBC and now concerned with wartime foreign broadcasts, was, like her friend Dorothy Wellesley, one of Vita Sackville-West's faithful retinue of ex-lovers, a species VW regarded with some disapproval. The proposed anthology—to which VW had been invited to contribute an essay about fiction (see above, 5 July 1940)—was never published.
6. 1: Ray Strachey died on 16 July. 2: Rose Macaulay dined with VW on 17 July. 3: *Roger Fry* was published on 25 July. 4 & 5: Mela Spira, whose husband Robert,

Wednesday 24 July

Yes those are things to write about; but I want at the moment, the eve of publication moment, to discover my emotions. They are fitful: thus not very strong—nothing like so strong as before The Years—oh dear nothing like. Still they twinge. I wish it were this time next week. There'll be Morgan, & Desmond. And I fear Morgan will say—just enough to show he doesn't like, but is kind. D. will certainly depress. The Times Lit Sup (after its ill temper about Reviewing) will find chinks. T. & T. will be enthusiastic. And—thats all. I repeat that 2 strains, as usual will develop: fascinating; dull; life like; dead. So why do I twinge? knowing it almost by heart. But not quite. Mrs Leh[man]n enthusiastic: John silent. I shall of course be sneered at by those who sniff at Bloomsbury. I'd forgotten that. But as L. is combing Sally I cant concentrate. No room of my own. For 11 days I've been contracting in the glare of different faces. It ended yesterday with the W.I.: my talk—it was talked—about the Dreadnought. A simple, on the whole natural, friendly occasion. Cups of tea; biscuits; & Mrs Chavasse, in a tight dress, presiding: out of respect for me, it was a Book tea. Miss Gardner had 3 Gs. pinned to her frock; Mrs Thompsett 3 weeks: & someone else a silver spoon.[7]

No I cant go on to Ray's death, about which I know nothing, save that that very large woman, with the shock of grey hair, & the bruised lip; that monster, whom I remember typical of young womanhood, has suddenly gone. She had a kind of representative quality, in her white coat & trousers; wall building, disappointed, courageous, without what? imagination?

Lady Oxford said that there was no virtue in saving; more in spending. She hung over my neck in a spasm of tears. Mrs Campbell [*unidentified*] has cancer. But in a twinkling she recovered & began to spend. A cold chicken she said was always under cover on the sideboard at my service. The country people send butter. She was beautifully dressed in a rayed

---

like thousands of other refugees in Britain, was interned as a precautionary measure when the threat of German invasion became manifest, appealed to VW to intercede on his behalf, and she enlisted the support of Lady Oxford, with whom she lunched on 17 July. 6: VW's sister-in-law Bella Southorn and her husband lunched with the Woolfs on 19 July. 7 & 8: Jack and Jeremy Hutchinson stayed the night at Monks House on 15 July, on the eve of the former's appearance as counsel for the prosecution in the trial at Sussex Assizes in Lewes of a Mrs Morgan of Brighton, found guilty on six counts of 'using an instrument . . . for a certain purpose.' 9: Hitler in his triumphant speech to the *Reichstag* on 19 July declared that, as the victor, 'speaking in the name of reason', he saw no reason why the war need continue, and appealed to Great Britain to capitulate.

7. For what has survived of VW's notes for her talk on the Dreadnought Hoax to the Rodmell Women's Institute, see *IQB*, Appendix E.

silk, with a dark blue tie; a dark blue fluted Russian cap with a red flap. This was given her by her milliner: the fruit of spending.

All the walls, the protecting & reflecting walls, wear so terribly thin in this war. There's no standard to write for: no public to echo back: even the 'tradition' has become transparent. Hence a certain energy & recklessness—part good—part bad I daresay. But its the only line to take. And perhaps the walls, if violently beaten against, will finally contain me.

a repetition I see

I feel tonight still veiled. The veil will be lifted tomorrow, when my book comes out. Thats what may be painful: may be cordial. And then I may feel once more round me the wall I've missed—or vacancy? or chill?

I make these notes, but am tired of notes—tire of Gide, tired of de Vigny notebooks. I want something sequacious now & robust. In the first days of the war I cd read notes only.[8]

Ray's hair stood up very vigorously on either side of the parting which lately she had made in the middle. Her bitterness at Oliver, whom she had loved, & did love, was perceptible—something tart about her; & as if some of the petals of what she hoped, as a girl, to be so yellow a sunflower—she was ambitious, self confident, was greedy & a little insensitive about 'fame'—as if these petals had withered & she cd. no longer be confident; was indeed disappointed, a little wounded, embittered; chiefly shown by her immense activity, as if always trying to get what she could not. And she grew so unwieldy; & cared so little for appearances; yet was envious, I guess, of the graces; & hadnt achieved altogether what her intention in disregarding the graces had been. I mean, she planned a great unconventional rough hewn figure; & it didnt altogether come off. She played patience endlessly. She had educated her children so carefully. Yet look what failures they both are. Christopher unimaginative; Barbara—oh, well she ran off the rails completely: B. was bitter against intellect—which Ray reverenced: yet had no aesthetic sense.[9] What else? Her humanity: offered to help when I was ill. Her competence. Her good nature. Her wisdom—yes, as she grew older, it was there. Perhaps at 70 she wd have created the legend of—the wise matriarch: have been surrounded, & central. But she died while it was in the rough, aged 53. Also a kind of rough radiance. Corpulent. Yet keen. Bright eyed. But I never knew her domestically. Always something

---

8. Alfred de Vigny's notes, *pensées*, &c were published posthumously as *Journal d'un poète* in 1867. 'Sequacious (a word Coleridge uses)': see *VI VW Letters*, no. 3617 to Ethel Smyth, 24 July 1940.

9. Cf. *Remarkable Relations* (1980) by Barbara Strachey, p. 300: 'Christopher, as expected, won prizes and scholarships at every turn . . .; but Barbara was in revolt . . .'

of the office—documents, overalls, interviews—about her. One of the people who was 'in love' in the old way. Oliver's letter asking her to see over some factory made her flush, at Firle in my little dining room. She tore it to scraps I think.[10] So I've written higgledypiggledy, about Ray. Her cordiality—& queer little quick voice: smoking: it used to be a pipe. Initiative[?], but no charm. Wrote without stopping. No form, no fineness. Her life much of a scramble & a fight: but in the office I guess very commanding, controlling & masterly.

Thursday 25 July

I'm not very nervous at the moment: indeed at worst its only a skin deep nervousness; for after all, the main people approve; still I shall be relieved *if* Morgan approves. That I suppose I shall know tomorrow. The first review (Lynd,) says: "deep imaginative sympathy . . . . makes him an attractive figure (in spite of wild phrases): There is little drama . . . . . at the same time those interested in modern art will find it of absorbing interest . . ." Then he goes on to mis-quote, having I daresay his whiskey by him.[11]

I shall settle in very happily I think to Coleridge after the splash is over. I expect some letters. But what is true, is that then I can write entirely to please myself: first a C.R: then PH: leaving spaces for odds & ends: for ex: an article for the pressing American lady. I'm thick in Mme Spira's affairs: she sobbed & left her strangled wool gloves behind her. I've heard from Margot & M. Storm Jameson—oh the bore of being kind![12] This war inflicts boredom endlessly. My little triumph today was that Flint [*Lewes grocer*] gave me extra tea. Now margarine is rationed; & I have a horrid skinflint morning ordering dinner, suspecting Louie who of course helps herself to this & that.

What a curious relation is mine with Roger at this moment—I who have given him a kind of shape after his death— Was he like that? I feel very much in his presence at the moment: as if I were intimately connected with him; as if we together had given birth to this vision of him: a child born of us. Yet he had no power to alter it. And yet for some years it will represent him.

10. See *I VW Letters*, no. 562 to Vanessa Bell, from Little Talland House, Firle, 6 April 1911: 'This morning . . . she had a letter from him asking her to go over some railway works. . . . She is either in love, or on the verge of it.'
11. See 'Books of the Week' by Robert Lynd, *New Chronicle*, 24 July 1940.
12. Margaret Storm Jameson, as President of the English Centre of the International PEN Club, was active in trying to help Jewish and anti-Nazi writers, and had also been appealed to by Mrs Spira on behalf of her interned husband.

Friday 26 July

I think I have taken, say a good second, judging from the Lit Sup review. No Morgan. Times say it takes a very high place indeed among biogs: Times say I have a genius for the relevant: Times (art critic I gather) goes on to analyse R.'s tones &c. Times intelligent, but not room for more.[13]

Its a nice quiet feeling now. With my Coleridge beneath me, & this over, as it really very nearly (how I hate that clash) is, I'm aware of something permanent & real in my existence. By the way, I'm rather proud of having done a solid work. I am content, somehow. But when I read my post its like putting my hand in a jar of leeches: Spira asking this; Douie soliciting books; John my L[eaning] T[ower] article; & so I've a mint of dull dreary letters to write.[14] But its an incredibly lovely— yes lovely is the word—transient, changing, warm, capricious summer evening. Also I won two games.

A large hedgehog was found drowned in the lily pool; L. tried to resuscitate it. An amusing sight. 2/6 is offered by the Govt. for live hedgehogs. I'm reading Ruth Benedict with pressure of suggestions— about Culture patterns—which suggests rather too much. Six vols of Aug. Hare also suggest—little articles.[15]

But I'm very peaceful, momentarily, this evening.

Saturday I suppose a no-review day. Immune is again the right word. No, John hasn't read it. When the 12 planes went over, out to sea, to fight, last evening, I had I think an individual, not communal BBC dictated feeling. I almost instinctively wished them luck. I should like to be able to take scientific notes of reactions. Invasion may be tonight or not at all—thats Joubert's summing up.[16] And—I had something else to say? but what. And dinner to get ready.

Sunday 28 July

Oh yes I see what this book is—its a refuge from Desmond. The mild kind avuncular Desmond. I've been beaten at bowls, & so the half paragraph turns to lead. Now if Morgan had written I shouldnt have

---

13. All the points VW notes come from 'Roger Fry. The Quaker in Art', a review in the *TLS*, 27 July 1940, written by *The Times* art critic Charles Marriott (1869-1957). (Although nominally published on Saturdays, the *TLS*—like other weeklies —appeared on Fridays.)

14. C. O. G. Douie (1896-1953), writer and civil servant, one-time Secretary of the Public Libraries Committee.

15. *Patterns of Culture* (1934) by Ruth Benedict. *The Story of My Life*, 6 volumes, 1896-1900, by Augustus Hare.

16. Air Marshal Sir Philip Joubert de la Ferté (1887-1965), Assistant Chief of Air Staff, gave regular broadcasts at this time.

turned it to lead. But I feel my irritation at being beaten fasten itself & phrase make—make the old phrases, for wh. God knows, there's no justification whatever today. Why do I mind being beaten at bowls? I think I connect it with Hitler. Yet I played very well. And, in an hours time, shall be repeating the other phrase wh. I made during the first game: a Season of calm weather. Such a curious peace; a satisfactory quiet. I shall see no one in London Yes for a moment I believe that I can compass a season of calm weather. Yet 'they' say the invasion is fixed for Aug. 16th. A season of calm weather is the crown for which I'm always pushing & shoving, swimming like the hedgehog who cuts his throat with his paws Nessa said yesterday at C[harlesto]n, if he swims. Angelica there: I diagnose strain; a little defiance, restlessness. And feel in Q. something heavy, mature, depressed. Almost a year he's been in the fields: all corn coloured & red poppied with his blue eyes for convolvulus. Judith & L. came on Monday. Thus our island will be invaded—my season of calm weather. Many ⟨an island⟩ a green isle—why cant I remember poetry? Clive silly & truculent about Auden & Isherwood.[17] I guess he'd already looked up his own name in R[oger]. Said he'd only read Margery['s Foreword]. And my family will accept this book in complete silence. 2 years hard work. But I shall hear eno' from 'the public'. Why dont we praise, or blame, each other? Has everything been said? Is it the repletion at the end of a party?

Queer, when its so tame after all, a book coming out, why one writes them? How much part does 'coming out' play in the pleasure of writing then? Each one accumulates a little of the fictitious V.W. whom I carry like a mask about the world.

[*Later*.] Waiting for the Sunday papers in which RF. will, or may, be disposed of by Desmond &, perhaps, Basil de Selincourt—looking up over the page to see if L. is coming across the orchard—does not favour the looking up of quotations in Coleridge's letters. I know that I shant get any superlatives either way. I know that Desmond (who very likely won't do it) will if he does, gently hum & haw something about Mrs Woolf's charm & sympathy & then proceed to give his own version of R. which will probably be more amusing than mine; & that'll fill his short column. Of course I am anxious partly to know how it strikes R.'s friends: thats an element not present in a novel review. Anyhow, how much less exacerbating this Sunday morning is than The Years Sunday

17. 'Many a green isle needs must be
    In the deep wide sea of misery,'
        Shelley, *Lines Written among the Euganean Hills*, 1818.
    Auden and Isherwood left England for America in January 1939; their intention to remain there, which gradually emerged after the outbreak of the war, provoked a crescendo of criticism in both the popular and quality press, and even in Parliament.

AUGUST 1940

morning. I remember coming out here in an ecstasy almost a bewilderment of relief when B. de S. for whose opinion I have hardly any respect, praised it—I thought too highly.[18] No, L. does not come.

Its a splendid summer morning, & Janet's white butterflies—the white birds she saw when she was dying—are all about the trees. It is 10.30 & I think I am calm eno' to return to Coleridge, until 11. when I shall allow myself to go indoors. I forgot, in the above analysis, to include the Frys—their reactions to good or bad reviews. That also tells.

[*Later.*] Yes, Desmond is, as always to me, slightly depressing. I divine that is that he feels I haven't given the familiar, the human, Roger—'our' Roger. That I've made a just & animated biography, stressing the public side, the intellect, the austerity & so on; but not been personal & ungirt enough. I think this is what L. felt. But then Nessa & Margery didn't. Anyhow there it is—& Desmond is going to write at greater length next week. Nothing in the Observer. So I return, not much depressed, not much exalted, to my Coleridge.[19]

Thursday 1 August

I was going to say, when Judith interrupted, the book is a dud to my friends: but seems selling well. This comment is made on coming back from London this lovely night: & a very good dinner, a Burma Cigar & am not a jot depressed. Indeed—he that is down need fear no fall &c.[1] —a dud, I'll explain later why I say this.

Friday 2 August

Complete silence surrounds that book. It might have sailed into the blue & been lost. "One of our books did not return" as the BBC puts it. No review by Morgan, no review at all. No letter. And tho' I suspect Morgan has refused, finding it unpalatable, still I remain—yes honestly, quiet minded, & prepared to face a complete, a lasting silence. And full— no not of ideas—I'm so jaded after Philip Morell, Pippa, & the London uproar—but with a sense of things forming, & freedom. So thats satisfactory.

About Philip—laid in a lemon coloured jersey in bed. Ott's drawing

18. See above, 14 March 1937.

19. Desmond MacCarthy gave brief praise to *Roger Fry* in his column 'Some Recent Books' in the *Sunday Times* of 28 July 1940; 'It is a book about which I have more to say . . . and shall probably succeed better in conveying next week the value of this biography.'

1. 'He that is down needs fear no fall,
    He that is low no pride.
 He that is humble ever shall
    Have God to be his guide.'
        · John Bunyan, *Shepherd Boy's Song.*

room cut in half. P. rather shaky, rather patched in complexion, & plausible, fluent & undistinguished. Reminisced: about Roger: a most ineffective man; a most unhappy man; his life so sordid. "No, I've not had a happy life. I wasted my time in politics. No we were very unhappy Ottoline & I at Garsington. Quarrelled often. Thought of separating. We were so unhappy we came here. Our last years were very happy." This said with his old rams watery smile. Cheerful enough, but only with Bridge & old memories. I think disillusioned about Ott. Tepid about her diaries. Thinks he's getting weaker & wont live through the winter. Things suddenly go black. Surrounded by polished furniture: too much furniture. Very flabby yet mildly affectionate. Showed me photographs: if I've the energy I'll get one copied for you. Then summoned Milly had out shawls pressed one—a coloured one I chose—on me. Outside Milly asked me to look at his bathroom, said "He's very lonely very lonely. He's too proud to ask people to come. None of the old friends come; only the family. Miss Julian does her best. But she's always been hard—she doesnt care for any of her ladyships things. She's no comfort. The Dr says dont be shocked if you go in & find him dead. I'm glad you encouraged him to play Bridge. I say after all whats the use of living without . . . . . . but he's better now. I put him straight to bed when he comes back. There is his place—in the dining room with a book rest in front of his plate."

I shook hands & walked off with my shawl.

Sunday 4 August

Just time, while Judith & Leslie finish their game, to record oh a great relief—Desmond's review really says all I wanted said.[2] The book delights friends & the younger generation say Yes, yes we know him; & its not only delightful but important. Thats enough. And it gave me a very calm rewarded feeling—not the old triumph, as over a novel; but the feeling I've done what was asked of me, given my friends what they wanted. Just as I'd decided I'd given them nothing but the materials for a book I hadnt written. Now I can be content: needn't worry what people think: for Desmond is a good bell ringer; & will start the others— I mean, the talk among intimates will follow, more or less, his lines. Herbert Read & MacColl have bit their hardest; put their case; now only Morgan remains, & perhaps a poisoned dart from W. Lewis. I thought I'd mentioned Read: polite to me; very mean & spiteful about R.[3]

2. Desmond MacCarthy's extended and laudatory review of *Roger Fry* appeared in the *Sunday Times* of 4 August 1940.

3. Herbert Read's review of *Roger Fry* appeared in *The Spectator*, 2 August 1940: see *M&M*, pp. 420-22; D. S. MacColl's mild bite—again at Roger rather than VW— occurs in the 'Books of the Day' feature in the *Observer*, 4 August 1940.

AUGUST 1940

Tuesday 6 August

Yes I was very happy again when I saw Clive's blue envelope at breakfast (with John) this morning. Its Clive almost—what?—devout— no quiet, serious, completely without sneer approving. As good in its way as the best of my books—the best biography for many years— The first part as good as the last & no break.[4] So I'm confirmed in what I felt, even when I had that beak pecking walk in March with a temperature of 101 with Leonard—confirmed in what I feel—that the first part is really more generally interesting, though less complex & intensified than the last. I'm sure it was necessary—as a solid pavement for the whole to stand on. So I'm really & truly immune, & feel, if only Louie's father hadnt died, & Mabel's lover hadnt gone to hospital so that I've all the cooking & washing up to do today, that I could go on to the next thing— to many next things. Is it an illusion that I'm freer & stronger, as a writer, than ever? Only now John persistently presses for my LT article; & the American lady—one never is free for more than a dogs chain length.

Men excavating gun emplacements in the bank. They look like little swarms of busy ants, as I walk. Cementing floors; sand bagging walls. Great lorries of material go bursting down the Roman Road. No one pays any attention—so blasé are we. Guns along the river, boughs for camouflage, excite no one. Its like the raising of the gallows tree, for an execution now expected in a week or fortnight. R. sells well. Talk of reprint.

Saturday 10 August

And then Morgan slightly damped me: but I was damp already from Leslie hum haw the night before & the day before & again tomorrow. So Morgan & Vita slightly damped: & Bob slightly elated & Ethel, & some old boy in the Spectator, attacking Read.[5] But Gods truth, thats the end of it all. No more reviews, & if I had solitude—no men driving stakes digging fresh gun emplacements & no neighbours, doubtless I cd. expand & soar—into PH. into Coleridge; but must first—damn John— re-write the LT.

Incessant company is as bad as solitary confinement—Angelica for 2 nights, adorable, oh yes, & intimate & mature, & I see so much more of her side when I talk to her—her so reasonable & lovely side—if it werent

4. Clive Bell's letter, written from Charleston on Sunday, is in MHP, Sussex. John Lehmann came to Monks House for the night on Monday 5 August.

5. E. M. Forster's review of *Roger Fry* appeared in the *NS&N*, 10 August 1940: see *M&M*, pp. 423-25. R. C. Trevelyan's and Ethel Smyth's letters, both of 7 August, are in MHP, Sussex and the Berg respectively. The letter in *The Spectator* of 9 August was from Sir Walter Langdon-Brown, from 1932-5 Regius Professor of Physic at Cambridge, an uncle of Maynard Keynes.

too, a delusion. But is love ever quite a delusion? Well J.'s is. I reduce myself to initials for discretion; but cant spin a word to catch a fly after these 10 days of people & people again. Now Mabel's here wh. adds to comfort but diminishes privacy. So thats my chart at the moment. No invasion. Large air flights—little white gnats this evening. Sales very good—2nd edition ordered. But I want sleep & silence.

Friday 16 August

Third edition ordered. L. said, at 37 on Wednesday "Its booming." The boom is dulled by our distance. And why does a word of tepidity depress more than a word of praise exalts? I dont know. I refer to Waley: I dont refer to Pamela—great work of art &c.[6] Well, Its taking its way. Its selling. Its done. And I'm writing PH. wh. leaves a spare hour. Many air raids. One as I walked. A haystack was handy. But walked on, & so home. All clear. Then sirens again. Then Judith & Leslie. Bowls. Then Mrs Ebbs &c to borrow table. All clear. I must make a stop gap for the last hour, or I shall dwindle, as I'm doing here. But PH. is a concentration —a screw. So I will go in, & read Hare & write to Ethel.

Very hot. Even out here.

[*Later.*] They came very close. We lay down under the tree. The sound was like someone sawing in the air just above us. We lay flat on our faces, hands behind head. Dont close yr teeth said L. They seemed to be sawing at something stationary. Bombs shook the windows of my lodge. Will it drop I asked? If so, we shall be broken together. I thought, I think, of nothingness—flatness, my mood being flat. Some fear I suppose. Shd we take Mabel to garage. Too risky to cross the garden L. said. Then another came from Newhaven. Hum & saw & buzz all round us. A horse neighed on the marsh. Very sultry. Is it thunder? I said. No guns, said L. from Ringmer, from Charleston way. Then slowly the sound lessened. Mabel in kitchen said the windows shook. Air raid still on, distant planes. Leslie playing bowls. I well beaten.

My books only gave me pain, Ch. Brontë said. Today I agree. Very heavy dull & damp. This must at once be cured. The all clear. 5 to 7. 144 down last night.[7]

6. Arthur Waley's full-page review of *Roger Fry* appeared in *The Listener* of 15 August. Pamela (b. 1902), married since 1923 to the Rumanian artist Micu Diamand, was Roger's only daughter.

7. In the Battle of Britain—the prelude to the intended invasion—the Luftwaffe suffered its heaviest reverses in the week ending 17 August, when the RAF claimed that 496 German aircraft were brought down. The air assault, particularly on Kent, Sussex, and Greater London, was maintained but, having failed to achieve mastery of the air over England, Hitler decided on 17 September to postpone, and later to call off, his plans to invade in 1940, and to concentrate on the destruction of London and other cities by night bombing.

AUGUST 1940

Monday 19 August

Yesterday, 18th, Sunday, there was a roar. Right on top of us they came. I looked at the plane, like a minnow at a roaring shark. Over they flashed—3, I think. Olive green. Then pop pop pop— German? Again pop pop pop, over Kingston. Said to be 5 Bombers hedge hopping on their way to London. The closest shave so far. 144 brought down—no that was last time. And no raid (so far) today. Rehearsal. I cannot read Remorse. Why not say so?[8]

Friday 23 August

Book flopped. Sales down to 15 a day since air raid on London. Is that the reason? Will it pick up? But I'm ravaged by Ann in house, Judith Leslie Eleanor Camilla in & out of house. Ann goes tomorrow. L. says he has a moral feeling of duty to young.[9]

The Woolfs drove to London on the morning of 26 August and returned to Monks House the following afternoon.

Wednesday 28 August

How I should like to write poetry all day long—thats the gift to me of poor Ann, who never reads poetry because she hated it at school. She stayed from Tuesday to Sunday night, to be exact; & almost had me down. Why? Because (partly) she has the artists temperament without being an artist. She's temperamental, but has no outlet. I find her charming; individual; honest, & somehow pathetic. Her curious obtusity, her slatiness of mind, is perceptible to her. And she hesitates. Ought one to make up? Richard says yes—I say no. The truth is she has no instinct for colour; no more than for music or pictures. A great deal of force & spirit & yet always at the leap something balks her. I can imagine her crying herself to sleep. So, having brought no rations, or book, she floundered on here. I called her, to mitigate her burden, My good dog, my Afghan hound—with her long too thick legs, & her long body; & the shock of wild unbrushed hair on top. I'm glad I'm so nice looking she said. And she is. But well it taught me, that week of unintermittent interruptions, bowls, tea parties & droppings in, what public school is like—no privacy. A good rub with a coarse towel for my old mind no doubt. And Judith & Leslie are about to play bowls. This is why, my

8. Rehearsal: of a play to be performed by the Rodmell Women's Institute. *Remorse*: a tragedy in blank verse by Coleridge.
9. Eleanor Clark and Camilla Ricardo, both undergraduates at Newnham, were friends of Judith Stephen and Leslie Humphrey, and were staying with them in a cottage they had rented in Rodmell for August.

first solitary morning, after London, & the protracted air raid—from 9.30 to 4am—I was so light so free so happy I wrote what I call PH poetry. Is it good? I suppose not, very.

I should say, to placate V.W. when she wishes to know what was happening in Aug. 1940—that the air raids are now at their prelude. Invasion, if it comes, must come within 3 weeks. The harrying of the public is now in full swing. The air saws; the wasps drone; the siren—its now Weeping Willie in the papers—is as punctual as the vespers. We've not had our raid yet, we say. Two in London. One caught me in the L. Library. There I sat reading in Scrutiny that Mrs W. after all was better than the young. At this I was pleased. John Buchan—"V.W is our best critic since M. Arnold & wiser & juster—" also pleased me.[10] I must write to Pamela. Sales a little better.

28th Aug. P.S. to the last page. We went out on to the terrace, began playing. A large two decker plane came heavily & slowly—L. said a Wellesley something. A training plane said Leslie. Suddenly there was pop pop from behind the Church. Practising we said. The plane circled slowly out over the marsh & back, very close to the ground & to us. Then a whole volley of pops (like bags burst) came together. The plane swung off, slow & heavy & circling towards Lewes. We looked. Leslie saw the German black cross. All the workmen were looking. Its a German; that dawned. It was the enemy. It dipped among the fir trees over Lewes & did not rise. Then we heard the drone. Looked up & saw 2 planes very high. They made for us. We started to shelter in the Lodge. But they wheeled & Leslie saw the English sign. So we watched—they side slipped glided swooped & roared for about 5 minutes round the fallen plane as if identifying & making sure—then made off towards London. Our version is that it was a wounded plane, looking for a landing. "It was a Jerry sure eno'" the men said: the men who are making a gun hiding by the gate. It wd have been a peaceful matter of fact death to be popped off on the terrace playing bowls this very fine cool sunny August evening.

Saturday 31 August

Now we are in the war. England is being attacked. I got this feeling for the first time completely yesterday. The feeling of pressure, danger horror. Vita rang up at 6 to say she cdn't come. She was sitting at S[issinghurs]t. the bombs were falling round the house. Theyd been fighting all day.

10. See *Scrutiny*, June 1940, R. G. Cox's review of *Folios of New Writing*: 'The most depressing thing about *New Writing* is its nullity . . . no work of any real distinction . . . In the previous decade there were at work Yeats, Lawrence, Mr Eliot, Mrs Woolf, Mr Forster, Mr T. F. Powys . . .' John Buchan's admiration is expressed in his *Memory Hold-the-Door*, 1940, p. 202.

I'm too jaded to give the feeling—of talking to someone who might be killed any moment. Can you hear that? she said. No, I cdnt. Thats another. That's another. She repeated the same thing—about staying in order to drive the ambulance—time after time, like a person who cant think. She'd heard that Christopher Hobhouse was killed by a bomb: that Cynthia North—so lovely like a young colt she was killed by a bomb she trod on.[11] It was very difficult talking. She said it was a comfort to talk. She broke off—Oh how I do mind this, & put the telephone down. I went & played bowls. A perfect quiet hot evening. Later the planes began zooming. Explosions. We were talking to Leslie & Judith & Pat Trench [*unidentified*]. To bed. Planes very close: explosions. Nessa says today there was a great blaze at Ripe. A tinkling sound in the field. Bomb cases found today. A great raid on London last night. Today quiet here. When I rang up St. after dinner, someone cut in with a call to Maldon. "Restricted service. Things very bad there just now." The feeling is that a battle is going on—a fierce battle. May last 4 weeks. Am I afraid? Intermittently. The worst of it ones mind wont work with a spring next morning. Of course this may be the beginning of invasion. A sense of pressure. Endless local stories. No—its no good trying to capture the feeling of England being in a battle. L. has just driven Judith & Leslie to the station. At last we shall be alone. Molly wont come. I daresay if I write fiction & Col[eridge] & not that infernal bomb article for USA, I shall swim into quiet water.[12] L. sleeps sound all through it every night.

Monday 2 September

There might be no war, the past 2 days. Only one raid warning. Perfectly quiet nights. A lull after the attacks on London. At Charleston yesterday a skeleton Memoir Club. We sat in the sun. It was hot. The apples hung red. Not a sound. Angelica & B. produced a sense of strain. Maynard what I call unredeemed Maynard, rather severe, snubbing, truculent. Talk about lives. Mine of Roger I gather is called by Maynard "The official life". 'Why not write the real life for the Memoir Club?' (thats why I thought him morose & savage.) Bunny said Biographies will always interest. Morgan said not to the next generation. The sensitive like ourselves wont interest them. I said autobiographies are their line. M. interested came over to me. We discussed Hugh. I said he was a

---

11. Christopher Hobhouse (1910-40), barrister and author and a close friend of Harold Nicolson, was killed in a bombing attack on Portsmouth on 26 August. Lady Cynthia Williams (1908-40), daughter of the Earl of Guilford, and her brother Lord North were both killed on 15 August by the explosion of a landmine on the South-East coast.

12. 'Thoughts on Peace in an Air Raid' (Kp C369): see above, 12 June 1940, n. 10.

prostitute. Q. said Derain was a prostitute. I read my Dreadnought notes, not very well. Lydia wdn't come. "She feels this is not the time for brains" said Maynard. Tired after bowls & writing my USA War article my mind jibs at recording. Yet talk is interesting. Nessa said artists always did what they could. Maynard said there'd be no change after the war. We shd. go back to where we were. Morgan lost his spectacles—found them in a book. Clive had been on Firle Tower & saw the flash at sea when the explosion came. Said it was a German big gun firing across Channel. Q. denied this. Bunny A. & Maynard walked off. I told Morgan how I'd tried being honest with Hugh. Hugh had snubbed Morgan. Talk about Penguins. Argument as to whether they're read.

So lovely an evening that the flat & the downs looked as if seen for the last time. No raid. Slept over Sara Coleridge. Letters from Ben (R. absorbing) from Bessie T. (a great biography). Letters I shd be answering instead of scribbling here.[1] It is perfect summer weather. A man stopped on the bank with all its battlements to say so. Mr Freeth showed me the fire engine: danger of incendiary bombs. Will Jansen paint the iron shed? He's a matter of fact chap. I urged camouflage if only on artistic grounds.[2] And so this page is perhaps unnecessarily filled

Thursday 5 September

Hot, hot, hot. Record heat wave, record summer if we kept records this summer. At 2.30 a plane zooms; 10 minutes later air raid sounds; 20 later, all clear. Hot, I repeat; & doubt if I'm a poet. HP [sic] hard labour. Brain w— no, I cant think of the word—yes, wilts. An idea. All writers are unhappy. The picture of the wor[l]d in books is thus too dark. The wordless are the happy: women in cottage gardens: Mrs Chavasse. Not a true picture of the wor[l]d; only a writers picture. Are musicians, painters happy? Is their world happier.

Now, in my nightgown, to walk on the marshes.

Saturday 7 September

An air raid in progress. Planes zooming. No, that one's gone over, very quick & loud. Cdnt see if it were English.

Ben Nicolson for the night. A very tall red faced obstinate tongue tied

---

1. *Coleridge Fille: A Biography of Sara Coleridge*, by Earl Leslie Griggs, which VW reviewed in the *NS&N*, 26 October 1940 (Kp C370). For Benedict Nicolson and *Roger Fry*, see below, 7 September 1940, n. 3. Bessie Trevelyan (1874-1957) was R. C. Trevelyan's Dutch wife; her letter is in MHP, Sussex; for VW's reply, see *VI VW Letters*, no. 3641.
2. Mr Freeth, foreman of South Farm, acted as Air Raid Warden in Rodmell.

apprehensive gentle but obdurate not very clever, slow indeed, serious however; reminding us of Vita (to look at) then Harold, then a touch queerly incongruously of Eddy. Very well mannered wh. perhaps increases difficulty. Very diffident. Coming from a large world. But speechless: till after dinner: when he developed his charge against Roger: that he didn't personify artists, & by omitting biography, intellectualised: so didnt reach the masses, "didnt show that Leonardo was thinking of a tree." I guess B.'s got hold of a crooked stick; & will produce (come peace) rather formless, many worded, literary books. Dressed as a private in big boots this morning.[3]

More planes over the house, going I suppose to London, which is raided every night. A fight no doubt in Kent.

Tuesday 10 September

Back from half a day in London—perhaps our strangest visit. When we got to Gower St. a barrier with Diversion on it. No sign of damage. But, coming to Doughty St. a crowd. Then Miss Perkins at the window. Meck S. roped off. Wardens there, not allowed in. The house about 30 yards from ours struck at one this morning by a bomb. Completely ruined. Another bomb in the square still unexploded. We walked round the back. Stood by Jane Harrison's house. The house was still smouldering. That is a great pile of bricks. Underneath all the people who had gone down to their shelter. Scraps of cloth hanging to the bare walls at the side still standing. A looking glass I think swinging. Like a tooth knocked out—a clean cut. Our house undamaged. No windows yet broken—perhaps the bomb has now broken them. We saw Sage Bernal with an arm band jumping on top of the bricks—who lived there?[4] I suppose the casual young men & women I used to see, from my window; the flat dwellers who used to have flower pots & sit on the balcony. All

3. Benedict Nicolson, now a gunner private stationed at Chatham, wrote to VW on 6 August 1940 about *Roger Fry*, criticising him for leading 'a very pleasant existence' while ignoring urgent political and social realities. VW's severe reply (*VI VW Letters*, no. 3627) brought a further letter (19 August) from Nicolson, claiming that his quarrel was 'not with art but with Bloomsbury' which 'despairing of educating the masses, ignored the stupidity and ignorance surrounding it to cultivate . . . exquisite sensibilities'. For VW's draft and reply of 24 August, and subsequent invitation to Monks House, see *VI VW Letters*, nos. 3633, 3634, and 3639. Nicolson's letters are in MHP, Sussex.

4. Jane Harrison (1850-1928), classical scholar and anthropologist; her house, where VW had visited her just before she died, was at 11 Mecklenburgh Street, leading off the Square. J. D. ('Sage') Bernal (1901-71), Professor of Physics at Birkbeck College, London, and Scientific Adviser to the Research and Experimental Department of the Ministry of Home Security.

now blown to bits— The garage man at the back—blear eyed & jerky told us he had been blown out of his bed by the explosion; made to take shelter in a church—a hard cold seat, he said, & a small boy lying in my arms. "I cheered when the all clear sounded. I'm aching all over." He said the Jerrys had been over for 3 nights trying to bomb Kings X. They had destroyed half Argyll Street, also shops in Grays Inn Road. Then Mr Pritchard ambled up. Took the news as calm as a grig. "They actually have the impertinence to say this will make us accept peace—!" he said: he watches raids from his flat roof & sleeps like a hog. So, after talking to Miss Perkins & Mrs Jackson (a bloodless sand hopper), but both serene—Miss P. had slept on a camp bed in her shelter—we went on to Grays Inn. Left the car & saw Holborn. A vast gap at the top of Chancery Lane. Smoking still. Some great shop entirely destroyed: the hotel opposite like a shell. In a wine shop there were no windows left. People standing at the tables—I think drink being served. Heaps of blue green glass in the road at Chancery Lane. Men breaking off fragments left in the frames. Glass falling. Then into Lincolns Inn. To the N.S. office: windows broken, but house untouched. We went over it. Deserted. Wet passages. Glass on stairs. Doors locked. So back to the car. A great block of traffic. The Cinema behind Mme Tussaud's torn open: the stage visible; some decoration swinging. All the R[egent's]. Park houses with broken windows, but undamaged. And then miles & miles of orderly ordinary streets—all Bayswater, & Sussex Sqre as usual. Streets empty. Faces set & eyes bleared. In Chancery Lane I saw a man with a barrow of music books. My typists office destroyed. Then at Wimbledon a Siren—people began running. We drove, through almost empty streets, as fast as possible. Horses taken out of the shafts. Cars pulled up. Then the all clear. The people I think of now are the very grimy lodging house keepers, say in Heathcote Street; with another night to face: old wretched women standing at their doors; dirty, miserable. Well—as Nessa said on the phone, its coming very near. I had thought myself a coward for suggesting that we shd. not sleep 2 nights at 37. I was greatly relieved when Miss P. telephoned advising us not to stay, & L. agreed.

Wednesday 11 September

Churchill has just spoken. A clear, measured, robust speech. Says the invasion is being prepared. Its for the next 2 weeks apparently if at all. Ships & barges massing at French ports. The bombing of London of course preparatory to invasion. Our majestic city—&c. which touches me, for I feel London majestic. Our courage &c. Another raid last night on London. Time bomb struck the Palace. John rang up. He was in Meck. Sqre the night of the raid. Wants the press moved at once. L. is to go up on Friday. Our windows are broken John says. He is lodging out somewhere. Meck. Sqre evacuated. A plane shot down before our eyes just before tea: over the [Lewes] race course; a scuffle; a swerve: then a plunge; & a burst of thick black smoke. Percy says the pilot baled out. We count now on an air raid about 8.30. Anyhow, whether or not, we hear the sinister sawing noise about then, which loudens & fades; then a pause; then another comes. "Theyre at it again" we say as we sit, I doing my work, L. making cigarettes. Now & then theres a thud. The windows shake. So we know London is raided again.

I decided today after tears from Mable (about L. & the electricity—the latest of many grievances) that she must go. She said—oh the usual things—about not giving him satisfaction; too nervous to speak to him. The poor tallow fleshed almost petrified woman; who can smile tho', & is unselfish (to me) but its no good.

Thursday 12 September

A gale has risen. Weather broken. Armada weather. No sound of planes today only wind. Terrific air traffic last night. But the raid beaten off by new London barrage. This is cheering. If we can hold out this week—next week—week after—if the weather's turned—if the force of the raids on London is broken—[5]

We go up tomorrow to see John about moving Press; to patch the windows, rescue valuables, & get letters—if that is we're allowed in the square. Oh, blackberrying I conceived, or remoulded, an idea for a Common History book—to read from one end of lit. including biog; & range at will, consecutively.

Friday 13 September

A strong feeling of invasion in the air. Roads crowded with army wagons: soldiers. Just back from half day in London. Raid, unheard by us, started outside Wimbledon. A sudden stagnation. People vanished. Yet some cars went on. We decided to visit lavatory on the hill; shut. So L. made use of tree. Pouring. Guns in the distance. Saw a pink brick shelter. That was the only interest of our journey—our talk with the man woman & child who were living there. They had been bombed at Clapham. Their house unsafe. So they hiked to Wimbledon. Preferred this unfinished gun emplacement to a refugee over crowded house. They had a roadmans lamp; a saucepan & cd boil tea. The nightwatchman

---

5. From 7 September until 3 November an average of 200 German bombers attacked London every night; from 10 September, instead of relying upon interception and directed anti-aircraft fire, the defensive tactic was transformed into a continuous barrage of anti-aircraft fire accompanied by a blaze of weaving searchlight beams—a measure immensely heartening to Londoners.

wdn't accept their tea; had his own. Someone gave them a bath. In one of the Wimbledon houses there was only a caretaker. Of course they cdn't house us. But she was very nice—gave them a sit down. We all talked. Middle class smartish lady on her way to Epsom regretted she cdnt house the child. But we wdn't part with her, they said—the man a voluble emotional Kelt, the woman placid Saxon. As long as she's all right we dont mind. They sleep on some shavings. Bombs had dropped on the Common. He a house painter. Very friendly & hospitable. They liked having people in to talk. What will they do? The man thought Hitler wd soon be over. The lady in the cocks hat said Never. Twice we left. More guns. Came back.

He laid rather a thin rug on the step for me to sit on. An officer looked in. "Making ready for the invasion" said the man, as if it were going off in about ten minutes.

At last started, keeping an eye on shelters & peoples behaviour. Reached Russell Hotel. No John. Loud gunfire. We sheltered. Started for Meck. Sqre: met John, who said the Sqre still closed; so lunched in the hotel. Decided the Press emergency—to employ Garden City Press—in 20 minutes. Raid still on. Walked to Meck. Sqre. Refused admittance. John told us the story of Monday night.[6] Bombs whistle, if they fall near. He heard two whistles. Looked out. A great blaze in Guilford St. Gas main struck & the Foundling shelter opposite Stephen hit. He decided he'd take shelter. Then an explosion. He went into Square & saw a tree where Byron Court had been. Also a great cloud of thick grey dust. Also a man walking slowly in his pyjamas. Then they were told to leave the Square. Later he met several young women at some Bar with hair, he thought, powdered—really the dust of the house. Some saved by an iron bar in the basement. Some its thought killed. They became merry. He rather white & shaky. Left him with distant guns firing—Started back. All clear in Maryleb[one] High St.

Saturday 14 September

A sense of invasion—that is lorries of soldiers & machines—like cranes—walloping along to Newhaven. An air raid is on. A little pop rattle wh. I take to be machine guns, just gone off. Planes soaring &

6. Because of the danger and damage in London, contingency plans to move the Hogarth Press and its staff to the Garden City Press at Letchworth in Hertfordshire were now expedited. John Lehmann's story of 'Monday night' (actually Sunday) and its aftermath is told in detail in his autobiography *I Am My Brother* (1960), pp. 78 ff. His flat was a few doors away from the Woolfs' on the north side of Mecklenburgh Square; the time-bomb which prevented their approach on 10 and 13 September was blown up a few days later making their house (and his) finally uninhabitable.

roaring. Percy & L. say some are English. Mabel comes out & looks. Asks if we want fish fried or boiled. As the result of a friendly cool talk, she's going to ask Flossie [*her sister*] about plans. They may set up outside the raid area. Anyhow, its settled, I think that she leaves here. A great relief. I like being alone in our little boat. I like provisioning & seeing alls shipshape & not having dependants. And must now write to Harry Stephen before bowls—a warm letter, couched in Stephenese, about Roger. Distant pops—a rapid little patter of sound over Newhaven way. Workmen on the hanger haystack—disguising a gun—said "Wish I were as sure of a thousand pounds as of winning the war." Complete confidence. Buck Palace bombed. Altar exposed; & in Eastbourne yesterday a church ruined & organ thrown on road. The BBC become rather sanctimonious over this.[7]

The great advantage of this page is that it gives me a fidget ground. Fidgets: caused by losing at bowls & invasion; caused by another howling banshee, by having no book I must read; & so on. I am reading Sevigné: how recuperative last week; gone stale a little with that mannered & sterile Bussy now. Even through the centuries his acid dandified somehow supercilious well what?—cant find the word—this manner of his, this character penetrates; & moreover reminds me of someone I dislike. Is it Logan? Theres a ceremony in him that reminds me of Tom.

I suggest supercilious

Theres a parched artificial cruelty &—oh the word! the word!—[8] Am I oversensitive to character, in writing? I think we moderns lack love. Our torture makes us writhe. But I cant go into that—a phrase that brings in old Rose [Macaulay], to whom I mean to write. One always thinks theres a landing place coming. But there aint. A stage, a branch, an end. I dislike writing letters of thanks about Roger. I've said it so many times. I think I will begin my new book by reading Ifor Evans, 6d Penguin. And whatever happens I will settle & sun on the moment. 58—not so many more. This is quite possible, in any condition. I sometimes think about violent death. Who's whistling in the churchyard? The Major says there was a landing, repulsed, at Bournemouth[?]. Keep out the war from this page, now & then. I'm reading Henry Williamson. Again I dislike him.[9]

7. Six bombs were dropped, one wrecking the chapel, on Buckingham Palace in a daylight raid on 12 September. The King and Queen, who saw the bombs fall, were unharmed.

8. Roger de Rabutin, Comte de Bussy (1618-93), a cousin of Mme de Sévigné; disgraced and exiled from court for his scandalous *Histoire amoureuse des Gaules* (1665), his many letters to her, though urbane, reveal a nature soured by disappointed ambition.

9. Ifor Evans, *A Short History of English Literature* (1940); *Goodbye West Country* (1937), a journal of his thoughts and occupations: by Henry Williamson (1895-1977), author of *Tarka the Otter*, *Salar the Salmon*, and many other books.

Sunday 15 September

No invasion yet. Rumours that it was attempted, but barges sunk with great loss. Via Maynard, via Major Gardner & Percy. Raids over Brighton this afternoon. Hornets (our own) swarmed over my head on the marsh. Sheep frightened. Its difficult to see the English white circle. Mabel goes tomorrow; so pray God the Church bells dont ring tonight.[10] Domestically, a great relief & peace, & expansion, it'll be tomorrow, into merry kitchen harum scarum ways. Now we go to our last Cook cooked dinner for I dont know how long. Could it be the end of resident servants for ever? This I pray this lovely fitful evening, as well as the usual Damn Hitler prayer. Carried wood; bowls; asked for Sara Coleridge, as tho the New Statesman were immortal.

Monday 16 September

Well, we're alone in our ship. A very wet stormy day. Mabel stumped off, with her bunions, carrying her bags at 10. Thank you for all your kindness, she said the same to us both. Also wd I give her a reference? "I hope we shall meet again" I said. She said Oh no doubt—thinking I referred to death. So that 5 years uneasy mute but very passive & calm relation is over: a heavy unsunned pear dropped from a twig. And we're freer, alone. No responsibility: for her. The house solution is to have no residents. but I'm stupid; have been dallying with Mr Williamson's Confessions, appalled by his ego centricity. Are all writers as magnified in their own eyes? He cant move an inch from the glare of his own personality—his fame. And I've never read one of those immortal works.

To Charleston this afternoon, after provisioning for our siege in Lewes. Last night we saw tinsel sparks here & there in the sky over the flat. L. thought they were shells bursting from the London barrage. Great air traffic all night—some loud explosions. I listened for Church Bells, thinking largely I admit, of finding ourselves prisoned here with Mabel. She thought the same. Said that if one is to be killed one will be killed. Prefers death in a Holloway shelter playing cards—naturally—to death here.

Tuesday 17 September

No invasion. High wind. Yesterday in the Pub. Library I took down a book of Peter Lucas's criticism. This turned me against writing my book. London Library atmosphere effused. Turned me against all lit crit; these so clever, so airless, so fleshless ingenuities & attempts to

10. i.e.: to signal that invasion was imminent.

prove—that T. S. Eliot, for example is a worse critic than F.L.L. Is all lit. crit. that kind of exhausted air?—book dust, London Library, air. Or is it only that F.L.L. is a second hand, frozen fingered, university specialist, don trying to be creative, don all stuffed with books, writer? Would one say the same of the Common Reader? I dipped for 5 minutes & put the book back depressed. The man asked What do you want Mrs Woolf? I said a history of English literature. But was so sickened, I cdn't look. There were so many. Nor cd I remember the name of Stopford Brooke.[11]

I continue, after winning two games of bowls. Our island is a desert island. No letters from Meck. No coffee. Papers between 3 & 4. Cant get on to Meck. when we ring up. Some letters take 5 days coming. Trains uncertain. One must get out at Croydon. Angelica goes to Hilton via Oxford.[12] So we, L. & I, are almost cut off. John agitated. Talks of L.'s "bravado": but L. hasnt spent a night in London. This irritates L. who says he will go up by train tomorrow. Happily he now postpones. I dont want to spend a day bomb dodging; train prisoned. We found a young soldier in the garden last night, coming back. "Can I speak to Mr Woolf?" I thought it meant billeting for certain. No. Could we lend a typewriter? Officer on hill had gone & taken his. So we produced my portable. Then he said: "Pardon Sir. Do you play chess?" He plays chess with passion. So we asked him to tea on Saturday to play. He is with the anti aircraft searchlight on the hill. Finds it dull. Cant get a bath. A straight good natured young man. Professional soldier? I think the son, say of an estate agent, or small shopkeeper. Not public school. Not lower class. But I shall investigate. "Sorry to break into your private life" he said. Also that on Saturday he went to the pictures in Lewes.[13]

Wednesday 18 September

"We have need of all our courage" are the words that come to the surface this morning; on hearing that all our windows are broken, ceilings down, & most of our china smashed at Meck. Sq. The bomb exploded. Why did we ever leave Tavistock?—whats the good of thinking that? We were about to start for London, when we got on to Miss Perkins who told us. The Press—what remains—is to be moved to

11. In his essay 'Modern Criticism' in *Studies French and English* (1934), F. L. Lucas devotes some eight pages to rather peevish abuse of T. S. Eliot as a critic. The Rev. Stopford Augustus Brooke (1832-1916) published several surveys of English literature; two editions of his *English Literature from AD 670 to AD 1832* were among the Woolfs' books (*Holleyman*, VS V pp. 21 and 55).
12. Hilton Hall was David Garnett's home, between Huntingdon and Cambridge.
13. He came to dinner on Sunday, 22 September, and played chess with LW; his name was Ken Sheppard.

Letchworth. A grim morning. How can one settle into Michelet & Coleridge? As I say, we have need of courage. A very bad raid last night on London. Waiting for the wireless. But I did forge ahead with PH all the same.

Thursday 19 September

Less need of courage today. I suppose the impression of Miss P.'s voice describing the damage wears off. Another loud night Another bad raid. Oxford Street now smashed. John Lewis, Selfridge, B[ourne] & H[ollingsworth], all my old haunts. Also British Museum forecourt. A gale & rain here. I picked blackberries, & became absorbed in my LP speech—dear—10 minutes talk—but how difficult—for tomorrow. No letters yet from M[ecklenburgh]. S[quare]. No parcels. Pippin [Woolf] wont come. I'm relieved. Percy is up to some swindle about honey. It costs us about 5/- a comb at this rate. He tervisagates in the usual way. Also has stolen wood.

Saturday 21 September

We've just bottled our honey. I'm in a rage. Nessa has told those d—d Anreps they can come to the [Rodmell] cottage for a fortnight. I walked to Piddinghoe & saw a wedding The clergyman in the vestry said: This page was signed in 1542—almost 400 years ago. 400 years hadnt chiselled those red shy yokels into a very sharp shape. The girl was townish, in pleated purple. The man red & coltish. He was seized by a friend in the porch who stuffed a whole bag of confetti between skin & shirt. "To make up for Brighton!" he said. Then the air raid went. I heard bombs on Brighton.

I have forced myself to overcome my rage at being beaten at Bowls & my fulminations against Nessa by reading Michelet:

As I told Ethel Smyth, one must drop a safety curtain over ones private scene. Michelet is my safety curtain. Posts still held up. No Buszard; no Times book; no answer from N.S. about Coleridge.[14] The train only goes so far as Peckham. (Theres the all clear, I rather think). Mrs Chavasse says someone left London at 6: arrived at 2 am. We go up on Monday to salvage & see John. Mabel is said to have nailed curtains over the windows. A bomb in Gordon Sqre. All windows at 46 broken. L. has written to ask the Bedfords to remit our rent [of 52 Tavistock Square]. If refused, we mean to tackle the Duke, & ventilate in the papers.

14. VW wrote to Ethel Smyth on 20 September: see *VI VW Letters*, no. 3646. Buszards, the Oxford Street restaurant and confectioners, probably supplied the Woolfs' sweet ration by post.

Very still & warm today. So invasion becomes possible. Smoke was going up like a picture on the house over the hill in Piddinghoe. The river high; all softly blue & milky: autumn quiet—12 planes in perfect order, back from the fight, pass overhead. Last night I read a potted version of my U S A article. Quentin very burly & male. Mrs West prefers not to have money. A woman shd. stay at home. Miss Gardner amiable & silly but handsome. Fears [*the postman*] admitted: the wage earner keeps a perk for himself. A scattered discussion. How odd if one cd strip the flesh & see the various motives function.[15]

Wednesday 25 September

It must have been the next day that the Anrep crisis happened. They had taken the cottage, Nessa told me, indefinitely: Helen & the 2 oafs. Then I lost my temper, more than for years. Sure enough they came on Monday. Had I time I would detail my great philosophic scheme for organising emotions for the length of their stay. Every fortnight a decorous tea. A letter to Helen explaining . . . & so on. Then, like a Star arising, Nessa wrote (we are cold & distant, after our wrangle) that they stay only a week. Well—I cannot now dissect my maneuvres. All day— Monday—in London I was composing my attitude; in the flat; dark; carpets nailed to windows; ceilings down in patches; heaps of grey dust & china under kitchen table; back rooms untouched. A lovely Septr day—tender—three days of tender weather— John came. We are moved to Letchworth. The Garden City was moving us that day. Roger surprisingly sells. The bomb in Brunswick Sqre exploded. I was in the bakers. Comforted the agitated worn women. Then letters, from Arthur Ponsonby & Lord Bicester & Christabel from the choked maw of the post office.[16] So home. And now, constricted by the Anreps in the village, I plan a tea say Saturday; clench my teeth, shut my eyes; & after that, to the peace of this empty house, & renewed country. Invasion again withdraws.

15. The Rodmell Labour Party met at Monks House on Friday 20 September; eight members were present. 'Mrs Woolf opened a discussion on Women and the War' (Minute Book, LWP, Sussex).

16. Arthur Ponsonby, Lord Ponsonby of Shulbrede (1871-1946), Leader of the Labour Party Opposition in the House of Lords, 1931-35, and an old friend of the Woolfs, wrote 'a very nice long letter about Roger'. (MHP, Sussex). Christabel Aberconway wrote on 12 September (MHP, Sussex) to ask VW to see Lord Bicester (1867-1956), Chairman of the Merchant Bankers Morgan, Grenfell & Co., who wished her to delete two sentences in *Roger Fry* concerning the millionaire J. Pierpont Morgan which gave great pain to his family. VW agreed to the deletions in principle, but in practice they were not made; the offending sentences are identified in *VI VW Letters*, no. 3653 to Donald Brace.

Thursday 26 September

A rather strained talk on the phone with Nessa. She hasn't forgiven the Anrep conversation;—damn Helen for once more moving herself into an impregnable position. However, Nessa held the Trump card. "Both our studios have been destroyed. The roofs fallen in. Still burning. Pictures burnt." So I had to pipe low. My fallen ceilings a trifle. Helen a mares nest. Our strategy was to invite the A.s & the B.s to the same tea. The A.s accept rapturously. So therell be 3 very unpleasant hours on Saturday. I must prepare my behaviour. Think of things to say. Gathering apples all the afternoon. German raider comes over. Shots fired at Asheham. Bombs towards Seaford. Writing to Ld Ponsonby I remain unmoved. Only a German bomber? Oh thats all—No I didn't look out— Consider this remark last year—still more, 10 years, still more 50 years ago. In flush with PH. thank God: & The Listener suggests a review. So I'm nose to the grindstone; the perfect antidote to Anreps.

I never mentioned Ken Sheppard, the unknown soldier. But must return to Michelet.

Sunday 29 September

A bomb dropped so close I cursed L. for slamming the window. I was writing to Hugh, & the pen jumped from my fingers.[17] Raid still on. Its like a sheep dog, chasing a fox out of the fold—you see them yapping & biting & then the marauder, dropping a bone, a bomb towards Newhaven, flies. All Clear. Bowls. Villagers at their doors. Cold. All now become familiar. I was thinking: (among other things) that this is a lazy life. Breakfast in bed. Read in bed. Bath. Order dinner. Out to Lodge. After rearranging my room (turning table to get the sun: Church on right; window left; a new very lovely view) tune up, with cigarette: write till 12; stop; visit L.: look at papers; return; type till 1. Listen in. Lunch. Sore jaw. Cant bite. Read papers. Walk to Southease. Back 3. Gather & arrange apples. Tea. Write a letter. Bowls. Type again. Read Michelet & write here. Cook dinner. Music. Embroidery. 9.30 read (or sleep) till 11.30. Bed. Compare with the old London day. Three afternoons someone coming. One night, dinner party. Saturday a walk. Thursday shopping. Tuesday going to tea with Nessa. One City walk. Telephone ringing. L. to meetings. KM. or Robson bothering—that was an average week; with Friday to Monday here.

I think, now we're marooned, I ought to cram in a little more reading. Yet why? A happy, a very free, & disengaged—a life that rings from one simple melody to another. Yes; why not enjoy this after all those years of the other? Yet I compare with Miss Perkins day. At 58 Miss P. may live as I do.

17. See *VI VW Letters*, no. 3649.

Anreps yesterday. Easy & familiar & friendly. The brats [*omission*] astonishingly rude to Helen, to whom therefore I relented. Both treat her as a menial, a servant, an imbecile. Both very callow, callous, rattling & over emphatic—unrestrained; embryos, unlicked cubs. Ba goes to the pub at night. Ba attacked Phoebe Poole [*an Oxford contemporary*]. She wants to go back to London. An undisciplined, unschooled & not very attractive or seductive mind. Crude & raw. Both of course young—& so have vitality. Helen their slave.

Nessa rang up. A statue & frigidaire alone salved.

Wednesday 2 October

Ought I not to look at the sunset rather than write this? A flush of red in the blue; the haystack in the marsh catches the glow; behind me, the apples are red in the trees. L. is gathering them. Now a plume of smoke goes from the train under Caburn. And all the air a solemn stillness holds.[1] till 8.30 when the cadaverous twanging in the sky begins; the planes going to London. Well its an hour still to that. Cows feeding. The elm tree sprinkling its little leaves against the sky. Our pear tree swagged with pears; & the weathercock above the triangular church tower above it. Why try again to make the familiar catalogue, from which something escapes. Should I think of death? Last night a great heavy plunge of bomb under the window. So near we both started. A plane had passed dropping this fruit. We went onto the terrace. Trinkets of stars sprinkled & glittering. All quiet. The bombs dropped on Itford Hill. There are two by the river, marked with white wooden crosses, still unburst. I said to L.: I dont want to die yet. The chances are against it. But theyre aiming at the railway & the power works. They get closer every time. Caburn was crowned with what looked a settled moth, wings extended—a Messerschmitt it was, shot down on Sunday.

I had a nice gallop this morning with Coleridge—Sara. I'm to make £20 with 2 articles. Books still held up. And Spiras free, & Margot writes to say 'I did it' & adds, "a long letter all about yourself & what you believe."[2] What do I? Cant at the moment remember. Oh I try to imagine how one's killed by a bomb. I've got it fairly vivid—the sensation: but cant see anything but suffocating nonentity following after. I shall think—oh I wanted another 10 years—not this—& shant, for once, be able to describe it. It—I mean death; no, the scrunching &

1. 'Now fades the glimmering landscape on the sight,
   And all the air a solemn stillness holds,'
   From Gray's *Elegy written in a Country Churchyard*.
2. Lady Oxford wrote on 26 September 1940 (MHP, Sussex): 'Dearest, beautiful Virginia, I got the man Robert Spira out at last! I *loathe* our vile treatment of aliens', and goes on to appeal for a long letter and a book.

scrambling, the crushing of my bone shade in on my very active eye & brain: the process of putting out the light,—painful? Yes. Terrifying. I suppose so—Then a swoon; a drum; two or three gulps attempting consciousness—& then, dot dot dot

Sunday 6 October

I snatch this page with Anreps & Ruth Beresford imminent to say—what?[3] Will it ever seem strange that L. & I walking on the marsh first look at a bomb crater: then listen to the German drone above: then I take 2 paces nearer L., prudently deciding that 2 birds had better be killed with one stone? They got Lewes at last yesterday. Eleven bombs Percy says—not one of em drawing blood; only sheds, graveyards & windows. We discount Percy. But its indisputable—the crater in the field by the line. Two or three crashes today. A very stormy huddled clouded day. Favourable for hiding planes. Wild geese on the river. So I say. L. says Cormorants. But my old St Ives sea sense scouts that.

I'm earning £30 this week. 2 Coleridges; Sitwells.[4] And cant help running them all into a book, in & out, round & round I shall thread a necklace through English life & lit. But no, I wont let myself reel it off. Never had a better writing season. P.H. in fact pleases me; & so little to do now. Many letters to write. Lord Bicester introduces the Morgans, who are deeply distressed by Roger. But I cant write with Anreps imminent. Praise be, they go tomorrow. Yet I like Baba—perking up so fresh & spouting through that crooked spout her nose: alive; foolish. Helen of course,—well, I dont like the suppliant; yet cant see how she cd. better it. The weak are the wrong doers, as old Waller [Jack Hills] once said. The drifters that foul the nets. Only—only—I see too many sides now, growing old. Whats she to do, being a drifter? Vita on Wednesday. I think I could stuff this hole—oh the Anreps—as I cant bowl in this gale—with Michelet. I'm tired of article writing.

Thursday 10 October

Rather flush of ideas, because I have had an idle day, a non-writing day—what a relief once in a way—a Vita talking day. About what? Oh the war; bombs; which house hit, which not; then Ben's attack;

---

3. Ruth Beresford (b. 1917), the second daughter of Saxon Sydney-Turner's Treasury colleague and friend J. B. Beresford, had been on the stage but was now doing war work, sharing a (bomb-blasted) flat in Brunswick Square with the editor of this diary. Igor Anrep was one of her many admirers.

4. *Two Generations* (1940) comprised chronicles written by two members of the Sitwell family edited and introduced by Osbert Sitwell; VW's notice, 'Georgiana and Florence', was printed in *The Listener*, 31 October 1940 (Kp C371).

then our books—all very ample easy & satisfying. She has a hold on life, knows plants & their minds & bodies, lunches with Prince Bernhart, makes a curtsey to the wrong man "I am Robert of Austria"—washes up with R. of A. & is generally slack & abundant & wholly without the little artists back kitchen smell, so perceptible in Helen, large & tolerant & modest, with her hands loosely upon so many reins: sons; Harold; garden; farm. Humorous too, & deeply, I mean awkwardly, dumbly affectionate. I'm glad that our love has weathered so well. She drove us to Lewes; a great storm; car incommoded; siren sounded as we left her at the crossroads. A wave of her hand; she drives off in her leggings brown velvet coat & yellow shirt grown, I suppose people wd. say, rather heavy & blowsy; her eyes less lustrous; her cheeks spread—but so careless of it all, it dont matter. So we walked home across the marsh. How free, how peaceful we are. No one coming. No servant. Dine when we like. Living near to the bone. I think we've mastered life rather competently.

I was thinking of Mabel's history. Her friend has died. Could I write it, how profoundly succulent it wd be. The cold pear shaped woman: her suppressed country childhood: no its her life with Charles that interests me. He was 'on his own.' Did a good deal of shady dealing I imagine. Lived in lodgings kept by an old lady near Elephant & Castle. Used to eat raw tripe—being from Yorkshire. A typical underworld card. He made a good deal at dog races. He wd take Mabel to race after race. How did they meet? He was life & romance to her. Why didnt they marry? Had he a wife? Every spare day I wd find him a solid red face grizzled man in his shirtsleeves—perhaps helping to wash up. His other passion was the Opera. He knew them all by heart. For hours they wd stand in a queue, at the Old Vic &c. She knew all the tunes. What a queer relationship—she so dumb & passive yet following him; maternally proud of him, to races, to plays: following the form of horses; always with something on. I gave him 3 lemons[?]; but I also made her come down here, when he was ill—Lord, the bloodless servitude of the domestic poor! Now she's been "as near death as can be"—the flats toppling on to their shelter. It is something like an Arnold Bennett novel the life of the bastard woman; her subterranean London life, with this 'friend' as she called him. Charles Stanford I think his name was—Charles will do—or wont do—She thought of him as of a small impetuous boy. Now his life is over; & no one will know more than I do about Charles & Mabel.

Saturday 12 October

I would like to pack my day rather fuller: most reading must be munching. If it were not treasonable to say so, a day like this is almost too—I wont say happy: but amenable. The tune varies, from one nice melody to another. All is played (today) in such a theatre. Hills & fields; I cant stop looking; October blooms; brown plough; & the fading & freshening of the marsh. Now the mist comes up. And one things 'pleasant' after another: breakfast, writing, walking, tea, bowls, reading, sweets, bed. A letter from Rose about her day. I let it almost break mine. Mine recovers. The globe rounds again. Behind it—oh yes. But I was thinking I must intensify. Partly Rose. Partly I'm terrified of passive acquiescence. I live in intensity. In London, now, or 2 years ago, I'd be owling through the streets. More pack & thrill than here. So I must supply that—how? I think book ⟨making⟩ inventing. And there's always the chance of a rough wave: no, I wont once more turn my magnifying glass on that. Scraps of memoirs come so coolingly to my mind. Wound up by those 3 little articles (one sent today) I unwound a page about Thoby.[5]

Fish forgotten, I must invent a dinner. But its all so heavenly free & easy—L. & I alone. We raised Louie's wages to 15/- from 12/- this week. She is as rosy & round as a small boy tipped. I've my rug on hand too. Another pleasure. And all the clothes drudgery, Sybil drudgery, society drudgery obliterated. But I want to look back on these war years as years of positive something or other. L. gathering apples. Sally barks. I imagine a village invasion. Queer the contraction of life to the village radius. Wood bought eno' to stock many winters. All our friends are isolated over winter fires. Letters from Angelica & Bunny &c. Chance of interruption small now. No cars. No petrol. Trains uncertain. And we on our lovely free autumn island. But I will read Dante, & for my trip thro' English lit book. I was glad to see the C.R. all spotted with readers at the Free Library to wh. I think of belonging.

Thursday 17 October

Our private luck has turned. John says Tavistock Sqre is no more. If thats so, I need no longer wake in the night thinking the Wolves luck has taken a downward turn. For the first time they were rash & foolish. Second, an urgent request from Harpers Bazaar for an article or story. So that tree, far from being barren, as I thought, is fruit bearing. And I've spent I dont know how much brain nerve earning £30 gs. with 3 little articles. But I say, the effort has its reward; for I'm worth, owing to that insect like conscience & diligence, £120 to the USA.[6]

5. See 'A Sketch of the Past' in *Moments of Being*, p. 117: 'I recover then today (October 12th 1940...) from these rapid notes only one actual picture of Thoby...'
6. In response to this urgent request transmitted through London from the New York office of *Harper's Bazaar*, VW sent them early in November her story 'The Legacy'—for which the impulse was her visit to Philip Morrell after Ottoline's

A perfect day—a red admiral feasting on an apple day. A red rotten apple lying in the grass; butterfly on it, beyond a soft blue warm coloured down & field. Everything dropping through soft air to rest on the earth. The light is now fading. Soon the Siren; then the twang of plucked strings . . . But its almost forgettable still; the nightly operation on the tortured London. Mabel wants to leave it. L. sawing wood. The funny little cross on the Church shows against the downs. We go up tomorrow. A mist is rising; a long fleece of white on the marshes. I must black out. I had so much to say. I am filling my mind slowly with E[lizabe]thans, that is to say letting my mind feed like the Red Admiral—the Siren, just as I had drawn the curtains. Now the unpleasant part begins. Who'll be killed tonight? Not us, I suppose. One doesn't think of that—save as a quickener. Indeed I often think our Indian summer was deserved: after all those London years. I mean, this quickens it. Every day seen against a very faint shade of bodily risk.

But to continue—Ly Oxford writes a crude grasping letter. Ethel, having done her usual trick—sympathy, I must have sympathy—forgets & owns she's alive, in fact, bustling; so why be taken in by the extroverts ever again? They scream to rouse an echo—like Hugh, Ethel must must be heard. Vita sent a broken po, & Jacobs sheep wool. Not an extrovert.[7] And I returned to PH today; & am to transfer my habitual note taking I think—what I do on odd days—to Random reading. The idea is, accumulate notes. Oh & I've mastered the iron curtain for my brain. Down I shut when I'm tied tight. No reading no writing. No claims, no 'must'. I walk—yesterday in the rain over the Piddinghoe down—a new line.

Sunday 20 October

The most—what?—impressive, no, thats not it—sight in London on Friday was the queue, mostly children with suitcases, outside Warren St tube. This was about 11.30. We thought they were evacuees, waiting for a bus. But there they were, in a much longer line, with women, men, more bags & blankets, sitting still at 3. Lining up for the shelter in the nights raid—which came of course. Thus, if they left the tube at 6 (a bad raid on Thursday) they were back again at 11. So to Tavistock Sq. With

---

death: see above, 12 May 1938—on the understanding that it was a firm commission, and offered also a character sketch of Ellen Terry. In the event, to VW's righteous indignation, *Harper's* rejected both: see below, 26 January 1941. The '3 little articles' were 'The Man at the Gate' (Kp C373); 'Sara Coleridge' (Kp C370); and 'Georgiana and Florence' (Kp C371).

7. Lady Oxford's letter of 9 October 1940 is in MHP, Sussex; Ethel Smyth's does not survive. For VW's thanks for the po etc see *VI VW Letters*, no. 3655.

a sigh of relief saw a heap of ruins. Three houses, I shd. say gone. Basement all rubble. Only relics an old basket chair (bought in Fitzroy Sqre days) & Penmans board To Let. Otherwise bricks & wood splinters. One glass door in the next door house hanging. I cd just see a piece of my studio wall standing: otherwise rubble where I wrote so many books. Open air where we sat so many nights, gave so many parties. The hotel not touched. So to Meck. All again litter, glass, black soft dust, plaster powder. Miss Talbot & Miss Edwards in trousers, overalls, & turbans, sweeping. I noted the flutter of Miss T.'s hands: the same as Miss Perkins. Of course friendly & hospitable in the extreme. Jaunty jerky talk. Repetitions. So sorry we hadnt had her card . . . to save you the shock. Its awful . . . Upstairs she propped a leaning bookcase for us. Books all over dining room floor. In my sitting room glass all over Mrs Hunter's cabinet—& so on.[8] Only the drawing room with windows almost whole. A wind blowing through. I began to hunt out diaries. What cd we salvage in this little car? Darwin, & the Silver, & some glass & china. Then, I on my chair hunting, Mabel came. As discreet & matronly as ever. Rather finer & sadder. I arranged that she shd. come here for a fortnight. She too almost, in her very trained servant way, overcome. Our house, she said, like a monkeys house. Hadnt had her clothes off since she left. And going to the hospital—here she paused. "You hear them whistling round you, you wonder is it our turn next?" The flats had fallen on top of her shelter. Anxious of course to sweep to recover my fur coat. I worked with her in the kitchen packing Duncan's glasses, Nessa's plates. Very friendly, devoted, her training as helper uppermost. Offered her fare. She refused. (And she hasnt come, greatly to our relief— Oh the pleasure of the empty house—of the ship in wh. we're the crew . . .) Then lunch off tongue, in the drawing room. John came. I forgot the Voyage of the Beagle. No raid the whole day. So about 2.30 drove home. L. says £10 wd cover our damage. Cheered on the whole by London. Damage in Bloomsbury considerable. 3 houses out in Caroline Place: but miles & miles of Hyde Park, Oxford & Cambridge Terrace, & Queens Gate untouched. Now we seem quit of London.

Plans for buying a house in Lewes & storing our furniture. Perhaps hiring rooms for our books at the Rectory. Exhilaration at losing possessions—save at times I want my books & chairs & carpets & beds—How I worked to buy them—one by one—And the pictures. But to be free of Meck. wd now be a relief. Almost certainly it will be destroyed—& our queer tenancy of that sunny flat over . . . In spite of the move & the expense, no doubt, if we save our things, we shall be

---

8. Miss Talbot and Miss Edwards were clerks in Dollman & Pritchard, the solicitors' office below the Woolfs' flat. Mrs Hunter was Ethel Smyth's sister; VW bought the cabinet at the sale of her effects: see *IV VW Diary*, 15 May 1931.

cheaply quit—I mean, if we'd stayed at 52 & lost all our possessions.
But its odd—the relief at losing possessions. I shd like to start life, in
peace, almost bare—free to go anywhere. Can we be rid of Meck tho'?

Nessa to tea yesterday. Talk of a farmhouse at Chalverton?—for A.
& B. I at once long to buy it—Checked by L. Tomorrow we go to
Lewes & house agents.

I must add that today is as hot as August: walked on downs; heard
gunfire at Dover?—shelling Calais; summer clothes; L. cleaning beds.
Too hot for fire. Mist rising, must black out.

[Tuesday 22 October][9]

Mabel has come. I thought I heard a rat gnawing when I came in from
the marsh. Strode into the kitchen & found her there. So all our solitude
is gone. There she is, passive, dependant. And how to make a move?
Seems impossible. The old weight of respectable damp despair is on me.
L. says she's positively cheered by Charles' death—after an operation at
Tooting. "I could envy him" she said to me this morning. "They say
I've grown fatter—sitting doing nothing"

To Lewes. Asked the rent of Yew Tree house—£110, with a view to
buying & storing. Denny Botten has rooms. Mrs Ebbs has a stable. Mrs
Ebbs always reads "your wife's books. But doesn't understand them—
for the beautiful English." I wish I didn't play bowls, & cd. settle in &
write calmly or read. As it is, in I rush, having irritated L. who said he
had bad luck; I won the 2nd game—too hasty to do more than black out
before dinner.

Mable somewhere secretively observant. The vast ideas that float are
never caught. I thought: how L. sees people in the mass: I singly. I
thought biography is like the rim of sea anemones left round the shore in
Gosse's Father & Son [1907]: I thought Beresford, Ruth's father, has
been killed by a bomb:[10] I thought, I will write supports & additions
for my old TLS articles; a good deal about manners, & our class; about
my rug (L. sneezes in the wc. I jump;) about a prayer for the V[ictoria]n
scene in P.H.; no reply from Harpers. Gramophone mended but bad;
if I wait the thought may return; a lovely almost a red admiral & apple
day; 24 vols of diary salved; a great mass for my memoirs.[11] The lazy

9. VW has dated this *23rd Oct.*; since the following entry is also dated *Wed. 23rd
   Oct.*, it seems probable that this was written on 22nd—when, according to LW's
   diary, they drove to Lewes.
10. J. B. Beresford, on Home Guard duty at the Treasury, was killed when it was hit
    by a bomb on 17 October.
11. LW, in his Preface to *A Writer's Diary* (1954), writes: 'When she died, she left 26
    volumes of diary, written in this kind of book in her own hand.' For details, see
    I VW Diary, Editor's Preface and Appendix I.

talk of pregnant women—to wit, Mrs Cruttenden in the bakers shop; lou[n]ged out & stood in the sun; & now I will light the fire, as L. comes in with the logs. And so, rug, reading, music, bed.

Wednesday 23 October

Heard the whistle of bombs for the first time today. About 5—windy cloudy: playing bowls. Suddenly heard a plane: suddenly heard a whistle. Like a toy pig escaping—rather: Then I saw smoke, over the field path. Then 4 separate thuds—said to be at Iford & by the new house opposite Northease. Went into village. What about the children, said Annie's sister in law. Then Annie & two children appeared. In the bus from Lewes they had seen the bombs fall near. No one hurt—as far as known. L. now holding agricultural meeting. How instinctive the mothers reaction is! The children . . . off she ran. Jaded with story spinning fr. an empty well in reply to 2 more letters from H[arper's]. B[azaar].

Saturday 26 October

"The complete Insider"—I have just coined this title to express my feeling towards George Trevelyan; who has been made Master of Trinity: whose history of England I began after tea (throwing aside Michelet vol. 15 with a glorious sense of my own free & easiness in reading now).[12] Herbert Fisher is another. So (with a 'perhaps') is Maynard. They are Romans not Greeks. I like outsiders better. Insiders write a colourless English. They are turned out by the University machine. I respect them. Father was one variety. I dont love them. I dont savour them. Insiders are the glory of the 19th century. They do a great service like Roman roads. But they avoid the forests & the will o the wisps.

Rather a harassed day yesterday—Leslie Humphreys: carrying the bust of Sir James.[13] He climbs. He's agile. He's communicative. But a bore— or will be—a garrulous bore. At the same time he part touched, part flattered me by his little private talk about Judith. How she refers "things to you & Leonard. You've got hold of something worth having." He pools his Bank balance with her: is proud, worshipping, of her; says she suffers, from a sense of guilt. Provides her I suppose with confidence &

12. G. M. Trevelyan was Master of Trinity College, Cambridge, from 1940-51; his *History of England* was published in 1926.

13. This was the bust of VW's grandfather Sir James Stephen (1789-1859) by the Scottish sculptor Alexander Munro (1825-71); see Leslie Stephen, *The Mausoleum Book* (1977), p. 99. Scorned by Vanessa and VW, it had been housed by Adrian Stephen, who now sent it for safety to Monks House—where it stood in an obscure corner of the garden until LW's death, when it was reclaimed by Adrian's daughter Ann.

the normal. But he irritated L.: & Mabel has trod on L.'s spectacles; &
the Frys will have her. Too cold for more.

Tuesday 29 October

Rather than wash my head I will here record (it has taken me 10
minutes to fit new sheets into this book) a London day. Up by train.
Saying a chill early morning good bye to Mabel, who's gone to Isabel
Fry [*one of Roger's sisters*]. Train luxurious & fast. Bus 18 waiting. Very
little new damage. City looked untouched. The flat wind swept. So
walked—all our part pitted & scarred. At 52 we saw the panels still
pendant—3 at least.[14] The scavenger talked to us about Sally—L.'s old
fine trusty crone. To buy wool. So round the squares home. Cold sausages
in the cold room. Salvaged a few books off the floor. Pritchard had his
gardener up with a spade. Much lamented our carpet inches deep in
plaster & glass. L. to the Fabians [*in Westminster*]. I by some hanky
panky on part of my watch so late—5 to the ½ hour in Piccadilly—had
to jump into a taxi. St James Church a shell; also the shop opposite.
Ruins in Leicester Sqre. Crater in front of the Palace. Willie & L. standing
outside Fabians. to Victoria. Air raid sounded. Sat there for ¾ hour. No
guns. So home. And how happy—several letters—one from the woman
gardener, who has never read anything so disgusting as p. 34 in R.F.;
book (E.F. Benson) from Times:[15] wood fire & thats all. Today I cycled
to Newhaven—City of the Dead. Sepulchred shops empty; silent, dour
men. Baker boasted of the raid—at 5.30 yesterday 25 Germans descended:
dropped 25 bombs—houses ruined—little girl killed. "And not a
Spitfire any where near . ." The gloomy self consequence of the newly↑
bombed. Home by Tarring Neville. The loveliest of low views.

Friday 1 November

A gloomy evening, spiritually: alone over the fire—L. in bed with
influenza cold: caught off Percy. So I am alone; & by way of conversation,
apply to this too stout volume.

My Times book this week is E. F. Benson's last autobiography—in
which he tried to rasp himself clean of his barnacles. I learn there the
perils of glibness. I too can flick phrases. He said "One must discover
new depths in oneself." Well I dont bother about that here. I will note,

14. i.e.: the decorations painted by Bell and Grant in 1924.
15. Rachel Dyce Sharp, of the Violet Nurseries, Henfield, and sister of the first editor
of the *New Statesman*, wrote to complain of a 'repulsive' passage about flogging
at his prep-school quoted by VW in *Roger Fry* (p. 28 in Penguin edition); see
VI VW Letters, no. 3676 and fn. The Times Book Club book was E. F. Benson's
Final Edition, an Informal Autobiography (1940).

tho', the perils of glibness. And add, considering how I feel in my fingers the weight of every word, even of a review, need I feel guilty?

The relics of my distracted morning—I had to ring up Miss Talbot—who was to come tomorrow—&c &c, were spent tightening that wretched £150 story, The Legacy.[1] Well, I combed & tidied it—so far as 'it' has any hair on its head. Then dipped into my memoirs: too circuitous & unrelated: too many splutters: as it stands. A real life has no crisis: hence nothing to tighten. It must lack centre. It must amble on. All the same, I can weave a very thick pattern, one of these days, out of that pattern of detail. Then I carried L.'s lunch. Then I pumped my bicycle. Then I rode to Lewes. I saw a chocolate velvet Bradfield, & slid past. Early in the morning Annie came, asked me to stand for W.I. Cttee. "No" I cried too violently. The poor dont understand humour. I repented; went round later & found her in the sunny parlour with all the sisters[?] artificial carnations, & said I would. For I could see, by the pleasure she felt when I offered to nominate her, that she takes this infernal dull bore seriously: its an excitement. Two white Penfold brats. They run out like dogs she said chasing them. If one lives in a village, one had better snatch its offerings.[2] Miss Talbot rang up. Sister too shy to come. Arranged both will come—oh dear—next week. And the raid was bad last night. At 3 am. a bomb dropped 2 doors off—seriously hurt a man. She said it was an English shell, unexploded. The Italians, she says, are practising: nosing in the dark—as they did t'other night here. This very simple self-conversation had better end with the page—paper being scarce, & so on.

I forgot to say that I heard of Hilda Matheson's death today from Ethel. But she calls up no image.[3]

Sunday 3 November

Yesterday the river burst its banks. The marsh is now a sea with gulls on it. L. (recovered) & I walked down to the hanger. Water broken, white, roaring, pouring down through the gap by the pill box. A bomb had exploded last month; old Thompsett told me it took a month to mend. For some reason (bank weakened Everest says by pill box) it burst again. Today the rain is tremendous. And gale. As if dear old nature were kicking up her heels. Down to the hanger again. Flood deeper & fuller. Bridge cut off. Water made road impassable by the farm. So all my marsh walks are gone—until? Another break in the bank. It comes over in a cascade: the sea is unfathomable. Yes, now it has

1. See above, 17 October 1940, n. 6.
2. Annie, see above, 5 September 1938, n. 4. VW was elected Treasurer of the Rodmell branch of the Women's Institute.
3. Hilda Matheson died in hospital on 30 October after a thyroid operation.

crept up round Botten's haystack—the haystack in the floods—& is at
the bottom of our field. Lovely if the sun were out. Medieval in the mist
tonight.[4]

T'other night cooking alone, Freeth came. Light showing. A plane
overhead (It was bright starlight). Later, P.C. Collins. Here I observed
the official bully. So 'rude': so rasping; the working man male dressed up.
Gave me a dressing down. Threatened. Scolded. What a chance to give
a lady a bit of his mind! When theyre not respectful, theyve no "manners"
to fall back on: only original—well not savagery, nor brutality: bully is
the fittest. Every night you show a light. No other house does. Next time
—prison, fine, indicated. I tried my lady battery on him. No good. Mr
Woolf in bed—thats why. No good. So I took notes of him too: useful
this breach in the bank of class manners. Anyhow we spent 4 hours
stitching curtains yesterday. L. still hanging. And Mary H. on the phone,
asking to bring Franzetti tomorrow. I am happy, quit of my money
making; back at P.H. writing in spurts: covering, I'm glad to say, a
small canvas. Oh the freedom—

Tuesday 5 November

The haystack in the floods is of such incredible beauty. . . When I
look up I see all the marsh water. In the sun deep blue, gulls caraway
seeds: snowberries[?]: atlantic flier: yellow islands: leafless trees: red
cottage roofs. Oh may the flood last for ever—a virgin lip; no bungalows;
as it was in the beginning. So we showed it to Mary & Mrs Hamilton
(an Italian; formerly married to Franchetti).[5] Now its lead grey with the
red leaves in front, our island sea. Caburn is become a cliff.

I was thinking: the University fills shells like H.A.L.F. & Trevelyan.
They are their product. Also: never have I been so fertile. Also: the old
hunger for books is on me: the childish passion So that I am very 'happy'
as the saying is: & excited by PH. This diary shorthand comes in useful.
A new style—to mix.

Yvonne knew Rezia. She now dreads germs. Covers her hands to
shake hands. A very dull life in the Palazzo Corsini. Nerino a doctor.
Was with the Huxleys & Sullivan when Ott & Pip came. Ott bathing
in pink tights with a great hat. I liked her when I found she was Italian.
Mary like a jennet—a mare with ears laid back. I liked her. Jimmy Sheehan
drinks. All the young English drink spirits.[6] I like wine. Air raids much

4. 'The Haystack in the Floods' is from *The Defence of Guenevere and other Poems*
(1858) by William Morris.
5. The Roman Countess Yvonne Pallavicini, formerly wife of the pianist Luigino
Franchetti, married the publisher Hamish Hamilton in 1940.
6. Lucrezia and Nerino Rasponi were Florentine friends of the Duckworths and
Stephens; in 1901 Rezia married the Principe Filippo Corsini, and they stayed with

less. Greeks holding out. Prospect more hopeful.[7] A crybaby letter from John. Doing the work of 3 men for 2½—all our fault. This his reaction to his own folly in poaching Auden. Auden has cried off—taking John's £100. Hamish Hamilton a publisher. Publishes Mrs Thirkell.[8] Mr Hanna arrives with L.'s [*A.R.P.*] armlet: violet silk with gold letters. Oh the black out wh. nips me in the bud. Miss Pound out with the Canadian. The Canadian playing a game in the road as I ordered dinner. Estimate from Carvills [of Lewes] for bringing furniture £25. No letters—only Denny.[9] And so to read George Trevelyan the perfect product of the Universities.

Thursday 7 November

Morgan asks if he may propose me for the L[ondon] L[ibrary] Committee. Rather to my pleasure I answered No. I dont want to be a sop—a face saver. This was a nice little finish to a meeting with EMF years ago in the L.L. He sniffed about women on Cttee. One of these days I'll refuse I said silently. And now I have.[10] Here is L. so I stop. Bad bombing last night—4 thuds: at 7—said to be Glyndebourne. London tomorrow Oh Lord the Talbots for the weekend.

1940[11]

37 Mecklenburgh Square existed till September. Then bombed. We went up every other week & slept there

---

the Stephens in the New Forest on their honeymoon journey. The Franchettis knew Aldous and Maria Huxley who in 1927 were living at Forte dei Marmi, where the Morrells and J. W. N. Sullivan (1886-1937), the writer on science and music, also visited them. James (Jimmy) Vincent Sheehan (1899-1975) was an American political journalist whom Duncan and Vanessa had seen a good deal of in Rome in 1931.

7. On 28 October Italian forces in Albania invaded Greece, but were repulsed and counter-attacked by the Greeks.

8. Auden had promised John Lehmann his next book of poems for the Hogarth Press in replacement for a travel book on America commissioned but never written, overlooking the fact he was contracted to Faber & Faber. Angela Thirkell (1890-1961) was a best-selling popular novelist.

9. Denny was the married name of Elizabeth Read who in 1933 lived in Rodmell and whose literary aspirations VW encouraged.

10. For VW's meeting with Forster in the London Library, see *IV VW Diary*, 9 April 1935.

11. In the Berg loose-leaf manuscript diary for 1940 (*Diary XXIX*), this summary, written on a separate sheet, is placed at the end of the year; it seems logically to belong here.

We had Mable.
Roger was published on 25th June.
The raids on London began in September.
France collapsed in June.
Raids here began in September.
There was the fear of invasion.
We were victorious over the Italians.
The Greeks were successful in Albania.
Herbert Fisher died
Ray Strachey died.
Humbert Wolfe died.
Hilda Matheson died.
Judith & Leslie stayed here for August.
Ann stayed with us.
Mabel left in October.
Louie takes on the house.
We go up only for the day.
L. arranges the vegetable growing.
Gives 12 W E A lectures.
I am Treasurer of the W I.
Morgan asked me to stand for L.L. Committee. I refused.

Tuesday 12 November

Chamberlain is dead: & if we hold on till March we have broken the back (or whatever the phrase is). These two facts sum up the papers. I could add about Greece . . . Hitler's speech . . . no: time goes so heavy & slow, that nothing marks the days. A bomb fell at lunch yesterday. There is nothing new. Eastbourne bombed. London. I am shirking, in these semi public utterances, the Talbot character. I had it on the tip of my tongue.[12] [omission]

Friday 15 November

As I cannot write if anyone is in the room, as L. sits here when we light the fire, this book remains shut. A natural slimming process. A screw over the end of P H. made me rather sink into the disillusions yesterday. We have been a bit pressed. Michael MacCarthy to lunch; L.'s [WEA] lecture; Nessa to lunch—2 hard shopping days, in one of wh. I bought blue serge slacks—all this has rattled my head; so I plunged into the past this morning; wrote about father; & then we walked in top

12. Neville Chamberlain died on Saturday 9 November; Miss Talbot (who was in fact married) came to Monks House from Saturday to Monday.

boots & trousers through the flood. Increased again. Lewes this evening with 2 lights showing looks like a harbour—like a French town spreading its skirts round a bay. I had a gaping raw wound too reading my essay in N.W. Why did I? Why come to the top when I suffer so in that light?[13]

Coventry almost destroyed. The usual traffic last night. All the hounds on their road to London. A bad raid there. When I am not writing fiction this fact seeps in. The necessity of living in the upper air. Then I tidied my room & threw masses on to the potato box for Louie. This also revives. I am a mental specialist now. I will enjoy every single day. We took 2 rooms at Botten's. I am always behindhand with letters. I am reading Read's Auty: a tight packed unsympathetic mind, all good cabinet making.[14] And pin my faith still to Trevy's history. And now return to that. Wind rising. So perhaps the traffic will be interrupted.

Sunday 17 November

I observe, as a curious trifle in mental history—I shd like to take naturalists notes—human naturalists notes—that it is the rhythm of a book that, by running in the head, winds one into a ball: & so jades one. The rhythm of PH. (the last chapter) became so obsessive that I heard it, perhaps used it, in every sentence I spoke. By reading the notes for memoirs I broke this up. The rhythm of the notes is far freer & looser. Two days of writing in that rhythm has completely refreshed me. So I go back to PH tomorrow. This I think is rather profound.

Butter stolen yesterday; Louie says "You are too well liked for any villager to take it— Had it been Mr Coates . . ." This flatters us. A fight over Knotts Bushes. 6 little companies of exclamation marks. Supposed to be the shrapnel after the air gun shell. Two loud explosions. A great chase, & all the farm out watching. Dumb Thompsett making wild attempts at comment. Flood even higher. And the plumes of the sky in the water—& the wild birds—& L. cut down the rusty funereal trees today. And I lost the saw. I cannot fix my mind to details. The butter disappeared when we were playing bowls. A mans voice heard, & the card of St Dunstan's found in the door. Assumption then that the voluntary Collector took it.

A Canadian soldier stole Peter's bicycle pump. Two Miss Pounds left the house holding nothing in their hands. Mrs Chavasse—I'm a lone woman—always sleeps in her shelter—a cellar, dripping wet—Lord!—

13. For VW's account of her father, see 'A Sketch of the Past' in *Moments of Being*, p. 123, dated 15 November. *Folios of New Writing*, which contained her essay 'The Leaning Tower', was published this month.
14. Herbert Read, *Annals of Innocence and Experience* (1940).

NOVEMBER 1940

Monday 18 November

These queer little sand castles, I was thinking; I was finishing Herbert
Read's autobiography this morning at breakfast. Little boys making sand
castles. This refers to H. Read; Tom Eliot; Santayana; Wells. Each is
weathertight, & gives shelter to the occupant. I think I can follow Read's
building; so far as one can follow what one cannot build. But I am the
sea which demolishes these castles. I use this image; meaning that owing
to Read's article on Roger, his self that built the castle is to me destructive
of its architecture. A mean, spiteful Read dwells outside. What is the
value of a philosophy which has no power over life? I have the double
vision. I mean, as I am not engrossed in the labour of making this
intricate word structure I also see the man who makes it. I should say it
is only word proof not weather proof. We have to discover the natural
law & live by it. We are anarchists: We take the leap (glory that is)
from what we know to the instinctive. This is his defence of romanticism,
of sur-realism. His selection from literature is: Flaubert, Henry James,
Blake, Wordsworth. All we at the moment can do is to make these
selections: like dogs seeking the grass that cures us. But of course, being
a tower dweller, Read then walls them in, others out. Plato of course did
not write reviews for The Spectator. I can thus endow him with a purity
that is impossible when I know that little Read attacks Roger. Little
Read is the image in the face of a pasty boardschool boy. Is this word
"little" inevitable of the living? I am carrying on, while I read, the idea of
women discovering, like the 19th century rationalists, agnostics, that
man is no longer God. My position, ceasing to accept the religion, is
quite unlike Read's, Wells', Tom's, or Santayana's. It is essential to
remain outside; & realise my own beliefs: or rather not to accept theirs.
A line to think out.

Saturday 23 November

Having this moment finished The Pageant—or Poyntz Hall?—(begun
perhaps April 1938) my thoughts turn, well up, to write the first chapter
of the next book (nameless). Anon, it will be called. The exact narrative
of this last morning should refer to Louie's interruption, holding a glass
jar, in whose thin milk was a pat of butter. Then I went in with her to
skim the milk off: then I took the pat & showed it to Leonard. This was
a moment of great household triumph.

I am a little triumphant about the book. I think its an interesting
attempt in a new method. I think its more quintessential than the others.
More milk skimmed off. A richer pat, certainly a fresher than that misery
The Years. I've enjoyed writing almost every page. This book was only
(I must note) written at intervals when the pressure was at its highest,
during the drudgery of Roger. I think I shall make this then my scheme:

if the new book can be made to serve as daily drudgery—only I hope to lessen that—anyhow it will be a supported on fact book—then I shall brew some moments of high pressure. I think of taking my mountain top—that persistent vision—as a starting point. Then see what comes. If nothing, it wont matter.

To lunch with B. & A. at Claverham yesterday.[15] B. was surly from the start. A. a little spotty. Also nervous. I got a little solitary gossip in the chimney corner. But its not the old family ease. B. suspects the family influence. B. dislikes the house. No room to swing a cat in he grumbled. "But I rather like the country." I, of course, at once saw the country as something I envied. We lost our way. Up a lane we went to a tree shadowed house, with a pond; & a swan; & a curious thatched barn, with small Gothic windows. I waited in the car. Such antiquity all gone to pieces. Some old farm waggons, some ploughs; a battered car in the yard. L. was wrongly directed. I knocked again; & an old buck in riding breeches—blue eyed, nair netted, munching her solitary lunch, came out. I noticed the ancient bits, walking sticks; & also the very fine panelled door. C[laverham]. farm house is in the fields. It has a pond. Long tracks of grass. Red plumed woods in the distance. And four hollow trees. Also a barn. I cd have fancied living there; it has a marble bath & W.C.: many rooms; thick walls; tiled passages; central heating. But they said it was betwixt & between: nothing in itself. When I think of Monks House when we took it—when I think of the E[arth] C[loset] in the garden; & the cane chair over a bucket, & the dogs barking; & how I hated the village—which has now become familiar & even friendly—arent I on the Cttee of the WI—dont I go to a meeting on Monday?—then I wd have given my eyes to live in Claverham, with the fields, & the green paths, & the farm horses ploughing. L. however saw none of this. In fact, A.'s position, with B. as her mentor, struck us both as almost grotesque—a distortion: a dream; for how can she endure Bottom. And when will she wake? So we drove back to the civilisation of Lewes, & I bought my cream separator: a sieve with which you skim the milk.

The flood is less today—as Q. & Elizabeth Watson lunch tomorrow to see it. No word from John. The L.T. article starred in a Lit. Sup. leader.[16] Am I again in favour? Yesterday a raider came popping over the hill: L. saw a smoke rise. In fact it was shot down at Tarring Neville. Louie says the country people "stomped" the heads of the 4 dead Germans into the earth.

15. Claverham was a farm house near Selmeston rented by Bunny and Angelica for some months.

16. 'The Leaning Tower' was pronounced 'a brilliant diagnosis' in a leader entitled 'ALL QUIET...' in the *TLS*, 23 November 1940, and was reviewed in the same issue under the heading 'The Tower Leans Left'.

Friday 29 November

Many many deep thoughts have visited me. And fled. The pen puts salt on their tails; they see the shadow & fly. I was thinking about vampires. Leeches. Anyone with 500 a year & education, is at once sucked by the leeches. Put L. & me into Rodmell pool & we are sucked—sucked—sucked. I see the reason for those who suck guineas. But life—ideas—thats a bit thick. We've exchanged the clever for the simple. The simple envy us our life. Last night L.'s lecture attracted Suckers. Gwen Thompsett is a sucker. (L. is getting logs so I cant write). From this to manners:—a thought to keep for my book.

John has written—wobbly: wants lime light & bouquets. 3rd imp. of Roger: & I not told.

Very busy this last week. To London: Bella & Tom. The last of 37 as a residence: furniture arrives on Monday. Leech Octavia asks to come. B. & A. tomorrow. Now I must read Ellen Terry.[17]

Friday 6 December

And then what they call real life broke in. Vans arrived in a deluge. Oh, we unpacked standing in the rain. And the Bottens did the dirty on us. Result: MH. gorged with old jugs & lidless pots. And the Christian room laden with 4 tons of old damp books.[1] Real life is a helter skelter, healthy for the mind doubtless. I cant climb up to the other life in a hurry. I see what a working womans life is. No time to think. A breeze ruffles the surface. No silence. I cannot concentrate upon E. Terry—partly because I'm not sure of my audience in Harper's.

Quentin last night; urbane & happy. Fears told us the story of South African war—war seen from the ground by the private. A childs eye view. Rather depressing—old papers, letters, notebooks: I'm going to bind the survivors tonight; & in coloured paper they may refresh my eye. All this writing—what a deluge of words I've let loose—on paper only: I mean not printed. And must now climb a low rung—Trevy—up towards my heights.

17. In preparation for her sketch of Ellen Terry for *Harper's Bazaar* (see above, 17 October 1940, n. 6), VW read her *Memoirs* (1933), edited by E. Craig and C. St John; Edward Gordon Craig's *Ellen Terry and her Secret Self* (1931); and *Ellen Terry and Bernard Shaw: a Correspondence* (1931).

1. Alarmed by the quantity of possibly inflammable furniture which arrived on 3 December, young Mr Botten only allowed the Woolfs to rent two instead of the three promised rooms in his farmhouse; their books, which came next day, were dumped in a storeroom at Mill House, once a shop, belonging to Mr Christian.

Sunday 8 December[2]

I have only five minutes after a struggle with Ellen Terry to say that the war—yes I have left only 5 minutes to fill in that omission—the war goes on; In ten years I shall ask, what was happening to the war? It is better. The Greeks are driving the Italians out of Albania. Perhaps this is the turning point in the war. But it dribbles out in such little drops. One cant always catch them. The war slowly enacts itself on a great scene: round our little scene. We spend 59 minutes here; one minute there. Badoglio has resigned. And if we beat Italy we beat Germany.[3] It is a cold windy winter day.

Monday 16 December

Exhausted with the long struggle of writing 2,000 about Ellen Terry,—interrupted by 4 days of furniture moving—distracted by the chaotic state of our possessions—oh the huddle & hideousness of untidiness—oh that Hitler had obliterated all our books tables carpets & pictures—oh that we were empty & bare & unpossessed—I take my pen to drawl & drowse a little. The year draws to an end; & I am harassed, damp: but I am relieved of a visit from Margot; & so will take the matter in hand: scrub & polish & discard: & make our life here as taut & bright & vigorous as it can be.

Its rather a hard lap: the winter lap. So cold often. And so much work to do. And so little fat to cook with. And so much shopping to do. And one has to weigh & measure. Then Kingsley comes & devours sugar & butter. I will write memoirs, I think: then Reading at Random. Measure, order, precision are now my gods. Even my hand shakes. We have the kitten. One day last week we lunched at Kings Cross with John. He was polite impersonal—the Prince Consort. A ceremonious lunch. Why are we hooked to that large, rather pretentious livid bellied shark? And must I spend my last years feeding his double row of teeth? I forget. I forget what I wished to say.[4]

K.M. effusive but less distasteful. He ruined 2 days, now I come to think of it. The sensitive plate of his mind only takes the surface. Yes, its like going to the films—the film of December 1940 talking to Kingsley. He reels off Bob Boothby: shelters; air raids; politics; not composed, but

2. VW has mistakenly dated this *Sunday Dec. 7th.*
3. Marshal Badoglio (1871-1956), Italian Chief of Staff since June 1940, resigned in December in protest against his country's invasion of Greece: an adventure now going badly for the Italians.
4. Kingsley Martin came for the night of Friday 13 December. On 10 December the Woolfs had driven to London and collected a blue short-haired kitten at King's Cross, where they met John Lehmann.

fluent. I sit with my eyes dazed.[5] Then at meals he scrapes & sops. I cook in the damp kitchen. And the village keeps tugging & jogging. The W I. party tomorrow. My old dislike of the village bites at me. I envy houses alone in the fields. So petty so teasing are the claims of Gardners & Chavasses. I dont like—but here I stop. Italy is being crushed. Laval dismissed. No raids lately. Margot asks me to lunch & has left me Voltaire in her will.[6]

Thursday 19 December

1940 is undoubtedly coming to an end. The shortest day comes this week: then the days draw out. It wd be interesting if I could take today, Thursday, & say exactly how the war changes it. It changes it when I order dinner. Our ration of margarine is so small that I cant think of any pudding save milk pudding. We have no sugar to make sugar puddings: no pastry, unless I buy it ready made. The shops don't fill till midday. Things are bought fast. In the afternoon they are often gone. Meat ration diminishes this week. Milk is so cut that we have to consider even the cats saucer. I spent an hour making butter from our skim of cream—a week's takings provides about ½lb. Petrol changes the day too. Nessa can only come here when she goes to Lewes shopping. All prices rise steadily. The screw is much increased since the summer. We buy no clothes but make do with the old. These are inconveniences rather than hardships. We dont go hungry or cold. But luxury is nipped off, & hospitality. It takes thought & trouble to feed one extra. The post is the most obvious inconvenience perhaps. It takes 2 days to get a London letter: 4 to get a parcel. Turkeys impossible. The pinch is said to be worse than last war. If it increases much we shall be hungry, I suppose. Economy on Mabel means less variety in food, more dusting & L. tidying. I bicycle to Lewes instead of driving. Then the black out—thats half an hour daily drudgery. We cant use the dining room after dark. These mornings L. breakfasts in the parlour by electric light. We dip into our great jars for pickled eggs & pretend they dont taste differently. We are of course marooned here by the bombs in London. This last week the raids are so few that we forget to listen for a siren.

5. Robert Boothby (b. 1900), MP, Parliamentary Secretary to the Ministry of Food in Churchill's government; a Select Committee of Enquiry had been set up by the Prime Minister to investigate his conduct with respect to claims against Czech financial assets in this country. After its adverse report in January 1941, Boothby resigned, although protesting his innocence.

6. Pierre Laval (1883-1945), Foreign Minister in the Vichy Government, a virulent enemy of Britain and an advocate of collaboration with the Nazis, exceeded the limits of Marshal Pétain's tolerance, and was ousted. (He returned to power in April 1942.) Lady Oxford's bequest was a bronze statuette of Voltaire by Houdon.

That used to come at 6.30 punctually. No bombs fall most nights. Beaverbrook warns us that early in Feb. not only raids but invasion will come. The Germans are said to be sending troops to occupy the recumbent Italy. Whats Hitler got up his sleeve next?—we ask.[7] A certain old age feeling sometimes makes me think I cant spend force as I used. And my hand shakes. Otherwise we draw breath as usual. And its a day when every bough is bright green & the sun dazzles me.

Friday 20 December[8]

Is there a difference of temperature between the morning mind & the evening? If so, it will be detected in the pages that come before this, the morning pages. We have been shopping in Brighton. It is a raw cold day, with the wind rising now. And I am mooning over my Shre. chapter in R[eading at] R[andom] trying to find some clue: some transition from the home to the host and hostess. Biblical prose I am thinking is not colloquial. But I wont work it out: rather give it an hour or so of dumb blind life & trust it will come to the top tomorrow. We bought a duck for our Xmas luncheon. We bought some buns & a wedge of cheese. I bought Eileen Power for 6d & regret not buying a new cigarette holder—mine being foul. Yesterday we went to the village school. They make things. If Raymond had been shown the spindly striped animals he wd have said they were prehistoric—invaluable Mycenean toys. I sat beside the flushed & cushioned Mrs Jansen; also beside Mrs Hanna, & invited Mrs Ebbs to tea, for she has a picture of the Dreadnought.

Sunday 22 December

How beautiful they were, those old people—I mean father & mother— how simple, how clear, how untroubled. I have been dipping into old letters & fathers memoirs. He loved her—oh & was so candid & reasonable & transparent—& had such a fastidious delicate mind, educated, & transparent. How serene & gay even their life reads to me: no mud; no whirlpools. And so human—with the children & the little hum & song of the nursery. But if I read as a contemporary I shall lose my childs vision & so must stop. Nothing turbulent; nothing involved: no introspection.

7. Lord Beaverbrook (1879-1964), Minister for Aircraft Production 1940-41, was a member of Churchill's War Cabinet. Italy was reeling not only from her reverses in Greece, but from her disastrous defeat in the Western Desert; driven from Egypt by the British offensive launched on 6 December, her remaining forces were now withdrawn within the defences of Bardia; but the story of her occupation by German troops was premature.

8. VW has dated this *Friday 20th Novr.*

DECEMBER 1940

[Tuesday 24 December]

I note with some dismay that my hand is becoming palsied. Why I
cant say. Can I make clear straight lines any more? It seems not. I write
this by way of an experiment, indeed its less palsied this morning, but
then I've been copying my Ms. of P.H., & am word drugged—but wont
go into that. And must go in & wash & dress for the Anreps & our
rather forced lunch party.

[Later] 24th Dec. Christmas Eve, & I didnt like to pull the curtains
so black were Leonard & Virginia against the sky. We lunched with
Helen; & again "I could have fancied living there".[9] An incredible loveli-
ness. The downs breaking their wave, yet one pale quarry; & all the
barns & stacks either a broken pink, or a verdurous green; & then the
walk by the wall; & the church; & the great tithe barn. How England
consoles & warms one, in these deep hollows, where the past stands
almost stagnant. And the little spire across the fields . . . We sat in a
ground floor garden room, untidy, littered, with the 2 oaves; & they had
a spread for us. So back through Lewes. And I worshipped the beauty of
the country, now scraped, but with old colours showing.

L. is now cutting logs, & after my rush of love & envy for Alciston
farm house, we concluded this is the perfect place. L. says it is exactly
right, for we needn't be cumbered with possessions here. Which reminds
me. We are very poor; & my hoard is 450: but must not be tapped again.
So I must write. Yes, our old age is not going to be sunny orchard
drowse. By shutting down the fire curtain, though, I find I can live in
the moment; which is good; why yield a moment to regret or envy or
worry? Why indeed?

Yesterday Octavia came with milk & cream; & Lady Oxford sent her
car down with the bust of Voltaire on a book. Very heavy. An extravagant
gesture on her part. And we saw the Keynes; & I cowered beneath his
pugnacious positive puritan ways— A blank wall of disapproval; till I
kissed him, on wh. he talked of Lydia, having a book about the ballet, in
his eager, stammering way. Questions of peace remains only, he says:
our victory certain. Churchill addressed the Italians.[10]

Sunday 29 December

There are moments when the sail flaps. Then, being a great amateur
of the art of life, determined to suck my orange, off, like a wasp if the

9. Helen Anrep had rented part of Court House Farm, Alciston, where there is one of
   the longest barns—170 ft—in Sussex.
10. The Woolfs went to tea at Tilton on Sunday 22 December; on 23 December
    Churchill broadcast to the Italians, reminding them of the long friendship between
    Britain and Italy and asserting that it was Mussolini alone who had led them to 'the
    horrid verge of ruin'.

blossom I'm on fades, & it did yesterday—I ride across the downs to the Cliffs. A roll of barbed wire is hooped on the edge. I rubbed my mind brisk along the Newhaven road. Shabby old maids buying groceries, in that desert road with the villas; in the wet. And Newhaven gashed. But tire the body & the mind sleeps. All desire to write diary here has flagged. What is the right antidote? I must sniff round. I think Mme de Sevigné. Writing to be a daily pleasure. Charleston dumb; Leslie vocal. Anreps lunched. I detest the hardness of old age—I feel it. I rasp. I'm tart.

> The foot less prompt to meet the morning dew,
> The heart less bounding at emotion new,
> And hope, once crush'd, less quick to spring again.

I actually opened Matthew Arnold & copied these lines [*from 'Thyrsis'*]. While doing so, the idea came to me that why I dislike, & like, so many things idiosyncratically now, is because of my growing detachment from the hierarchy, the patriarchy. When Desmond praises East Coker, & I am jealous, I walk over the marsh saying, I am I; & must follow that furrow, not copy another. That is the only justification for my writing & living.

How one enjoys food now: I make up imaginary meals.

— 1941 —

1941

Snow fell in Sussex as the new year began, and it was very cold. VW's diary (DIARY XXX) is written in a stationer's ring-back notebook retrieved from the mass of their books salvaged from Mecklenburgh Square, now piled up in a storeroom in the village.

Wednesday 1 January

On Sunday night, as I was reading about the great fire, in a very accurate detailed book, London was burning. 8 of my city churches destroyed, & the Guildhall. This belongs to last year. This first day of the new year has a slice of a wind—like a circular saw. Leslie H. came to lunch; said um-um so often I nearly goggled; he was discussing the foundations of communism, having come chiefly to pick L.'s brain. Gossip in between; then old Octavia came, with her market womans basket. Great white bottles of milk & cream. L. looking at the comet. Rather a strong moon, & so cant identify the constellation. Mrs Coleridge Taylor tapped at the door; about a concert.[1] And now its close on cooking time. This book was salvaged from 37: I brought it down from the shop, with a handful of Elizabethans for my book, now called "Turning a Page". A psychologist would see that the above was written with someone, & a dog, in the room. To add in private: I think I will be less verbose here perhaps—but what does it matter, writing too many pages. No printer to consider, no public.

Thursday 9 January

A blank. All frost. Still frost. Burning white. Burning blue. The elms red. I did not mean to describe, once more, the downs in snow; but it came. And I cant help even now turning to look at Asheham down, red, purple, dove blue grey, with the cross so melodramatically against it. What is the phrase I always remember—or forget. Look your last on all things lovely.[2]

Yesterday Mrs Dedman was buried upside down. A mishap. Such a

---

1. Mrs Coleridge Taylor, a musician and wife of the composer Samuel Coleridge Taylor's son Hiawatha, lived up Mill Lane at Rodmell.
2. 'Look thy last on all things lovely,
   Every hour—'

   Walter de la Mare, *Fare Well*, iii.

heavy woman, as Louie put it, feasting spontaneously upon the grave.[3] Today she buries the Aunt whose husband saw the vision at Seaford. Their house was bombed by the bomb we heard early one morning last week. And L. is lecturing & arranging the room. Are these the things that are interesting? that recall; that say Stop you are so fair? Well, all life is so fair, at my age. I mean, without much more of it I suppose to follow. And t'other side of the hill there'll be no rosy blue red snow. I am copying P.H. I am economising. I am to spend nothing. One day, 11 years ago I spent £2.2 on glass jars. That was the loosening of the purse— & I said it was difficult.[4] Is it difficult now to string tight? The great change isnt that but the change to the country. Miss Gardner instead of Elizabeth Bowen. Small beer. But, space, silence; & time. I can sit down to a book. This I havent done since 1924, I suppose when we went to 52: & the scrimmage began. Oh but I'm so tormented by the evening beauty, & I assure you Asheham down is purple pink. And the smoke, rolling like a convoluted—should I dare to say bowel?—is incandescent. Juliette has a boy. Elaine has the measles;[5] & to conclude the marsh is of the colour & substance of an opaque emerald. Many mad letters from adoring women. I never like or respect my admirers, always my detractors. Desmond's book has come. Dipping I find it small beer. Too Irish, too confidential, too sloppy & depending upon the charm of the Irish voice. Yet I've only dipped, I say to quiet my critical conscience, which wont let me define things so easily. Bardia taken.[6]

Wednesday 15 January

Parsimony may be the end of this book. Also shame at my own verbosity, which comes over me when I see the 20 it is—books shuffled together in my room. Who am I ashamed of? Myself reading them.

I answered David Cecil's silly sneer at Lytton & Mrs Woolf, withdrawing from life to cultivate their art in quiet. The little man I suppose justifies himself by sneering at us.[7] Then Joyce is dead—Joyce about a

---

3. Mrs Dedman died on 7 January, aged 74; she and her husband both worked occasionally for the Woolfs when the latter first came to Rodmell in 1919.
4. For VW's colloquy 'before I can unbend my old penurious muscles', see *III VW Diary*, 13 April 1929; but some glass jars were acquired eleven years before *that*: see *I VW Diary*, 23 July and 7 October 1918.
5. VW wrote next day to the nine-year-old Elaine Robson: see *VI VW Letters*, no. 3677.
6. Desmond MacCarthy's latest book was *Drama* (1940). British and Australian troops captured Bardia (and the greater part of four Italian divisions) on 5 January.
7. David Cecil's article has not been traced; his distressed letter of excuse and apology (undated and scarcely legible) in reply to VW's (uncollected) letter is in MHP, Sussex.

fortnight younger than I am. I remember Miss Weaver, in wool gloves, bringing Ulysses in type script to our tea table at Hogarth House. Roger I think sent her. Would we devote our lives to printing it? The indecent pages looked so incongruous: she was spinsterly, buttoned up. And the pages reeled with indecency. I put it in the drawer of the inlaid cabinet. One day Katherine Mansfield came, & I had it out. She began to read, ridiculing: then suddenly said, But theres some thing in this: a scene that should figure I suppose in the history of literature. He was about the place, but I never saw him. Then I remember Tom in Ottoline's room at Garsington saying—it was published then—how could anyone write again after achieving the immense prodigy of the last chapter? He was for the first time in my knowledge, rapt, enthusiastic. I bought the blue paper book, & read it here one summer I think with spasms of wonder, of discovery, & then again with long lapses of intense boredom. Shanks borrowed it; saying it must be hidden from Bowen Hawkesford. This goes back to a pre-historic world. And now all the gents are furbishing up opinions, & the books, I suppose, take their place in the long procession.[8]

We were in London on Monday. I went to London Bridge. I looked at the river; very misty; some tufts of smoke, perhaps from burning houses. There was another fire on Saturday. Then I saw a cliff of wall, eaten out, at one corner; a great corner all smashed; a Bank; the Monument erect; tried to get a Bus; but such a block I dismounted; & the second bus advised me to walk. A complete jam of traffic; for streets were being blown up. So by tube to the Temple; & there wandered in the desolate ruins of my old squares: gashed; dismantled; the old red bricks all white powder, something like a builders yard. Grey dirt & broken windows; sightseers; all that completeness ravished & demolished. So to Buszards where, for almost the first time, I decided to eat gluttonously. Turkey & pancakes. How rich, how solid. 4/- they cost. And so to the L.L. where I collected specimens of Eng. litre. & heard from Mr Cox how he sat over the kitchen fire at Kingston.[9]

8. James Joyce—born 2 February 1882—died in Zurich on 13 January 1941. For Harriet Weaver's visit to Hogarth House, see *I VW Diary*, 18 April 1918. VW made no contemporary record of Katherine Mansfield's reactions to the typescript of *Ulysses*, nor of T. S. Eliot's enthusiasm at Garsington: though see *II VW Diary*, 26 September 1922. *Ulysses* was published by Shakespeare & Co in Paris in February 1922; VW bought a copy in April, which in September that year she lent to the poet Edward Shanks who was carrying on a flirtation with the then Rodmell rector's daughter.

9. Frederick James Cox (1865-1955) joined the staff of the London Library before VW was born; he became the unavoidable custodian of access to and information upon the riches within.

JANUARY 1941

Monday 20 January

I will be curt, compressed. A mood like another. Back from a damp, perhaps rather strained, visit to Charleston. Nessa & Quentin; Adrian has almost died of pneumonia. Nessa apprehensive, on guard, when I spoke of Angelica's dirt. Search for epidiascope in Lewes. Fruitless. Lecture tomorrow.[10] 5 small trout for lunch. Octavia's cream. Talk of soup making. Reading Gide. La Porte Etroite [1909] feeble, slaty, sentimental.

Visit from Oliver Strachey. All stocky gloom. Flogged my brain for topics. Lighted on the war. Civilisation over for 500 years. "And my life is at an end." Enter two breezy brisk colleagues. He shares a sitting room.[11] I lost several pages of PH. I say to Nessa, Do you find painting gets slower? Yes. One can do more. And money? Never think of it. And Helen? She does nothing. I like being alone. How can one do nothing? Duncan coming & Clive. All the same MH is somehow cheerful. Q. has an offer of a draughtsman job at Dorking. Better than farm work. The Girls school at Lewes is behind Ann of Cleves House, a large, tiled, swept, clamorous place. The headmistress large & tight, practical. "No one knows we exist" she said.[12] I am reading—oh all lit. for my book. No answer from David, or Harper's Bazaar. And Ethel's letters go unread—oh dear.

Sunday 26 January

A battle against depression, rejection (by Harper's of my story & Ellen Terry) routed today (I hope) by clearing out kitchen; by sending the article (a lame one) to N.S.: & by breaking into PH 2 days, I think, of memoir writing.[13]

This trough of despair shall not, I swear, engulf me. The solitude is great. Rodmell life is very small beer. The house is damp. The house is

---

10. VW had persuaded Angelica to give an illustrated talk on 'The Stage' to the Rodmell Women's Institute on 21 January.
11. Oliver Strachey had been recalled from retirement to work as a cryptographer in the War Office Cipher Department at Woburn in Bedfordshire, where he was billeted. Vanessa brought him to tea at Monks House on 17 January.
12. VW had probably tried to borrow an epidiascope from Miss Abbott, headmistress of the County School for Girls in Southover, for Angelica's lecture.
13. *Harper's Bazaar*'s London office wrote on 21 January 1941 to say New York did not want 'The Legacy', 'but are tremendously keen to publish something', and returned both VW's mss (LWP, Sussex, II D 1b). For her letters of remonstrance (possibly written by LW?) see *VI VW Letters*, nos. 3681 and 3688. 'Ellen Terry' appeared in the *NS&N* on 8 February 1941; 'The Legacy' was posthumously published in *The Haunted House and Other Stories* (Kp A28).

untidy. But there is no alternative. Also days will lengthen. What I need is the old spurt. "Your true life, like mine, is in ideas" Desmond said to me once. But one must remember one cant pump ideas. I begin to dislike introspection. Sleep & slackness; musing; reading; cooking; cycling; oh & a good hard rather rocky book—viz: Herbert Fisher. This is my prescription. We are going to Cambridge for two days. I find myself totting up my friends lives: Helen at Alciston without water; Adrian & Karin; Oliver at Bedford, & adding up rather a higher total of happiness. There's a lull in the war. 6 nights without raids. But Garvin says the greatest struggle is about to come—say in 3 weeks—& every man, woman dog cat even weevil must girt their arms, their faith—& so on.[14]

Its the cold hour, this, before the lights go up. A few snowdrops in the garden. Yes, I was thinking: we live without a future. Thats whats queer, with our noses pressed to a closed door. Now to write, with a new nib, to Enid Jones.[15]

Friday 7 February[1]

Why was I depressed? I cannot remember.

We have been to Charlie Chaplin. Like the milk girl we found it boring. I have been writing with some glow. Mrs Thrale is to be done before we go to Cambridge.[2] A week of broken water impends. Cambridge; then Elizabeth Bowen; then Vita & Enid Jones. Helen has repaid me £25. Do I like her better for it? I think so. The snow came back. Marshes in the thaw a swamp. We were in London [on 5 February], & had to come home, owing to a bomb, by Dorking; the car was locked at Martin's [garage]; we dined at the White Hart—poor soup & oxtail; London streets are very empty—Oxford Street a wide grey ribbon. My red purse bag stolen & L. gave me another. At Charleston Clive was stockish, like a Bell. I said "What a risk Nessa ran marrying him!" The Sitwells are proving their existence as poets in the Law Courts—This is

14. In a signed article in *The Observer*, 26 January 1941, the editor J. L. Garvin wrote: 'Everything tells us that the iron orchestra is working up to fortissimo. Every single man and woman of us must awaken quietly to the knowledge that the crisis of our lives . . . must arise between now and Easter.'

15. See *VI VW Letters*, no. 3684 to the writer Enid Bagnold (Lady Jones, 1889-1981) who lived at Rottingdean, inviting her to lunch with Vita Sackville-West on 18 February.

1. VW has dated this *Friday 7th Jan.*

2. The Woolfs saw Chaplin's *The Great Dictator* in Lewes. VW's review of *Hester Lynch Piozzi (Mrs Thrale)*, 1941, by the American scholar J. L. Clifford, appeared in the *NS&N* of 8 March 1941 (Kp C374).

despicable but delightful.[3] And what else? [Ellen] Terry appears today in the N.S. The Italians are flying. The 3rd week in March is fixed for invasion. Now black out, & perhaps write to Mary. No I think read— what? I must tune up for my Elizabethans.

On Tuesday 11 February the Woolfs drove to London in the morning and went on by an afternoon train to Cambridge, where they stayed at the Bull Hotel, going after dinner to visit Pernel Strachey at Newnham College. Next morning they went to see the Hogarth Press in its wartime home with the Garden City Press at Letchworth, and returned to Cambridge to dine with Dadie Rylands. They travelled home via London on Thursday 13 February.

Sunday 16 February

In the wild grey water after last weeks turmoil. I liked the dinner with Dadie best. All very lit up & confidential. I liked the soft grey night at Newnham. We found Pernel in her high ceremonial room, all polished & spectatorial. She was in soft reds & blacks. We sat by a bright fire. Curious flitting talk. She leaves next year.

Then Letchworth—the slaves chained to their typewriters, & their drawn set faces, & the machines—the incessant more & more competent machines, folding, pressing, glueing & issuing perfect books. They can stamp cloth to imitate leather. Our Press is up in a glass case. No country to look at. Very long train journeys. Food skimpy. No butter, no jam. Old couples hoarding marmalade & grape nuts on their tables. Conversation half whispered round the lounge fire. Eth Bowen arrived two hours after we got back, & went yesterday; & tomorrow Vita; then Enid; then perhaps I shall re-enter one of my higher lives. But not yet.

Wednesday 26 February

My 'higher life' is almost entirely the Elizabethan play. Finished Pointz Hall, the Pageant: the Play—finally Between the Acts this morning.[4] Flora & Molly have just gone; leaving me to ask this bitter bright spring day, why they came?

Yesterday in the ladies lavatory at the Sussex Grill at Brighton I heard: She's a little simpering thing. I dont like her. But then he never did

3. Hamilton Fyfe, in a review of *Edith Sitwell's Anthology* in *Reynolds' News* of 11 February 1940, adverted to the undeserved vogue of the Sitwells in the nineteen-twenties, concluding: 'Now oblivion has claimed them . . .' The Sitwells' libel action against the paper was heard on 5 February 1941 before Mr Justice Cassels, who awarded them damages of £350 each.

4. VW now gave the typescript of *Between the Acts* to LW to read.

care for big women. (So to Bert) His eyes are so blue. Like blue pools. So's Gert's. They have the same eyes, only her teeth part a little. He has wonderful white teeth. He always had. Its fun having the boys . . . If he dont look out he'll be court martialed.

They were powdering & painting, these common little tarts, while I sat, behind a thin door, p—ing as quietly as I could.

Then at Fuller's. A fat, smart woman, in red hunting cap, pearls, check skirt, consuming rich cakes. Her shabby dependant also stuffing. Hudson's van unloading biscuits opposite. The fat woman had a louche large white muffin face. T'other was slightly grilled. They ate & ate. Talked about Mary. But if she's very ill, you'll have to go to her. Youre the only one. . . . But why should she be? . . . I opened the marmalade but John doesnt like it—And we have two pounds of biscuits in the tin upstairs. . . . Something scented, shoddy, parasitic about them. Then they totted up cakes. And passed the time o' day with the waitress. Where does the money come to feed these fat white slugs? Brighton a love corner for slugs. The powdered the pampered the mildly improper. I invested them in a large house in Sussex Sqre. We cycled. Irritated as usual by the blasphemy of Peacehaven. Helen has fallen through, I mean the house I got her with Enid Jones, the day Enid lunched here, with Vita; & I felt so untidy yet cool; & she edgy & brittle.[5] No walks for ever so long. People daily. And rather a churn in my mind. And some blank spaces. Food becomes an obsession. I grudge giving away a spice bun. Curious—age, or the war? Never mind. Adventure. Make solid. But shall I ever write again one of those sentences that gives me intense pleasure? There is no echo in Rodmell—only waste air. I spent the afternoon at the school, marbling paper. Mrs D. discontented. & said, Theres no life in these children, comparing them with Londoners, thus repeating my own comment upon that long languid meeting at Chavasses. No life: & so they cling to us. This is my conclusion. We pay the penalty for our rung in society by infernal boredom.

Saturday 8 March

Just back from L.'s speech at Brighton.[1] Like a foreign town: the first spring day. Women sitting on seats. A pretty hat in a teashop—how fashion revives the eye! And the shell encrusted old women, rouged, decked, cad[a]verous at the tea shop. The waitress in checked cotton.

No: I intend no introspection. I mark Henry James's sentence: Observe perpetually. Observe the oncome of age. Observe greed. Observe my

---

5. Helen Anrep had to leave her rooms at Alciston, which were requisitioned by the military, and VW was trying to find her some alternative: she came to tea on 22 February.

1. LW lectured to the WEA on 'Common Sense in History'.

own despondency. By that means it becomes serviceable. Or so I hope.[2] I
insist upon spending this time to the best advantage. I will go down with
my colours flying. This I see verges on introspection; but doesn't quite
fall in. Suppose, I bought a ticket at the Museum; biked in daily & read
history. Suppose I selected one dominant figure in every age & wrote
round & about. Occupation is essential. And now with some pleasure I
find that its seven; & must cook dinner. Haddock & sausage meat. I
think it is true that one gains a certain hold on sausage & haddock by
writing them down.

Last night I analysed to L. my London Library complex. That sudden
terror has vanished; now I'm plucked at by the H. Hamilton lunch that
I refused. To right the balance, I wrote to Stephen & Tom: & will write
to Ethel & invite myself to stay; & then to Miss Sharp who presented me
with a bunch of violets.[3] This to make up for the sight of Oxford Street
& Piccadilly which haunt me. Oh dear yes, I shall conquer this mood.
Its a question of being open sleepy, wide eyed at present—letting things
come one after another. Now to cook the haddock.

*Life at Monks House kept on in its outwardly restricted and monotonous
fashion, with teatime visits and visitors (Angelica and Bunny, the Hutchinsons
and Mrs Hamilton, Octavia Wilberforce), with LW lecturing, with shopping
and cooking and air raid warnings. On 14 March VW and LW went by
train to London for the day, and lunched in Westminster with John
Lehmann, who learned that VW had completed a new novel,* Between the
Acts. *On 20 March she sent him the typescript with a deprecatory letter
asking him to decide if it should be published, as she and LW differed: she
felt it was too slight and sketchy. On 18 March LW had noted that VW
was not well; on 20 March Vanessa came to tea and, obviously worried by
her sister's condition, wrote on reaching home urging her to be sensible, and
to trust her and Leonard's advice. In VW's answer, written probably on
23 March, she admits that 'this horror began' in the last few weeks and
that she is certain she is going mad again and will not recover* (VI VW
Letters, *no. 3708*). *That day, Sunday, the Woolfs went to see Mrs Chavasse
in the village. The following day, the last on which she wrote in her diary,
Leonard noted in his: 'V. slightly better'.*

2. Cf. 'Henry James' in Desmond MacCarthy's *Portraits* (1931), p. 155: 'He had been
   describing to me the spiral of depression which a recent nervous illness had compelled him . . . to descend. . . . "But it has been good . . . for my genius." Then he
   added, "Never cease to watch whatever happens to you." '
3. VW's letter to Stephen Spender must be no. 3587 in *VI VW Letters*, there wrongly
   dated 1940; that to T. S. Eliot is no. 3698; and to Ethel Smyth, inviting herself to
   stay for a night in April, no. 3699 dated 10 March. Rachel Dyce Sharp (see above,
   29 October 1940, n. 15) was at LW's lecture in Brighton, and subsequently wrote
   enthusiastically about it to VW (MHP, Sussex).

Monday 24 March

She had a ⟨face⟩ nose like the Duke of Wellington & great horse teeth & cold prominent eyes. When we came in she was sitting perched on a 3 cornered chair with knitting in her hands. An arrow fastened her collar. And before 5 minutes had passed she had told us that two of her sons had been killed in the war. This, one felt, was to her credit. She taught dressmaking. Everything in the room was red brown & glossy. Sitting there I tried to coin a few compliments. But they perished in the icy sea between us. And then there was nothing.

A curious sea side feeling in the air today. It reminds me of lodgings on a parade at Easter. Everyone leaning against the wind, nipped & silenced. All pulp removed.

This windy corner. And Nessa is at Brighton, & I am imagining how it wd be if we could infuse souls.

Octavia's story. Could I englobe it somehow? English youth in 1900.

Two long letters from Shena & O. I cant tackle them, yet enjoy having them.

L. is doing the rhododendrons . . .

John Lehmann had written enthusiastically to VW about Between the Acts, *which he had already announced for Spring publication by the Hogarth Press; but her doubts and depression gaining ground, she wrote apologetically to tell him she had decided it was too silly and trivial and that she would revise it for publication in the autumn* (VI VW Letters, no. 3709, 27? March). *LW, alarmed by her state of mind and health and the ominous signs of breakdown, now persuaded her to see Octavia Wilberforce as a doctor as well as a friend, and took her to Brighton for this purpose on Thursday 27 March. The following morning Virginia drowned herself in the tidal river Ouse; Leonard found her stick on the bank near the swing bridge at Southease; her body was found some three weeks later on the further side of the same stretch of water. It was cremated on 21 April, and Leonard buried her ashes beneath one of the great elms at the edge of the bowling lawn in Monks House garden.*

ABBREVIATIONS EMPLOYED FOR BOOKS, JOURNALS AND COLLECTIONS

Berg
: The Henry W. and Albert A. Berg Collection of English and American Literature in the New York Public Library.

DNB
: The Dictionary of National Biography.

Holleyman
: Holleyman & Treacher Ltd: *Catalogue of Books from the Library of Leonard and Virginia Woolf, taken from Monks House, Rodmell, and 24 Victoria Square, London, and now in the possession of Washington State University.* Privately printed, Brighton, 1975.

HP Checklist
: *A Checklist of The Hogarth Press, 1917-38*, compiled by J. Howard Woolmer. Hogarth Press, London, 1976.

Kp
: B. J. Kirkpatrick: *A Bibliography of Virginia Woolf.* Third edition, Oxford University Press, 1980.

LW
: Leonard Woolf: *Autobiography . . .*, volumes I-V. Hogarth Press, London, 1960-69.

LWP, Sussex
: *Leonard Woolf Papers, c. 1885-1969.* University of Sussex Library Catalogue, 1980.

MHP, Sussex
: *Monks House Papers.* University of Sussex Library Catalogue, 1972.

M&M
: Robin Majumdar and Allen McLaurin, editors: *Virginia Woolf. The Critical Heritage.* Routledge & Kegan Paul, London, 1975.

NS&N
: *The New Statesman and Nation.* (Weekly).

QB
: Quentin Bell: *Virginia Woolf. A Biography*, volume I (1882-1912) and II (1912-1941). Hogarth Press, London, 1972.

TLS
: *The Times Literary Supplement.* (Weekly).

VW
: Virginia Woolf.
  The Letters of Virginia Woolf, volumes I-VI, edited by Nigel Nicolson and Joanne Trautmann. Hogarth Press, London, 1975-80.
  The Diary of Virginia Woolf, volumes I-IV, edited by Anne Olivier Bell. Hogarth Press, London, 1977-82.

NOTE: unless otherwise indicated, the *Uniform Edition* of The Works of Virginia Woolf, published in London by the Hogarth Press and in the United States by Harcourt Brace Jovanovich, is that used for reference.

APPENDIX I

BIOGRAPHICAL OUTLINES

ANREP, Helen, *née* Maitland (1885-1965). Born in California, she studied music in Europe, and associated with Augustus John and his Bohemian circle; in 1917 she married the Russian mosaicist Boris von Anrep (1883-1969) by whom she had had two children, Anastasia ('Baba') and Igor, and whom she finally left in 1926 to live as his wife with Roger Fry in Bloomsbury. After the latter's death in 1934, she moved to Charlotte Street, WC1, where, until the war began, she dispensed generous support and advice to a younger generation of artists. It was Helen Anrep, together with Roger Fry's sister and executor Margery Fry, who had prevailed upon VW to write his life, an undertaking which was one of her major preoccupations between 1935 and its publication in July 1940.

BELL, Clive (Arthur Clive Heward, 1881-1964), art critic. Of a wealthy philistine family, he was a Cambridge contemporary and friend of Lytton Strachey and of Thoby Stephen, whose sister Vanessa he married in 1907, becoming the brother-in-law and a close confidant of VW, particularly before her own marriage in 1912. A great Francophile, sociable, gallant, and hospitable, he had an independent establishment at 50 Gordon Square, but shared Charleston as a country family home with his wife and children and Duncan Grant. His influence and opinions were chiefly disseminated through his numerous contributions to the *NS&N*; the only book he published in the period covered by this volume of VW's Diary was *Enjoying Pictures* (1934).

BELL, Vanessa ('Nessa'), *née* Stephen (1879-1961), painter, VW's beloved sister. She married Clive Bell in 1907, and their sons were Julian Heward (1908-37) and Quentin Claudian Stephen (b. 1910). After a liberating love affair in 1911 with Roger Fry, whose lifelong friendship she retained, she lived and worked from about 1914 with the artist Duncan Grant; their daughter Angelica Vanessa was born on Christmas Day, 1918. Vanessa made Charleston in Sussex a country home for all her family, and since 1928 also had a small cottage near Cassis in Provence; in London she and Duncan Grant occupied adjacent studios at no. 8 Fitzroy Street, WC1. See *Vanessa Bell*, a biography by Frances Spalding, 1983.

ELIOT, Thomas Stearns (1888-1965), American-born poet, critic, and dramatist; educated at Harvard and Oxford Universities, he worked in a London bank until 1925, when he joined the publishers Faber & Faber, from whence he continued to edit *The Criterion*, the literary periodical he founded in 1922. He became a British subject in 1927, and in that year was received into the Anglican Church. His impulsive marriage in 1915 to Vivienne Haigh-Wood (1888-1947) had been unhappy and destructive, and in 1933 he had left her. The Woolfs had known him since 1918, and in spite of great differences of outlook, he remained one of their most cherished and respected friends.

FORSTER, Edward Morgan (1879-1970), novelist, educated at King's College, Cambridge, and, like LW, a member of the Cambridge Conversazione Society (the 'Apostles'). His last novel, *A Passage to India*, was published in 1924, but he continued to write and publish criticism and stories, and was active as a speaker, a broadcaster, and a supporter of civil liberties and liberal causes. He lived partly with his mother at Abinger Hammer, Surrey, and had a *pied-à-terre* in Brunswick Square, Bloomsbury. His dearest friend was a policeman, R. J. Buckingham, whom he met in 1927 and who, with his wife May, became Forster's lifelong support and help.

GARNETT, David ('Bunny', 1892-1981), only child of the publisher's reader Edward Garnett and his wife Constance, translator of the Russian classics. As a pacifist, he worked on the land during the First War, living at Charleston with Duncan Grant and Vanessa Bell and her sons, and was there when their daughter Angelica was born at Christmas 1918. His first novel, *Lady into Fox* (1922), was an unexpected success, and thereafter he lived by his pen; he was a regular contributor to the *NS&N*, of which he was literary editor from 1932-35. His wife, Ray Marshall, whom he married in 1921, died in 1940, and in 1942 he married Angelica with whom, somewhat to the distress of her parents, he had been living for some time.

GRANT, Duncan James Corrowr (1885-1978), artist, only child of Major Bartle Grant of the Indian Army, youngest brother of Lady Strachey, with whose family of ten children Duncan was largely brought up in London. He was one of the inmates of the shared house, 38 Brunswick Square, in which VW and LW lived before their marriage. Gifted, improvident, charming, and attractive to both sexes—though his many affairs were almost invariably with his own—from about 1914 until her death he lived and worked with Vanessa Bell and was the father of her daughter Angelica, b. 1918. His reputation and success reached its peak in the 1930s.

KEYNES, John Maynard (1882-1946), economist, Fellow and Bursar of King's College, Cambridge, and one of the Woolfs' oldest friends. In 1916, while working for the Treasury, he took over the lease of the Bells' house at 46 Gordon Square, which remained his London home, though shortly after his marriage in 1925 to the Russian ballerina Lydia Lopokova (1891-1981), he also took a 99-year lease of Tilton, the neighbouring farm to Charleston, where his assumption of the role of country gentleman caused his irreverent friends to refer to him as The Squire of Tilton. A man of extraordinary intelligence and vitality, his revolutionary economic theories, brilliantly expounded in books, articles, and speech, commanded increasing respect and acceptance, and in 1940 he was asked to rejoin the Treasury; in 1942 he was made a peer. He was a collector of books and paintings, a great supporter of the arts, and founded the Cambridge Arts Theatre in 1936.

LEHMANN, John Frederick (b. 1907), poet, publisher, and editor; educated at Eton and Cambridge, where he became a close friend of Julian Bell. In 1931 he joined the Hogarth Press as trainee manager, but the strain of working under LW and the allurements of freedom and a life in Vienna led to his leaving after eighteen months. In April 1938 he returned as partner, buying VW's half-share in the Hogarth Press, and thenceforward undertook an increasing share in its management in consultation with LW, with VW continuing to read and advise on mss. Lehmann brought with him to the Hogarth Press the hard-cover literary magazine *New Writing* which he founded and had edited since 1936, and a new series was started in the autumn of 1938.

MacCARTHY, Desmond (1877-1952), literary journalist, drama critic, and editor, graduate of Trinity College, Cambridge, and an Apostle; and with his wife Molly (*née* Mary Warre-Cornish, 1882-1953—like VW a niece by marriage of Thackeray's daughter Lady Ritchie), old and dear friends of the Woolfs. Desmond was literary editor of the *New Statesman*, 1920-27, editor of *Life and Letters*, 1928-33, and from 1928 senior literary critic of the *Sunday Times*. His genius for words and ideas, which gave rise among his many friends to the highest expectations of literary greatness, emerged largely in conversation, to their immediate if transient pleasure. Molly, also a writer, was afflicted by deafness. They had three children, Michael (1907-73), a farmer; Rachel (1909-82), who in 1932 married Lord David Cecil; and Dermod (b. 1911), who became a doctor.

MORRELL, Lady Ottoline, *née* Cavendish-Bentinck (1873-1938), half-sister of the 6th Duke of Portland, hostess and patroness of the arts. In 1902 she married Philip Morrell (1870-1943), barrister and Liberal MP, 1906-18. In 1915 the Morrells moved to Garsington Manor, Oxfordshire, which they made a refuge for pacifists and a resort for writers, artists, and intellectuals; VW had often been their guest there. In 1927 they returned to Bloomsbury, to live at 10 Gower Street, where Lady Ottoline resumed her pre-war Thursday evening At Homes. Her later years were marred by painful ill-health. See Appendix II: VW's obituary tribute in *The Times*. The Morrells' only child, their daughter Julian (b. 1908), married and left home in 1928.

MORTIMER, Raymond (1895-1980), critic and man of letters, graduate of Balliol College, Oxford. VW had known him since 1923, when he was serving his literary apprenticeship under Desmond MacCarthy on the *New Statesman*; from 1935-1947, with a short war-time interruption, he was literary editor of the *NS&N*. A passionate and informed Francophile and traveller, he was a particular friend of Clive Bell, of Harold Nicolson, and of Francis Birrell (1889-1935).

RYLANDS, George Humphrey Wolferstan ('Dadie', b. 1902), scholar of Eton and of King's College, Cambridge. In July 1924 he came as apprentice manager to the Hogarth Press in Tavistock Square, hoping to combine this with work on a fellowship dissertation, but by the end of the year he withdrew. He returned to Cambridge in 1927 on his election as Fellow of King's, and there put down his roots, serving the college and the University in several capacities, including that of Lecturer of English Literature; his particular interest was in drama, and he was responsible for many University stage productions. Always one of the attractions of Cambridge for VW, his hospitality bore extravagant fruit in the luncheon party described in *A Room of One's Own*.

SACKVILLE-WEST, Victoria Mary ('Vita', 1892-1962), poet, novelist, and biographer, only child of the 3rd Baron Sackville whose estates and Elizabethan mansion Knole in Kent she was by reason of her sex debarred from inheriting. She was the wife of the one-time career diplomat Harold Nicolson (1886-1968), writer and broadcaster and from 1935-45 National Labour MP for West Leicester. Although both were instinctively and actively homosexual, their marriage was cemented by lasting love and two children, Benedict (1914-78) and Nigel (b. 1917). The love affair between Vita and VW, of which *Orlando* (1928) was the issue, had since been transmuted into an enduring friendship, while Vita found other women lovers. In 1930 she and Harold had bought the derelict Sissinghurst Castle in Kent, and devoted their imagination and resources into breathing new life into its fabric and gardens.

SMYTH, Dame Ethel (1858-1944), composer, author, and feminist. She studied music in Leipzig and, the daughter of an army general, was a vigorous campaigner both for the performance of her own compositions and for the cause of women's rights. Reading *A Room of One's Own* fired her with the desire to meet its author, which she did in 1930 and thereafter, in spite of her age and her deafness, was one of VW's most devoted, demanding, irresistable and intimate friends, engendering a prolific correspondence between them. She lived at Coign, a house she built near Woking, with a dog and a maid, but was a resolute visitor. Ethel Smyth published several volumes of reminiscences, and continually sought VW's help and advice on her writing.

APPENDIX II

LADY OTTOLINE MORRELL

From *The Times* (early editions only) of 28 April 1938.
Virginia Woolf writes:—
The remarkable qualities of Ottoline Morrell—her originality, her courage, the personal ascendancy that created so memorable a society—have already been noted in your columns. Still the desire remains to testify, however imperfectly, to the splendid use she made of those rare gifts of fortune and of character. The great lady who suddenly appeared in the world of artists and writers immediately before the War easily lent herself to caricature. It was impossible not to exclaim in amazement at the strangeness; at the pearls, at the brocades, at the idealisms and exaltations. Again, with what imperious directness, like that of an artist intolerant of the conventional and the humdrum, she singled out the people she admired for qualities that she was often the first to detect and champion, and brought together at Bedford Square and then at Garsington, Prime Ministers and painters, Bishops and freethinkers, the famous and the obscure! Whether she sat at the head of her table against a background of pale yellow and pomegranate, or mused at Garsington with her embroidery on her lap and undergraduates at her feet, or held on her way down the Tottenham Court Road like a Renaissance princess listening to inaudible music while the passers by stared, she created her own world. And it was a world in which conflicts and collisions were inevitable; nor did she escape the ridicule of those whom she befriended.

But beneath this exotic appearance, sometimes so odious to her—"Look at my hands!" she once protested. "How ugly they are!"—there was a complex nature. She boasted, whether fancifully or not, of a French washerwoman among her ancestresses. Certainly there was a raciness in her refinement; a democratic spirit which led her not only to flout the conventions of the world, but to keep her house bravely open during the War to the unpopular and the friendless. It was that inner freedom, that artist's vision, that led her past the decorated drawing-room with all its trappings to the actual workshop where the painter had his canvas, and the writer his manuscript. The "great hostess" was very humble in the presence of those who could create beauty; and very generous; and very sincere. For beneath the glamour which she created as inevitably as the lily pours out scent, there was a diffident and shrinking spirit. As the years passed this became more and more apparent. Deafness had grown upon her and she was often ill. She accepted such trials with aristocratic, or, it may be, with devout composure. She made no more efforts to gather the many coloured reins into her own hands; to drive her team with reckless courage through a world that, she felt, was destroying all she cherished. Rather she was content to sit back in the corner of her sofa working at her embroidery still, but no longer presiding. There in the evening, alone, even lovelier in her black than in her brocade, she would talk of the people she had known; of some new poem she had liked; of some unknown poet she had met; and of London, whose beauty she loved; and of that English country that was so dear to her—the country round Welbeck; and of the eccentricities of her forebears; of the old Duke who dug the tunnels; and how she had run through the great rooms as a child discovering pictures; and of the ardours and failures of her life; and of Shelley and Keats—until at last, at last, it was time to go from the room which she had made so beautiful.

Index to the Diary

operative, 116; his play suppressed?, 179 & n; Eliot disappointed in, 192; goes to America, 307 & n; breaks promise to Hogarth Press, 337 & n; *ref*: 182; *Letters From Iceland*, 107 & n; *On the Frontier*, 179 & n

Auppegard, Normandy home of Ethel Sands and Nan Hudson: 171, 172n

Austen, Cassandra: 277

Austen, Jane: masterly . . . Mistressly, 277; talked of by Desmond, 280; *Emma*, 98; *Sense and Sensibility*, 274, 277

Austria: Hitler invades, 129 & n

Ayshford-Ayre, Mrs: 289, 290n

Bach, J. S.: 7, 238

Bagenal, Barbara, *née* Hiles: loving Tomlin, 48 & n; *ref*: 22n, 67, 116

Bagenal, Judith: 22 & n, 116, 247

Bagenal, Nicholas: 22n, 67, 116

Bagnold, Enid (Lady Roderick Jones): 355 & n, 356, 357

Baker, Mary: 50 & n

Baldwin, Stanley: on the King, 11; on Newnham Fund, 21 & n; awful speech, 35 & n; & abdication crisis, 39, 40, 41; *ref*: 150n

Balestier, Carrie (Mrs Rudyard Kipling): 28

Balzac, Honoré de: VW reading, 77, 80, 291 & n; *La Comédie humaine*, 291n

Baring, Maurice: 92 & n, 210

Barnes, George: 31 & n, 83, 84

Bartholomew, Mrs, of Rodmell: 159

Bartholomew, Percy: to the rescue, 100 & n; & village rumour, 162; gives notice, 230; irritates LW, 250; spraying trees, 271; flirting, 275; sees wounded arriving, 284; & Arras hell, 289; weeding & rumouring, 290; annoys LW, 301; spots planes, 320; war rumours *via*, 321; 'tervisagates', 323; discounted, 327; gives LW flu, 334; *ref*: 73, 90, 262, 285

Bates, Sir Percy: and *Q. Mary* agitation, 14 & n

Beaverbrook, Lord: 345 & n

Bedford, Duchess of ('The Flying Duchess'): 72 & n

Beerbohm, Florence, *née* Kahn: 184

Beerbohm, Max: Duncan Grant meets, 6 & n; VW does not, 13; VW records his dinner-party talk, 183-5

Beethoven: 156

Belgium: the fat on the fire, 245 & n; invasion of, 284 & n; English refugees from, 290

Bell, Angelica: a room of her own, 15 & n; a sensation . . ., 20; a Turgenev heroine, 22; discusses 4/8 time, 25; & roast turkey, 48; her Brighton story, 96; Julian's death, & after, 104, 105; plays bowls, 106; reads aloud, 108; real, 109; on Sissinghurst excursion, 111; silent & decisive, 117; to Cassis, 121, 125, back from, 126; met at Chekhov play, 128; her stage triumph, 139 & n; finished at Islington, 146; in *Lysistrata*, 156, 157n; talked about Julian—her sobriety & depth, 158; in *Gammer Gurton . . .*, 162 & n; giving up stage, 164; to tea, 170; Cassis-bound, 171; is 'perfect' writes Duncan, 186; silent & reserved, 190; VW's £100 to, 192; sang a song, 199; on Richard Llewelyn Davies, 203; in nursing home, 220; better, 221; in bed, 225; moody, 228; & allowance, 237; hides . . . a butterfly, 242; doesn't count, 246; her 21st birthday, 257; silent, not disapproving, 269; puts VW to bed, 271; her 'affair' with Bunny, 282 & n; no more gossiping, 283; Bunny lurches in with, 299; strain diagnosed, 307; 'her side' seen, 310-11; & strain, 314; goes to Hilton, 322 & n; letter from, 329; farmhouse for?, 332, 341 & n; & 'Bottom' the mentor, 341; her lecture, 354 & n; *ref*: 21, 110, 134, 150, 173, 191, 233, 234, 243, 315, 343, 358

Bell, Clive: for Biographical Note *see* Appendix I; in Paris, 14; on *Queen Mary* decorations, 22 & n; VW lunches with, 35 & n, 36, 37; democratic about Mrs Simpson, 39 & n; remarks dearth of deaths, 47; lunch with, 50 & n; in France with Janice, 106; Julian something like, 110; deflated, 117; Bobo flinches from, 129 & n; influenza attacks, 132; at Charleston, 134, 139; balderdash . . . rampant, 140; ignored Bussy, 158; writing on war, 159 & n; some sensibility still, 163; at historic

Memoir Club meeting, 169; prefers the country, 171; at Charleston, 174; Woolfs to dine with, 186; dinner with, 190; quarrelsome & peevish, 191; painting & music discussed, 199; ebullient, dancing with Bobo, 203; reads memoir, truculent about Roger, 212-13 & n; suppressed by Nessa?, 213; talk of Gertler, 221; & doctors, 223; testy at Charleston, 230 & n; the best over, 231; grumbling, 236; says everyone wants peace, 242; abrupt & truculent, 244; away, 247; after-dinner guest, 268; in political argument, 269; unease at ill-adjusted dress, 280; his night, 282; sullen, 299; truculent about Auden & Isherwood, 307; approves *Roger Fry*, 310 & n; on Firle Tower, 315; stockish, Bell-like, 355; *ref*: 4, 7, 21, 66 & n, 93, 150, 180, 225, 354; 'Inside the Queen Mary: A Business Man's Dream', 22 & n; 'Dr Freud on Art', 213n; *Warmongers*, 159n

Bell, Sir Hugh: 278 & n

Bell, Julian: sends Vanessa Chinese silk, 15 & n, Vanessa's defensiveness over his essay on Roger, 51 & n; to enlist for Spain, 54 & n; home from China, 67; grown a man, 68; his problem, 69; depressed, 73, 77; peppery & pithy, obstinately set on Spain, 79-80; his Chinese spoils, 81 & n; qualifies contentment, 83; bitter against Bloomsbury, 86; gone to Spain, 93 & n; no news of, 94; near Madrid, 101; gingerly remarks about . . ., 102; his death, & after, 104-5 & n; Eliot & his essays, 105 & n, 108 & n; 'stalks beside me', 107; his queer power over Nessa, 108; Hart & Cochrane on his death, 109 & n, 113-14; on War, 110 & n; but for his death . . ., 111; what he would say now, 115; not thought of as dead, 121-2; & anxiety, 125; his 30th birthday, 126; Mauron on, 126-7 & n; why is he not here?, 131; 'not there', 139, 146; effect on Vanessa, 148; Maynard on, 154 & n; anniversary of his death, 156; his ghost, 164; dreamt of, 172; dreamt of, sniping article on, 199 & n; killed for 'this', 206; in background?, 226; reading, 260; since his death . . ., 272;

ref: 84, 108n, 114n, 159, 361; *Julian Bell: Essays, Poems and Letters, 1938*, 51n, 105n, 154n, 199n

Bell, Oliver: 211 & n

Bell, Quentin: & roast turkey, 48; to dinner, 54, in gum boots, 55; to dine, 74; praises *Years*, 75; dumbfounded by the major, 104; & Julian's death, 104, 105; plays bowls, 106; helps Vanessa, 108; on Sissinghurst excursion, 111; dry & merry, 116; to dine, 128; 'They' will take him, 131; imparts news of Ott's death, 135; at Charleston, 146; conscript?, & birthday, 162; to paint table, 164, 166; & all the horror, 166, 170; at historic Memoir Club meeting, 168-9; Cassisbound, 171; price of table, 192; for weekend, 225; & potting shed, 228; Maynard's tractor driver, 233 & n; to eat grouse, 234; plaster of Paris for, 238; & Bradfield, 239 & n; hides from Gages, 242; in spite of, 243; doesn't count, 246; a rosy sun, 261; in political argument, 269; *remembering Moore*, 286; over, 291; heavy, mature, depressed, 307; calls Derain a prostitute, 315; very burly & male, 324; & flood lunch, 341; urbane & happy, 342; offered draughtsman job, 354; *ref*: 11, 21, 63, 99n, 110, 139, 173, 189, 230, 276, 284, 361

Bell, Vanessa: for Biographical Note *see* Appendix I; tea with, 6; & London Group crisis, 9 & n; holds back democracy, 12; to *Hedda Gabler*, receives silk, 15 & n; her potters' party, 20; discusses 4/8 time, 25; a spell of writing with required, 36; & Tonks, 47n; & Tomlin's death, 48; turns to steel at talk of Julian, 51 & n, in submerged mood, 54 & n; artistic collaborator, 57 & n, illustrated incidents, 58; doesn't want VW, 63; LW critical of, 68; to tea, 71; for *Years*, 80; Julian's shadow over, 80; visit to, 81; '32 Recent Paintings by . . .', 85 & n; long natural gossip with, 91; at Charleston . . ., 94; at Albert Hall meeting, 98, 99n; & Julian, & politics, 102; Julian's death, & after, 104, 105n; 'shall never be happy again', 106; cannot write about, 107; reminiscent of father, & Julian's power, 108;

Emery, Kathleen, of Rodmell: 164 & n, 285, 288
Empire Review: 75
Enfield, Dorothy, *née* Hussey: 203 & n
Erasmus: 240
Étoile, restaurant: 82 & n
Evans, Ifor: *A Short History of English Literature*, 320 & n
Evening Standard: Arnold Bennett in, 16 & n, 256 & n; *Years* reviewed in, 70 & n; & *3 Gns* snarled at, 149 & n; its Peace placard, 170; & Third Class conversation, 241
Everest, Louie, *née* West: enchanted, 75 & n; butting ram, 100; gruesome tales, 161, 162n; her verdict on war, 168; & the carpenter, 170; missed PM, 175; and price of clothes, 231; gives LW cold, 245; happy obscurity with, 246; to dentist, 250, 251-2; usual strain with Mabel, 272; attends church, 274; no news of brother, 289; anxiety over father, 290; & Duke's death, 291; agog about Harry, 297; picking fruit, 299; toothless, agog, 299; & skinflint suspicions, 305; her father's death, 310; wage rise for, 329; takes on house, 338; & potato box, butters Woolfs parsnips, 339; & triumphant pat, 340; on country ways, 341; buries aunt, 352; *ref*: 250, 257, 300, 335
Everest, Mrs: 297

Fabian Society: 265 & n
Farrell, Sophia: 22 & n, 192, 198
Faulkner, William: praises *Years*, 91
Fears, Mr, Rodmell postman: 324, 342
Fielding, maid to Lady Colefax: 26, 27, 28
Finland: attacked by Russia, 248 & n; Red rout in, 264; unidentified correspondent, 269; & peace, 272 & n
Firle Place, Sussex: Monks House preferred to, 197 & n
Fisher, Emmeline: 281 & n
Fisher, Herbert: 281 & n
Fisher, H. A. L.: wants to see VW, 171 & n; knocked senseless, 279 & n; dies, 280; remembered, 281 & n, 282; 'insider', 333; University product, 336; in death toll, 338; & rather rocky book, 355; *ref*: 283
Fisher, Mary: 100 & n, 283

Fisher, Admiral Sir William, of Dreadnought fame: 100 & n
Fitzgerald, Edward: *Dictionary of Madame de Sevigné*, 133 & n
Flaubert, Gustave: 25, 240 & n, 340
Flavinda (fict): 228 & n
Fleming, Peter: 282
Flint, Lewes grocer: 233, 305
Flossie *see* Riley, Flossie
Forster, E. M.: for Biographical Note *see* Appendix I; no post-op news of, 4 & n, 5 & n; & Bugger crew, 6; going on well, 15; Woolfs drive him home, 23 & n; VW might appeal to, 30; can always ask, 31; Isherwood admires, 59; at Memoir meeting—and T. E. Lawrence, 82; almost weeps, 83; & Spanish Relief, 98, indifferent, 99; grown a fat man?, 101; Day Lewis prefers, 117; Pelicans & Buggers, 120; & letters, 129; Rose Macaulay on, 130 & n; & pageant, 139, 156 & n; on Hitler, & anti-Fascism, 142 & n; on Goldie, 162 & n; at historic Memoir Club meeting, 167-8; his 'Credo' praised, 169 & n; not a patch on, 188; his reputation higher, & communist group, 189; on communism, & libel, 205 & n; keeps diary?, 244; has tea brought up, 280; & *Roger Fry*—dislike anticipated, 303, *if* he approves, 305, no Morgan, if Morgan, 306, no Morgan, 308, only Morgan, 309, slightly dampening, 310 & n; on biographies, 314; & Hugh Walpole, 315; & London Library committee—VW's 'nice little finish', 337 & n, 338; *ref*: 257, 292; 'England's Pleasant Land', 156n; 'Two Cheers for Democracy', 169n
Forster, Alice Clara ('Lily', EMF's mother): 23 & n
Forum, The, N.Y. periodical: 175 & n, 249 & n, 250, 251, 263
France: in alliance?, 33; to visit in May, 79; if France fights . . ., 168; a few days in?, 215; Brittany & Normandy, 219; fighting continues in, 298; *ref*: 53, 87, 91, 106, 131, 171, 267
Franchetti *see* Hamilton Mrs
Franco: & Churchill, 35; winning, 199; at Barcelona, 201; recognised, 206 & n. *See also under* Spain
Frankau, Gilbert: 258 & n

376

Freeth, Mr, of Rodmell: 315, 336
Freud, Anna: 202 & n, 205
Freud, Martin: 155 & n, 191, 202, 264
Freud, Sigmund: at Hampstead, 202 & n;
dies, 238 & n; his papers, his publishers, 243 & n; VW reading, 248;
gulping up, 249; finds upsetting, 250;
on Groups, 252 & n; VW going to
read, 266; reading, 299; *Civilisation
and its Discontents*, 250n; *The Future
of an Illusion*, 250n; *Group Psychology*,
252n
Freund, Gisèle, photographer: 220 & n
Fry, Sir Edward: 215
Fry, Helen, née Combe: 172, 269, 270n
Fry, Isabel: 334
Fry, Joan Mary: 60 & n, 276
Fry, Julian: 58 & n, 59, 60 & n-61
Fry, Margery ('Ha'): phones with request, 58 & n; favours *Years*, 71;
snubs over sales, 83; dines tomorrow,
134 & n; VW writing to please, 186;
& Fry biography, 266, 270, 271; 2 or
3 hours with, 267; 'unbounded admiration', 272 & n, 308; entering her
corrections, 274, 277; to meet Helen?,
275; brain creased after, 276; says
knitting's useless, 277; *ref*: 227, 307
Fry, Roger: memorial fund for, 16 & n;
Mauron on, 35 & n; Julian Bell on,
51 & n; & Julian Fry, 60 & n, 61;
when he died . . ., 104, 106; trusted
life, 110; his birthplace visited, 115,
116; family & past, 131; Cambridge
letters, 139, 141; difficult to recover,
144; Gumbo on his biography, 155;
& Rothenstein compared, 156 & n;
ignored Bussy—Bussy on, 158; his 2
lives . . ., & Trevelyan, 159 & n; &
Metropolitan Museum, 166; 'how I
bless Roger,' 167; & eternal moment,
168; in VW's dream, 172; & Helen, &
Nessa, 172, 173; & Oxford Slade
Professorship, 173 & n; trying to see
like, 174-5; & PIP, 176; how to show
one cared, 181; Max on, 183; paying
debt to, 186; his letters to his father,
189; how we used to talk, 191; debt
to, 200; Nessa's Berlin letters to, 204;
Cambridge letters, 212; Clive on, 213
& n; MacColl on, 226 & n; his love
affairs, 230; lectures published at last,
240 & n; *Transformations*, & Hannay,
260, 261; that iridescent man, 266;

loves & character, 267; some extravagance about, 269; reactions to
biography, 271-2 & n; LW's dissympathy with?, 271; restored to
Nessa, 272; his pictures, 279; Desmond remembers, 280; was he like
that?, 305; Read spiteful about, 309 &
n; Ben Nicolson's charge, 316 & n;
ref: 256, 309, 353; *The Artist and
Psycho-Analysis*, 213n; *Last Lectures*,
240n; *Transformations*, 260, 262. *See
also under* Woolf, Virginia: (7) Her
own published books: *Roger Fry: A
Biography*
Furse, Katherine, née Symonds: 229 & n

Gage, 6th Viscount: 197n, 242
Garbo, Greta: 27
Gardner, Diana, of Rodmell: 104, 182,
261, 301, 303, 324, 344, 352
Gardner, Major, of Rodmell: 104 & n,
264, 320, 321
Garnett, David ('Bunny'): for Biographical Note *see* Appendix I; & shock of
regret, 68, 69n; reviews *Years*, 70 &
n; at Memoir Club meeting—to do
T. E. Lawrence, 82 & n; & Spanish
Relief, 99; to tea, 149; reads Memoir,
155, 156n; hears memoir, 169; at
Charleston, 228; VW offered his
NS&N page, 240 & n; his 'affair' with
Angelica, 282 & n; lurches in, 299;
produces strain, 314; letter from, 329;
farmhouse for?, 332; dislikes house,
suspects family, 341 & n; 'Bottom'
the mentor, 341; tomorrow, 342; *ref*:
315, 358
Garnett, Edward: 15 & n
Garvin, J. L.: 355 & n
Garvin, Viola: 256 & n
Gathorne-Hardy, Robert: 140 & n
George V: probably dying, 8 & n, 9;
dead, 10; America mourns, Japan
weeps, 11; democracy swarms, 12
George VI: 42n, 84
Germany: elbowed by Simpson, 39;
attacked by Budberg, 53; divides
Poland, 239 & n; Desmond's plan for,
279; how to beat, 343
Gertler, Mark: at Ott's memorial service,
136 & n; to dine, 219 & n; upon his
suicide, 221 & n; Kot on, 287
Gibbon, Edward: bicentenary article on,
39 & n, 44, wants polishing, 48;

polishing, 51; brooding over, 69; needs too much screw, 72; *must* send today, 79; article on his aunts, 80 & n, 84, 86; & Keynes, 82; & Ott, 98; & death, 161; *ref*: 56, 59, 80, 91

Gide, André: his journal read, 227 & n; & fashionable dodge, 229; lucidity & logic of, 244; conglobulates, 263; tired of, 304; reading, 354; *La Porte étroite*, 354

Giffard, H. S., 1st Earl of Halsbury: *The Laws of England*, 301 & n

Gillies, William: 249 & n

Girton College, Cambridge: 92 & n

Gluck: 238

Glyndebourne: 148, 149, 337

Goering: 168

Gogol, Nikolai: article on?, 273

Goldenveizer, A. B.: *Talks With Tolstoi*, 273 & n

Goldsmith, Oliver: 62

Gollancz, Victor: on LW's *Barbarians*, evasive & dishonest, 220 & n; prevaricating, 221; letter-war with, 223

Gordon Square: Basque refugees in, 97; sitting in, 157; bomb in, 323

Gordon Square, No. 37: 48

Gordon Square, No. 46: Roger at, in 1910, 167; all windows broken at, 323

Gordon Square, No. 50: Clive's notice to, 171; to leave, 188; leaving, 193

Gosse, Edmund: *Father and Son*, 332

Graf Spee, pocket battleship: into the jaws of death at Montevideo, 251 & n

Graham, Dr George, of Harley Street: 55 & n

Graham, John L.: *The Good Merchant*, 106 & n

Graham-Harrison, Francis: 206 & n

Graham-Harrison, Sir William, former Treasury counsel: & Saxon's dinner, 101 & n

Grant, Duncan: for Biographical Note *see* Appendix I; on Bugger crew—che*z* Colefax, 6 & n; London Group crisis, 9 & n; in death trudge, 11; and *Queen Mary* agitation, 14 & n; to *Hedda Gabler*, 15; going to Spain, 20; & Tomlin's death, 47, 48 & n; his *I Tatti* memoir, 82 & n; in France, 91; & Spanish Relief, 98; Julian's death & after, 104; gives VW brooch, 116; 'Recent Works by . . .',

120 & n; picture purchased, 121 & n; at Cassis, 125; dining, 128; at Ott's memorial service, 136; on W. Rothenstein, 156; unreasonable about him, 157 & n; Cassis-bound, 171; & *Roger Fry*, 173; in complete bliss, 186 & n; argumentative, amusing, 190; his £40 carpet, 190 & n; his £30 picture, 192; as blond prince, 203; at Analysts' dinner, 208; allegiance to, 214; upon Gertler's suicide, 221; & skin diseases, 223; bubbling, & Ottoline portrait, 225, 226n; pobbling, 226; & 480 canvases, 228; his aunt Violet, 231; and suicide, 239; sells to Queen, 247 & n; his table's effect, 265; wants cigarettes, 269; buoyed up by, 274; sees air battle, 284; over, 291; angry at Bunny over Angelica, 292; like an onion, 299; his glasses packed, 331; coming, 354; *ref*: 7, 106, 117, 158

Grant, Ethel (Mrs Bartle Grant, Duncan's mother): at *Hedda Gabler*, 15 & n

Grant family: 236 & n

Grant Duff, Shiela: 133 & n

Graves, Robert: & Laura Riding, 269 & n

Graves, Sally *see* Chilver, Elizabeth

Gray, Thomas: churchyard elegy quoted, 326 & n; *The Progress of Poetry*, quoted, 76-7 & n

Greece: 153, 338

Greenwood, Arthur: & England's duty, 233 & n

Grey, Earl: monument to, 65 & n

Griffiths, Miss, of Hogarth Press: 288, 291

Grigson, Geoffrey: 16 & n

Grosvenor, The Hon. Mrs Norman: 18 & n

Group Theatre: LW's *Hotel* for?, 180; *ref*: 131n

Guedalla, Philip: 147

Gwynne, Neville, of Piddinghoe: 92 & n, 257 & n

Hackett, Francis: 140 & n

Haig, Field-Marshall Earl: 152 & n

Halifax, Lord: 34 & n, 231 & n

Hallowes, Miss, Joseph Conrad's secretary-nurse: 258 & n

Hambourg, Mark, pianist, and wife: 205 & n

Hambro, Winifred: swallowed by Loch Ness, 154 & n

Hamilton, Gerald: 264 & n

Huxley, Maria: 336 & n
Hyde Park: 69, 102, 118, 219
Hyde Park Gate, No. 22: 85, 103
Hyndman, Tony: & Spender & Spain, 56 & n

Ibsen, Henrik: *The Doll's House*, 14, 15n; *Hedda Gabler*, 15 & n; *The Master Builder*, 15n, 20 & n, 21 & n
Ilbert, Sir Courteney: 281 & n
International Brigade: 54n, 56n. *See also under* Spain
Isherwood, Christopher: rather a find, & Auden, 59 & n; visits, 78; asks favour, bound for Madrid?, 100 & n; & Hogarth cooperative, 116, 121; begins to boom, 118; begs story . . ., 118 & n; highest place for, 130 & n; talking at Press, 156; play suppressed?, 179 & n; can't promise to Sibyl, 182; & Max, 183; Eliot disappointed in, 192; to America, 307 & n; *Lions and Shadows*, 130n; *On the Frontier*, 179 & n; *Sally Bowles*, 118 & n
Italy: set on war, 6 & n; King of, stiffens Mussolini?, 177; nips off Albania, 213 & n; to enter war?, 292; declares war, 294 & n; if we beat . . ., 343 & n; being crushed, 344; recumbent, 345 & n; Churchill broadcasts to, 346 & n

Jaloux, Edmond: 61 & n
James, Henry: & Colefax, 28; Ott reads, 98; & Dickens, 215; & 'Leaning Tower', 267; 'observe perpetually', 357 & n; *ref*: 340
Jameson, (Margaret) Storm: 126 & n, 147, 305 & n
Janson, Guy, of Rodmell: 162, 163n, 176, 315
Japan: 110 & n, 264
Jeans, James: *The Mysterious Universe*, 107 & n
John, Augustus: 48 & n, 144
John, K.: on *3 Gns*, 149 & n
Johnson, Dr: 62, 146 & n
Jones, Alice: 132n, 164
Jones, Dr and Mrs Ernest: 86 & n
Jongh, Ada de: 106 & n
Joubert de la Ferté, Air Marshal Sir Philip: 306 & n
Jowett, Benjamin: 136
Joyce, James: upon his death, 352-3 & n; *Ulysses*, 353 & n

Joyce, William (Lord Haw-Haw): 283 & n, 295

Kapp, Edmond X.: 99 & n
Kapp, Yvonne: dry & merry, 116
Kent, Duke of: 81
Kernahan, Coulson: Max on, 184 & n; *God and the Ant*, 184 & n
Keynes, Geoffrey: 219 & n
Keynes, John Maynard: for Biographical Note *see* Appendix I; enthusiastic about *Years*, 76, VW's 'best book'— his heart condition, 77; for *Years*, 80, 82; at Memoir Club meeting, praises VW's Gibbon, 82; bad news, no news, 90 & n; ill—but better, 91; recumbent, on Bentham's evil, 129 & n; may jibe at *3 Gns* . . ., 147, very critical?, 163; rather grim, 164; his Early Beliefs, 168, 169 & n; to tea, 178; Munich—a put-up job, 179 & n; approves LW's *Hotel*, 180; & Christmas reunion, 193; his father 'dying', 198 & n; Plesch's cure for, & failing optimism, 213 & n; employs Quentin, 233 & n; Shaw produces heart attack, 240 & n; recorded for posterity, 255 & n, 256; reads Walpole, 258; what of his optimism now?, 283; truculent, on biography, 314; & Lydia's opinion, 315; war rumours *via*, 321; 'insider' (perhaps), 333; disapproving puritan, kissed, 346; *ref*: 44, 47, 122, 252; 'Mr Chamberlain's Foreign Policy', 179n; *Two Memoirs*, 169n
Keynes, John Neville: 198 & n, 255
Keynes, Margaret, *née* Darwin: 95 & n, 219 & n
Kilvert, Rev. Francis: his *Diary*, 228 & n
Kipling, Rudyard: his death, 8 & n; quoted, 62 & n
Klein, Melanie: 208 & n, 209
Knight, Dame Laura: 193 & n
Koteliansky, S. S.: same as ever . . ., 18 & n; solitude mania, 71 & n; for *Years*, 80; & Sarton, 96 & n; & uncompromising severity, 221; VW's cotranslator, 273 & n; 'the mad', 287; *Talks With Tolstoi*, 273n

Labour Party: LW attends special meeting of, 17; meetings at Rodmell, 20, 54, 74, 104 & n, 116, 213, 248, 324 & n; its young men, 35; gossips about

King, 40; Ann Stephen on, 97; diddled over Spain, 114 & n; hemming & hawing, 131; Rodmell cabal against, 162; & Czechoslovakia, 173; LW liaises for, 174; meeting tonight, 207; & landowner's attitude, 257; VW's 10-minute talk for, 323

Lamb, Charles: & Max, 184 & n; LW's resemblance to, 273 & n

Lane, Allen: VW snubs, 120 & n

Lang, Cosmo Gordon, Archbishop of Canterbury: Wells on, 53 & n

Lange, Miss, Hogarth Press manager: 52 & n, 54, 82, 121, 127

Laval, Pierre: 344 & n

Lawrence, Susan: 134 & n

Lawrence, T. E.: his letters, 82 & n; Duncan against, 190; *The Letters of T. E. Lawrence*, 190n

Leaf, Charlotte M. ('Lotta'): 83 & n

League of Nations: Hitler's re-entry proposal, 16 & n; LW urges support for, 17 & n; Lord Cecil on, 33 & n

Lean, Tangye: 207 & n

Leavis, Q. D. ('Queenie'): On *3 Gns*, 165 & n; cancelled, 166

Left Review, The: 80 & n

Lehmann, Beatrix: 110 & n, 254n, 269 & n

Lehmann, John: for Biographical Note *see* Appendix I; & Hogarth cooperative, 116; & *New Writing*, 118 & n; eager to buy Press, 121; 'our Partner', 127 & n, 128; & Vienna, 133; saddened & hammered, 134; much impressed, 137; first breach with?, 138; angry letter to . . ., 155 & n; talking at Press, 156; to combat, 157; to tea, 158; to see tomorrow, 169; suppose him called up . . ., 170; to transport Press?, 175 & n; making scenes, 190; reports on OM stakes, 193; 'temperamental', 193; questions regarding, 199; depressed, 200; cocktail at, 208; talk about future, 218; to lunch, 222; baffled, 230; at Wimbledon, 233; and grouse, 234; sandwiches with, 236; a bit coarse, & his poems, 239; pans out well, 247; Spender at war with, 251; eager & boyish, 264; . . . how unlike, 269; to bring friend, 275, 276 & n; lunch with, & rations dodge, 278; wishes to come, 285; offered India Office job, 295; lunches, 297; & *Roger Fry*,

silence anticipated, 303; soliciting 'Leaning Tower', 306, —damn John, 310; wants Press moved at once, 317, 318, 319 & n; agitated, irritates LW, 322; up to see, 323; Press moved, 324; sends crybaby letter about Auden, 337 & n; no word from, 341; wants limelight, 342; 'The Prince Consort', 343; and *Between the Acts*, 358, 359; *ref*: 8, 219, 237, 239, 242, 283, 292, 331

Lehmann, Mrs: 162, 282, 303

Lehmann, Rosamond (Mrs Wogan Phillips): 36 & n, 37, 47, 142 & n, 208, 247 & n

Leopold, King of the Belgians: 288 & n

Letchworth: Hogarth and the Garden City Press: 319 & n, 324, 356

Lewes: clever people from, 20; Bells met in, 22; fireworks at, 31 & n, 33; in hot weather, 99; opera-goers in, 149; & pump threat, 162; its tradespeople indifferent, 232; flurry of shoppers in, 233; VW cycles to, 243; very empty, 262; Desmond speculates regarding, 280; listening in, 300; provisioning in, 321; pictures in, 322; 'eleven' bombs on?, 327; & house-buying plans, 331, 332; VW rides to, 335; civilisation of, 341; Girls' school at, 354 & n; *ref*: 23, 73, 107, 172, 250, 273, 299, 313, 328, 333, 337, 344, 346

Lewis, E. D.: 257 & n, 262

Lewis, Katherine ('Katie'): 119 & n, 120, 121, 205 & n

Lewis, Percy Wyndham: hot mean reading, 117 & n; exacerbation from, 119; Eliot portrait row, 139 & n; decapitated by, 188; poisoned dart from?, 309; *Blasting and Bombardiering*, 117n

Lewis, John, & Co Ltd: 9, 10n, 11

Liberal Party: 174

Life and Letters, periodical: 75 & n, 201 & n

Listener, The, periodical: doesn't review *Years*, 71, snubs it, 75 & n; will pass, 77; talk for, 81; LW writes to, 119 & n; Joe slave to, 120; on *3 Gns*, 148 & n; review for, 260 & n; suggests review, 325; *ref*: 22n, 31, 263

Liverpool University: offers VW honorary doctorate, 206

Llewelyn-Davies: *see* Davies, Llewelyn

Lloyd, Mr, dog breeder: 81 & n

Lockhart, J. G.: 152 & n

Loeb, Janice: at Clive's, 66 & n; lashing out, 187, 188; giving tongue, 199; in a great nose, 203; her petrol coupons, 244 & n, & car, 255, 259; ref: 74, 106, 117, 171

London: whole connoisseurship of, 14; unenthusiastic audience?, 15; gay & garrulous, 39; how quiet, 50; too tight, too hot, 90; strenuous days in, 93; hectic, 94; Basque refugees in, 97 & n; odious, 106; back in, 112; reciting Stevenson in, 113 & n; ecstasy near Blackfriars, 141; visits to, 164; tomorrow, 169; single-room future in, 171; crowded, 174; sanity after, 175; respite for, 176; evacuation arrangements, 177; & menagerie vision, 178; longed for, 179; tired after, 180; straight back to, 182; its politics, 200; German planes over?, 211; macaroni from, 215; bitter cold in, 217; & cost of living, 218; back to uproar, 219; intrudes fairly vigorously, 220; not a nice season in, 226; & pressure, 228; tomorrow, 229; 'seemed cheery', 231; frightening?, 234; balloons over, brigandage in, 236; Mabel on, restless for, 238; all agog, 240; safe week in, 241; & first day of war, 242; recedes, 244; a day in, 245; & back, 246; 'London technique', 257; reaction after?, 260; unable to go to, 262; can't even imagine, 263; silent, couchant, 267; adventures in, 267-70; too feverish in, 270; on Monday, 275, 276; whom meeting?, 277; on Tuesday, & muddy streets, 279; a room for Desmond in?, 280; & crowded diary, 282; company in, 283; going to, to be bombed, 285; exodus to, 286; 3 days in, 287; raid on conceived, 288; and clean air, 290; wiped out . . ., 292; skeletal diary of, 297; back from, 299; safe & solid, 300; extreme jadedness of, 302; shall see no one in, 307; uproar, 308; bombers bound for, 312, & raids, 313; great raid on, 314; raided every night, Square hit, 316, other bomb damage, 317, raided again, & new barrage, 318 & n, seen from Rodmell?, 321; & LW's 'bravado', about to start for, 322; a very bad raid, 323; attitude composed in, 324; & Rodmell comparison, 325, 329; planes going to, 326; & Mabel's subterranean life, 328; tortured, after all those years—& shelter queue, 330; cheered by, quit of, 331; hounds on road to, 339; last of residence in, 342; marooned from, 344; burning, churches destroyed, 351; ravished & demolished, 353; very empty, theft in, 355; ref: 17, 24, 25, 49, 67, 73, 74, 78, 80, 87, 104, 108, 148, 166, 199, 226, 230, 232, 250, 252, 264, 266, 337, 356

London Group: crisis meeting, Vanessa & Duncan beaten, 9 & n

London Library: & gas mask trials, 174; Jack Hills remembered at, 198; looking up quotes at, 278; during air raid, 313; its atmosphere effused, 321; Morgan & committee offer, 337 & n; & Mr Cox, 353 & n; & VW's complex, 358; ref: 199, 338

London School of Economics: 22

Lopokova, Lydia (Mrs Maynard Keynes): a great success, 14, 15n; anxious about Maynard, 77; like a peasant, deplores the age, 129; reports Maynard's attitude to 3 Gns, 163; 'we all put up with you', 163; 'now boys & girls', 169; to tea, 178; very congenial, 179; approves LW's Hotel, 180; & Christmas reunion, 193; & Maynard's treatment, 213; hostile to wives, 215; provokes laughter, 251; elf-like, & posterity, 255-6; not time for brains, 315; Maynard talked of, 346; ref: 21n, 44, 47, 64n, 122, 252

Loti, Pierre: 88

Lowell, James Russell: 113 & n; 'The Biglow Papers', quoted, 115 & n

Lucas, F. L. ('Peter'): left out, 119 & n; gossip about, 205; his Journal—no excuse, 227 & n, & fashionable dodge, 229; inspires aversion to criticism, 321; don trying to be creative, 322 & n

Lucas, Prudence, née Wilkinson: 119 & n, 205, 227 & n

Lugton, Nurse: her words, 246 & n

Lyall, Sir Alfred: Trevelyan's choice, 82 & n

Lynd, Robert (Y.Y.): 148 & n, 221, 245 & n, 305 & n

Lynd, Sylvia: on 3 Gns, 145 & n; ref: 147

Lyon, A. Neil: 55 & n, 116

serious illness—a rash, 191; prefers Monks House, 197; buries Mitz, 198; talked, 199; questioned, exacerbated, to cocktail, 201; with Freud, 202; & brother Harold, 205; in from Cranium, 207 & n; & German visitor, 208 & n; back improving, all rash, 210; abnormal, normal, 212; sees Miss Robins, 214; rash improving, 215; dismal Mrs W. tea, 216; bargains for Mecklenberg, 219; drawn in, 220; his mother's death, 223; & Ottoline epitaph, 225, 226n; gloomy, 226; his hobby, 227; his Kingsley anecdotes, 228; bags fruit trees, 233; reports on Newhaven, 238; painted by Vanessa, 240, 243; & dog's rib, 243; catches cold, 245; on detachment, 248; irritated by Percy, 250; buys mackintosh, 251; skates, 252, 259; on his mother, 255; glooming, 256; with Sally, 263; bachelor buffy friend dies, 266; sees heraldic bird, 267; has barometer, lends pound, 270; makes rock garden—most rational & revealing about *Roger Fry*, 271; like Lamb, & smouldering, 273 & n; works all afternoon, 274; needled by Miss Robins, 278; fish for, 279; & whore, 283; petrol for suicide, & Fire Watching, 284; discusses fruit, 285; on the English genius, 288; & lower orders, 291; his coolness, 293; as he would say, 295; & air raid practice, 297; annoyed with Percy, reads Giffard, 301; gives away saucepans, 302; & drowned hedgehog, 306; & Battle of Britain, 311; & moral duty to the young, 312; identifies aircraft, 313; sleeps sound, 314; makes use of tree, 318; spots planes, 320; 'bravado' irritation, & chess partner, 322; writes for remittance, 323; gathers apples, 326, 329; saws wood, 330; assesses damage, 331; cleans beds, sees in the mass, sneezes in WC, 332; comes with logs, 333; holds agricultural meeting, 333; irritated, 334; recovers, 335; hanging blackout curtains, 336; & ARP armlet, 337; & Victory digging, 338; cuts down trees, 339; wrongly directed, didn't see, 341; getting logs, 342; tidying, breakfasting, 344; cutting logs, 346;

looking at comets, 351; doing rhododendrons, 359

(2) *The Hogarth Press and literary work*: interviews Miss Hepworth, 51; wants *3 Gns* by autumn, 59; orders more *Years*, 69; & BBC series, 81; & Hogarth stock, 81-2; & novel for Press, 107; Press to die off, 113; & the Young Brainies, 116; 'Does Education Neutralise Thought?', & *Listener* letter, 119 & n; dropped by Lane, 120 & n; writing his play, 133 & n, 159; *3 Gns* publicity quotes, 154 & n; talking with Lehmann etc, 156; no hurry for Fry, 161; in event of war, 175; his play read to Keyneses, 180; Gollancz commissions book, 183 & n; his play for Group?, 183 & n; second *Deluge* volume, 197, 198n; published 239; abuse & Lehmann, 200; & book-production students, 206; galloping through *Barbarians*, 215, and Gollancz's misgivings, & his dishonesty, 220 & n, letter war, 223; & *NS&N*, 240; *Deluge* reviewed, 242, Desmond praises, 246 & n, sells slowly, 247; reactions to *Barbarians*, 247, 248; down from his book, 255; printing, 261; reading proofs, 271; Robins Ms for, 278 & n; finishes book, 285; & Austen Chamberlain's life, 295 & n; & Press move, 317

(3) *Political activities and opinions*: besieged about Europe, 16; supports League, 17 & n; on isolationism, 33; & abdication crisis, 38; fighting 'no good', 57; talks about India, 58; & Spanish Relief, 98n; enraged with Labour, 114 & n; to write politics?, 115; usual hectic negotiations, 131; consulted by Kingsley, 132; what Kingsley says, 142, 165, 211; & village cabal, 162; & Hitler—very black, 164; discussions with H. Nicolson, 173 & n, 176; Kingsley begs, Labour-Liberal liaison, 174; the next screw, 201; out at Fabians, 204; & Sir John Maynard's memo, 217 & n; pessimistic about Hitler, 232; better to win, 233; & WEA lectures, 244 & n, 263, 338, 352, 357; discusses Fabian treatise, 265; attends meetings, 325; goes to Fabians, 334; Leslie picks his brain, 351

approves, 127, not so much, 133, less excited . . ., 141, predicts angry men, 146; & Allen Lane, 120 & n; each installed, 120; kidney worry, 121, 122, prostate?, normal, 125, indescribable relief, 126, imminence of sample, 128; absolutely normal, 172; our last brilliant season, 130; our week's treat, 138; Ka's help recalled, 143; and Hogarth House, 145; old or middle-aged?, 149; northern holiday begun, 150; VW shows letter, 155; L. shows sensibilities, 159, and sunset, 161; 'I like this in L.', 167; crisis not discussed, 167; 'We . . . can make out', 170; longings discussed, 179; & dependence, & table clearing, 180; & Helen's overdraft, L. very divine, 181; L. 'my inviolable centre', 183; to inspect house, 185; walking together, an end, 186; the cigar quarrel, 187; renewed anxieties, 188; L.'s birthday, 189; breaking in upon him, talk of death, 190; his serious illness?—a rash, 191; & VW's mixed motives, 210; to Eliot's play, 211n; L. fonder? . . ., one of the facts, 216; L. drawn in, 220; 'compared with me', 223; dumpish moviegoers, 225; & glooms, 226; VW's greenhouse guilt, 227, & L.'s adroitness, & happy reconciliation, 228; up & down, 232; standing by, 233; walking terrace, 234; calculating income, 237; alone together, 239; playing bowls, 240; happy obscurity, 226; & legacy, VW takes back place, 247; L. subtle & wise, 248; foolish, for once, 259; L. smiles, 269, explains barometer, 270, gives severe *Roger Fry* lecture—VW detached, interested, 271; what he felt, 308; usual strain, 272; poor L., 273; in spite of L., 274; pair of elms, 274 & n, 277, 346; bowling & reading, 276; happy as bank holiday clerks, 278; alone, 290; & lower orders, 291; coolness, doldrums, 293; queasy friendship feeling, discussed with L., 294; as L. would say, 295; L. said . . ., 301; L. coming?, 307, does not come, 308; beak-pecking remembered, 310; in Battle of Britain, 311 & n; in agreement, 317; working, making cigarettes, 318; almost cut off, 322;

L. cursed, & visited, 325; VW doesn't want to die, 326, . . . prudent marsh bird . . ., geese or cormorants?, 327; alone, 329; L. checks impulse, sees differently, has bad luck, 332, his lunch carried, 335; here he is, 337; L. & the diary, 338, 342; great household triumph, 340; on Angelica's position, 341; & leech pool, 342; Monks House—exactly right, 346; L. replaces bag, 355; & VW's London Library complex, 358

(4) *Diversions, parties and travel*: invited to Cambridge, 5-6; tea with Vanessa: buggery discussed, 6; death of George V, 10, 11, 12; to Canterbury cathedral, 11; to Chaplin's *Modern Times*, and *A Doll's House*, 14; *Hedda Gabler*, 15; political reunions, 17; to E. Bowen, 18; *The Master Builder*, 20; with E. M. Forster to Abinger, Colefax visits, 23; to Lords, 25; tea with Lady Colefax, 26-8; Lewes fireworks, 31; dinner with Adrian, 32; Lord Robert Cecil to tea, 33-5; lost in Wimbledon, 35-6; lunch with Clive, lunch at Claridges, 36, 37; Abdication crisis, 38, 39, 40-1, 42-4; to Wilberforce and Robins, 48-50; funeral of Miss West, 51-2; H. G. Wells at the Hutchinsons, 52-3; Stephen Spender to tea, 56-7; *Uncle Vanya*, 57; Isherwood and Sally Chilver to dine, 59; Julian Fry to dine, 60-1; Desmond MacCarthy talks seven hours, 62-3; walk at Cockfosters, 66; dinner at Charleston: return of Julian, 68; strange story from Bina Gardens, 71; to Janet Case, 76; Hugh Walpole: his scabrous tales, 78; a political evening, 79-80; to the Opera, 81; Memoir Club meeting, 82-3; a youthful party, 86; tour in France, 87-90; Desmond MacCarthy: his burst of intimacy, 91-2; London hectic, 93-4; Albert Hall meeting, 98-9; dinner with Ann and Richard, 100; a pious excursion, 102; Mrs Woolf plaintive at Worthing, 103; opinions of shell-shocked major, 104; T. S. Eliot at Monks House, 111-12; Spenders to dine, 115; City walks, 119, 131, 132-3, 203; *Trial of a Judge*, 131; Ottoline Memorial Service, 135-6;

Lady Simon to tea, 137-8; visits to Philip Morrell, 140, 309; dinners with Mrs Woolf, 147, 182, 183; two weeks in North Britain, 150-4; a specimen day, 156; to the Ballet, 157; to *Lysistrata*, 158; Memoir Club meeting, 168-9; London in crisis, 174-5; Max Beerbohm at Lady Colefax's, 183-5; *Twelfth Night*, 190; 'debauched' evening with Clive, 191, 211-12; T. S. Eliot to dinner, 192-3; to Hertford House, 200; visit to Freud, 202; Adrian's party, 202-3; to Polytechnic, 206; to Vanessa, 207; Psycho-Analysts' dinner, 208; lunch with Diana Cooper, 209; T. S. Eliot and others entertained, 211; Memoir Club meeting, 212; tea with Mrs Woolf, 216; a wedding observed, 218; Day-Lewis, 218; Mrs Woolf's funeral, 224; London in wartime, 236, 242, 246, 249, 257-8, 267, 277, 282, 287, 297, 299-300, 301, 316, 318-19, 324, 330-1, 334, 353; Hogarth Press staff at Monks House, 237; Spender at Monks House, 238-9; also T. S. Eliot, 245, Eddy Sackville-West, 246, John Lehmann, 247, 264; *Importance of Being Earnest*, 258; Hugh Walpole to tea, 158-9; Desmond MacCarthy to dinner, 279-80; Lady Colefax to tea, 280; Penshurst, 296-7; E. Bowen at Monks House, 299; Memoir Club meeting, 314; Vita at Monks House, 327-8; lunch with Bunny and Angelica, 341; lunch with John Lehmann, 343; Kingsley Martin spoils two days, 343; Oliver Strachey at Monks House, 354; visit to Cambridge and Letchworth, 356

(5) *Domestic matters*: fainting girl succoured, 19; must tidy up, 50; improvements at Monks House, 130, 135, 159, 160, 165, 167; village life, 164; life without electricity, 179, 262; bookcase acquired, 186; philanthropic budget, 192; all pipes frozen, 197; leaving 52 Tavistock Square, 219, 220, 225; for Mecklenburgh Square, 226; greenhouse at Monks House, 227, 228, 229; Percy gives notice, 230; chaos at Mecklenburgh Square, 230, 231; black-out, 234; income, 237; Mabel comes and goes, 238, 246, 318,

320, 321, 328, 332, 334; Jack Hills' legacy, 247, 249, 250; wartime motoring, 250; rations and prices, 263; butter all eaten by guests, 277; must make money, 300; Louie's wages raised, 329; possessions stored and removed, 331-2, 339, 342, 343; shortages, 343; 'we are poor', 346; economising, 352; on haddock and sausage meat, 358

(6) *Literary activities*: reading *The Trumpet Major*, 4; on Hardy, 5, Borrow, 6, Dickens, 13, Flaubert's letters, 25; *Sunday Times'* Book Show, 29, 119; *Daily Worker* article, 30, 32; difficulties of reviewing, 32; Gibbon, 44, 48, 51, 69, 72; broadcasting, 77, 79, 80, 83; little articles ruin one's time, 81; dream as subject for story?, 95; *Love for Love*, a masterpiece, 97; large offers from Janet Case, 102-3; large offers from New York, 107; new novel foreseen, 114; snub to Pelicans, 120; Chateaubriand, 120; 'Horace Walpole' sketch for America, 144; work for *TLS*, 144-5; concerning biography, 187; Chaucer and Mme de Sévigné, 197; Delacroix journals, 199; transactions with U.S. publishers, 200, 201, 231, 262, 272, 278; new novel 'described', 201; Henry Taylor's story, 204; critical work planned, 205; Chaucer, T. S. Eliot, and Mme de Sévigné, 209; *Family Reunion* won't do, 210; Dickens analysed, 214; inner censors, 229; journalism, 240, 245; speech of business men recorded, 241; Gerald Heard discussed, 243; a little memoir, 248; the diary a necessity, 251; advice from Maynard Keynes, 256; *Sense and Sensibility* discussed, 277; lecture for Women's Institute, 280; masses of Coleridge and Wordsworth letters, 289; in the mood for memoirs, 293; Coleridge, 300; writers unhappy, 315; Herbert Read, his autobiography, 340

(7) VW's published books:
A Room of One's Own: & *Three Guineas*, 134, 193
Between the Acts (provisionally entitled 'Pointz Hall'): summer's night, 133 & n; all life, all art, 135; so

absorbed in, 137; to become a play, 139; airy world of, 141; mood used up, 144; writing gaily, 149; difficult passage in, 154; & violent oscillation, 155; wild ideas—to end with a play, 159; rather enjoy doing, 160; & threat of war, 162; to lay aside, 166; kicking heels with, 171; rather absorbed in, 172; enjoyed intensely, 179; can't screw, 180; little poems for, 180; anything in it?, 189; 120 pages written, 193; the Barn scene, 199; in full flood, & lyric vein, 200; one day's happiness with, 205; several pages of, 207; Eliot & drama idea, 18th century scene, 210; Flavinda's speech, 228 & n; affects head?, 229; made up a little, 259; threshed & threshed, 289; strain to write, scraps, orts etc, 290; could finish, 293; can be finished, 294; & the last lap, 298; to fix upon, 299; better finish, 300; first a CR, then . . ., 305; expand & soar into, 310; a concentration, a screw, 311; poetry— is it good?, 313; did forge ahead, 323; in flush with, 325; pleases me, 327; returned to, 330; Victorian scene in, 332; writing in spurts, excited by, 336; screw, & disillusions, 338; its obsessive rhythm, profound observations on, 339; finished, triumphant about, 340; copying—word-drugged, 346; copying, 352; several pages lost, 354; finally 'Between the Acts', 356 & n

Common Reader, The: in Penguin, 137, 183 & n; depressed by, 322; spotted with readers, 329

Flush: & after, 188

Night and Day: 188

Orlando: & book-production students, 206 & n; & Bennett, 256 & n

'Pointz Hall' (*Between the Acts*, see above)

Roger Fry: A Biography: now to do, 4 & n; instead of *Years*, 5; unable to do, 13; congenial ramble about, 22; a form for?, 30; fitted out for, 65; strategy regarding, 91; waiting, 100; this autumn, 105; to start?, 131; two pages written, 132; with help of memoirs, 133 & n; surrounds me, 134; relieve myself of, 135; all my mind to, can't attend to, 137; eyes ache with, 138; solid world of, 141; can't broach, retyping, 144; freshener before, 149; distracted from, 154; appalling grind, 155; work at, 156; & my abstracting power, 157; assiduous truth, 159; won't go on doing, 161; to brew more, 162; thorough good book, 163; strung into a ball with, 164; too detailed & flat, 165; too jaded for, 169; stopping, 170; all that fact, 171; chapter sketched, 172-3, & written by mistake, 173 & n; burden, 178; incapable of, 179; screwed up over, 179; can't screw, 180; long grind, 182; when I have done, 187; started again, 190; semi-drudgery, 191; brought to 1919, joyless & unprogressive, 193; & Josette chapter, 197; holiday from, 199; lyric vein, verification politics, 200; head protests at, 204; holiday from, 205; last word, first sketch, 207; to re-write, 209; put aside, 210; fiddling again with, 212; rate of revising, 213, 215; Clifton passage, 214; marriage chapter, 216; dried up about, 217; PIP chapter, appallingly difficult, 220, grind of, 222, cross about, & pleasure—Omega chapter, 225; mind running on, & concluding quote, 226 & n; to rest from, 228; Symonds, & *Vision & Design*, 229 & n; & love affairs, 230; to force brain, 234; steep grind, 235; seems hopeless, 239; all copied out, 240; masterfully pulled together, 241; 'the Roger fort', 221; flying off from, 242; 'Transformations', 243; cannot rewrite last page, 246; first chapter sent, 246; screwing at, 247; a failure, 248; finer work?, 249; all unseen, 250; titivating, 252; 'the old bird', 255; to attack Omega, 258; filled the cistern?, 259; reeling off, 260; titivating, 264; teeth into, shivers anticipated, 266; must send to Margery, 270; LW, & Vanessa on, 271-2 & n; Duncan on, & Margery, 272 & n; hanging over me, 273; when I'm quit of, 274; to the printer?, 275; to be quit of, 276; Brace shies at, 278; & scale of feelings, 284; Brace accepts, 289; & *Pointz Hall*, 290; voice dormant under, 291; no proofs, 292; what lies behind, & LW's coolness, 293; forgotten about,

299; reviewed by Lynd, 305 & n; a good second—*TLS*, 306 & n; Clive and, 307; a dud . . . selling well, 308; MacCarthy on, 308 & n, 309 & n; Read & MacColl on, 309 & n; Clive . . . approving, 310 & n; booming—third edition, & Pamela Diamand, 311; official life—Keynes, 314; Ben & Bessie on, 315 & n; Harry Stephen about, 320; 'thank you' letters disliked, 320; surprisingly sells, 324; deletions requested, 324 & n; J. P. Morgan distressed by, 327; p. 34—so disgusting, 334 & n; further reflections on Read, 340, drudgery of, 340; 3rd impression of, 342; *ref*: 35, 44, 115, 147, 338

Three Guineas (provisionally called 'Answers to Correspondents' or 'Letters to an Englishman'): next book, 3 & n; not to think of, 4; final form?, 18 & n; 'Two Guineas', 22; 'making up', 29; begun, & liked, 35; can't stop thinking, 52; writing hard, 54; absorption in, 55; LW wants, 59; off again, 61; racing metaphor regarding, 62, 65, 79, 112; entirely imbued in, 62; university part of, 64; too jaded with, 66; strain of, 67; praise distracts from, 67; way prepared for, 68, 76; Professional chapter of, 69; must begin again, 70; held up—pressing for speech, 71; flames up at war talk, 80; to pounce on, hostility anticipated, 84; got going with, 90; dreaming of, 91; & Cambridge women, 92 & n; conduct &c, 94; good quote for, . . . final chapter, 95; preaching & practice, 96; back to . . ., 99; Second Guinea, 100, 101; stop thinking about, 102; to storm last section?, 103; to finish, 105; ready for, 109; & Julian's essay, 111; last page of?, sizzling since Delphi, 112 & n; revising 1st Guinea, 118; such intentness, 119; what reception for?, 120; 2nd Guinea finished, 122; last chapter 'finished', 125; LW gravely approves, 127; Outsider & notes, 5 hours a day at, 128 & n; privately bored with, summary of, 130 & n; excites bookseller, 131; and LW?, 133; & *A Room* . . ., 134, 193; & freedom, & *TLS*, 137 & n; what will

they say to?, 139; expectations, dreads, omens, 141; reactions, 145 & n, sneer enthusiasm, enthusiasm sneer, 146; coming out day, 147 & n-148 & n; & *Years*—one book, 148; taken seriously, on the whole, 149 & n; taken from the life, 149-150 & n; & Vita, 149, 151, 157 & n, 158, 182; bad review by G. M. Young, 153, 154n; & Pippa on, 154; & violent oscillation, selling well, 155; strikes rock of rage, 155; its indirect results, 156; 6,000 broached, 157; dogs, education, schoolmasters, 161; & Keynes, & a counterblast?, 163 & n; American's enthusiasm, Q. Leavis's violence, 165 & n; Jane Walker's applause, 166 & n; said what I wanted, 170; letters and sales, 173; disliked by Helen, 181; read by young, 182; queers critical pitch, 188; want to sum up, 191; summed up, 193; nothing like so bad, & nun's letter, 219 & n; Shena Simon &, 248; admired by soldier & distracted woman, 250, 251n; failure in US, 269; *ref*: 44, 132, 154n

To the Lighthouse: Quentin on, 75; in Everyman, 183 & n; *ref*: 70 & n

The Voyage Out: & acute despair, 17; & precipice, 24 & n

The Waves: LW prefers *Years*, 30; & French translation, 60 & n, 61; Keynes and, 77; attacked in *Scrutiny*, 91 & n; Sarton on, 96; & *Pointz Hall*, 179; and after . . ., 188

The Years: final revision, 3; 'bony excrescence', 3; feeble twaddle, 8; last chapter left behind, 11; Richmond scene, & Eleanor in Oxford Street, 13 & n; to printer, 15; enough of, 16; a happy effect of, 17; best scene, first proofs, 18; to interpolate & rub out, 24; near precipice, LW actually likes, 28; his judgment, 30; must immerse in, 31; worst pages done, 33; a lesson on scenes, 36; taut, real, strenuous, 38; a failure, 44; litter of, 50; publication date of, 52, uneasy prelude to, 54; appreciated in *Observer*, 55 & n; anticipations, 58; Desmond carries off, 62; not even recommended, 64; fatal day approaching, 66; *TLS*,

Printed in the United States
30721LVS00005B/1

9 780156 260404